D1649190

American Casebook Series
Hornbook Series and Basic Legal Texts
Nutshell Series

of

WEST PUBLISHING COMPANY
P.O. Box 3526
St. Paul, Minnesota 55165
December, 1979

ACCOUNTING

Fiflis and Kripke's Teaching Materials on Accounting for Business Lawyers, 2nd Ed., 684 pages, 1977 (Casebook)

ADMINISTRATIVE LAW

Davis' Cases, Text and Problems on Administrative Law, 6th Ed., 683 pages, 1977 (Casebook)

Davis' Basic Text on Administrative Law, 3rd Ed., 617 pages, 1972 (Text)

Davis' Police Discretion, 176 pages, 1975 (Text)

Gellhorn's Administrative Law and Process in a Nutshell, 336 pages, 1972 (Text)

Mashaw and Merrill's Introduction to the American Public Law System, 1095 pages, 1975, with 1978 Supplement (Casebook)

Robinson and Gellhorn's The Administrative Process, 928 pages, 1974 (Casebook)

ADMIRALTY

Healy and Sharpe's Cases and Materials on Admiralty, 875 pages, 1974 (Casebook)

AGENCY—PARTNERSHIP

Crane and Bromberg's Hornbook on Partnership, 695 pages, 1968 (Text)

Henn's Cases and Materials on Agency, Partnership and Other Unincorporated Business Enterprises, 396 pages, 1972 (Casebook)

Reuschlein and Gregory's Hornbook on the Law of Agency and Partnership, 625 pages, 1979 (Text)

Seavey's Hornbook on Agency, 329 pages, 1964 (Text)

Seavey and Hall's Cases on Agency, 431 pages, 1956 (Casebook)

AGENCY—PARTNERSHIP—Continued

Seavey, Reuschlein and Hall's Cases on Agency and Partnership, 599 pages, 1962 (Casebook)

Steffen and Kerr's Cases and Materials on Agency-Partnership, 4th Ed., approximately 860 pages, December, 1979 (Casebook)

Steffen's Agency-Partnership in a Nutshell, 364 pages, 1977 (Text)

ANTITRUST LAW

Gellhorn's Antitrust Law and Economics in a Nutshell, 406 pages, 1976 (Text)

Oppenheim and Weston's Cases and Comments on Federal Antitrust Laws, 3rd Ed., 952 pages, 1968, with 1975 Supplement (Casebook)

Oppenheim and Weston's Price and Service Discrimination under the Robinson-Patman Act, 3rd Ed., 258 pages, 1974 (Casebook—reprint from Oppenheim and Weston's Cases and Comments on Federal Antitrust Laws, 3rd Ed., 1968)

Posner's Cases and Economic Notes on Antitrust, 885 pages, 1974 (Casebook)

Sullivan's Handbook of the Law of Antitrust, 886 pages, 1977 (Text)

See also Regulated Industries, Trade Regulation

BANKING LAW

See Regulated Industries

BUSINESS PLANNING

Painter's Problems and Materials in Business Planning, 791 pages, 1975, with 1978 Supplement (Casebook)

CIVIL PROCEDURE

Casad's Res Judicata in a Nutshell, 310 pages, 1976 (Text)

CIVIL PROCEDURE—Continued

Cound, Friedenthal and Miller's Cases and Materials on Civil Procedure, 2nd Ed., 1186 pages, 1974 with 1978 Supplement (Casebook)

Cound, Friedenthal and Miller's Cases on Pleading, Discovery and Joinder, 643 pages, 1968 (Casebook)

Ehrenzweig and Louisell's Jurisdiction in a Nutshell, 3rd Ed., 291 pages, 1973 (Text)

Federal Rules of Civil-Appellate-Criminal Procedure—West Law School Edition, 342 pages, 1979

Hodges, Jones and Elliott's Cases and Materials on Texas Trial and Appellate Procedure, 2nd Ed., 745 pages, 1974 (Casebook)

Hodges, Jones and Elliott's Cases and Materials on the Judicial Process Prior to Trial in Texas, 2nd Ed., 871 pages, 1977 (Casebook)

Kane's Civil Procedure in a Nutshell, 271 pages, 1979 (Text)

Karlen's Procedure Before Trial in a Nutshell, 258 pages, 1972 (Text)

Karlen and Joiner's Cases and Materials on Trials and Appeals, 536 pages, 1971 (Casebook)

Karlen, Meisenholder, Stevens and Vestal's Cases on Civil Procedure, 923 pages, 1975 (Casebook)

Koffler and Reppy's Hornbook on Common Law Pleading, 663 pages, 1969 (Text)

McBaine's Cases on Introduction to Civil Procedure, 399 pages, 1950 (Casebook)

McCoid's Cases on Civil Procedure, 823 pages, 1974 (Casebook)

Park's Computer-Aided Exercises on Civil Procedure, 118 pages, 1976 (Coursebook)

Shipman's Hornbook on Common-Law Pleading, 3rd Ed., 644 pages, 1923 (Text)

Siegel's Hornbook on New York Practice, 1011 pages, 1978 (Text)

See also Federal Jurisdiction and Procedure

CIVIL RIGHTS

Abernathy's Cases and Materials on Civil Rights, approximately 665 pages, January 1980 (Casebook)

Lockhart, Kamisar and Choper's Cases on Constitutional Rights and Liberties, 4th Ed., 1244 pages plus Appendix, 1975, with 1979 Supplement (Casebook)—reprint from Lockhart, et al. Cases on Constitutional Law, 4th Ed., 1975

Vieira's Civil Rights in a Nutshell, 279 pages, 1978 (Text)

COMMERCIAL LAW

Bailey's Secured Transactions in a Nutshell, 377 pages, 1976 (Text)

Epstein and Martin's Basic Uniform Commercial Code Teaching Materials, 599 pages, 1977 (Casebook)

Henson's Hornbook on Secured Transactions under the U.C.C., 2nd Ed., 504 pages, 1979 with 1979 P.P. (Text)

Murray's Commercial Law, Problems and Materials, 366 pages, 1975 (Coursebook)

Nordstrom and Clovis' Problems and Materials on Commercial Paper, 458 pages, 1972 (Casebook)

Nordstrom and Lattin's Problems and Materials on Sales and Secured Transactions, 809 pages, 1968 (Casebook)

Nordstrom's Hornbook on Sales, 600 pages, 1970 (Text)

Selected Commercial Statutes, 1277 pages, 1979

Speidel, Summers and White's Teaching Materials on Commercial and Consumer Law, 2nd Ed., 1475 pages, 1974 (Casebook)

Stone's Uniform Commercial Code in a Nutshell, 507 pages, 1975 (Text)

Uniform Commercial Code, Official Text with Comments, 994 pages, 1978

UCC Article Nine Reprint, 128 pages, 1976

Weber's Commercial Paper in a Nutshell, 2nd Ed., 361 pages, 1975 (Text)

White and Summers' Hornbook on the Uniform Commercial Code, 2nd Ed., approximately 1202 pages, January, 1980 (Text)

COMMUNITY PROPERTY

Huie's Texas Cases and Materials on Marital Property Rights, 681 pages, 1966 (Casebook)

Verrall's Cases and Materials on California Community Property, 3rd Ed., 547 pages, 1977 (Casebook)

COMPARATIVE LAW

Langbein's Comparative Criminal Procedure: Germany, 172 pages, 1977 (Casebook)

CONFLICT OF LAWS

Cramton, Currie and Kay's Cases-Comments-Questions on Conflict of Laws, 2nd Ed., 1021 pages, 1975 (Casebook)

Ehrenzweig's Treatise on Conflict of Laws, 824 pages, 1962 (Text)

Ehrenzweig's Conflicts in a Nutshell, 3rd Ed., 432 pages, 1974 (Text)

CONFLICT OF LAWS—Continued

Goodrich and Scoles' Hornbook on Conflict of Laws, 4th Ed., 483 pages, 1964 (Text)

Scoles and Weintraub's Cases and Materials on Conflict of Laws, 2nd Ed., 966 pages, 1972, with 1978 Supplement (Casebook)

CONSTITUTIONAL LAW

Engdahl's Constitutional Power in a Nutshell: Federal and State, 411 pages, 1974 (Text)

Ginsburg's Constitutional Aspects of Sex-Based Discrimination, 129 pages, 1974 (Casebook)—reprint from Davidson, Ginsburg and Kay's Cases on Sex-Based Discrimination, 1974

Lockhart, Kamisar and Choper's Cases-Comments-Questions on Constitutional Law, 4th Ed., 1664 pages plus Appendix, 1975, with 1979 Supplement (Casebook)

Lockhart, Kamisar and Choper's Cases-Comments-Questions on the American Constitution, 4th Ed., 1249 pages plus Appendix, 1975, with 1979 Supplement (Casebook)—reprint from Lockhart, et al. Cases on Constitutional Law, 4th Ed., 1975

Lockhart, Kamisar and Choper's Cases and Materials on Constitutional Rights and Liberties, 4th Ed., 1244 pages plus Appendix, 1975, with 1979 Supplement (Casebook)—reprint from Lockhart, et al. Cases on Constitutional Law, 4th Ed., 1975

Miller's Presidential Power in a Nutshell, 328 pages, 1977 (Text)

Nowak, Rotunda and Young's Hornbook on Constitutional Law, 974 pages, 1978, with 1979 pocket part (Text)

Vieira's Civil Rights in a Nutshell, 279 pages, 1978 (Text)

William's Constitutional Analysis in a Nutshell, 388 pages, 1979 (Text)

CONSUMER LAW

Epstein's Consumer Protection in a Nutshell, 322 pages, 1976 (Text)

Kripke's Text-Cases-Materials on Consumer Credit, 454 pages, 1970 (Casebook)

McCall's Consumer Protection, Cases, Notes and Materials, 594 pages, 1977, with 1977 Statutory Supplement (Casebook)

Schrag's Cases and Materials on Consumer Protection, 2nd Ed., 197 pages, 1973 (Casebook)—reprint from Cooper, et al. Cases on Law and Poverty, 2nd Ed., 1973

Selected Commercial Statutes, 1277 pages, 1979

CONSUMER LAW—Continued

Spanogle and Rohner's Cases and Materials on Consumer Law, 693 pages, 1979 (Casebook)

Uniform Consumer Credit Code, Official Text with Comments, 218 pages, 1974

CONTRACTS

Calamari & Perillo's Cases and Problems on Contracts, 1061 pages, 1978 (Casebook)

Calamari and Perillo's Hornbook on Contracts, 2nd Ed., 878 pages, 1977 (Text)

Corbin's Text on Contracts, One Volume Student Edition, 1224 pages, 1952 (Text)

Freedman's Cases and Materials on Contracts, 658 pages, 1973 (Casebook)

Fuller and Eisenberg's Cases on Basic Contract Law, 3rd Ed., 1043 pages, 1972 (Casebook)

Jackson's Cases on Contract Law in Modern Society, 1404 pages, 1973 (Casebook)

Keyes' Government Contracts in a Nutshell, 423 pages, 1979 (Text)

Reitz's Cases on Contracts as Basic Commercial Law, 763 pages, 1975 (Casebook)

Schaber and Rohwer's Contracts in a Nutshell, 307 pages, 1975 (Text)

Simpson's Hornbook on Contracts, 2nd Ed., 510 pages, 1965 (Text)

COPYRIGHT

Nimmer's Cases and Materials on Copyright and Other Aspects of Law Pertaining to Literary, Musical and Artistic Works, Illustrated, 2nd Ed., 1023 pages, 1979 (Casebook)

See also Patent Law

CORPORATIONS

Hamilton's Cases on Corporations—Including Partnerships and Limited Partnerships, 998 pages, 1976, with 1979 Case and Statutory Supplement (Casebook)

Henn's Cases on Corporations, 1279 pages, 1974, with 1974 Statutes, Forms and Case Study Supplement (Casebook)

Henn's Hornbook on Corporations, 2nd Ed., 956 pages, 1970 (Text)

Jennings and Buxbaum's Cases and Materials on Corporations, 5th Ed., 1156 pages, 1979 (Casebook)

CORRECTIONS

Krantz's Cases and Materials on the Law of Corrections and Prisoners' Rights, 1130 pages, 1973, with 1977 Supplement (Casebook)

CORRECTIONS—Continued

Krantz's Law of Corrections and Prisoners' Rights in a Nutshell, 353 pages, 1976 (Text)

Model Rules and Regulations on Prisoners' Rights and Responsibilities, 212 pages, 1973

Popper's Post-Conviction Remedies in a Nutshell, 360 pages, 1978 (Text)

CREDITOR'S RIGHTS

Epstein's Debtor-Creditor Law in a Nutshell, 2nd Ed., approximately 322 pages, December, 1979 (Text)

Epstein and Landers' Debtors and Creditors: Cases and Materials, 722 pages, 1978, with 1979 Supplement (Casebook)

Riesenfeld's Cases and Materials on Creditors' Remedies and Debtors' Protection, 3rd Ed., 795 pages, 1979 with 1979 Statutory Supplement (Casebook)

Selected Bankruptcy Statutes, 351 pages, 1979

CRIMINAL LAW AND CRIMINAL PROCEDURE

Cohen and Gobert's Problems in Criminal Law, 297 pages, 1976 (Problem book)

Davis' Police Discretion, 176 pages, 1975 (Text)

Dix and Sharlot's Cases and Materials on Criminal Law, 2nd Ed., 756 pages, 1979 (Casebook)

Federal Rules of Civil-Appellate-Criminal Procedure—West Law School Edition, 342 pages, 1979

Grano's Problems in Criminal Procedure, 171 pages, 1974 (Problem book)

Heymann and Kenety's The Murder Trial of Wilbur Jackson: A Homicide in the Family, 340 pages, 1975 (Case Study)

Israel and LaFave's Criminal Procedure in a Nutshell, 2nd Ed., 404 pages, 1975 (Text)

Johnson's Criminal Law: Cases, Materials and Text on Substantive Criminal Law in its Procedural Context, 878 pages, 1975, with 1977 Supplement (Casebook)

Kamisar, LaFave and Israel's Cases, Comments and Questions on Modern Criminal Procedure, 4th ed., 1572 pages, plus Appendix, 1974, with 1980 Supplement (Casebook)

Kamisar, LaFave and Israel's Cases, Comments and Questions on Basic Criminal Procedure, 4th Ed., 790 pages, 1974, with 1980 Supplement (Casebook)—reprint from Kasimar, et al. Modern Criminal Procedure, 4th ed., 1974

LaFave's Modern Criminal Law: Cases, Comments and Questions, 789 pages, 1978 (Casebook)

LaFave and Scott's Hornbook on Criminal Law, 763 pages, 1972 (Text)

CRIMINAL LAW AND CRIMINAL PROCEDURE—Continued

Loewy's Criminal Law in a Nutshell, 302 pages, 1975 (Text)

Saltzburg's American Criminal Procedure, Cases and Commentary, approx. 1270 pages, December, 1979 (Casebook)

Uniform Rules of Criminal Procedure—Approved Draft, 407 pages, 1974

Uviller's The Processes of Criminal Justice: Adjudication, 2nd Ed., 700 pages, 1979. Soft-cover reprint from Uviller's The Processes of Criminal Justice: Investigation and Adjudication, 2nd Ed. (Casebook)

Uviller's The Processes of Criminal Justice: Investigation and Adjudication, 2nd Ed., 1320 pages, 1979 with 1979 Statutory Supplement (Casebook)

Uviller's The Processes of Criminal Justice: Investigation, 2nd Ed., 650 pages, 1979. Soft-cover reprint from Uviller's The Processes of Criminal Justice: Investigation and Adjudication, 2nd Ed. (Casebook)

Vorenberg's Cases on Criminal Law and Procedure, 1044 pages, 1975, with 1979 Supplement (Casebook)

See also Corrections, Juvenile Justice

DECEDENTS ESTATES

See Wills, Trusts and Estates

DOMESTIC RELATIONS

Clark's Cases and Problems on Domestic Relations, 2nd Ed., 918 pages, 1974, with 1977 Supplement (Casebook)

Clark's Hornbook on Domestic Relations, 754 pages, 1968 (Text)

Kay's Sex-Based Discrimination in Family Law, 305 pages, 1974 (Casebook)—reprint from Davidson, Ginsburg and Kay's Cases on Sex-Based Discrimination, 1974

Krause's Cases and Materials on Family Law, 1132 pages, 1976, with 1978 Supplement (Casebook)

Krause's Family Law in a Nutshell, 400 pages, 1977 (Text)

Paulsen's Cases and Selected Problems on Family Law and Poverty, 2nd Ed., 200 pages, 1973 (Casebook)—reprint from Cooper, et al. Cases on Law and Poverty, 2nd Ed., 1973

EDUCATION LAW

Morris' The Constitution and American Education, 833 pages, 1974 (Casebook)

EMPLOYMENT DISCRIMINATION

Cooper, Rabb and Rubin's Fair Employment Litigation: Text and Materials for Student and Practitioner, 590 pages, 1975 (Coursebook)

EMPLOYMENT DISCRIMINATION—

Continued

Player's Cases and Materials on Employment Discrimination Law, approximately 825 pages, December, 1979 (Casebook)

Player's Federal Law of Employment Discrimination in a Nutshell, 336 pages, 1976 (Text)

Sovern's Cases and Materials on Racial Discrimination in Employment, 2nd Ed., 167 pages, 1973 (Casebook)—reprint from Cooper et al. Cases on Law and Poverty, 2nd Ed., 1973

See also Women and the Law

ENVIRONMENTAL LAW

Currie's Cases and Materials on Pollution, 715 pages, 1975 (Casebook)

Federal Environmental Law, 1600 pages, 1974 (Text)

Hanks, Tarlock and Hanks' Cases on Environmental Law and Policy, 1242 pages, 1974, with 1976 Supplement (Casebook)

Rodgers' Hornbook on Environmental Law, 956 pages, 1977 (Text)

See also Natural Resources and Water Law

EQUITY

See Remedies

ESTATE PLANNING

Casner and Stein's Estate Planning under the Tax Reform Act of 1976, 456 pages, 1978 (Coursebook)

Lynn's Introduction to Estate Planning, in a Nutshell, 2nd Ed., 378 pages, 1978 (Text)

EVIDENCE

Broun and Meisenholder's Problems in Evidence, 130 pages, 1973 (Problem book)

Cleary and Strong's Cases, Materials and Problems on Evidence, 2nd Ed., 1124 pages, 1975 (Casebook)

Federal Rules of Evidence for United States Courts and Magistrates, 325 pages, 1979

Kimball's Programmed Materials on Problems in Evidence, 380 pages, 1978 (Problem book)

Lempert and Saltzburg's A Modern Approach to Evidence: Text, Problems, Transcripts and Cases, 1231 pages, 1977 (Casebook)

Lilly's Introduction to the Law of Evidence, 486 pages, 1978 (Text)

McCormick, Elliott and Sutton's Cases and Materials on Evidence, 4th Ed., 1088 pages, 1971 (Casebook)

McCormick's Hornbook on Evidence, 2nd Ed., 938 pages, 1972, with 1978 pocket part (Text)

EVIDENCE—Continued

Rothstein's Evidence in a Nutshell, 406 pages, 1970 (Text)

FEDERAL JURISDICTION AND PROCEDURE

Currie's Cases and Materials on Federal Courts, 2nd Ed., 1040 pages, 1975, with 1978 Supplement (Casebook)

Currie's Federal Jurisdiction in a Nutshell, 228 pages, 1976 (Text)

Federal Rules of Civil-Appellate-Criminal Procedure—West Law School Edition, 342 pages, 1979

Forrester and Moye's Cases and Materials on Federal Jurisdiction and Procedure, 3rd Ed., 917 pages, 1977 (Casebook)

Merrill and Vetri's Problems on Federal Courts and Civil Procedure, 460 pages, 1974 (Problem book)

Wright's Hornbook on Federal Courts, 3rd Ed., 818 pages, 1976 (Text)

FUTURE INTERESTS

See Wills, Trusts, and Estates

HOUSING AND URBAN DEVELOPMENT

Berger's Cases and Materials on Housing, 2nd Ed., 254 pages, 1973 (Casebook)—reprint from Cooper et al. Cases on Law and Poverty, 2nd Ed., 1973

See also Land Use

INDIAN LAW

Getches, Rosenfelt and Wilkinson's Cases on Federal Indian Law, 660 pages, 1979 (Casebook)

INSURANCE

Keeton's Cases on Basic Insurance Law, 2nd Ed., 1086 pages, 1977

Keeton's Basic Text on Insurance Law, 712 pages, 1971 (Text)

Keeton's Case Supplement to Keeton's Basic Text on Insurance Law, 334 pages, 1978 (Casebook)

Keeton's Programmed Problems in Insurance Law, 243 pages, 1972 (Text Supplement)

INTERNATIONAL LAW

Friedmann, Lissityzyn and Pugh's Cases and Materials on International Law, 1205 pages, 1969, with 1972 Supplement (Casebook)

Jackson's Legal Problems of International Economic Relations, 1097 pages, 1977, with Statutory Supplement (Casebook)

Kirgis' International Organizations in Their Legal Setting, 1016 pages, 1977 (Casebook)

INTRODUCTION TO LAW

Dobbyn's So You Want to go to Law School, Revised First Edition, 206 pages, 1976 (Text)

Kinyon's Introduction to Law Study and Law Examinations in a Nutshell, 389 pages, 1971 (Text)

See also Legal Method and Legal System

JUDICIAL ADMINISTRATION

Carrington, Meador and Rosenberg's Justice on Appeal, 263 pages, 1976 (Casebook)

Nelson's Cases and Materials on Judicial Administration and the Administration of Justice, 1032 pages, 1974 (Casebook)

JURISPRUDENCE

Christie's Text and Readings on Jurisprudence—The Philosophy of Law, 1056 pages, 1973 (Casebook)

JUVENILE JUSTICE

Fox's Cases and Materials on Modern Juvenile Justice, 1012 pages, 1972 (Casebook)

Fox's Juvenile Courts in a Nutshell, 2nd Ed., 275 pages, 1977 (Text)

LABOR LAW

Gorman's Labor Law-Unionization and Collective Bargaining, 914 pages, 1976 (Text)

Leslie's Labor Law in a Nutshell, 403 pages, 1979 (Text)

Nolan's Labor Arbitration Law and Practice in a Nutshell, 358 pages, 1979 (Text)

Oberer, Hanslowe and Anderson's Cases and Materials on Labor Law—Collective Bargaining in a Free Society, 2nd Ed., 1168 pages, 1979, with 1979 Statutory Supplement (Casebook)

See also Employment Discrimination, Social Legislation

LAND FINANCE—PROPERTY SECURITY

Bruce's Real Estate Finance in a Nutshell, 292 pages, 1979 (Text)

Maxwell, Riesenfeld, Hetland and Warren's Cases on California Security Transactions in Land, 2nd Ed., 584 pages, 1975 (Casebook)

Nelson and Whitman's Cases on Real Estate Finance and Development, 1064 pages, 1976 (Casebook)

Osborne's Cases and Materials on Secured Transactions, 559 pages, 1967 (Casebook)

Osborne, Nelson and Whitman's Hornbook on Real Estate Finance Law, 3rd Ed., 885 pages, 1979 (Text)

LAND USE

Beuscher, Wright and Gitelman's Cases and Materials on Land Use, 2nd Ed., 1133 pages, 1976 (Casebook)

Hagman's Cases on Public Planning and Control of Urban and Land Development, 1208 pages, 1973, with 1976 Supplement (Casebook)

Hagman's Hornbook on Urban Planning and Land Development Control Law, 706 pages, 1971 (Text)

Wright and Webber's Land Use in a Nutshell, 316 pages, 1978 (Text)

See also Housing and Urban Development

LAW AND ECONOMICS

Manne's The Economics of Legal Relationships—Readings in the Theory of Property Rights, 660 pages, 1975 (Text)

See also Regulated Industries

LAW AND MEDICINE—PSYCHIATRY

King's The Law of Medical Malpractice in a Nutshell, 340 pages, 1977 (Text)

Sharpe, Fiscina and Head's Cases on Law and Medicine, 882 pages, 1978 (Casebook)

LEGAL RESEARCH AND WRITING

Cohen's Legal Research in a Nutshell, 3rd Ed., 415 pages, 1978 (Text)

How to Find the Law With Special Chapters on Legal Writing, 7th Ed., 542 pages, 1976. Problem book available (Coursebook)

Rombauer's Legal Problem Solving—Analysis, Research and Writing, 3rd Ed., 352 pages, 1978 (Casebook)

Statsky's Legal Research, Writing and Analysis: Some Starting Points, 180 pages, 1974 (Text)—reprint from Statsky's Introduction to Paralegalism, 1974

Statsky and Wernet's Case Analysis and Fundamentals of Legal Writing, 576 pages, 1977 (Text)

Weihofen's Legal Writing Style, 2nd Ed., 332 pages, 1980 (Text)

LEGAL CLINICS

Freeman and Weihofen's Cases and Text on Clinical Law Training—Interviewing and Counseling, 506 pages, 1972 (Casebook)

LEGAL PROFESSION

Aronson's Problems in Professional Responsibility, 280 pages, 1978 (Problem book)

Mallen and Levit's Legal Malpractice, 727 pages, 1977 (Coursebook)

LEGAL PROFESSION—Continued

Mellinkoff's The Conscience of a Lawyer, 304 pages, 1973 (Text)

Mellinkoff's Lawyers and the System of Justice, 983 pages, 1976 (Casebook)

Pirsig and Kirwin's Cases and Materials on Professional Responsibility, 3rd Ed., 667 pages, 1976, with 1977 Supplement (Casebook)

LEGAL HISTORY

See Legal Method and Legal System

LEGAL METHOD AND LEGAL SYSTEM

Aldisert's Readings, Materials and Cases in the Judicial Process, 948 pages, 1976 (Casebook)

Fryer and Orentlicher's Cases and Materials on Legal Method and Legal System, 1043 pages, 1967 (Casebook)

Greenberg's Judicial Process and Social Change, 666 pages, 1977 (Coursebook)

Kempin's Historical Introduction to Anglo-American Law in a Nutshell, 2nd Ed., 280 pages, 1973 (Text)

Kimball's Historical Introduction to the Legal System, 610 pages, 1966 (Casebook)

Leflar's Appellate Judicial Opinions, 343 pages, 1974 (Text)

Mashaw and Merrill's Introduction to the American Public Law System, 1095 pages, 1975, with 1978 Supplement (Casebook)

Murphy's Cases and Materials on Introduction to Law—Legal Process and Procedure, 772 pages, 1977 (Casebook)

Smith's Cases and Materials on the Development of Legal Institutions, 757 pages, 1965 (Casebook)

Statsky's Legislative Analysis: How to Use Statutes and Regulations, 216 pages, 1975 (Text)

LEGISLATION

Davies' Legislative Law and Process in a Nutshell, 279 pages, 1975 (Text)

Nutting and Dickerson's Cases and Materials on Legislation, 5th Ed., 744 pages, 1978 (Casebook)

Statsky's Legislative Analysis: How to Use Statutes and Regulations, 216 pages, 1975 (Text)

LOCAL GOVERNMENT

McCarthy's Local Government Law in a Nutshell, 386 pages, 1975 (Text)

Michelman and Sandalow's Cases-Comments-Questions on Government in Urban Areas, 1216 pages, 1970, with 1972 Supplement (Casebook)

Stason and Kauper's Cases and Materials on Municipal Corporations, 3rd Ed., 692 pages, 1959 (Casebook)

LOCAL GOVERNMENT—Continued

Valente's Cases and Materials on Local Government Law, 928 pages, 1975 (Casebook)

MASS COMMUNICATION LAW

Gillmor and Barron's Cases and Comment on Mass Communication Law, 3rd Ed., 988 pages, 1979 (Casebook)

Ginsburg's Regulation of Broadcasting: Law and Policy Towards Radio, Television and Cable Communications, 741 pages, 1979 (Casebook)

Zuckman and Gayne's Mass Communications Law in a Nutshell, 431 pages, 1977 (Text)

MORTGAGES

See Land Finance—Property Security

NATURAL RESOURCES LAW

Rodger's Cases on Energy and Natural Resources Law, 995 pages, 1979 (Casebook)

See also Environmental Law & Water Law

OFFICE PRACTICE

Binder and Price's Legal Interviewing and Counseling: A Client-Centered Approach, 232 pages, 1977 (Text)

Edwards and White's Problems, Readings and Materials on the Lawyer as a Negotiator, 484 pages, 1977 (Casebook)

Freeman and Weihofen's Cases and Text on Clinical Law Training—Interviewing and Counseling, 506 pages, 1972 (Casebook)

Shaffer's Legal Interviewing and Counseling in a Nutshell, 353 pages, 1976 (Text)

Strong and Clark's Law Office Management, 424 pages, 1974 (Casebook)

OIL AND GAS

Hemingway's Hornbook on Oil and Gas, 486 pages, 1971, with 1978 pocket part (Text)

Huie, Woodward and Smith's Cases and Materials on Oil and Gas, 2nd Ed., 955 pages, 1972 (Casebook)

See also Natural Resources

PARTNERSHIP

See Agency—Partnership

PATENT LAW

Choate's Cases and Materials on Patent Law, 1060 pages, 1973 (Casebook)

See also Copyright

POVERTY LAW

Brudno's Poverty, Inequality, and the Law: Cases-Commentary-Analysis, 934 pages, 1976 (Casebook)

POVERTY LAW—Continued

Brudno's Cases on Income Redistribution Theories and Programs, 480 pages, 1977 (Casebook)—reprint from Brudno's Cases on Poverty, Inequality and the Law, 1976

Cooper, Dodyk, Berger, Paulsen, Schrag and Sovern's Cases and Materials on Law and Poverty, 2nd Ed., 1208 pages, 1973 (Casebook)

LaFrance, Schroeder, Bennett and Boyd's Hornbook on Law of the Poor, 558 pages, 1973 (Text)

See also Social Legislation

PRODUCTS LIABILITY

Noel and Phillips' Cases on Products Liability, 836 pages, 1976 (Casebook)

Noel and Phillips' Products Liability in a Nutshell, 365 pages, 1974 (Text)

PROPERTY

Aigler, Smith and Tefft's Cases on Property, 2 volumes, 1339 pages, 1960 (Casebook)

Bernhardt's Real Property in a Nutshell, 425 pages, 1975 (Text)

Browder, Cunningham, Julin and Smith's Cases on Basic Property Law, 3rd Ed., 1447 pages, 1979 (Casebook)

Burby's Hornbook on Real Property, 3rd Ed., 490 pages, 1965 (Text)

Chused's A Modern Approach to Property: Cases-Notes-Materials, 1069 pages, 1978 (Casebook)

Cohen's Materials for a Basic Course in Property, 526 pages, 1978 (Casebook)

Donahue, Kauper and Martin's Cases on Property, 1501 pages, 1974 (Casebook)

Hill's Landlord and Tenant Law in a Nutshell, 319 pages, 1979 (Text)

Moynihan's Introduction to Real Property, 254 pages, 1962 (Text)

Phipps' Titles in a Nutshell, 277 pages, 1968 (Text)

Smith and Boyer's Survey of the Law of Property, 2nd Ed., 510 pages, 1971 (Text)

Uniform Land Transactions Act, Uniform Simplification of Land Transfers Act, Uniform Condominium Act, 1978 Official Text with Comments, 462 pages, 1978

See also Housing and Urban Development, Land Finance, Land Use

REAL ESTATE

See Land Finance

REGULATED INDUSTRIES

Morgan's Cases and Materials on Economic Regulation of Business, 830 pages, 1976, with 1978 Supplement (Casebook)

REGULATED INDUSTRIES—Continued

Pozen's Financial Institutions: Cases, Materials and Problems on Investment Management, 844 pages, 1978 (Casebook)

White's Teaching Materials on Banking Law, 1058 pages, 1976, with 1976 Statutory Supplement (Casebook)

See also Mass Communication Law

REMEDIES

Cribbet's Cases and Materials on Judicial Remedies, 762 pages, 1954 (Casebook)

Dobbs' Hornbook on Remedies, 1067 pages, 1973. (Text)

Dobbs' Problems in Remedies, 137 pages, 1974 (Problem book)

Dobbyn's Injunctions in a Nutshell, 264 pages, 1974 (Text)

McClintock's Hornbook on Equity, 2nd Ed., 643 pages, 1948 (Text)

McCormick's Hornbook on Damages, 811 pages, 1935 (Text)

O'Connell's Remedies in a Nutshell, 364 pages, 1977 (Text)

Van Hecke, Leavell and Nelson's Cases and Materials on Equitable Remedies and Restitution, 2nd Ed., 717 pages, 1973 (Casebook)

York and Bauman's Cases and Materials on Remedies, 3rd Ed., 1250 pages, 1979 (Casebook)

REVIEW MATERIALS

Ballantine's Problems

Smith's Review

SECURITIES REGULATION

Ratner's Securities Regulation: Materials for a Basic Course, 2nd Ed., approximately 1062 pages, December, 1979, with 1979 Supplement (Casebook)

Ratner's Securities Regulation in a Nutshell, 300 pages, 1978 (Text)

SOCIAL LEGISLATION

Brudno's Income Redistribution Theories and Programs: Cases-Commentary-Analysis, 480 pages, 1977 (Casebook)—reprint from Brudno's Poverty, Inequality and the Law, 1976

Cohen's Cases and Materials on Law and Social Control: The Processes of Deprivation of Liberty, approximately 825 pages, December, 1979 (Casebook)

Cooper and Dodyk's Cases and Materials on Income Maintenance, 2nd Ed., 449 pages, 1973 (Casebook)—reprint from Cooper et al. Cases on Law and Poverty, 2nd Ed., 1973

LaFrance's Welfare Law: Structure and Entitlement in a Nutshell, 455 pages, 1979 (Text)

LAW SCHOOL PUBLICATION—Continued

SOCIAL LEGISLATION—Continued

Malone, Plant and Little's Cases on the Employment Relation, 1055 pages, 1974, with 1977 Supplement (Casebook)

See also Poverty Law

SURETYSHIP

Osborne's Cases on Suretyship, 221 pages, 1966 (Casebook)

Simpson's Hornbook on Suretyship, 569 pages, 1950 (Text)

TAXATION

Chommie's Hornbook on Federal Income Taxation, 2nd Ed., 1051 pages, 1973 (Text)

Chommie's Review of Federal Income Taxation, 90 pages, 1973 (Text)

Hellerstein and Hellerstein's Cases on State and Local Taxation, 4th Ed., 1041 pages, 1978 (Casebook)

Kahn and Gann's Corporate Taxation and Taxation of Partnerships and Partners, 1107 pages, 1979 (Casebook)

Kragen and McNulty's Cases and Materials on Federal Income Taxation, 3rd Ed., Vol. 1, 1270 pages, 1979 (Casebook)

Kramer and McCord's Problems for Federal Estate and Gift Taxes, 206 pages, 1976 (Problem book)

Lowndes, Kramer and McCord's Hornbook on Federal Estate and Gift Taxes, 3rd Ed., 1099 pages, 1974 (Text)

McCord's 1976 Estate and Gift Tax Reform-Analysis, Explanation and Commentary, 377 pages, 1977 (Text)

McNulty's Federal Estate and Gift Taxation in a Nutshell, 2nd Ed., 488 pages, 1979 (Text)

McNulty's Federal Income Taxation of Individuals in a Nutshell, 2nd Ed., 422 pages, 1978 (Text)

Rice's Problems and Materials in Federal Estate and Gift Taxation, 3rd Ed., 474 pages, 1978 (Casebook)

Rice and Solomon's Problems and Materials in Federal Income Taxation, 3rd Ed., 675 pages, 1979 (Casebook)

Rose and Raskind's Advanced Federal Income Taxation: Corporate Transactions-Cases, Materials and Problems, 955 pages, 1978 (Casebook)

Selected Federal Taxation Statutes and Regulations, 1415 pages, 1979

Soboloff's Federal Income Taxation of Corporations and Stockholders in a Nutshell, 374 pages, 1978 (Text)

TORTS

Green, Pedrick, Rahl, Thode, Hawkins, Smith and Treece's Cases and Materials on Torts, 2nd Ed., 1360 pages, 1977 (Casebook)

TORTS—Continued

Green, Pedrick, Rahl, Thode, Hawkins, Smith, and Treece's Advanced Torts: Injuries to Business, Political and Family Interests, 544 pages, 1977 (Casebook)—reprint from Green, et al. Cases and Materials on Torts, 2nd Ed., 1977

Keeton's Computer-Aided and Workbook Exercises on Tort Law, 164 pages, 1976 (Coursebook)

Keeton and Keeton's Cases and Materials on Torts, 2nd Ed., 1200 pages, 1977 (Casebook)

Kionka's Torts in a Nutshell: Injuries to Persons and Property, 434 pages, 1977 (Text)

Malone's Torts in a Nutshell: Injuries to Family, Social and Trade Relations, 340 pages, 1979 (Text)

Prosser's Hornbook on Torts, 4th Ed., 1208 pages, 1971 (Text)

Shapo's Cases on Tort and Compensation Law, 1244 pages, 1976 (Casebook)

See also Products Liability

TRADE REGULATION

Oppenheim and Weston's Cases and Materials on Unfair Trade Practices and Consumer Protection, 3rd Ed., 1065 pages, 1974, with 1977 Supplement (Casebook)

See also Antitrust, Regulated Industries

TRIAL ADVOCACY

Bergman's Trial Advocacy in a Nutshell, 402 pages, 1979 (Text)

Hegland's Trial and Practice Skills in a Nutshell, 346 pages, 1978 (Text)

Jean's Trial Advocacy (Student Edition), 473 pages, 1975 (Text)

McElhaney's Effective Litigation, 457 pages, 1974 (Casebook)

TRUSTS

See Wills, Trusts and Estates

WATER LAW

Trelease's Cases and Materials on Water Law, 3rd Ed., 828 pages, 1979 (Casebook)

See also Natural Resources & Environmental Law

WILL, TRUSTS AND ESTATES

Atkinson's Hornbook on Wills, 2nd Ed., 975 pages, 1953 (Text)

Averill's Uniform Probate Code in a Nutshell, 425 pages, 1978 (Text)

Bogert's Hornbook on Trusts, 5th Ed., 726 pages, 1973 (Text)

Clark, Lusky and Murphy's Cases and Materials on Gratuitous Transfers, 2nd Ed., 1102 pages, 1977 (Casebook)

WILL, TRUSTS AND ESTATES
—Continued

Gulliver's Cases and Materials on Future Interests, 624 pages, 1959 (Casebook)

Gulliver's Introduction to the Law of Future Interests, 87 pages, 1959 (Casebook)

Halbach (Editor)—Death, Taxes, and Family Property: Essays and American Assembly Report, 189 pages, 1977 (Text)

Mennell's Cases and Materials on California Decedent's Estates, 566 pages, 1973 (Casebook)

Mennell's Wills and Trusts in a Nutshell, 392 pages, 1979 (Text)

Powell's Cases on Trusts and Wills, 639 pages, 1960 (Casebook)

Simes' Hornbook on Future Interests, 2nd Ed., 355 pages, 1966 (Text)

WILL, TRUSTS AND ESTATES
—Continued

Turrentine's Cases and Text on Wills and Administration, 2nd Ed., 483 pages, 1962 (Casebook)

Uniform Probate Code, 5th Ed., Official Text With Comments, 384 pages, 1977

WOMEN AND THE LAW

Davidson, Ginsburg and Kay's Text, Cases and Materials on Sex-Based Discrimination, 1031 pages, 1974, with 1978 Supplement (Casebook)

See also Employment Discrimination

WORKMEN'S COMPENSATION

See Social Legislation

*

ADVISORY BOARD
AMERICAN CASEBOOK SERIES
HORNBOOK SERIES AND BASIC LEGAL TEXTS
NUTSHELL SERIES

JESSE H. CHOPER

Professor of Law
University of California, Berkeley

DAVID P. CURRIE

Professor of Law
University of Chicago

HARRY T. EDWARDS

Professor of Law
University of Michigan

RUTH B. GINSBURG

Professor of Law
Columbia University

YALE KAMISAR

Professor of Law
University of Michigan

WAYNE R. LaFAVE

Professor of Law
University of Illinois

RICHARD C. MAXWELL

Professor of Law
University of California, Los Angeles

ARTHUR R. MILLER

Professor of Law
Harvard University

CHARLES ALAN WRIGHT

Professor of Law
University of Texas

HANDBOOK

ON

SECURED TRANSACTIONS

UNDER THE
UNIFORM COMMERCIAL CODE

SECOND EDITION

By

RAY D. HENSON

Professor of Law, University of California,
Hastings College of the Law

HORNBOOK SERIES

ST. PAUL, MINN.
WEST PUBLISHING CO.
1979

RECEIVED
MAR 2 4 1992
MSU - LIBRARY

KF
1050
.H45
1979

COPYRIGHT Ⓒ 1973 By WEST PUBLISHING CO.

COPYRIGHT Ⓒ 1979 By WEST PUBLISHING CO.

All rights reserved

Printed in the United States of America

Library of Congress Cataloging in Publication Data

Henson, Ray D   1924–
       Handbook on secured transactions under the uniform commercial code.
       (Hornbook series)
       Includes index.
       1. Security (Law)—United States. I. Title. II. Series.
KF1050.H45 1979   346'.73'074   78–26098

ISBN 0–8299–2023–4

Henson Secured Transactions 2d Ed. HB
1st Reprint—1980

THIS BOOK IS DEDICATED TO MY STUDENTS

PAST

PRESENT

FUTURE

WITH RESPECT, AFFECTION, AND GRATITUDE

*

PREFACE TO THE SECOND EDITION

There have been more reported Code cases since the first edition of this book appeared in 1973 than there were in all of the years before that time. Quite apart from the number of cases, some of the litigated issues are of considerable interest, and an effort has been made to deal with all of the significant developments, with ample citation of authority.

In some ways a second edition of a book in an evolving field is harder to put together than a first edition. I am most grateful for the invaluable assistance of Mrs. Joan Long, who for several years has had the unenviable task of transcribing my handwriting into the typed manuscript. No one could have had a better research assistant than Stephen D. Holz, Hastings '78, who has also learned to read my handwriting in the course of checking my work. Surely no law school could possibly have a finer library staff than Hastings, and while my gratitude goes to each and every member of that staff, I am especially grateful to Dan F. Henke, the Librarian, and to Robert Berger, Assistant Librarian. Perhaps it is one of those things that is usually understood even if unspoken, but one's associates mean a very great deal in life, and the delightful, diverse, erudite, marvelous faculty at Hastings have contributed much to me and to my work.

RAY D. HENSON

San Francisco
December, 1978

*

PREFACE TO THE FIRST EDITION

This book is a product of two decades as a lawyer and two years as a law professor. My outlook on a branch of law that I have been involved with for so long could never be academic, as that word is so often used, and yet I hope that through the years I have managed to maintain a somewhat broad perspective and a certain detachment. No one wishes to be accused of mumpsimus.

Be that as it may, this book is meant to be a practical guide to Article 9 with some academic overtones. There is no effort at exhaustive citation of cases, since the advent of the Commercial Code has made readily accessible in several sources essentially all cases dealing with any given section. Some cases are clearly wrong, some are clearly right, many are simply trivial. The problem lies in trying to figure out what a complicated statute means, and in general that meaning should be extricated from the statute itself.

The changes made by the 1972 revisions of Article 9 are featured throughout this book. The Revised Article 9 was passed by the Illinois General Assembly in the spring of 1972, and it will undoubtedly achieve the nationwide acceptance of the original Code. In any case, where changes were made problems were thought to exist. These problems may have been real in the sense of being raised by judicial interpretation or misinterpretation, or theoretical in the sense of being raised in law review articles, or they may have arisen because the language of the 1962 Code was thought to be less clear than it might have been. But whatever the reasons for them, the revisions are extremely important, and they are important without regard to whether or when they are enacted by any state.

It has been my privilege to have known many of the persons connected with the Code in its formative stages. They have influenced me in a variety of ways, and I owe a great deal to them; a few of those names cannot be left out. My respect for the Father of the Uniform Commercial Code, the late William A. Schnader of Philadelphia, is as great as I could accord to any man, for in addition to his enormous abilities and the endless energy he expended on behalf of the Code, he was very kind to me. To Walter D. Malcolm, of Boston, I owe a great deal, and my regard for him is unbounded. When he decided to retire as Chairman of the Uniform Commercial

PREFACE TO THE FIRST EDITION

Code Committee of the Corporation, Banking and Business Law Section of the American Bar Association, he recommended me to the Chairman of the Section as his successor. His faith meant a lot to me. In time and through fate, this opportunity to serve the bar led to the Chairmanship of the Section of Corporation, Banking and Business Law of the American Bar Association. I believe that a lawyer should serve his profession, and I am grateful for the opportunities that I have been given to serve. I count it a privilege to have served as Chairman of the Commercial Code Committees of the Chicago, Illinois State, and American Bar Associations.

Through more years than I sometimes wish to remember William B. Davenport of the Chicago Bar has been a friend of mine. We are still friends after doing three books together, and that says a good bit for his charity and kindness. Bill has been kind enough to read several chapters in this book, and I appreciate that along with many other things.

When Dean (now Judge) Charles W. Joiner called me in Chicago in 1970 to see if I would be interested in teaching law at Wayne State University, I did not hesitate very long. And I am glad I didn't. It has been my privilege to know some very fine students who are becoming excellent lawyers, and apparently year by year one meets yet more fine young people who in turn will become fine lawyers, just as each spring the earth renews itself. I am grateful for this opportunity. I hope that somehow, perhaps quite indirectly, I can impart to them the joy of law and the privilege that I have always felt that it is to be a lawyer.

Some of my students have helped me considerably with this book, and I gratefully acknowledge my debt to: John G. Cameron, Jr., Wayne '74; Joseph M. Malinowski, Wayne '72, now of the Los Angeles Bar; Richard U. Mosher and William M. Moss, Wayne '72, now of the Detroit Bar; and John E. Rennels, Wayne '74. But every line in this book came from my pen. It may be that some of the ideas are owed to others and are not appropriately acknowledged, but at least in my case this is inadvertent, if true. Sometimes it becomes difficult to determine just where an idea originated, and occasionally it may be justifiable, although ungracious, to fail to check every possible source in the interest of adding one more footnote. After a time there are rather few original ideas in the Code world, but then there are rather few original ideas anywhere.

Some of the material in this book originally appeared in somewhat different form in and is reprinted through the courtesy of the editors of: The Business Lawyer, Catholic University Law Review, Columbia

PREFACE TO THE FIRST EDITION

Law Review, Georgia Law Review, Law Notes of the American Bar Association's Young Lawyers Section, Marquette Law Review, New York University Law Review, Notre Dame Lawyer, University of Illinois Law Forum, University of Miami Law Review, and William and Mary Law Review.

While an ethical question might be raised about a member of the Article 9 Review Committee writing a book about Article 9, I have followed (very distantly) in the footsteps of an eminent scholar or two in producing such a work, and perhaps in legal circles a precedent stands until it is authoritatively overruled. In no case does anything in this book depend on inside information not available to anyone researching the subject.

Naturally I hope that this book will be useful to students, lawyers, and judges. It is an honest effort to do some hard thinking, often in dark places. But I have been around too long and have been too critical of too many books to have many illusions left. Anyway, as Holmes told us, "Certainty generally is illusion."

RAY D. HENSON

Detroit
June, 1973

*

SUMMARY OF CONTENTS

*

TABLE OF CONTENTS

TABLE OF CONTENTS

PART II. PERFECTION BY FILING

PART III. PERFECTION BY POSSESSION; TEMPORARY PERFECTION

PART IV. PERFECTION BY ATTACHMENT

TABLE OF CONTENTS

CHAPTER 5. PRIORITIES

CHAPTER 6. PROCEEDS

CHAPTER 7. RIGHTS OF LIEN CREDITORS, INCLUDING THE TRUSTEE IN BANKRUPTCY

TABLE OF CONTENTS

CHAPTER 8. FIXTURES

CHAPTER 9. MULTISTATE TRANSACTIONS

CHAPTER 10. DEFAULT

TABLE OF CONTENTS

CHAPER 11. A SIMPLE SECURITY AGREEMENT: FORM AND CONTENT

†

HANDBOOK

OF THE

LAW OF SECURED TRANSACTIONS

CHAPTER 1

A BRIEF HISTORY OF THE UNIFORM COMMERCIAL CODE

Table of Sections

§ 1–1. How the Code Started

It is, of course, true that the author of a history determines who figures in his writings. This does not mean that the literary work is accurate or more than one man's view, nor is this even important unless a number of people come to accept the particular version as true. Various people have written their own versions of how the Uniform Commercial Code began, and since some of these accounts omit the man who really was responsible for it all, a tribute to a great man is in order.

William A. Schnader of Philadelphia first proposed the idea of a Uniform Commercial Code in 1940, when he was President of the National Conference of Commissioners on Uniform State Laws, and the Commissioners were meeting in Philadelphia. To give General Schnader credit for this is only to pay him a portion of the honor he is due. The Commissioners approved the project, and, when it appeared to be more than they could take on, the American Law Institute joined. It appears to be the fact that only the possibility of fashioning a Uniform Commercial Code kept the Institute from dissolution during the troubled days of World War II. But the two organizations kept going and their joint effort is the most widely accepted and most influential work that either group has ever promulgated.

Some think of the young and the professors as visionaries. This is not accurate when applied to the field of commercial law. In this field it is quite generally the practitioners of experience who come up with the most "radical" ideas.

It took a man with the background and stature of General Schnader to suggest that Commercial Law was one subject and that it could be dealt with in one statute. This idea may be taken for granted today but it was new in 1940. In those days there were separate acts governing—and separate courses covering—Sales and, as it was then called in law school, Bills and Notes. (It should also be remembered that many state constitutions prohibit more than one subject being covered in one act.) Probably no school had a separate course in secured transactions in personal property; and documents of title, investment securities, and bank deposits and collections were generally unknown quantities to students, no matter how important they might be the minute after graduation. Students could spend hours worrying about whether odd language used in 1673 created a negotiable instrument or the rights of the "owner" of negotiable paper as against a thief, but the practicalities of bulk sales were untouched. A revolution in law and in outlook can be credited to General Schnader.

Not only was the idea of the Uniform Commercial Code due to General Schnader, the fact that the Code ever reached completion and became the law of 49 states, the District of Columbia, and the Virgin Islands was due primarily to his political sagacity and persistence. There was plenty of help from the practicing bar—the vital contribution of the Code Committee of the American Bar Association's Section of Corporation, Banking and Business Law under the Chairmanship of the great Boston lawyer, Walter D. Malcolm, deserves special praise—and the law professors did their part, but the one indispensable guiding spirit was William A. Schnader. No recipient of the American Bar Association's Medal ever did more to change and improve American law, and probably no one else could have done what he did.

The Chief Reporter for the Code through the years was that delightful gentleman and great academic authority on commercial law, the late Professor Karl N. Llewellyn. The Associate Chief Reporter was Professor Soia Mentschikoff. The Associate Reporters for Article 9 were Professor Grant Gilmore, who has written a witty, definitive treatise on Article 9, and Professor Allison Dunham, who appears to have abandoned commercial law in favor of real property law and whose insights are having great impact in a field where they are urgently needed.

The impetus toward a broad, all-encompassing Commercial Code arose because of a proposal in 1938 by the Merchants Association of New York City for a federal sales act to govern interstate sales.[1] The mere suggestion of such an act caused concern to the Commissioners on Uniform Laws, for they had sponsored the Uniform Sales Act in 1906 and this Act had apparently become dated. (Nor was the prospect of one law governing intrastate sales and another governing interstate sales generally interesting to the bar in those days). The Commissioners were also considering then a revision of the Uniform Negotiable Instruments Law, which was the first uniform law the Commissioners had sponsored and which dated from 1896. The NIL, as it was always called, no longer deserved to be called "uniform" for over 80 sections were no longer uniform among the states, because of local amendments or local judicial interpretations. The Commissioners had also sponsored other acts in the commercial law field, such as the Uniform Bills of Lading Act, the Uniform Warehouse Receipts Act, the Uniform Stock Transfer Act, the Uniform Trust Receipts Act, the Uniform Conditional Sales Act, and the Uniform Chattel Mortgage Act. Some of these acts were widely adopted, some were not, and the chattel mortgage act was not passed by any state.

The long and careful drafting of the Code began in 1942 and was primarily accomplished between 1945 and 1952. The story of this work and the many eminent judges, lawyers, and law professors associated with it is told in the Comment to the Title of the Code in the 1962 Official Text with Comments.[2]

The Code was first passed by Pennsylvania in 1953. This was an act of faith by the Pennsylvania legislature, and it is fair to say that their faith reflected confidence in the late General Schnader, the late Judge Herbert F. Goodrich of the United States Court of Appeals for the Third Circuit who was then also Director of the American Law Institute, and the many Pennsylvania lawyers who had given so much to the cause. Indeed, the devotion of so many lawyers from all

1. *See* Malcolm, The Uniform Commercial Code in the United States, 12 Int'l & Comp.L.Q. 226 (1963), in ABA, Uniform Commercial Code Handbook 1 (1964); *see generally* Schnader, Pennsylvania and the Uniform Commercial Code, 37 Temp.L.Q. 265 (1964); Schnader, A Short History of the Preparation and Enactment of the Uniform Commercial Code, 22 U.Miami L.Rev. 1 (1967).

2. *See also* Mentschikoff, The Uniform Commercial Code: An Experiment in Democracy in Drafting, 36 A.B.A.J. 419 (1950); Mentschikoff, Uniform Commercial Code—20 Years After, N.Y.S.Bar Assn., Proceedings of Annual Meeting, Section of Banking, Corp. & Bus.Law, Jan. 1972, p. 37.

over the country to the cause of the Code is without parallel in our legal history.

While Pennsylvania accepted the Code on faith, New York referred the Code to its Law Revision Commission. The Commission spent much time, effort, and money in a study of the Code and eventually suggested changes. During this period the Code's sponsors were also restudying the Code, and it was being given a thorough testing in the laboratory of Pennsylvania. Various changes were approved by the Sponsoring Organizations (i. e., the ALI and the Commissioners) which resulted in the 1958 Official Text, which Pennsylvania promptly enacted in place of the earlier version. The march was under way, and the ultimate result has been the enactment of the Code in every jurisdiction of the United States except Louisiana.

§ 1–2.   The Work of the Permanent Editorial Board

Today, more than ever before, it is of great importance that a commercial law be uniform. Amendments to take care of purely local problems may be accepted without creating national difficulty, but multitudinous local changes, often intended simply as a matter of language rather than substance, are a matter of intense national concern. Because so many states were making so many changes in the Code at the time it was enacted—few if any of which were really necessary as the example of Pennsylvania and other states with "pure" Codes testified—the Sponsoring Organizations created the Permanent Editorial Board for the Uniform Commercial Code in 1961. The Board's primary function was to bring about and to maintain uniformity in the Code and to that end the Board was authorized to approve amendments (1) if it was shown that a Code provision was unworkable or required amendment; (2) if court decisions had rendered the correct interpretation of a provision doubtful and an amendment could clear up the doubt; (3) if new commercial practices rendered existing provisions obsolete or made new provisions desirable; or (4), which is no longer significant, if amendments would lead to a wider enactment of the Code.

The Board's Report No. 1 was issued in 1962 and the amendments suggested by the Board resulted in the 1962 Official Text, which became the generally adopted version, subject to local changes. The Board appointed three subcommittees and in time issued three reports, approving some amendments and some optional sections but disapproving most of the local changes made by enacting states.

In Report No. 3, issued in 1966, the Board noted that 337 non-uniform amendments had been made to Article 9. While many amendments were trivial, 47 of the 54 sections in Article 9 had in fact been changed in the various states. Because of "this distressing situation," as the Board termed it, it was decided to appoint an Article 9 Review Committee to restudy Article 9 in depth. The Review Committee met many times over a period of four years. Two Preliminary Drafts were published for criticism. The Final Report was issued in 1971. While a great may changes are proposed in Article 9, the basic structure has been durable and is retained.[3] Professor (now Mr. Justice) Robert Braucher of Massachusetts served as Reporter and Professor Homer Kripke of New York served as Associate Reporter for this project. Two more able and dedicated men could not have been found. The members of the Article 9 Review Committee were: Professor Herbert Wechsler of New York City, Director of the American Law Institute, chairman; Joe C. Barrett, of Jonesboro, Arkansas; Carl W. Funk of Philadelphia; the Honorable John S. Hastings of Chicago, then Chief Judge of the United States Court of Appeals for the Seventh Circuit; Robert Haydock, Jr., of Boston; Ray D. Henson of Chicago (now of San Francisco); Harold Marsh, Jr., of Los Angeles; William Curtis Pierce of New York City; Professor Millard H. Ruud then of the University of Texas Law School; and the Honorable Sterry R. Waterman, Judge (now Senior Judge) of the United States Court of Appeals for the Second Circuit. Professor Grant Gilmore and Peter F. Coogan served as Consultants.

The Review Committee's Final Report was accepted by both Sponsoring Organizations with amendments, and the ultimate result is the 1972 Official Text.

3. *See* Braucher, Coogan, Davenport, Gilmore, and Kripke, A Look at the Work of the Article 9 Review Committee, 26 Bus.Law. 307 (1970).

CHAPTER 2

THE INTERPRETATION OF THE UNIFORM COMMERCIAL CODE

Table of Sections

§ 2–1. General Observations on the Interpretation of Statutes

No doubt there are certain canons of statutory construction which are being taught in law schools and which, when thought to be useful, are even mentioned by courts. But for various reasons, the proper interpretation of the Uniform Commercial Code may be approached as a somewhat new proposition to be examined. The matter of how to approach the theoretically proper solution to a problem is quite closely allied with what is in fact being done in this field, and the propriety of the "is" must be weighed against the balance of the "ought."

A re-examination of some standard jurisprudential guides to legal interpretation [1] reinforces a pre-existing belief that there are no guides of any genuine importance. Certain old maxims are still occasionally paraded in opinions,[2] but it is evident that they are simply thrown in as buttresses and have in no way been relied upon as significant aids to interpretation.

Part of the difficulty with canons of construction is an attempt to generalize them. As Mr. Justice Holmes was fond of pointing out, the

---

1. *See, e. g.,* E. Bodenheimer, Jurisprudence: The Philosophy and Method of the Law, 347–386, (1962); B. Cardozo, The Nature of the Judicial Process, (1921); W. Friedman, Legal Theory 401–464, (4th ed. 1960); J. Gray, The Nature and Sources of the Law, (2d ed. 1921); D. Lloyd, Introduction to Jurisprudence, 386–406 (1959); J. Salmond, Jurisprudence, 151–161, (11th ed., G. Williams ed. 1957). *See also* C. Fifoot, Judge and Jurist in the Reign of Queen Victoria, 129–133 (1959). Compare, J. Frank, Courts on Trial 292–309, (1949); L. Hand, The Spirit of Liberty 103–110 (1960); K. Llewellyn, The Bramble Bush, 70–91, (1951); K. Llewellyn, Jurisprudence: Realism in Theory and Practice, (1962); A. Ross, On Law and Justice, 75–169, (1959); E. Patterson, Jurisprudence: Men and Ideas of the Law 421–425, 559–594, (1953).

2. *See, e. g.,* "expressio unius est exclusio alterius" in Biddle v. State Beverage Dept., 187 So.2d 65, 67 (Fla. 1966); Steinfeld v. Jefferson County Fiscal Court, 312 Ky. 614, 616, 229 S.W.2d 319, 320 (Ct.App.1950); *Cf.* Dick v. Roberts, 8 Ill.2d 215, 218, 133 N.E.2d 305, 308 (1956); Galloway v. Truesdell, 83 Nev. 13, 422 P.2d 237, 246 (1967).

chief end of man may be to frame general propositions, but no general proposition is worth a damn.[3] Certain canons have a degree of validity in some cases but not in all. For example, looking for the "intent of the legislature" [4] is clearly appropriate in construing acts where the legislature had a very obvious reason for passing a bill, but it is absurd to think that any legislature had any intent whatsoever as to an obscure point covered by the Uniform Commercial Code. An enacting legislature clearly intended to pass the Code in the form in which it was enacted and, except where local variations were made, it meant for an act sponsored by the National Conference of Commissioners on Uniform State Laws and the American Law Institute to be interpreted as the act itself specified, with the aid of the Official Comments.[5]

3. *See, e. g.*, 1 Holmes—Pollock Letters 118; *id.* Vol. 2 at 13, 59 (Howe ed., 2d ed. 1961).

4. In determining whether section 10 of the Uniform Trust Receipts Act created a lien or a priority, a distinguished federal court stated: "The legislative interest is crystal clear." *In re* Crosstown Motors, Inc., 272 F.2d 224, 226 (7th Cir. 1959), *certiorari denied sub nom.* Commercial Credit Corp. v. Allen, 363 U.S. 811, 80 S.Ct. 1246, 4 L.Ed.2d 1152 (1960). (That is, the use of the "priority" foreclosed further thought.) Since the UTRA was, and was always conceded to be, exceedingly difficult to understand, it seems most probable that when the Illinois General Assembly passed that act in 1935 no thought at all was given to the question at issue. Indeed, the Illinois legislature would have been most prescient had it, in 1935, anticipated the famous 1938 amendments to the Bankruptcy Act which precipitated the Crosstown problem. It is very likely that most instances of judicial reliance on legislative intent are as inapposite as the reliance in Crosstown. According to Mr. Justice Holmes, "We do not inquire what the legislature meant; we ask only what the statute means." O. Holmes, The Theory of Legal Interpretation, Collected Legal Papers 203, 207 (1920).

5. The use of the term "Official Comments" may be questioned under the 1962 Code—the term is used in the 1972 Code—but it seems appropriate to describe those comments drafted by the Code's sponsors which appear with the Official Text of the Code, and it distinguishes them from the local comments which appear in the annotated statutes of the various Code states. But *see* Skilton, Some Comments on the Comments to the Uniform Commercial Code, 1966 Wis.L. Rev. 597. While the Official Comments are not entitled to the weight accorded to the officially enacted statute and the Comments are occasionally inaccurate, as the Definitional Cross References are sometimes incomplete, nevertheless the value of the comments is considerable. For example, the Comments to § 6–102 states what should be clear from the language of the statute "that among the enterprises not subject to Article 6— Bulk Transfers are "hotels, restaurants, and the like whose principal business is the sale not of merchandise but of services." In the face of this clear interpretation, it was decided in Pennsylvania that Article 6 applied to a bulk transfer of a restaurant and bar. Zinni v. One Townships Line Corp., 36 Pa.D. & C.2d 297, 53 Del.Co. 11, 3 UCCRep. 305 (1965). In a similar situation, a New York court refused to follow such a clearly erroneous interpretation of the Code. Kane-Miller Corp. v. Tip Tree Corp., 60 Misc.2d 776, 303 N.Y.S.2d 273 (1969). A new statute clearly deserves to be interpreted on its own terms.

Enactment was an act of faith: faith in the Code's sponsors and what they were trying to do.

Whether we choose to admit it or not, it is impossible to explain how we understand and interpret law. There is no dearth of explanations, but as serious efforts to understand mental processes, they can be little more than failures with occasionally stimulating but often limited appeal.[6]

If we are trained to believe that "statutes in derogation of the common law must be strictly construed," it may be difficult to realize that this is merely an enshrined remark which may have been pertinent in explaining one result once, but which has in fact no validity at all. It would be exceedingly undemocratic and even arrogant to think that this canon had any real basis; it is just the opposite of the proper judicial attitude. It is a cliché which is used as a substitute for thinking and no more than that.

Law without language is inconceivable, and statutes are of course written language. The important words carry a certain amount of freight with them, for we are accustomed to using certain words in certain ways. We respond to them more or less automatically. For that reason it was a step forward when, for instance, "conditional sale" and "chattel mortgage" were abandoned in favor of "secured trans-

---

6. This statement is believed to be true, and it is made after a number of personal ventures into the field. But the fact that a question cannot be answered in a scientific sense does not necessarily mean that such a question should not be asked. We can sometimes learn much by exploring the unknowable. However, it helps if we understand the problems involved in communication or else we may think that we are answering questions when they have no particular answers. These problems are not peculiar to law. In fact, lawyers have contributed very little of any importance to the understanding of "meaning," although the problem is of singular significance to law. Some books of general value are: J. Austin, Philosophical Papers (J. Urmson and G. Warnock eds. 1961); A. Ayer, Philosophy and Language (1960); P. Bridgman, The Logic of Modern Physics (1927); R. Brown, Words and Things (1958); R. Carnap, The Logical Syntax of Language (1937); W. John-son, People in Quandaries (1940); S. Hayakawa, Language in Thought and Action (1949); A. Korzybski, Science and Sanity (4th ed. 1958); S. Langer, An Introduction to Symbolic Logic (2d ed. 1953); A. Levi, Philosophy in the Modern World (1959); G. Moore, Some Main Problems of Philosophy (1953); C. Morris, Signs, Language and Behavior (1955); C. Ogden and I. Richards, The Meaning of Meaning (8th ed. 1946); W. Quine, From a Logical Point of View (1953); B. Russell, Human Knowledge: Its Scope and Limits (1948); G. Ryle, Dilemmas (1956); G. Ryle, The Concept of Mind, (1949); P. Strawson, Individuals (1959); H. Weinberg, Levels of Knowing and Existence (1959); A. Whitehead, Symbolism, Its Meaning and Effect (1927); L. Wittgenstein, Philosophical Investigations (Anscombe trans. 1953); L. Wittgenstein, Tractatus Logico-Philosophicus (1922). As may be obvious from the titles, these books explore different routes toward somewhat similar goals.

action." [7] New terms encourage fresh thinking, but there are limits beyond which even new terms become impractical. To encourage uniformity in interpretation, the defined terms in the Code must be carefully studied. Some circularity is unavoidable even in a dictionary and, of course, not every term is defined in the Code. A criticism frequently encountered is that certain concepts such as "commercially reasonable" are not defined; but the critics have apparently never tried to imagine a definition of such concepts, for they are undefinable except for giving selective examples of conduct which does or does not conform.[8] The law is full of such concepts: justice, due process, equitable, fair comment, valid. Such concepts, even though not definable in a significant sense, can ordinarily be applied in a factual context, and they then became meaningful.

But even words which are cogently defined are not significant in isolation. It is their use in a sentence, and ultimately in the broader act, that makes them meaningful. On the basis of knowledge and experience and fresh study brought to bear on a given statutory provision, we can see if it applies or how it applies in a given factual context.

When we interpret the Code, we must remember that it is not a constitution that we are expounding.[9] For obvious reasons, the

---

7. Article 9's abolition of the distinction between "title" and "lien" had to go to the Court of Appeals for the Second Circuit for a vindication. *See In re* Yale Express System, Inc., 370 F.2d 433 (2d Cir. 1966).

> We would indeed be myopic if we failed to recognize the revolution in commercial law that the Uniform Commercial Code has occasioned in the states. It would be incongruous for the federal courts, historically the leaders in the development of the law, to continue to employ anachronistic distinctions to determine whether a creditor is entitled to redeem property held by the trustee when the overwhelming number of states have succeeded in bringing their laws more into line with commercial reality.

Id. at 437 (Kaufman, J.).

8. *See* § 9–507(2) for examples of what is "commercially reasonable." Another undefined term is "new value," of which examples are given in § 9–108.

All section references not otherwise identified are to the 1962 Official Text of the Uniform Commercial Code.

9. Chief Justice Marshall's famous expression "[I]t is a constitution we are expounding," McCulloch v. Maryland, 4 Wheat. (17 U.S.) 316, 407 (1819), was often referred to by Mr. Justice Frankfurter. *See, e. g.,* Frankfurter, John Marshall and the Judicial Function, 69 Harv.L.Rev. 217, 218 (1955) in F. Frankfurter, Of Law and Men 3, 5 (1956); F. Frankfurter, with Phillips, Felix Frankfurter Reminisces 166 (1960); F. Frankfurter, Mr. Justice Holmes and the Supreme Court 28 (1938). No one since the great days of Mr. Justice Holmes has written as perceptively on statutory construction as Justice Frankfurter. *See* Frankfurter, Some Reflections on the Reading of Statutes, 47 Colum.L.Rev. 527 (1947). *See also* Friendly, Mr. Justice Frankfurter and the Reading of Statutes, in Felix Frankfurter: The Judge 30 (W. Mendelson ed. 1964).

English have been deeply concerned with statutory interpretation, while we have been principally preoccupied with constitutional interpretation. But if the problems are not the same, they are not totally dissimilar.

While it is difficult to change the Constitution by amendment, it is also difficult to secure uniform enactment of officially sponsored amendments to uniform legislation.[10] In fact, it seems to be impossibly difficult to secure the uniform enactment of a uniform act in the first place.[11]

§ 2–2. The Code's Provisions on Interpretation

The Code contains express provisions on its own interpretation. Section 1–102 provides:

(1) This Act shall be liberally construed and applied to promote its underlying purposes and policies.

(2) Underlying purposes and policies of this Act are

(a) to simplify, clarify and modernize the law governing commercial transactions;

(b) to permit the continued expansion of commercial practices through custom, usage and agreement of the parties;

(c) to make uniform the law among the various jurisdictions.

This command from the enacting legislature is entitled to complete acceptance, recognition and enforcement by every court.[12] The

---

10. Since no prior uniform acts were kept up-to-date by officially sponsored amendments, our experience is limited, but officially approved amendments to the Code have not been widely enacted.

11. As of November, 1966, there were 337 non-uniform amendments to various sections of art. 9; 47 of the 54 sections have been non-uniformly amended, some by as many as thirty states. This appalling situation contributed to the appointment of a special Review Committee to restudy Article 9 in depth. Permanent Editorial Board for the Uniform Commercial Code, Rep.No. 3 X–XI (1967). While we hope the experience will not be repeated, in times past uniform acts have been warped by divergent judicial interpretations as well as by unofficial amendments. Eighty sections of the NIL had different interpretations in different states as a result of conflicting court decisions. Malcolm, General Background, Concepts, and Coverage of the Uniform Commercial Code in The Illinois Uniform Commercial Code 4, 5 (1962).

12. See Hawkland, Uniform Commercial "Code" Methodology, 1962 U.Ill. L.F. 291. Compare Hicks, Uniformity of the Commercial Code, 8 B.C.Ind. & Com.L.Rev. 568 (1967). See also Hillman, Construction of the Uniform Commercial Code: UCC Section 1–103 and "Code" Methodology, 18 B.C.Ind. & Com.L.Rev. 655 (1977).

personal predilections of a particular judge are not properly part of the interpretative process.

It is the legislature's function to reflect the will of the people through enactments, and it is the courts' function to properly interpret and enforce what the legislature has enacted except where constitutional inhibitions prohibit such action.

Is there any reason why the Code should not "be liberally construed and applied to promote its underlying purposes and policies"? There is none. If the legislature so commands, the courts must obey. There is no excuse—certainly no reason—for doing anything else.

Commerce is moving faster than ever before. There is no reason why commercial law should lag behind. The Code achieved its object of simplifying, clarifying and modernizing the law as of the time of its promulgation, but the courts must assist in permitting "the continued expansion of commercial practices" in such fields as bank credit cards, which were unknown thirty years ago. The Code provides the basic mechanism for credit cards, but the parts were not geared to handle this product, although the agreements of the parties should be given a decent scope in which to operate within commercially reasonable limits.[13]

The purpose of making the law uniform can only be understood to mean: making the law uniformly correct within the aims and purposes of the Code's sponsors. It would be absurd to suggest that if the first decision on a particular point were clearly wrong, every later court should follow that holding in order to make the law's interpretation uniform. Insofar as the Code's provisions themselves are uniform throughout the country, as about half of them are,[14] it is understandable that some courts will differ as to interpretation; and it is somewhat misleading to suggest that a holding of the Orphan's Court of Allendale or a referee in Portland—or indeed any court other than the United States Supreme Court—determines the interpretation of a law for any broader area than the court's limited jurisdiction or, within limits, for parties other than those before the court in the case de-

---

13. *See* Davenport, Bank Credit Cards and the Uniform Commercial Code, 1 Val.U.L.Rev. 218 (1967).

14. As of November, 1966, there were about 750 non-uniform amendments among the 49 jurisdictions which had then enacted the Code. Of the Code's 399 sections, 195 had not been amended by any state and 76 sections were amended by only a single state. *See* Schnader, The Uniform Commercial Code—Today and Tomorrow, 22 Bus. Law. 229, 230–31 (1966). Of course, it must be remembered that many amendments to the Code are trivial (and inexcusable for that reason) and others were thought necessary to meet purely local problems.

cided. Courts change interpretations; even dissents sometimes become the law. A decision has precedential value for other jurisdictions only when it meets acceptable criteria of quality.

It is important to note a third provision of section 1–102:

(3) The effect of provisions of this Act may be varied by agreement, except as otherwise provided in this Act and except that the obligations of good faith, diligence, reasonableness and care prescribed by this Act may not be disclaimed by agreement but the parties may by agreement determine the standards by which the performance of such obligations is to be measured if such standards are not manifestly unreasonable.

And a fourth:

(4) The presence in certain provisions of this Act of the words "unless otherwise agreed" or words of similar import does not imply that the effect of other provisions may not be varied by agreement under subsection (3).

While these provisions insure judicial scrutiny of what the parties do—actually the parties' agreement is probably evidenced by contracts of adhesion in most cases—by imposing a standard of "manifestly unreasonable," there is room for some play in the joints. An over-reaching secured party cannot extract the last drop of the debtor's blood just by getting his signature on an agreement,[15] but the parties may agree on rather routine points, such as how many days' notice must be given after default under a security agreement and before a sale of the collateral.[16] The over-riding obligation of good faith has far more importance than has yet been recognized in the cases or perhaps in lawyers' briefs since courts normally seem to choose between arguments presented rather than searching for other and different grounds.

---

15. It was clearly improper for a referee in bankruptcy to transport the doctrine of unconscionability, as applied to sales transactions in § 2–302, into secured transactions not arising out of sales and governed by Article 9. See In re Dorset Steel Equipment Co., 2 UCC Rep.Serv. 1016 (E.D.Pa. 1965) and In re Elkins-Dell Manufacturing Co., 2 UCC Rep.Serv. 1021 (E.D.Pa.1965), both vacated and remanded, 253 F.Supp. 864 (E.D.Pa. 1966) (The district judge expressly declined to find § 2–302 applicable to agreements other than sales contracts. He did, however, recognize an independent doctrine of unconscionability which, on a proper factual determination, would be a legitimate reason for disallowing a claim in bankruptcy). See also American Home Improvement, Inc. v. MacIver, 105 N.H. 435, 201 A.2d 886 (1964).

16. See § 9–504(3).

It is to be hoped that the offer of the Permanent Editorial Board to provide, if requested, amicus briefs in cases at the appellate level will be accepted in those instances where the proper interpretation of the Code may be doubtful or a conflict of policy, as between the Code and the Bankruptcy Act, may be thought to exist.[17]   But what if a court requests an amicus brief and then does not accept the Board's view?[18]   The chances are that the court's interpretation of the Code will be erroneous and that other courts will not, like the Internal Revenue Service on occasion, "acquiesce."

While rarely acknowledged, much commercial law is purely a matter of private contact.   There is, indeed, remarkably little litigation in this area, and of the little litigation that there is, few cases are of transcendent importance to anyone except the litigants.   Disagreements among major lenders with millions of dollars at stake rarely proceed beyond negotiation and into the court house; these lenders are more interested in amicable solutions to problems than in finding out who is "right."   If a contract is clearly drafted and if it clearly covers the point at issue, litigation is almost unknown.   The primary function of a commercial lawyer is to give advice.

§ 2–3.   Litigation Under Article 9

The litigation under Article 9 has produced few examples of the outré except for a certain number of decisions coming out of the bankruptcy courts.   At the appellate level, most opinions reflect an awareness of the value of the Code, the work that went in to it, the contin-

17. As of November 1966, only two requests for briefs amici curiae had been received by the Board. *See* Dezendorf, How the Code's Permanent Editorial Board is Functioning, 22 Bus. Law. 227, 228 (1966).   Since that time *amicus* briefs have been filed in, e. g., In re Portland Newspaper Publishing Co., 271 F.Supp. 395 (D.C.Or.1967), and in the appeal, *sub nom.* DuBay v. Williams, 417 F.2d 1277 (9th Cir. 1969); and in Grain Merchants of Indiana, Inc. v. Union Bank & Savings Co., 408 F.2d 209 (7th Cir. 1969) certiorari denied 396 U.S. 827, 90 S.Ct. 75, 24 L.Ed. 2d 78; and in James Talcott, Inc. v. Franklin Nat. Bank, 292 Minn. 277, 194 N.W.2d 775 (1972).   Several courts have had the benefit of *amicus* briefs by the Commissioners on Uniform State Laws for the states involved. *See, e. g.*, National Cash Register Co. v. Firestone & Co., 346 Mass. 255, 256, 191 N.E.2d 471, 472 (1963); Norton v. National Bank of Commerce, 240 Ark. 143, 144, 398 S.W.2d 538, 539 (1966).

18. In a sense this happened in Norton v. National Bank of Commerce, 240 Ark. 143, 398 S.W.2d 538 (1966), where the Supreme Court of Arkansas requested an amicus brief from Joe C. Barrett, Esq., a Commissioner on Uniform State Laws from Arkansas, and Mr. Barrett was assisted by the Permanent Editorial Board in the preparation of his brief.   240 Ark. at 144, 398 S.W.2d at 539.   According to one commentator, "[I]t seems clear that this case should not be followed by the next court to consider the problem." Ambrosini, Debtor's Right to Notice Upon Disposition of Collateral, 8 B.C. Ind. & Com.L.Rev. 267, 272 (1967).

uing efforts of its sponsors to keep it up-to-date and uniform, and a genuine desire to interpret the Code as its sponsors think it should be interpreted.[19]

While the importance of bankruptcy courts as a testing ground for the Code's secured transactions can be overemphasized, it is nonetheless inescapably true that if a secured transaction is involved in a bankruptcy proceeding, the transaction must be enforced or the collateral is lost to the secured party. The overwhelming number of secured transactions will be retired in accordance with the contracts involved; if the situation were otherwise, our economy would collapse. But when a debtor goes into bankruptcy, if the secured party cannot enforce his right to the collateral, the terms of the agreement between the parties are then rewritten at the worst possible time, from the secured party's point of view. Where the secured party has made an improper filing, aside from situations where the error was mechanical, trivial, and not really misleading to third parties, then we need not be especially concerned with his fate.[20] If he has given proper notice to the world of his interest in the collateral and the transaction is then not enforced, our concern takes on another dimension.

What happens in fact in bankruptcy courts is of the highest importance to secured creditors. It is also impossible to determine in detail. We know isolated instances, but we do not know, we cannot know, how every case is handled. Indeed, such a mass of material would be unassimilable. The decisions are not officially reported, but enough Code cases are unofficially reported to give us an insight into how solutions are approached at this level. (No one could seri-

19. *See, e. g., In re* Yale Express Systems, Inc., 370 F.2d 433, 436 n. 2 (2d Cir. 1966) (Kaufman, J.); United States v. Wegematic Corp., 360 F.2d 674, 676 (2d Cir. 1966) (Friendly, J.); *In re* Excel Stores, Inc., 341 F.2d 961, 963 (2d Cir. 1965) (Medina, J.); Appeals of General Electric Co., 73 I.D. 95, 3 UCC Rep.Serv. 510 (U.S. Dept. of Int., Board of Contract Appeals, 1966); Appeal of Productions Unlimited, Inc., VACAB–541, 3 UCC Rep. Serv. 620 (Veterans Administration Contract Appeals Board, 1966). On the Code as a source of federal common law, see particularly United States v. Hext, 444 F.2d 804 (5th Cir. 1971). On the background of the Code, *see* Braucher, The Legislative History of the Uniform Commercial Code, 58 Colum.L.Rev. 798 (1958); Malcolm, The Uniform Commercial Code in the United States, 12 Int'l & Comp.L.Q. 226 (1963) in ABA, Uniform Commercial Code Handbook 1 (1964); Schnader, Pennsylvania and the Uniform Commercial Code, 37 Temp.L.Q. 265 (1964); Mentschikoff, Uniform Commercial Code—20 Years After, N.Y.S. Bar Assn., Proceedings of Annual Meeting, Section of Banking, Corp., & Bus.Law, Jan. 1972, p. 37.

20. There have been far too many cases involving obviously improper filings. *See, e. g., In re* Advertising Distributors of America, Inc., 2 UCC Rep. Serv. 548 (N.D.Ohio 1965) (in bankruptcy); *In re* Causer's Town & Country Super Market, Inc., 2 UCC Rep. Serv. 541 (N.D.Ohio 1965); In re Falkof, 2 UCC Rep.Serv. 731 (D.Mass. 1963).

ously recommend reporting all trial level decisions because, aside from unmanageable volume, reported opinions of trial courts are often perfunctory, not necessarily well reasoned, and of little or no precedential value when the courts are below the level of the federal district courts.)

On the basis of the opinions available for study, we know that some bankruptcy judges are sympathetic to the aims of the Code or that, in any event, they see it as their duty to enforce secured transactions properly handled in accordance with state law. We also know that a considerable number are not sympathetic to the Code or to secured credit in general, and that they will find some basis for setting aside almost any secured transaction that comes before them.[21] We cannot know how many secured transactions have been compromised in bankruptcy because so little was involved that the attorneys for the secured party have felt the only practical answer was to accept a percentage of the value of the collateral rather than spend the time and money required for a review to secure the proper result; that such compromises are, in a sense, forced on secured parties is not open to serious doubt, although the proposition cannot be proved by objective evidence.

It is not acceptable in these times for courts, any courts, to thwart the expressed purposes of a modern commercial law. The Uniform Commercial Code is too important to the economy of our country for judicial disagreement with its aims to be manifested in clearly wrong decisions. When the Code has been enacted by a legislature, it should be interpreted as the Code's sponsors intended, unless a legislature has made an amendment to achieve a different result, and we may hope that local amendments will be held to a minimum. The importance of uniform commercial law cannot be over-emphasized.

---

21. Readers of E. Berne, Games People Play (1964), might suggest that the game is called Kick the Code, or I'll Have the Last Word (Most of The Time) No Matter What You Think.

CHAPTER 3

THE SECURITY AGREEMENT

Table of Sections

§ 3–1. What Article 9 Covers

Unless the transaction is specifically excluded by Section 9–104, Article 9 applies, according to Section 9–102(1), to all consensual security interests in personal property and fixtures, and to sales of accounts, contract rights, and chattel paper. The reason for covering sales of certain kinds of collateral, as well as secured transactions involving those kinds of collateral, is that it is often difficult to determine whether a transaction is meant as a sale or as security, since both are likely to be phrased in terms of assignment, and the consequences are the same to third parties. Even between the parties to the agreement, sales and assignments for security are treated the same in Article 9 except for certain consequences on default.

In the 1972 Official Text the term "contract rights" has been dropped so that this kind of collateral will be either accounts or general intangibles.

The basic test for the application of Article 9 is whether the transaction is *intended* to create a security interest. In most instances it will be obvious if a secured transaction is intended, but occasionally it will not be clear, and in any event "security interest" is a defined term. Like all defined terms in the Code, its definition must be carefully examined.

16

The definition of "security interest" is broad enough to include certain transactions which the parties have labelled consignments or leases and which the parties may not have thought of as secured transactions, but which will be treated as such under the Code.[1]   On the other hand, when the payment of one obligation has been contractually subordinated to the payment of another, this subordination has been expressly declared not to create a security interest under Section 1–209, which was added to the Code as an optional provision in 1966.[2]

As expressed in Section 9–102(2):

> This Article applies to security interests created by contract including pledge, assignment, chattel mortgage, chattel trust, trust deed, factor's lien, equipment trust, conditional sale, trust receipt, other lien or title retention contract and lease or consignment intended as security. This Article does not apply to statutory liens except as provided in Section 9–310.

Statutory liens, which Article 9 does not cover except for the priority provision of Section 9–310, do not arise by reason of a contract between the parties creating them. They arise because a statute or a common law rule says that in certain circumstances a lien arises, as, for example, where a mechanic performs services on a motor vehicle and is given by statute a right to retain possession of the vehicle until paid for the work.

The various kinds of contractually created security interests to which Article 9 is said to apply are the pre-Code devices in use in the different states, although not all states recognized all of the listed varieties.

The pledge is as old as recorded history and is still in use, as the presence of pawnbrokers attests. In this transaction the debtor borrows money by physically transferring to a secured party the possession of the property to be used as security, and the property will be returned if the debt is repaid. Since the debtor does not retain the use of pledged goods, this security device has obvious disadvantages from the debtor's point of view. The pledge is still widely used, however, and it works satisfactorily in many cases, as, for example, where stock certificates are pledged with a bank as security for a loan.

In the typical chattel mortgage situation before the Code, an owner of chattels could borrow money by giving a security interest in the goods to the chattel mortgagee. The writing by which this was accomplished was called a chattel mortgage, and the interest created by the writing was also called a chattel mortgage, which led to some confusion. The mortgage was recorded in its entirety in the appropri-

---

1. *See* §§ 3–12 and 3–13 *infra.*   **2.** *See* § 5–20 *infra.*

ate public office. As in the case of a real estate mortgage, the mortgagor continued in possession of the mortgaged property, but public notice was given of the mortgagee's interest in the goods. Sometimes goods were acquired by giving the seller or a third party financer a chattel mortgage on the goods to secure the unpaid balance of the purchase price, and this amounted to the creation of what the Code calls a purchase money security interest.[3] It also meant that the debtor-mortgagor acquired title to the goods, and under pre-Code law the location of title often had important consequences.[4] Any purchase money chattel mortgage transaction could probably have been handled as a conditional sale in which the seller of the goods retained title to them until they were paid for, or the seller could transfer its interest to a financer who retained title until payment in full. Since the seller (or assignee) had "title," in years gone by it seemed only natural for the seller to repossess the goods on the buyer's default, and this attitude had important repercussions. The location of title is immaterial under Section 9–202. Aside from those few states which had enacted the Uniform Conditional Sales Act, no public recording was generally required in the United States to give notice to third parties that the buyer in possession did not have unencumbered ownership.

While the chattel mortgage and conditional sale may have functioned adequately in the realm of consumer financing, they were either not so suitable or even not allowable under the law of various states for some commercial financing. It might have been sensible to use these devices for the acquisition of furniture or machinery of a manufacturing corporation, for whatever goods of this kind the corporation acquired could have been suitably described in a writing which might have been recorded, but these devices could not work in their traditional ways when, for example, chocolate was being financed for a candy manufacturer, or refrigerators were being financed for a retailer who acquired them for sale to consumers.

Trust receipt financing developed at common law in the Eastern states to facilitate the importation of goods, and eventually this form of financing was recognized in the complicated Uniform Trust Receipts

---

3. § 9–107.

4. *See, e. g., In re* Lake's Laundry, Inc., 79 F.2d 326 (2d Cir. 1935), certiorari denied *sub nom.* Lake's Laundry v. Braun, 296 U.S. 622, 56 S.Ct. 144, 80 L.Ed. 442 (1935). As Judge Learned Hand remarked in his dissent in *Lake's Laundry,* "It seems to me a barren distinction, though indubitably true, that title does not pass upon a conditional sale; 'title' is a formal word for a purely conceptual notion; I do not know what it means and I question whether anybody does, except perhaps legal historians. The relations resulting from conditional sales are practically the same as those resulting from mortgages; I would treat them as the same when we are dealing with the reorganization of the debtor's property." 79 F.2d at 328–329.

Act promulated in 1933. Under the Act, three parties were required in a transaction. There had to be a seller of the goods, a financer who paid the seller for the goods and who was called an entruster, and a buyer of the goods, called a trustee, who received the goods under a trust receipt. Under this arrangement a manufacturer could not directly retain a security interest in goods supplied to a distributor or retailer, and this necessitated the existence of a third party financer, which might be a finance subsidiary of the seller created for this purpose.[5] The financer entrusted the goods to the buyer as trustee, and the buyer, who did not have title, in turn disposed of the goods and, in the usual case, accounted to the entruster for the agreed upon release amount. For example, an automobile dealer might receive in trust cars from the manufacturer which had been financed by a bank which entrusted them to the dealer as trustee on the understanding that when any car was sold the dealer would pay to the bank a specified amount for the bank to release that car from the trust. While the statutory system was complicated, the form of financing served an important purpose in its day, and a number of provisions in Article 9 have their genesis in the Uniform Trust Receipts Act.

There was no uniform act covering factor's liens, but, following the lead of New York, many states adopted such statutes in the years after 1911. There was much diversity among the various factors' lien acts,[6] but in general the acts facilitated financing a manufacturer's work in process and resulting inventory.

While accounts receivable financing has long been of great importance in our economy, no uniform act covered this field before the Code. When goods are sold on credit, various problems arise. The seller may need cash sooner than the buyer is obligated to pay; a dishonest seller might assign the right to payment to several financers. Or a buyer might become insolvent before payment was made. Who bore the risk of loss? In the form of financing called "factoring," the purchaser of the account ordinarily assumed the credit risk without recourse against the seller, and the buyers were notified to pay the financer, so that this was called "notification" financing. In nonnotification financing, the accounts were assigned as security for a loan; the seller remained liable to pay the financer; the credit risk remained with the seller if its purchasers did not pay, and these purchasers were not informed of the assignment.[7] Under the Code this

---

5. *See, e. g., In re* United Thrift Stores, Inc., 363 F.2d 11 (3d Cir. 1966).

6. For interpretative decisions, *see, e. g.,* Manchester Nat'l Bank v. Roche, 186 F.2d 827 (1st Cir. 1951); *In re* Comet Textile Co., 15 F.Supp. 963 (S. D.N.Y.1936), affirmed 91 F.2d 1008 (2d Cir. 1937); Colbath v. Mechanicks Nat'l Bank, 96 N.H. 110, 70 A.2d 608 (1950).

7. *See generally* Greenberg, Inventory and Accounts Receivable Financing, 1956 U.Ill.L.F. 601.

kind of collateral is called "accounts" [8] but the definition is narrower than the usual view of accounts receivable, so that it is essential to check the Code definitions and use the Code terminology correctly. Moreover, the Code covers both security interests in accounts assigned as security and sales of those accounts to an assignee, and this dual coverage is expressed in the title of Article 9 and in Section 9–102(1) (b).

In Section 9–102(3) there is a rather confusing provision which states:

> The application of this Article to a security interest in a secured obligation is not affected by the fact that the obligation is itself secured by a transaction or interest to which this Article does not apply.

The most obvious application of this provision is in a situation where a mortgagee of real estate in turn borrows money and pledges the mortgage note for security. Article 9 has nothing to do with the mortgage itself, nor would it govern a sale of the note, but it does cover a security interest in the pledged note, which is an instrument in Article 9 terminology. Before Comment 4 to Section 9–102 was amended in 1962, it contained an erroneous suggestion that Article 9 also governed a pledge of the mortgage. The Comments in the Official Text with Comments editions of the Code should always be cautiously read because they are not officially enacted in any state, and they may contain occasional lapses. But the fact that inaccuracies have been written by experts should suggest to those working with the Code that it may often be difficult to understand and interpret.

§ 3–2. Excluded Transactions

Transactions excluded by § 9–104 are set forth below as they appear in the 1972 Official Text with deletions in brackets and new language italicized:

This Article does not apply

(a) to a security interest subject to any statute of the United States [such as the Ship Mortgage Act, 1920,] to the extent that such statute governs the rights of parties to and third parties affected by transactions in particular types of property; or

(b) to a landlord's lien; or

8. § 9–106.

(c) to a lien given by statute or other rule of law for services or materials except as provided in Section 9–310 on priority of such liens; or

(d) to a transfer of a claim for wages, salary or other compensation of an employee; or

[(e) to an equipment trust covering railway rolling stock; or]

(e) to a transfer by a government or governmental subdivision or agency; or

(f) to a sale of accounts [, contract rights] or chattel paper as part of a sale of the business out of which they arose, or an assignment of accounts [, contract rights] or chattel paper which is for the purpose of collection only, or a transfer of a [contract] right *to payment under a contract* to an assignee who is also to do the performance under the contract *or a transfer of a single account to an assignee in whole or partial satisfaction of a preexisting indebtedness;* or

(g) to a transfer of an interest in or claim in or under any policy of insurance, *except as provided with respect to proceeds (Section 9–306) and priorities in proceeds (Section 9–312);* or

(h) to a right represented by a judgment *(other than a judgment taken on a right to payment which was collateral)*; or

(i) to any right of set-off; or

(j) except to the extent that provision is made for fixtures in Section 9–313, to the creation or transfer of an interest in or lien on real estate, including a lease or rents thereunder; or

(k) to a transfer in whole or in part of [any of the following:] any claim arising out of tort; [any deposit, savings, passbook or like account maintained with a bank, savings and loan association, credit union or like organization.]; or

(l) *to a transfer of an interest in any deposit account (subsection (1) of Section 9–105), except as provided with respect to proceeds (Section 9–306) and priorities in proceeds (Section 9–312).*

The reason for most of these exclusions is obvious: they do not involve consensual security in a commercial setting. There are, however, a number of federal statutes operating in the field, and to the extent that they regulate the transaction, they preempt the Code; to the extent that they do not regulate the transaction, the Code applies. Some of the federal acts basically go no further than providing a place of filing.

The Federal Aviation Act [9] may have preempted the field of recordation of interests in aircraft, but in the absence of a broader federal act, the validity of the underlying transaction and the resolution of certain priorities among conflicting interests are governed by the Code.[10]

The Ship Mortgage Act of 1920 [11] covers the formal requirements of preferred ship mortgages and the means for giving public notice of their existence by recording the mortgage with the collector of customs of the port of documentation and by indorsing the mortgage on the vessel's documents.[12] The preferred status follows from compliance with the Act's requirements if the mortgage covers "any vessel of the United States (other than a towboat, barge, scow, lighter, car float, canal boat, or tank vessel, of less than twenty-five gross tons)." [13] Vessels of the United States are "vessels registered pursuant to law . . . ." [14] and this requires that the vessels be built in this country and owned by a United States citizen.[15] Where the mortgage does not come under the federal act, either because of a technical failure of compliance with the terms of the act or because of the vessel's size or for any other reason, then resort may be had to state law.[16] Construction financing of ships is accommodated by the Code; [17]

9. 49 U.S.C.A. § 1403 et seq. With this act, compare the Federal Motor Vehicle Lien Act, 49 U.S.C.A. § 313 (1970). See generally Sigman, The Wild Blue Yonder: Interests in Aircraft Under Our Federal System, 46 So.Cal.L.Rev. 316 (1973).

10. Feldman v. Philadelphia Nat'l Bank, 408 F.Supp. 24 (E.D.Pa.1976); Feldman v. Chase Manhattan Bank, N.A., 368 F.Supp. 1327 (S.D.N.Y.1974), reversed on other grounds 511 F.2d 468 (2d Cir. 1975); American Aviation, Inc. v. Aviation Ins. Managers, Inc., 244 Ark. 829, 427 S.W.2d 544 (1968); International Atlas Services, Inc. v. Twentieth Century Aircraft Co., 251 Cal.App.2d 434, 59 Cal.Rptr. 495 (1967), certiorari denied 389 U.S. 1038 (1968); Southern Jersey Airways, Inc. v. National Bank of Secaucus, 108 N.J.Super 369, 261 A.2d 399 (1970); Idabel Nat'l Bank v. Tucker, 544 P.2d 1287 (Okl.App.1975).

11. 41 Stat. 1000–1008 (1920), 46 U.S.C. A. §§ 911–961. The specific reference to

this act has been deleted in Revised § 9–104(a).

12. 46 U.S.C.A. §§ 921, 922.

13. 46 U.S.C.A. § 922.

14. 46 U.S.C.A. § 221.

15. R. C. Craig Ltd. v. Ships of Sea Inc., 345 F.Supp. 1066 (S.D.Ga.1972).

16. See generally Gilmore and Black, The Law of Admiralty 718–727 (2d ed. 1975); James Stewart & Co. v. Rivara, 274 U.S. 614, 47 S.Ct. 718, 71 L.Ed. 1234 (1927); McCorkle v. First Pennsylvania Banking & Trust Co., 459 F. 2d 243 (4th Cir. 1972); North American Continental Co. v. The El Cuis, 107 F.Supp. 436 (E.D.N.Y.1952); Security Bank of Oregon v. Levens, 480 P.2d 706 (Or.1971).

17. Traditionally ship construction financing where a security interest is

and where there is an assignment of payments earned or to be earned under a charter for the use or hire of a vessel, those rights to payment will be contract rights under the 1962 Code or accounts under the 1972 Code,[18] and the Code applies to both assignments for security and sales of such collateral.[19]

Where a federal statute provides for national registration or filing of security interests, compliance with that act is necessary for perfection under the Code.[20]　However, most federal legislation in this area is a bit sketchy,[21] and a reference to state law would seem to be necessary in order to resolve the inherent problems arising from secured transactions covering such property.

It is possible that a security interest in a tenant's goods may be granted to a landlord in the lease,[22] in which case filing would be required to perfect the security interest of the lessor created by the contract.[23]　However, in the usual situation where a landlord is asserting an interest in a tenant's goods, the interest claimed will be a non-contractual landlord's lien, and this interest is excluded from Article 9 by Section 9–104(b), which appears to refer to both common law and statutory landlord's liens, since such a lien, if statutory, would be excluded in any case by Section 9–102(2).　In the event of a conflict between the holder of a security interest and a landlord asserting a landlord's lien, the priority is not resolved by Section 9–310 and apparently a reference to non-Code law would be necessary.[24]

---

involved has been accomplished by means of a chattel mortgage (a security interest in Code terminology). *See* Rodgers, Ship Construction Financing —Particularly Legal Problems Relating to Security Under American Law, 12 Bus.Law. 142 (1957). *See also* Simpson, Ship Financing—A Panel Discussion, 13 Bus.Law. 145 (1958); Pidot, Private Financing of Ship Construction with Government Insurance, 12 Bus.Law. 157 (1957); Jackson, Financing Marine Equipment Under Title XI: New Developments and Procedures, 28 Bus.Law. 1197 (1973).

18. § 9–106, Revised § 9–106.

19. § 9–102(1), Revised § 9–102(1).

20. § 9–302(3)(a), Revised § 9–302(3)(a); § 9–302(4), Revised § 9–302(4).

21. As to patents, see § 35 U.S.C.A. § 261; as to copyrights under the former act, see 17 U.S.C.A. §§ 28, 30, and under the act effective as of January 1, 1978, see 17 U.S.C.A. § 205.

22. *See, e. g.*, Goldie v. Bauchet Properties, 15 Cal.3d 307, 124 Cal.Rptr. 161, 164, 540 P.2d 1, n. 2 (1975); Dunham's Music House, Inc. v. Asheville Theatres, Inc., 10 N.C.App. 242, 178 S.E 2d 124 (1970).

23. *In re* King Furniture City, Inc., 240 F.Supp. 453 (E.D.Ark.1965). In the absence of proper Code filing, a trustee in bankruptcy of the lessee would have priority over the lessor under § 9–301(1)(b) and Bankruptcy Act, § 70c. *In re* Leckie Freeburn Coal Co., 405 F.2d 1043 (6th Cir. 1969).

24. In Harney v. Spellman, 113 Ill.App. 2d 463, 251 N.E.2d 265 (1969), the property was consumer goods, and the contest was between a purchase money secured party and a landlord claiming the goods under the Landlord-Tenant Act, Ill.Rev.Stat.1967 Ch. 80, § 16. The landlord was given priority on the ground that the security interest was

Section 9–310 resolves the conflict between the holder of a security interest in goods and a person who is in possession of goods and who has furnished services or materials in the ordinary course of business with respect to the goods—i. e., an artisan's or mechanic's lien, in general terms—by giving priority to the person in possession who has provided the materials or services, unless the lien is created by statute and the statute provides priority for the secured party.[25] The provision in Section 9–104(c) excludes from Article 9's coverage any other aspect of these liens, whether they are common law or statutory. While the excluded liens are those "arising from work intended to enhance or preserve the value of the collateral," [26] which should exclude such liens as landlord's liens,[27] there may be some gray area here where inclusion or exclusion is less than crystal clear.[28]

The exclusion of transfers of claims "for wages, salary, or other compensation of an employee" [29] refers generally to wage assignments executed by employees in connection with loans, and an independent contractor is not an employee for purposes of this exclusion.[30] Wage assignments are generally regulated by statute and may be entirely forbidden.[31]

The 1962 Code excluded equipment trusts covering railway rolling stock but this exclusion was deleted in the 1972 Code. The only reason for the original exemption of equipment trusts was pressure from some railroad interests. In substance, rather than form, equipment trusts are substantially similar to conditional sales of rolling stock, which have always been covered by the Code, and in all cases filing is

---

not perfected and therefore subordinate to the landlord's lien. The court's holding may have been correct on the basis of non-Code law, but the court did not realize that a purchase money security interest in consumer goods of the kind involved was perfected without the necessity of filing under § 9–302(1)(d). *See also* Universal C.I.T. Credit Corp. v. Congressional Motors, Inc., 246 Md. 380, 228 A.2d 463 (1967); *In re* Einhorn Bros. Inc., 171 F.Supp. 655 (D.C.E.D.Pa.1959), affirmed 272 F.2d 434 (3d Cir. 1959); Firestone Tire & Rubber Co. v. Dutton, 205 Pa.Super. 4, 205 A.2d 656 (1964); Beneficial Finance Co. of Amarillo v. Van Shaw, 476 S.W.2d 772 (Tex.Civ.App.1972); Associates Financial Services of Texas, Inc. v. Solomon, 523 S.W.2d 722 (Tex.Civ.App.1975). *Cf.* United States (Treasury Dept. I.R.S.) v. Globe Corp., 113 Ariz. 44, 546 P.2d 11 (1976).

25. Municipal Equipment Co. v. Butch & Son Deep Rock, 185 N.W.2d 756 (Iowa, 1971). *Cf.* Fruehauf Corp. v. Huntington Moving & Storage Co., —— W.Va. ——, 217 S.E.2d 907 (1975).

26. Official Comment, § 9–310.

27. *Compare* Bank of North America v. Kruger, 551 S.W.2d 63 (Tex.Civ.App. 1977) with *In re* Einhorn Bros., Inc., 171 F.Supp. 655 (D.C.E.D.Pa.1959), affirmed 272 F.2d 434 (3d Cir. 1959).

28. *See* Hasid Jobbing House, Ltd. v. Stolzar, 8 U.C.C.Rep.Serv. 234 (N.Y. Sup.Ct.1970) (attorney's retaining lien).

29. § 9–104(d).

30. Massachusetts Mut. Life Ins. Co. v. Central Penn. Nat'l Bank, 372 F.Supp. 1027 (E.D.Pa.1974).

31. *See, e. g.*, Cal.Civ.Code, § 2983.7.

presumably required by Section 20(c) of the Interstate Commerce Act.[32]

In place of the deleted exclusion of equipment trusts of railway rolling stock in the 1972 Code, there has been inserted an exclusion for transfers by a government or governmental subdivision or agency. This will eliminate the application of Article 9 to transactions where governmental agencies borrow money and grant security interests in, for example, sewer, electricity, or water charges as collateral.

While Article 9 does not by its terms apply to sales of general intangibles, it does apply to sales of accounts and chattel paper and, in the 1962 Code but not in the 1972 Code, to sales of contract rights. (The term "contract rights" has been eliminated in the 1972 Code.) Where sales of accounts or chattel paper (or contract rights under the 1962 Code) are made as part of a sale of the business from which this collateral arose, this transfer is excluded from Article 9.[33] Similarly assignments for the purposes of collection only are excluded.[34] Under the 1962 Code a transfer of a contract right to a person who is to perform the contract is excluded,[35] but under the 1972 Code, reflecting the elimination of "contract rights" as a kind of collateral, transfers of rights to payment under a contract are excluded where the assignee is to perform the contract, and transfers of a single account in whole or partial satisfaction of a preexisting debt are excluded.[36] The exclusions are intended to be of transfers which do not involve ordinary commercial financing transactions.[37]

Insurance policies can, in a sense, serve as collateral, by assigning an interest in a matured or unmatured policy—that is, by assigning a claim to insurance proceeds which have become payable but which

32. 49 U.S.C.A. § 20c.

33. *Cf.* Dynair Electronics, Inc. v. Video Cable, Inc., 55 Cal.App.3d 11, 127 Cal. Rptr. 268 (1976).

34. United States v. Mercury Motor Express, Inc., 294 F.Supp. 919 (S.D.Ga. 1968); Feldman v. Philadelphia Nat'l Bank, 408 F.Supp. 24 (E.D.Pa.1976).

35. American East India Corp. v. Ideal Shoe Co., 400 F.Supp. 141 (E.D.Pa. 1975).

36. This statutory result was reached under the 1962 Code in Lyon v. Ty-Wood Corp., 212 Pa.Super. 69, 239 A. 2d 819 (1968) principally on the basis that the assignment of an account by a debtor to a creditor was not *intend-*

ed as security, and Article 9 applies to transactions which are intended to create security, under § 9–102(1)(a), rather than assignments in satisfaction of debts. *See also* Spurlin v. Sloan, 368 S.W.2d 314 (Ky.Ct.App. 1963). Both opinions are subject to the criticism under the 1962 Code that Article 9 applies to sales of accounts, as well as to security interests in accounts created by assignment, and the opinions do not seem to be cognizant of this. *See also* Consolidated Film Industries v. United States, 403 F. Supp. 1279 (D.Utah 1975), reversed 547 F.2d 533 (1977).

37. Official Comment 6 to § 9–104; Bramble Transportation, Inc. v. Sam Senter Sales, Inc., 294 A.2d 97 (Del. Super.1971).

have not been paid or by changing a beneficiary to transfer a potential interest to a creditor, as might be done in the case of life insurance. As has been pointed out, ". . . this exclusion applies only to situations where the parties to a security agreement attempt to create a direct security interest in an insurance policy by making the policy itself the immediate collateral securing the transaction." [38] Insurance companies maintain records in which these transfers can be recorded, and apparently such a system works satisfactorily. Where several creditors have been assigned interests in insurance policies, peculiar problems may arise when the creditors, or some of them, have not been named loss payees or a notice of their interest may or may not be properly given to the insurance company. The result in *National Bedding & Furniture Industries, Inc.* v. *Clark* [39] can be explained on the basis that the secured party's interest in the destroyed collateral was transferred to the insurance proceeds, even without the secured party's having been named loss payee on the policy in accordance with the requirements of the security agreement, and thus was entitled to priority over some judgment creditors who had received an assignment of the policy proceeds after the collateral was destroyed. This result would be clear under Revised Section 9–306(1); the rationale in the opinion for the result reached is not expressed in the terms suggested. As some additional language in Revised Section 9–104(g) makes clear, when the insurance is casualty insurance covering primary collateral and the collateral is destroyed, the provisions of Section 9–306 on proceeds and Section 9–312 on priorities are applicable.

While judgment creditors sometimes assign interests in the judgments for various reasons, this is not an ordinary form of commercial collateral, and such assignments are excluded from Article 9 except where, under the 1972 Code, the judgment is based on a right to payment which was collateral. (The exception would cover a situation where an account has been assigned as collateral and the assignee-secured party has sued the account debtor on the account and recovered judgment.) Since Article 9 does not apply to a right represented by a judgment, the effectiveness of the assignment of a judgment and the time when it becomes perfected will be governed by the non-Code law of the state.[40]

The right of set-off is excluded from Article 9 by Section 9–104(i). The most common right of set-off, perhaps, is the right exercised by a bank against its depositor when the depositor has borrowed from the

---

38. PPG Industries, Inc. v. Hartford Fire Ins. Co., 531 F.2d 58, 60 (2d Cir. 1976). Cf. *In re* Thrasher, 21 UCC Rep.Serv. 1420 (E.D.Tenn.1977) (in bankruptcy).

39. 252 Ark. 780, 481 S.W.2d 690 (1972). *See* § 6–8 *infra*.

40. *In re* Law Research Service, Inc. v. Martin Lutz App. Print. Inc., 498 F.2d 836 (2d Cir. 1974).

bank and has, in time of need, funds on deposit which the bank can use to apply toward the debt. Banks have occasionally run into difficulty in enforcing this right of set-off as against deposits in which a third party claims a perfected security interest as proceeds.[41] Whether a right of set-off exists depends on the non-Code law of the state,[42] but the right is old in our law and it is recognized by the Bankruptcy Act.[43] The right of set-off exists in more contexts than that of the bank-customer relationship,[44] of course, and it does not depend on the existence of a security interest.[45]

Since Article 9 basically covers only security interests in personal property and fixtures,[46] Section 9–104(j) perhaps unnecessarily but certainly specifically excludes interests in or liens on real estate including leases and rents arising under leases. When rents under leases are assigned to financers, as probably will be done in connection with mortgages of income-producing real estate, compliance with applicable state non-Code law is necessary for the protection of the assignee, but a Code filing is meaningless.[47] Rental income under real property leases is not a kind of collateral recognized under Article 9, and it certainly is not an "account" which must arise from the sale or lease of goods or the rendition of services.[48] Where a note secured by a real property mortgage is pledged for security, the Code applies to the pledge of the note but does not apply to the mortgage.[49] In states,

41. See, e. g., Brown & Williamson Tobacco Corp. v. First Nat'l Bank of Blue Island, 504 F.2d 998 (7th Cir. 1974); First Nat'l Bank in Grand Prairie v. Lone Star Life Ins. Co., 524 S.W.2d 525 (Tex.Civ.App.1975). See also First Wisconsin Nat'l Bank v. Midland Nat'l Bank, 76 Wis.2d 662, 251 N.W.2d 829 (1977) (involving a certificate of deposit which had been pledged).

42. Morrison Steel Co. v. Gurtman, 113 N.J.Super. 474, 274 A.2d 306 (1971).

43. Bankruptcy Act, § 68a, 11 U.S.C.A. § 108a.

44. See, e. g., City of Vermillion, S. D. v. Stan Houston Equipment Co., 341 F.Supp. 707 (D.S.D.1972).

45. Associates Discount Corp. v. Fidelity Union Trust Co., 111 N.J.Super. 353, 268 A.2d 330 (1970).

46. § 9–102(1)(a).

47. In re Bristol Associates, Inc., 505 F.2d 1056 (3d Cir. 1974). In this excellent opinion Judge Adams reviews thoroughly the background and solution of this problem. See also Marcelletti & Son Constr. Co., Inc. v. Mill-Creek Township Sewer Authority, 313 F.Supp. 920 (W.D.Pa.1970).

48. § 9–106. But see United States v. PS Hotel Corp., 404 F.Supp. 1188 (E. D.Mo.1975), affirmed 527 F.2d 500 (8th Cir. 1975) where it was said that an assignee of "accounts receivable" arising from a motel operation who had perfected under the Code was entitled to priority over a real estate claimant whose rights arose under an assignment in a lease. If the "accounts receivable" arose from motel room rentals, the collateral would not be "accounts" as that term is defined in § 9–106, and the decision would appear to be wrong on that point, but the source of the "accounts receivable" is unclear.

49. § 9–102(3). See Commerce Union Bank v. May, 503 S.W.2d 112 (Tenn. 1973); Riebe v. Budget Financial Corp., 264 Cal.App.2d 576, 70 Cal. Rptr. 654 (1968).

such as Illinois, where the beneficiary's interest under a land trust is considered to be personal property, if the beneficiary creates a security interest in the beneficial interest, this will be a general intangible under the 1962 Code and subject to the perfection rules of Article 9,[50] but this transfer will be perfected without filing under Revised Section 9–302(1)(c).

Clause (k) of Section 9–104 of the 1962 Code and clauses (k) and (*l*) of the 1972 Code exempt transfers of tort claims and of interests in deposit accounts (except for application of the proceeds provisions of Section 9–306 and the priorities rules of Section 9–312). There has been virtually no litigation as to the tort claim exemption.[51] There has been some litigation over the deposit account exemption. Under the 1962 Code the exemption applied to a transfer of a "deposit, savings, passbook or like account maintained with a bank, savings and loan association, credit union or like organization."[52] This has been changed in the revised version by using the newly defined term "deposit account" for the exclusion,[53] and the definition of the term excepts accounts evidenced by certificates of deposit.[54] The newly enunciated exception was implicit in the earlier provision, and a certificate of deposit is an instrument[55] which is subject to the rules of Article 9.[56] If a transaction comes within the exception, the effect of the transfer must be determined by non-Code law.[57] Where proceeds of collateral are deposited in a bank account, a secured party having a perfected security interest in proceeds should be able, in appropriate circumstances, to follow its interest into the debtor's bank account, and this is not excluded by Section 9–104.[58]

50. Levine v. Pascal, 94 Ill.App.2d 43, 236 N.E.2d 425 (1968).

51. In *In re* Ore Cargo, Inc., 544 F.2d 80 (2d Cir. 1976) the court said that § 9–104(k) specifically excluded tort claims, and that such a claim, which was not known to the secured party when the security agreement was made, was not covered by a standard security agreement. *See also* Arkwright Mut. Ins. Co. v. Bargain City, U.S.A., Inc., 373 F.2d 701, 704 (3d Cir. 1967) certiorari denied 389 U.S. 825 (1967) where in footnote 9 the court said that the assignment of a tort claim against the United States, arising out of an airplane accident, was excluded from Article 9 by § 9–104 (k); and Grise v. White, 355 Mass. 698, 247 N.E.2d 385 (1969), where the court did not decide whether the transfer was excluded by § 9–104.

52. § 9–104(k).

53. Revised § 9–104(*l*).

54. Revised § 9–105(1)(e).

55. § 9–105(1)(g), Revised § 9–105(1)(i).

56. Southview Corp. v. Kleberg First Nat'l Bank, 512 S.W.2d 817 (Tex.Civ. App.1974).

57. Walton v. Piqua State Bank, 204 Kan. 741, 466 P.2d 316 (1970).

58. Domain Industries, Inc. v. First Security Bank & Trust Co. 230 N.W. 2d 165 (Iowa 1975); Commercial Discount Corp. v. Milwaukee Western Bank, 61 Wis.2d 671, 214 N.W.2d 33 (1974); *In re* JCM Cooperative, Inc., 8 UCC Rep.Serv. 247 (W.D.Mich.1970) (in bankruptcy).

Many states have broadened some exclusions and added others. The effect of these changes is sometimes clear and sometimes conjectural.

§ 3–3. "Debtor"

The term "debtor" as defined in Section 9–105(1)(d) normally means "the person who owes payment or other performance of the obligation secured." There are occasions when the collateral is owned by a third party who is willing to make it available as security or where the property has been transferred to a person who has not assumed the debt, and in such cases "debtor" may include the owner of the collateral as well as the person who is obligated on the debt or performance. Section 9–112 deals specifically with the rights of the owner of collateral who is not the "debtor," where this fact is known to the secured party, and the rights of the owner are particularly important on default. The term "debtor" means the owner of the collateral in a provision dealing with the collateral, or the obligor in a provision dealing with the obligation, or both if the context requires a dual application. If the transaction is subject to Article 9, the term also includes the seller of accounts, contract rights, and chattel paper, but the term "contract rights" has been eliminated in Revised Article 9.

In the ordinary secured transaction it will be obvious who the debtor is. But there are occasionally some situations where this is not so clear. Section 9–504(3) requires notice to the "debtor" in certain circumstances before the secured party can proceed to dispose of the collateral after default. Where the secured party repossessed the collateral immediately prior to the debtor's bankruptcy, notice to the debtor-bankrupt, sent after the bankruptcy petition was filed, has been held to be sufficient,[59] but notice to the debtor-bankrupt, rather than to the trustee, has been held to be inadequate where the repossession occurred after the bankruptcy petition was filed.[60] As the date of the filing in bankruptcy, the trustee became vested with the bankrupt's title to the property,[61] and the secured party was aware of the filing. Accommodation indorsers of a secured note have been held to be debtors entitled to notice of a proposed disposition after default.[62]

---

59. *In re* Senters, 9 UCC Rep.Serv. 922 (S.D. Ohio 1970) (in bankruptcy).

60. *In re* Frye, 9 UCC Rep.Serv. 913 (S.D.Ohio 1970) (in bankruptcy). *See also In re* Hughes, 12 UCC Rep.Serv. 982 (D.C.E.D.Tenn.1973) (in bankruptcy).

61. Bankruptcy Act, § 70a, 11 U.S.C.A. § 110a.

62. T & W Ice Cream, Inc. v. Carriage Barn, Inc. v. Terwilleger, 107 N.J.Super. 328, 258 A.2d 162 (1969). *See generally* § 10–11 *infra*.

In *Norton* v. *National Bank of Commerce of Pine Bluff*[63] a consumer bought an automobile from a car dealer under a conditional sale contract which the dealer subsequently assigned to a bank under a recourse financing arrangement. On the consumer's default, the bank repossessed the car and sold it without notice to the bank or to the consumer, and subsequently the bank sought to recover a deficiency from the dealer. While the result in the case may be defensible for various reasons, the court was in error in thinking that the car dealer was a "debtor" as to the conditional sale contract, for which the automobile was security, and therefore entitled to notice as "debtor" under Section 9–504(3) before the car was disposed of. The dealer was a debtor under the financing arrangement with the bank as to the chattel paper which was the subject of the transaction between them, and the chattel paper as such was not being disposed of. The result in the case may have been reached because of the prior course of dealing between the parties.[64]

Where a person has been in possession of goods under circumstances other than as owner—that is, as lessee, for example—and then enters into a purchase money security arrangement with a secured party to acquire ownership of the goods, the application of Section 9–312(4) has been somewhat uncertain because of its requirement that, for priority over conflicting security interests, a purchase money security interest in collateral other than inventory must be perfected when the "debtor receives possession of the collateral or within ten days thereafter." On the stipulated facts, possession of the goods was acquired some time before the possessor was technically a "debtor" or the goods were "collateral." The cases have gone both ways in resolving the priority problem,[65] but the problem of determining the meaning of "debtor" would appear to be a crucial factor in applying the priority rule.

§ 3–4. "Secured Party"

Under Section 9–105(1)(i), the term "secured party" means a person who holds a security interest. This includes a seller of collateral who has retained a security interest as well as a lender who has taken a security interest or the assignee of either of them. If the sale is subject to Article 9, the term also means the purchaser of

---

63. 240 Ark. 143, 398 S.W.2d 538 (1966).

64. § 1–205(1).

65. Compare Brodie Hotel Supply, Inc. v. United States, 431 F.2d 1316 (9th Cir. 1970) and *In re* Ultra Precision Industries, Inc., 503 F.2d 414 (9th Cir. 1974) with North Platte State Bank v. Production Credit Ass'n, 189 Neb. 44, 200 N.W.2d 1 (1972). *See also In re* Automated Bookbinding Services, Inc., 471 F.2d 546 (4th Cir. 1972); Fan-Gil Corp. v. American Hospital Supply Corp., 49 Mich.App. 106, 211 N.W.2d 561 (1973).

accounts, contract rights, or chattel paper, but "contract rights" has been dropped in Revised Article 9. In large financing transactions where there may be a number of holders of debt obligations, their representative, if there is one, is the secured party. The representative will usually be a trustee if there is a trust indenture in an equipment trust agreement or the like.

If a conditional seller of goods, who is a secured party, transfers the contract, or the note and contract, as the case may be, for his own financing purposes,—the transfer may be a sale or an assignment for security—the assignee is then the secured party and the conditional seller is now a debtor for the purposes of the new transaction, and the original debtor is now an "account debtor" as defined in Section 9–105(1)(a).

§ 3–5. "Collateral"

As defined in Section 9–105(1)(c), "collateral" is the property subject to a security interest. It also includes accounts, contract rights, and chattel paper which have been sold, if the sale is subject to Article 9, but the term "contract rights" has been eliminated from Revised Article 9. The collateral may be owned by the debtor or by a third party who has made it available as security.[66] The provisions of Article 9 are applicable regardless of whether the debtor or the secured party has "title" to the collateral; that is, in the case of goods, for example, it does not matter whether a seller has retained title to the goods or whether a lender has taken a security interest in the goods to secure a loan and the title is in the debtor or a third party who has made the goods available as security.

Collateral is a general term for any personal property or fixtures standing as security. Collateral is usually divided into three classes which are in turn subdivided: goods (which may be inventory, consumer goods, equipment, or farm products), intangibles (accounts, general intangibles, and contract rights, which are eliminated as a separate kind of collateral by Revised Article 9), and semi-intangibles (instruments, documents, and chattel paper). Arguably fixtures are a fifth class of goods, but in any event goods which have become fixtures could, prior to affixation, have been put into one of the categories of goods recognized by the Code.

The same item of goods may fall into different classes under Section 9–109 at different stages during the life of the goods. In

---

66. *See, e. g.*, Grace v. Sterling, Grace & Co., 30 A.D.2d 61, 289 N.Y.S.2d 632 (1968), where securities were pledged and then repledged.

the hands of its manufacturer, a refrigerator held for sale would be inventory, as it would also be when the refrigerator is in the possession of a retailer and displayed in a showroom for ultimate sale. If the refrigerator were bought for use in a physician's office, it would be equipment, while it would be consumer goods if bought for use in a consumer's home.

If a consumer bought a refrigerator from a dealer for personal use on conditional sale, the refrigerator would be collateral and the conditional sale contract would be the security agreement. If the dealer in turn, to secure financing from a bank, assigned the conditional sale contract to its financer, the collateral in this situation is the conditional sale contract which would be categorized as chattel paper. This distinction has sometimes not been recognized by the courts.[67]

When property becomes "collateral" has occasionally been a crucial question particularly in connection with the application of the purchase money priority rule of Section 9–312(4).[68] *What* property is collateral has also been an occasionally troublesome problem. In *Shaffer* v. *Davidson*[69] an individual borrowed some money from another individual, executing a note to evidence the obligation. Apparently the lender required an accommodation maker, and Mrs. Davidson served this role. The note was secured by a chattel mortgage on the borrower's car, but there was no filing of a financing statement nor any lien notation on the automobile's certificate of title which was physically held by the secured party. When the borrower and the car disappeared, the lender attempted to enforce the liability of Mrs. Davidson as an accommodation maker of the note, but without success. The court viewed the chattel mortgage as collateral in the form of chattel paper, and thought that the lender had discharged Mrs. Davidson by unjustifiably impairing the collateral by failing to note the lien on the certificate of title.[70] The chattel mortgage should have been recognized as the security agreement and the automobile as the collateral. Since the lender retained possession of the title certificate, it is not clear how a notation of a lien on the certificate would have prevented the disappearance of the vehicle or how this failure impaired the collateral.

---

67. *See, e. g.*, Norton v. National Bank of Commerce, 240 Ark. 143, 398 S.W. 2d 538 (1966); Shaffer v. Davidson, 445 P.2d 13 (Wyo.1968).

68. *See* text at n. 65 *supra* in § 3–3.

69. 445 P.2d 13 (Wyo.1968).

70. § 3–606(1) provides: "The holder discharges any party to the instrument to the extent that without

such party's consent the holder . . .

(b) unjustifiably impairs any collateral for the instrument given by or on behalf of the party or any person against whom he has a right of recourse."

Under § 3–415(5), if an accommodation party pays the instrument, he "has a right of recourse on the instrument against" the accommodated party.

§ 3-6. Basic Requirements of the Security Agreement

It is a fundamental provision of Article 9 that "Except as otherwise provided by this Act a security agreement is effective according to its terms between the parties, against purchasers of the collateral and against creditors."[71] While most security agreements will, as a matter of custom or necessity, be written, the term "security agreement" is defined as "an agreement which creates or provides for a security interest,"[72] and "agreement" is in turn defined basically as the "bargain of the parties in fact."[73] There is, then, no statutory requirement that *all* security agreements be written. But as a matter of compliance with Article 9's statute of frauds provisions, which is necessary for the security interest to be enforceable against anyone, the security agreement must be in writing except where the collateral is pledged.[74] The 1962 Code contained the anomalous possibility of having an attached security interest which was not enforceable even against the debtor because the provision on attachment merely required an "agreement" (in addition to two other requirements) whether the collateral was or was not pledged.[75] This insignificant conflict has been corrected in Revised Article 9 by combining the attachment provision and the statute of frauds provisions into Revised Section 9-203(1).

While the security agreement will generally be effective in accordance with its terms, both between the parties and against third parties, there are two important exceptions: if the Code itself specifies rules which cannot be displaced or if other statutes make certain contractual provisions illegal, no agreement of the parties will override

---

71. § 9-201.

72. § 9-105(1)(h). Revised § 9-105(1)(*l*).

73. § 1-201(3). *See* Estate of Beyer v. Bank of Pennsylvania, 449 Pa. 24, 295 A.2d 280 (1972) for the importance of a "course of dealing".

74. § 9-203(1). Technically, the requirements refer to enforceability against the debtor or third parties, so it is theoretically possible that an issue might be raised under the 1962 Code as to the enforceability of an oral security agreement against a secured party who does not have possession of the collateral and who has not advanced funds but might arguably be forced to do so; this possibility is remote and it is not available under Revised § 9-203(1).

The terms "written" and "writing" include any "intentional reduction to tangible form". § 1-201(46). On the use of a tape recording to satisfy Article 8's statute of frauds provision, *see* Ellis Canning Co. v. Bernstein, 348 F.Supp. 1212 (D.C.Colo.1972).

A security interest in personal property may be created in a mortgage or lease of real estate. *See* United States v. Baptist Golden Age Home, 226 F. Supp. 892 (W.D.Ark.1964) (real estate mortgage); Dunham's Music House Inc. v. Ashville Theaters, Inc., 10 N.C. App. 242, 178 S.E.2d 124 (1970) (real estate lease). *See also In re* Florio, 24 U.C.C.Rep.Serv. 415 (D.R.I.1978) (in bankruptcy).

75. § 9-204(1).

such rules or statutes, for the Code does not validate any practice which is illegal under other statutes.[76] Examples of statutes which proscribe certain practices are: usury laws, small loan laws, and retail installment sales acts. Such statutes may also prescribe, as well as proscribe, certain forms of contractual agreements. If listed in Section 9–203(2) (or Section 9–203(4) of the Revised Code) these statutes will control in the event of any conflict with the Code. The Code of each state must be consulted to see what statutes are given this effect. It must be borne in mind that the Code is not social legislation, as that term is generally used, and there may be a variety of acts, especially in the field of consumer protection, which must be consulted to see if a conflict exists.

Among the provisions in the Code which cannot be changed by agreement are these: Section 1–102(3) which states that the obligations of good faith, diligence, reasonableness, and care prescribed by the Code cannot be disclaimed although the parties may set their own standards for the performance of these obligations if the standards are not manifestly unreasonable; Section 9–301 which states to whose rights an unperfected security interest is subordinated; Section 9–307 which states the rights of buyers of goods vis-a-vis secured parties; Section 9–312 which states priority rules where there are conflicting security interests in the same collateral; Part 5 of Article 9 which states procedures on default which in general may not be waived or varied if they give rights to the debtor or impose duties on the secured party.[77]

§ 3–7. Two Exceptions to the Statute of Frauds Requirements

There are two exceptions to the usual Article 9 requirements for the enforceability of security interests under Section 9–203(1): one involves the security interest of a collecting bank under Section 4–208 and the other concerns security interests arising under Article 2 as provided in Section 9–113.

A bank is given a security interest in an item and any accompanying documents, or the proceeds of either, when credit given for a deposited item has been used, or when credit has been made available for withdrawal as of right, or if the bank has made an advance against

---

76. § 9–201. *See* Lyles v. Union Planters Nat. Bank, 239 Ark. 738, 393 S.W.2d 867 (1965); First Nat. Bank of Millville v. Horwatt, 192 Pa.Super. 581, 162 A.2d 60 (1960).

77. § 9–501(3). *See* Nelson v. Monarch Investment Plan of Henderson, Inc., 452 S.W.2d 375 (Ky.App.1970).

an item.[78] This security interest extends to all items and accompanying documents, and their proceeds, which are received at one time when any credit which has been given is withdrawn or applied in part.[79] If the collecting bank receives final settlement for an item, the security interest terminates.[80] Until the bank receives final settlement (or gives up possession of the item or accompanying documents for purposes other than collection), the security interest continues and is subject to Article 9 except that no signed security agreement otherwise required by Section 9–203(1) is necessary, no filing is required for perfection, and the security interest has priority over conflicting perfected security interests in the item or the documents or the proceeds of either.[81]

Ordinarily a collecting bank will give only provisional credit for a deposited item, and the customer will have no right to withdraw funds represented by that item, before final settlement by the payor bank.[82] There are times, however, when the collecting bank will allow a customer to withdraw funds, whether by agreement or unintentionally, before an item is finally paid.[83] In such cases, the bank has a security interest in the item [84] and has given value to the extent of its security interest, for purposes of determining its status as a holder in due course.[85]

Section 9–113 recognizes security interests arising under Article 2 and states that they are subject to Article 9 "except that to the extent

78. § 4–208(1).

79. § 4–208(2).

80. *Id.*

81. § 4–208(3).

82. *See* § 4–213.

83. A bank may pay an item, and change the customer's account, when the item is otherwise properly payable but creates an overdraft. § 4–401(1). See also § 4–212(1); Citizens Nat. Bank of Englewood v. Fort Lee Sav. & Loan Ass'n, 89 N.J.Super. 43, 213 A.2d 315 (1965).

84. § 4–208. *See* Waltham Citizens Nat. Bank v. Flett, 353 Mass. 696, 234 N.E.2d 739 (1968).

85. §§ 3–303(a), 4–209. The requirements that must be met for one to be a holder in due course are stated in § 3–302. *See* Citizens Nat. Bank of Englewood v. Fort Lee Sav. & Loan Ass'n, 89 N.J.Super. 43, 213 A.2d 315 (1965). In Bowling Green, Inc. v. State Street Bank and Trust Co., 425 F.2d 81 (1st Cir. 1970), the court decided that a security interest of the Article 9 variety was a security interest for the purposes of § 4–209, and that this section was not limited by § 4–208. The security interest in issue arose in a check, which was deposited, as proceeds of collateral subject to a security interest. The depositary bank was the secured party under a chattel paper financing arrangement. Part of the proceeds of the check went to the depositary bank as a credit against an overdraft (permitted by the bank in reliance on the promised deposit so that the depositor could pay its workers) and this could fit within § 4–208(1)(a); and the balance of the proceeds was set off against a considerable debt due to the bank.

that and so long as the debtor does not have or does not lawfully obtain possession of the goods," [86] a security agreement is not necessary to make the security interest enforceable, no filing is required for perfection, and the secured party's rights on default are governed by Article 2.[87] If the buyer lawfully obtains possession of the goods, compliance with Article 9 is necessary for the seller to have a perfected security interest in them.[88]

Although the usual Article 2 security interest will be the seller's, it is possible for a buyer to have a security interest in goods which he has received, in order to secure any payments made or expenses reasonably incurred in connection with the goods, if he has rightfully rejected the goods or justifiably revoked his acceptance of them.[89] The buyer may hold the goods and resell them to recover payments and allowable expenses but he is not authorized to retain estimated damages and must account to the seller for any funds received on the sale in excess of the amount of his security interest.[90]

The seller of goods reserves a security interest in them if the goods are shipped under a negotiable bill of lading or if they are shipped to the seller or his nominee under a non-negotiable bill.[91] The unpaid seller has remedies analogous to those of a secured party in certain circumstances where the buyer becomes insolvent or fails to make payments due on or before delivery of the goods,[92] but the seller's interest is not denominated an Article 2 security interest unless the buyer does not have possession of the goods or they are subject to the documents described above.[93] If the seller reserves title to the goods shipped or delivered to the buyer, he has only a security interest,[94] and if the buyer has received the goods, the provisions of Article 9 apply [95] regardless of the location of "title." [96]

---

86. § 9–113.

87. *Id. See In re* Kokomo Times Publishing & Printing Corp., 301 F.Supp. 529 (S.D.Ind.1968), Steelman v. Associates Discount Corp., 7 UCC Rep. Serv. 697 (Ga.Ct.App.1970).

88. Pitt v. Raymond, 11 UCC Rep.Serv. 870 (D.Or.1972); First Nat'l Bank of Elkhart County v. Smoker, 153 Ind. App. 71, 286 N.E.2d 203 (1972); Stumbo v. Paul B. Hult Lumber Co., 444 P.2d 564 (Or.1968); Valley Bank & Trust Co. v. Gerber, 526 P.2d 1121 (Utah 1974).

89. § 2–711(3). *See* Lanners v. Whitney, 247 Or. 223, 428 P.2d 398 (1967).

90. *Id*; § 2–706(6).

91. §§ 2–401(2), 2–505(1). *See also* § 1–201(37).

92. §§ 2–702, 2–703, 2–705. Where a financing agency (defined in § 2–104 (2)) is involved, *see* §§ 2–506(1), 2–707.

93. §§ 9–113, 2–505(1).

94. § 2–401(2). *See In re* DeVita Fruit Co. v. FCA Leasing Corp., 473 F.2d 585 (6th Cir. 1973); First Nat'l Bank of Elkhart County v. Smoker, 153 Ind. App. 71, 286 N.E.2d 203 (1972).

95. § 9–113.

96. § 9–202. *See In re* Samuels & Co., Inc., 526 F.2d 1238 (5th Cir. 1976).

§ 3–8. Formal Requisites

The formal requisites of a security agreement are minimal. If the collateral is not pledged, the debtor must have signed a security agreement which describes the collateral and, in addition, if the collateral is crops or oil, gas or minerals to be extracted or timber to be cut, a description of the land concerned must be included.[97] The land description is required only for crops or timber in Revised Article 9.[98]

In the 1962 Code there is a provision stating that in describing collateral, the word "proceeds" alone is sufficient to cover proceeds of any kind.[99] This sentence has been dropped from the subsection dealing with the formal requisites of a security agreement in the revised version of Article 9, and new subsection 9–203(3) states: "Unless otherwise agreed a security agreement gives the secured party the right to proceeds provided by Section 9–306." The right to proceeds is a matter of contract between the parties, but proceeds are almost always claimed and the intention of the parties to cover proceeds is presumed under the 1972 Code unless the contrary is stated. It was, however, by no means clear that proceeds had to be claimed in the security agreement under the 1962 Code in order to have an enforceable security interest in them. Certainly no such claim was needed to have a security interest in identifiable proceeds during the ten days after their receipt,[1] and after ten days the security interest depended on perfection by filing or possession.[2]

Section 9–110 states that any description of real or personal property is sufficient, whether or not it is specific, if it reasonably identifies what is described.

Where there is a difference between the description of collateral in the financing statement and the description in the security agreement, the narrower description should ordinarily be controlling. The security agreement is the contract between the parties, and the security interest of the secured party extends only to the collateral in which the debtor has granted such an interest. The secured party's interest probably cannot be enlarged as a matter of contract between the parties, by a broader description in the financing statement, where the collateral is required to be described by item or type under Section 9–402(1), but in any event so far as third parties are concerned the

97. § 9–203(1). *See, e. g.,* Peoples' Bank v. Pioneer Food Industries, Inc., 253 Ark. 277, 486 S.W.2d 24 (1972).

98. Revised § 9–203(1)(a).

99. § 9–203(1)(b).

I. § 9–306(2), (3).

2. § 9–306(3).

narrower description ought to be controlling.[3] So far as the requirements of the Code are concerned, such general descriptions as "all
goods," [4] "all equipment," [5] "inventory" [6] or the like should be adequate to satisfy the requirements of Section 9–203. Where there
are internal inconsistencies in the description of the collateral, a court
may properly construe the description to restrict the secured party's
interest to what is clearly and unequivocally described.[7]

§ 3–9. Financing Statement as Security Agreement

The formal requisites of a financing statement set forth in Section 9–402(1) of the 1962 Code include the minimal requirements for
a security agreement contained in Section 9–203(1), except for a
reference to oil, gas, minerals, and timber, and this omission had
been cured in the revised version of Section 9–402. In the usual
situation, a financing statement need contain only the names of
the parties, their addresses, a description of the collateral by item or
type, and in the 1962 Code the signatures of both parties but in the
1972 Code only the signature of the debtor.[8]

The Code does not require the use of any magic words in order to
create a security interest. It is usual to state in a security agreement
that the debtor "grants" a security interest in described collateral to
the secured party, and this terminology will not appear on most
financing statements currently in use. The omission could easily be
supplied by slightly more printing or typing,[9] if it were thought to be
desirable for the financing statement to serve as a security agreement, but the mere fact that granting clauses are traditional does not
mean that they are immutable. The Code requires no such terminology, and there is no reason why a standard form of financing statement
could not serve as a security agreement at least when accompanied by

---

3. *See* § 4–7 *infra*.

4. *See, e. g.*, James Talcott, Inc. v.
Franklin Nat'l Bank of Minneapolis,
292 Minn. 277, 194 N.W.2d 775 (1972).

5. *See, e. g.*, United States v. First
Nat'l Bank in Ogallala, Nebraska, 470
F.2d 944 (8th Cir. 1973); National
Cash Register Co. v. Firestone & Co.,
346 Mass. 255, 191 N.E.2d 471 (1963).
But *cf.* Mammouth Cave Production
Credit Ass'n v. York, 429 S.W.2d 26
(Ky.Ct.App.1968).

6. *See, e. g., In re* Platt, 257 F.Supp.
478 (E.D.Pa.1966).

7. *See, e. g., In re* Mitchell v. Shepherd
Mall State Bank, 458 F.2d 700 (10th
Cir. 1972). If the security agreement
provides that it covers collateral "as
per attached listing" or the like and
nothing is attached, no collateral is
covered. J. K. Gill Co. v. Fireside
Realty, Inc., 262 Or. 486, 499 P.2d 813
(1972).

8. *See generally* §§ 4–5–4–10 *infra*.

9. Cheek v. Caine & Weiner Co., Inc.,
335 F.Supp. 1319 (C.D.Cal.1971) (security interest was perfected when filed
financing statement stated: "This document is also intended to be a security agreement.")

a note.[10] Of course the note might itself constitute the security agreement.[11]

If it is intended that a financing statement serve as a security agreement, there would have to be an obligation to be secured, and this will ordinarily be evidenced by a note which will state the amount and terms of the loan, and the fact that the note is secured. It may well be the case that in essentially every instance where the issue is raised whether a financing statement may be a security agreement the proper issue should be whether the note itself constitutes the security agreement, as it could if it complied with the Code's simple requirements.[12]

If a financing statement signed by the debtor is on file and a loan has in fact been made, the most reasonable explanation for the filing is that the debtor intended to grant a security interest in the described collateral. Indeed, no other explanation comes readily to mind. Third

---

10. *See, e. g.,* Drysdale v. Cornerstone Bank, 562 S.W.2d 182 (Mo.App.1978); Evans v. Everett, 279 N.C. 352, 183 S.E.2d 109 (1971); *In re* Center Auto Parts, 6 UCC Rep.Serv. 398 (C.D.Cal.1968) (in bankruptcy); First Nat'l Bank & Trust Co. of Augusta v. McElmurray, 120 Ga. 134, 169 S.E.2d 720 (1969) (dictum); First Nat'l Bank & Trust Corp. of America, 130 Ga.App. 896, 204 S.E.2d 781 (1974). *Cf. In re* Amex-Protein Development Corp., 504 F.2d 1056 (9th Cir. 1974); Morey Machinery Co., Inc. v. Great Western Industrial Machinery Co., 507 F.2d 987 (5th Cir. 1975); *In re* Wambach, 343 F.Supp. 73 (N.D. Ill.1972), affirmed 484 F.2d 572 (7th Cir. 1973); Komas v. Small Business Administration, 71 Cal.App.3d 809, 139 Cal.Rptr. 669 (1977). *Contra,* American Card Co. v. H.M.H. Co., 97 R.I. 59, 196 A.2d 150 (1963) (leading case for this view); Mid-Eastern Electronics, Inc. v. First Nat'l Bank of Southern Maryland, 380 F.2d 355 (4th Cir. 1967); L and V Co. v. Asch, 267 Md. 251, 297 A.2d 285 (1972); Crete State Bank v. Lauhoff Grain Co., 195 Neb. 605, 239 N.W.2d 789 (1976).

11. In *In re* Broward Auto Brokers, Inc., 11 UCC Rep.Serv. 402 (S.D.Fla. 1972) (in bankruptcy), the lien was noted on a vehicle's title certificate and the note described the vehicle as collateral, but the absence of a separate security agreement was fatal to the secured party in a bankruptcy proceeding. This kind of result would not seem to be supportable. No third party was or could have been misled, and the intention of the parties was clear. *But see* Peterson v. Ziegler, 39 Ill.App.3d 379, 350 N.E.2d 356 (1976). *See also* First County Nat'l Bank & Trust Co. v. Canna, 124 N.J.Super. 154, 305 A.2d 442 (1973).

12. In Transport Equipment Co. v. Guaranty State Bank, 518 F.2d 377 (10th Cir. 1975), it was apparently held that a security interest was perfected by the secured party's taking possession of the collateral, but that an earlier filed financing statement was not effective to perfect the security interest because there was no separate security agreement. It would seem that if filing would not perfect the security interest because of an alleged lack of the necessary security agreement, then possession will be of no more value. The requirement of an agreement for attachment, which is necessary for perfection, will not be met by possession any more than it was by filing. (The agreement might have been found on other bases, perhaps, had the court been so inclined.) The court cited § 9–203(1)(a) as giving the secured party an enforceable se-

parties must rely on what the public files disclose and surely have no right to take advantage of the subsequently discovered fact that there is no writing labelled "Security Agreement," so long as the terms of the arrangement can be reasonably established, as they probably can be in a note. Where leases have been said to create security interests, it is most unlikely that the leases have contained any traditional words granting the lessor a security interest, but this has never, nor should it have, impeded courts from concluding in the proper circumstances that a lease may in fact be a security agreement.[13] Of course, where a lease is intended by the parties to create a security interest and there is a proper filing, the security interest will be perfected even though the lease contains no words of grant.[14] This result has properly been reached under the 1962 Code, and it is expressly provided for in Revised Section 9–408.

The mere filing of a financing statement does not necessarily mean that a secured transaction has been entered into, but if there is a secured transaction in fact, then the security agreement may be the financing statement. The Code expressly states that a security agreement may be filed as a financing statement if it meets the statutory requirements and is signed by both parties under the 1962 Code[15] or by the debtor alone under the revised version.[16] The filing fee is likely to be higher if the filing is not on a standard form, however.[17]

§ 3–10. The Security Agreement as a Contract

The function of the security agreement is to evidence the contract the parties have made. The length and complexity of the agreement will ordinarily vary with the amount of money that is involved. The security agreement might in form be a lease or conditional sale contract or consignment agreement.

The agreement will normally state what the events of default are, and it is not unusual to find a list of remedies available to the secured party on default, although this is pointless, at least in most cases,

curity interest, but this was solely a statute of frauds provision in the 1962 Code; it did not state the requirements for attachment which are in § 9–204(1); the requirements are combined in Revised § 9–203(1).

13. *In re* Walter W. Willis, Inc., 313 F. Supp. 1274 (N.D.Ohio 1970). *See generally* § 3–12 *infra.*

14. *In re* Walter W. Willis, Inc., 313 F. Supp. 1274 (N.D.Ohio 1970).

15. § 9–402(1).

16. Revised § 9–402(1).

17. This is expressly provided for in Revised § 9–403(5), but there have been amendments to the 1962 Code in various states to achieve this end.

insofar as the list is merely a repetition of the provisions in Part 5 of Article 9 which would govern in any event. However, the parties may agree on the standards to measure the performance of their rights and duties on default, if the standards are not manifestly unreasonable, and the security agreement is the place to do this.[18] For example, if provided in the security agreement, the secured party may require the debtor to assemble the collateral at a designated place which is reasonably convenient,[19] and the number of days' notice which will be considered reasonable before the secured party disposes of the collateral may be agreed on,[20] provided always that these standards are not manifestly unreasonable.[21]

If after-acquired property is to be included as collateral, if future advances are to be made, or if the debtor is to have complete liberty in dealing with the collateral, the security agreement is where these matters should be provided for.

§ 3–11. Security Interest

The term "security interest" basically means a contractual interest in personal property or fixtures which secures payment on performance of an obligation.[22] It also includes the interest of a buyer of accounts, chattel paper, or contract rights if the transaction is subject to Article 9.[23]

Most of the time a security interest will be created by a writing designed for the purpose which will often be designated a security agreement, but it might also be called a conditional sale contract or a retail installment sale contract or a chattel mortgage. Sometimes a contract called a lease or a consignment will in fact be a security agreement, or it will be treated as one and a security interest will arise. Generally, however, when a security interest is created it is because the parties obviously intended this and took the usual steps to achieve the result.

---

18. § 9–501(3).

19. § 9–503.

20. §§ 9–501(3), 9–504(3). *See* Motor Contract Co. v. Sawyer, 8 UCC Rep. Serv. 1122 (Ga.Ct.App.1971).

21. §§ 1–102(3), 9–501(3).

22. §§ 1–207(37), 9–102(2). *See* also Revised § 9–102(1)(a).

23. § 1–207(37). Article 9 applies to sales of accounts, contract rights, and chattel paper unless the sales are excluded by § 9–104. § 9–102(1)(b). (The term "contract rights" has been dropped from Revised Article 9.) *See* § 9–104(f). Revised § 9–104(f).

In no ordinary sense does a sale of accounts or chattel paper (or contract rights under the 1962 Code) create a security interest, but most of these sales are treated as if they did create a security interest and they are subject to Article 9. This is basically because third parties would otherwise have no way of knowing what kind of arrangement there was and they are left in much the same position in either case. Either a sale or a security transfer of these kinds of collateral will probably be phrased in terms of "assignment." Either might involve recourse against the assignor. The only time when a difference is really material is on default, when the debtor (or assignor) is liable for a deficiency or entitled to a surplus only if the security agreement provides for this, if the transaction was a sale rather than a secured transaction.[24]

A buyer of goods acquires a "special property" in them, under Section 2–401(2), when they are identified to a contract of sale; this is not in itself a security interest.[25] If the buyer wants a security interest, he must comply with Article 9, and where the buyer is making payments on goods being manufactured he might often be well advised to file a financing statement and regularize a security interest in the goods. Otherwise, if the seller becomes insolvent, he may have no effective remedy either by way of reaching the goods or recovering his payments. Certainly the remedy of Section 2–502 is almost always going to be illusory where the buyer pays in installments over a period of time since it conditions the buyer's rights on, inter alia, the seller's insolvency within ten days after receipt of the first installment of the price.

Where a seller of goods reserves or retains "title" to goods after they are shipped or delivered to the buyer, all that this amounts to is a security interest.[26] Aside from goods such as automobiles which may be subject to certificates of title, it is doubtful whether there is a more meaningless but ingrained legal concept than that of "title."[27] A conditional seller does, of course, retain "title" to goods, but in most instances he must do something to give public notice of this reservation if he expects third parties to be affected by the security interest.

---

24. *See* §§ 9–502(2), 9–504(2).

25. § 1–201(37).

26. *Id.*

27. Judge Learned Hand said: "It seems to me a barren distinction, though indubitably true, that title does not pass upon a conditional sale; 'title' is a formal word for a purely conceptual notion; I do not know what it means and I question whether anybody does, except perhaps legal historians." *In re* Lake's Laundry, 79 F.2d 326, 328 (2d Cir. 1935), certiorari denied *sub nom.* Lake's Laundry v. Braun, 296 U.S. 622, 56 S.Ct. 114, 80 L.Ed. 422 (1935).

When the seller ships goods under a non-negotiable document naming himself or a nominee as consignee, or when he ships under a negotiable bill of lading, he reserves a security interest in the goods.[28] If the shipment is to the buyer's order, the seller's rights are quite tenuous.[29] If the shipment is to the order of the seller or his nominee, the seller has, as a practical matter, done the best he can do in these circumstances.[30] These Article 2 security interests are covered by Section 9–113.[31]

In Section 9–107 a "purchase money security interest" is defined as one which is taken or retained by the seller to secure the unpaid balance of the purchase price or one which is "taken by a person who by making advances or incurring an obligation gives value to enable the debtor to acquire rights in or the use of collateral if such value is in fact so used." The security interest of the seller commonly arises in conditional sale contracts, where the buyer agrees to pay for goods over a period of time in installments and the seller, by contract, retains "title" to the goods until they are fully paid for. If, as often happens, the seller assigns its interest under the contract to a financer, the financer would also have a purchase money security interest. Since many third parties such as credit unions, banks, or consumer finance companies, finance the purchase of goods for consumers or financial institutions finance the acquisition of goods for business entities, the purchase money security interest also exists in these instances provided it can be shown that the value given went to the seller. This usually requires that the financer must make a check payable to the seller, or to the seller and buyer jointly; crediting the buyer's account with the purchase price, while the buyer pays with a personal check, probably will not result in a purchase money security interest.

While a purchase money security interest taken or retained by a seller ordinarily will arise at the time the contract of sale is entered into, there have been instances where sellers have been said to have purchase money security interests which arose as a result of contracts entered into at a later date.[32] This result, while perhaps surprising

---

28. § 2–505(1).

29. On the seller's right to stop the goods in transit, *see* § 2–705. If the buyer receives the goods and payment is due and demanded on delivery, the buyer's right to retain the goods, as against the seller, is under §§ 2–507 (2) conditional on making payment, but if the buyer in turn sells the goods, the sub-purchaser is very likely to take good "title" under § 2–402 as against the first seller.

30. In general, the bailee must deliver the goods to the person entitled to them under the document, under § 7–403. Section 7–502 specifies the rights acquired by "due negotiation," which is defined in § 7–501(4).

31. *See* § 3–2 supra this Chapter.

32. *See, e. g.,* Mayor's Jewelers of Ft. Lauderdale, Inc. v. Levinson, 39 Ill. App.3d 16, 349 N.E.2d 475 (1976); *In*

and contrary to the usual practices, is defensible on the face of the statutory language. That is, even though the security interest arises after the buyer has acquired goods on open credit, if the security interest is taken by the seller for part or all of the purchase price, it meets the technical requirements of Section 9–107.[33] Presumably this problem might arise when a seller and a buyer are initially overly optimistic about the buyer's ability to pay cash after some credit period, and the buyer simply cannot pay.[34] While the seller in such cases may in fact have no right to repossess the goods, if they have been sold on open credit, and might have simply a contract claim for the purchase price, the buyer may be willing to grant the seller a security interest in the circumstances, and the security interest will be purchase money and, in the case of consumer goods, no filing will be necessary for perfection under Section 9–302(1)(d).

If a lease or consignment is intended to be a secured transaction, it obviously creates a security interest and is subject to Article 9. This effect is also achieved in some cases where it is not necessarily contemplated by the parties and these problems must be considered in some detail.

§ 3–12. Leases

No doubt an agreement labeled "Lease" is usually exactly what it purports to be, but for many years it has not been uncommon for some parties to enter into what is called a lease when in fact the transaction amounts to a conditional sale.[35]

If a secured transaction is the real aim of the parties, compliance with Article 9 is necessary. If a legitimate lease is created, no filing is required. Whether a lease is intended as security is not always obvious but it is perfectly clear to everyone that there is no reason whatsoever to assume that anyone owns absolutely and free of security interests whatever property he may possess, beginning with the telephone.

The Code provides a rather loose standard for determining whether a lease creates a security interest. It is by no means obvious, when many problems are considered, how the standard could be tightened

---

re Robertson, 6 UCC Rep.Serv. 266 (E. D.Tenn.1969) (in bankruptcy).

33. The transaction might run into problems under §§ 9–301(2) or 9–312(4), depending on other facts.

34. See, e. g., In re Yale Express System, Inc., 370 F.2d 433 (2d Cir. 1966), where this problem arose in a bankruptcy context.

35. See, e. g., Lucas v. Campbell, 88 Ill. 447 (1878).

without requiring a filing for all leases, or all leases running longer than perhaps thirty days (including renewals), and this seems to be presently unacceptable in some quarters. The Code states:

> Whether a lease is intended as security is to be determined by the facts of each case; however, (a) the inclusion of an option to purchase does not of itself make the lease one intended for security, and (b) an agreement that upon compliance with the terms of the lease the lesser shall become or has the option to become the owner of the property for no additional consideration or for a nominal consideration does make the lease one intended for security.[36]

The end result of a conditional sale is that when the buyer finishes paying for the goods, he owns them, or has "title" to them.[37] If a nominal lessee ends up as owner, then the transaction is the same in substance, no matter what the difference in form.[38] Where the effect of a transaction is to create a security interest, Article 9 applies without regard to the location of title.[39]

Unfortunately the modern phenomenon of leasing equipment or consumer goods is too new for some courts to appreciate the financial facts of life. Even if a lease is a perfectly legitimate lease from the perspective of the lessor and lessee, there may be a considerable incentive in a bankruptcy proceeding to find that a secured transaction has resulted and that it is invalid for want of filing,[40] if the problem arises in bankruptcy as often happens. Any lease of consequence must provide a monetary return roughly equivalent to a conditional sale to enable the lessor to finance the acquisition and purchase price of the goods he is leasing. But if the lessee has no option to buy them for a nominal consideration, there is no basis for determining that a

---

36. § 1–201(37).

37. Where there is an option to purchase at any time for the balance of the rent, a security interest is created. General Electric Credit Corp. v. Bankers Commercial Corp., 244 Ark. 984, 429 S.W.2d 60 (1968).

38. Avis Rent-A-Car System, Inc. v. Franklin, 82 Misc.2d 66, 366 N.Y.S.2d 83 (1975). Brandes v. Pettibone Corp., 79 Misc.2d 651, 360 N.Y.S.2d 814 (N.Y. Sup.Ct.1974). *But see* Szabo Food Service, Inc. of North Carolina v. Balentine's, Inc., 285 N.C. 452, 206 S.E.2d 242 (1974).

39. § 9–202. The abolition of distinctions based on form has had a broad effect in many areas, including the seller's right of reclamation in bankruptcy. *See, e. g., In re* Yale Express System, Inc., 370 F.2d 433 (2d Cir. 1966).

40. In *In re* Transcontinental Industries, Inc., 3 UCC Rep.Serv. 235 (N.D. Ga.1965) (in bankruptcy), what appears to have been an ordinary commercial leasing transaction, at least in the context of its time, was treated as creating a security interest which was unperfected for lack of filing, in a bankruptcy proceeding.

security interest is created.[41] What is a nominal consideration is not always evident although 1% or even 5% of the purchase price might clearly so qualify.[42] If 20% of the price had to be paid in any event, this would not be a nominal sum in one sense—that is, in relation to the total price—although it might be in dollars.[43] In all cases where there is an option to purchase, the rent paid in one degree or another will be credited toward the purchase price, even though the price is the market value, or a comparable objective price, determined at the time the option is exercised.[44]

41. *In re* Telemax Corp., 12 UCC Rep. Serv. 742 (S.D.N.Y.1973); *In re* Lockwood, 16 UCC Rep.Serv. 195 (D.Conn. 1974) (in bankruptcy). To make a lease one intended for security, the option must be part of the original transaction and not a subsequent and apparently unrelated event. Leaseamerica Corp. v. Kleppe, 405 F.Supp. 39 (N.D.Iowa 1975).

42. Where the purchase price was approximately 10% of the lease rental and the market value of the goods would be substantially in excess of this amount, the lease was said to amount to a conditional sale contract because the debtor's "only sensible course" would be to purchase the goods. *In re* Washington Processing Co., Inc., 3 UCC Rep.Serv. 475 (S.D. Cal.1966) (in bankruptcy). *See also* Percival Constr. Co. v. Miller & Miller Auctioneers, Inc., 532 F.2d 166 (10th Cir. 1976). But a purchase price of 10% of the initial cost of the goods has been held not to be a "nominal consideration" as a matter of law in Granite Equipment Leasing Corp. v. Acme Pump Co., 165 Conn. 364, 335 A.2d 294 (1973), and therefore the lease was not a disguised security agreement; while a purchase price of $1000, which would have been approximately 10% of the estimated value of the goods at the end of the lease term, was held to be nominal in Peco, Inc. v. Hartbauer Tool & Die Co., 262 Or. 573, 500 P.2d 708 (1972), and the test adopted for "nominal" was a comparison of the option price with the market value of the goods at the time the option could be exercised. *See also* McGalliard v. Liberty Leasing Co. of Alaska, 534 P.2d 528 (Alaska 1975). Where the option price in each of two leases was $1.00, or a total of $2.00,

and the total rental was $73,303.32, the consideration was nominal and the leases were held intended for security in James Talcott, Inc. v. Franklin Nat'l Bank of Minneapolis, 292 Minn. 277, 194 N.W.2d 775 (1972).

43. *See, e. g., In re* Wheatland Electric Products Co., 237 F.Supp. 820 (W.D. Pa.1964) (not nominal consideration where, in one lease, 70% of rent paid could be applied toward not more than 75% of purchase price; dictum); *In re* Alpha Creamery Co., Inc., 4 UCC Rep.Serv. 794 (W.D.Mich.1967) (in bankruptcy) (not nominal where option price was approximately 32% of list price); *In re* Oak Manufacturing, Inc., 6 UCC Rep.Serv. 1273 (S.D.N.Y.1969) (in bankruptcy) (option price nominal where it was approximately 9% of aggregate lease payments and approximately 13% of fair market value); Xerox Corp. v. Smith, 67 Misc.2d 752, 325 N.Y.S.2d 682 (N.Y.Civ.Ct.1971) (bona fide lease where rental payments were applied toward purchase price but in any event option price was in excess of 50% of total price of goods). But if a percentage of the rent paid could be applied toward the purchase price and this would in fact aggregate the price over the term of the lease, a security interest would be created, without regard to the amount of rent actually paid at the time the issue is raised. Stanley v. Fabricators, Inc., 459 P.2d 467 (Alaska 1969); *In re* Jim Wilson, Inc., 17 UCC Rep.Serv. 1104 (E.D.Tenn.1975) (in bankruptcy). *See also* Citizens & Southern Leasing, Inc. v. Atlanta Federal Savings & Loan Ass'n, 23 UCC Rep.Serv. 741 (Ga.App.1978).

44. Leases have received a considerable amount of attention in the law re-

In any case, if there is absolutely no option to purchase the goods, there is no basis in the Code for finding a security interest even though the lease extends over the probable useful life of the goods.[45] An option contained in a side agreement should be entitled to as much weight as if it were in the lease, or even more.[46]

The parties to a legitimate lease will often be most reluctant to file a financing statement showing themselves as debtor and secured party. This can have unfortunate implications in income and perhaps even property tax situations,[47] as well on financial statements. The major advantage of filing is in the event of bankruptcy when even a bona fide lease by any standards may nevertheless be termed a secured transaction with the result that the lessor's interest is invalid in the absence of filing. A new Section 9–408 has been added to Revised Article 9 to allow the parties to file a financing statement as lessor and lessee, rather than as secured party and debtor, and in the event

---

views. *See, e. g.*, Hiller, Security Aspects of Chattel Leases in Bankruptcy, 34 Fordham L.Rev. 439 (1966); Kripke, Fairberg, Kemirich, Levinson, & Whiteside, Getting Down to Earth on Equipment Leasing, 12 Prac.Law. 9 (Jan. 1966); Leary, Leasing and Other Techniques of Financing Equipment Under the U.C.C., 42 Temp.L.Q. 217 (1969); Del Duca, Evolving Standards for Distinguishing a "Bona Fide Lease" from a "Lease Intended as Security," 75 Com.L.J. 218 (1970); Hawkland, The Proposed Amendments to Article 9 of the U.C.C.—Part 5: Consignments and Equipment Leases, 77 Com.L.J. 108 (1972).

45. In re Telemax Corp., 12 UCC Rep. Serv. 742 (S.D.N.Y.1973); Diaz v. Goodwin Brothers Leasing, Inc., 511 S.W.2d 680 (Ky.1974).

46. *See, e. g., In re* Willis, Inc., 313 F.Supp. 1274 (N.D.Ohio 1970). The problem of the Parol Evidence Rule, § 2–202, can of course be raised here, but it would seem to defeat the purpose of the Rule if it could be used to exclude evidence which in fact explains what the transaction is all about. *But see In re* Atlanta Times, 259 F.Supp. 820 (N.D.Ga.1966), affirmed sub nom. Sanders v. National Acceptance Co., 383 F.2d 606 (5th Cir. 1967). Where a trustee in bankruptcy attempted to introduce oral evidence of an agreement to purchase leased goods and the lease itself was otherwise complete and unambiguous, such evidence was said to be improper in the absence of "some writing sufficient to indicate that a contract for sale" was made under § 2–201(1). *In re* Financial Computer Systems, Inc., 474 F.2d 1258 (9th Cir. 1973). But parol evidence was held admissible to show the intention of the parties in *In re* A. & T. Kwik-N-Handi, Inc., 13 UCC Rep.Serv. 960 (M.D.Ga.1973) (in bankruptcy). *See also In re* Polaris Industries, Inc., 14 UCC Rep.Serv. 182 (E.D.Tenn.1973) (in bankruptcy); *In re* First Baptist Church of Margate, Florida, 17 UCC Rep.Serv. 1098 (S.D. Fla.1975) (in bankruptcy). Where a lease admittedly was intended to create a security interest but the option to purchase for no consideration at end of term was oral, a security interest was found to exist and to be perfected by a filing in *In re* Walter W. Willis, Inc., 313 F.Supp. 1274 (N. D.Ohio 1970).

47. *But see* Hoover Equipment Co. v. Board of Tax Roll Corrections of Adair County, 436 P.2d 645 (Okl.1967) where, apparently for state constitutional reasons, equipment was leased to a county and, over the lessor's protest, the equipment remained the lessor's property for purposes of an ad valorem tax assessment even though the lessor had assigned its interest to various state and national banks.

the transaction is determined to be for security, this filing constitutes perfection.[48] The filing is not in itself to be a factor in determining whether the lease is intended for security. If parties take advantage of this provision, it should go a long way towards curing a continuing problem in bankruptcy. Even under the 1962 Code the parties could be identified parenthetically as lessor and lessee, even though their names appear in boxes designated secured party and debtor on the financing statement. This would be protection for the lessor on the lessee's insolvency and at the same time it would give public notice of how the parties looked at the transaction.

If the transaction is, and is intended to be, a true lease in its inception, a filing under Revised Section 9–408 may arguably not be effective to perfect a security interest which might be created at a later point in time if the lessee and lessor were to agree that the lessee should become the owner of the goods subject to the retention of a security interest by the lessor-seller. That section is intended to protect the interest of the lessor in the leased goods where, despite the views of the parties to the transaction, a court decides that a security interest has been created; it does not in terms cover the situation where in fact a true lease exists and the parties subsequently change the nature of the transaction by their own action.

While the Code does not in terms cover leases of goods, in addition to sales of or security interests in them, Article 2 expressly covers "transactions in goods," [49] rather than sales alone and some cases have by analogy extended the provisions of Article 2 to lease transactions.[50]

If a lease comes within Article 9, and a financing statement is properly filed, the rights and remedies on default will be governed by Part 5 of Article 9.[51] If a pure lease is involved, the procedures on default will presumably be a matter of private contract covered by the lease itself.[52]

---

48. This result was recognized under the 1962 Code by way of dictum in *In re* Lockwood, 16 UCC Rep.Serv. 195 (D.Conn.1974) (in bankruptcy).

49. § 2–102.

50. *See, e. g.*, KLPR TV, Inc. v. Visual Electronics Corp., 327 F.Supp. 315 (W.D.Ark.1971) (warranties of merchantability and fitness provided in §§ 2–314 and 2–315 were applicable to lease); Baker v. Seattle, 79 Wash.2d 198, 484 P.2d 405 (1971) (limitation of liability in lease ineffective when not conspicuous because unconscionable by analogy to §§ 2–316(2) and 2–719(3)).

51. Dynalectron Corp. v. Jack Richards Aircraft Co., 337 F.Supp. 659 (W.D. Okl.1972).

52. Avis Rent-A-Car System Inc. v. Franklin, 76 Misc.2d 310, 350 N.Y.S.2d 579 (1973); McGuire v. Associates Capital Services Corp., 133 Ga.App. 408, 210 S.E.2d 862 (1974).

§ 3–13. Consignments

If a consignment is intended as security, it falls under Article 9,[53] since it is simply a form of inventory financing, but not all consignments have this end in view. Some consignments apparently are used even today as a means by which the consignor can control the price at which the goods are sold by the consignee.

The problems arise under Section 2–326(3) which provides:

Where goods are delivered to a person for sale and such person maintains a place of business at which he deals in goods of the kind involved, under a name other than the name of the person making delivery, then with respect to claims of creditors of the person conducting the business the goods are deemed to be on sale or return. The provisions of this subsection are applicable even though an agreement purports to reserve title to the person making delivery until payment or resale or uses such words as "on consignment" or "on memorandum." However, this subsection is not applicable if the person making delivery

(a) complies with an applicable law providing for a consignor's interest to be evidenced by a sign, or

(b) establishes that the person conducting the business is generally known by his creditors to be substantially engaged in selling the goods of others, or

(c) complies with the filing provisions of the Article on Secured Transactions (Article 9).

Goods are on "sale or return" if they are delivered primarily for resale but may be returned even though they comply with the contract.[54] Unless Section 2–326(3) is complied with, the consigned goods are subject to the claims of the buyer's creditors.[55] Since essentially no states have laws authorizing the posting of signs to give public notice of the consignor's interest—and posting a sign in the absence of such a statute would be meaningless[56]—and since no well-advised consignor would rely on general knowledge that a consignee is substantially engaged in selling the goods of others, it is clear that the filing provisions of Article 9 must be complied with if the consignor

---

53. §§ 1–201(37), 9–102(2).

54. § 2–326(1)(b).

55. § 2–326(2). *See* Mann v. Clark Oil & Refining Corp., 302 F.Supp. 1376 (E.D.Mo.1969), affirmed 425 F.2d 736 (8th Cir. 1970); *In re* De'Cor Wallcovering Studios, Inc., 8 UCC Rep.Serv. 59 (E.D.Wis.1970) (in bankruptcy).

Compare In re Mincow Bag Co., 29 A. D.2d 400, 288 N.Y.S.2d 364 (1968), affirmed 24 N.Y.2d 776, 300 N.Y.S.2d 115, 248 N.E.2d 26 (1969). *See also In re* Gross Mfg. & Importing Co., 328 F.Supp. 905 (D.N.J.1971).

56. *See e. g.*, Interstate Tire Co. v. United States, 12 UCC Rep.Serv. 948 (D.Ariz.1973).

is to be protected from the consignee's creditors. While the rule is clear, it has adumbrations which are not.

Under Section 2–326(2), goods held on "sale or return" are subject to the claims of the buyer's creditors unless Section 2–326(3) is complied with. The term "creditor" is defined in Section 1–201(12) to include "a general creditor, a secured creditor, a lien creditor and any representative of creditors . . . ." Where a secured party has a perfected security interest in a seller's inventory and the security interest extends, as it normally would, to after-acquired property, consigned goods will fall under this security interest in the absence of an Article 9 filing, even if the transaction amounts to a "true" consignment, under the 1962 Code [57] (and more than filing is required by Revised Section 9–114). (If the consignee goes into bankruptcy, the consignor's interest would also be cut off.)[58] While Section 9–204(1) and Revised Section 9–203(1) require for attachment that there must be an agreement (signed by the debtor in Revised Section 9–203(1)), value must have been given, and the debtor must have rights in the collateral, only the issue of "rights in the collateral" would seem to create a possible problem. (There is ordinarily no problem of an agreement in this context, and "value" is broadly defined in Section 1–201(44).) Since Section 2–326(2) subjects consigned goods to the claims of the consignee's creditors, absent compliance with Section 2–326(3), it would appear that the consignee indeed has rights in the collateral.[59]

If the consignment is in fact a form of inventory financing and is subject to Article 9, then Section 9–312(3) must be complied with. Since this is a form of purchase money financing, the consignor will be entitled to priority over earlier filed conflicting security interests which cover after-acquired inventory if, but only if, the consignor has filed a financing statement and given notice to earlier secured parties before the debtor-consignee receives the goods that the consignor claims a purchase money security interest in described collateral.[60] Because third parties, whether prior secured parties or creditors, are in much the same position whether or not secured inventory financing is intended by a consignment, substantially similar rules are contained

---

57. Nasco Equipment Co. v. Mason, 291 N.C. 145, 229 S.E.2d 278 (1976). General Electric Credit Corp. v. Town & Country Mobile Homes, Inc., 22 UCC Rep.Serv. 1255 (Ariz.App.1977).

58. *In re* Bro Cliff, Inc., 8 UCC Rep. Serv. 703 (W.D.Mich.1971) (in bankruptcy) (where the secured party filed a termination statement instead of a financing statement).

59. Sussen Rubber Co. v. Hertz, 19 Ohio App.2d 1, 249 N.E.2d 65, 48 O.O.2d 12 (1969).

60. § 9–312(3). The rules have been clarified in Revised § 9–312(3) but remain basically the same.

in Revised Article 9 for true consignments,[61] but filing is permitted under designations of consignor and consignee rather than secured party and debtor.[62] Under the 1962 Code, if a secured transaction, is not created, filing under Article 9 protects the goods from the consignee's creditors and Article 2 governs the transaction otherwise.[63]

It is perhaps the essence of a true consignment, under the Code as well as under pre-Code law, that the consignee is not obligated to pay for consigned goods unless they are sold;[64] if unsold, they may be returned to the consignor. If there is no obligation owing, there is nothing to secure, and there is no secured transaction. But whatever reason the parties may have for the transaction is peripheral, and creditors are in the same situation regardless of the private arrangement between the consignor and consignee. For this reason under Revised Article 9 notice and filing are required in any consignment to preserve the priority of the consignor's interest.

§ 3–14. Assignments of Rights Under Contracts

The basic rule of Section 9–318 is:

(1) Unless an account debtor has made an enforceable agreement not to assert defenses or claims arising out of a sale as provided in Section 9–206 the rights of an assignee are subject to:

   (a) all the terms of the contract between the account debtor and assignor and any defense or claim arising therefrom; and

61. Revised § 9–114. If the consignor does not file and give the required notice, his interest is subordinate to those who would be entitled to priority if the goods were the debtor's property. This brings in the priority rules of § 9–312 but not the rules of § 9–301, since a security interest is not involved. Section 2–326 states when the goods are subject to the claims of the buyer's creditors, and "creditor" is defined in § 1–201(12) to include a general creditor, a secured creditor, a lien creditor, and any representative of creditors.

62. Revised § 9–408.

63. *Compare* Hawkland, Consignment Selling Under the Uniform Commercial Code, 67 Com.L.J. 146 (1962) and Hawkland, The Proposed Amendments to Article 9 of the U.C.C.—Part 5:

Consignments and Equipment Leases, 77 Com.L.J. 108 (1972) *with* Duesenberg, Consignment Distribution Under the Uniform Commercial Code, Bankruptcy and Antitrust Considerations, 2 Val.U.L.Rev. 227 (1968) and Duesenberg, Consignments Under the U.C.C.; A Comment on Emerging Principles, 26 Bus.Law. 565 (1970). Some of the controversy in the two most recent articles cited above revolves around Columbia Int. Corp. v. Kempler, 46 Wis.2d 550, 175 N.W.2d 465 (1970). Probably the leading case decided under the Code is General Electric Co. v. Pettingell Supply Co., 347 Mass. 631, 199 N.E.2d 326 (1964). *See also* Vonins, Inc. v. Raff, 101 N.J.Super. 172, 243 A.2d 836 (1968).

64. *See In re* Miller, 545 F.2d 916 (5th Cir. 1977).

(b) any other defense or claim of the account debtor against the assignor which accrues before the account debtor receives notice of the assignment.

The "account debtor" referred to is defined in Revised Section 9–105(1)(a) as a "person who is obligated on an account, chattel paper or general intangible," and "contract right" is included in the 1962 Code definition.

In the commercial world—leaving to one side consumer transactions—in some types of cases it would be common for buyers or lessees of goods to agree not to assert against an assignee any claims which might be asserted against the seller or lessor, and this kind of an agreement is normally effective where the assignment is taken for value, in good faith, and without notice of claims or defenses.[65] It would be highly unlikely in a commercial setting that a financer would accept an assignment where the buyer or lessee is known to have defenses to payment, since this probably amounts to buying a law suit in which the financer is bound to lose a certain amount of money even if the effort to win some money is successful. Since most commercial sellers and lessors of goods need constant financing to operate, it is probable that their security arrangements or leases will contain "hell or high water" clauses under which the buyers or lessees waive the right to assert any defenses to payment against an assignee,[66] although these claims could still be asserted against the assignors who sold or leased the goods.

A defense which could be asserted against a holder in due course could, however, be asserted against an assignee. These defenses are stated in Section 3–305, and they relate basically to the validity of the underlying transaction. Where there is no express agreement not to assert defenses, if the buyer signs both a negotiable instrument and a security agreement, the buyer has in effect made an agreement not to assert defenses against an assignee, aside from defenses available against a holder in due course,[67] since a holder in due course could probably enforce the note.

Where the assignment is of payments due under a construction contract or some other kinds of contracts, it is quite likely that there will be no provision relating to the waiver of defenses in the underlying contract. If there is no such waiver, then the assignee's rights will be subject to defenses or claims arising out of the underlying

65. § 9–206(1). *See* B.V.D. Co., Inc. v. Marine Midland Bank-New York, 60 A.D.2d 544, 400 N.Y.S.2d 63 (1977).

66. However, such clauses are not always enforced. *See, e. g.,* Chemical

Bank v. Penny Plate, Inc., 144 N.J. Super. 390, 365 A.2d 945 (1976).

67. § 9–206(1).

contract which has been assigned [68] and to any other defenses or claims which accrue before the account debtor has received notification [69] of the assignment,[70] but the assignee is not obligated to perform the contract which has been assigned, nor does the assignment impose contract or tort liability on the assignee for the assignor's acts or omissions.[71] While the defenses or claims to which the assignee is subject may arise before or after the assignment if they relate to the contract assigned, defenses or claims arising out of other relationships must have accrued before notice of the assignment was received if they are to be asserted against the assignee. While the meaning of "accrue" may not be free from doubt, it has been held that a claim accrues when a cause of action comes into existence; that is, when a breach of contract occurs in this context.[72] However, the use of the words "defense or claim arising" from the assigned contract, to which the assignee is subject, suggests a defense when the assignee is asserting an affirmative right to payment. It would not seem that the assignee should be subjected to the possibility of having to pay back to the account debtor any funds the account debtor has paid to the assignee, if events should, after payment, give the account debtor a claim against the assignor.[73] The account debtor could, of course,

68. *See* James Talcott, Inc. v. H. Corenzwit & Co., 76 N.J. 305, 387 A.2d 350 (1978); Ertel v. Radio Corp of America, —— Ind.App. ——, 354 N.E.2d 783 (1976). *See also* Finance Co. of America v. United States Fidelity & Guaranty Co., 277 Md. 177, 353 A.2d 249 (1976); Investment Service Co. v. North Pacific Lumber Co., 261 Or. 43, 492 P.2d 470 (1972); James Talcott, Inc. v. Brewster Sales Corp., 16 UCC Rep.Serv. 1165 (N.Y.Sup.Ct.1975); Associates Loan Co. v. Walker, 76 N.M. 520, 416 P.2d 529 (1966). The right to the assigned funds may be subject to statutory liens under the law of some states. *See e. g.,* Panhandle Bank & Trust Co. v. Graybar Electric Co., Inc., 492 S.W.2d 76 (Tex.Civ.App.1973). *See also* Nat'l Bank of Detroit v. Eames and Brown, 396 Mich. 611, 242 N.W.2d 412 (1976).

69. *See* § 1–201(26). The filing of a financing statement will not comply with the requirement that the account debtor must receive notification of the assignment. *In re* Chase Manhattan Bank v. State of New York, 48 App.Div.2d 11, 367 N.Y.S.2d 580 (1975). Actual knowledge of a partner is notice to the partnership. Gateway Nat'l Bank of Chicago v. Saxe, Bacon & Bolan, 40 A.D.2d 653, 336 N.Y.S.2d 668 (1972).

70. American East India Corp. v. Ideal Shoe Co., 400 F.Supp. 141 (E.D.Pa. 1975); Fall River Trust Co. v. B. G. Browdy, Inc., 346 Mass. 614, 195 N.E. 2d 63 (1964); Commercial Savings Bank v. G. & J. Wood Products Co., Inc., 46 Mich.App. 133, 207 N.W.2d 401 (1973).

71. § 9–317. *See* Farmers Acceptance Corp. v. DeLozier, 178 Colo. 291, 496 P.2d 1016 (1972); Black v. Sullivan, 48 Cal.App.3d 557, 122 Cal.Rptr. 119 (1975); Brandes v. Pettibone Corp., 79 Misc.2d 651, 360 N.Y.S.2d 814 (N.Y. Sup.Ct.1974). *Cf.* Massey-Ferguson Credit Corp. v. Brown, —— Mont. —— 567 P.2d 440 (1977).

72. Seattle-First Nat'l Bank v. Oregon Pacific Industries, Inc., 262 Or. 578, 500 P.2d 1033 (1972).

73. *Compare* James Talcott, Inc. v. Brewster Sales Corp., 16 UCC Rep. Farmers Acceptance Corp. v. DeLozier, Serv. 1165 (N.Y.Sup.Ct.1975) with 178 Colo. 291, 496 P.2d 1016 (1972). *See also* Massey-Ferguson Credit Corp. v. Brown, —— Mont. ——, 567 P.2d 440 (1977); Benton State Bank v. Warren, 263 Ark. 1, 562 S.W.2d 74 (1978).

assert a claim against the assignor based on breach of warranty or breach of some contractual obligation, but it would not appear correct to extend the statute to give an affirmative right to the account debtor to recover payments made to the assignee. The fair implication to be drawn from Section 9–317 in this context would suggest that an assignee should not be liable for the assignor's acts or omissions, and to read Section 9–318 to impose such liability would seem to be unwarranted.

Experience growing out of the Second World War demonstrated the necessity of occasional contract modifications or substitutions, and the practical impossibility of securing advance consent of numerous assignees to such modifications. The effect of Section 9–318(2) is to recognize that modifications may be made and to give the assignee corresponding rights under the modified or substituted contract, provided the changes are made in good faith and in accordance with reasonable commercial standards. The original assignment may, however, provide that any modification or substitution will be a breach, and the change cannot affect assigned rights to payment previously earned.

A term in a contract prohibiting the assignment of money to become due with performance of the contract is ineffective under Section 9–318(4),[74] and a failure to recognize the assignee's rights may subject the account debtor to double payment. After the account debtor has received notification of the assignment, if the notice requires future payments to be made to the assignee, then this must be complied with.[75] A reasonable identification of the rights assigned is necessary,[76] if the assignment is to be effective, and the account debtor may request reasonable proof of the assignment, and if such proof is not forthcoming, the account debtor may continue to pay the assignor.[77] If the account debtor simply ignores the assignment and later claims the notice was not sufficiently explicit, the failure to demand more detailed information may be an important factor in the

74. *See, e. g.,* General Electric Supply Co. v. Epco Constructors, Inc., 332 F. Supp. 112 (S.D.Tex.1971).

75. Marine Nat'l Bank v. Airco, Inc. v. Craneways, Inc., 389 F.Supp. 231 (W. D.Pa.1975); American Bank of Commerce v. City of McAlester, 555 P.2d 581 (Okl.1976); Bank of Commerce v. Intermountain Gas Co., 96 Idaho 29, 523 P.2d 1375 (1974).

76. In Citizens State Bank of Corrigan v. J. M. Jackson Corp., 537 S.W.2d 120 (Tex.Civ.App.1976), invoices sent to the account debtor by the assignor said: "Make all checks payable to Citizens State Bank and Jetero Underground Utility Contractors, Inc." and this suggestion was ignored by the account debtor. It was held that the notation did not give the account debtor notice of the assignment of the right to payment to the bank and it did not identify the bank's rights. *See also* Surety Savings & Loan Co. v. Kanzig, 53 Ohio St.2d 108, 372 N.E.2d 602, 7 O.O.3d 187 (1978); John Deere Co. v. Neal, 544 S.W.2d 514 (Tex.Civ. App.1976); S & W Trucks, Inc. v. Nelson Auction Service, Inc., 80 N.M. 423, 457 P.2d 220 (1969).

77. § 9–318(3).

assignee's favor,[78] or if the account debtor makes some, but not all, of the required payments to the assignee, then there may be liability to the assignee for the balance even though the payments made may have equalled the assignor's loan since the assignee is not obligated to the account debtor to apply payments made to the repayment of the loan.[79]

It may sometimes be difficult to determine when an organization "receives notification," although this term is amplified in Sections 1–201(26) and (27). Clearly it is not prudent to hand a notice of assignment to a clerk,[80] although such a person might be the one to open a notice delivered by mail, but the organization notified ought to have reasonable internal procedures for transmitting communications or else it should be liable to third parties who have relied on procedures that "due diligence" would dictate to ordinarily prudent persons. It may, of course, make some difference in result when the person notified is a church rather than a municipal corporation or business organization.[81]

---

78. Marine Nat'l Bank v. Airco, Inc. v. Craneways, Inc., 389 F.Supp. 231 (W. D.Pa.1975).

79. Florida First Nat'l Bank at Key West v. Fryd Constr. Corp., 245 So.2d 883 (Fla.App.1970).

80. *See* Bank of Salt Lake v. Corporation of the President of the Church of Jesus Christ of Latter-Day Saints, 534 P.2d 887 (Utah 1975).

81. *Compare* Bank of Salt Lake v. Corporation of the President of the Church of Jesus Christ of Latter-Day Saints, 534 P.2d 887 (Utah 1975) with American Bank of Commerce v. City of McAlester, 555 P.2d 581 (Okl.1976).

CHAPTER 4

PERFECTION

Table of Sections

PART I. ATTACHMENT

PART I. ATTACHMENT

§ 4–1. Basic Requirements of Perfection

"A security interest is perfected when it has attached and when all of the applicable steps required for perfection have been taken . . . . If such steps are taken before the security interest attaches, it is perfected at the time when it attaches." [1] Depending on the kind of collateral and the arrangement between the parties, it may be that the security interest is automatically perfected at the moment it attaches and no additional steps need be taken; or the filing of a financing statement or certificate of title notation may be necessary; or perhaps possession must be transferred.

A perfected security interest is not, however, necessarily good against all third parties. Purchasers of the collateral may in some cases take free of a security interest which has been perfected, and there may be conflicting perfected security interests in the same collateral.

If any act is required for perfection and it is taken before all of the events necessary for attachment have occurred, then perfection will occur when the last of the events necessary for attachment happens. For example, a financing statement may be filed before the parties have entered into an agreement or before the secured party gives value or before the debtor acquires rights in the collateral, so that perfection would occur only when the last of these events takes place.

§ 4–2. Attachment

Three events are necessary for attachment: there must be an agreement, value must have been given, and the debtor must have rights in the collateral.[2] In the 1962 Code there is no requirement that the agreement [3] be in writing, although for the security interest to be

---

1. § 9–303(1).

2. § 9–204(1). *See* Evans Products Co. v. Jorgensen, 245 Or. 362, 421 P.2d 978 (1966). *See also* Revised § 9–203(1), (2). On "rights in the collateral," see Avco Delta Corp. Canada Ltd. v. United States, 459 F.2d 436 (7th Cir. 1972); Rex Financial Corp. v. Mobile America Corp., —— Ariz.App. ——, 580 P.2d 8, 23 UCC Rep.Serv. 788 (1978). On the necessity for an agreement, see Flor-

ida Nat'l Bank at Lakeland v. State, 350 So.2d 365 (Fla.App.1977).

3. "Agreement" is defined in § 1–201 (3). *See In re* Reinard, Inc., 1 UCC Rep.Serv. 424 (W.D.Pa.1961) (in bankruptcy.) A security interest cannot attach before the security agreement is executed by the debtor. Ranchers and Farmers Livestock Auction Co. v. First State Bank of Tulia, Texas, 531 S.W.2d 167 (Tex.Civ.App.1975).

enforceable against the debtor or third parties a written agreement signed by the debtor is required where the collateral is not pledged.[4] This inadvertent failure to mesh the provisions on attachment with the statute of frauds provision has been cured in the revised version of Article 9, and for both attachment and enforceability the agreement must be written except the case of a pledge.[5]

In the ordinary situation the agreement will be on a form supplied by a lender or seller, and it will be labelled "Security Agreement," "Conditional Sale Contract," or the like. In the unusual situation, the essentials of an agreement in traditional terms may or may not be pieced together from different sources. In one case a financing statement together with a stipulation for judgment was held sufficient to constitute a security agreement, but the financing statement said on its face: "This document is also intended as a security agreement."[6] This no doubt effectuated the intention of the parties, but it is doubtful that the financing statement alone would have been sufficient because it did not show the amount of the obligation, nor would the stipulation alone have been adequate because it did not identify the collateral. In another case a promissory note which stated on its face: "This note is secured by a certain financing statement," was read together with the financing statement to constitute the agreement.[7] Since a financing statement may describe collateral but clearly cannot be collateral, the court took an understanding and enlightened view of the transaction. On the other hand, a bankruptcy court refused to read together a note, which did not refer to any other writing, and an application for a motor vehicle certificate of title which showed a lien holder, to find a security agreement.[8] There

---

4. § 9–203(1). *See* Girard Trust Corn Exchange Bank v. Warren Lepley Ford Inc. (no. 2), 13 Pa.D. & C.2d 119 (1957). For an anomalous case arising under the 1962 Code, see Mayor's Jewelers of Ft. Lauderdale, Inc. v. Levinson, 39 Ill.App.3d 16, 349 N.E.2d 475 (1976). In this case a husband in Illinois ordered from a Florida jeweler a 2.5 carat diamond ring for his wife as a 25th wedding anniversary gift. The husband received the ring, notified the jeweler that he approved of it, and presented it to his wife, all on July 15. Not until October 28 did the husband sign the conditional sale contract, when he was at the seller's store in Florida. The husband subsequently filed bankruptcy, and the wife on the following March 14, pledged the ring with the husband's lawyer as security for his fee in the bankruptcy proceeding. The Florida jeweler was successful in an effort to recover the ring.

Apparently, the court thought the security interest had attached and was perfected, the ring being consumer goods, even though the security interest was not enforceable against anyone until the husband signed the security agreement (conditional sale contract) some months after the attachment and perfection. The wife was not a "buyer" under § 9–307(2); nor did that section apply to the lawyer.

5. The provisions of §§ 9–203(1) and 9–204(1) have been combined in Revised § 9–203(1).

6. Cheek v. Caine & Weiner Co., Inc., 335 F.Supp. 1319 (C.D.Cal.1971).

7. *In re* Center Auto Parts, 6 UCC Rep. Serv. 398 (C.D.Cal.1968).

8. *In re* Harmon, 6 UCC Rep.Serv. 1280 (D.Conn.1969) (in bankruptcy). *Cf. In re* Wambach, 484 F.2d 572 (7th Cir. 1973).

have been many cases reaching various results, mostly relating to whether there is a security agreement, but an even more basic question is whether there is an agreement necessary for attachment, signed by the debtor. In general, the agreement for attachment will be the security agreement, of course, and it would appear that such an agreement ought to be found, where necessary, by tying together a number of writings where the congeries of events could not sensibly indicate anything other than the existence of a security interest, which will certainly be the case where a financing statement signed by the debtor is properly filed to give public notice and a secured transaction in fact exists.

The term "value" is broadly defined in Section 1–201(44). A person gives value for rights if they are acquired in return for a binding commitment to extend credit or for an extension of immediately available credit,[9] or if they are acquired as security for a claim or in satisfaction of a claim,[10] or if they arise by accepting delivery pursuant to a purchase contract, or if the rights are acquired in return for any consideration sufficient to support a simple contract.[11]

When the debtor has rights in the collateral is, on the other hand, a more difficult matter.[12] Most of the time it will be perfectly obvious when and whether the debtor has rights in the collateral, for he will either own the collateral when the agreement for security is made or he will be acquiring the collateral from the seller.[13] Article

9. *See, e. g., In re* King-Porter Co., Inc., 446 F.2d 722 (5th Cir. 1971); *In re* United Thrift Stores, Inc., 363 F.2d 11 (3d Cir. 1966); Honea v. Laco Auto Leasing, Inc., 80 N.M. 300, 454 P.2d 782 (1969).

10. *See, e. g.,* United States v. Big Z Warehouse, 311 F.Supp. 283 (S.D.Ga. 1970); *In re* Samuels & Co., Inc., 526 F.2d 1238 (5th Cir. 1976); *In re* Platt, 257 F.Supp. 478 (E.D.Pa.1966); *In re* Barney v. Rigby Loan & Inv. Co., 344 F.Supp. 694 (D.Idaho 1972); Hillman's Equipment, Inc. v. Central Realty, Inc., 144 Ind.App. 18, 242 N.E.2d 522 (1968), reversed on other grounds 253 Ind. 48, 246 N.E.2d 383 (1969); Stumbo v. Paul B. Hult Lumber Co., 251 Or. 20, 444 P.2d 564 (1968); Sherburne Corp. v. Carter, 143 Vt. 411, 340 A.2d 82 (Vt.1975); *In re* John G. Kain Co., Inc., 11 UCC Rep.Serv. 886 (E.D.Tenn. 1972) (in bankruptcy).

11. *See, e. g.,* Miller's Shoes & Clothing v. Hawkins Furniture & Appliance,

Inc., 300 Minn. 460, 221 N.W.2d 113 (1974).

12. *See, e. g.,* Avco Delta Corp. Canada Ltd. v. United States, 459 F.2d 436 (7th Cir. 1972); Branch v. Steph, 389 F.2d 233 (10th Cir. 1968); Douglas-Guardian Warehouse Corp. v. Esslair Endsley Co., 10 UCC Rep.Serv. 176 (W. D.Mich.1971); Cain v. Country Club Delicatessen of Saybrook, Inc., 25 Conn.Sup. 327, 203 A.2d 441 (1964); Swets Motor Sales, Inc. v. Pruisner, 236 N.W.2d 299 (Iowa 1975); Evans Products Co. v. Jorgensen, 245 Or. 362, 421 P.2d 978 (1966); Chrysler Corp. v. Adamatic, Inc., 59 Wis.2d 219, 208 N. W.2d 97 (1973). *Cf.* Zions First Nat'l Bank v. First Security Bank of Utah, 534 P.2d 900 (Utah 1975).

13. *See* First Nat'l Bank of Elkhart County v. Smoker, 153 Ind.App. 71, 286 N.E.2d 203 (1972). *See also* Galleon Industries, Inc. v. Lewyn Machinery Co., Inc., 50 Ala.App. 334, 279 So.2d 137 (1973).

2 provides various guides for sales transactions, although it will not always be clear when a buyer acquires rights in the goods.[14]

Unfortunately Section 9–204(2) of the 1962 Code had some explicit rules for determining when a debtor had no rights in collateral, and the rules were either obvious (and superfluous), antiquarian (and unnecessary), or accurate enough but subject to misinterpretation. These provisions have been dropped in the revised version of Article 9. Except for the owners of private lakes or the few who find treasure in a statutory codification of Low v. Pew,[15] it would be difficult to imagine rights in fish until caught.[16] Nor would most farmers assume that they had rights in crops before they were planted. And no businessman would suppose that he had such collateral as a contract right or account before he had a contract. The great problem created by Section 9–204(2) was the provision that a debtor had no rights in an account until it came into existence. The rule might have been self-evidently correct, insofar as a specific account was concerned, but it created some conceptual problems for some bankruptcy lawyers when accounts were financed on a continuing basis and the debtor became bankrupt within four months of the time any of the accounts became subject to the security interest. While the conceptual difficulty of some lawyers did not extend to the courts,[17] it was simpler to expunge a needless provision than to continue to wave a red flag.

An attached security interest is simply one which is enforceable between the parties.[18] It may also (but not necessarily) be enforceable against third parties.

§ 4–3. Postponed Attachment

A security interest attaches when there is agreement, value is given, and the debtor has rights in the collateral—unless explicit agreement postpones the time of attaching.[19] Normally it would be desirable for the security interest to attach and be perfected at the earliest possible time, particularly if the debtor is in difficulty and insolvency is a distinct possibility. However, in certain kinds of loans such as those made by banks and insurance companies to finance companies, which are normally unsecured, the lender would have a cer-

---

14. *See, e. g.*, § 2–501(1), whose clause (c) will present problems in dealing with "unborn young" of elephants.

15. 108 Mass. 347, 11 Am.Rep. 357 (1871).

16. These examples are from § 9–204(2) (a)–(d).

17. *See* §§ 7–9 to 7–12 infra.

18. Bramble Transportation, Inc. v. Sam Senter Sales, Inc., 294 A.2d 97 (Del.1971), affirmed 294 A.2d 104 (Del. 1972).

19. § 9–204(1), Revised § 9–203(2).

tain amount of leverage if on a technical default a security interest in the borrower's accounts receivable or other collateral were to attach, pursuant to the loan agreement, and be perfected, pursuant to a previously filed financing statement. The mere existence of a filed financing statement would not perfect the security interest if the time of attachment were postponed under the security agreement, but whenever the security interest attached, as on the happening of an event of default, it would be perfected. So long as bankruptcy did not occur within four months of the date of attachment and perfection, no attack on the grounds of a preference could be sustained.

This kind of security interest is analogous to the English, Scottish, and Canadian floating charge, except that the floating charge is an equitable interest recognized in bankruptcy, which is not ordinarily possible in the United States. A debtor who has granted a floating charge on his assets may dispose of those assets free of the charge until a default causes the charge to crystallize or attach to those assets then subject to the charge.[20] The concept of postponed attachment introduces a somewhat similar possibility into our law, although a security interest that becomes effective only on bankruptcy would be valueless in the United States. The legal theory involved is quite different but the effects of the floating charge and a so-called floating lien on inventory and accounts are substantially similar.

In *In re Dolly Madison Industries, Inc.*,[21] stock was placed in an escrow with an agreement stating that if the purchaser of the stock defaulted and did not cure the default within five days after receipt of notice of the default, the escrow agent would deliver the certificates to the seller, "*whereupon* seller's rights and obligations . . . shall be those of a secured party . . . ." This language was said to postpone the time of attachment of the security interest until the requirements of the escrow agreement were met,[22] and in this case the uncured default occurred more than six months after a Chapter X Bankruptcy Reorganization petition was filed, so that the seller's rights were inferior to the rights of the trustee. This case is no doubt correct in the reading of the escrow agreement, and the case illustrates the hazard, from the secured party's point of view, of conditioning default and rights flowing therefrom on the giving of no-

---

20. *See* L. Gower, Modern Company Law 78–80, 420–434 (3rd ed. 1969). The "floating charge" was recognized in Pennsylvania Co. for Insurance on Lives and Granting Annuities v. United Railways of Havana and Regla Warehouses, 26 F.Supp. 379 (D.C.Me. 1939).

21. 351 F.Supp. 1038 (E.D.Pa.1972).

22. *Cf. In re* Copeland, 531 F.2d 1195 (3d Cir. 1976), where the language in the pledge agreement was said not to postpone the time of attachment but rather to establish a procedure to enforce the security interest on default. *See also* Allegaert v. Chemical Bank, —— F.2d ——, 24 U.C.C.Rep.Serv. 426 (S.D.N.Y.1978).

tice and the receipt of that notice by the debtor; it also suggests that, from the seller's side it would have been preferable to cast the transaction as a secured transaction from its inception, so that the security interest would have been perfected from the time of the pledge.

PART II. PERFECTION BY FILING

§ 4–4. Perfection by Filing: Excepted Transactions

The basic rule is that filing is required for perfection of all security interests except for those excepted from this requirement in Section 9–302(1). The exceptions are:

(1) Security interests in collateral which is pledged under Section 9–305: letters of credit and advices of credit, goods, instruments, money (under the 1972 Official Text), negotiable documents, and chattel paper.

(2) Security interests in instruments and documents temporarily perfected for 21 days under the rules of Section 9–304(4) and (5) or interests in proceeds for 10 days under Section 9–306(3).

(3) Under the 1962 Official Text, purchase money security interests in farm equipment costing not over $2500. This exception is deleted in the 1972 Official Text. In no case did it apply to fixtures or motor vehicles.

(4) Under the 1972 Official Text, but not under the 1962 Code, security interests created by assignments of beneficial interests in trusts or decedents' estates.

(5) Purchase money security interests in consumer goods, subject to certain exceptions in the case of motor vehicles and fixtures.

(6) An assignment of accounts (and contract rights under the 1962 Code) which alone or when aggregated with other assignments to the same assignee does not transfer a significant part of the assignor's outstanding accounts (or contract rights).

(7) Security interests arising under Article 2, or security interests of collecting banks arising under Section 4–208.

(8) Under the 1962 Code, security interests which may be filed or registered under a federal system or under a state system of central filing or certificate of title notation where such notation is required (or, in an alternative provision, where it is optional). Under the 1972 Code, the exception goes to security interests in property which is subject to a statute or treaty of the United States providing for na-

tional or international registration or certificates of title or which specifies a different place for filing from that specified in the Code; and to any specifically enumerated state statutes providing certificates of title covering various classes of goods, except during any time when the goods are inventory.

(9) Under the 1972 Official Text, assignments for the benefit of creditors and subsequent transfers by the assignee.

The most significant exceptions to Code filing for perfection are obviously purchase money security interests in consumer goods, collateral which is subject to certificate of title notation, and pledged collateral.

§ 4–5. The Financing Statement

While a copy of the security agreement may be filed as a financing statement if it meets the requirements of Section 9–402(1), it is customary to file a standard form of financing statement which contains the minimum statutorily required information.[23] The only required information in most cases will be the names [24] and addresses [25] of the debtor and secured party and a description of the collateral.[26] Under the 1962 Code both parties must sign the financing statement,[27] although under the 1972 Official Text only the debtor must sign.[28] If the security interest has been duly perfected but changes in circum-

---

23. From the filing officer's point of view—and from the secured party's point of view if the filing officer transcribes, accurately one hopes, information from a non-uniform to a uniform form—it is preferable that standard forms be used. The revised version of Article 9 follows some state variations in allowing a justified higher fee when non-standard forms are filed. See Revised § 9–403(5). *See generally* Kripke and Felsenfeld, Secured Transactions: A Practical Approach to Article 9 of the Uniform Commercial Code, 17 Rutgers L.Rev. 168, 172–74 (1962).

24. *See* § 4–6 infra.

25. A post office box has been held to be a sufficient address for the secured party. Silver v. Gulf City Body & Trailer Works, 432 F.2d 992 (5th Cir. 1970). The absence of a residence address for an individual debtor, where a state modification of § 9–402(1) required this information, was found to

be immaterial where the debtor's mailing address and the address of his chief place of business, where the collateral was located, were given; this met the "substantial compliance" test of § 9–402(5). Lines v. Bank of California, 467 F.2d 1274 (9th Cir. 1972). An address for the debtor in a state different from that in which the security interest was filed was held adequate in *In re* De-Flectronics, Inc., 4 UCC Rep.Serv. 450 (D.Conn.1967) (in bankruptcy). *See also In re* Bankrupt Estate of Smith, 508 F.2d 1323 (5th Cir. 1975); Goldie v. Bauchet Properties, 124 Cal.Rptr. 161, 540 P.2d 1 (1975).

26. § 9–402(1). A sufficient form is set out in § 9–402(3).

27. § 9–402(1). If there are two secured parties, both must sign. *In re* Murray, 2 UCC Rep.Serv. 667 (D.Ore. 1964) (in bankruptcy).

28. Revised § 9–402(1).

stances dictate the filing of a new financing statement, probably only the secured party need sign.[29]

The purpose of a financing statement is simply to give notice to the world that designated parties have entered into a secured transaction covering described collateral. The details must be learned from the parties.[30] While the appearance of the financing statement forms

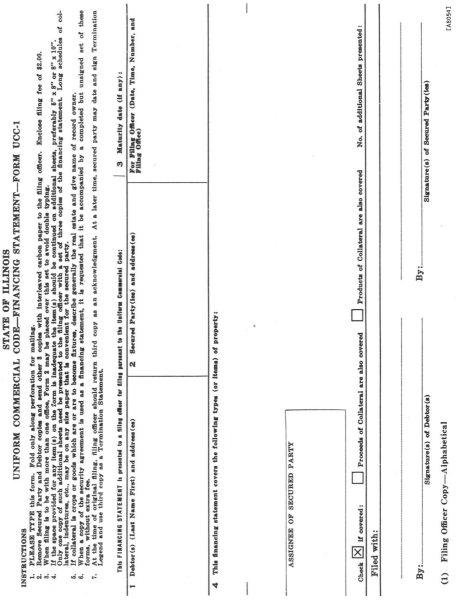

---

29. *See* § 9–402(2), Revised § 9–402(2). *See also In re* Parks, 16 Ohio Misc. 135, 45 Ohio Op. 109 (1968); Ky.Att'y Gen.Op. No. 65–570, 2 UCC Rep.Serv. 1007 (1965).

30. The Code provides no mechanism for the merely curious to learn the details of a secured transaction from the secured party. Where the details are of legitimate interest third par-

will vary somewhat from state to state, the following form is representative of those used under the 1962 Code.

The following form is used in California under the 1972 Code:

This FINANCING STATEMENT is presented for filing pursuant to the California Uniform Commercial Code.

1. DEBTOR (LAST NAME FIRST—IF AN INDIVIDUAL)	1A. SOCIAL SECURITY OR FEDERAL TAX NO.

1B. MAILING ADDRESS	1C. CITY, STATE	1D. ZIP CODE

2. ADDITIONAL DEBTOR (IF ANY) (LAST NAME FIRST—IF AN INDIVIDUAL)	2A. SOCIAL SECURITY OR FEDERAL TAX NO.

2B. MAILING ADDRESS	2C. CITY, STATE	2D. ZIP CODE

3. DEBTOR'S TRADE NAMES OR STYLES (IF ANY)	3A. FEDERAL TAX NUMBER

4. SECURED PARTY	4A. SOCIAL SECURITY NO., FEDERAL TAX NO. OR BANK TRANSIT AND A.B.A. NO.
NAME	
MAILING ADDRESS	
CITY STATE ZIP CODE	

5. ASSIGNEE OF SECURED PARTY (IF ANY)	5A. SOCIAL SECURITY NO., FEDERAL TAX NO. OR BANK TRANSIT AND A.B.A. NO.
NAME	
MAILING ADDRESS	
CITY STATE ZIP CODE	

6. This FINANCING STATEMENT covers the following types or items of property **(include description of real property on which located and owner of record when required by instruction 4).**

7. CHECK IF APPLICABLE ☒   7A. ☐ PRODUCTS OF COLLATERAL ARE ALSO COVERED   7B. DEBTOR(S) SIGNATURE NOT REQUIRED IN ACCORDANCE WITH INSTRUCTION 5(a) ITEM: ☐ (1) ☐ (2) ☐ (3) ☐ (4)

8. CHECK IF APPLICABLE ☒   ☐ DEBTOR IS A "TRANSMITTING UTILITY" IN ACCORDANCE WITH UCC § 9105 (1) (n)

9.
►
SIGNATURE(S) OF DEBTOR(S)

DATE:

TYPE OR PRINT NAME(S) OF DEBTOR(S)

►
SIGNATURE(S) OF SECURED PARTY(IES)

TYPE OR PRINT NAME(S) OF SECURED PARTY(IES)

11. Return copy to:

NAME
ADDRESS
CITY
STATE
ZIP CODE

CODE 1 2 3 4 5 6 7 8 9 0

10. THIS SPACE FOR USE OF FILING OFFICER (DATE, TIME, FILE NUMBER AND FILING OFFICER)

(1) FILING OFFICER COPY   FORM UCC-1—FILING FEE $3.00 Approved by the Secretary of State

[B9508]

ties may use the procedures set up by § 9–208 under which the debtor may request information which he may pass on to interested persons. If the secured party provides erroneous information which is justifiably relied on, he may be estopped to deny its accuracy under § 1–103.

It is crucial that the financing statement be promptly and properly filed when it is received by the appropriate office. While some secured parties may visit the filing office to go through the files and learn what is filed against their debtors, it is more likely that employees of lawyers or professional organizations may conduct the searches or else the procedure of Section 9–407(2) will be relied on. Section 9–407(2) provides that, on request, the filing officer will issue a certificate showing filings against particular debtors. Where the certificate contains erroneous information which is detrimentally relied on, there should be liability on the filing officer to compensate the secured party.[31] Since presentation of the financing statement and tender of the filing fee or acceptance of the statement by the filing officer will constitute filing under Section 9–403(1), it is highly important that filing officers perform their work expeditiously and accurately. If the filing office improperly files or indexes a financing statement, the security interest will nevertheless be perfected,[32] but third parties can be seriously misled.

Revised Section 9–402(1) contains an added sentence stating: "A carbon, photographic or other reproduction of a security agreement or a financing statement is sufficient as a financing statement if the security agreement so provides or if the original has been filed in this state." While it may be difficult to think of any objection to filing a photocopy of a financing statement, in early days such a filing was said to be a nullity because it had not been "signed."[33] This view would appear to be baseless even under the earlier Code,[34] but the problem—and it may well be a problem in states requiring dual filing, if a sufficient number of financing statements have not been executed and the debtor is subsequently recalcitrant—has been resolved by the 1972 Official Text.

§ 4–6. The Parties' Names

Where the debtor is a corporation, the corporate name is the only possible name to be used on the financing statement.[35] At first glance

31. *See* Hudleasco, Inc. v. State, 90 Misc.2d 1057, 396 N.Y.S.2d 1002 (N.Y. Ct.Claims, 1977). *See also In re* Fowler, 407 F.Supp. 799 (W.D.Okl. 1975); *In re* May Lee Industries, Inc., 380 F.Supp. 1 (S.D.N.Y.1974), affirmed 501 F.2d 1407 (2d Cir. 1974).

32. *In re* Royal Electrotype Corp., 485 F.2d 394 (3d Cir. 1973).

33. *In re* Kane, 1 UCC Rep.Serv. 582, 55 Berks.Co.L.J. 1 (E.D.Pa.1962) (in bankruptcy).

34. *See* § 4–9 *infra.*

35. *Cf. In re* Green Mill Inn, Inc., 474 F.2d 14 (9th Cir. 1973) where the "substantial compliance" provision of § 9–402(5) (Revised § 9–402(8)) saved a filing in which the debtor's name was shown as "Taylor, Maxime" but the signature line showed the debtor's signature as "Green Mill Inn, Inc., by Maxime Taylor, President" and in fact the debtor was the corporate entity; however, the Secretary of State's office through cross-indexing under both names provided actual notice to anyone interested, and no one could in fact have been misled or prejudiced.

this might seem to be true of an individual whose legal name would seem to be the only choice for the name to be shown, and the problem will usually be just that simple. However, some individuals operate businesses as sole proprietorships under names other than their own. While it would be proper to show both the individual's name and the name under which he does business, the use of a d/b/a name alone is not ordinarily adequate and it can be misleading to other creditors.[36] Moreover, an individual can do business under any number and variety of assumed names so that the only acceptable name to be used as basic notice on a financing statement is the individual's proper name.[37] The 1962 Code was silent on this problem, but the revised version of Article 9 requires the name of the individual, although acknowledging that trade names may be added.[38]

But if individuals can do business under assumed names, partnerships may become incorporated, corporations can change their names, and the entity of the corporate debtor can be changed by merger or otherwise.[39] This problem was not dealt with in the 1962 Code,[40]

See also In re Sport Shack, 383 F. Supp. 37 (N.D.Cal.1974); In re Hatfield Const. Co., 10 UCC Rep.Serv. 907 (M.D.Ga.1971) (in bankruptcy).

36. See, e. g., Douglas-Guardian Warehouse Corp. v. Esslair Endsley Co., 10 UCC Rep.Serv. 176 (W.D.Mich.1971); In re Leichter, 471 F.2d 785 (2d Cir. 1972); See also In re Firth, 363 F. Supp. 369 (M.D.Ga.1973); In re Hill, 363 F.Supp. 1205 (N.D.Miss.1973); In re Fowler, 407 F.Supp. 799 (W.D.Okl. 1975); In re Merrill, 9 UCC Rep.Serv. 757 (D.Neb.1971) (in bankruptcy); In re Wishart, 10 UCC Rep.Serv. 1296 (W.D.Mich.1972) (in bankruptcy); In re Jones, 11 UCC Rep.Serv. 249 (W.D. Mich.1972) (in bankruptcy).

37. See, e. g., In re Thomas, 310 F.Supp. 338 (N.D.Cal.1970).

38. Revised § 9–402(7).

39. This problem was apparent from the beginning in a very famous case but it was not raised until it reached the Court of Appeals for the 9th Circuit, and the court refused to consider it. DuBay v. Williams, 417 F.2d 1277 (9th Cir. 1969). See In re Portland Newspaper Publishing Co., Inc., 3 UCC Rep.Serv. 194, 196–199 (D.C.Ore.1966) (in bankruptcy). See also Siljeg v. National Bank of Commerce of Seattle, 509 F.2d 1009 (9th Cir. 1975); Inter Mountain Ass'n of Credit Men v. Villager, Inc., 527 P.2d 664 (Utah 1974). Cf. Borg-Warner Acceptance Corp. v. Bank of Marin, 36 Cal.App.3d 286, 111 Cal.Rptr. 361 (1973).

40. A filing under the pre-incorporation name of the debtor was held sufficient to continue perfection after incorporation in Borg-Warner Acceptance Corp. v. Bank of Marin, 36 Cal.App. 3d 286, 111 Cal.Rptr. 361 (1973), under an earlier California version of § 9–402(1). See also In re Sofa Centre, Inc., 18 UCC Rep.Serv. 536 (M.D.Fla. 1975) (in bankruptcy). In In re A–1 Imperial Moving & Storage Co., Inc., 350 F.Supp. 1188 (S.D.Fla.1972), a financing statement was filed on April 9, 1971, under the name A–1 Imperial Moving and Storage Company, Inc., said by the court to have been an unregistered trade name, and subsequently the debtor's name was changed, after incorporation, to 6105 Corporation, and it was subsequently changed to A–1 Imperial Moving and Storage Company, Inc. on January 24, 1972, prior to bankruptcy on May 22, 1972. The financing statement was held to be effective only as of January 24, 1972, which would appear to create possible preference problems. It is difficult to see why the original

and it probably has not been covered by any statute prior to the 1972 Official Text of Article 9. Revised Section 9–402(7), provides that if the debtor changes his name (for individuals may change their names by marriage or legal procedure) [41] or if an organization changes its name, identity, or corporate structure, and the change causes the financing statement to become seriously misleading, the filing is not effective to perfect a security interest in collateral acquired more than four months after the change, unless a new appropriate financing statement is filed during that period. Such a financing statement may be signed by the secured party alone.[42]

In the case of a partnership, the partnership name should be shown, although the names of the partners may be added.[43] This was generally assumed to be the case under the 1962 Code, and it is specifically recognized in the revised Code. The rules stated above would apply to a change of a partnership into a corporation. The term "organization," which is used in Revised Section 9–402(7) to cover changes in debtors other than individuals, is a defined term,[44] and

filing should not have been effective on April 9, 1971, and, if then effective, it should have been effective thereafter, since nothing in the 1962 Code— or indeed in the Revised Code, on these facts—provides otherwise. With this holding, *compare* Continental Oil Co. v. Citizens Trust & Savings Bank, 57 Mich.App. 1, 225 N.W.2d 209 (1975), affirmed 397 Mich. 203, 244 N.W.2d 243 (1976); *In re* The Grape Arbor, Inc., 6 UCC Rep.Serv. 632 (E.D.Pa. 1969) (in bankruptcy), and *In re* Pasco Sales Co., Inc., 77 Misc.2d 724, 354 N.Y.S.2d 402 (N.Y.Sup.Ct.1974). In *In re* Kalamazoo Steel Process, Inc., 503 F.2d 1218 (6th Cir. 1974), it was held that a filing under the debtor's correct name as of that time was not effective to continue the perfection of the security interest when the debtor subsequently changed its name to the former name of the secured party, which in turn had changed its name (but not to the former name of the debtor), so that on the debtor's subsequent bankruptcy the trustee took superior rights under § 70c of the Bankruptcy Act. The decision seems to rest basically on a presumed lack of good faith on the part of the secured party, invoking § 1–203 and § 1–201 (19). The facts are admittedly a bit peculiar, but it is not entirely clear that the result should be reached in the absence of showing that there real-

ly was a lack of good faith. *Compare In re* Kittyhawk Television Corp., 516 F.2d 24 (6th Cir. 1975), in which perfection was said to continue despite a change in the debtor's name from "Kittyhawk Broadcasting Corporation" to "Kittyhawk Television Corporation;" Fliegel v. Associated Capital Co. of Delaware, Inc., 272 Or. 434, 537 P.2d 1144 (1975); *In re* Tri-Cities Music Centers, Inc., 4 Bkcy.Ct.Dec. 36 (E.D.Tenn.1978) (in bankruptcy).

41. *See, e. g., In re* Gac, 11 UCC Rep. Serv. 412 (W.D.Mich.1972) (in bankruptcy), where a financing statement filed under the debtor's married name was held effective in her bankruptcy following a divorce, after which she resumed her former name.

42. Revised §§ 9–402(2)(d), 9–402(7).

43. Revised § 9–402(7). *See In re* Lockwood, 16 UCC Rep.Serv. 195 (D.Conn. 1974) (in bankruptcy).

44. § 1–201(28): " 'Organization' includes a corporation, government or governmental subdivision or agency, business trust, estate, trust, partnership or association, two or more persons having a joint or common interest, or any other legal or commercial entity."

it should include all debtors who are not individuals. In any case, the intent of the revision is clear, and the intent should be carried out even in instances where the application of the words may be less than commanding.

Since financing statements are indexed under the debtor's name [45] and not under the name of the secured party, a mistake in the secured party's name would ordinarily be unimportant.[46] A mistake also is unlikely in view of the fact that the secured party prepares most financing statements and can be counted on to supervise the typing of its name or the use of a name stamp, if forms containing a printed name are not available. In any case substantial—not exact—compliance with the financing statement requirements is all that is required for an effective filing, and the statement will be effective even though it contains minor errors, if they are not seriously misleading.[47] The

---

45. § 9–403(4). The leading decision on a slightly incorrect debtor's name is *In re* Excel Stores, Inc., 341 F.2d 961 (2d Cir. 1965). *See also In re* Nara Non Food Distributing, Inc., 66 Misc. 2d 779, 322 N.Y.S.2d 194 (N.Y.Sup.Ct. 1970), affirmed 36 A.D.2d 796, 320 N. Y.S.2d 1014 (1971); *In re* Hatfield Const. Co., 10 UCC Rep.Serv. 907 (M. D.Ga.1971) (in bankruptcy); *In re* Reeco Electric Co., Inc., 415 F.Supp. 238 (D.Me.1976); Sherman v. Upton, Inc., — S.D. —, 242 N.W.2d 666 (1976). *Cf.* John Deere Co. of Baltimore, Inc. v. William C. Pahl Const. Co., Inc., 59 Misc.2d 872, 300 N.Y.S.2d 701 (N.Y. Sup.Ct.1969), ("Ranelli Construction, Inc." instead of "Ranalli Construction, Inc." was seriously misleading and ineffective). Where the names of the parties were transposed on the financing statement, the filing was held ineffective in *In re* Uptown Variety, 6 UCC Rep.Serv. 221 (D.Or.1969) (in bankruptcy). *Compare In re* Raymond F. Sargent, Inc., 8 UCC Rep.Serv. 583 (D.Me.1970) (in bankruptcy) (showing debtor's name as "Raymond F. Sargent Co., Inc." instead of "Raymond F. Sargent, Inc." was seriously misleading and ineffective) with *In re* Raymond F. Sargent, Inc., 8 UCC Rep. Serv. 746 (D.Me.1970) (in bankruptcy) (where box for debtor's name on financing statement showed "Sargent Raymond F. Inc." but signature was "Raymond F. Sargent, Inc." filing was effective).

46. *See, e. g., In re* Wilco Forest Mach., Inc., 491 F.2d 1041 (5th Cir. 1974); *In re* Colorado Mercantile Co., 299 F. Supp. 55 (D.Colo.1969). The secured party of record may in fact be a representative of a group of secured parties, which is recognized by § 9–105(1) (i) and Revised § 9–105(1)(m), or a nominee, a practice approved in *In re* Cushman Bakery, 526 F.2d 23 (1st Cir. 1975).

47. § 9–402(5), Revised § 9–402(8). *See e. g., In re* French, 317 F.Supp. 1226 (E.D.Tenn.1970) (omission of address of debtor and secured party not minor errors); *In re* Grandmont, 310 F.Supp. 968 (D.C.Conn.1970) (omission of date of security agreement minor error); *In re* Brawn, 6 UCC Rep.Serv. 1031 (D.Me.1969) (in bankruptcy) (misspelling of Brown for Brawn not minor error in debtor's name); *In re* Antekeier, 6 UCC Rep.Serv. 1027 (W.D.Mich.1969) (in bankruptcy) (omission of description of collateral not minor error); *In re* Esquire Produce Co., 5 UCC Rep. Serv. 257 (E.D.N.Y.1968) (in bankruptcy) (one digit mistake in serial number of motor vehicle was minor error); *In re* Vielleux, 5 UCC Rep.Serv. 277 (D.Conn.1967) (in bankruptcy) (mistake of over one year in date of security agreement not minor error); *In re* Tomlin, 2 UCC Rep.Serv. 197 (E.D. Ky.1963) (omission of serial number of motor vehicle not minor error). *See also In re* Mount, 5 UCC Rep.

Code does not deal specifically with errors in the secured party's name, but of course it is not an error to file a financing statement showing either the original secured party who has assigned its interest or the assignee as the secured party. Section 9–302(2) specifically recognizes that no filing is required in the case of an assignment by a secured party to continue the effectiveness of a perfected security interest against creditors of or transferees from the original debtor; if it is the assignor who gets into financial trouble, the assignee would be well advised to file an assignment, however. Absent unusual circumstances, there would appear to be no problem where the secured party of record is a nominee rather than the real secured party [48] or the principal secured party,[49] when there are various creditors involved in the secured transaction. The definition of "secured party" points to the Code's attitude toward this problem when it provides: "When the holders of obligations issued under an indenture of trust, equipment trust agreement or the like are represented by a trustee or other person, the representative is the secured party." [50] There are, however, limits, and a filed financing statement naming one secured party was held not to perfect claims of companies related to the secured party where these claims were assigned to the secured party of record after bankruptcy was filed by the debtor.[51] It would be possible to consider the secured party of record as the agent of the related companies, but in the circumstances the transactions at issue were subject to dispute as to attachment as well as perfection, particularly where the claims were assigned after bankruptcy. A different situation is presented when collateral has been pledged; but "floating secured parties" can be expected to provoke an unfavorable reaction whether justifiable or not.

§ 4–7. Description of Collateral

The basic provision of Article 9 in this area states that " . . . any description of personal property . . . is sufficient whether

Serv. 653 (S.D.Okla.1968) (in bankruptcy) (both good faith and commercial reasonableness considered in determining whether an error in a financing statement is minor); Clarke Floor Machine Div. of Studebaker Corp. v. Gordon, 7 UCC Rep.Serv. 363 (Super. Ct., Md., 1970) (non-misleading error in secured party's name minor).

48. *In re* Cushman Bakery, 16 UCC Rep.Serv. 897 (D.Me.1975). *See also In re* Wilco Forest Mach., Inc., 491 F. 2d 1041 (5th Cir. 1974).

49. *See, e. g., In re* King-Porter Co., Inc., 446 F.2d 722 (5th Cir. 1971); *In*

re Colorado Mercantile Co., 299 F. Supp. 55 (D.Colo.1969); Bramble Transp. Inc. v. Sam Senter Sales, Inc., 294 A.2d 97 (Del.1971), affirmed 294 A. 2d 104 (Del.1972). In the case of participations, the lead bank may be shown as secured party although it may not be the major lender, but this filing should be sufficient to perfect the security interest as to all participants. Heights v. Citizens Nat'l Bank, 463 Pa. 48, 342 A.2d 738 (1975).

50. § 9–105(1)(i), Revised § 9–105(1)(m).

51. *In re* E. A. Fretz Co., Inc., 565 F.2d 366 (5th Cir. 1978).

or not it is specific if it reasonably identifies what is described." [52] The collateral must be described in both the security agreement and the financing statement. The requirement for the security agreement is simply that it contain a "description of the collateral," [53] where the collateral has not been pledged, but the requirement for the financing statement is that it must contain "a statement indicating the types, or describing the items, of collateral." [54] This last provision is supplemented by a statement that: "A financing statement substantially complying with the requirements of this section is effective even though it contains minor errors which are not seriously misleading." [55] The effect of these provisions is to create a system of notice filing. That is, the filing must give notice to the public that a security interest exists in collateral,[56] but the specific items may or may not be described, or, if they are described, slight inaccuracies are tolerable if they are not misleading.[57] This system was designed in reaction to holdings of some older cases where the slightest mistake, misleading to no one, invalidated the filing.[58] When an item

52. § 9–110. *See* United States v. Antenna Systems, Inc., 251 F.Supp. 1013 (D.C.N.H.1966) ("all furniture fixtures and equipment now owned and hereinafter acquired by Borrower" reasonably identified certain collateral covered by security agreement as required by § 9–110); *In re* Esquire Produce Co., 5 UCC Rep.Serv. 257 (E. D.N.Y.1968) (in bankruptcy) ("1966 Ford" sufficient description under 9–110); *In re* Hodgin, 7 UCC Rep.Serv. 612 (W.D.Okl.1970) (in bankruptcy) ("1969 Fiat" insufficient to describe 1969 Toyota); *In re* Richards, 7 UCC Rep.Serv. (W.D.Mich.1970) (in bankruptcy) (type of collateral or goods is necessary to description under § 9–110); *In re* Kowalski, 202 F.Supp. 897 (D.C.Conn.1968).

53. § 9–203(1)(b), Revised § 9–203(1)(a).

54. § 9–402(1), Revised § 9–402(1). Where the financing statement said "various equipment, see Schedule 'A' attached hereto" but Schedule A was inadvertently not attached, the description was still held adequate, in *In re* Stegman, 15 UCC Rep.Serv. 225 (S.D.Fla.1974). But where the financing statement said merely "See attached description of property" and there was no attached description, the filing was properly held ineffective in *In re* Antekeier, 6 UCC Rep.Serv. 1027 (W. D.Mich.1969) (in bankruptcy).

55. § 9–402(5), Revised § 9–402(8).

56. Where a 1968 Chevrolet Impala was accurately described in the security agreement, the description "passenger automobile" in the financing statement was held adequate to perfect the security interest in *In re* Stephens, 8 UCC Rep.Serv. 597 (W.D.Okl.1970) (in bankruptcy). As it was expressed in Marine-Midland Bank—Eastern National Ass'n v. Conerty Pontiac-Buick, Inc., 77 Misc.2d 311, 352 N.Y.S.2d 953 (1974): "The description need only inform, it need not educate." *See also In re* Laminated Veneers Co., Inc., 471 F.2d 1124 (2d Cir. 1973). *Cf. In re* Fairway Wholesale, Inc., 21 UCC Rep. Serv. 1429 (D.Conn.1977) (in bankruptcy).

57. Describing a 1969 Toyota as a "1969 Fiat" in the financing statement resulted in an unperfected security interest in *In re* Hodgin, 7 UCC Rep. Serv. 612 (W.D.Okl.1970) (in bankruptcy). *Cf.* McGehee v. Exchange Bank & Trust Co., 561 S.W.2d 926, 23 UCC Rep.Serv. 816 (Tex.Civ.App.1978).

58. For an example of the kind of judicial interpretation the Code was counteracting, see General Motors Accept. Corp. v. Haley, 329 Mass. 559, 109 N.E.2d 143 (1952). Here the "error" was showing a party as "E. R. Miller Company" when the correct

is sufficiently described in fairly general terms but a serial number is added, it is quite simple for a typist to make a mistake in typing the number but it seems unfair to penalize a secured party for a mistake that in fact misled no one. In the days when there were not so many automobiles on the highways, a description of "one new Jordan Touring car, Number 6552" in a chattel mortgage was held ineffective to perfect the lien that was good against a purchaser when the serial number was in fact 6557.[59] In such circumstances it seems reasonably clear that anyone should have notice by virtue of the general description, if the mortgage files were consulted, and few, if any, would in fact check serial numbers when individuals are involved. The trend under the Code is to follow rather liberally the "substantial compliance" test of Section 9–402(5) or Revised Section 9–402(8),[60] which is the proper judicial approach to this kind of legislation.

It must be noted, however, that descriptions of collateral are required both in the financing statement and in the security agreement.[61] Depending on circumstances, the description in the security agreement is likely to be far more detailed than the one in the financing statement, for the former is the contract between the parties while the latter simply gives notice of the arrangement to the world. All that the financing statement is required to contain is "a statement indicating the types, or describing the items, of collateral." [62] Whether the description used is general or specific—that is, by type or by item—depends on a number of variables, but the collateral should be described specifically where feasible.

If all of the debtor's equipment is collateral, it should be sufficient to state "equipment" [63] in the blank on the financing statement. If

---

name was "E. R. Miller Co., Inc."; it was held that the error did not impart constructive notice to lien creditors. Under the Code a somewhat similar error was found minor and inconsequential in *In re* Nara Non Food Distributing Inc., 66 Misc.2d 779, 322 N. Y.S.2d 194 (1970), affirmed 36 A.D.2d 796, 320 N.Y.S.2d 1014 (1971).

59. Wise v. Kennedy, 248 Mass. 83, 142 N.E. 755 (1924).

60. *See, e. g.,* Still Associates, Inc. v. Murphy, 358 Mass. 760, 267 N.E.2d 217 (1971) in which the court refused to follow the view expressed in Wise v. Kennedy, 248 Mass. 83, 142 N.E. 755 (1924), and found a filing effective where one digit was incorrect in a ten-digit serial number. *See also* City Bank and Trust Co. v. Warthen Serv-

ice Co., 91 Nev. 293, 535 P.2d 162 (1975); Central Nat'l Bank & Trust Co. of Enid v. Community Bank & Trust Co. of Enid, 528 P.2d 710 (Okl. 1974); Bank of North America v. Bank of Nutley, 94 N.J.Super. 220, 227 A.2d 535 (1967); *In re* Esquire Produce Co., Inc., 5 UCC Rep.Serv. 257 (E. D.N.Y.1968) (in bankruptcy) (a description of "1966 Ford" was found a sufficient description, and one wrong digit in a serial number was a harmless error).

61. *See* § 9–203(1)(b), Revised § 9–203 (1)(a); § 9–402(1), Revised § 9–402(1).

62. § 9–402(1). *See* James Talcott, Inc. v. Franklin Nat. Bank, 292 Minn. 277, 194 N.W.2d 775 (1972).

63. The use on a financing statement of a defined Code term for collateral

two typewriters are being financed for a large business, they probably should be specifically described on the financing statement, as they certainly would be in the security agreement; to claim "equipment" in these circumstances probably will result in the secured party's having to release [64] the collateral that is not in fact included so that the debtor may obtain additional financing elsewhere. However, on these facts if a second financer did lend against an item of equipment and a financing statement was duly filed identifying the collateral, that second secured party would have a security interest subordinate to that of the first secured party if the first secured party and the debtor subsequently entered into a new or amendatory security agreement which included this same additional collateral, under the first to file rule in Section 9–312(5)(a); the second secured party had notice of the claim of the prior secured party by reason of the filing.

Over-reaching in the description of collateral is a particularly acute problem in the case of consumers. A description of "all consumer goods" in a financing statement sounds ominous. It may, however, be accurate. If it is too broad, as being beyond the collateral described in the security agreement, then the security agreement's description should restrict and control the financing statement's description. In any event, Section 9–204(4)(b) or Revised Section 9–204(2) will prevent the application of a security interest to after-acquired consumer goods, in most instances. But apart from its psychological aspects, there is no legal reason under the Code why the description "consumer goods" is not an adequate description in a financing statement or a security agreement on both.[65] The term

should cover any collateral of that kind which the debtor has during the period the statement is effective, if this is what the parties intend as evidenced by the security agreement, subject to § 9–204(4), Revised § 9–204(2). *See, e. g.,* National Cash Register Co. v. Firestone & Co., 346 Mass. 255, 191 N.E.2d 471 (1963), the leading case in this area. On "equipment" as adequate, *see e. g.,* United States v. Crittenden, 563 F.2d 678 (5th Cir. 1977); Maryland Nat'l Bank v. Porter-Way Harvester Mfg. Co., 300 A.2d 8 (Del. 1972); James Talcott, Inc. v. Franklin Nat'l Bank of Minneapolis, 292 Minn. 277, 194 N.W.2d 775 (1972).

64. The procedure for releasing collateral is in § 9–406, Revised § 9–406.

65. Where a security agreement showed as collateral "All of the consumer goods . . ." followed by an em-

bracive listing of goods in the printed portion of the agreement and a detailed typed list of such goods, and the filed financing statement described the collateral as "all of the consumer goods . . . located at Debtor's address shown above," the descriptions were held to be adequate in *In re* Turnage, 493 F.2d 505 (5th Cir. 1974). *See also In re* Trumble, 5 UCC Rep.Serv. 543 (W.D.Mich.1968) (in bankruptcy); *In re* Thompson, 8 UCC Rep.Serv. 1407 (W.D.Wis.1971) (in bankruptcy). Contra *In re* Lehner, 427 F.2d 357 (10th Cir. 1970); *In re* Bell, 6 UCC Rep.Serv. 740 (D.Colo.1969) (in bankruptcy); *In re* Woods, 9 UCC Rep.Serv. 116 (D.Kan.1971), all apparently holding that "consumer goods" in a financing statement is an inadequate description. There can be no support for these opinions and they would seem to be incorrect; but tech-

covers a recognized type of goods under Section 9–109, and all that Section 9–402(1) requires is a description by type on the financing statement. There may, however, be problems under the federal Truth in Lending Act.[66]

The concept of general intangibles may present peculiar problems. Since the term "general intangibles" is defined in Section 9–106 to include any personal property not otherwise categorized, it may be adequate to state simply "general intangibles" in the security agreement, and this is certainly a description by "type" that should suffice for the financing statement. The term would be reasonable where the debtor intends to grant a security interest in various kinds of business collateral which can be sensibly described plus miscellaneous collateral which cannot be so easily identified but which is perhaps necessary for the functioning of the business. By negative inference, it would appear that the use of this term in the security agreement would have been considered an adequate description in a number of cases.[67]

No kind of detailed description could be more accurate than "all household goods" or "all equipment" or "all inventory"[68] at a particular location if in fact this general description is correct. In the ordinary usage of English, "inventory" or "accounts" includes after-acquired collateral and means whatever at any time can properly be classified as inventory or accounts within the Code's definition of the term.[69] These kinds of collateral obviously must and do change. Even

nically all the 10th Circuit decided in *In re* Lehner was that the court was not convinced that the district court was "clearly wrong" and accordingly the judgment of the district court was affirmed in a per curiam opinion. The three cases all arose out of bankruptcy proceedings.

66. *See, e. g.,* Pollock v. General Finance Corp., 535 F.2d 295 (5th Cir. 1976); Tinsman v. Moline Beneficial Finance Co., 531 F.2d 815 (7th Cir. 1976); Sneed v. Beneficial Finance Co., 410 F.Supp. 1135 (D.Hawaii 1976). *Cf.* Anthony v. Community Loan & Investment Corp., 559 F.2d 1363 (5th Cir. 1977).

67. *See, e. g.,* United States v. Antenna Systems, Inc., 251 F.Supp. 1013 (D. N.H.1966); *In re* Emergency Beacon Corp., 23 UCC Rep.Serv. 766 (S.D.N.Y. 1977) (in bankruptcy).

68. *See* Borg-Warner Acceptance Corp. v. Wolfe City Nat'l Bank, 544 S.W.2d 947 (Tex.Civ.App.1976) ("all inventory of goods including . . ." held ade-

quate); *In re* Goodfriend, 2 UCC Rep. Serv. 160 (E.D.Pa., 1964) ("inventory . . . contained in the Kiddy and Women's Wear Shop" held adequate description). *See also* Evans Products Co. v. Jorgensen, 245 Or. 362, 421 P.2d 978 (1966) ("inventory" held adequate description); Goodall Rubber Co. v. Mews Ready Mix Corp., 7 UCC Rep. Serv. 1358 (Wis.Cir.Ct.1970) ("equipment" held adequate description to include steel curb and gutter forms).

69. As to inventory, *see In re* Goodfriend, 2 UCC Rep.Serv. 160 (E.D.Pa. 1964); Evans Products Co. v. Jorgensen, 245 Ore. 362, 421 P.2d 978 (1966). As to accounts, *see* Girard Trust Co. v. Strickler, 458 F.2d 435 (4th Cir. 1972); South County Sand & Gravel Co. v. Bituminous Pavers Co., 256 A.2d 514 (R.I.1969), *reversed on other grounds,* 274 A.2d 427 (1971). *See also* Matthews v. Arctic Tire, Inc., 262 A.2d 831 (R.I.1970). As to "accounts receivable," *see In re* Varney Wood Products, Inc., 458 F.2d 435 (4th Cir. 1972).

equipment changes, by way of deterioration as well as by disposition and replacement.

Where there is a discrepancy between the description in the security agreement and that in the financing statement, the narrower description should control as far as third parties are concerned.[70]   (As between the parties to the transaction, the security interest should be enforceable as created in the security agreement under Section 9–201, unless there are difficulties going to the validity of the contract.)   As against the world, the secured party has perfected an interest only in collateral described in the financing statement provided it is described in a security agreement,[71] and as between the debtor and the secured party the security interest as a matter of contract covers only what is described in the security agreement.   While occasional questions have been raised about over-broad descriptions in the financing statement, particularly in the consumer area, there would seem to be no legitimate issue to be raised here because the financing statement simply gives notice to the world, and a too-broad notice is, if anything, beneficial to third parties because it gives them warning to stay away.   In no event can the security interest extend beyond the collateral in which the debtor has granted a security interest to the secured party.

There are many kinds of collateral, and generalizations are difficult.   It must be constantly kept in mind that the financing statement simply gives notice of the arrangement between the parties, that it is by no means the same as the contract between the parties (such as the pre-Code recorded chattel mortgage would have been).   While nothing excuses over-reaching by the secured party, if the result of finding a financing statement invalid because of a technical mistake is simply to benefit third parties who have in no way been misled— and they are not likely to have been misled to their detriment in extending credit by a too-broad description of collateral—then the result is plainly wrong and clearly unjust.

§ 4–8. Real Estate Descriptions

Where the financing statement is required to contain a real property description, the provisions from Sections 9–110 and 9–402 on suf-

---

70. *See, e. g., In re* Mitchell v. Shepherd Mall State Bank, 458 F.2d 700 (10th Cir. 1972); *In re* Marta Cooperative, Inc., 344 N.Y.S.2d 676 (N.Y.Co. Ct.1973).

71. In Kapp v. United States, 20 UCC Rep.Serv. 1355 (N.D.Ill.1976), the secured party was found to be entitled to priority over a subsequently filed federal tax lien when the financing statement claimed "all present and future accounts, contract rights, chattel paper, general intangibles and instruments . . ." and the collateral in issue was a relocation payment in connection with a condemnation, which was said to be a general intangible. The opinion contains no reference to the description in the security agreement, but perhaps it can be assumed to be the same as the description in the financing statement.

ficiency and minor errors are applicable. Under the 1962 Code real property descriptions are required on financing statements covering crops and fixtures,[72] and the description used should be adequate for the statements to be properly indexed in the real estate records.[73] This may mean a legal description in some areas, while a street address or popular name may be enough in others.[74]

Under the revised version of Article 9, real property descriptions are required when the collateral is crops, or timber to be cut, or minerals (including oil and gas) and accounts arising from their sale at the point of extraction, or if the financing statement is to be filed as a fixture filing.[75] Except for crops, it is required that the statement show on its face that this kind of collateral is covered and that it is to be filed in the real estate records.[76] This is intended to eliminate certain idiosyncratic practices of a few local filing officers who did not, because it was not unequivocally clear under the 1962 Code that they

---

72. § 9–402(1). *See* United States v. Big Z Warehouse, 311 F.Supp. 283 (S.D.Ga.1970); *In re* Mount, 5 UCC Rep.Serv. 653, (S.D.Ohio 1968) (in bankruptcy).

73. The intention of § 9–401(1) is that such filings should be placed in the real estate records as a mortgage would be.

74. It is probably advisable to use both a legal description and an informal designation if both are known; in case there is a typographical error in one, the filing officer may still be able to identify the right property. In rural areas the descriptions are likely to be somewhat less formal than city lawyers might expect. For an illustrative pre-Code case, *see* State Bank of Eureka v. Lynn L. Banta, Inc., 44 Ill.App.2d 325, 194 N.E.2d 669 (1963) where an adequate real property description for a crop mortgage was: ". . . real estate, situated and being in the County of Marshall and State of Illinois, to wit: 253 acres that I have rented from William Barth and is located about 1 mile north of Washburn, Illinois." *See also* United States v. Big Z Warehouse, 311 F.Supp. 283 (S.D.Ga.1970). *But see* Piggott State Bank v. Pollard Gin Co., 243 Ark. 159, 419 S.W.2d 120 (1967). Any standard form of fi-

nancing statement which follows the model set out in § 9–402(3) contains a blank in which real estate concerned is to be described when the collateral is crops or fixtures. While a street address may be an adequate description, according to Home Savings Ass'n v. Southern Union Gas Co., 486 S.W.2d 386 (Tex.Civ.App.1972) (dictum), the complete absence of a description in the proper place will not suffice, and this absence in the designated blank is not cured by giving an address of the debtor in a preceding space on the form for the debtor's name and address even if that is in fact where the fixtures are kept. *Id.; In re* Shepherd, 14 UCC Rep.Serv. 249 (W.D.Va. 1974) (in bankruptcy).

75. Revised § 9–402(1), (5).

76. While a security interest in crops would naturally identify the collateral in that way, it is not specifically required by Revised § 9–402(5) that this fact be shown on the financing statement as it is for the other kinds of collateral covered by that Section. In the few states which adopted the first alternative version of § 9–401(1), there is no requirement that a security interest in crops be locally filed, nor does the revised version of that alternative so require.

had to, file some financing statements in the real estate records. If the debtor does not have an interest of record in the real estate, in those cases where a real property description must be given, the name of the record owner must be shown on the financing statement.[77] This is important in areas where grantor-grantee records, rather than tract records, are kept.

§ 4–9. Signatures of the Parties

The 1962 Code requires that the financing statement be signed by both the debtor and the secured party.[78] Clearly only the signature of the debtor is of any importance, and the requirement of signing by the secured party has been eliminated in the revised version of Article 9.[79] Since by definition "signed" in Section 1–201(39) "includes any symbol executed or adopted by a party with present intention to authenticate a writing," it was possible for an astute court to find that the secured party had adopted its name in the body of the financing statement as a signing.[80] The Code has never required that the statement be manually subscribed, although this is the usual thing for the parties to do and spaces are provided for this purpose on all standard forms.

Ordinarily where a corporation is a party, the financing statement will be signed by an agent on behalf of the corporation, and the name of the party in interest will be obvious because the corporate name will be written or printed on one line with "By" and a place for an agent's signature on the following line. Occasionally the standard procedure is not followed and, especially in bankruptcy proceedings, litigation may follow to declare the security interest valid or invalid, as the case may be. In one well reasoned case, the secured party's execution was found to have been adequate where the secured party's name, "Raven Industries, Inc." was handwritten in the space labelled "Secured Party," on the financing statement but no agent's signature followed; and on behalf of the debtor, an officer signed his name, under it writing the name and address of the corporate debtor.[81] As the court pointed out, the financing statement was properly indexed in the Secretary of State's Office, and it clearly provided adequate notice to anyone searching the files.

77. Revised § 9–402(5).

78 § 9–402(1).

79. Revised § 9–402(1).

80. The leading case supporting this position is Benedict v. Lebowitz, 346 F.2d 120 (2d Cir. 1965). *See also* Allo-

way v. Stuart, 385 S.W.2d 41 (Ky. 1964); *In re* Horvath, 1 UCC Rep. Serv. 624 (D.Conn.1963) (in bankruptcy). *Cf.* Plemens v. Didde-Glaser, Inc., 244 Md. 556, 224 A.2d 464 (1966). *Contra, In re* Carlstrom, 3 UCC Rep.Serv. 766 (D.Me.1966) (in bankruptcy).

81. *In re* Sport Shack, 383 F.Supp. 37 (N.D.Cal.1974).

Where a financing statement contained a trade name in the box for the debtor's name and address but it was properly executed by the individual debtor, this was held to be adequate in a bankruptcy case because all that Section 9–402(1) of the 1962 Code required was that the financing statement be "signed by the debtor" and give the debtor's mailing address.[82] This decision is particularly liberal since an inquiry to the Secretary of State's Office failed to disclose the filing of this financing statement in the name of the individual debtor, although it was indexed under the debtor's trade name. As the court pointed out, all that Section 9–403(1) requires for filing is the presentation of the financing statement and tender of the filing fee, so that a security interest could in fact be perfected even though the financing statement was never indexed. In another bankruptcy proceeding it was held adequate where the financing statement showed the debtor's correct corporate name except for the absence of "Inc." at the end of the name, and it was signed by an agent without any indication of the agent's capacity or without showing the principal's name in the signature space.[83]

To eliminate certain questions about the necessity of a manual signature on a financing statement, the revised Code allows the filing of a "carbon, photographic or other reproduction of a security agreement or a financing statement" if the security agreement provides for it or if the original statement has been filed in the particular state.[84] This eases the secured party's problem in cases where dual filing is required although its necessity was not realized at the time the transaction was entered into, and the debtor is subsequently unavailable or recalcitrant. The signature of the secured party alone is not sufficient

---

82. *In re* Bengtson, 3 UCC Rep.Serv. 283 (D.Conn.1965) (in bankruptcy).

83. *In re* A & T Kwik-N-Handi, Inc., 12 UCC Rep.Serv. 765 (M.D.Ga.1973) (in bankruptcy). *See also In re* Williams, 16 UCC Rep.Serv. 240 (N.D.Ala.1974) (in bankruptcy) (financing statement was effective where corporate secured party's name and address were shown at top of form but the signature space was blank as to the corporate name with an agent's signature on the next line, and the secured party submitted evidence of the agent's authority); Sherman v. Upton, Inc., — S.D. —, 242 N.W.2d 666 (1976); *In re* Reid Communications, Inc., 21 UCC Rep. Serv. 1436 (W.D.Va.1977) (in bankruptcy).

84. Revised § 9–402(1). This procedure was satisfactory in some states under the 1962 Code. *See, e. g.,* N.Mex. Att'y Gen.Opinion No. 62–126, 1 UCC Rep.Serv. 748 (1962); Wyo.Att'y Gen. Opinion No. 26, 1 UCC Rep.Serv. 799 (1962); Va.Att'y Gen.Opinion, 3 UCC Rep.Serv. 248 (1965); Mo.Att'y Gen. Opinion No. 402 (1965) No. 49 (1966), 3 UCC Rep.Serv. 552 (1966); Fla.Att'y Gen.Opinion No. 067–6, 4 UCC Rep. Serv. 273 (1967). *Contra, In re* Kane, 1 UCC Rep.Serv. 582 (E.D.Pa.1962) (in bankruptcy) (local filing of photocopy of financing statement insufficient even though original copy filed centrally).

on a financing statement where the second filing is a purely intrastate requirement for perfection of a security interest in original collateral.[85]

While the debtor must normally sign the financing statement to perfect the original security interest, in certain other cases the statement may be signed only by the secured party. These are principally situations where the debtor's cooperation is unlikely. The secured party alone may sign the financing statement when it is filed to perfect a security interest in collateral moved into a second state from a state where it was already subject to a security interest, and the financing statement discloses this fact. (The security interest need not have been perfected in the state from which the collateral was removed.) The secured party alone may sign when the filing is to perfect a security interest in proceeds, if the security interest in the original collateral was perfected and if the statement describes the original collateral.[86] These two situations were covered in the 1962 Code and they are continued in the revised Code.

Three further instances are contained in the 1972 Official Text where only the secured party need sign: where the debtor's location is changed to a second state, if the financing statement contains this fact; where the filing is to perfect a security interest in collateral as to which a filing has lapsed; where the filing is to perfect a security interest in collateral acquired after a change of the debtor's name, identity, or corporate structure.[87]

§ 4–10. Maturity Date

The usual form of financing statement used under the 1962 Code contains a blank in which a maturity date may be stated. If the maturity date given is five years or less, the financing statement is effective until the stated date plus sixty days. If no maturity date is stated or if the obligation is stated to be payable on demand, the financing statement is effective for five years from the date of filing.[88]

---

85. *See* § 9–402(2), Revised § 9–402(2). Section 9–401 contains two alternative versions of subsection (3). The first alternative provides that a proper filing continues to be effective even though the debtor's residence, place of business, or the location of the collateral or its use changes. *See, In re* Gildner, 6 UCC Rep.Serv. 973 (W.D. Mich.1969) (in bankruptcy), (regarding place); *In re* Morton, 9 UCC Rep. Serv. 1147 (D.Me.1971) (in bankruptcy) (regarding use). The second alternative requires refiling within four months after such a change (except that a change in use does not impair the effectiveness of the original filing) and the secured party may sign the financing statement filed in the new county; the signature of the debtor is not required. *See In re* Armstrong, 7 UCC Rep.Serv. 781 (W.D.Okla.1970) (in bankruptcy).

86. § 9–402(2), Revised § 9–402(2).

87. Revised § 9–402(2).

88. § 9–403(2). *See In re* Cantrill Const. Co., 418 F.2d 705 (6th Cir.

Unless a continuation statement is filed before the end of the effective period, the effectiveness of the financing statement lapses and the security interest becomes unperfected unless it is perfected without filing,[89] as it would be if the secured party were then in possession of the collateral.[90]

It apparently has been the almost universal practice not to insert a maturity date on the financing statement, with the result that almost all statements are effective for five years. This practice is recognized in the 1972 Official Text of Article 9, which makes filed financing statements effective for five years.[91] Of course, if the obligation is retired before the end of the five-year period and no further loans are contemplated, a termination statement can be filed to evidence that a security interest no longer exists.[92]

In two unusual situations the five-year period does not apply: to real estate mortgages filed as fixture filings [93] and to financing statements in which the debtor is, and is stated to be, a transmitting utility.[94] In both instances the statement is effective until an appropriate filing is made to terminate it.

§ 4–11. Lapse

Unless a continuation statement is filed before the time when the financing statement ceases to be effective, lapse occurs.[95] In most cases this will mean that the security interest becomes unperfected. It will, in any case, become unperfected by filing, although if the secured party is then in possession of the collateral, the perfection will continue.[96]

1969); Mid-Eastern Electronics, Inc. v. First Nat'l Bank of Southern Maryland, 455 F.2d 141 (4th Cir. 1970).

89. *Id. See* Commercial Credit Corp. v. National Credit Corp., 251 Ark. 702, 473 S.W.2d 881 (1971). In states requiring dual filing, if the dates on the two statements are inconsistent, no doubt the earlier date (or under the 1962 Code, perhaps the earlier date plus sixty days) will be the limit for the period of perfection. *See In re* Cohen, 4 UCC Rep.Serv. 22 (E.D.Pa. 1967) (in bankruptcy).

90. § 9–303(2). The requirements for filing continuation statements are in § 9–403(3). Each continuation statement is effective for five years, and there is no limit on the number which may be filed.

91. Revised § 9–403(2). *But see* § 9–403 (6).

92. *See* § 9–404, Revised § 9–404.

93. Revised § 9–403(6). *See also* Revised §§ 9–313(1)(b), 9–402(6).

94. Revised § 9–403(6). *See also* Revised §§ 9–105(1)(n), 9–401(5).

95. § 9–403(2), Revised § 9–403(2). A late filed continuation statement will not continue perfection and it will not reperfect the security interest because the continuation statement does not meet the requirements of a financing statement. *See In re* Vodco Volume Development Co., Inc., 567 F.2d 967 (10th Cir. 1978) (result based on local amendment to § 9–403(3)).

96. § 9–303(2).

The effect of lapse on third party interests was uncertain under pre-Code law and has been subject to some disagreement under the 1962 Code. Circular priority problems can arise if a lapsed security interest is said to continue to be prior to a second security interest, which is the only effective security interest when, for example, bankruptcy intervenes. Suppose A has a filed, perfected security interest in X's equipment, and then B is granted a security interest in the same equipment and it is properly perfected. Then A's interest lapses by expiration of time, and X files a petition in bankruptcy while B's interest is still effective. Clearly the trustee in bankruptcy will be subject to B's security interest. But if A is said to be entitled to priority over B, even though A's interest is now unperfected, then A has priority over B, B has priority over the trustee, and the trustee has priority over A.[97]

As between competing security interests, the usual justification for giving priority to the first filed, but lapsed, security interest over the second filed, but still effective, security interest, is that the second party knew that he had a junior interest when he entered into the transaction and there is no reason to give him more than he bargained for.[98] Whatever the merit of this resolution of the problem, it was not explicitly accepted by the 1962 Code [99] and it is explicitly rejected by the 1972 Code. In Revised Section 9–403(2) it is stated: "If the security interest becomes unperfected upon lapse, it is deemed to have been unperfected as against a person who became a purchaser or lien creditor before lapse."[1] Since the term "purchaser" includes secured parties as well as buyers,[2] a junior secured party's interest will rise to the top when a prior party's interest lapses,[3] and a buyer who purchased subject to a security interest will take free of it when lapse occurs. Whether judgment lienors should be able to take advantage of lapse was a matter of disagreement between the

97. While the Bankruptcy Act was amended to avoid the particular problem raised in *In re* Quaker City Uniform Co., 238 F.2d 155 (3d Cir. 1956), certiorari denied 352 U.S. 1030, 77 S. Ct. 595, 1 L.Ed.2d 599 (1957), the opinion is instructive in the sorts of problems circular priority situations can engender.

98. *See In re* Andrews, 172 F.2d 996 (7th Cir. 1949). *See generally* 1 G. Gilmore, Security Interests in Personal Property § 21.6 (1965).

99. Regardless of whatever interpretation the statutory language may be capable of, Comment 3 to § 9–403 takes the position that if the first secured party's security interest lapses, the second interest rises to the top— i. e., takes priority—if it continues to be perfected by filing or otherwise. *See also* Comment 7 to § 9–103, 1962 Official Text.

1. *See also* Revised §§ 9–103(1)(d)(i), 9–103(3)(e). *Cf.* Revised § 9–103(2)(d).

2. § 1–201(32), (33).

3. In Mastan Co., Inc. v. Orax Realty Corp., 20 UCC Rep.Serv. 1076 (N.Y. Sup.Ct.1976), it appears to have been

Article 9 Review Committee and the Permanent Editorial Board. The inclusion of lien creditors was made by the Board.

A new provision in the 1972 Code prevents lapse of a security interest during the debtor's insolvency proceedings by continuing the effectiveness of a financing statement, which would otherwise have lapsed during these proceedings, until sixty days after the proceedings end.[4] That a filed financing statement remains effective during insolvency proceedings, despite the expiration of its effective period, may be thought to be law at the present time but the issue has been difficult to resolve, and this resolution will now be clear.[5]

§ 4–12. Amendments to the Financing Statement

Both the debtor and the secured party are required to sign a writing which amends a financing statement. An amendment does not extend the period of the financing statement's effectiveness, and added

held that a lapsed security interest continues to have priority over a subsequently perfected security interest whose holder had knowledge of the earlier security interest prior to its lapse. If the case holds this, it is clearly wrong. It is possible, however, that the first secured party took possession of the collateral before its filing lapsed and that by retaining possession its perfection continued under § 9–312. The opinion is not clear on this point.

4. Revised § 9–403(2). This change would have been helpful to the secured party in Eastern Indiana Production Credit Ass'n v. Farmers State Bank, 31 Ohio App.2d 252, 287 N.E.2d 824 (1972), where the first secured party to file lost his priority by failing to file a continuation statement during the debtor's bankruptcy proceedings, and the interest was held to lapse.

5. There has been some disagreement on this point. Apparently this provision was thought to be unnecessary by Mr. Levenberg, in an article critical of the Article 9 amendments proposed by the Review Committee. Levenberg, Comments on Certain Proposed Amendments to Article 9 of the Uniform Commercial Code, 56 Minn.L. Rev. 117, 125–26 (1971). The criticism was answered by Professor Kripke. Kripke, Mr. Levenberg's Criticism of the Final Report of the Article 9 Review Committee: A Reply, 56 Minn.

L.Rev. 805, 811 (1972). The merit of Revised § 9–403(2) was demonstrated, about the time Professor Kripke's article appeared, in Eastern Indiana Production Credit Ass'n v. Farmers State Bank, 31 Ohio App.2d 252, 287 N.E.2d 824 (1972), where the secured party's interest was held to have lapsed on a failure to file a continuation statement after the intervention of bankruptcy. *Contra, In re* South County Motel Corp., 19 UCC Rep.Serv. 1254 (D.R.I.1976) (in bankruptcy), holding that the effectiveness of the financing statement does not lapse at the end of the Code's stated period when bankruptcy has intervened, relying in part on Isaacs v. Hobbs Tie and Timber Co., 282 U.S. 734, 51 S.Ct. 270, 75 L.Ed. 645 (1931). *See also In re* Sheets, 7 UCC Rep.Serv. 893 (W.D. Okl.1970) (in bankruptcy), arising under Alternative Subsection (3) of § 9–401 requiring refiling within four months after a debtor moves from one county to another. In this case the debtor filed a bankruptcy petition within four months of moving from one county to another, and the secured party did not refile in the second county within four months of removal, with the result that the trustee in bankruptcy was held to take superior rights under § 70c of the Bankruptcy Act when the perfected security interest lapsed at the end of the four-month period.

collateral is covered only from the date the amendment is filed.[6] Probably the only time an amendment would be filed, as a practical matter, is when collateral is to be added. Whether there is any merit in an amendment, good only for the remaining period of the original filing's effectiveness, versus an original financing statement which would be good for five years, is an open question in the abstract.

If collateral is to be released, a form signed only by the secured party may be used,[7] and the same is the case where a filing is made to show a change in the debtor's location under the 1962 Code [8] or in location, identity, or corporate structure under the revised version.[9]

§ 4–13. Termination Statements

When there is no secured obligation outstanding and no commitment to make one, the secured party is required to send the debtor a termination statement, if this is demanded in writing. If the original secured party has assigned his security interest and the termination statement is signed by one other than the secured party of record, written evidence of the assignment must be provided. Where the secured party does not comply with a proper demand within ten days, he is liable to the debtor for $100 and also for any loss caused to the debtor by his failure.[10]

These basic provisions in the 1962 Code are carried forward with some elaboration, principally mechanical and for the filing officer's guidance, in the 1972 Code. One significant change in the 1972 Code is in the area of consumer financing where the secured party will be required within a month after the debtor is entitled to a termination statement or within ten days after a written demand from the debtor to file a termination statement with the filing officer or officers with whom financing statements were filed.[11] The requirement of *filing*

---

6. § 9–402(4), Revised § 9–402(4). The revised version makes explicit requirements which were implicit in the 1962 Code.

7. § 9–406. Revised § 9–406. *But see* Credit Plan, Inc. v. Hall, 9 UCC Rep. Serv. 514 (Okl.Ct.App.1971) (nothing in §§ 9–404 or 9–406 prohibits the oral release of a security interest or the oral giving of consent to a sale of the collateral by the debtor.) *Cf.* § 9–306(2).

8. § 9–402(2).

9. Revised § 9–402(2).

10. § 9–404. *See* Tyler v. Eastern Discount Corp., 55 Misc.2d 1002, 286 N. Y.S.2d 948 (1968).

11. Revised § 9–404(1). This provision might have avoided the problem raised in *In re* Hagler, 10 UCC Rep.Serv. 1285 (E.D.Tenn.1972) (in bankruptcy), where a finance company loaned money to a consumer, secured by a perfected security interest in household furniture, and then a second finance company made a loan to the consumer and took a security interest in the same goods, learning subsequently of the first company's security interest which the second company paid with-

a termination statement, rather than merely sending one to the debtor, is intended for the protection of consumers who might not be aware of the advisability of filing such a statement if it were merely mailed to them. Of course most consumer financing is probably purchase money and often involves automobiles, so that either no Code filing is required for perfection or else certificate of title laws govern the mechanics of perfection and this provision is not in terms applicable; but in those cases where a Code filing has been made, this change is helpful.

§ 4–14. Real Estate Mortgage as a Fixture Filing

Under both the 1962 and 1972 Codes, fixtures may be encumbered in a real estate mortgage.[12]   Fixtures in existence at the time a mortgage is given will normally be covered by the mortgage, and there is no purpose to be served in filing a separate financing statement.

Under the 1972 Code a duly recorded mortgage will be effective as a fixture filing if the goods which are or are to become fixtures to the identified real estate are described by item or type in the mortgage and if the mortgage meets the standard requirements of a financing statement,[13] which most ordinary mortgages would, at least if the addresses of the parties were given. Perhaps the most prevalent ' use of this possibility will be in the financing of improvements through second or third mortgages on the real estate.

A real estate mortgage which is effective as a fixture filing remains effective until the mortgage is discharged.[14] The five-year limitation does not apply.

§ 4–15. Transmitting Utilities

In 1964 a Transmitting Utility Place of Filing Act was semi-officially proposed for enactment by states which had no legislation

out, however, requesting or receiving a termination statement. The consumer debtor then borrowed more money from the first company. The debtor then filed a wage earner proceeding under Chapter XIII of the Bankruptcy Act. In a contest between the two finance companies, the court found that the second company was entitled to priority in the collateral, relying heavily on Coin-O-Matic Service Co. v. Rhode Island Hospital Trust Co., 3 UCC Rep.Serv. 1112 (R.I.Super.Ct. 1966), which is generally conceded to be an erroneous decision. Clearly under § 9–312(5) priority should have been in the order of filing, and the first finance company to file ought to have prevailed. The second company should have been certain, when it paid off the original loan of the first company, that the debtor received and filed a termination statement; this would be required by good business practice.

12. § 9–313(1), Revised § 9–313(3).

13. Revised § 9–402(6). Under Revised § 9–402(1), only the debtor need sign the financing statement.

14. Revised § 9–403(6).

concerning filings by the covered corporations. The basic reason was to provide relief from needless multiple filings, of no value to anyone, for utilities doing business over wide areas, without amending the Code. The principal problem was fixtures, for the Code required filing in every county where any fixtures were located, even though there was not the remotest likelihood that any prospective financer would be misled by a failure to file in the records of Astabula County or the like. (One must not, of course, confuse the political potency of local recorders with the value of their records to the public they supposedly serve.) This Act had some acceptance,[15] although occasionally there have been amendments to the Code to effect the intended result.[16] The substance of this Act has been incorporated into the 1972 revisions.

The term "transmitting utility" means "any person primarily engaged in the railroad, street railway or trolley bus business, the electric or electronics communications business, the transmission of goods by pipeline, or the transmission or the production and transmission of electricity, steam, gas or water, or the provision of sewer service."[17]

The revised Code provides for central filing of all security interests in collateral, including fixtures, of a transmitting utility, and such a filing constitutes a "fixture filing"[18] so that local filing in every county will no longer be necessary. This provides a saving to the utility (and its customers) as well as a more efficient means for creditors to learn of outstanding security interests. Only central filing would be required in any case for collateral other than fixtures, under any official alternative in Section 9–401(1), even under the 1962 Code.

The financing of utilities is ordinarily long term. There is no reason, as there is with ordinary financing transactions, to limit the effectiveness of financing statements to five years in order to permit filing officers to clear their files, and no purpose would be served by requiring the filing of continuation statements. Casual financing does not occur here. A provision in the revised Code states that a filed financing statement, which says that the debtor is a transmitting utility is effective until a termination statement is filed.[19] The real estate concerned need not be described.[20]

15. See, e. g., Rev.Code Mont.1947, §§ 87A–9–302.1, 87A–9–302.2.

16. See, e. g., Ky.–KRS 355.9–302(5); Vernon's Ann.Mo.Stat. § 400.9–302(5).

17. Revised § 9–105(1)(n).

18. Revised § 9–401(5).

19. Revised § 9–403(6).

20. Revised § 9–402(5).

§ 4–16. What Constitutes Filing

The Code very plainly states that "Presentation for filing of a financing statement and tender of the filing fee or acceptance of the statement by the filing officer constitutes filing under this Article."[21] Since there are important consequences to filing and a failure of a filing officer to perform his duties properly may be costly to secured parties, this section is of considerable importance. The filing is effective from the time the statement is presented or accepted, without regard to delays in indexing. The liability imposed on filing officers, if any, for failure to perform their duties may be regulated by statute, and local laws should be consulted.

Where a copy of the original security agreement is presented for filing, as may be done under Section 9–402(1), it is quite likely that the filing officer will prepare and insert in the files a standard size financing statement. This form will clearly not be signed by the parties or either of them. Nevertheless, this indicates an "acceptance of the statement by the filing officer" and therefore is a filing under Section 9–403(1).[22] If the form submitted for filing does not meet the requirements for a financing statement contained in Section 9–402 and is not accepted by the filing officer, this should not be considered a filing under Section 9–403(1) which provides in part that "Presentation for filing of a financing statement and tender of the filing fee . . constitutes filing . . ." This provision must be read to require a conforming form,[23] at least insofar as this relates to the effectiveness of the filing in its technical aspects. If there are minor errors in the form but it is accepted by the filing officer, it may very well, if properly indexed, be adequate to give notice to the public, and the errors may be excused under the last subsection of Section 9–402.

Where federal registration or filing is required or where a state requires certificate of title notation for perfection, the statute regulating the applicable procedure must be consulted to determine what constitutes filing.

---

21. § 9–403(1). *See In re* Royal Electrotype Corp., 485 F.2d 394 (3d Cir. 1973); *In re* May Lee Industries, Inc., 380 F. Supp. 1 (S.D.N.Y.1974), affirmed 501 F.2d 1407 (2d Cir. 1974); *In re* Bengston, 3 UCC Rep.Serv. 283 (D.Conn. 1965) (in bankruptcy); *In re* Smith, 10 UCC Rep.Serv. 730 (W.D.Okl.1971) (in bankruptcy). *See also In re* Mutual Board & Packaging Corp., 342 F.2d 294 (2d Cir. 1965) ("filing" effective from time received even though filing officer erroneously refused to accept the writing) (based on pre-Code New York law which was similar to Code on this point); *In re* Kern, 443 F. Supp. 219 (D.Kan.1977) (dictum). The filing fee tendered must be correct to invoke this section. *See* In re Fidler, 24 UCC Rep.Serv. 465 (D.Or.1978) (in bankruptcy).

22. *In re* Thibodeau, 19 UCC Rep.Serv. 1250 (D.Me.1976) (in bankruptcy).

23. *In re* Smith, 205 F.Supp. 27 (E.D. Pa.1962).

§ 4–17. Where to File

Section 9–401(1) gives three alternative provisions regulating the places to file. The law of each state must be consulted to see which alternative was chosen, the filing offices selected, and whether there are any local variations beyond this point.

In the first alternative, the 1962 Code provides for fixture filings to be made locally in the office where a mortgage on the real estate would be filed or recorded and all other filings are to be made in a central office, which is usually the Secretary of State's office. This alternative was chosen by very few states.[24]

In the second alternative, the 1962 Code provides for local filing for fixtures, crops, consumer goods, and farm-connected collateral (such as farm equipment, farm products and collateral arising on the sale of such products), and central filing in all other cases. This was the most widely adopted alternative.

The third alternative is the same as the second except that where filing in a central office is required, local filing is also required where the debtor has a place of business in only one county, or if the debtor has no place of business in the state but resides in the state, then filing is also required in the county of his residence. This dual filing requirement is of no known benefit to anyone except local recorders.

These alternatives remain basically unchanged in the redraft except that each alternative now contains a provision for local filing where the collateral is timber to be cut, or minerals or the like (including oil and gas) and accounts arising from a sale at the point of extraction (all as provided in revised Section 9–103(5)), and the fixture provision is now stated in terms of a financing statement filed as a fixture filing where the collateral is goods which are or to become fixtures.[25]

These filing provisions are not applicable if the matter is governed by Sections 9–302(3) and (4), specifying overriding federal or state statutes and their effect, and a security interest may in some cases be perfected without filing under Section 9–302(1).

In general terms, the Code provides local filing for essentially local transactions, such as those involving consumers and those in some way touching the land, and central filing for business transactions.

---

24. *See* 3 Uniform Laws Annotated—
Uniform Commercial Code 238 (1968).

25. Revised § 9–401(1).

§ 4–18. The Debtor's Residence

The second and third alternative versions of Section 9–401(1) provide that in the case of farm-connected collateral or consumer goods, there must be a filing in the county of the debtor's residence (or if the debtor is a non-resident of the state in the county where the goods are kept) and where the collateral is crops there must also be a filing in the county where the crops are growing or to be grown if that county is different from the debtor's county of residence.[26]

In the case of consumer goods, this provision ordinarily creates no particular problems. Some debtors are, however, quite mobile. So long as the filing is in the county where the debtor actually resides at the time the security interest attaches, the filing should perfect the security interest then and thereafter even though the debtor subsequently moves to another locality. If the filing is in a county where the debtor claims to have a permanent residence but does not then reside, the filing would be ineffective,[27] although dual filing in both counties is a simple solution to the problem. If a debtor's mailing address is in one county but the residence is in another, filing in the county of the mailing address presumably would not be effective.[28] There are times when the secured party simply has to investigate the facts or else assume the risk of inaccurate information provided by the debtor. There have been serious problems, however, in the case of farm-connected collateral. The covered collateral is farm equipment, farm products, and accounts (and contract rights under the 1962 Code) and general intangibles "arising from or related to the sale of farm products by a farmer . . . ."[29]

If all farm-debtors were what they are so often pictured as—that is, ordinary individuals tilling their own soil—the questions would be few and readily resolvable. But many farm-debtors today are business corporations. Where they reside is not so clear. It is hoped that this issue will be resolved by a new Section 9–401(6) in the 1972 Official Text which provides that for purposes of determining the place to file, "the residence of an organization is its place of business if it has one or its chief executive office if it has more than one place of business." A similar provision appears in Revised Section 9–103(3)(d).

26. United States v. Hughes, 340 F. Supp. 539 (N.D.Miss.1972); United Tobacco Warehouse Co., Inc. v. Wells, 490 S.W.2d 152 (Ky.1973).

27. *In re* Pelletier, 5 UCC Rep.Serv. 327 (D.Me.1968) (in bankrutcy). *See also* In re Knapp, 575 F.2d 341 (2d Cir. 1978).

28. *See, e. g., In re* Baker, 4 UCC Rep. Serv. 723 (E.D.Wis.1967) (in bankruptcy), where the debtor's post office address was in Illinois but his residence was in an adjoining county in Wisconsin. *See also In re* Kalinoski, 13 UCC Rep.Serv. 387 (W.D.Wis.1973) (in bankruptcy).

29. § 9–401(1), alternatives two and three.

§ 4–19. Fixture Filings

The 1962 Code requires for perfection of a security interest in a fixture that a filing be made "in the office where a mortgage on the real estate concerned would be filed or recorded." [30] While the language might seem clear enough to require a filing officer to file fixture financing statements in the real estate records, this provision has sometimes been interpreted rather literally: filing in the same office, but not in the same records, was all that was required. In any case, filing was not required for priority of the fixture financer over real estate interests existing at the time the goods were affixed; attachment alone was sufficient. [31] The exemptions from filing for purchase money security interests in consumer goods and in farm equipment costing not more than $2500 were not available if the goods were fixtures. [32]

A filing in the real estate records will not perfect an interest in goods which are not fixtures, [33] of course, and if the parties agree that goods will remain personal property even though attached to real estate, arguably as fixtures, a filing only in the real estate records may result in an unperfected security interest, [34] but filing both in the real estate records (as against third parties) and in the proper chattel security office (as between the parties) ought to be adequate. If the goods are determined to be fixtures, a filing in the chattel records will not be effective, at least as against persons without notice. [35]

As redrafted, the filing provisions refer to a financing statement filed as a fixture filing, which is to be filed in the office where a real estate mortgage would be filed or recorded. [36] It is made clear that filing officers must index fixture filings under the names of the debtor and any owner of record shown on the statement as if they were mortgagors in a real estate mortgage, and the statements are to be indexed as if they were mortgages. [37] The term "fixture filing" [38] is introduced into the 1972 Official Text for purposes of priority under Section 9–313. If the secured party is not concerned about priority against real

---

30. § 9–401(1). *See generally* Kratovil, Financing Statements for Fixture Filings, 23 Bus.Law. 1210 (1968).

31. § 9–313(2).. *See, e. g.*, Karp Bros. Inc. v. West Ward Sav. & Loan Ass'n, 440 Pa. 583, 271 A.2d 493 (1970).

32. § 9–302(1)(c), (d).

33. *In re* Park Corrugated Box Corp., . 249 F.Supp. 56 (D.N.J.1966).

34. Cain v. Country Club Delicatessen, 25 Conn.Super. 327, 203 A.2d 441

(1964) ; *In re* Nelson, 6 UCC Rep.Serv. 854 (D.Utah 1968) (in bankruptcy), affirmed 6 UCC Rep.Serv. 857 (D.Utah 1969).

35. Tillotson v. Stephens, 195 Neb. 104, 237 N.W.2d 108 (1975).

36. Revised § 9–401(1).

37. Revised § 9–403(7).

38. Revised § 9–313(1)(b).

estate interests, filing in the chattel records will perfect his security interest against other parties, or in the case of a purchase money security interest in consumer goods, no filing at all will be required,[39] for fixtures will now be treated like any other consumer goods except motor vehicles.[40]

A financing statement filed as a fixture filing, where the debtor is not a transmitting utility, must state that it covers fixtures, must state that it is to be filed in the real estate records, and it must contain a description of the real estate which is adequate to permit proper filing. Where the debtor does not have an interest of record in the real estate, the name of the record owner must be given.[41] The redrafted version makes every reasonable effort to assure that financing statements intended as fixture filings will be properly indexed and handled in the real estate records. To conform to local practices, certain optional language is suggested in the applicable provisions,[42] and enacting states may come up with further refinements. Local tinkering with an intricate and well-drafted and complicated statute is not a pastime to be recommended to any but adepts, however.

§ 4–20. Consigned or Leased Goods

While some consignments and leases of goods are plainly, aside from the label attached, intended as security, others are clearly legitimate transactions as described. But even legitimate consignments and leases may, for whatever reasons, be invalidated as disguised secured transactions if the debtor becomes bankrupt. Lessors and consignors have long wished to have a means of filing, perhaps exclusively for reasons of protection if the debtor becomes bankrupt, without compromising the tax or other aspects of their transaction, as might happen if a financing statement labelled the parties "debtor" and "secured party." In any event, all consignments require filing for safety whether or not inventory financing is the aim under the 1962 Code,[43] and under the revision all consignments are subject to similar rules regardless of the purpose of the transaction.[44]

A new section has been added to the 1972 Official Text permitting a filing using "consignee" and "consignor" and "lessee" and "lessor"

39. Revised § 9–313(4)(c), (d).

40. Revised § 9–302(1)(d). *But see* Revised § 9–313(4)(c), (d).

41. Revised § 9–402(5).

42. See Revised §§ 9–402(5), 9–403(7).

43. § 2–326(3). *See, e. g.,* American Nat'l Bank of Denver v. Tina Marie Homes, Inc., 28 Colo.App. 477, 476 P. 2d 573 (1970).

44. Revised §§ 9–114, 9–312(3).

rather than "debtor" and "secured party." [45] While mere filing is not to be a factor in determining whether the transaction is in fact intended as security, if a security interest is found to exist, it will be perfected by the filing if it has otherwise attached.[46] If utilized, this provision will eliminate a trap for the unwary.

The 1972 Official Text does not require filing for all leases, as it does in substance for all consignments. Whether it should have done so is another question. No one would suggest that the telephone company should have to file to protect its interest in a subscriber's phone, nor that a car rental company should file to protect itself in case a renter goes bankrupt on the one day when he rents a car. Beyond this point the issues become more difficult to resolve if one is determined, contrary to experience, to insist that third parties have a right to assume that debtors own outright all property in their possession. Aside from purchase money exceptions, these matters are difficult to solve by legislative fiat unless, for instance, it is said that all leases of more than a limited duration must be protected by filed financing statements. The continuing development of leases is presently too uncertain to be tied into a strait jacket from which escape would be difficult. As it stands, the Code leaves a bit of room for some play in the joints, as Justice Holmes put it.[47]

§ 4–21. When to File

"A security interest is perfected when it has attached and when all of the applicable steps required for perfection have been taken." [48] If filing is required for perfection and a financing statement has been filed before attachment has occurred, then perfection takes place when the last of the events necessary for attachment happens.[49] It is often advisable for a financing statement to be filed and for a search of the records to be made, in order to be certain that the filed financing statement is the only one on record claiming the designated collateral, before the secured party advances value. In a number of instances the first secured party to file is entitled to priority if there are conflicting perfected security interests in the same collateral.[50]

---

45. Revised § 9–408.

46. *Id*.

47. Tyson & Bro. United Theatre Ticket Offices v. Banton, 273 U.S. 418, 446, 47 S.Ct. 426, 433, 71 L.Ed. 718 (1927) (dissenting opinion).

48. § 9–303(1).

49. *In re* United Thrift Stores, Inc., 242 F.Supp. 714 (D.N.J.1965), affirmed 363 F.2d 11 (3d Cir. 1966).

50. § 9–312(5)(a), Revised § 9–312(5)(a). Most states have adopted optional § 9–407 which provides a mechanism for obtaining information from filing officers, but the liability of the filing officers for providing inaccurate information is a non-Code problem.

§ 4–22. Claims to Proceeds and Products; Accessions

If the secured party claims an interest in the proceeds or products of collateral, this may be indicated on the face of standard forms of financing statements by checking a box before the proper word. This is a part of the form set out in Section 9–402(3) of the 1962 Code. The provision for proceeds has been dropped from this form in revised Article 9 because the right to proceeds given by Revised Section 9–306 is now treated as part of the consensual agreement the parties entered into.[51] Under this provision no claim to proceeds need be made on the financing statement and it would have no particular effect if it were made. If certain kinds of proceeds are being financed, the collateral should be inclusively described on the statement, as by claiming "inventory and accounts." Under the 1962 Code, however, a claim to proceeds would cover identifiable proceeds of any kind.

The basic reason for claiming "products" is to follow a security interest into finished goods where a portion of a manufacturing process is being financed. The principal recognition of a claim to a product in Article 9 is in Section 9–315(1)(b), which provides that if the financing statement covering the original goods also covers the product into which they have been manufactured, processed or assembled, the security interest in the original goods continues in the product.[52] Where the financing statement claims "products", a security interest in the goods as accessions cannot be claimed.[53] If various suppliers of a radio manufacturer were to claim a security interest in the financed parts and their product, they would share in the manufactured goods in that ratio which the cost of their goods bears to the cost of the total product.[54] Where a claim to the goods which are installed in or affixed to other goods is maintained, the rules of priority follow those for fixtures under the 1962 Code.[55] Such claims would be for the goods as accessions.[56]

---

51. Revised § 9–203(3).

52. § 9–315 appears to have been cited in very few cases, and in no case was it properly applicable on the facts: First Security Bank of Utah v. Zions First Nat'l Bank, 537 P.2d 1024 (Utah 1975); Sowards v. State, 137 Ga.App. 423, 224 S.E.2d 85 (1976); First Nat'l Bank of Brush v. Bostron, —— Colo. App. ——, 564 P.2d 964 (1977). The section applies to goods which have become part of a product or mass, not to ordinary goods which are part of ordinary inventory. The *Bostron* case recognized, properly, that a security

interest in cattle feed, including products, did not extend to the cattle fed.

53. § 9–315(1).

54. § 9–315(2).

55. § 9–314. *Compare* Mills-Morris Automotive v. Baskin, 224 Tenn. 697, 462 S.W.2d 486 (1971), *with* Wooden v. Michigan Nat. Bank, 117 Ga.App. 852, 162 S.E.2d 222 (1968), and Municipal Equipment Co. v. Butch & Son Deep Rock, 185 N.W.2d 756 (Iowa 1971). *See*

56. See note 56 on page 93.

The problem of accessions arises infrequently, judging from reported cases, but an obvious instance of the difficulty arises where a motor vehicle is being financed by a secured party and the debtor in possession of necessity acquires a new engine or new tires for the vehicle with a security interest being reserved by the seller of the goods because of the debtor's inability to pay cash. If the debtor then defaults as to both secured parties, which one is entitled to priority as to the engine or tires? Obviously a repossessing secured party who has financed the vehicle wants a completely equipped vehicle which can in turn be resold in an effort to recover the unpaid balance of the loan. Equally obviously the unpaid seller of the tires or engine wants to repossess its goods, or presumably its loss will be total. No doubt such a seller in the usual case will be a garage owner who could have asserted a mechanic's lien had the vehicle been retained in the garage owner's possession until payment, but the lien would be lost when the goods were released to the owner of the vehicle,[57] leaving only a claim for the purchase price unless a security interest has been reserved.

If the seller of the engine or tires reserved a security interest at the time the goods were installed, the seller should prevail over the vehicle's secured party, with a right to remove the accessions.[58] Conversely, if the sale were on open credit with no security interest reserved, or if the seller acquired a security interest after installation of the goods, then the financer of the vehicle should prevail.[59] If the security interest in the accession is not properly perfected, however, those third parties identified in Section 9–314(3), including a trustee in bankruptcy as a lien creditor, will have priority over the secured party.[60]

---

also Ford Motor Credit Co. v. Howell Bros. Truck & Auto Repair, Inc., 57 Ala.App. 46, 325 So.2d 562 (1975); International Atlas Services, Inc. v. Twentieth Century Aircraft Co., 251 Cal.App.2d 434, 59 Cal.Rptr. 495 (1967), certiorari denied 389 U.S. 1038 (1968); In re Venango Limestone Co., Inc., 1 UCC Rep.Serv. 591 (W.D.Pa.1960) (in bankruptcy), affirmed 1 UCC Rep. Serv. 602 (W.D.Pa.1960); In re Williams, 12 UCC Rep.Serv. 990 (E.D.Wis. 1973) (in bankruptcy).

56. § 9–314.

57. § 9–310. If the statute creating the lien subjected it to a perfected security interest, the secured party would prevail even if the garage owner retained possession of the vehicle. Municipal Equipment Co. v. Butch & Son Deep Rock, 185 N.W.2d 756 (Iowa 1971).

58. § 9–314(1). See International Atlas Services, Inc. v. Twentieth Century Aircraft Co., 251 Cal.App.2d 434, 59 Cal.Rptr. 495 (1967), certiorari denied 389 U.S. 1038 (1968) (dictum).

59. § 9–314(2). See Ford Motor Credit Co. v. Howell Bros. Truck & Auto Repair, Inc., 57 Ala.App. 46, 325 So.2d 562 (1975).

60. In re Williams, 12 UCC Rep.Serv. 990 (E.D.Wis.1973) (in bankruptcy). If the alleged accession is held not to be one, and the security interest in the goods has been properly perfected, the secured party will prevail over a subsequent purchaser of the whole. Mills-Morris Automotive v. Baskin, 224 Tenn. 697, 462 S.W.2d 486 (1971).

§ 4–23. Change in Debtor's Residence or Place of Business, or in Location or Use of Collateral

Section 9–401(3) has two alternative versions. In both a change in the use of the collateral does not impair the effectiveness of the original filing. In the first alternative the filing also continues to be effective even though the debtor's residence or place of business or the location of the collateral changes.[61] In the second alternative the effectiveness continues only for four months unless a financing statement, which may be filed in the new county when signed by the secured party alone, is filed within that period.[62] These provisions relate only to intrastate transactions.

§ 4–24. Improper Filings

It is always possible that a secured party in good faith[63] may file in the wrong place, or at least not in all of the right places where dual filing is required in some states. The Code provides that such a filing is effective with regard to any collateral as to which it was proper and also as against any person who had knowledge[64] of the financing statement.[65] While knowledge plays a very minor part in the rules of Article 9,[66] it does seem fair that anyone who knows of a filed financing statement, even if it is improperly filed, should take subject to it; and where dual filing is required,[67] filing in only one place should not be effective except against parties with knowledge because the security interest is not perfected. The knowledge element has been eliminated in Revised Section 9–301(1)(b) so that an unperfected security interest is subordinate to the rights of a lien creditor which arise before perfection, without regard to whether the lien creditor knew of the unperfected security interest.[68]

In *In re Babcock Box Co.*,[69] a bankruptcy case arising in a state where dual filing was required, the central filing was proper but the

---

61. *See In re* Bankrupt Estate of Smith, 508 F.2d 1323 (5th Cir. 1975).

62. *See In re* Armstrong, 7 UCC Rep. Serv. 781 (W.D.Okl.1970) (in bankruptcy); *In re* Sheets, 7 UCC Rep.Serv. 893 (W.D.Okl.1970) (in bankruptcy). The second alternative in § 9–401(3) was adopted in very few states.

63. " 'Good faith' means honesty in fact in the conduct or transaction concerned." § 1–201(19).

64. "Knowledge" means actual knowledge. *See* § 1–201(25). *See also* § 1–201(27).

65. § 9–401(2).

66. *See* Felsenfeld, Knowledge as a Factor in Determining Priorities Under the Uniform Commercial Code, 42 N.Y.U.L.Rev. 246 (1967).

67. § 9–401(1), Third Alternative.

68. *See also* Revised § 9–301(3).

69. 200 F.Supp. 80 (D.Mass.1961).

local filing was not although done in good faith, and the trustee in bankruptcy had knowledge of the filings. It was held that under Section 70c of the Bankruptcy Act the trustee, regardless of personal knowledge, had the status of a hypothetical creditor without knowledge—it was not shown that all creditiors had knowledge of the improper filing—and therefore took priority over an unperfected security interest. According to the court, "§ 9–401(2) merely makes the *lien* effective, despite the failure to make proper filing as to persons having actual knowledge of the contents of the financing statement. It does not make the improper filing effective as to anyone who does not have such knowledge and hence the lien cannot be said to have been perfected."[70] It would appear that if the lien (i. e., security interest) was effective against persons with knowledge of the improper filing, then it would follow that the security interest was perfected as to such persons. If the Code provision meant anything else, it would appear to be meaningless. Despite the perhaps infelicitous language of the opinion, the result might be justified on the basis that Section 9–401(2) makes the security interest effective against a *person* with knowledge of the improperly filed financing statement, and the definition of "person" in Section 1–201(30) does not include a trustee in bankruptcy or any other representative of creditors, but only individuals and organizations. Whether or not there is an improper filing, the security interest is good between the parties under Section 9–201, and the only point of Section 9–401(2) must be directed toward third parties,[71] although perhaps not such third parties as representatives of creditors.[72] In the 1962 Code the representative of creditors is in terms bound by the knowledge of the represented creditors if they all have knowledge of an unperfected security interest,[73] but it seems totally improbable that absolutely all creditors of anyone would have knowledge of any unperfected security interest, if one includes such creditors as the telephone company or a public utility. In any case, the knowledge provision affecting lien creditors has been dropped in the 1972 Code,[74] and a distinction must be drawn between a representative of creditors, such as a trustee in bankruptcy, and other secured parties. Knowledge of a prior security interest, which has not been perfected and which the secured party

---

70. *Id.* at 81 (emphasis added). On this point, compare Chrysler Credit Corp. v. Bank of Wiggins, 358 So.2d 714 (Miss.1978) with First Nat'l Bank & Trust v. First Nat'l Bank of Greybull, —— F.2d ——, 24 UCC Rep.Serv. 46 (10th Cir. 1978).

71. *See In re* Davidoff, 351 F.Supp. 440 (S.D.N.Y.1972).

72. *See In re* Scholl, 6 UCC Rep.Serv. 1116 (W.D.Wis.1969) (in bankruptcy).

73. §§ 9–301(1)(b) and (3). See *In re* Komfo Products Corp., 247 F.Supp. 229 (E.D.Pa.1965). Of course, if there is no showing that any creditors or the trustee knew of an improper filing, there would seem to be no basis for invoking § 9–401(2). *In re* Hyde, 6 UCC Rep.Serv. 979 (W.D.Mich.1969) (in bankruptcy).

74. Revised §§ 9–301(1)(b) and (3).

made no effort to perfect, would not affect the priority of a subsequent secured party who did perfect a security interest in the same collateral.[75]

While improper filings may sometimes be effective, there is a good faith requirement, but good faith alone is hardly sufficient to invoke Section 9–401(2) when the filing is not proper as to any collateral [76] and it is not shown that the target person, against whom effectiveness is sought, had knowledge. Where the security agreement and financing statement cover collateral of various kinds and filings must be made in different offices in order to comply with the requirements of Section 9–401(1), the first part of Section 9–401(2) makes the filing effective for collateral as to which it is proper, even though the filing is not proper for all of the collateral; [77] the second part of the Section makes the filing effective against persons with knowledge of the contents of the financing statement [78] even though the filing is improper.[79] Where knowledge is not shown and the erroneous filing is not proper as to any of the claimed collateral, the security interest is simply unperfected and the secured party's good faith is immaterial,[80] or if a filing is made in only one of two required offices, the secured party's good faith will not matter and the security interest will not be effective,[81] at least if the knowledge provision cannot be invoked, and "knowledge" means actual, not constructive, knowledge.[82]

75. *See, e. g.,* Bloom v. Hilty, 427 Pa. 463, 234 A.2d 860 (1967).

76. Larson Co. v. Pevos, 18 Mich.App. 171, 170 N.W.2d 924 (1969).

77. *In re* Rutland Tile Center, Inc., 5 UCC Rep.Serv. 1115 (D.Vt.1968) (in bankruptcy).

78. Being informed by the debtor that a security interest exists is sufficient knowledge. *In re* Davidoff, 351 F. Supp. 440 (S.D.N.Y.1972).

79. State of Missouri v. Kerr, 509 S.W. 2d 61 (Mo.1974) (financing statement filed in only one of two required offices was effective against state tax lien when state's tax representative had knowledge of financing statement before lien was filed).

80. *In re* Campbell, 3 UCC Rep.Serv. 889 (S.D.Ohio 1966) (in bankruptcy); *In re* Worldwide Handbag Co., Inc., 4 UCC Rep.Serv. 608 (N.Y.Sup.Ct.1967)

(involving assignee for the benefit of creditors as lien creditor); *In re* Village Variety & Garden Shop, Inc., 4 UCC Rep.Serv. 607 (D.Or.1967) (in bankruptcy); *In re* Baker, 4 UCC Rep.Serv. 723 (E.D.Wis.1967) (in bankruptcy); *In re* Kalinoski, 13 UCC Rep. Serv. 387 (W.D.Wis.1973) (in bankruptcy). *See also* Meadows v. Bierschwale, 516 S.W.2d 125 (Tex.1975); National Bank of Royal Oak v. Frydlewicz, 67 Mich.App. 417, 241 N.W.2d 471 (1976).

81. *In re* Hurt Enterprises, Inc., 321 F. Supp. 1307 (W.D.Va.1971); *In re* Luckenbill, 156 F.Supp. 129 (E.D.Pa. 1957); *In re* Lux's Superette, Inc., 206 F.Supp. 368 (E.D.Pa.1962); *In re* Golden Kernel, Inc., 5 UCC Rep.Serv. 43 (E.D.Pa.1968) (in bankruptcy); *In re* Computer Careers Institute, Inc., 9 UCC Rep.Serv. 930 (E.D.Tenn.1971) (in bankruptcy). *See also In re* P. S. Products Corp., 435 F.2d 781 (2d Cir. 1970).

82. § 1–201(25).

§ 4–25. Assignments of Security Interests

Many secured transactions are entered into with the understanding that the secured party will assign his interest. Most conditional sales are financed, in one way or another, by third party financers, not by the sellers.

Standard forms of financing statements will have a space in which an assignment may be shown,[83] or a form for assignments may be used.[84]

An account debtor may continue to pay the assignor until he has been properly notified of an assignment and, if requested, reasonable proof of the assignment must be furnished.[85]

While a filed assignment is not necessary, where a perfected security interest is assigned, to continue the perfection as against creditors of the original debtor or his transferees,[86] a filed assignment is necessary to protect the assignee against claims of the assignor's creditors.

Ordinarily the secured party or assignee shown on the financing statement will be the real party in interest, but this is not invariably the case. The secured party shown on the financing statement may be an agent or a trustee [87] (particularly where there are several secured parties) or a nominee.[88] The interest of such persons can, of course, be properly transferred without any changes being shown in the public records, and the rights of creditors of the debtor will not be prejudiced, since the security interest has been made public regardless of the identity of the actual secured party in interest at the time that this may become a matter of concern. This view corresponds with what is generally assumed to be the law when a negotiable note secured by a mortgage has been duly negotiated to a holder in due

---

83. *See* Marco Finance Co. v. Solbert Industries, Inc., 534 S.W.2d 469 (Mo. App.1975).

84. *See* § 9–405(2).

85. § 9–318(3). A letter stating "You are authorized to pay . . ." certain sums to assignees has been held insufficient as an assignment. S & W Trucks, Inc. v. Nelson Auction Service, Inc., 8 N.M. 423, 457 P.2d 220 (1969). *See* Marine Nat'l Bank v. Airco, Inc., 389 F.Supp. 231 (W.D.Pa. 1975).

86. § 9–302(2). *In re* Davidoff, 10 UCC Rep.Serv. 725 (S.D.N.Y.1972) (in bankruptcy).

87. *See* § 9–105(1)(i), Revised § 9–105(1) (m) (second sentence). The agency need not be disclosed in the financing statement. Industrial Packaging Products Co. v. Fort Pitt Packaging International, Inc., 399 Pa. 643, 161 A.2d 19 (1960).

88. *See In re* Cushman Bakery, 526 F.2d 23 (1st Cir. 1975).

course; that is, the security follows the note, without regard to changes in the public records.[89]

Section 9–318(1) provides:

> Unless an account debtor has made an enforceable agreement not to assert defenses or claims arising out of a sale as provided in Section 9–206 the rights of an assignee are subject to
>
> (a) all the terms of the contract between the account debtor and assignor and any defense or claim arising therefrom; and
>
> (b) any other defense or claim of the account debtor against the assignor which accrues before the account debtor receives notification of the assignment.

Section 9–206 allows a buyer or lessee of goods to give a waiver of defenses against the seller or lessor which will be enforceable by an assignee, unless a statute or decision establishes a different rule for consumers, and where a buyer executes both a negotiable instrument and a security agreement as part of the same transaction, the buyer makes such a waiver because Article 3 would give a holder in due course of the note the right to enforce the note despite such personal defenses as failure of consideration.[90] Leaving to one side the consumer cases arising out of sales, this provision is probably effective in accordance with its terms in business transactions.

In a business context, the parties may effectively agree that the buyer's defenses or claims cannot be asserted against the seller's assignee, but if there is no explicit agreement on the point, the assignee takes subject to the terms of the assigned contract and defenses or claims arising under that contract [91] and also subject to other defenses or claims which the account debtor (ordinarily in this context the buyer of goods) has against the assignor if the defenses or claims have "accrued" before the account debtor is notified of the assignment. Presumably in this provision the term "claims" includes set-offs,[92]

89. Under the Code, *see, e. g.*, Ragge v. Bryan, 249 Ark. 164, 458 S.W.2d 403 (1970).

90. See § 3–305 on the rights of a holder in due course, and compare § 3–306 on the rights of one who is not a holder in due course. The effect of § 3–305 in consumer cases is circumscribed in many instances because of state law outside the Code or by federal rules where the notes arise out of sale transactions. *See, e. g.*, 15 U.S.C.A. § 1666i, 16 C.F.R. 433 (1977).

91. Associates Loan Co v. Walker, 76 N.M. 520, 416 P.2d 529 (1966). *See also* James Talcott, Inc. v. Brewster Sales Corp., 16 UCC Rep.Serv. 1165 (N. Y.Sup.Ct.1975).

92. Investment Service Co. v. North Pacific Lumber Co., 261 Or. 43, 492 P.2d 470 (1972); Farmers Acceptance Corp. v. DeLozier, 178 Colo. 291, 496 P.2d 1016 (1972).

and "accrued" refers to the time when a cause of action came into existence,[93] so that it would not be possible for an account debtor, when sued, to assert against an assignee a right of set-off arising under an unrelated contract when the right had not arisen before the account debtor was notified of the assignment.[94] This limitation may perhaps be justified on the basis that it is necessary if businesses are to receive financing, and the account debtors have remedies directly against the persons they did business with, that is, the assignors. In any case, these limitations do not relate to rights growing out of the assigned contract.

The statute specifies no particular form of notification in Section 9-318(1)(b), so presumably the rule of Section 1-201(26) would be applicable, and the account debtor would "receive notification" if the notice is brought to his attention or to the attention of a proper employee.[95] However, until the notice is received, the account debtor may continue to pay the assignor and will not be liable twice for payments made between the time of the assignment and the time of the receipt of notice.[96] Nor will the account debtor be liable to the assignee for payments made to the assignor after notice of the assignment has been received if in fact the account debtor has claims against the assignor under the contract in excess of the amounts improperly paid to the assignor rather than the assignee.[97] If a notice has been given to the account debtor, payments should then be made to the assignee, and the assignee is under no obligation to apply the first money received to the immediate repayment of the loan,[98] which might make it difficult for a contractor to continue performance and to keep paying workers and suppliers. It is not advisable for the account debtor to make future payments to others than the assignee

93. Seattle-First Nat'l Bank v. Oregon Pacific Industries, Inc., 262 Or. 578, 500 P.2d 1033 (1972).

94. Fall River Trust Co. v. B. G. Browdy, Inc., 346 Mass. 614, 195 N.E.2d 63 (1964). *See also* American East India Corp. v. Ideal Shoe Co., 400 F.Supp. 141 (E.D.Pa.1975). *Cf.* James Talcott, Inc. v. Sacks Woolen Co., Inc., 18 UCC Rep.Serv. 534 (N.Y.Sup.Ct.1975).

95. *See* Bank of Salt Lake v. Corporation of the President of the Church of Jesus Christ of Latter-Day Saints, 534 P.2d 887 (Utah 1975); Gateway Nat'l Bank of Chicago v. Saxe, Bacon & Bolan, 40 A.D.2d 653, 336 N.Y.S.2d 668 (1972). *See also* §§ 1-201(25), 1-201 (27). The filing of a financing statement is not "notice." *In re* Chase

Manhattan Bank (N.A.) v. State of New York, 48 A.D.2d 11, 367 N.Y.S.2d 580, 357 N.E.2d 366 (1975).

96. § 9-318(3). *See* Commercial Savings Bank v. G & J Wood Products Co., Inc., 46 Mich.App. 133, 207 N.W.2d 401 (1973). If no notice is ever given, the account debtor is of course protected in paying the assignor rather than the assignee. First Finance Co. v. Akathiotis, 110 Ill.App.2d 377, 249 N.E. 2d 663 (1969).

97. Ertel v. Radio Corp. of America, —— Ind.App. ——, 354 N.E.2d 783 (1976).

98. Florida First Nat'l Bank at Key West v. Fryd Construction Corp., 245 So.2d 883 (Fla.App.1971).

on the thought that the assignee has been paid enough to repay the loan or on some other basis, unless the assignee is prepared to pay twice [99] or has an agreement with the assignee. There is no requirement that the notification be given by the assignee, but it is likely that a financial institution, the usual assignee in these cases, would be better prepared with the proper forms for the purpose. In any event where the notification on the bottom of invoices sent by the assignor to the account debtor stated that checks in payment were to be made jointly payable to a designated bank and the assignor, this was said in one case to be insufficient notice of the assignment.[1] The notation did not state that there had been an assignment nor reasonably identify the assignee's rights, as required by Section 9–318 (3); nor, indeed, were the parties identified as assignor and assignee. While it seems reasonable to conclude that the notification was not legalistically done, it hardly seems reasonable for a corporate account debtor to ignore this notice with impunity, as the court allowed, when the statute authorizes the account debtor to demand reasonable proof of the assignment, and no such demand was made. Had the bank sent its own notice of the assignment, presumably this problem could not have been raised. Insofar as the case involved a notice given one day before the loan was made and one day before the security agreement was executed, it would seem dubious to suggest that the account debtor "could not be put on notice of an assignment prior to the time that that assignment existed," [2] for that was in fact what was done, and the notice was simply ignored. Common sense should not be left at the courthouse door.

Changes have been made in subsections (2), (3), and (4) of Section 9–318 in the 1972 Code principally to reflect the fact that "contract right" has been dropped in the revised version of Article 9, but also to obviate problems that might arise because an "account debtor," to which the subsections refer, is defined in Section 9–105(1)(a) to mean a person obligated on an account, chattel paper, or general intangible, while the language in the earlier version referred to accounts and contract rights as the subjects of assignment. The earlier language of Section 9–318(3), for example, authorized the account debtor to pay the assignor until the account debtor received notification of the assignment of the *account*; what very probably had been assigned, in most cases, would have been a contract right which would ripen into an account when the underlying contract was performed but which was not an account at the time of the assignment. This problem was raised in one case and resolved by the court's determination

---

99. Bank of Commerce v. Intermountain Gas Co., 96 Idaho 29, 523 P.2d 1375 (1974).

1. Citizens State Bank of Corrigan v. J. M. Jackson Corp., 537 S.W.2d 120 (Tex.Civ.App.1976).

2. *Id.* at 121.

that in the circumstances the arrangement reasonably identified the rights assigned, as required by Section 9–318(3).[3] Under Revised Section 9–106, reflecting the dropping of the term "contract right," an account includes a right to payment whether or not earned by performance, if it is a right to payment for goods sold or leased or services rendered not evidenced by an instrument or chattel paper.

As a result of experience during World War II, it became obvious that modifications of assigned contracts were sometimes necessary, particularly in the field of government contracts. This experience is behind Section 9–318(2) which allows good faith modifications, if commercially reasonable, even though notification of the assignment has been given, so long as the assigned right to payment has not yet been earned, and the assignee's rights continue in the modified contract. While it might not usually be advisable to so provide, the contract of assignment could make modification a breach, which would give the assignee the rights and remedies of a secured party under Part 5 of Article 9.

If a contract between the contract debtor and the assignor contains a term prohibiting an assignment, the term is ineffective,[4] according to Section 9–318(4), and if an assignment is made, it presumably is enforceable. However, in order for the assignee to be entitled to recover anything, there must be something owing to the assignor. What the section permits is an assignment of money due or becoming due under a contract—the contract itself may not be assignable— so that if the assignor, perhaps because of a failure to perform or perform properly, has nothing coming due, the assignee will get nothing or in fact may have to repay money which has been received.[5] In construction contracts there may well be mechanic's lien claims which will come ahead of the assignee's right to collect.[6] The assignee ordinarily will be in no better position than the assignor.

---

3. Marine Nat'l Bank v. Airco, Inc., 389 F.Supp. 231 (W.D.Pa.1975).

4. *See, e. g.*, Florida First Nat'l Bank at Key West v. Fryd Construction Corp., 245 So.2d 883 (Fla.App.1971). *Contra*, Mingledorff's, Inc. v. Hicks, 133 Ga. App. 27, 209 S.E.2d 661 (1974), where the court enforced a no-assignment clause in a contract for the installation of heating and air conditioning systems apparently on the ground that the contract was basically for services, not the sale of goods, and the court thought that § 9–318(4) applied only to goods. However, the term "account" is defined in § 9–106 as including rights to payment for services rendered which are not evidenced by instruments or chattel paper, as well as rights to payment for goods sold or leased.

5. Farmers Acceptance Corp. v. DeLozier, 178 Colo. 291, 496 P.2d 1016 (1972).

6. Panhandle Bank & Trust Co. v. Graybar Electric Co., Inc., 492 S.W.2d 76 (Tex.Civ.App.1973).

PART III. PERFECTION BY POSSESSION; TEMPORARY PERFECTION

§ 4–26. What Collateral May be Pledged

Section 9–305 states that a security interest in goods, instruments, negotiable documents, chattel paper, or letters of credit and advices of credit[7] may be perfected by the secured party's taking possession of the collateral.[8] To this list the redraft of Article 9 has added "money."[9] While not expressly stated, it is inherent in this provision that possession by an agent is possession by the secured party.

---

7. *See* § 5–116(2)(a), Revised § 5–116(2)(a). When in the revised version of Article 9 "contract right" was dropped and "account" was expanded to cover most of what would have been contract rights, § 5–116(2)(a) had to be amended to conform, by a substitution of terms. To effectuate the use of "back to back" letters of credit, § 5–116 provides, in part, that while the right to draw under a credit can be transferred or assigned only when the credit expressly says so, the beneficiary may assign his right to proceeds before performance even though the credit says that it is nontransferable or nonassignable, and this is the assignment of a "contract right" ("account" under Revised Article 9) and it is governed by Article 9 except that an assignment is ineffective until the letter of credit or advice of credit is delivered to the assignee, and the delivery constitutes perfection under Article 9. This provision coordinates with § 9–305.

8. In Lee v. Cox, 18 UCC Rep.Serv. 807 (M.D.Tenn.1976), another class of collateral was apparently added: an unpaid seller of Arabian horses, who had retained the registration papers pending payment in full, was allowed to retain those papers even though the horses were to be sold in a bankruptcy proceeding and the horses would bring a higher price with the registration papers. This result apparently was reached because of the terms of the contract of sale, which had not been performed, and not because Article 9 recognized a pledge of these papers as creating a security interest in any kind of collateral. The registration papers are not really analogous to a motor vehicle certificate of title, since the horses could be sold without the papers and the buyer would take good title. The security interest was held not to be perfected in *In re* Bialk, 16 UCC Rep.Serv. 519 (W.D.Mich.1974) (in bankruptcy), where the collateral was medals and coins kept in a bank safe deposit box to which the debtor had given the secured party the keys. The bailee-bank had no notice, and the debtor could have had the box opened without presenting the keys if a fee were paid. The secured party was said not to have possession under § 9–305.

9. It was an understandable oversight in the drafting of Article 9 that coins of numismatic value were not provided for. If the coins were spendable (or if not, for that matter), a pledge was the only sensible way of perfecting a security interest in them, and yet they did not in terms fall under § 9–305 since they were expressly excluded from the definition of goods in § 9–105(1)(f) and were not otherwise covered. While accommodated in the 1972 Official Text, the 1962 Official Text was indeed superficially at fault here, leading one referee in bankruptcy to the absurd conclusion that there was no perfected security interest in spendable numismatic coins which had been pledged, that they were general intangibles and no security interest in them could be perfected except by filing (and there was no filing). This result was reversed in an excellent opinion by Judge Regan in *In re* Midas Coin Co., Inc., 264 F.Supp. 193 (E.D.Mo.1967), *affirmed sub nom.* Zuke v. St. Johns Community Bank, 387 F.2d 118 (8th Cir. 1968). *See also In re* Burnett, 21 UCC Rep.Serv. 1471 (D.R.I.1977) (in bankruptcy).

There is no relation back when perfection is by possession,[10] and the perfection continues only so long as possession is retained.[11] But if the security interest was perfected by some other means before possession was transferred, the perfection would continue.[12] This might be the case where there was a filed security interest in goods and the debtor pledged them with the secured party just before the filing lapsed, or at any time during the five year period for that matter; or if the secured party had a purchase money security interest in a painting sold to a consumer and the consumer later pledged the painting with the secured party; or if the security interest was first perfected by a pledge and then there was a filing and the secured party released the goods to the debtor.

But a pledge will not perfect a security interest if the events required for attachment have not occurred.[13] That is, there must have been an agreement, value must have been given, and the debtor must have rights in the collateral under Section 9–204(1) or Revised Section 9–203(1). In *Transport Equipment Co.* v. *Guaranty State Bank,*[14] a security interest was considered to be unperfected by filing because the financing statement contained no "granting" clause and there was no security agreement although there was a promissory note, the details of which are not disclosed in the opinion.[15] However, when the secured party took possession of the collateral this was held to perfect the security interest. The requirement of an "agreement" under Section 9–204(1) or Revised Section 9–203(1) is no more met in the case of a mere pledge than it is when there is a filed financing statement but no separate security agreement. Admittedly it would seem only reasonable that a taking of possession of collateral implies the existence of an agreement for security, but the same is true of the filing of a financing statement where in fact there is an obligation to be secured. The agreement may be oral where the goods are pledged while it must be in writing and signed by the debtor where the debtor retains possession of the collateral,[16] but in any event for attachment there

---

10. § 9–305. The reference to relation back is simply intended to make it clear that the Code intends no reversion to the days when a belated transfer of possession perfected a security interest as of the time when it was created. *See In re* Granite City Co-operative Creamery Ass'n, 7 UCC Rep. Serv. 1083 (D.Vt.1970) (in bankruptcy). Such problems once arose in bankruptcy and have long been matters of ancient history. *See, e. g.*, Sexton v. Kessler, 225 U.S. 90, 32 S.Ct. 657, 56 L.Ed. 995 (1912). *See* Bankruptcy Act, § 60a(7).

11. Except for interests temporarily perfected for 21 days under § 9–304(5). *See In re* Washington Processing Co., Inc., 3 UCC Rep.Serv. 475 (S.D.Cal.

1966) (in bankruptcy). If unregistered securities are pledged, their release may result in liability for the pledgee under Rule 10(b)–5. *See* Mallis v. Federal Deposit Ins. Corp., 568 F.2d 824 (2d Cir. 1977), certiorari dismissed 435 U.S. 381, 55 L.Ed. 357, 98 S.Ct. 1117 (1978).

12. § 9–303(2).

13. § 9–303(1).

14. 518 F.2d 377 (10th Cir. 1975).

15. As to these matters, *see* § 3–9 *supra*.

16. These are statute of frauds provisions in § 9–203(1) and Revised § 9–203(1).

must be an agreement under either version of the Code, and the court's resolution of the problems involved may deserve fresh thinking when a similar problem arises in the future. The implications do not so much go to the pledge problem as to the use of a financing statement (or a financing statement and note) as a security agreement, but the case does underscore the necessity of an agreement even in the case of a pledge, and the decision seems to rest on some unstated assumption that there must be an agreement when the secured party takes possession of the collateral, which is no doubt true, but perhaps no truer in the case of a pledge than where a financing statement is filed.

A special sort of problem can arise where there is an unperfected security interest in goods, and the goods are repossessed (or possessed for the first time) by the secured party just before the debtor files a bankruptcy petition. If the act of repossession is treated as the perfection of a security interest, then we have a "transfer" [17] on account of an antecedent debt and, other elements being present, a preference under the Bankruptcy Act,[18] which probably can be set aside.[19] It would seem, however, that the secured party is not in fact perfecting a security interest in the usual sense but rather exercising rights on the debtor's default as given in Part 5 of Article 9, although the exercise by the secured party of the right to take possession of the collateral after default is often analyzed as perfection of the security interest when there has been no prior perfection.[20] In *In re Bye* [21] a

---

17. Bankruptcy Act, § 1(30), 11 U.S.C.A. § 1(30).

18. Bankruptcy Act, § 60a(1), 11 U.S. C.A. § 96(a)(1).

19. Bankruptcy Act, § 60b, 11 U.S.C.A. § 96(b).

20. *See, e. g.,* Engelsma v. Superior Products Mfg. Co., 298 Minn. 77, 212 N.W.2d 884 (1973) (dictum); Barry v. Bank of New Hampshire, 113 N.H. 158, 304 A.2d 879 (1973). In Porter v. Searle, 228 F.2d 748 (10th Cir. 1955), a pre-Code case, when a buyer refused to execute what would now be a security agreement and financing statement after a transfer of possession of the goods, it was held that the seller's repossession was not to perfect the security interest but to discharge it. (The case involves what would now be an unperfected security interest but what was then treated as an equitable lien, an analysis that would no longer appear to be feasible under Bankruptcy Act, § 60a(6), and the Code.) In Kulik v. Albers, Inc., 91 Nev. 134, 532 P.2d 603 (1975), a secured party with

an unperfected security interest took possession of collateral, apparently by voluntary transfer from the debtor in satisfaction of the debt, prior to the levy of execution under a third party claim against the debtor, and this was held to be a fraudulent conveyance under the Uniform Fraudulent Conveyance Act. Since the debtor's antecedent debt to the secured party was satisfied, it would appear that the secured party had given "fair consideration" under § 3 of the Uniform Fraudulent Conveyance Act so that there would have been no ground for the levying creditor to attack the transfer under that Act. Apparently the taking of possession of the collateral by the secured party was treated as a perfection of the security interest, but if so this would seem to preclude a levying creditor acquiring superior rights under § 9–301(1)(b), contrary to the court's holding. *See also* Raleigh Industries of America, Inc. v. Tassone, 74 Cal.App.3d 692, 141 Cal. Rptr. 641 (1977).

21. 5 UCC Rep.Serv. 656 (D.Minn.1968) (in bankruptcy).

sole proprietorship and a bank entered into a security agreement covering certain collateral but the bank failed to perfect its security interest by filing in both offices required by local law. The bank took possession of the collateral within four months of the date when the debtor filed his bankruptcy petition, and this was held to have been a perfection of the security interest, and thus a "transfer" which, occurring within four months of bankruptcy, created a preference, other elements being present.[22] It would seem that the "transfer" as defined in Section 1(30) of the Bankruptcy Act took place when the security agreement was entered into, but for the purposes of the preference provision of Section 60a(1), the "transfer" takes place when, according to Section 60a(2), the transfer becomes "so far perfected that no subsequent lien upon such property .   .   . could become superior to the rights of the transferee," and in the case of an unperfected security interest this moment cannot occur as long as the debtor has possession of the goods, in the absence of proper filing, where the goods are equipment because used in the debtor's business. Whatever the analysis that may be appropriate for bankruptcy preference purposes, it would seem that, at least absent bankruptcy, where a secured party takes possession, after default, of goods subject to an unperfected security interest, that is not a perfection of the security interest but a method of realizing on the collateral under Part 5 of Article 9. If a preference attack by the trustee did not succeed, perhaps because the secured party did not have reasonable cause to believe the debtor was insolvent at the time the goods were repossessed, there would appear to be no basis for challenge under Section 70c of the Bankruptcy Act so long as the repossession is prior to the filing in bankruptcy,[23] and the possession may be that of someone other than the actual secured party.[24]

There is no explanation in the Code of what is meant by *"taking possession of the collateral,"* which is the term used in Section 9–305. This term may have been chosen originally because it seems to be appropriately apposite to the priority rules of Section 9–312(4) and Section 9–301(2) (at least as revised) which are based on when the debtor *"receives possession of the collateral."* In the usual cases where collateral is pledged, it will be physically transferred from the debtor to the secured party, and the concept of taking possession will present no problem. Where the secured party has possession of the collateral at the time the secured transaction is entered into and then on some basis the goods thereafter reach the debtor's premises before a filing

---

22. *See In re* Gross Mfg. & Importing Co., Inc., 328 F.Supp. 905 (D.N.J.1971).

23. *In re* Char, 15 UCC Rep.Serv. 509 (S.D.N.Y.1974) (in bankruptcy).

24. *In re* Simpson, 4 UCC Rep.Serv. 243 (W.D.Mich.1966) (in bankruptcy).

is made, the secured party clearly may have a serious problem if third party rights intervene and there is no filing within ten days to comply with Sections 9–301(2) or 9–312(4). If the collateral were inventory, a problem could arise under Section 9–312(3). Quite apart from the matter of "receiving" or "taking," "possession" itself is an undefined concept in Article 9 but it would appear ordinarily to mean actual physical possession,[25] although some kinds of collateral in at least some circumstances may not be readily susceptible of physical possession.[26]

There is a sentence in Section 9–305 which states: "If such collateral other than goods covered by a negotiable document is held by a bailee, the secured party is deemed to have possession from the time the bailee receives notification of the secured party's interest."[27] In this sentence "such collateral" refers to every kind of collateral in which a security interest can be perfected by possession, and that covers all categories except accounts and general intangibles (and contract rights under the 1962 Code).[28] The meaning of this provision is clear insofar as "bailee" means the kind of person referred to in Article 7: a person who issues a warehouse receipt, bill of lading, or other document of title acknowledging possession of goods and contracting to deliver them.[29] In the case of goods held by a warehouseman

---

25. Compare the definition in § 2–103(1) (c): " 'Receipt' of goods means taking physical possession of them."

26. *See, e. g.,* Blumenstein v. Phillips Ins. Center, Inc., 490 P.2d 1213 (Alaska 1971), where a conditional seller of a small sailing vessel failed to perfect a security interest and then attempted to retake possession (in some sense) after receiving a "quitclaim deed" from the defaulting buyer, but the seller's efforts were made only after the rights of an attaching creditor had arisen. On the facts it probably would not have mattered what the conditional seller did by way of belatedly repossessing the vessel, but one can imagine some practical problems in retaking possession of a boat in Nome, Alaska, as winter approaches. *See also In re* Republic Engine & Mfg. Co., 3 UCC Rep.Serv. 655 (N.D.Ohio 1966) (in bankruptcy).

27. *See* Estate of Hinds, 10 Cal.App.3d 1021, 89 Cal.Rptr. 341 (1970) (pointing out that § 9–305 does not require that the secured party *send* notice to the bailee—in this case an escrowee—but

that the notice be received). While a debtor cannot be considered a bailee for purposes of § 9–305, *In re* De-Flectronics, 4 UCC Rep.Serv. 450 (D. Conn.1967) (in bankruptcy), an attorney for the debtor was recognized as a bailee for such purposes in Barney v. Rigby Loan & Inv. Co., 344 F.Supp. 694 (D.Idaho 1972). *Contra,* Stein v. Rand Construction Co., Inc., 400 F. Supp. 944 (S.D.N.Y.1975). *See also In re* Copeland, 531 F.2d 1195 (3d Cir. 1976); *In re* Miller, 545 F.2d 916 (5th Cir. 1977); Heinicke Instruments Co. v. Block, 14 UCC Rep.Serv. 167 (D.Or.1974).

28. If goods are subject to a filed, perfected security interest at the time the bailee takes possession, the first perfected security interest is entitled to priority. Douglas-Guardian Warehouse Corp. v. Esslair Endsley Co., 10 UCC Rep.Serv. 176 (W.D.Mich. 1971).

29. § 7–102(1)(a). Probably only goods (as defined in § 9–105(1)(f), Revised § 9–105(1)(h)) could be covered by documents of title in the normal course

under a non-negotiable document of title, receipt of notification of the secured party's interest in any case constitutes perfection,[30] without regard to the possessory aspect. If "bailee" is used in a broader sense—and nowhere in Article 9 is it restricted to the Article 7 definition[31]—the problems may become complicated, as, for example, where securities are kept with a depositary and then are used for collateral for loans by third parties.

§ 4-27. Goods

While pledges of consumer goods may be rare, they are not unknown, as pawnbrokers can attest. Pledges are possible but unlikely in the case of equipment, which it is probably necessary for the debtor to retain if his business is to continue to operate. Pledges are fairly common in the case of inventory, and they often take the form of a field warehouse, although goods can be stored in any warehouse with the secured party holding a non-negotiable receipt issued to him or a negotiable receipt issued or indorsed to him, or he may notify the warehouseman of his interest if a negotiable receipt is not outstanding.

If there is a filed security interest covering the goods at the time possession is transferred, the pledgee's interest will be subordinate. In the case of equipment, where a purchase money security interest may be perfected by filing within ten days after the debtor receives possession of the goods, a pledgee might take subject to a security interest which is not on file at the time the goods are pledged. It is always advisable for a pledgee to search the appropriate files before accepting the goods and making the loan; business experience may suggest further precautions.

of events. While nothing in Article 9 restricts the use of "bailee" to the definition in Article 7, the same could be said of Article 2 where in fact the usage would seem to be so restricted. *See, e. g.,* § 2-503(4). *See* Stanley v. Fabricators, Inc., 459 P.2d 467 (Alaska 1969).

30. § 9-304(3). *See* Philadelphia Nat. Bank v. Irving R. Boody Co., 1 UCC Rep.Serv. 560 (Funk, Arbitrator 1963). *See also* Funk, Trust Receipt v. Warehouse Receipt—Which Prevails When They Cover the Same Goods? 19 Bus. Law. 627 (1964).

31. The president of the debtor corporation could not, for purposes of § 9-305, serve as bailee to hold collateral, and such possession resulted in an unperfected security interest in *In re* North American Builders, Inc., 320 F.Supp. 1229 (D.Neb.1970). The bailee must be an independent person, as a professional bailee would be, and not the debtor or a relative of the debtor or an officer of the debtor. *See In re* Black Watch Farms, Inc., 9 UCC Rep. Serv. 151 (S.D.N.Y.1971) (in bankruptcy).

§ 4–28. Field Warehouses

Field warehouses are used for business, not legal reasons.[32] Any time a field warehouse is used, the secured party could and for maximum protection probably should perfect his security interest by filing. Field warehouses are used so that the secured party can maintain a control over the debtor's inventory for business purposes. In the ordinary case, a professional warehouseman will establish a warehouse on the debtor's premises, probably by fencing off a portion of the debtor's premises, signs will be posted, and non-negotiable receipts for the goods will be issued to the secured party. The secured party may authorize the warehouseman to release goods to the debtor at a certain rate or in certain daily quantities or in whatever situations satisfy the parties. Specified amounts of raw materials may be released, for example, in a manufacturing process, when agreed quantities of finished products are produced. The custodian in charge of the field warehouse will usually be a former employee of the debtor who temporarily serves in the new capacity and who is now paid by the warehouseman. The possibilities for fraud are apparent, but the interest of field warehousemen in protecting their business reputations is such that this form of security control continues to be used even though it is not legally necessary under the Code. A somewhat relaxed form of field warehousing known as "certified inventory control" has also been used,[33] and filing for perfection is probably necessary if this system is used; it is certainly prudent.

§ 4–29. Instruments

In general, security interests in instruments can be perfected only by taking possession.[34] There is a 21-day period of perfection without filing or taking possession which begins to run at the time of attach-

---

32. Before the Code, field warehouses did serve a legal function, at least when scrupulously maintained. *See* Skilton, Field Warehousing as a Financing Device, 1961 Wis.L.Rev. 221, 403, Birnbaum, Form and Substance in Field Warehousing, 13 Law & Contemp.Prob. 579 (1948), Friedman, Field Warehousing, 42 Colum.L.Rev. 991 (1942). Thanks to the notoriety generated by the so-called Salad Oil Swindle of the early 1960's, some of the practices of field warehousing are better known than they once were, but an aura of esoterica remains. *See* Proctor & Gamble Distributing Co. v. Lawrence American Field Warehousing Corp., 16 N.Y.2d 344, 266 N.Y.S.2d 785, 213 N.E.2d 873, 21 A.L.R.3d 1320 (1965); Krause v. American Guarantee & Liability Ins. Co., 22 N.Y.2d 147, 292 N.Y.S.2d 67, 239 N.E.2d 175 (1968); Heimann v. American Express Co., 53 Misc.2d 749, 279 N.Y.S.2d 867 (1967).

33. *See* Davenport & Henson, Secured Transactions—II at 70–71 (1966).

34. § 9–304(1), Revised § 9–304(1). A secured party in possession may in some circumstances be subject to considerable liability under § 9–207. *See, e. g.,* Reed v. Central Nat. Bank

ment, if the interest arises for new value under a written security agreement.[35]   Since the term "instrument" includes securities,[36] as well as negotiable and non-negotiable paper,[37] this provision may well be used when, if federal law permits, a lender finances the acquisition of securities; it will rarely be used to finance a borrower's acquisition of commercial paper.

Where the secured party has a perfected security interest in an instrument by a pledge, the interest remains perfected for 21 days if the secured party delivers the instrument to the debtor for sale or exchange or presentation, collection, renewal or registration of transfer.[38]   Where a note or a bond or a debenture or stock may be pledged to secure payment of an obligation, this provision allows the secured party to maintain his interest for 21 days after releasing the collateral while the debtor sells or presents and collects the instrument.   A bona fide purchaser [39] of a security or a holder in due course [40] who acquired a negotiable instrument would, however, take free of the secured party's claim.[41]

Since subsequent financers could qualify for these positions, the primary protection of this provision arises if the debtor becomes bankrupt within the 21-day period.

of Alva, 421 F.2d 113 (10th Cir. 1970) (involving convertible debentures); Grace v. Sterling, Grace & Co., 30 A.D. 2d 61, 289 N.Y.S.2d 632 (1968) (involving repledged convertible debentures); Traverse v. Liberty Bank & Trust Co., 5 UCC Rep.Serv. 535 (Mass.Super.Ct. 1967) (involving convertible debentures).   An interesting case involving "possession" is *In re* Chapman, 5 UCC Rep.Serv. 649 (W.D.Mich.1968) (in bankruptcy).

35.   § 9–304(4).

36.   *In re* Copeland, 531 F.2d 1195 (3d Cir. 1976). § 8–321 of Revised Article 8—Investment Securities (officially approved in 1978) requires a transfer of a "security," as defined in Article 8, to the secured party or a person designated by the secured party for enforceability and attachment of the security interest.   The rules of this section on attachment and perfection of security interests in certificated and uncertificated securities effectively overrule some sections of Article 9.

37.   § 9–105(1)(g), Revised § 9–105(1)(i). *See* Stein v. Rand Const. Co., Inc., 400 F.Supp. 944 (S.D.N.Y.1975) (certificate of deposit).

38.   § 9–304(5)(b). The perfection lapses if the debtor is allowed to keep possession of the instrument beyond the 21-day period. McIlroy Bank v. First Nat. Bank of Fayetteville, 252 Ark. 558, 480 S.W.2d 127 (1972).

39.   §§ 8–301, 8–302.

40.   §§ 3–302, 3–305, 1–201(20).

41.   § 9–309. One could not be a holder in due course of a negotiable instrument, under § 3–302(1)(c), if he knew the instrument was claimed by a prior secured party, although filing of a financing statement would not be notice in itself. *See* §§ 9–309 (last sentence), 3–304(5), 1–201(25). Thus a purchaser of non-negotiable paper under § 9–308 could acquire priority in circumstances where, having notice, a purchaser of negotiable paper could not. This has been changed in Revised § 9–308 so that purchasers of all "instruments" are treated the same. *See* Felsenfeld, Knowledge as a Factor in Determining Priorities Under the Uniform Commercial Code, 42 N.Y.U.L.Rev. 246, 265–70 (1967).

Under the 1962 Code there is a subtle inconsistency between the provisions of Sections 9–304(1) and 9–306. The former states that a security interest in instruments can be perfected only by possession except for the 21-day perfection discussed above; the latter states that the secured party has a continuing perfected security interest in identifiable proceeds arising on the disposition of collateral, and this security interest continues automatically for ten days after receipt of the proceeds and beyond that time if proceeds are claimed on a filed financing statement.[42] Thus Section 9–306 provides for a filed perfected security interest in instruments as proceeds, although this is done only in general terms. Here again, however, the security interest could be defeated by some third parties.[43]

This inconsistency has been eliminated in the 1972 Official Text by adding to Section 9–304(1) a reference to Section 9–306, which has also been changed so that a security interest in instruments cannot be perfected beyond ten days by filing as to proceeds.[44] This is not a matter of major importance in any case.

§ 4–30. Negotiable Documents

The usual method of perfecting a security interest in negotiable documents of title is by possession.[45] While filing is a possible means,[46] in ordinary circumstances—absent bankruptcy, that is—filing is worthless because the document represents the goods,[47] and a holder to whom a negotiable document of title has been duly negotiated will take priority over an earlier security interest perfected by filing, for filing is not notice to a holder in these circumstances.[48] It is quite fundamental that a negotiable document represents the goods it covers, and a security interest in the goods is perfected by perfecting a security interest in the document,[49] and the only sensible means of perfection is by possession.

There is a 21-day period of automatic perfection from the time of attachment when a security interest in a negotiable document arises for new value under a written security agreement.[50] This kind of

---

42. § 9–306(2), (3).

43. §§ 9–308, 9–309.

44. Revised § 9–306(3).

45. § 9–305.

46. § 9–305.

47. § 7–502(1).

48. § 9–309. *See* United States v. Hext, 444 F.2d 804, 814 n. 34 (5th Cir. 1971).

49. § 9–304(2).

50. § 9–304(4).

interest can arise where a lender advances the funds necessary to pay a draft accompanied by a negotiable document, in accordance with the terms of a security agreement between the lender and the debtor. This kind of transaction is not ordinarily susceptible to double financing. After the 21-day period, perfection would depend on filing or possession of the document.[51]

Where a secured party has a security interest in a negotiable document perfected by possession, the interest will continue to be perfected for 21 days if the document is released to the debtor so that he may sell or make necessary preliminary arrangements to dispose of the goods.[52] A clause has been added to this provision in the redraft to state that priority between conflicting security interests in the goods is subject to Section 9–312(3)[53] and a correlative provision has been inserted into Section 9–312(3). The purpose of these changes is to insure that prior filed inventory financers receive notice of the purchase money financing before the debtor receives the goods, if in fact inventory financing is the object of the documentary transaction. Under the 1962 Code if a secured party holding a negotiable document covering inventory released that document to the debtor so that he could obtain possession of the goods for the purpose of sale as inventory in the absence of notice to prior secured parties under Section 9–312(3), it is probable that the financer of goods subject to the document would have priority under Section 9–312(5)(b) because his security interest in the goods was perfected originally by possession of the document, and priority is determined in the order of perfection when the conflicting interests are not all perfected by filing. The security interests of earlier inventory financers arguably might not attach, and therefore could not be perfected, before the debtor received possession of the goods, for prior to that time he may have had no rights in them.

§ 4–31. Chattel Paper

While a security interest in chattel paper may be perfected by filing,[54] the safest procedure is to take possession of it.[55] If the paper is left with the debtor, the secured party runs the risk that the debtor

51. § 9–304(6).

52. § 9–304(5)(a).

53. Revised § 9–304(5)(a).

54. § 9–304(1). But a filed, perfected security interest in a lease as chattel paper does not result in a perfected

security interest in the leased goods, at least where a "true lease" is involved and different filing offices are involved for the security interests as in a multistate transaction. *In re Leasing Consultants, Inc.*, 486 F.2d 367 (2d Cir. 1973).

55. § 9–305.

will sell the paper to a third party who will give new value for it and take possession of it in the ordinary course of his business. Such a purchaser will take priority (1) over an earlier filed security interest if he has no knowledge of it or (2) over a security interest in the paper claimed merely as proceeds of inventory even though he knows that the specific paper is subject to such a security interest.[56] If chattel paper is to be left with the debtor, the secured party can stamp it to show his interest so that no one could subsequently buy it without knowledge [57] that it is subject to a security interest.

In Section 9–308 there is a cross-reference to Section 9–304 which is followed by a parenthetical expression: "permissive filing and temporary perfection." Section 9–308 deals with both chattel paper and non-negotiable instruments (or simply instruments under the 1972 Official Text), and this presumably explains the double-barrelled parenthetical reference which is half wrong in every joint application. That is, there is no permissive filing as to instruments and there is no temporary perfection as to chattel paper in Section 9–304.

PART IV. PERFECTION BY ATTACHMENT

§ 4–32. Purchase Money Security Interests in Consumer Goods

No filing is required to perfect a purchase money security interest in consumer goods, if they are neither fixtures nor motor vehicles required to be licensed.[58] This security interest, which is automatically perfected on attachment,[59] will be effective against everyone except a buyer who buys without knowledge of the security interest, for value, and for his own personal, family, or household purposes; if protection against such a buyer is desired, filing is required.[60] There is no time limit to the effectiveness of the automatically perfected interest, as there is in the case of a filed interest.

---

56 § 9–308, Revised § 9–308.

57. § 1–201(25).

58. § 9–302(1)(d). This provision has been changed in a number of states in important ways. *Cf.* Revised § 9–302(1)(d). *See* White-Sellie's Jewelry Co., Inc. v. Goodyear Tire & Rubber Co., 477 S.W.2d 658 (Tex.Civ.App. 1972); *In re* Nicolosi, 4 UCC Rep.Serv. 111 (S.D.Ohio 1966) (in bankruptcy).

59. *See* Mayor's Jewelers of Ft. Lauderdale, Inc. v. Levinson, 39 Ill.App.3d 16, 349 N.E.2d 475 (1976) for a case involving unusual facts under the 1962 Code, discussed in § 4–2 *supra*. However, if the purchase money security agreement also includes other goods previously purchased but not completely paid for, this consolidation may result in an unperfected security interest as to all of the goods. *See In re* Manuel, 507 F.2d 990 (5th Cir. 1975).

60. § 9–307(2). *See* Everett Nat. Bank v. Deschuiteneer, 109 N.H. 112, 244 A.2d 196 (1968); Malaley v. Colonial Trading Co., 6 UCC Rep.Serv. 746 (Pa. C.P.1969).

This provision can be justified in a variety of ways, but perhaps the simplest justification is that we live in an economy that is dependent on installment buying by consumers. Many consumers do not qualify for time sales on unsecured credit, and sellers simply will not sell to them except on conditional sale. The Code provision allows both sides to get what they want: the buyer can receive the goods immediately, and the seller has a security interest which is effective on attachment. If the seller is willing to take the risk of the consumer selling to a neighbor, he need not bother to file, or he can carry non-filing insurance, which has been available for many years. No one could possibly imagine that consumers today own all of the goods in their possession free of liens so that old-fashioned arguments about apparent ownership fall on deaf ears when made by third party creditors who claim to have believed the debtor "owned" all the goods he possessed.

Some states have varied the Code's provisions by inserting dollar limits for the purchase price of consumer goods in which a security interest can be automatically perfected. Where this has been done, is the time price or the cash price to be used in determining whether the security interest is perfected automatically or filing is required? Either view is probably justifiable in the absence of a clear statute.[61] If a consumer's goods are removed from a state where perfection of the security interest was automatic to one where a filing is required because the goods have a purchase price in excess of the statutory limit for automatic perfection, a failure to file in the state of removal within four months will probably result in an unperfected security interest.[62] If both states have the uniform version of the Code, no

---

61. Where the cash price was below and the time price above the limit where filing was required, the higher price was considered the purchase price in *In re* Smith, 9 UCC Rep.Serv. 950 (E.D.Wis.1971) (in bankruptcy). *See also In re* La Rose, 7 UCC Rep. Serv. 964 (D.Conn.1970) (in bankruptcy), reaching the same conclusion (dictum) as to farm equipment having a time purchase price in excess of the $2500 limitation in § 9–302(1)(c). A similar problem could be raised when several items are purchased at the same time, none of them individually costing as much as the statutory limitation but all of them collectively costing in excess of the limitation. In an apparently unreported decision involving consumer goods a bankruptcy court concluded that the statutory limitation applied to the aggregate value of all of the goods. *See In re* Smith, *supra*, at p. 952. This result may be defensible but it is debatable. The contrary view prevailed in a case involving the $2500 limitation for farm equipment, International Harvester Credit Corp. v. American Nat'l Bank of Jacksonville, 296 So.2d 32 (Fla.1974), but note the cogent arguments presented in the dissenting opinion, *id.* at 37–39.

62. The four-month period comes from § 9–103(3), Revised (§§ 9–103(1)(d), (2)(b). *See In re* Atchison, 6 UCC Rep. Serv. 258 (E.D.Wis.1969) (in bankruptcy).

filing is necessary in the state of removal to continue the perfection of the security interest.[63]

It may not be entirely clear on the face of Section 9–307(2) that it is intended to protect only those consumers who buy goods directly from other consumers, where the secured party is relying on automatic perfection and has not filed a financing statement. But the provision requires "consumer goods" and that term is defined in Section 9–109 as goods ". . . used or bought for use primarily for personal, family or household purposes." This clearly excludes the possibility of covering inventory (in the hands of a merchant) which will in time become consumer goods if purchased by a consumer for personal use. The person who takes free of an unfiled (but perfected) security interest is a buyer without knowledge of the security interest in whose hands the goods will be consumer goods, since the language of Section 9–307(2) tracks with the definition in Section 9–109. The term "buyer" is not defined in Article 9 but apparently the term should be understood in its ordinary sense of "a person who buys or contracts to buy goods."[64] Certainly the term is used to mean something different from "purchaser" which is quite broadly defined in Section 1–201. In any event the term "buyer" has been correctly interpreted as not including a successful bidder at an execution sale [65] or a trustee in bankruptcy.[66]

Filing is required for a consumer's fixtures [67] and for motor vehicles required to be licensed.[68] Presumably all motor vehicles, using that term with its usual connotations, must be licensed, but the local state motor vehicle act must be consulted on this point.

There is an ever-increasing abundance of consumer protection legislation, and it must be emphasized that the Code regulates only the security aspects of consumer transactions. While local statutes in

---

63. *In re* Marshall, 10 UCC Rep.Serv. 1290 (N.D.Ohio 1969) (in bankruptcy).

64. § 2–103(1)(a).

65. National Shawmut Bank of Boston v. Vera, 352 Mass. 11, 223 N.E.2d 515 (1967).

66. *In re* Kretzer, 1 UCC Rep.Serv. 369 (E.D.Pa.1955) (in bankruptcy). Problems have arisen, however, where the same collateral, along with additional collateral as it is purchased, continues to serve as security. *See generally* § 5–18 *infra; In re* Jackson, 9 UCC Rep.Serv. 1152 (W.D.Mo.1971) (in bankruptcy), *In re* Brouse, 6 UCC Rep. Serv. 471 (W.D.Mich.1969) (in bankruptcy). In add-on transactions there obviously is some difficulty in the secured party's attempt to claim a purchase money security interest in all of the collateral. *See In re* Manuel, 507 F.2d 990 (5th Cir. 1975).

67. *See* § 9–401(1). *Cf.* Revised § 9–302 (1)(d).

68. *See* § 9–302(3)(b), (4). *See* Harper v. Avco Financial Services, Inc., 124 Ga.App. 6, 183 S.E.2d 89 (1971). As to mobile homes, *see In re* Merrill, 9 UCC Rep.Serv. 755 (D.Neb.1971) (in bankruptcy); Recchio v. Mfrs. & Traders Trust Co., 8 UCC Rep.Serv. 565 (N.Y.App.Div.1970); *cf.* George v. Commercial Credit Corp., 440 F.2d 551, 8 UCC Rep.Serv. 1315 (7th Cir. 1971).

existence when the Code was passed may be enumerated in Section 9–203(4), which specifically states that in case of conflict such statutes control over the Code, it is entirely possible that later statutes may not have been inserted into that section by amendment and they still would be held to supersede any inconsistent Code provision.

The 1972 Official Text has amended Section 9–302(1)(d) by eliminating the requirement of filing for consumers' fixtures in all cases in favor of requiring a "fixture filing" when priority over real estate interests is required. A purchase money security interest in a fixture will be automatically perfected in the same way that a security interest in any other consumer goods (other than motor vehicles) would be: the security interest would be perfected without filing against lien creditors, for example, but for priority over certain real estate interests, as provided in Revised Section 9–313, a fixture filing would be necessary.

A further revision changed the provision on motor vehicles from requiring filing in the case of vehicles "required to be licensed" to requiring it for those "required to be registered." The result of a recent flurry in the field of motor vehicle certificate of title legislation is that almost all states now require title certificates, and all states should. In any case, presumably ordinary motor vehicles will be registered whether or not they are certificated.

§ 4–33. Purchase Money Security Interests in Farm Equipment

The 1962 Official Text of Section 9–302(1)(c) provides for automatic perfection of purchase money security interests in farm equipment costing not more than $2500, but states that filing is required for fixtures and for motor vehicles required to be licensed. The entire provision has been deleted in the 1972 Official Text, so that the usual rules as to filing will apply. The deletion of this provision required a corresponding deletion in Section 9–307(2) which, in the 1962 Code, provided that a buyer of farm equipment originally costing not more than $2500 in which the security interest could have been automatically perfected would take free of the security interest if he purchased the equipment for his own farming operations without knowledge of the security interest and for value, unless the secured party had filed a financing statement. This protection for a farmer buying from a neighbor is the same as that given a consumer-buyer from a consumer-seller.

Apparently the thought behind the $2500 exemption for farm equipment was to facilitate farm credit for relatively small items, by analogy to consumer transactions. The $2500 figure was lowered in many states—$500 was a popular substitute—but the provision, regardless of the dollar limit, has often been said to inhibit credit to farmers. The reason given is that a lender, such as a local bank, cannot be assured that an item of equipment proposed as collateral is free of liens or has not been put together by a number of components all of which are subject to automatically perfected purchase money security interests. This seems a bit far-fetched but it has been repeated so many times that it has been generally accepted, although it would seem likely that a farmer could produce bills of sale for items of such value if they were to be used as collateral.

In those states having a dollar limitation for exemption from filing, where the undisputed price of the goods is below the limit, there should be no problem.[69] If the cash price is less than the limit but the time price is higher than the limit, the time price may be properly treated as the purchase price for goods in fact bought on time, so that the security interest is not automatically perfected on purchase and filing is required.[70] Where several items are bought at one time and each item is below the dollar limitation but all of the items taken together exceed the limitation, either result is possible.[71] If the purchase price of farm equipment exceeds the dollar limitation but a down payment is made and the resulting balance is below the limitation, a strict adherence to the "purchase price" language of Section 9–302(1)(c) would suggest that filing is required for perfection.[72]

The term "farm equipment" is not defined in the Code. Section 9–109 defines goods as " 'equipment' if they are used or bought for use primarily in business (including farming . . .)," so if an item is in fact used in farming operations it presumably would be farm equipment even if it were owned by someone who was not a farmer.[73]

69. Lonoke Production Credit Ass'n v. Bohannon, 238 Ark. 206, 379 S.W.2d 17 (1964).

70. *In re* La Rose, 7 UCC Rep.Serv. 964 (D.Conn.1970) (in bankruptcy) (dictum).

71. *See* International Harvester Credit Corp. v. American Nat'l Bank of Jacksonville, 296 So.2d 32 (Fla.1974), holding that the individual prices control.

72. Mammoth Cave Production Credit Ass'n v. York, 429 S.W.2d 26 (Ky.1968).

73. Citizens Nat'l Bank in Ennis v. Sperry Rand Corp., 456 S.W.2d 273 (Tex.Civ.App.1970). To the same effect, see Sequoia Machinery, Inc. v. Jarrett, 410 F.2d 1116 (9th Cir. 1969), where the analogous expression "equipment used in farming operations" in § 9–401(1) was in issue. *See also In re* Anderson, 6 UCC Rep.Serv. 1284 (S.D.Ohio 1969) (in bankruptcy).

CHAPTER 5

PRIORITIES

Table of Sections

§ 5-1. Introduction

Some of the common, or relatively common, problems in secured transactions are discussed here in terms of priorities because, as a practical matter, this is how they are ordinarily raised. This material involves a rather basic review of Article 9 principles with a few elaborations.

In the 1962 Code, Section 9–312(1) states that the "rules of priority" contained in a number of specifically identified sections govern where applicable. This led to some disagreement as to whether rules stated in the referenced sections stated rules of priority or of perfection or just what they meant.[1] There was no satisfactory means of

---

1. According to Professor Gilmore: "The Article 9 treatment of priority problems will appear to the neophyte to constitute an impenetrable maze. A sequence of eleven sections (§§ 9–306 to 9–316) is exclusively devoted to this subject, and other sections outside the sequence are relevant in some priority situations." G. Gilmore, Security Interests in Personal Property 656 (1965). *Compare* Kripke, Suggestions for Clarifying Article 9: Intangibles, Proceeds, and Priorities, 41 N.Y.U.L. Rev. 687 (1966) *with* Henson, Counter-

resolving these differences on the basis of the language in the 1962 Code, and to some extent, and at least superficially, these disagreements are swept under the rug by Revised Section 9–312(1) which says that "rules of priority stated in other sections" in Part 3 and those in Sections 4–208, 9–103, and 9–114 will govern where applicable. While this revised language resolves no arguments under the 1962 Code, if it settles any under the 1972 Code, the detailed rules under the 1972 Code are considerably clarified and simplified. In any event, the only proper way to read a section of a statute is from its beginning, and if a priority conflict is resolved by any other section in Part 3 of Article 9, or by the other specifically cross-referenced sections, or by the first four subsections of Section 9–312, the residual provisions of Section 9–312(5) will not come into play.

If the priority problem is not specifically dealt with elsewhere, or if purchase money security interests do not qualify for the expressly stated priorities in subsection (3) and (4) of Section 9–312, we come to the residual rules of Section 9–312(5) which determine priority (a) in the order of filing where both security interests are perfected by filing (regardless of the time of attachment), (b) in the order of perfection where both interests are not perfected by filing (regardless of the time of attachment), and (c) in the order of attachment where neither is perfected. Strangely enough, no rule is stated to cover the case where one interest is perfected and the competing interest is not, although the answer would seem to be clear; alternatively this problem is answered by Section 9–312(5)(b) by providing priority in the "order of perfection"[2] although it would appear that the language is directed to a situation where both interests are perfected.

Revised Section 9–312(5) resolves residual conflicts by these rules:

(a) Conflicting security interests rank according to priority in time of filing or perfection. Priority dates from the time a filing is first made covering the collateral or the time the security interest is first perfected, whichever is earlier, provided there is no period thereafter when there is neither filing nor perfection.

suggestions Regarding Article 9: A Reply to Professor Kripke, 42 N.Y. U.L.Rev. 74 (1967). For an authoritative discussion of priority problems, *see generally* W. Davenport and D. Murray, Secured Transactions 305–362 (1978).

2. *See* Bloom v. Hilty, 427 Pa. 463, 234 A.2d 860 (1967). Section 9–301(1)(a) says that an unperfected security interest is subordinate to the rights of persons entitled to priority under § 9–312.

(b) So long as conflicting security interests are unperfected, the first to attach has priority.

Revised Section 9–312(6) provides that the date of filing or perfection for collateral is also the date of filing or perfection as to proceeds.

Some of the obvious and less obvious problems flowing from these provisions are dealt with in the material which follows.

§ 5–2. Consumer Goods

Consumer goods are defined as goods "used or bought for use primarily for personal, family or household purposes" in Section 9–109. In purchase money situations the goods will be "bought for use" and the automatically perfected security interest should remain perfected even though their use subsequently changes.[3] In non-purchase money situations the use of the goods at the time the security interest attaches should govern, and the security interest must be perfected by filing, which would remain effective even though the use changes.[4] That is, if a lawyer bought a television set on time for use in her home, the security interest would be automatically perfected, and the security interest should remain perfected even though the television set is taken to the lawyer's office where it would be classified as equipment. In any event, some types of goods are capable of various kinds of use, at least if the debtor is a sole proprietor of a business or a professional person, and the primary use should be controlling in a non-purchase money situation or the primary purpose for which the goods were bought for use in purchase money transactions.[5] If the secured party relies on the debtor's representation as to the use or proposed use of goods—and no other course of conduct would ordinarily be feasible—then such reliance, if misplaced, appears to be at the secured party's peril.[6]

3. *See In re* Barnes, 11 UCC Rep.Serv. 670 (D.Me.1972) (in bankruptcy). (Consumer goods subsequently used as equipment, but security interest properly perfected in consumer goods held effective as to equipment in bankruptcy); *In re* Morton, 9 UCC Rep.Serv. 1147 (D.Me.1971) (in bankruptcy).

4. *See* § 9–401(3) provides that a filing made in the proper place continues to be effective even though the use of the collateral thereafter is changed, if the use controlled the original filing.

5. The purchase price of the goods or their size should be immaterial. An airplane costing $23,955 was held to be consumer goods in Commercial Credit Equipment Corp. v. Carter, 83 Wash.2d 136, 516 P.2d 767 (1973), in which opinion the court expressly disapproved of the holdings in *In re* Sprague, 4 UCC Rep.Serv. 702 (N.D. N.Y.1966) (in bankruptcy), and *In re* Vinarsky, 4 UCC Rep.Serv. 707 (N.D. N.Y.1966) (in bankruptcy), both of which cases involved mobile homes of considerable size which were held not to be consumer goods, at least in part, it would appear, because they could not be "consumed."

6. *See In re* McClain, 447 F.2d 241 (10th Cir. 1971) (security interest properly

In February A buys a color television set for use in his home. It is sold by X Co. on conditional sale but no financing statement is filed.

While X Co. retained possession of the television set, it was inventory, but when A received possession it became consumer goods. The same television set would be equipment if used to amuse waiting clients in a lawyer's office.[7]

X Co., by use of a conditional sale contract, retained a purchase money security interest [8] in the television set, and it was perfected without filing.[9] In terms, the conditional sale contract would probably state that X Co. retained title to the goods until the purchase price was paid in full, but in fact under the Code X's interest would be limited to a security interest,[10] and the provisions of Article 9 would apply without regard to where "title" might be located.[11]

Had Z Credit Union advanced the funds that were used for the purchase of the television set, as by making a check payable to the seller, Z would have a purchase money security interest perfected without filing, but Z would have to be sure that the funds it advanced were used to buy the goods.[12]

A sells the television set to B, a neighbor who knows nothing of X's security interest and who pays A the agreed price.

B will take free of X's security interest.[13] As a practical matter B probably would not know of X's security interest if X had filed a financing statement, but if there had been a filing, B would take subject to X's interest.[14] There has to be some means for a seller or

---

perfected for use "in business," which was the use debtor represented would be made of the goods, held unperfected in debtor's bankruptcy because of filing in improper office, where goods were always used as consumer goods, according to parol evidence).

7. § 9–109. It is perhaps unnecessary to point out that the occasionally heard or seen expression "a consumer good" is a solecism which is not likely to become acceptable English usage at any foreseeable time. When used as a synonym for chattels, "goods" has no singular form.

8. § 9–107(a).

9. § 9–302(1)(d), Revised § 9–302(1)(d).

10. § 2–401(1).

11. § 9–202.

12. § 9–107(b).

13. § 9–307(2). *See* Everett Nat'l Bank v. Deschuiteneer, 109 N.H. 112, 244 A. 2d 196 (1968) (dictum). While a trustee in bankruptcy often seems to possess a variety of guises, a trustee is not a "buyer" for purposes of § 9–307 (2), according to *In re* Ten Brock, 4 UCC Rep.Serv. 712 (W.D.Mich.1966) (in bankruptcy). The term "buyer" is not defined in the Code although "buyer in ordinary course of business" is defined in § 1–201(9).

14. § 9–307(2).

financer to protect itself against dishonest debtors, even though this may be at the expense of relatively innocent consumers. Consumer buyers should be as aware as anyone could be that other consumers often buy on time and may well not have paid for the goods they are selling. They could demand the original bill of sale before paying for goods that are being bought from a fellow consumer.

Z Credit Union makes a loan to A secured by the television set as collateral.

This is not a purchase money security interest as stated. The interest of Z would be subordinate to X Co.'s purchase money security interest for, assuming that Z filed to perfect its security interest, priority would be determined in the order of perfection under Section 9–312 (5)(b), and the same result would be reached under Revised Section 9–312(5)(a). The security interest of X Co. would be effective only to the extent of the unpaid balance of obligations due to X, so if there were an "equity" it would be available to satisfy Z's claim. The debtor may encumber his interest in the goods, even though the creation of a second security interest may be a default under the first security agreement.[15]

Y, a judgment creditor, levied on the television set while it it was in A's possession

Since X's security interest was perfected at the time it arose and even before A received possession of the goods, Y could never have become a lien creditor before perfection of X's security interest and Y will be subordinate to X. Section 9–301 deals with this problem in somewhat arguably ambiguous terms which may not be so arguably ambiguous on close analysis. Subsection (1) gives priority to lien creditors over unperfected security interests, while subsection (2) contains a grace period for filing with concomitant priority to the purchase money secured party if he files before or within ten days after the debtor receives possession of the goods. (Subsection 9–301(1)(b) of the 1962 Code limits priority to lien creditors "without knowledge" whose rights arise before perfection, but the knowledge requirement is omitted in the 1972 Code.) Since this security interest is always perfected and no filing is ever required, the lien creditor is clearly subordinate to the purchase money security interest. The subordination of unperfected security interests stated in Section 9–301(1) implies that a perfected security interest is not so subordinated, and the opening words—"Except as otherwise provided in subsection (2)"—have

15. § 9–311.

the purpose of giving priority through a ten-day grace period for filed purchase money security interests which would otherwise be subordinate under subsection (1)'s rules.

While a lien creditor may pursue the debtor's interest in the collateral,[16] it may often be true that the debtor will have very little equity in the goods. Nothing in Article 9 authorizes a sale free and clear of the perfected security interest,[17] and no doubt very few would bid very much at an execution sale when the sale is subject to the security interest. Moreover, depending on the terms of the security agreement covering default, it is quite likely that the secured party will be entitled to possession of the goods on the debtor's default,[18] so a purchaser at an execution sale may be buying a law suit.[19] In general, any sale of the collateral on execution must be subject to a perfected security interest.[20]

> The television set does not work properly and A takes it to a repair shop where the repairman replaces various parts and allegedly performs much labor.

So long as the repairman retains possession of the set, if he has a lien by statute or common law he is entitled to priority unless the lien is statutory and the statute provides otherwise.[21] A judicial rule

---

16. *See, e. g.,* Fitchburg Yarn Co. v. Wall & Co., Inc., 46 A.D.2d 763, 361 N.Y.S.2d 170 (1974) (involving accounts); Shaw Mudge & Co. v. Sher-Mart Mfg. Co., Inc., 132 N.J.Super. 517, 334 A.2d 357 (1975) (involving accounts).

17. *But see* Maryland Nat'l Bank v. Porter-Way Harvester Mfg. Co., 300 A.2d 8 (Del.1972), holding that the security interest is extinguished on an execution sale and the sale proceeds are to be distributed on the basis of priority of liens in the property. The decision appears to be clearly incorrect and seems to represent a reluctance to recognize an obvious change wrought by the Code in Delaware law on this point. For another incorrect decision holding that a sale to satisfy delinquent taxes extinguishes a prior perfected security interest, giving the purchaser clear title, see Moorehead v. John Deere Industrial Equipment Co., — Colo. —, 572 P.2d 1207 (1977).

18. Ford Motor Co. v. City of New York, 14 UCC Rep.Serv. 211 (N.Y.Sup. Ct.1974). *But see* First Nat'l Bank of

Glendale v. Sheriff of Milwaukee County, 34 Wis.2d 535, 149 N.W.2d 548 (1967).

19. *See, e. g.,* Murdock v. Blake, 26 Utah 2d 22, 484 P.2d 164 (1971) (levying creditor liable in conversion to secured party); Royal Store Fixture Co. v. New Jersey Butter Co., 114 N.J.Super. 263, 276 A.2d 153 (1971) (levying creditor liable in conversion).

20. Citizens Bank of Lavaca v. Perrin & Sons, Inc., 253 Ark. 639, 488 S.W.2d 14 (1972); Powell v. Whirlpool Employees Federal Credit Union, 42 Mich. App. 228, 201 N.W.2d 683 (1972).

21. § 9–310. *See, e. g.,* United States v. Crittenden, 563 F.2d 678 (5th Cir. 1977); Gulf Coast State Bank v. Nelms, 525 S.W.2d 866 (Tex.1975); Mousel v. Daringer, 190 Neb. 77, 206 N.W.2d 579 (1973) (agister's lien); Manufacturers Acceptance Corp. v. Gibson, 220 Tenn. 654, 422 S.W.2d 435 (1967); Forrest Cate Ford v. Fryar, 62 Tenn.App. 572, 465 S.W.2d 882 (1970). *Compare* Smith v. Eastern Airmotive Corp., 99 N.J.Super. 340, 240

does not override this priority; only an express statutory provision can. The basic principle is that a repairman who contributes to the continuing value of goods is, subject to meeting these provisions of the Code, entitled to priority over a security interest. These rules apply to any goods and not just to consumer goods.

As the Official Comment to Section 9–310 makes clear, the liens given priority are those "arising from work intended to enhance or preserve the value of the collateral . . ." This language would show that the ordinary landlord's lien was not intended to be included, and this has been generally recognized by the courts.[22]

> On March 1, A changes his residence from State G to State H, moving the television set along with other household goods to State H. On March 15, he sells the television set to a neighbor who knows nothing of X's security interest in State G and who pays value.

The neighbor will take free of X's security interest under Section 9–307(2), but X's security interest is perfected in State G without filing and will continue to be perfected in State H without filing and without regard for the four-month period of reperfection specified by Section 9–103(3)[23] unless a positive act is required for continued perfection in State H. While the third sentence of this subsection is not as clear as it might be, this is the only reasonable reading of it. If State H happens to have amended its Code to require filing for purchase money security interests in consumer goods above a certain dollar amount and if the television set had a purchase price over that

A.2d 17 (1968) with Southern Jersey Airways, Inc. v. National Bank of Secaucus, 108 N.J.Super. 369, 261 A.2d 399 (1970) (both involving state mechanic's liens on aircraft versus security interests recorded under the Federal Aviation Act). *Cf.* National Trailer Convoy Co. v. Mount Vernon Nat'l Bank & Trust Co., 420 P.2d 889 (Okl.1966); Commonwealth Loan Co. v. Berry, 2 Ohio St.2d 169, 207 N.E.2d 545, 31 O.O.2d 321 (1965). Although common law possessory liens may now be rare, a common law mechanic's lien for automobile repairs was found to exist in Nat'l Bank of Joliet v. Bergeron Cadillac, Inc., 38 Ill.App.3d 598, 347 N.E.2d 874 (1976), despite extensive statutory lien provisions. According to the dissent, the majority's cases in support of such lien were from 1860, 1914, and 1916, and the lien raises constitutional issues. *Cf.* Ford Motor Credit

Co. v. Howell Bros. Truck & Auto Repair, Inc., 57 Ala.App. 46, 325 So.2d 562 (Ala.App.1975). *See also* Fruehauf Corp. v. Huntington Moving and Storage Co., 217 S.E.2d 907 (W.Va.1975); Balzer Machinery Co. v. Klineline Sand & Gravel Co., 533 P.2d 321 (Or. 1975).

22. *See, e. g., In re* Einhorn Bros., Inc., 171 F.Supp. 655 (E.D.Pa.1959), affirmed 272 F.2d 434 (3d Cir. 1959); Bank of North America v. Kruger, 551 S.W. 2d 63 (Tex.Civ.App.1977); Peterson v. Ziegler, 39 Ill.App.3d 379, 350 N.E.2d 356 (1976). *But see* Nicholson's Mobile Home Sales, Inc. v. Schramm, —— Ind. App.2d ——, 330 N.E.2d 785 (1975) (involving an innkeeper's lien on a mobile home).

23. *See In re* Marshall, 10 UCC Rep. Serv. 1290 (N.D.Ohio 1969) (in bankruptcy).

limit, then the security interest should be perfected for four months in State H but not beyond that time unless there is a filing in the state of removal before the expiration of four months.[24] If a filing were required in State H and none was made within four months, then any purchaser of the television set during this period should take free of the lapsed security interest at the end of the four-month period. This is by no means a universally accepted result under the 1962 Code, but Section 9–103(3) can be read to produce this result in conjunction with Section 9–403(2). In any event, this would seem to be the proper result, and it would be required under Revised Section 9–103(1)(d).

While the security interest of X Co. would not, presumably, have expired by its terms shortly after removal of the television set to State H, Section 9–103(3) would appear to give a four-month period of perfection in the state of removal without regard to an earlier expiration in State G. This possibility does not exist under Revised Section 9–103(1)(d)(i).[25]

> Instead of selling his television set to a neighbor on March 15 in State H, A borrows some money from B Bank on that date and grants the Bank a security interest in the television set. B Bank promptly files a financing statement in the proper office.

Unless State H has amended its Code to require some positive act for perfection of purchase money security interests in consumer goods, the security interest of X Co. should continue until it expires, or until the statute of limitations runs. During this time the interest of B Bank should always be subordinate to that of X Co. If some positive act of reperfection is required in State H and X Co. does nothing, then X's security interest will lapse four months after removal and the interest of B Bank will be entitled to priority after that time. This result should be reached under the 1962 Code,[26] and it is required by the 1972 Code.[27] After lapse a lien creditor stands in the same position as a secured party in these circumstances.

> A bought a car in State G on February 1. It was financed by Bank B, whose security interest was duly noted on a certificate of title issued by State G. On March 1, A moved to State H and sold the car to P on March 15.

24. *See In re* Atchison, 6 UCC Rep. Serv. 258 (E.D.Wis.1969) (in bankruptcy).

25. *See generally* § 9–5 *infra.*

26. §§ 9–103(3), 9–403(2).

27. Revised §§ 9–103(1)(d), 9–403(2).

P would take subject to the interest of Bank B if P purchased while the car was subject to the certificate of title issued by State G. If by any possible means A managed to get a clean certificate of title issued by State H which showed no liens, then P should take free of Bank B's security interest under the language of Section 9–103(4) which makes perfection depend on the law of the state issuing the certificate of title which covers the vehicle. The vehicle would no longer be covered by State G's certificate of title when a certificate is issued by State H, and Section 9–103(4) appears to make perfection depend on the law of the state whose certificate is outstanding when the issue of priority arises. When a certificate of title is outstanding, subsection (4) and not the other preceding subsections of Section 9–103 governs conflicts, and there is no provision for a four-month continued perfection after removal in (4).[28]

Under Revised Section 9–103(2)(d), if P were a consumer he would take free of the security interest created in State G if he paid value and took delivery without knowing of B's interest and after issuance of a clean certificate of title. If P were an automobile dealer, however, he would buy the car subject to Bank B's security interest. Bank B's interest would be effective against an automobile dealer for four months after removal even though a new and clean certificate of title had been issued by State H, and if a new certificate were not issued in State H, the perfection given by State G's certificate of title would continue so long as State G's certificate was outstanding. If the security interest in State G were perfected otherwise than by certificate of title notation—as by filing or, in some states where there are non-uniform amendments to Section 9–302(1)(d), by automatic perfection in the case of purchase money security interests in cars sold to consumers—there will be a four-month period of perfection in State H (even if the security interest expires earlier in State G). However, if the security interest lapses, a "purchaser" in State H will take priority even though he purchased during the period when the security interest was effective and if there is a buyer in State H (other than an automobile dealer) who buys after State H issues a clean certificate of title and he pays value and takes delivery without knowledge of the security interest, he will take priority over Bank B.

There may be some question about the term "clean certificate" in these circumstances. The language of Revised Section 9–103(2)(d) states that the "clean" certificate must "not show that the goods are

28. *See* §§ 9–8 and 9–9 *infra.*

subject to the security interest or that they may be subject to security interests not shown on the certificate. . . ." The practice of the various states is by no means uniform in the issuance of new certificates of title. While any new certificate should show any security interests noted on a surrendered certificate, this may not invariably be done, and if the car has come from a non-title state, the certificate may or may not show that it is subject to possible liens. There might be a code number indicating that the car came from another state that would be meaningful to automobile dealers but not to others who are not in the business. The Code provision should be broadly read to protect the innocent—i. e., consumers and other buyers in State H (other than automobile dealers) and secured parties in State G.

There may be times when considerable reliance may be placed on the Article 2 rules. If a person has purchased an automobile from a dishonest seller, paid the price, and taken possession, but the purchaser has not received the title certificate, perhaps relying on the seller to get a new certificate issued in the purchaser's name, a serious problem arises where the dishonest seller immediately enters into a security agreement with a lender and the lender is shown on the new certificate of title when issued. As between the lender, whose interest is perfected, and the purchaser who has nothing to show as to ownership, which party prevails? If the view is taken that the purchaser of the vehicle acquired title to the goods under Article 2,[29] then the seller arguably had nothing left to give to the secured party.[30] One of the requirements for attachment is that the debtor must have rights in the collateral,[31] and attachment is necessary for perfection.[32] This view runs counter to the usual view that a certificate of title can be relied on, but the local certificate of title law must be consulted, as well as the Code.

§ 5–3. Equipment

According to Section 9–109(2), goods are

"equipment" if they are used or bought for use primarily in business (including farming or a profession) or by a debtor who is a non-profit organization or a governmental subdivision or agency or if the goods are not included in the definitions of inventory, farm products or consumer goods.

---

29. *See* § 2–401(2).

30. *See* Nat'l Exchange Bank of Fond du Lac v. Mann, 81 Wis.2d 352, 260 N. W.2d 716 (1978); Stroman v. Orlando

Bank & Trust Co., 239 So.2d 621 (Fla. App.1970).

31. § 9–204(1), Revised § 9–203(1)(c).

32. § 9–303(1).

"Equipment" encompasses those things which are relatively permanent in the life of a business: desks, chairs, machinery, and so on. The *business* may be a sole proprietorship, a partnership, or America's largest corporations; and farming and the professions are covered. While there is no problem about covering a physician's or surgeon's professional tools, or a lawyer's office furnishings and books, it has been a long time since the three recognized professions were divinity, medicine, and law. In these days practically everyone from fan dancers on up (or down, as the case may be) considers herself or himself a member of a profession, and there is no need to rely on etymological niceties in interpreting the definition of equipment. It should cover any goods used in business or work which are financible by their owners or users, as well as goods owned by nonprofit organizations and governmental units. This is a residual definition and it includes any goods not covered by the definitions of inventory, farm products, or consumer goods, which are the other three recognized categories.

It is no doubt standard practice for anyone lending against equipment already owned by a debtor to check in the appropriate filing office to be sure that there are no earlier filings before making a loan. If there is an earlier filing claiming "equipment" of the debtor, a lender knows that his interest in the collateral will be subordinate to the earlier interest under Section 9–312(5) [33] unless a subordination agreement is entered into pursuant to Section 9–316.[34]

If the security interest in equipment is a purchase money interest, Section 9–312(4) gives a ten-day grace period for perfection, which normally will be by filing, after the debtor receives possession [35] of the goods, and if the security interest is perfected within this time it will have priority over any conflicting security interests whether arising through after-acquired property clauses in earlier transactions or by non-purchase money filings during this time. Revised Section 9–312(4) gives this same priority to proceeds of the equipment too.

---

33. National Cash Register Co. v. Firestone & Co., 346 Mass. 255, 191 N.E.2d 471 (1963).

34. The subordination agreement may be oral, according to A–W–D, Inc. v. Salkeld, —— Ind.App. ——, 372 N.E.2d 486 (1978) (dictum).

35. "Receives possession" is not directly defined but "receipt" of goods is defined in § 2–103(1)(c) as taking physical possession of them. Where the goods have to be assembled, difficult problems can arise. *See, e. g., In re Automated Bookbinding Services, Inc.,* 471 F.2d 546 (4th Cir. 1972).

If a seller or a third party advancing the funds for the purchase of goods fails to file within ten days after the debtor receives the goods, the purchase money priority is lost and priority will be determined according to the rules of Section 9–312(5). This will usually mean that priority is determined in the order of filing, so that an earlier filed financer of equipment claiming after-acquired goods would have priority over a later purchase money financer who did not file within ten days.

It is not impossible that perfection by a secured party who is a purchase money financer might first be by possession although both secured parties have filed, but this is extremely unlikely with equipment unless it is financed by a purchase money financer under documents of title. Where both security interests are perfected by filing, Section 9–312(5)(a) gives priority in the order of filing, apparently without regard to the possibility that the earlier interest may first have been perfected by possession. Revised Section 9–312(5)(a) gives priority in the order of filing *or* perfection, depending on which occurs first, so long as there is no interval thereafter when the interest is unperfected, so that an interest perfected first by possession would have priority if there were a later filing before the goods were released to the debtor.

It is possible that there might be double purchase money financing of equipment. That is, a third party financer might advance the down payment used to purchase goods and the seller might retain a security interest for the balance. Assuming both parties file promptly, it would appear that this is a case not covered by Section 9–312(4) because both parties filed within the allowed ten days and the section applies only where a purchase money security interest conflicts with another ordinary security interest, not with another purchase money security interest. This would throw the problem into Section 9–312(5) where priority would be determined in the order of filing. It would seem that the more reasonable result would be, by analogy to Section 9–315(2), that each purchase money security interest would rank equally according to the proportion of the purchase price each advanced, but this does not appear to be an admissible result in these circumstances when the collateral is equipment.

Where a purchase money financer of equipment still has a security interest in an item of equipment that is traded-in on new equipment subsequently acquired and whose purchase is financed on a purchase money basis, the problems are difficult. The new equipment is clearly, to some extent at least, proceeds of the old under Section 9–

306(1), and the earlier security interest continues into the new goods. Arguably, the earlier security interest continues with its same priority if a security interest in proceeds was claimed in a filed financing statement, under Sections 9–306(2) and (3) and Section 9–312(6), with help from the same sections as revised. This is true because the problem is not expressly solved by Section 9–312(4) of either version of the Code and, if priority is resolved in the order of filing, under both versions of Section 9–312(5) the earlier purchase money security interest would have been filed first, it would have been continuously perfected, and it would be entitled to priority.

> On March 1, as consideration for a loan, B Co. granted to Bank A a security interest in all of the equipment, then owned and thereafter acquired, located at its plant in K City, and a financing statement was filed that day in the proper office. On March 15 S Co. sold a cutting machine to B Co. on conditional sale with 10% of the purchase price paid down. The machine was delivered on March 15. A financing statement was filed in the proper office on March 30. On June 1, B Co. defaulted under its security agreements with Bank A and S Co.

Had S Co. filed its financing statement in the proper office before B Co. received possession of the machine or within ten days after possession was taken, S Co. would have been entitled to priority for its purchase money security interest under Section 9–312(4). Since S Co. is not entitled to the purchase money priority because of late filing, the priority problem must be resolved under Section 9–312(5), and Bank A will be entitled to priority over S Co. in the cutting machine.[36]

> On March 1, as consideration for a loan, B Co. granted to Bank A a security interest in all of its equipment, then owned and thereafter acquired, located at its plant in K City, and a financing statement was filed that day in the proper office. At this date B Co. had possession of a cutting ma-

---

36. National Cash Register Co. v. Firestone & Co., Inc., 346 Mass. 255, 191 N.E.2d 471 (1963); James Talcott, Inc. v. Franklin Nat'l Bank of Minneapolis, 292 Minn. 277, 194 N.W.2d 775 (1972); American Nat'l Bank & Trust Co. of Sapulpa v. National Cash Register Co., 473 P.2d 234 (Okl.1970); National Cash Register Co. v. Mishkin's 125th St. Inc., 65 Misc.2d 386, 317 N.Y.S.2d 436 (N.Y.Sup.Ct.1970); Merchants Nat'l Bank of Manchester v. McCarthy, 16 UCC Rep.Serv. 1139 (Mass.App. Div.1975). *But see* International Harvester Credit Corp. v. American Nat'l Bank of Jacksonville, 296 So.2d 32 (Fla.1974), reaching the inexplicable result that the first secured party's priority over a late-filing purchase money secured party is limited to the debtor's equity in the after-acquired property; note the vigorous dissent of Chief Justice Carlton, *id.* at 35, 39–46.

chine which it was then leasing from S Co. On March 15,
B Co. entered into a contract with S Co. by which S Co.
agreed to sell and B Co. agreed to purchase the cutting machine, the purchase price to be paid over a period of twelve
months, with S. Co. retaining title to the machine until it
was fully paid for. The lease had contained no option by
which B Co. could purchase the machine, and no portion of
the rental payments were, under the lease, applicable to any
purchase. S Co. filed a financing statement in the proper
office on March 15. On June 1 B Co. defaulted under both
security agreements.

While this is a purchase money transaction between B Co. and
S Co., under the terms of Section 9–107(a), it may not fit easily
under Section 9–312(4). On one analysis of these facts, B Co. had
"received possession" [37] of the machine some time prior to the execution of the contract of sale and the creation of the security interest
so that it would be impossible for S Co. to have priority since the
terms of Section 9–312(4) cannot be complied with; that is, the security interest cannot be perfected at the time the debtor "receives
possession of the collateral or within ten days thereafter," for the
debtor received possession in the sense of physical control of the machine under a lease.[38] If this approach is taken, it becomes necessary
for S Co. to take possession of the cutting machine and then to redeliver it to B Co. in order to be eligible for the purchase money
priority. Otherwise, if priority is determined under Section 9–312
(5), S Co. will lose to Bank A, since the Bank was the first to file.
While it would not appear proper to determine priority in the order
of perfection of the security interest in the cutting machine on these
facts, the security interests of both Bank A and S Co. in the machine
apparently are perfected at the same time, and this problem is not
resolved by Section 9–312. The time of perfection should not be
used because both of the security interests are perfected by filing.

It is possible to take the position that B Co. does not become a
"debtor" as to S Co. and the goods do not become "collateral" until
such time as the security agreement between those parties is entered
into. If this approach is taken, then S Co. is entitled to priority under Section 9–312(4) if S Co. files before or within ten days after

37. While "receives possession" is not
defined in Article 9, § 2–103(1)(c)
states: " 'Receipt' of goods means taking physical possession of them."

38. *See* James Talcott, Inc. v. Associates Capitol Co., Inc., 491 F.2d 879 (6th

Cir. 1974); *In re* Automated Bookbinding Services, Inc., 471 F.2d 546
(4th Cir. 1972); North Platte State
Bank v. Production Credit Ass'n of
North Platte, Nebraska, 189 Neb. 44,
200 N.W.2d 1 (1972) (involving
cattle).

the contract of sale is entered into.[39]   While either solution of the problem may be feasible, giving priority to S Co. on the facts stated seems to be the better answer.   It at least avoids requiring S Co. to repossess and to redeliver the goods in order to achieve priority, and this activity, if deemed necessary, would result in added costs, which would necessarily be passed on without any obvious benefit to anyone.

> On March 1, as consideration for a loan, B Co. granted to Bank A a security interest in all of its data processing equipment, then owned and thereafter acquired, located at its plant in K City   A financing statement was filed that day in the proper office in which the collateral was described as "equipment." On March 15 B Co. and F Finance Co. entered into an agreement under which F Finance Co. loaned $50,000 to B Co. and B Co. granted to F a security interest in a cutting machine, then on the premises of B Co.'s plant in K City.   F Finance Co. had examined a copy of the security agreement between B Co. and Bank A, the copy being provided by B Co.   A financing statement covering "one Z Brand cutting machine No. 1234" was filed in the proper office on March 15.   On April 1 B Co. needed more money, and B Co. and Bank A entered into another security agreement under which Bank A made a new loan and the collateral was described in the agreement as "one Z Brand cutting machine No. 1234."   No new financing statement was filed.   On July 1 B Co. defaulted under all three security agreements.

The transactions here are not purchase money, so the priority problem will be resolved under Section 9–312(5).   Since Bank A filed first claiming "equipment," Bank A will have priority over F Finance Co.   Both secured parties are claiming collateral which is equipment; both security interests are perfected by filing.   Priority is determined in the order of filing on these facts, without regard to which security interest attached first, and clearly the security

39. *In re* Ultra Precision Industries, Inc., 503 F.2d 414 (9th Cir. 1974); Brodie Hotel Supply, Inc. v. United States, 431 F.2d 1316 (9th Cir. 1970); Fan-Gil Corp. v. American Hospital Supply Corp., 49 Mich.App. 106, 211 N.W.2d 561 (1973).   The 4th Circuit in *Automated Bookbinding Services, supra,* distinguished that fact situation from *Brodie, supra,* by saying that in *Brodie* the debtor had physical control before the goods were sold to him while in *Automated* the goods were in the debtor's possession at a date in advance of the ten-day period for filing, as they were although the goods had to be assembled, and the secured party took the reasonable position that tender of delivery did not take place until installation was completed, which was within the ten-day period.   The 9th Circuit followed *Brodie* in *Ultra Precision, supra,* where the facts were arguably roughly comparable to *Automated.*   This seems to be an issue where the circuits are in conflict.

interest of F Finance Co. attached first and was in fact perfected first as to the cutting machine, but Bank A had filed first as to equipment, and F Finance Co., as a prudent lender, would be obligated to search the files, which would reveal what Bank A claimed, before taking its security interest. Had F searched the files and discovered Bank A's financing statement claiming "equipment," a release of the cutting machine could have been obtained and filed pursuant to Section 9–406, or the two secured parties could have entered into a subordination agreement under Section 9–316. There would not appear to be any basis for invoking estoppel against Bank A, under Section 1–103, on the facts stated.[40]

While the suggested resolution has ample Code and case authority for support,[41] the first case to decide a somewhat similar controversy gave priority to the Finance Co. in the example above, and this solution was not reached without the court's awareness of scholarly opinions to the contrary. This case, which was *Coin-O-Matic Service Co.* v. *Rhode Island Hospital Trust Co.,*[42] came down when Article 9 was being redrafted, and in the Final Report of the Review Committee it was stated: "The Committee considered drafting a provision emphasizing its disagreement with the *Coin-O-Matic* line of cases, but concluded that the existing Code is clear enough, and should not be disturbed just to override some lower court cases."[43] There is no requirement in Section 9–204(5) or Revised Section 9–204(3) that future advances be made pursuant to a commitment in order to be entitled to a priority based on the original filing, and this priority is spelled out in Revised Section 9–312(7).

On March 1, as consideration for a loan B Co. granted to Bank A a security interest in existing equipment at a stated

---

40. In United States v. Thompson, 272 F.Supp. 774 (E.D.Ark.1967), it would appear that estoppel must have been the underlying thought behind the opinion, although the doctrine was not referred to, when the court gave priority to an unperfected security interest in equipment over a perfected security interest created between family-controlled entities. There is no basis for citing § 9–312, as the court did, in giving priority to the unperfected security interest on the ground that the other security interest was not filed at or within ten days after delivery of the equipment. The doctrine of estoppel was properly rejected in Mammoth Cave Production Credit Ass'n v. York, 429 S.W.2d 26 (Ky.1968), where the purchase money secured party did not file a financing statement within ten days after the debtor received the goods nor, indeed, for nearly two years thereafter.

41. *See, e. g., In re* Rivet, 299 F.Supp. 374 (E.D.Mich.1969); Thorp Finance Corp. of Wisconsin v. Ken Hodgins & Sons, 73 Mich.App. 428, 251 N.W.2d 614 (1977); *In re* Merriman, 4 UCC Rep.Serv. 234 (S.D.Ohio 1967) (in bankruptcy). *See generally* § 5–19 *infra.*

42. 3 UCC Rep.Serv. 1112 (R.I.Super. Ct.1966).

43. Review Committee for Article 9 of the Uniform Commercial Code, Final Report, p. 227 (1971).

address. No financing statement was filed. On March 15 F Finance Co. made a loan to B Co. and took a security interest in the same equipment. F Finance Co. filed a financing statement in the proper office on March 15. On June 1, B Co. defaulted under both security agreements.

F Finance Co. is entitled to priority in the equipment under Section 9–312(5) as the first to perfect.[44] On the facts stated Bank A never perfected its security interest. If this resolution is not expressly mandated by Section 9–312(5), perhaps because that section appears on its face to require that both security interests must be filed or perfected, the result can be reached via Section 9–301(1)(a) which subordinates an unperfected security interest to persons entitled to priority under Section 9–312, and the clear import of Section 9–312(5) is that the perfected security interest is entitled to priority over the unperfected security interest since it is entitled to priority over a subsequently perfected security interest. Would it matter if F Finance Co. knew of Bank A's prior, unperfected security interest? Apparently not.[45] Nothing in Section 9–312(5) makes the application of the priority rules depend on knowledge. Bank A's problem arises because of its own fault in not filing a financing statement in a timely manner. While an issue might be raised as to the Finance Co.'s good faith,[46] so long as the Finance Co. advanced funds against the collateral, its security interest should be effective to that extent.

§ 5–4. Inventory

Inventory is quite broadly defined in Section 9–109(4) and the term covers goods

> . . . held by a person who holds them for sale or lease or to be furnished under contracts of service or if he has so furnished them, or if they are raw materials, work in process or materials used or consumed in a business. Inventory of a person is not to be classified as his equipment.

---

44. See, e. g., In re Samuels & Co., Inc., 526 F.2d 1238 (5th Cir. 1976); Witmer v. Kleppe, 469 F.2d 1245 (4th Cir. 1972); Aetna Casualty & Surety Co. v. J. F. Brunken & Son, Inc., 357 F. Supp. 290 (D.S.D.1973).

45. See, e. g., In re Smith, 326 F.Supp. 1311 (D.Minn.1971); In re Miller, 14 UCC Rep.Serv. 1042 (D.Or.1974) (in bankruptcy); In re Gunderson, 4 UCC Rep.Serv. 358 (S.D.Ill.1967) (in bankruptcy). See also First Nat'l Bank & Trust Co. of Vinita, Oklahoma v. Atlas Credit Corp., 417 F.2d 1081 (10th Cir. 1969); H. and Val. J. Rothschild, Inc. v. Northwestern Nat'l Bank of St. Paul, 242 N.W.2d 844 (Minn.1976); Bloom v. Hilty, 427 Pa. 463, 234 A.2d 860 (1967).

46. See §§ 1–102(3), 1–201(19). But see Thompson v. United States, 408 F.2d 1075 (8th Cir. 1969).

This definition covers more than most people would ordinarily think of as inventory, since the term is generally used to refer to goods held for sale, whether by a manufacturer, a wholesaler or distributor, or a retailer. The broad Code definition makes it possible to finance a manufacturer and to have an effective security interest through all stages of the manufacturing process, from the raw materials through the work in process into the finished goods. Goods held for lease are included, as are presumably goods which are in fact leased, although leased goods are not in terms within the definition. (The definition, insofar as it refers to goods out of the debtor's control, seems to cover only goods "furnished" under contracts of service, in addition to goods to be so furnished.) Materials used or consumed in the business are included, such as shipping crates kept for use in transporting a manufacturer's or seller's products, or the gasoline held for use in such a person's trucks. Inventory is not something intended to be kept permanently by a debtor in the operation of a business; it is fairly transitory, intended for sale or lease or consumption as the business is carried on.

Under Section 9–307(1) a buyer in ordinary course of business will usually take free of a security interest created by his seller,[47] and the definition of "buyer in ordinary course of business" in Section 1–201(9) is usually thought to have the effect of restricting the application of Section 9–307(1) to inventory. The definition of "inventory" in Section 9–109(4) requires that such goods be "held by a person who holds them for sale . . . " but may the person holding the goods be someone other than the seller? If the goods are in the possession of a secured party by way of pledge, may the debtor sell them to a buyer who will take free of the security interest? It has been held that the answer is yes.[48]

Admittedly neither Section 9–307(1) nor Section 1–201(9) uses the term "inventory"—if these sections did, the problem raised here

---

47. Buyers in ordinary course of used goods take a risk that the goods may have been traded-in or disposed of by a former owner while subject to an earlier security interest perfected by filing, and such buyers will not take free of these interests. *See* First American Bank of North Beach, Florida v. Hunning, 218 Va. 530, 238 S.E.2d 799 (Va.1977). They take free only of interests created by their sellers. *See* Rex Financial Corp. v. Mobile America Corp., 23 UCC Rep. Serv. 788 (Ariz.App.1978).

48. Tanbro Fabrics Corp. v. Deering Milliken, Inc., 39 N.Y.2d 632, 385 N.Y.S.2d 260, 350 N.E.2d 590 (1976). *See* Kripke, Should Section 9–307(1) of the Uniform Commercial Code Apply Against a Secured Party in Possession? 33 Bus.Law. 153 (1977); Kreindler, The Uniform Commercial Code and Priority Rights between the Seller in Possession and a Good Faith Third Party Purchaser, 82 Com. L.J. 86 (1977), Birnbaum, Section 9–307(1) of the Uniform Commercial Code Versus Possessory Security Interests—A Reply to Professor Kripke, 33 Bus.Law. 2607 (1978); Gottlieb, Section 9–307(1) and *Tanbro Fabrics*: A Further Response, 33 Bus.Law. 2611 (1978).

would not be possible, since the seller is not holding the goods and the secured party is here holding the goods for security, not for sale —and the point at issue raises a problem with the drafting of Section 9–307(1) that is, in part, caused by the failure to use the defined term "inventory."

It is, of course, true that buyers of inventory often do not buy goods which the seller has on display. The seller may display a model and deliver the item sold, such as a refrigerator, from a warehouse. Or the sale may be made through the mail or over the telephone. So that the buyer has not directly relied on the seller's possession of goods on display as being available for sale. In these cases a secured party probably can usually rely on tracing its security interest into the proceeds arising on sale.

While the problem in the *Tanbro* case [49] may be peculiar to the textile industry, it seems improper that a security interest perfected by possession can be wiped out by the debtor's sale to a third party of collateral the debtor does not possess and has no right to sell. Had a financing statement been filed, presumably the result would have been the same. This seems to leave an area where, no matter what the secured party does, a buyer from the debtor will prevail, at least if an issue of good faith cannot be successfully raised. The result can, however, be justified, as it was by the New York Court of Appeals, by one reading of the provisions of Section 9–307(1).

If two secured parties file against the same debtor claiming "inventory" or, if a more specific description is used, claiming the same type of inventory, priority would be resolved in the order of filing under Section 9–312(5)(a). If one secured party has filed on a debtor's inventory, that does not eliminate the possibility of the debtor getting new financing elsewhere. There is always the possibility of competing secured parties entering into a subordination agreement pursuant to Section 9–316, for they may adjust their relative priorities in any manner that they agree,[50] since in any case their interests will be ahead of third party liens acquired subsequently. There is also the possibility of the second secured party achieving priority because of purchase money financing which complies with Section 9–312(3): the security interest is perfected (ordinarily by filing) and prior secured parties are properly notified before the debtor receives pos-

49. Tanbro Fabrics Corp. v. Deering Milliken, Inc., 39 N.Y.2d 632, 385 N.Y. S.2d 260, 350 N.E.2d 590 (1976).

50. Or the subordination agreement may confirm the priorities established by filing, as in Borg-Warner Acceptance Corp. v. First Nat'l Bank of Pipestone, 307 Minn. 20, 238 N.W.2d 612 (1976). The subordination agreement need not be in writing to be binding. A–W–D, Inc. v. Salkeld, — Ind.App. —, 372 N.E.2d 486 (1978) (dictum).

session of the goods that this financing is about to take place.[51] The purchase money secured party might be the seller or distributor of the inventory who retains a security interest in the goods or a financial institution which advances the funds that directly go to make the acquisition possible.

No doubt Section 9–312(3) has worked adequately in practice but there are some problems. The most obvious problem is that the section does not state how long the required notification is effective, when given by the purchase money financer to earlier secured parties. It is specified that the notification must be received (in accordance with Section 1–201(26)) by the other secured parties before the debtor receives the goods, it must state that the notifying party has or expects to acquire a purchase money security interest in the goods, and the inventory must be described by item or type. If the financing is to continue over a period of time, it would be prudent to state this in the notice, and the notice should be effective for the five years that the filing will be effective,[52] but this is not specified in the 1962 Code. It is expressly stated in Revised Section 9–312(3)(c).

A minor problem is resolved by Revised Section 9–312(3)(b) when it requires that the purchase money financer must give notification in writing to persons who had *filed* financing statements covering the same kinds of inventory before the purchase money secured party filed or before the 21-day period of temporary perfection begins to run under Section 9–304(5) which allows goods represented by a negotiable document or goods held by a bailee who has not issued a negotiable document to be released to the debtor for specified purposes, with perfection continuing for 21 days. Section 9–312(3) in the 1962 Code requires notification to prior secured parties who are "known" to the purchase money secured party, as well as to those who have filed, which can create some uncertainty when the financing begins with documents of title.

It was debatable under the 1962 Code how to solve the priority problem where there was first a financer of inventory who had filed and then a subsequent purchase of inventory was financed by a second secured party who acquired a purchase money interest by paying against a negotiable document of title which was then released to the

---

51. In the absence of notice, the earlier filed security interest will be entitled to priority. *In re* Tri-Cities Music Centers, Inc., 22 UCC Rep.Serv. 254 (E.D.Tenn.1977) (in bankruptcy).

52. Fedders Financial Corp. v. Chiarelli Bros., Inc., 221 Pa.Super. 224, 289 A.2d 169 (1972).

debtor in order for him to acquire the goods. When goods are subject to a negotiable document of title, a security interest in the goods is perfected by perfecting a security interest in the document, under Section 9–304(2), which was done here by possession, and that perfected security interest continues for 21 days after the document is surrendered to the debtor to enable the debtor to get possession of the goods for specified purposes related to processing or sale. Section 9–312(3)(b) may be read as applying only where the purchase money financer has perfected by filing since it speaks of "the date of the filing made by" him, or it may be read as alternatively covering (1) a situation where notice must be given by non-filing purchase money financers to non-filing prior "known" secured parties or (2) a case where all parties have filed, and if so read it does not cover our problem. If the documentary purchase money inventory financer does not give notice to the earlier inventory financer, who has priority? If the problem is treated as coming within Section 9–312(3), then the earlier financer apparently is entitled to priority. Revised Sections 9–312(3)(b) and 9–304(5)(a) resolve the issue that way, in the absence of the notice which is now clearly required. However, an alternative answer under the 1962 Code would be that the purchase money financer is entitled to priority, even without having given notice, since Section 9–309 provides that nothing in Article 9 limits the rights of "a holder to whom a negotiable document of title has been duly negotiated," and such a holder takes "priority over an earlier security interest even though perfected." (Section 7–503(1) does limit the rights of holders to whom documents of title are duly negotiated, but it has no application here because the holder of the filed security interest had no interest in these goods before the document was issued.) Section 9–303(2) states that if a security interest is perfected in one manner, as by possession of a negotiable document, and is subsequently perfected in some other way, as by the provisions of Section 9–304(5), the security interest is deemed to be continuously perfected if there was no period when it was unperfected. By these combined provisions, the purchase money financer would have priority in the inventory, unless there is authority to reverse priorities in the Code once the debtor receives the goods, and the 1962 Code need not in any situation be read to reverse priorities once they are established.

Because Section 9–306 provides for a perfected security interest to continue in identifiable proceeds, there has been considerable discussion about whether the purchase money inventory financer's priority continued in accounts arising when inventory was sold so as to take priority over an earlier accounts financer.[53] This issue is resolved in Revised Section 9–312(3) by giving the purchase money security interest priority over conflicting security interests in the same collateral and "in identifiable cash proceeds received on or before delivery of the inventory to a buyer" provided the required steps are taken. Since the cash must be received before the debtor gets the goods, the cash cannot be proceeds of an account, and since the cash must be identifiable, the priority is probably restricted to checks, unless the secured party is extremely agile and assiduously polices the debtor's conduct of his business. (Under Revised Section 9–306(1), the term "cash proceeds" includes "deposit accounts," which is defined in Revised Section 9–105(1)(e), but this possibility presents a problem in tracing, since the proceeds must be identifiable, or in the event of insolvency the deposit account must contain only proceeds.) This priority does not extend to traded-in goods. Whether it should is a debatable matter, but the traded-in goods will in turn become inventory and presumably they will fall under the earlier security interest, which seems a bit odd. They will surely be taken for antecedent debt, for the purposes of Section 60 of the Bankruptcy Act, and it is presently unclear what effect this provision will have in the purchase money secured party's maintaining a continuously perfected security interest in changing collateral if the debtor goes into bankruptcy, since there will be a release of collateral without a corresponding priority in the substituted collateral, although presumably the perfection continues.

On March 1, in consideration of a loan of $300,000 B Co. granted to Bank A a security interest in all of B Co.'s inventory then owned and thereafter acquired. A financing statement was filed in the proper office. On April 1 B Co. and S Credit Co. entered into an agreement under which S Credit Co. would finance B Co.'s acquisition of inventory described as "RCA merchandise: stereos, radios, televisions or any combination there-

53. In *In re* Mary Grey Hosiery Mills, Inc., 20 UCC Rep.Serv. 1060 (W.D.Va. 1976) (in bankruptcy), a financer of inventory and proceeds prevailed over a subsequent accounts financer, although the facts are a bit peculiar and the court cites § 9–308 which is not in point. *Compare* Henson, Priorities Under the Uniform Commercial Code, 41 Notre Dame Law 425, 431–32 (1966) *with* Kripke, Suggestions for Clarifying Article 9: Intangibles, Proceeds, and Priorities, 41 N.Y.U.L.Rev. 687, (1966), and Henson, Countersuggestions Regarding Article 9: A Reply to Professor Kripke, 42 N.Y.U.L.Rev. 74, 75–77 (1967). The issue of a purchase money inventory financer's priority in accounts as against an earlier inventory financer's interest in the accounts was discussed but left for consideration on remand in *In re* Mid State Wood Products Co., 323 F.Supp. 853 (N.D.Ill.1971). As to complying with the notice requirement of § 9–312(3) orally, *see* GAC Credit Corp. v. Small Business Administration, 323 F.Supp. 795 (W.D.Mo.1971) (this holding is questionable).

of," and this description also appeared on a financing statement filed in the proper office on April 1. On April 2 a senior vice president of S Credit Co. called a senior vice president of Bank A in charge of the Bank's inventory financing department, and the Bank A vice president was told over the telephone that S Credit Co. intended to finance B Co.'s acquisition of RCA merchandise on a purchase money basis. At this time, no such merchandise had been financed but subsequent shipments were financed by S. By July 1 B Co. was in default under the security agreements with Bank A and S Credit Co.

Since Bank A had a filed and perfected security interest in B Co.'s inventory, the RCA merchandise would be subject to that security interest when acquired. Whether Bank A or S Credit Co., which also had a perfected security interest in that RCA merchandise, would be entitled to priority in the described goods is a matter which may well be resolved in different ways under the 1962 and 1972 versions of Article 9. Assuming that both parties adequately described the collateral in their financing statements, is a telephone call an adequate "notification" for purposes of Section 9–312(3)(b) and (c) of the 1962 Code? It has been held that oral notification is adequate under Sections 1–201(25) and (26).[54] Aside from problems of proof when notices are given orally, there appears to be no reason why such a notice is inadequate under the 1962 Code. However, under, Revised Section 9–312(3)(b) the notification must be in writing, and this is surely the only prudent way to proceed under the 1962 Code. Had S Credit Co. not filed and given proper notice to Bank A before B Co. received the goods, under either version of the Code Bank A would have priority in the goods S Credit Co. financed.[55] If the requirements of Section 9–312(3) are not complied with by the purchase money financer, the problem should be resolved under Section 9–312(5).

§ 5–5. Agricultural Collateral

To anyone searching through Article 9 to find rules governing priorities in agricultural collateral, it might appear that Section 9–312(2) is an important provision. It states:

A perfected security interest in crops for new value given to enable the debtor to produce the crops during the production

---

54. GAC Credit Corp. v. Small Business Administration, 323 F.Supp. 795 (W. D.Mo.1971).

55. *See* Borg-Warner Acceptance Corp. v. First Nat'l Bank of Pipestone, 307 Minn. 20, 238 N.W.2d 612, (1976); Evans Products Co. v. Jorgensen, 245 Or. 362, 421 P.2d 978 (1966); Manufacturers Acceptance Corp. v. Penning's Sales, Inc., 5 Wash.App. 501, 487 P.2d 1053 (1971); National Bank & Trust Co. v. Moody Ford, Inc., 149 Ind.App. 479, 273 N.E.2d 757 (1971); Sears, Roebuck & Co. v. Detroit Federal Sav. & Loan Ass'n, 79 Mich.App. 378, 262 N.W.2d 831 (1977).

season and given not more than three months before the crops become growing crops by planting or otherwise takes priority over an earlier security interest to the extent that such earlier security interest secures obligations due more than six months before the crops become growing crops by planting or otherwise, even though the person giving new value had knowledge of the earlier security interest.

This section has turned out to be substantially meaningless.[56] It was no doubt first adopted on the supposition that it would enable a poor farmer to borrow money to plant current crops by giving a new value secured party a security interest in them which would have priority over a long overdue earlier security interest. If the section is ineffectual, there was no movement to delete it or restate it during the period when Article 9 was being revised, and it remains in Revised Article 9 without change. A priority conflict between competing agricultural financers which does not involve crops or, if it involves crops does not come within Section 9–312(2), will be resolved by the other priority rules of Section 9–312.[57]

Section 9–312(2) relates to crops, as do several other sections in Article 9. Growing crops are specifically included in the definition of "Goods" in Section 9–105; harvested crops would be covered in the all-inclusive language of the definition: "all things which are movable at the time the security interest attaches . . ." with listed exceptions. The unborn young of animals are also covered. (Unhatched fowl are left out.) In the revised version, the definition also includes "standing timber which is to be cut and removed under a conveyance or contract for sale."[58] It should also be noted that a contract for the sale of growing crops (and timber to be cut, under the 1972 Code) apart from the land is a contract for the sale of goods under Article 2, whether the buyer or the seller is to sever the subject of the sale.[59]

---

56. *But see* United Tobacco Warehouse Co., Inc. v. Wells, 490 S.W.2d 152 (Ky.1973).

57. United States v. Minster Farmers Co-op. Exchange, Inc., 430 F.Supp. 566 (N.D.Ohio 1977).

58. *Cf.* Barry v. Bank of New Hampshire, 112 N.H. 226, 293 A.2d 755 (1972).

59. § 2–107(2), Revised § 2–107(2). The requirement of § 2–107(1) that the sale

of timber is a sale of goods only if the timber is to be severed by the seller has been changed in the 1972 Code, by the deletion of "timber" from Revised § 2–107(1) and by adding a reference in Revised § 2–107(2) so that a sale of growing timber is a sale of goods whether it is severed by either the buyer or the seller. There is no change in § 2–107(3) which makes the provisions of the section "subject to any third party rights provided by the law relating to realty records . . ." Sales of timber or growing crops may

In other words, the Code follows general pre-Code law in recognizing crops as goods which may be the subjects of sales or security interests apart from the land on which they are growing. It would seem to be clear that a real estate mortgagee who intends to claim an interest in crops which has priority over subsequently granted security interests in the crops as personalty will have to comply with the Article 9 requirements as to filing. (The real estate mortgage may be sufficient as a security agreement.)[60] It would be improvident for a real estate mortgagee to rely on a standard form of mortgage covering "rents, issues, and profits" or the like. If a real estate mortgagee filed a financing statement claiming a security interest in crops, the filing would be effective for five years (unless under the 1962 Code a maturity date of less than five years was stated) but there is no provision making the security interest effective without periodic refilings if the mortgage runs for twenty years.

Section 9–204(2)(a) of the 1962 Code states that for purposes of that section, the debtor has no rights "in crops until they are planted or otherwise become growing crops, in the young of livestock until they are conceived." This provision has been deleted in the 1972 Code, and in any case it said nothing that would not otherwise be true. This section deals with attachment in the 1962 Code and, after providing that after-acquired collateral may secure all obligations covered by the security agreement, goes on to state an exception:[61]

No security interest attaches under an after-acquired property clause

have to be recorded in the real estate records to protect the buyer against a purchaser of the real estate. *See generally* Coogan and Mays, Crop Financing and Article 9: A Dialogue with Particular Emphasis on Problems of Florida Citrus Crop Financing, 22 U. Miami L.Rev. 13 (1967).

60. A security agreement covering crops or timber to be cut is required to contain a description of the land concerned, in addition to describing the collateral. This is a statute of frauds provision, and compliance is necessary for the security interest to be enforceable against the debtor or third parties. § 9–203(1)(b), Revised § 9–203(1)(a). A real estate mortgage would meet this requirement of a security agreement and it would be "signed" by the debtor, but it would not be signed by the secured party as is normally required in the case of a financ-

ing statement under §§ 9–402(1) and (2) but not under Revised § 9–402(1). A real estate mortgage might or might not have the addresses of the parties required by § 9–402(1). Under § 9–110 any description of real estate is sufficient "if it reasonably identifies what is described." This conforms to pre-Code requirements for chattel mortgages on crops which, since they were not filed in the real estate records, did not usually contain meticulous descriptions of the land on which the crops were to be grown or were growing.

61. § 9–204(4)(a). This provision is eliminated in Revised Article 9. It was omitted when the Code was enacted in California, Hawaii, Iowa, and New Jersey, and the period was extended from one year to two to seven years in Georgia, North Carolina, Oregon, and Texas.

(a) to crops which become such more than one year after the security agreement is executed except that a security interest in crops which is given in conjunction with a lease or land purchase or improvement transaction evidenced by a contract, mortgage or deed of trust may if so agreed attach to crops to be grown on the land concerned during the period of such real estate transaction . . .

This provision was dropped from Revised Article 9 because it is in practical effect meaningless. While after-acquired property clauses covering crops are restricted to one year's operation in security agreements in the case of pure crop mortgages, a filed financing statement covering crops may be effective for five years, and priority is assured by filing, leading to a meaningless annual execution of security agreements.[62]

The most difficult questions arise under Section 9–307(1) which provides:

A buyer in ordinary course of business (subsection (9) of Section 1–201) other than a person buying farm products from a person engaged in farming operations takes free of a security interest created by his seller even though the security interest is perfected and even though the buyer knows of its existence.

The term "farm products" is considerably broader than crops since goods are

"farm products" if they are crops or livestock or supplies used or produced in farming operations or if they are products of crops or livestock in their unmanufactured states (such as ginned cotton, wool-clip, maple syrup, milk and eggs), and if they are in the possession of a debtor engaged in raising, fat-

---

62. *See* United States v. Gleaners & Farmers Co-op. Elevator Co., 481 F. 2d 104 (7th Cir. 1973). *Cf.* United States v. Busing, 7 UCC Rep.Serv. 1120 (E.D.Ill.1970), where the court apparently did not realize that a previously filed financing statement perfected a series of security interests under various security agreements so that on such basis the United States would have been entitled to priority over a party claiming a subsequent security interest (on what basis is un-clear) who was held to be a buyer in ordinary course taking subject to the government's security interest under § 9–307(1), and § 9–201 was said to determine priorities. *See also* Gulf Oil Co. U. S. v. First Nat'l Bank of Hereford, 503 S.W.2d 300 (Tex.Civ.App. 1973); United States v. Minster Farmers Co-op. Exchange, Inc., 430 F.Supp. 566 (N.D.Ohio 1977); First Security Bank of Utah v. Wright, 521 P.2d 563 (Utah 1974).

tening, grazing or other farm operations. If goods are farm products they are neither equipment nor inventory.[63]

In the most trivial application, these sections provide that a tourist buying tomatoes in August from a farmer's roadside stand buys them subject to an existing crop mortgage (assuming there is one) rather than taking free of an inventory security interest as she would do in other circumstances involving inventory. Here the tomatoes are in an unmanufactured state, they are bought from the farmer who raised them, and they are bought from the debtor who granted a security interest in the crop to a secured party. These implications would never occur to a buyer and they would never be pursued by a secured party. If the tomatoes were processed into tomato preserves by the farmer's wife and sold in jars at the stand, they would not be farm products but inventory, and a buyer at the stand would take free of the security interest.

The problems intensify if the sale is, for example, of a daily supply of milk to a milk dealer who may in turn sell the milk to a dairy.[64] While one financing a herd of cattle would perhaps not be likely to claim a security interest in milk as a product, and authority to sell the milk on a daily basis might be implied where it is not expressly given (since the milk must be disposed of), there are obvious problems here, theoretical though they may be.

The difficulties are aggravated where the security interest is in an annual crop such as wheat which the debtor sells to a grain elevator in violation of a security agreement,[65] and the elevator in turn sells

---

63. § 9–109(3). Goods used or bought for use primarily in farming will be equipment under § 9–109(2) if they are not farm products, although if the farmer holds certain goods, such as harvesting equipment, for lease or to be furnished under contracts of service, the goods should be inventory. Chickens were held to be livestock in United States v. Pete Brown Enterprises, Inc., 328 F.Supp. 600 (N.D.Miss. 1971), since the definition of "farm products" includes eggs as products of livestock; see also Official Comment 4 to § 9–109. Feed-lot steers in possession of a debtor who was fattening them were held to be farm products rather than inventory in *In re* Cadwell, Martin Meat Co., 10 UCC Rep.Serv. 710 (E.D.Cal.1970) (in bankruptcy).

64. Milk check financing is discussed in Coates, Farm Secured Transactions Under the UCC, 23 Bus.Law. 195, 207–08 (1967). This article deals with many problems in a practical and helpful way. When the milk reaches a dealer or dairy, it will become inventory under § 9–109(4). An interesting cotton problem arose in United States v. Hext, 444 F.2d 804 (5th Cir. 1971). This opinion was described as a tour de force in Kennedy, Secured Transactions, 27 Bus.Law. 755, 766 (1972).

65. Overland Nat'l Bank of Grand Island v. Aurora Co-op. Elevator Co., 184 Neb. 843, 172 N.W.2d 786 (1969) (involving milo).

to a manufacturer of breakfast cereal which subsequently sells to distributors, and ultimately retailers sell the cereal to consumers. Under the Code, the farmer's secured party could follow the wheat into the hands of the consumer (although surely not profitably beyond that point), since even buyers in ordinary course take free only of security interests created by their sellers, not of security interests further back in the chain. The breakfast cereal is a product of the original wheat and the original security interest presumably can be traced.[66]

A number of problems have arisen in connection with sales of cattle by farmers,[67] although there has been no case where a farmer's financer tried to reclaim steaks from a dinner table.[68]

What the Code provides is relatively clear; whether it is the right answer is another matter. Indeed, whether there is a right answer here, is not obvious. Some buyers from farmers think it is absolutely essential that they take free of security interests, as other buyers of inventory do, but some financers of farmers think it is just as essential that their security interests be protected.[69] At one stage in the re-

---

66. § 9–306(2). If the right steps were taken to claim "products" in the financing statement, this might be an instance where § 9–315 could be utilized, although apparently no cases have yet applied that section in this context.

67. But a contract to sell cattle, where nothing has been done beyond that point, is not a "sale, exchange or other disposition" under § 9–306(2). Weisbart & Co. v. First Nat'l Bank of Dalhart, 568 F.2d 391 (5th Cir. 1978).

68. In Clovis Nat. Bank v. Thomas, 77 N.M. 554, 425 P.2d 726 (1967), where the debtor sold cattle without the secured party's written consent as required in the security agreement, the secured party was found to have waived its rights under the agreement by past conduct, and it could not maintain an action in conversion against the commission house handling the sale when the debtor did not apply the proceeds towards reduction of the loan. *See also* Planters Production Credit Ass'n v. Bowles, 256 Ark. 1063, 511 S.W.2d 645. *Contra*, Garden City Production Credit Ass'n v. Lannan, 186 Neb. 668, 186 N.W.2d 99 (1971). *See* Burlington Nat. Bank v. Strauss, 50 Wis.2d 270, 184 N.W.2d 122 (1971).

See also In re Cadwell, Martin Meat Co., 10 UCC Rep.Serv. 710 (E.D.Cal. 1970) (in bankruptcy). Cf. United States v. Greenwich Mill & Elevator Co., 291 F.Supp. 609 (N.D.Ohio 1968). In United States v. Topeka Livestock Auction, Inc., 392 F.Supp. 944 (N.D. Ind.1975) an auctioneer was held liable in conversion to the secured party for selling livestock which was subject to a perfected security interest. Disagreeing with *Clovis* and containing numerous citations to authorities is Central California Equipment Co. v. Dolk Tractor Co., —— Cal.App.3d ——, 144 Cal.Rptr. 367 (1978).

69. This is the position of the United States, which is an extremely important financer of agricultural collateral, and all taxpayers have an interest here. This may be one of those areas where, no matter what state law says, the interest of the United States will be protected under federal law. *See* United States v. McCleskey Mills, Inc., 409 F.2d 1216 (5th Cir. 1969); United States v. Big Z Warehouse, 311 F. Supp. 283 (S.D.Ga.1970). *See generally* Dolan, Section 9–307(1): The U.C.C.'s Obstacle to Agricultural Commerce in the Open Market, 72 Nw.U.L.Rev. 706 (1978).

drafting of Article 9, the words "other than a person buying farm products from a person engaged in farming operations" were deleted from Section 9–307(1),[70] but this language was restored eventually by the Permanent Editorial Board.[71]

The 1962 Code provides that a purchase money security interest in farm equipment costing not more than $2500, except for fixtures and licensed motor vehicles, is automatically perfected on attachment without filing.[72] A correlative provision in Section 9–307(2) states that where the original purchase price of farm equipment was not more than $2500, a buyer will take free of a perfected security interest if he buys without knowledge of the security interest, for value, and for his own farming operations, unless a financing statement has been filed before the purchase. The $2500 amount has been reduced in a number of states, generally to $500 in both sections. Although the purpose of the provisions was to facilitate farm credit, by analogy to consumer credit,[73] the provisions appear not to have worked to the benefit of farmers, and both have been eliminated in Revised Article 9.

The most significant case in this area arose from the bankruptcy of a meat packer, Samuels & Co., Inc. of Dallas, Texas.[74] The tortuous, if not torturous, course of this litigation[75] ultimately produced an opinion which is undoubtedly correct in its interpretation of the Code, despite vigorous dissent,[76] and it has also prompted a considerable amount of federal[77] and state legislation[78] designed to pro-

---

70. *See* Review Committee for Article 9 of the Uniform Commercial Code, Preliminary Draft No. 2, pp. 16, 81 (1970).

71. Permanent Editorial Board for the Uniform Commercial Code, Review Committee for Article 9, Final Report 101, 209 (1971).

72. § 9–302(1)(c).

73. *See* §§ 9–302(1)(d), 9–307(2). These provisions are retained with alterations in Revised § 9–302(1)(d) in the Revised Code.

74. *In re* Samuels & Co., Inc., 526 F.2d 1238 (5th Cir. 1976). The opinion was originally written as a dissent in 510 F.2d 139 at 154, and its appearance is extremely unusual in the Federal Reporter since the substantive opinion of the Fifth Circuit begins, "I dissent." 526 F.2d at 1241.

75. *In re* Samuels & Co., Inc., 483 F.2d 557 (5th Cir. 1973); reversed and remanded, *sub nom.* Mahon v. Stowers, 416 U.S. 100 (1974); *In re* Samuels & Co., Inc., 510 F.2d 139 (5th Cir. 1975), reversed on rehearing *en banc* in 526 F.2d 1238 (5th Cir. 1976).

76. 526 F.2d at 1249.

77. See the 1976 amendments to the Packers and Stockyards Act, 7 U.S. C.A. § 181 et seq., particularly §§ 196, 228b and 228c.

78. The statutes of any state concerned should be consulted, but the act effectively amending the Code will probably appear elsewhere in the statutes. It is possible that such state statutes may create statutory liens which are invalid under Bankruptcy Act § 67c.

duce a different result on such facts even though the side ramifications of the new legislation may take some time to unfold.

The basic facts were these: For some time C.I.T. Corporation had been financing the meat packing operation of Samuels, and C.I.T. had a perfected security interest in Samuels' inventory and after-acquired property, including livestock purchased for slaughter and processing. For eleven days in May of 1969 various cattle farmers had delivered cattle to Samuels with the understanding that they would be paid after slaughtering when the carcasses were inspected, graded, and weighed. These sellers did not reserve or perfect purchase money or any other security interests under Article 9. On May 23, 1969, C.I.T. learned that Samuels was going to file a plan of arrangement under Chapter 11 of the Bankruptcy Act, and C.I.T. refused to advance additional funds for cattle then in Samuels' hands. Samuels did file on May 23, and ultimately ended in straight bankruptcy. The cattle sellers received checks which were never paid.

Ignoring the Article 2 aspects of the case, it should be clear that when the cattle sellers delivered their cattle to Samuels without reserving a security interest, the cattle became subject to C.I.T.'s perfected security interest. The sellers could have protected their interest by complying with Section 9–312(3), but this they did not do, so that under Section 9–312(5) C.I.T. was entitled to priority in what, by this stage of the proceedings, was proceeds.

While on the facts of this case the sellers were, in Judge Godbold's words, "little fellows" and the lender was a large financial corporation, "the next seller may be a tremendous corporate conglomerate engaged in the cattle feeding business, and the next lender a small town Texas bank." [79] The implication is that the courts should apply the law as passed by the legislature rather than engage in judicial amendments to the statute which may result in a supposedly equitable solution in the case at hand but not in other cases.

§ 5–6. Accounts

An account, according to Section 9–106, is a "right to payment for goods sold or leased or for services rendered which is not evidenced by an instrument or chattel paper." Undoubtedly there are few oral leases of goods, but there are many sales of goods on open account, such as the ordinary charge account sales. Conditional sales or sales involving promissory notes are not included in the definition.

It seems to be generally accepted that the right to payment may be for both goods sold *and* services rendered, despite the use of the

---

79. 526 F.2d at 1242.

disjunctive "or" in the definition of "account." [80] This becomes an issue particularly in the case of contractors engaged in the construction business, where the right to payment, when earned, will often arise from a combination of labor and materials added to the premises. While materials added during construction may not usually be thought of as "goods sold" by the contractor to the owner of the property—a view which might create occasional difficulty in the fixture area [81]—this position seems to be taken without any particular analysis of the conceptual problem in connection with the assignment of accounts by contractors.

A security interest in accounts can be perfected only by filing, with the rare exception of an assignment which alone or with others to the same assignee does not transfer a significant part of the assignor's outstanding accounts, as to which no filing is needed for perfection.[82] It would be an oversight to rely on this provision.

Article 9 covers sales of accounts as well as assignments of accounts for security, and sales must comply with the same rules as secured transactions, since the interest of a buyer of accounts is a "security interest" if it is not excluded from Article 9.[83] The exclusions are for sales of accounts as part of the business out of which they arose, or an assignment for collection only.[84] The reason for covering both sales and assignments for security is that third parties are in the same situation no matter which arrangement the parties have made, and both kinds of transactions are likely to be phrased in terms of assignment, and it is occasionally difficult to be certain just what the parties really intended.

The 1972 Code eliminates "contract rights" as a class of collateral, so insofar as contractual rights to payments relate to goods sold or leased or services rendered and are not evidenced by an instrument or chattel paper, they are accounts before as well as after they are earned by performance.[85] This change led to a concomitant change in Re-

80. *See, e. g.,* Pine Builders, Inc. v. United States, 413 F.Supp. 77 (E.D.Va. 1976); Richmond Crane Rigging & Drayage Co., Inc. v. Golden Gate Nat'l Bank, 27 Cal.App.3d 968, 104 Cal.Rptr. 277 (1972).

81. *See* § 8–3 *infra* at n. 52 and accompanying text.

82. § 9–302(1)(e). The exception providing perfection without filing for isolated assignments which are not significant was misapplied in *In re First General Contractors, Inc.,* 12 UCC Rep.Serv. 762 (S.D.Fla.1971) (in bankruptcy), although the result is

appealing here. *See* E. Turgeon Constr. Co. v. Elhatton Plumbing & Heating Co., Inc., 110 R.I. 303, 292 A. 2d 230 (1972).

83. § 1–201(37). *See* Major's Furniture Mart, Inc. v. Castle Credit Corp., Inc., 449 F.Supp. 538 (E.D.Pa.1978).

84. § 9–104(f).

85. Revised § 9–106. This section makes rights to payments, earned or unearned, under ship charters and incidental rights (whatever they may be) accounts rather than contract rights.

vised Section 9–104(f) which excludes transfers of contractual rights to payments to an assignee who is also to perform the contract, and also excluded is a transfer of a single account in whole or partial satisfaction of a preexisting indebtedness to the assignee.[86]

Since filing is required for perfection of security interests in accounts, where there are conflicting security interests in accounts as primary collateral priority should be resolved in the order of filing,[87] or if only one is filed, it should be entitled to priority.

> A grants a security interest in his accounts to X and X files; A then grants a security interest in inventory and the proceeds of the inventory, including accounts, to Y and Y files. Is X or Y entitled to the accounts when trouble comes?

It is not theoretically impossible for a secured party to have a purchase money security interest in accounts—as where Bank B advances funds to Financer C to enable C to purchase the accounts of A—but this is one step back of the transaction at hand, and a purchase money security interest in accounts is not possible in the context of a retail operation where the accounts arise from sales of inventory which may be financed on a purchase money basis.[88]

If this conflict between a financer of accounts and a subsequent financer of inventory and proceeds (including accounts) is not resolved by subsections (3) or (4) of Section 9–312, is it resolved by subsection (5)? If it is, does the accounts financer win? Perhaps the most appealing answer is that the accounts financer does win because he was the first to file as to the collateral in which a conflict exists, and this answer will be required by Revised Section 9–312 because the purchase money inventory financer's priority extends only to identifiable cash proceeds received on or before delivery of goods to a buyer under subsection (3) or if the transaction is not purchase money, presumably subsections (5) and (6) will give the same result since the inventory financer's proceeds claim will be second in time of filing.

---

86. This change may have been motivated by a desire to avoid the problem (and misinterpretation of the Code) found in Spurlin v. Sloan, 368 S.W.2d 314 (Ky.App.1963). *See also* Lyon v. Ty-Wood Corp., 212 Pa.Super. 69, 239 A.2d 819 (1968). *Cf.* E. Turgeon Constr. Co. v. Elhatton Plumbing & Heating Co., Inc., 110 R.I. 303, 292 A.2d 230 (1972).

87. § 9–312(5)(a); Revised § 9–312(5)(a).

88. *See* Northwestern Nat'l Bank Southwest v. Lectro System, Inc., —— Minn. ——, 262 N.W.2d 678 (1977).

Alternatively, Section 9–312(1) states that specified rules of priority govern where applicable, including "Section 9–306 on proceeds and repossessions." Section 9–306(2) provides that, in the case of inventory, a security interest continues in identifiable proceeds received by the debtor, and Section 9–306(3) states that the security interest in the proceeds is a continuously perfected security interest where the filed financing statement covered proceeds. Because a security interest cannot attach until a debtor has rights in the collateral, under Section 9–204(1), and he has no rights in a specific account until it comes into existence, under Section 9–204(2)(d), the rights of the accounts financer would presumably be subordinate in these circumstances to the continuously perfected security interest of the financer of inventory and proceeds, including accounts. It may be questioned whether the provisions of Sections 9–306(2) and (3) state priority rules, but in any case they state rules, and these rules would be relatively meaningless in this context if they were not applied to give priority to a continuously perfected security interest, in the absence of clear provisions to the contrary elsewhere.

> In order to obtain necessary financing to perform a construction contract with H Co., A Contracting Co. entered into a security agreement with B Bank, granting to the Bank a security interest in contract rights and accounts under the 1962 Code (or simply accounts under the 1972 Code) arising under the contract with H Co. A financing statement was filed in the proper office. During construction, A subcontracted some of the work to S Co., which filed a mechanic's lien. The lien was filed against the real property of H Co. on which the construction was located.

Should H Co. pay B Bank the amount due under the construction contract, at least to the extent of its security interest, or should it pay S Co. the amount of its claim first before paying anything to B Bank? While there is considerable diversity in the mechanics' lien laws of the several states, it is probable that any such statute will give a lien good against the affected real estate to a mechanic who performs labor or furnishes materials in connection with construction on real estate if specified procedures are followed. If this is so, the owner of the real estate will wish to make certain that such a lienor is duly paid. But on the facts stated, is B Bank entitled to satisfy its security interest first on the ground that its interest predated the effectiveness of the mechanic's lien?

This is clearly not a case that comes under Section 9–310. That section regulates priority between a mechanic's lienor and a secured party with an interest in *goods,* in situations where the mechanic's lienor has furnished services or materials with respect to the goods subject to the security interest, such as repairs to an automobile which is subject to a security interest. Here the mechanic's lien affects real estate and the security interest is in accounts (and contract rights under the 1962 Code).

Indeed, the priority problem is not resolved by Article 9, since the mechanic's lien is against real estate, and the lienor has, on the facts stated, taken no steps to obtain a security interest in personal property. So far as appears, the contract was fully performed by A Contracting Co. although it may be assumed that funds received from B Bank were diverted to purposes other than paying S Co., a not uncommon situation judging from reported cases. But B Bank has perfected its security interest in the collateral and has a right to whatever payment is due from H Co. to A Contracting Co.[89] This would leave H Co. with its real estate subject to a mechanic's lien despite having paid for a lien-free construction job, and this is not a happy situation, although if H Co. had been reasonably prudent it would have required A Contracting Co. to provide payment and performance surety bonds to insure that the contract was properly performed and that there would be no liens against the property. If such bonds were in fact required, as would normally be the case, this would throw the loss on the insurance company writing the bonds.

The facts stated above were basically the situation in *Citizens Fidelity Bank & Trust Co.* v. *Fenton Rigging Co.*[90] In that case the court gave priority to the subcontractor, S Co. The court was of the opinion that when the mechanics' lien was filed by the subcontractor, the owner became "directly obligated," in the court's words, to pay the "sums claimed." It is difficult to see how this direct liability could be said to arise under the mechanics' lien law of the state involved,[91] since the statute creates a lien on property, not an obligation to pay, and the lien, in case of cost overruns, could not exceed the contract price. But since it was held that the obligation to pay the subcontractor arose on the contractor's failure to make the payment due and the filing of the mechanics' lien, the amount due to the subcontractor "ceased to be a part" of the bank's collateral, which

---

89. While the facts are different from the example in the text and the opinion has demonstrable flaws, in National Bank of Detroit v. Eames & Brown, Inc., 50 Mich.App. 447, 213 N.W.2d 573 (1973), the court recognized that a prior perfected security interest was entitled to priority over one claiming under the state's so-called Building Contract Fund Act, not because Article 9 determines the priority but rather because the Article 9 perfected security interest left nothing for a later claimant to acquire rights in or at least nothing that such a claimant did acquire rights in on the facts in the case.

90. 522 S.W.2d 862 (Ky.1975).

91. Ky.—KRS 376.010 (Bobbs-Merrill 1972).

was said to be "accounts receivable," so that "the amounts due did not become subject" to the security interest of Bank B. While the statute relates the mechanics' lien back from the time of filing to the time when the work was commenced, nevertheless the lien is on the land and improvements and not on the money coming due to the prime contractor from the owner, in which the bank had a perfected security interest as proceeds of the account, which would in turn have been proceeds of a contract right under the 1962 Code, and no doubt the collateral ought to have been described as "contract rights [under an identified contract] and proceeds." Under the 1972 Code the collateral would have been correctly described as accounts and proceeds.

> In order to obtain the necessary financing to perform a construction contract with H Co., A Contracting Co. entered into a security agreement with B Bank, granting to the Bank a security interest in contract rights and accounts under the 1962 Code (or simply accounts under the 1972 Code) arising under the contract with H Co. A financing statement was filed in the proper office. Because it was required by the construction contract, A obtained payment and performance bonds from S Surety Co. under which S assured that the construction would be duly completed and paid for. In the application for the bond A assigned to S a security interest in contract rights and accounts arising under the construction contract under the 1962 Code (or simply accounts under the 1972 Code). No financing statement was filed. During the course of construction A became insolvent, and it was necessary for S to complete the construction.

As between S Surety Co. and B Bank, who is entitled to any retained funds and to progress payments which were earned under the contract with H Co. after S took over the construction? If this problem were treated purely as a priority problem under Article 9, B Bank would be entitled to all payments coming due under the construction contract because, under Section 9–312(5), B was the only secured party to file and perfect a security interest in the collateral, although both B and S had received security interests in the same collateral. However, it has long been recognized that this fact situation creates peculiar problems that have not been thought susceptible to a statutory solution.[92] It would be possible for sureties to file to perfect their security interests but they have refused to do so, in part, apparently, because of very practical difficulties in doing this when thousands of bonds are constantly being written all over the country.

---

92. *See* Canter v. Schlager, 358 Mass. 789, 267 N.E.2d 492 (1971) for a brief history of the Code's early days when a statutory solution was attempted and then dropped.

Moreover, if the financer and the surety both filed, in every case an impasse would result which would require negotiation for resolution, and this would not be economically feasible. The construction of a major project requires both an interim financer and a surety if the project is to be undertaken, and the project must be satisfactorily completed free and clear of liens if the permanent lender is to make a mortgage loan in accordance with the commitment to lend which makes the project possible.

The doctrine of subrogation provides perhaps the most satisfactory solution to the problem, and it now seems to be rather generally accepted despite early cases which took the view that the surety's right to payment was a Code security interest which was unperfected in the absence of filing,[93] a view which of course has substance if the surety's claim is solely based on the terms of an assignment of money to come due under the construction contract. But as was pointed out in *Jacobs* v. *Northeastern Corp.*:[94] "Rights of subrogation, although growing out of a contractual setting and ofttimes articulated by the contract, do not depend for their existence on a grant in the contract, but one created by law to avoid injustice. Therefore, subrogation rights are not 'security interests' within the meaning of Article 9." If subrogation can be used, " . . . the surety may stand in the shoes of either (1) the contractor whose obligations are discharged, (2) the owners to whom it was bound, or (3) the subcontractors whom it paid."[95] On this approach, the surety should prevail over the contractor's trustee in bankruptcy, where the contractor has filed a bankruptcy petition, regardless of which provision of the Bankruptcy Act the trustee may be relying on.[96] The

93. *See, e. g.,* United States v. G. P. Fleetwood & Co., Inc., 165 F.Supp. 723 (W.D.Pa.1958).

94. 416 Pa. 417, 429, 206 A.2d 49, 55 (1965).

95. Canter v. Schlager, 358 Mass. 789, 794, 267 N.E.2d 492, 496 (1971), relying on Pearlman v. Reliance Ins. Co., 371 U.S. 132 (1962). *See also* National Surety Corp. v. State Nat'l Bank of Frankfort, 454 S.W.2d 354 (Ky.1970); Pembroke State Bank v. Balboa Ins. Co., 144 Ga.App. 609, 241 S.E.2d 483 (1978).

96. *See* Canter v. Schlager, 358 Mass. 789, 267 N.E.2d 492 (1971). In United States v. G. P. Fleetwood & Co., Inc., 165 F.Supp. 723 (1958), the court seemed to feel that because the appli-cation for the performance bond was executed within four months before the contractor's bankruptcy, the assignment to the surety was a preference. (The case was not based on subrogation.) While this seems to be dubious, in any event even if there were a preference under Bankruptcy Act, § 60a, it is highly unlikely that any surety would knowingly enter into a bond on behalf of a contractor known to be insolvent so that the preference could probably not be set aside under Bankruptcy Act, § 60b, but this problem (which also involves an issue as to when the "transfer" to the surety took place) is eliminated by the subrogation approach. *See In re* J. V. Gleason Co., Inc., 452 F.2d 1219 (8th Cir. 1971). *Cf.* Maryland Casualty Co. v. Mullett, 295 F.Supp. 875 (W.D.Pa.1969).

end result usually seems to be that the financing bank keeps what it has received and the surety gets the rest.[97]

The recognition of the equitable doctrine of subrogation in this area—or legal subrogation, as it is sometimes called—obviates a conceptual problem under the Code, as well as a very real problem for sureties. Subrogation can be imported into this area by virtue of Section 1–103, which provides that the principles of law and equity supplement the Code provisions, unless displaced by particular provisions of the Code, and by the better view this principle has not been supplemented. Indeed, since the time of *French Lumber Co., Inc.* v. *Commercial Realty & Finance Co., Inc.,*[98] the doctrine of subrogation has taken on unsuspected vitality.

If the surety's right to payment is treated as subject to Article 9, what kind of security interest could it be? It could possibly be considered as a contract right under the 1962 Code or an account under the 1972 Code on the ground that it is a "right to payment" which is not evidenced by an instrument or chattel paper, and yet it is not really a right to payment arising under a contract in the sense meant by Section 9–106. That is, the surety's right to payment arises because the contractor (whose work has been performed by the surety) did not do the work called for by the contract, and therefore, the contractor's efforts never resulted in a right to payment, and the definitions of Section 9–106 do not fit. What the surety has done is to perform the work under the contract because an entirely separate agreement imposes that obligation. But if the surety has a right to payment, arguably it is excluded by Section 9–104(f) as a transfer of a right to payment to an assignee who is to perform the contract, and yet the surety never expects to have to perform the construction contract when the surety agreement is entered into. The simplest solution is the one generally adopted; that is, to assume the surety's rights arise outside the Code under the doctrine of subrogation.

If the surety is granted a security interest in the contractor's equipment, in the application for the bond, then it will be necessary for the surety to file a financing statement if it hopes to prevail over other secured parties claiming properly perfected security interests in the equipment.[99]

§ 5–7. Contract Rights

The term "contract right" is defined in Section 9–106 to cover "any right to payment under a contract not yet earned by performance

97. *See, e. g.,* National Shawmut Bank v. New Amsterdam Casualty Co., 411 F.2d 843, 848 (1st Cir. 1969).

98. 346 Mass. 716, 195 N.E.2d 507 (1964).

99. Aetna Casualty & Surety Co. v. J. F. Brunken & Son, Inc., 357 F.Supp. 290 (D.S.D.1973); *In re* Merts Equipment Co., 438 F.Supp. 295 (M.D.Ga. 1977).

and not evidenced by an instrument or chattel paper."[1] For example, a manufacturer agrees to produce and deliver quantities of goods over a period of time, for which the buyer will pay on delivery. The manufacturer can borrow against these future payments, which are contract rights. In this kind of situation, the contract rights when earned will become accounts because the right to payment arises out of goods sold.[2] (If the contract involved royalty payments, when earned they would become general intangibles.) A financer would probably claim contract rights and proceeds on a financing statement. A priority problem could arise if there were an accounts financer in the picture, with as much resulting uncertainty as in the case of the accounts versus inventory and proceeds problem discussed under Accounts.[3] It is in any case somewhat unclear whether rights to payment under construction contracts turn into accounts when earned because of uncertainty whether those contracts involve "goods sold or leased or . . . services rendered" as required by Section 9–106 for an account, but it is generally assumed that they do.[4]

While "contract rights" seems like a useful concept, the only Code provision discriminating in terms between an account and a contract right is Section 9–318(2) which allows the modification of an assigned contract where the contract right has not become an account. This Section has been redrafted to reflect the elimination of "contract right" from Revised Article 9. Indeed, even the title of Article 9 has had to be changed, since the Article under the 1962 Code covered sales as well as assignments for security of contract rights.

Priority conflicts involving contract rights as such should be minimal, since priority will be determined in the order of filing under Section 9–312(5), if both security interests are perfected by filing. The

1. In Consolidated Film Industries v. United States, 403 F.Supp. 1279 (D. Utah 1975), reversed on other grounds 547 F.2d 533 (10th Cir. 1977) the right of a distributor to receive future royalties from the performances of a motion picture under a contract not then completed was held to be a contract right; on this analysis the right to royalties would probably be an account under the 1972 Code, as a right to payment for goods leased not yet earned by performance. A lessee's right to the return of a security deposit has been treated as a contract right in United States v. Samel Refining Corp., 461 F.2d 941 (3d Cir. 1972); presumably it would be a general intangible under Revised § 9–106. See also Dynair Electronics, Inc. v. Video Cable, Inc., 55 Cal.App.3d 11, 127 Cal.Rptr. 268 (1976); Art-Camera-Pix, Inc. v. Cinecom Corp., 64 Misc.2d 764, 315 N.Y.S.2d 991 (N.Y.Sup.Ct. 1970); Continental Finance, Inc. v. Cambridge Lee Metal Co., Inc., 56 N.J. 148, 265 A.2d 536 (1970).

2. See Marine Nat'l Bank v. Airco, Inc., 389 F.Supp. 231 (W.D.Pa.1975).

3. See § 5–6.

4. See Rudolph, Financing on Construction Contracts Under the Uniform Commercial Code, 5 B.C.Ind. & Com.L.Rev. 245 (1964).

conflicts arise as the contract is performed and the rights to payment are earned. The problems here are analogous to those arising between financers of accounts and financers of inventory who claim proceeds, except that here the first financer would claim accounts or general intangibles and the second financer would claim contract rights and proceeds (or accounts or general intangibles or both).[5]

With the elimination of "contract right," the definition of "account" in Revised Section 9–106 has been broadened to include rights to payment whether or not earned by performance, but the rights must still be for goods sold or leased or services rendered not evidenced by an instrument or chattel paper. Some rights to payment will now be general intangibles, whether or not earned.

§ 5–8. Chattel Paper

The term "chattel paper" is defined in Section 9–105(1)(b) to cover "a writing or writings which evidence both a monetary obligation and a security interest in or a lease of specific goods. . . ." Where there is both a security agreement or lease and an instrument or a series of instruments, the aggregate is chattel paper. (Since this definition on its face would cover ship charters and the like, they are expressly excluded.) The most ordinary kinds of chattel paper are conditional sale contracts and non-purchase money security agreements of the type that used to be called chattel mortgages.[6] Promissory notes may be used in both kinds of transactions, and when they are, both the notes and the agreements together constitute chattel paper. Article 9 applies to both security interests in and sales of chattel paper, as is made expressly clear by the title to Article 9 and by

5. In Citizens Fidelity Bank & Trust Co. v. Fenton Rigging Co., 522 S.W. 2d 862 (Ky.1975), there was a contest between a subcontractor which filed a mechanic's lien and a financing bank which apparently had a perfected security interest in the prime contractor's accounts, and the lienor was given priority in the fund payable to the contractor by the owner of the property on which the construction was being performed. While the opinion is not as clear as it might have been, the decision seems to rest on the idea that the mechanic's lienor's rights fastened on to the contract rights so that when they became accounts on performance and thus subject to the bank's security interest, the lienor's interest would have priority and the bank's rights would be subject to the prior interest. Had the bank claimed contract rights and accounts under the 1962 Code, rather than accounts, a different issue would have been presented. This case is discussed from a different perspective in § 5–6 *supra*.

6. Occasionally some courts have been confused about "collateral." *See, e. g.,* Shaffer v. Davidson, 445 P.2d 13 (Wyo. 1968) where the court treated a chattel mortgage, which was the security agreement, as chattel paper collateral, when the collateral was in fact an automobile.

Section 9–102(1)(b), and the term "security interest" covers all sales of chattel paper, according to Section 1–201(37), unless the transaction is excluded from Article 9 by Section 9–104(f). The exclusions cover a sale of chattel paper as part of a sale of the business out of which it arose or an assignment purely for collection.

A security interest in chattel paper may be perfected by filing. [7] This presents the superficially anomalous possibility of perfecting a security interest in instruments, as part of chattel paper, by filing rather than taking possession. [8] A security interest in chattel paper may be perfected by possession,[9] and this is the most effective means of assuring priority to the secured party.

If a security interest in chattel paper is perfected by filing, it is possible that the paper may be sold or subjected to a security interest where the buyer or financer gives new value and takes possession of the paper without knowing of the filed interest. If this happens, such a person takes priority over the filed security interest under Section 9–308.[10] Moreover, such a "purchaser" [11] will take priority over the filed security interest even though he knows of it if the filed interest claims chattel paper "merely" as proceeds of inventory,[12] as where an inventory financer claims a security interest in inventory and proceeds but is not in fact financing the proceeds.

There are obvious possibilities for improper conduct by a debtor if chattel paper is left in his possession, and if an instrument is separated from a security agreement it may well be acquired by one who will take priority over the filed financer under either Section 9–308 or 9–309. If chattel paper, for whatever the reason, is left with the debtor, it can be stamped to show an assignment of the paper to the secured

---

7. § 9–304(1).

8. A security interest in instruments as such may be perfected only by possession. § 9–304(1). But there are possibilities of temporary perfection under §§ 9–304(4) and (5), and security interests in instruments as proceeds may be perfected by filing as to proceeds under § 9–306. The term "instruments" is broadly defined in § 9–105(1)(g), Revised § 9–105(1)(i). Where the security interest is perfected by filing, various third parties may acquire priority over the filed security interest.

9. § 9–305.

10. *See, e. g.*, American State Bank v Avco Financial Services of the United States, Inc., 71 Cal.App.3d 774, 139 Cal.Rptr. 658 (1977).

11. "Purchaser" is defined in § 1–201 (33).

12. *See, e. g.*, Associates Discount Corp. v. Old Freeport Bank, 421 Pa. 609, 220 A.2d 621 (1966); Rex Financial Corp. v. Great Western Bank & Trust, 23 Ariz.App. 286, 532 P.2d 558 (1975); Chrysler Credit Corp. v. Sharp, 288 N. Y.S.2d 525, 56 Misc.2d 261 (Sup.Ct. 1968).

party, so that it cannot be transferred to a purchaser who does not know of the secured party's interest, although this presents difficulties in the case of chattel leases which may be executed in multiple original copies. If there are multiple executed copies, this fact can be indicated on the face of each copy, with a notation stating that the original has been assigned to a designated secured party. Where the financing is handled on a continuing basis, these precautions will be a matter of form. If the transaction is isolated, as it might be if a great deal of money were involved, the secured party would be well advised to take possession of the paper rather than merely filing.

> M Company leased machines from L Leasing Co. for use in M's manufacturing plant. In order to acquire the machine for leasing, it was necessary for L to arrange financing with B Bank, and under the security agreement between B and L, L granted to B a security interest in the lease, and a financing statement was filed in the proper office claiming a security interest in chattel paper consisting of an identified lease.

The leases are properly described as chattel paper, under the definition of that term in Section 9–105(1)(b), when they are used as security for the lessor's financing, and this is the case whether the leases are true leases or disguised conditional sales.[13]

While a security interest in chattel paper may be perfected by filing, according to Section 9–304(1), if a filing is made and the leases are left in the lessor's possession, the secured party runs the risk that a dishonest lessor may transfer the lease to a bona fide purchaser of the paper who pays value and takes possession of the lease in the ordinary course of business without actual knowledge that there has been a filing, and such a purchaser will take priority over the secured party under Section 9–308. The purchaser, under the definition of that term in Section 1–201, may be a buyer or a secured party. If a lease is left in the debtor's possession under the terms of the agreement between L and B in the example above, the paper could be stamped to show that the lessor's interest has been assigned to the financer so that no third party could take possession of the lease without knowledge of the assignment.

Will B Bank, as the lessor's financer, want a security interest in the goods subject to the lease or will it be adequate from B's point of view to rely simply on an assignment of the lease in the security agreement? This depends on an evaluation of the credit risks in-

---

13. *See* § 1–201(37) and § 3–12 *supra*.

volved.[14] If the lease between M and L is in fact a disguised conditional sale and a financing statement has been filed—or if in any event a financing statement has been filed pursuant to Revised Section 9–408—then B as the lessor's financer may be shown on the financing statement as an assignee or a separate assignment may be filed. Neither act is required to protect B as assignee against creditors of the lessee, under Section 9–302(2), but an assignment of record is necessary to protect B against creditors of the lessor, if an interest in the goods is material to B.[15] If a true lease is involved and B as a secured party is concerned about a security interest in the goods, then L as lessor-owner may be required to execute a financing statement as debtor showing B Bank as secured party. If the lease contains an unconditional promise to pay the rentals to the lessor's assignee and the lessee's credit rating is high enough, the secured party may not require a security interest in the goods, regardless of the security interest versus true lease question.

§ 5–9. Instruments

While it may be doubted that very many negotiable instruments are (by themselves and apart from security agreements) pledged for security,[16] the term "instrument" also includes securities [17] and non-negotiable paper evidencing a right to the payment of money if the paper "is not itself a security agreement or lease and is of a type which is in ordinary course of business transferred by delivery with any necessary indorsement or assignment." [18]

---

14. A perfected possessory security interest in chattel paper does not perfect a security interest in the underlying collateral. Nicholson's Mobile Home Sales, Inc. v. Schramm, — Ind. App. —, 330 N.E.2d 785 (Ind.App. 1975). *Cf. In re* Western Leasing, Inc., 17 UCC Rep.Serv. 1369 (D.Or. 1975) (in bankruptcy).

15. *See In re* Leasing Consultants, Inc., 486 F.2d 367 (2d Cir. 1973) where both the lessor and the lessee became involved in bankruptcy proceedings.

16. A promissory note was pledged as security in *In re* Chapman, 5 UCC Rep.Serv. 649 (W.D.Mich.1968) (in bankruptcy). The requirements for a negotiable instrument are set out in § 3–104(1). *See also* McIlroy Bank v. First Nat'l Bank of Fayetteville, 252 Ark. 558, 480 S.W.2d 127 (1972).

17. *See, e. g., In re* Sportsland, Inc., 17 UCC Rep.Serv. 1333 (D.Mass.1975) (in

bankruptcy). The term "security" is defined in § 8–102(1)(a), and it includes far more than stock certificates. A revised version of Article 8, primarily necessitated by the move to a certificateless society, was approved by the American Law Institute in 1978. On adoption, Revised Article 8 will have a considerable impact in the area of security interests in securities. *See* particularly Revised § 8–321. The revision of Article 8 involves corresponding amendments to §§ 9–103, 9–105, 9–203, 9–302, 9–304, 9–305, 9–309, and 9–312.

18. § 9–105(1)(g), Revised § 9–105(1)(i). A certificate of deposit was held to be an instrument in First Nat'l Bank in Grand Prairie v. Lone Star Life Ins. Co., 524 S.W.2d 525 (Tex.Civ.App. 1975).

A security interest in instruments, unless they are part of chattel paper, can be perfected only by possession [19] except for instances of temporary perfection under subsections (4) and (5) of Section 9–304 and except where the security interest is claimed in the instruments as proceeds under Section 9–306.[20]

Section 9–304 gives temporary perfection for 21 days to security interests in instruments, without possession in the secured party, in two circumstances. The first is where the interest arises for new value under a written security agreement, as when a bank lends money to enable a customer to purchase stock, where some time will normally elapse between payment and delivery of the certificate registered in the name of the buyer. The second is where there is a security interest perfected by possession and the secured party releases the instrument to the debtor so that it can be sold or exchanged (as where the debtor must sell and deliver a stock certificate in order to get the funds necessary to repay a bank loan or where a certificate must be exchanged as in the case of a merger) or where the delivery is for presentation, collection, renewal or registration of transfer. If a note is pledged, it will be necessary to present it for payment if it becomes due during the period when it is security for another obligation, and a release for that purpose does not deprive the secured party of a perfected security interest.[21]

While the security interest in instruments is temporarily perfected during the 21-day period, a bona fide purchaser of a security [22] or a holder in due course [23] who takes a negotiable instrument will take priority over the security interest,[24] and the secured party must look to the proceeds of the sale to satisfy the security interest. The necessity for this rule is perhaps most obvious in the case of a stock certificate

---

19. There may be two security interests granted to two different secured parties in the same instrument, and possession by one of the secured parties can be effective to perfect both security interests. *In re* Chapman, 5 UCC Rep.Serv. 649 (W.D.Mich.1968) (in bankruptcy). Possession by a bailee, such as a bank, is more usual. *See, e. g., In re* Copeland, 531 F.2d 1195 (3d Cir. 1976). Where the escrow holder was a lawyer who had represented both parties, the lawyer was held not to be an agent of the secured party for the purpose of holding the instrument and perfecting a security interest in it. Stein v. Rand Constr. Co., Inc., 400 F.Supp. 944 (S.D.N.Y.1975).

20. § 9–304(1), Revised § 9–304(1).

21. The security interest lapses after 21 days, where a note is released by a secured party to the debtor. McIlroy Bank v. First Nat'l Bank of Fayetteville, 252 Ark. 558, 480 S.W.2d 127 (1972).

22. *See* §§ 8–301 and 8–302.

23. *See* §§ 3–302(1) and 3–305.

24. § 9–309.

pledged with a bank where the stock must be sold to pay the loan, and the bank releases the stock to the debtor who delivers it to a broker who sells it. The ultimate buyer could hardly be expected to take subject to an earlier security interest. Paper collateral embodying rights, such as negotiable instruments or stock certificates, is traditionally treated as if the paper itself reified the rights. The 21-day period is chosen because of Section 60 of the Bankruptcy Act, which allows a 21-day relation back for perfection in certain circumstances, and Section 9–304(6) requires compliance with the applicable provisions of Article 9 if perfection is to continue beyond the 21-day period. If the security interest is perfected in a timely manner, then perfection is continuous under Section 9–303(2).

In the 1962 Code, Section 9–308 gives priority over a temporarily perfected security interest to a purchaser of a non-negotiable instrument who gives new value and who takes possession in the ordinary course of business if the purchaser is without knowledge that the instrument is subject to a security interest. Where a purchaser is aware that an instrument is claimed merely as proceeds of inventory, he will not take priority over the inventory financer, whether the instrument is negotiable or not (and a purchaser could not be a holder in due course if he were aware of the claim) [25] while a purchaser of chattel paper, including instruments, could take priority over the inventory financer in these circumstances.[26] This anomaly is corrected in Revised Section 9–308, which covers "instruments" whether negotiable or not and which restates the provisions of Section 9–308 in clearer language. Under Revised Section 9–308 a purchaser of an instrument who gives new value and takes possession in the ordinary course of his business will have priority over a security interest which is temporarily perfected under Section 9–304 or perfected because the instrument is proceeds under Section 9–306 if he does not know of the security interest, and he will have priority over a security interest in the instrument claimed merely as proceeds of inventory under Section 9–306 even if he knows the instrument is subject to that claim.

B Bank financed the operation of X Construction Co. and took a security interest in X's accounts and their proceeds. A financing statement was filed in the proper office. Sub-

---

25. *See* §§ 3–302(1)(c), 1–201(25). Filing of a financing statement does not in itself constitute notice to a person who would otherwise be a holder in due course. § 3–304(5), § 9–309 (last sentence).

26. *See* Felsenfeld, Knowledge as a Factor in Determining Priorities Under the Uniform Commercial Code, 42 N.Y.U.L.Rev. 246 (1967).

sequently X persuaded P Co. to pay a bill then due for labor and materials by giving to X a promissory note which X subsequently negotiated to a supplier, R Co. in payment of a bill.   As between R Co. and B Bank who is entitled to receive the payment due under the note at maturity?

The note from P Co. is identifiable proceeds of an account under Section 9–306(1), and B Bank's security interest in accounts and proceeds is a perfected security interest which continues from the account into the promissory note made by P Co. under Section 9–306 (2).   However, if the note is a negotiable instrument under Section 3–104(1), then under Section 9–309 a holder in due course—that is, a person meeting the requirements of Section 3–302(1)—will take free of B Bank's security interest in the note as proceeds of an account.   As expressed in the last sentence of Section 9–309, "Filing under this Article does not constitute notice of the security interest to . . . " a holder in due course. So far as appears from the facts given, R Co. is a holder in due course of the note, and R Co. is entitled to priority over B Bank's perfected security interest.[27]

While Section 9–308 of the 1962 Code would not apply to a situation where the note is negotiable, Revised Section 9–308 applies to both negotiable and non-negotiable instruments. However, for a purchaser of an instrument to take priority over a claimant to the note as proceeds, the purchaser would have to give new value and take possession of the note in the ordinary course of business, without knowledge that the specific paper is subject to a security interest. (Clause (b) of Section 9–308 is not in point here because B Bank's claim is not based on the note's being proceeds of inventory.)   While R Co. took the note by purchase under Section 1–201(32) and would be a purchaser under Section 1–201(33), the note was taken in payment of a bill, so new value was not given, and the purchase of such notes would presumably not be in the ordinary course of business for suppliers of construction companies.

§ 5–10.   Documents of Title

In ordinary circumstances, when we talk of documents of title we mean either bills of lading or warehouse receipts, but the term is more

---

27.   The fact situation in the text is based on Citizens Valley Bank v. Pacific Materials Co., 263 Or. 557, 503 P. 2d 491 (1972), and so is the resolution of the problem. *See also* North Central Kansas Production Credit Assn. v. Boese, 19 UCC Rep.Serv. 179 (D. Kan.1976), where a check was negotiated to a holder in due course, although payment was stopped by the drawer, and the check was also claimed by a cattle financer as proceeds arising from the sale of cattle; the holder in due course was a Las Vegas establishment known as Fremont Casino Corporation.

broadly defined in the Code,[28] and these documents may be either negotiable or non-negotiable. Priority problems involving documents will normally arise in connection with inventory financing, although they can arise in cases of equipment or farm collateral financing.

While goods are held by the issuer of a negotiable document, a security interest in the goods is perfected by perfecting a security interest in the document,[29] and while this may be done by filing,[30] possession,[31] is the only safe means so far as competing secured parties are concerned. Filing is not notice of the security interest to a holder to whom a negotiable document of title has been duly negotiated,[32] and he will take priority over the security interest.[33] This makes it advisable for a financer to lend against negotiable documents, rather than non-negotiable documents. A financer who has acquired a negotiable warehouse receipt by due negotiation can then have a non-negotiable receipt issued in his name to facilitate inventory financing thereafter through the use of delivery orders. A 21-day period of temporary perfection is provided by Section 9–304(4) for a security interest in negotiable documents running from the time of attachment, to the extent the interest arises for new value under a written security agreement.

Where goods are held by a bailee who has not issued a negotiable document for them, a security interest in the goods can be perfected by filing as to the goods, or by the issuance of a document in the secured party's name,[34] or by the bailee's receipt of notification of the secured party's interest,[35] and receipt of notification by the bailee is deemed to be possession by the secured party.[36]

28. *See* § 1–201(15). The definition of "document" in § 9–105(1)(e) simply refers to the definition in § 1–201(15), but this definition has been expanded in Revised § 9–105(1)(f) to include receipts covered by § 7–201(2) for distilled spirits and agricultural commodities. The most interesting documentary financing problems under the Code are discussed in Funk, Trust Receipt vs. Warehouse Receipt—Which Prevails When They Cover the Same Goods? 19 Bus.Law. 627 (1967) and Douglas-Guardian Warehouse Corp. v. Esslair Endsley Co., 10 UCC Rep.Serv. 176 (W.D.Mich.1971). *See also In re* Fairfield Elevator Co., Inc., 14 UCC Rep.Serv. 96 (S.D.Iowa, 1973) (in bankruptcy). A recent article of seminal importance is Dolan, Good Faith Purchase and Warehouse Receipts: Thoughts on the Interplay of Articles 2, 7, and 9 of the UCC, 30 Hastings L.J. 1 (1978).

29. § 9–304(2).

30. § 9–304(1).

31. § 9–305.

32. *See* §§ 7–501(4), 7–502, 7–503.

33. § 9–309.

34. Stanley v. Fabricators, Inc., 459 P. 2d 467 (Alaska 1969). *See also* Lofton v. Mooney, 452 S.W.2d 617 (Ky.1970).

35. § 9–304(3).

36. § 9–305 (second sentence).

Where there is a perfected security interest in a negotiable document or in goods held by a bailee who has not issued a negotiable document, the security interest will be temporarily perfected for 21 days if the secured party makes the goods or documents available to the debtor for the purposes specified in Section 9–304(5) (a), such as sale or dealing with the goods in preparation for sale. While the priority rules may be unclear under the 1962 Code where the goods become inventory, under the 1972 Code the purchase money financer must comply with the provisions of Section 9–312(3) to have priority over an earlier inventory financer claiming after-acquired inventory of the type involved and, among other things, this requires giving notice to the earlier financer before the debtor receives the goods.

> B Bank financed the purchase of a shipment of rugs for X Rug Store by paying a draft drawn to the seller's order by the seller on the buyer, X, which the seller had indorsed and delivered to the seller's bank along with a bill of lading under which the shipment of rugs was consigned to the order of the seller. The bill of lading was also indorsed to the seller's bank. Both the draft and the bill of lading were duly negotiated by the seller's bank to B Bank. On May 1, B Bank by contractual arrangement with X Rug Store, indorsed and released to X the bill of lading, and X received the rugs on surrender of the document to the carrier that day. The rugs were placed in X's store for sale on May 2. On May 3 S Finance Company made an advance pursuant to agreement and filed a financing statement in proper form claiming a security interest in X's rugs and their proceeds. On May 4 B Bank filed a financing statement in proper form claiming a security interest in X's rugs and their proceeds.

B Bank has a purchase money security interest in X's rugs under Section 9–107(a), and the security interest was originally perfected by taking possession of the negotiable document pursuant to Section 9–305 while the goods were in the carrier's possession. Under Section 9–304(5) (a), B Bank's security interest remained perfected when it released the document to X so that X could obtain possession of the rugs for ultimate sale, and the security interest remained perfected for 21 days. Under Section 9–303(2) B Bank's perfected security interest continued beyond the 21 day period because of B's filing.

Under the 1962 Code B Bank's security interest in the rugs is entitled to priority over S Finance Co.'s security interest because B's interest was perfected first under Section 9–312(5)(b), and Section 9–312(6) requires that for the priority rules of Section 9–312(5) a security interest perfected by a means other than filing is to be treated at all times as if perfected by such other means, in this case by possession of the negotiable document. The same result would be reached under Revised Section 9–312(5)(a).

Since this transaction involves inventory financing in the context of the problem, what effect does Section 9–312(3) have? Under the 1962 Code B's purchase money security interest was perfected when X received possession of the rugs, so B would be entitled to priority unless B somehow learned of S's interest before B filed.

Even if B learned of S's interest before B filed, it would in terms be impossible for B to comply with Section 9–312(3)(b) because S's interest arose after the debtor received possession of the collateral, so this should be one of those "cases not governed by other rules" and therefore subject to Section 9–312(5). Under the Revised Code the problem would again be covered by Revised Section 9–312(5) because Revised Section 9–312(3)(b) requires notice to the holder of the conflicting security interest only where the conflicting interest is filed before the beginning of the 21-day period of temporary perfection of Section 9–304(5); or alternatively, Revised Section 9–312(3) could be said to govern and to give priority to the purchase money secured party because the purchase money security interest was perfected under Revised Section 9–304 when the debtor received possession of the inventory as clause (a) of Section 9–312(3) requires, and the balance of the section is inapplicable on these facts. Revised Section 9–304(5)(a) refers problems of priority in the goods to Revised Section 9–312(3), although the former section governs perfection.

Suppose B Bank had not filed until 12 days after X had received possession of the rugs. If X sold a rug to a consumer on conditional sale the day the shipment was received by X, with a small cash down payment, would B or S be entitled to the proceeds? Under Section 9–307(1) the consumer as a buyer in ordinary course of business would take free of the security interests of B and S, and those security interests would continue in the identifiable proceeds. B's perfected security interest in the conditional sale contract would lapse ten days after it was received by X, under Section 9–306(3) because B had not at that time filed anything, and then S's priority would be clear as to the chattel paper. Had S immediately taken possession of the conditional sale contract, S might in any case have qualified for priority under Section 9–308, although on the facts stated it would seem that S would not meet the requirements of that section in that new value would appear not to have been given for the chattel paper since it is claimed merely as proceeds of inventory. If B Bank filed 12 days after X received the goods, B's priority in the inventory of rugs would continue, as would B's priority in the identifiable proceeds of rugs sold in the preceding ten days.

X Store received some inventory in which Bank B, having properly filed, has a perfected security interest. Subsequently these goods are placed in a warehouse.

If a negotiable warehouse receipt is issued by the warehouse to X and X duly negotiates [37] the receipt to Bank C as collateral for a loan, is Bank C entitled to priority over Bank B in the goods? Section 9–309 provides that nothing in Article 9 limits the rights of a holder to whom a negotiable document of title has been duly negotiated, and such a holder takes priority over an earlier perfected security interest; filing is not notice to the holder of the earlier security interest. Section 7–501 specifies the requirements of "due negotiation," and Section 7–502 states the rights acquired by such a due negotiation—the rights include title to the document and title to the goods—but the rights given by Section 7–502 are subject to Section 7–503. Under Section 7–503 if goods are subject to a perfected security interest at the time they are put in a warehouse, as in the example above, and the warehouseman issues a document, the document confers no right in the goods against the secured party if the secured party neither authorized the storage, sale, or disposition of the goods (with a cross-reference to Section 9–307) nor acquiesced in the procurement of the document. Since the goods are inventory, it would ordinarily be the case that Bank B had indeed authorized X Store to sell the goods in the ordinary course of business, or in the language of the statute had given the debtor, X Store, "power of disposition." It is also quite possible that B Bank could be said to have "acquiesced in the procurement" of a document of title, if the Store had no facilities for storage and it was known that the goods would be warehoused. However, it does not appear from the facts stated that B Bank "delivered or entrusted" the goods or "any document of title covering them" to X Store, as Section 7–503(1)(a) requires, so that this section would provide that the document conferred no rights in the goods to Bank C as against Bank B. If this is so, under Section 9–312(5) priority would be determined in the order of perfection, so that Bank B's security interest would be satisfied first and Bank C would come second. Priority would be determined under Section 9–312(5) because Bank C's security interest is clearly not a purchase money security interest and Section 9–312(3) could not apply.

If X Store, having warehoused the goods, had obtained from the warehouseman a non-negotiable receipt in the name of Bank C

---

37. Aside from other requirements specified in § 7–501, negotiable documents must be "duly negotiated" in the regular course of business or financing, under § 7–501(4), and according to Official Comment 1, a negotiation by a tramp or a professor would not be due negotiation. *See also* Official Comment 1 to § 7–503 which appears to put "truck drivers or petty clerks" in the same category.

pursuant to a financing arrangement, Bank C would have a perfected security interest in the goods under Section 9–304(3) but Bank C's interest would be subordinate to Bank B's filed security interest under Section 9–312(5)(b) or Revised Section 9–312(5)(a) since priority would be determined in the order of perfection, and Bank B's interest was perfected first by filing.[38]

If at the time X Store received the inventory, Bank B had a filed financing statement of record but Bank B and X Store had not then entered into a security agreement, and if the goods were then put into a warehouse which issued a non-negotiable receipt to X Store which then transferred the receipt to Bank C as security for a loan, who would have priority if Bank B and X Store subsequently entered into a security agreement? Section 9–312(5)(b) would give priority in the order of perfection, where both security interests are not perfected by filing, which would mean that Bank C would have priority over Bank B if Bank C complied with Section 9–304(3) and had a document issued in its name or notified the bailee or filed before Bank B entered into the security agreement with X Store to perfect its security interest pursuant to Section 9–303(1). Revised Section 9–312(5)(a) would appear to give priority to Bank B, as the first to file, but if this is the solution under Revised Article 9, then it appears to conflict with the Section 7–504(1) where the transferee of a document which has been delivered but not duly negotiated acquires the title and rights that the transferor had to convey. At the time X Store transferred the document to Bank C, there was no security agreement between X Store and Bank B so that X Store could have transferred all of its rights in the goods to Bank C, leaving nothing for Bank B. If X Store had no rights left in the goods which could have been transferred to Bank B, then there could have been no attachment of the purported security interest between X Store and Bank B, and the filing would presumably be a nullity.

If Bank C had bought the goods and if a non-negotiable receipt had been issued in its name between the time when Bank B filed and the time when Bank B entered into a security agreement with X Store, Bank C would appear to prevail over Bank B under Section 7–504, and nothing in Article 9 would provide to the contrary. Buyers in ordinary course would be protected by Section 9–307(1), although Bank C would probably not be such a person; and if Bank C is not a buyer in ordinary course, it may still not be entitled to protection under Section 9–301(1)(c) because it has not "received delivery" of the collateral but only of a receipt covering the goods. Since this conflict does not arise between secured parties, it is not resolved by Sec-

---

38. *See* Philadelphia Nat'l Bank v. Irving R. Boody Co., Inc., 1 U.C.C.Rep. Serv. 560 (Arbitrator, 1963). *See generally* Dolan, Good Faith Purchase and Warehouse Receipts: Thoughts on the Interplay of Articles 2, 7, and 9 of the U.C.C., 30 Hastings L.J. 1978.

tion 9–312. Nor is it covered by Section 9–306(2) because there is no security interest at the time the goods are sold to Bank C. This may be one of those problems coming within Section 9–201 which provides that "except as otherwise provided by this *Act*, a security agreement is effective according to its terms between the parties, against purchasers of the collateral and against creditors." (Emphasis added.) The subsequent security agreement of Bank B can cover only what X Store then had to convey, which would be nothing under Section 7–504 if X Store has already conveyed its interest in the goods to Bank C in a way that protects that buyer.

§ 5–11. General Intangibles

While the term "general intangibles" is somewhat confusingly defined,[39] it is a residual classification of collateral. Article 9 applies to any transaction intended to create a security interest in personal property unless the transaction is expressly excluded in Section 9–104 (and to sales of accounts, contract rights, and chattel paper). There are certain kinds of transactions where the collateral fits into no spefic category recognized by Article 9,[40] so it is necessary to have a catch-all classification into which any left-out financible rights will fall.

The category of general intangibles was originally thought to cover only relatively exotic transactions such as rights to payment under performance or exhibition contracts, or assignments of royalties under patent or copyright agreements.[41] The category covers more, including rights to the repayments of unsecured loans not evidenced by notes and payments to dealers for retroactive volume discounts. But sales of general intangibles are not included in Article 9.[42]

Among the kinds of collateral which have been held to be general intangibles are the following: a liquor license,[43] a refundable lease se-

---

39. § 9–106 says: " 'General intangibles' means any personal property (including things in action) other than goods, accounts, contract rights, chattel paper, documents, and instruments." In Revised § 9–106 "contract rights" is dropped and "money" is added.

40. *See* United States v. Antenna Systems, Inc., 251 F.Supp. 1013 (D.N.H. 1966) for an interesting case where certain kinds of collateral—blueprints, drawings, bids, proposals, cost estimates—were held to be general intangibles; this was not the only possible result, however. This was a bankruptcy case. *See also* Nunne-maker Transportation Co. v. United California Bank, 456 F.2d 28 (9th Cir. 1972).

41. Except to the extent excluded by § 9–104(a).

42. *See In re* Joseph Kanner Hat Co., Inc., 482 F.2d 937 (2d Cir. 1973).

43. Bogus v. American Nat'l Bank, 401 F.2d 458 (10th Cir. 1968); Gibson v. Alaska Alcoholic Beverage Control Bd., 377 F.Supp. 151 (D.Alaska 1974). *See also* Paramount Finance Co. v. United States, 379 F.2d 543 (6th Cir. 1967).

curity deposit,[44] a security interest in a patent application,[45] an assignment for security of a beneficial interest in a land trust,[46] a trademark,[47] rights arising under cable television installation agreements,[48] business books and records and the right to manufacture or sell certain kinds of equipment.[49]

There are instances of assignments for security of contract rights where, when earned, the right to payment is a general intangible, rather than an account. An example is an assignment, to secure a loan, of royalties to be paid under a patent licensing contract over a period of time. With the abolition of "contract rights" under Revised Article 9, these rights to payments will presumably be general intangibles before as well as after they are earned.

There have been suggestions that such contractual rights as the right to require that collateral be insured or maintained in good condition or not removed from a designated place, or a secured party's right to receive periodic financial statements from the debtor, and other such covenants might be viewed as general intangibles. This seems highly improbable, since contractual promises of these kinds have no value as collateral in themselves, they are not "personal property" covered by Article 9, and they are purely ancillary promises which, if breached, might allow an acceleration of the obligation or perhaps be enforceable by specific performance. This kind of conceptual confusion led to a rather odd—possibly helpful, probably mean-

---

44. United States v. Samel Refining Corp., 313 F.Supp. 684 (E.D.Pa.1970), affirmed 461 F.2d 941 (3d Cir. 1972). The district court and the court of appeals both held that a security deposit under a lease of real estate was a contract right, and the district court said that when the lease deposit became refundable, it became a general intangible, perfected under a claim to contract rights and proceeds in a filed financing statement. Since the category of "contract rights" has been dropped from Revised Section 9–106, this kind of deposit (if the view of these courts is accepted) would have to be either an account or a general intangible. It surely could not be an account, which must arise from rights to payment for goods sold or leased or for services rendered. In any event, the security interest in the rent deposit was actually perfected by possession, since the lessor deposited the sum in an escrow account in a financial institution.

45. Holt v. United States, 13 U.C.C. Rep.Serv. 336 (Dist.Col.1973).

46. Levine v. Pascal, 94 Ill.App.2d 43, 236 N.E.2d 425 (1968). Under Revised § 9–302(1)(c) "a security interest created by an assignment of a beneficial interest in a trust or a decedent's estate" is perfected without filing.

47. *In re* Magnum Opus Electronics, Ltd., 19 U.C.C.Rep.Serv. 242 (S.D.N.Y. 1976) (in bankruptcy) (the name involved was a trademark under state law).

48. Dynair Electronics, Inc. v. Video Cable, Inc., 55 Cal.App.3d 11, 127 Cal. Rptr. 268 (1976).

49. *In re* Emergency Beacon Corp., 23 UCC Rep.Serv. 766 (S.D.N.Y.1977) (in bankruptcy).

ingless, and surely harmless—amendment to Section 9–106 in 1966, in which rights to payment under ship charters were expressly stated to be contract rights—changed to accounts in the 1972 Code—and "all rights incident to the charter or contract" were included. The comment following the Section states that the specific language was designed to prevent splitting up rights to the payment of money from ancillary rights by making them all the same kind of collateral. It would be interesting to see a secured party attempt to realize on one of the ancillary covenants if it were treated as collateral within the provisions of Part 5 of Article 9 governing default.

Priority conflicts involving general intangibles are not likely to be bountiful outside of bankruptcy, and if a secured party has made a proper and timely filing, there should be no difficulty in bankruptcy. The principal problem lies in recognizing general intangibles, claiming them in financing statements, and drafting a meaningful security agreement covering them when they are collateral.

§ 5–12. Future Advances in General

Future advances are specifically authorized by Section 9–204(5) which provides: "Obligations covered by a security agreement may include future advances or other value whether or not the advances or value are given pursuant to commitment." [50] This section appears in Part 2 of Article 9, and, as the title to this Part indicates, the provision relates to the security agreement, not to the financing statement which is not required to disclose any arrangement concerning future advances.[51]

The express statutory provision eliminates any doubt as to the validity of future advances between the parties, but there may be some problems when the rights of third parties are concerned.[52] While it would seem to be merely prudent drafting to cover future advances in a security agreement if they are contemplated, the language of Section 9–204 need not be read to require this, although the Comments following that section state that future advances are covered "when the security agreement so provides."[53] This suggests that they are

---

50. This provision is § 9–204(3) in Revised Article 9, and a parenthetical phrase has been added to refer to the new definition of "pursuant to commitment" in § 9–105(1)(k).

51. Moody Day Co. v. Westview Nat'l Bank, 452 S.W.2d 572 (Tex.Civ.App. 1970).

52. The pre-Code development in this area is illuminatingly discussed in 2 G. Gilmore, Security Interests in Personal Property 916–931 (1965).

53. But see Kimbell Foods, Inc. v. Republic Nat'l Bank of Dallas, 401 F. Supp. 316 (N.D.Tex.1975) where the court likened the future advance

covered *only* when the security agreement so provides, and this is not what the statutory language necessarily says.

The Official Comment to Section 9–204 states that "this subsection validates the future advance interest, provided only that the obligation be covered by the security agreement." It is debatable whether this comment is an accurate exposition of the statutory language. In many instances the matter may be academic, however, for reasons discussed in § 5–19, Refinancing Without Refiling, but the language quoted above has apparently been influential in some cases.[54] The better view would seem to be that future advances made pursuant to subsequent loan agreements are entitled to the same priority as the first advance,[55] and this rule is codified in Revised Section 9–312(7).

§ 5–13.   Future Advances—Competing Secured Parties

As between competing secured parties, the priority of the future advance lender should normally be determined by Section 9–312(5). Where both security interests are perfected by filing, then priority is determined by the order of filing. If Bank A files a financing statement covering equipment on February 1, Bank B files and advances funds on February 15, and Bank A makes its loan on March 1, Bank A as the first to file clearly has priority over Bank B. If Bank A had

---

clause in a security agreement to a "dragnet" clause and concluded that the collateral would protect future advances only where they were "of the same class as the primary obligation . . . ." This decision was reversed in 557 F.2d 491 (5th Cir. 1977). On the matter of enforcing "dragnet" clauses, see *In re* Riss Tanning Corp., 468 F.2d 1211 (2d Cir. 1972); *In re* Iredale's Ltd., 476 F.2d 938 (9th Cir. 1973). However, even though the security agreement may be broadly enough phrased that collateral for one loan may secure other past and future debts, if this is not the intention of the parties in the particular circumstances their intention will prevail. John Miller Supply Co., Inc. v. Western State Bank, 55 Wis.2d 385, 199 N.W.2d 161 (1972); Hancock County Bank v. American Fletcher Nat'l Bank & Trust Co., 150 Ind.App. 513, 276 N.E.2d 580 (1971). In *In re* Zwicker, 8 U.C.C.Rep.Serv. 924 (W.D.Wis.1971) (in bankruptcy), the security agreement provided that the collateral would secure "present and future debts, obligations, and liabilities of whatever nature," and even though

the note was paid, for which the collateral had been given, when the security interest was not terminated the collateral was held to secure future advances, in this case overdrafts on the debtor's bank account.

54. *See, e. g.*, Texas Kenworth Co. v. First Nat'l Bank of Bethany, 564 P. 2d 222 (Okl.1977), where the court seems also to have relied on some discredited cases such as Coin-O-Matic Service Co. v. Rhode Island Hospital Trust Co., 3 U.C.C.Rep.Serv. 1112 (R.I. Super.Ct.1966) and on one case, *In re* Rivet, 4 U.C.C.Rep.Serv. 1087 (E.D. Mich.1967) (in bankruptcy), which was reversed in 299 F.Supp. 374 (E.D.Mich. 1969).

55. *See, e. g.*, James Talcott, Inc. v. Franklin Nat'l Bank of Minneapolis, 292 Minn. 277, 194 N.W.2d 775 (1972). *See also* Kimbell Foods, Inc. v. Republic Nat'l Bank of Dallas, 557 F.2d 491 (5th Cir. 1977); National Bank of Northern New York v. Shaad, 60 A.D. 2d 774, 400 N.Y.S.2d 965 (1977).

made a loan on February 1 and had made a further loan on March 1, whether or not pursuant to a commitment, Bank A would again have priority over Bank B, and the priority would extend to both loans.[56] If Bank A had filed a financing statement on February 1 but had made neither a loan nor a commitment to make one, and if Bank B had made a loan and taken possession of the collateral on February 15, then if A made a loan on March 1, B would have priority over A because B's security interest was perfected first. In this last instance, Section 9–312(5)(b) would determine priority in the order of perfection since both were not perfected by filing. B's security interest was perfected by taking possession of the collateral, but A's security interest was not perfected until March 1 when he advanced value. Only at this time would the requirements of Section 9–303(1) be met, for the security interest could not have attached earlier.[57] This result will be changed in Revised Section 9–312(5) by determining priority in the order of "filing or perfection," so that Bank A would win. Revised Section 9–312(7) gives to future advances the same priority that the first advance has, if the future advances are made while the security interest is perfected by filing or possession, or if the commitment is made before or during the period of perfection. The last sentence of Revised Section 9–312(7) states: "In other cases a perfected security interest has priority from the date the advance is made." The words "in other cases" refer to instances where future advances are made while the security interest is not perfected by filing or possession. These will be the rare cases where there is a temporarily perfected security interest under Section 9–304, and during this period of temporary perfection a competing secured party acquires a security interest when he has no way, through filing or possession by the first secured party, of knowing of his competitor's existence. Here the priority of the advance dates only from the time when it is made. This may result in the first secured party having, in a sense, two security interests, with the second (representing the advance) being subordinate to the security interest of the second secured party.

A different set of problems would arise if the collateral were chattel paper. If Bank A filed a financing statement covering chattel pa-

56. *See* Kimbell Foods, Inc. v. Republic Nat'l Bank of Dallas, 557 F.2d 491 (5th Cir. 1977). This result may be somewhat debatable under the 1962 Code but it is clearly required by Revised § 9–312(7). *See* Coogan, Article 9 of the Uniform Commercial Code: Priorities Among Secured Creditors and the "Floating Lien," 72 Harv.L. Rev. 838, 866–68 (1959) for a contrary view as to the result under the 1962 Code.

57. *See* § 9–204(1), Revised §§ 9–203(1), (2). *Cf.* Estate of Beyer v. Bank of Pennsylvania, 449 Pa. 24, 295 A.2d 280 (1972).

per on February 1 but did not advance any funds or make a commitment to do so, and if Bank B lent funds on the security of a pledge of the chattel paper on February 15, then if Bank A advanced funds on March 1, Bank B would have priority over Bank A. While a security interest in chattel paper may be perfected either by filing [58] or taking possession,[59] where the perfection is by filing a purchaser for new value who takes possession in the ordinary course of business and without knowledge that the paper is subject to a security interest takes priority over an earlier filed interest; [60] a secured party is a "purchaser" as that term is defined in Section 1–201(33).

§ 5–14.   Future Advances and Lien Creditors Under the 1962 Code

There has been some discussion about who has priority when a security interest is perfected by filing on, for example, February 1, an execution lien arises on February 15, and the secured party makes a future advance on March 1.[61]   Since by hypothesis the events necessary for attachment—that is, there was an agreement, the secured party gave value, and the debtor had rights in the collateral [62]—had occurred on or before February 1, when the security interest was perfected, one solution is to say that the lien creditor could not come ahead of the March 1 advance.[63]   Nothing in Article 9 would give a lien creditor priority over a perfected security interest, which is what we have.   Section 9–301(1) gives a lien creditor priority over a security interest only if he becomes a lien creditor before perfection.   It appears here that the security interest was duly perfected on February 1, although the amount of the loan, for which the collateral was security, varied thereafter.[64]

---

58. § 9–304(1).

59. § 9–305.

60. § 9–308, Revised § 9–308(a).

61. *Compare* 2 G. Gilmore, Security Interests in Personal Property 935–939 (1965) *with* Coogan, Article 9 of the Uniform Commercial Code: Priorities Among Secured Creditors and the "Floating Lien," 72 Harv.L.Rev. 838, 866–68 (1959). *See* Ege, Priority of Future Advances Lending Under the Uniform Commercial Code, 35 U.Chi. L.Rev. 128 (1967).

62. § 9–204(1), Revised § 9–203(1).

63. *See* Friedlander v. Adelphi Mfg. Co., Inc., 5 UCC Rep.Serv. 7 (N.Y.Sup. Ct.1968), where the judgment creditor became a lien creditor under local law on issuance of execution, and not on the subsequent levy of execution by the sheriff, and the secured party was entitled to priority for future advances made after judgment was recovered and execution was issued but not levied. *See also* Marine Midland Bank-Eastern Nat'l Ass'n v. Conerty Pontiac-Buick, Inc., 77 Misc. 2d 311, 352 N.Y.S.2d 953 (1974).

64. Where a security interest was perfected by proper filing, the loan was repaid, and a new loan later was made on the same collateral immediately prior to the debtor's bankruptcy, the secured party prevailed over the trustee in bankruptcy even though there originally was no commitment to

Alternatively it may be suggested that the lien creditor's rights will have priority over the future advance. This approach gains support from Section 9–311 which provides:

> The debtor's rights in collateral may be voluntarily or involuntarily transferred (by way of sale, creation of a security interest, attachment, levy, garnishment or other judicial process) notwithstanding a provision in the security agreement prohibiting any transfer or making the transfer constitute a default.

One possible deduction from this section is that a lien creditor can indeed reach the debtor's equity in property by legal process and, that having been done, the secured party's subsequent advance would be subordinated to the lien creditor's rights. But the point of the section seems to be to state what would in any case be true: that the debtor's equity can be voluntarily transferred or involuntarily reached by creditors, and that there is nothing whatsoever that the secured party can do to prevent this, although the happening of such an event might—and probably would—be made a default under the security agreement. However, if the debtor has transferred his rights in the collateral on February 1 to secure a loan which may thereafter fluctuate in amount, the application of Section 9–311 is less clear.

Does it matter whether the future advance is made pursuant to commitment? Nothing in Section 9–204(5) makes the validity of the advance depend on a commitment to make it. In determining priority, does it matter whether the advance was made pursuant to a "binding commitment" or was merely voluntary? Professor Gilmore finds the distinction in this context between voluntary and obligatory advances to be essentially meaningless.[65] Part of the reason for this conclusion is that one of the requirements for attachment under Section 9–204(1)—and attachment is necessary for perfection under Section 9–303(1)—is that value must be given, and the definition of "value" in Section 1–201(44) states that value is given for rights if they are acquired "(a) in return for a binding commitment to extend credit . . .; . . . or (d) generally in return for any consideration sufficient to support a simple contract." In the time sequence of our hypothetical, the March 1 future advance should come ahead of

---

make the new loan, in *In re* Glawe, 6 UCC Rep.Serv. 876 (E.D.Wis.1969) (in bankruptcy). *See also In re* Zwicker, 8 UCC Rep.Serv. 924 (W.D. Wis.1971) (in bankruptcy).

65. 2 G. Gilmore, Security Interests in Personal Property 938 (1965).

the February 15 execution lien if on February 1 the secured party either made a "binding commitment" to make an advance or in fact made an advance on that date; if he did neither, his security interest would have been perfected only on March 1 when an advance was made, since prior to that date he had not given value under either clause (a) or clause (d) of Section 1–201 (44).

§ 5–15. Lien Creditors and the 45-day Rule on Future Advances Under the 1972 Code

In the revised version of Article 9 two 45-day provisions have been added to delineate the effect of future advances. They are Revised Sections 9–301 (4) and 9–307 (3). The first states a rule affecting lien creditors, and the second concerns buyers who are not buyers in ordinary course of business. There is another provision, related to these two, in Revised Section 9–312 (7) covering priorities among conflicting security interests when future advances are made.

Revised Section 9–301 (1) (b) states that an unperfected security interest is subordinate to the rights of a person who becomes a lien creditor before the security interest is perfected. (This is, however, subject to the ten-day grace period for filing with respect to purchase money security interests as specified in Secton 9–301 (2).) As "lien creditor" is defined in Section 9–301 (3), the term includes those acquiring liens by attachment (in a non-Code sense) or levy or the like, or an assignee for the benefit of creditors, a trustee in bankruptcy, or a receiver in equity. The revised definition eliminates any element of knowledge on the part of the representative of the creditors, and this element has also been eliminated from Revised Section 9–301 (1) (b).

Revised Section 9–301 (4) reads:

> A person who becomes a lien creditor while a security interest is perfected takes subject to the security interest only to the extent that it secures advances made before he becomes a lien creditor or within 45 days thereafter or made without knowledge of the lien or pursuant to a commitment entered into without knowledge of the lien.

The principal purpose of this section is to provide for the priority over a federal tax lien of future advances made within 45 days after a tax lien is filed. It has, of course, a broader effect.

There is some reluctance to allow a secured party to enlarge his security interest vis-a-vis lien creditors after their liens have arisen, but if future advances are made the debtor's estate is increased and presumably this in turn may benefit the lien creditors even as the secured party claims his security interest for the advances. In any case the lien creditors probably will not be coming out any worse— and theoretically equally—as a result of the future advances.

The language of Revised Section 9–301(4) is intended to give an unquestioned priority to a future advance secured party for 45 days after the lien creditor's rights arise. This period was chosen to conform to the requirements of the Federal Tax Lien Act of 1966.[66] The language of the provision goes on, however, to give priority beyond the 45-day period if the future advance is made without knowledge of the lien or if the advance is made "pursuant to a commitment" which was made without knowledge of the lien—or at least this is what the language may be thought to say. An argument might be made that the provision is worded in such a way as to reduce the 45-day period if knowledge of the lien is acquired and an advance is made with knowledge of the lien before the end of the 45 days. That is, each "or" clause might be given equal and independent weight with time being measured from the same point rather than sequentially. For federal tax lien purposes it is necessary that the priority of the advances be assured for 45 days after the lien is filed and, this being the purpose of Section 9–301(4), it should be interpreted to provide this result.

§ 5–16.   The Federal Tax Lien

The United States is given a lien for taxes "upon all property and rights to property, whether real or personal, "belonging to a person who neglects or refuses to pay any tax after demand,[67] and the lien arises when the assessment is made.[68] Since the lien continues until the tax liability is satisfied or expires, it covers after-acquired property.[69] Quite apart from other unpleasant ramifications, the tax lien may have disastrous consequences in financings where future advances are involved, and these matters are covered by the Federal Tax Lien Act of 1966.[70]

---

66. Pub.L. No. 89–719, 80 Stat. 1125 (1966). See United States v. Trigg, 465 F.2d 1264, 1270 n. 5 (8th Cir. 1972) (dictum).

67. 26 U.S.C.A. (I.R.C.1954) § 6321.

68. Id., § 6322.

69. Id. See Glass City Bank of Jeanette, Pa. v. United States, 326

U.S. 265, 66 S.Ct. 108, 90 L.Ed. 56 (1945).

70. Pub.L. No. 89–719, 80 Stat. 1125 (1966). This Act has been much commented on. See, e. g., Plumb, The New Federal Tax Lien Law, 22 Bus. Law. 271 (1967); Plumb, Federal Liens and Priorities—Agenda for the Next Decade, 77 Yale L.J. 228, 605, 1104 (1967, 1968); Coogan, The Effect

While the federal tax lien attaches to the debtor's "property," it is not always by any means clear just what "property" the debtor has which may be subject to the lien.[71] Since state law is the usual source of property rights, that law normally must be the guide to whether the debtor does or does not have property rights which can be reached by a lien.[72] When the debtor's property is subject to a perfected security interest,[73] presumably only his equity can be reached,[74] and in the case of purchase money security interests his equity may be *de minimus* when the lien attaches.[75]

Because of obvious inequities if there are no exceptions to the federal tax lien, the lien is not valid against "any purchaser, holder of a security interest, mechanic's lienor, or judgment lien creditor" until notice of the lien is filed.[76] Moreover, even though a notice is filed,

of the Federal Tax Lien Act of 1966 Upon Security Interests Created Under the Uniform Commercial Code, 81 Harv.L.Rev. 1369 (1968); Creedon, Assignments for Security and Federal Tax Liens, 37 Fordham L.Rev. 537 (1969).

71. If a security interest is unperfected, the tax lien has priority. United States v. Trigg, 465 F.2d 1264 (8th Cir. 1972); Fred Kraus & Sons, Inc. v. United States, 369 F.Supp. 1089 (N.D.Ind.1974); Nevada Rock & Sand Co. v. United States Treasury, I. R. S., 376 F.Supp. 161 (D.Nev.1974); L. B. Smith, Inc. v. Foley, 341 F.Supp. 810 (W.D.N.Y.1972); Interstate Tire Co. v. United States, 12 UCC Rep.Serv. 948 (D.Ariz.1973); Community Bank of East Peoria v. Meister Bros., Inc., 12 Ill.App.3d 1004, 299 N.E.2d 589 (1973).

72. Aquilino v. United States, 363 U.S. 509, 80 S.Ct. 1277, 4 L.Ed.2d 1365 (1960), on remand 10 N.Y.2d 271, 219 N.Y.S.2d 254, 176 N.E.2d 826; United States v. Durham Lumber Co., 363 U.S. 522, 80 S.Ct. 1282, 4 L.Ed.2d 1371 (1960); United States v. Bess, 357 U.S. 51, 78 S.Ct. 1054, 2 L.Ed.2d 1135 (1958). These cases are discussed at length in Creedon, Assignments for Security and Federal Tax Liens, 37 Fordham L.Rev. 535 (1960). *See also* Texas Oil & Gas Corp. v. United States, 466 F.2d 1040, 11 UCC Rep. Serv. 575 (5th Cir. 1972); *In re* Riss Tanning Corp., 468 F.2d 1211, 11 UCC Rep.Serv. 601 (2d Cir. 1972); Avco Delta Corp. Canada Ltd. v. United

States, 459 F.2d 436 (7th Cir. 1972); Centex Const. Co. v. Kennedy, 332 F. Supp. 1213 (S.D.Tex.1971).

73. If the security interest (even though purchase money) is not perfected, the federal tax lien will have priority. L. B. Smith, Inc. v. Foley, 341 F.Supp. 810 (W.D.N.Y.1972). *See also* Interstate Tire Co. v. United States, 12 UCC Rep.Serv. 948 (D.Ariz.1973). This seems to be the result required by § 9–301(1)(b) and Revised § 9–301 (1)(b). If there has been a proper levy on the taxpayer's property, it will be entitled to priority over a subsequently filed tax lien. Asher & Vandenburgh v. United States, 570 F.2d 682 (7th Cir. 1978).

74. § 9–311. *See* Valentine v. United States, 23 UCC Rep.Serv. 778 (S.D. Ohio 1977). Where the collateral was destroyed by fire and casualty insurance proceeds became payable before federal tax liens were filed, the secured party was held entitled to the insurance proceeds in PPG Industries, Inc. v. Hartford Fire Ins. Co., 531 F.2d 58 (2d Cir. 1976).

75. *See, e. g.*, General Motors Acceptance Corp. v. Wall, 239 F.Supp. 433 (W.D.N.C.1965); United States v. Lebanon Woolen Mills Corp., 241 F.Supp. 393 (D.N.H.1964).

76. 26 U.S.C.A. (I.R.C.1954) § 6323(a). As to the United States as a lien creditor under § 9–301(3), *see, e. g.*, United States v. Trigg, 465 F.2d 1264 (8th Cir.

the lien will not be valid in stated circumstances against certain persons who have no actual notice or knowledge of it such as purchasers of securities, purchasers of motor vehicles, and purchasers of personal property at retail who purchase in the ordinary course of business.[77]

There are, however, some very difficult questions in the area of future advances. If a lender makes advances pursuant to an existing security agreement, is he protected after a tax lien is filed? Is he protected whether or not he was obligated to make the advances? Does it matter that he did not know of the tax lien? Is he protected or not depending on whether the security agreement was entered into before or after the tax lien was filed? Does it matter when the advances are made?

Section 6323(c)(1) of the Internal Revenue Code provides:

> To the extent provided in this subsection, even though notice of a lien imposed by section 6321 has been filed, such lien shall not be valid with respect to a security interest which came into existence after tax lien filing but which—
>
> (A) is in qualified property covered by the terms of a written agreement entered into before tax lien filing and constituting—
>
> > (i) a commercial transactions financing agreement,
> >
> > (ii) a real property construction or improvement financing agreement, or
> >
> > (iii) an obligatory disbursement agreement, and
>
> (B) is protected under local law against a judgment lien arising, as of the time of tax lien filing, out of an unsecured obligation.

It is not entirely fair to ignore the "real property construction or improvement financing agreement" since it does not necessarily deal entirely with real property in terms which are beyond our scope. It includes improvements to real property, which might include fixtures, and it covers "raising or harvesting of a farm crop or the raising of livestock or other animals,"[78] which come within the definition of

---

1972); L. B. Smith, Inc. v. Foley, 341 F. Supp. 810 (D.C.N.Y.1972). The revised 1966 Uniform Federal Tax Lien Registration Act, promulgated by the National Conference of Commissioners on Uniform State Laws, has been widely enacted. *See* 7 Uniform Laws Annotated 381 (Master Edition, 1970).

77. 26 U.S.C.A. (I.R.C.1954) § 6323(b).

78. *Id.*, § 6323(c)(3)(A)(iii).

"farm products" in Section 9–109(3). This rather mongrel definition may intimate some of the difficulties to be found in the Tax Lien Act of 1966, whose most obvious purpose was to amend Section 6323 of the Internal Revenue Code to make it responsive to society's needs in part as expressed in the Uniform Commercial Code. It is however, difficult to mesh provisions of two statutes when they cover the same things in different language or do not cover the same things in similar language.

As a matter of draftsmanship, it is doubtful that the tax lien should be stated to be "not valid" against certain interests when "subordinate" to those interests would surely be more accurate.

In any case, for the tax lien not to be "valid," the competing "security interest" which comes "into existence after tax lien filing" must be in "qualified property" and covered by a written agreement entered into before the tax lien filing, which agreement (for present purposes) must be a "commercial transactions financing agreement" or an "obligatory disbursement agreement" and under state law the security interest must be protected "against a judgment lien arising, as of the time of tax lien filing, out of an unsecured obligation." It is essential that the advances be made within 45 days after the tax lien filing if the security interest is to be protected, and the advances must be made without knowledge of the filing of the lien.[79]

The term "security interest" is differently defined in Section 6323 (h)(1)[80] from the definition of the Uniform Commercial Code in Section 1–201(37), and the Internal Revenue Code provides:

> The term "security interest" means any interest in property acquired by contract for the purpose of securing payment or performance of an obligation or indemnifying against

---

79. 26 U.S.C.A. (I.R.C.1954) § 6323(d) provides:

Even though notice of a lien imposed by Section 6321 has been filed, such lien shall not be valid with respect to a security interest which came into existence after tax lien filing by reason of disbursements made before the 46th day after the date of tax lien filing, or (if earlier) before the person making such disbursements had actual notice or knowledge of tax lien filing, but only if such security interest—

(1) is in property (A) subject, at the time of tax filing, to the lien imposed by section 6321, and (B) covered by the terms of a written agreement entered into before tax lien filing, and

(2) is protected under local law against a judgment lien arising, as of the time of tax lien filing, out of an unsecured obligation.

80. As to accounts under the 1972 Code, see Pine Builders, Inc. v. United States, 413 F.Supp. 77 (E.D.Va.1976). *Cf.* Continental Finance, Inc. v. Cambridge Lee Metal Co., Inc., 100 N.J. Super. 327, 241 A.2d 583 (1968) decided under the 1962 Code.

loss or liability. A security interest exists at any time (A) if, at such time, the property is in existence and the interest has become protected under local law against a subsequent judgment lien arising out of an unsecured obligation, and (B) to the extent that, at such time, the holder has parted with money or money's worth.

Perhaps the most obvious problems in the Revenue Code's definition are the requirements of protection against judgment liens arising out of unsecured obligations and measuring the extent of the interest by the holder's having parted with "money or money's worth." Under Revised Section 9–301(1) a perfected security interest would have priority over the rights of a "lien creditor" which arise after perfection—perhaps we can ignore the element of knowledge on the part of the lien creditor and assume the same requirements under the 1962 Code—but a lien creditor, under Section 9–301(3) must acquire a lien "by attachment, levy, or the like," and this will normally require more than simply recovering a judgment. But a perfected security interest would surely come ahead of a judgment lien in any case where it has priority over a lien creditor. The test of "money or money's worth" is difficult to evaluate. There is no problem if a loan has been advanced but it is not easy to decide how this test is met in the case of future advances which are not unequivocally obligatory, but under Revised Section 9–301(4) the advances must be made "pursuant to a commitment" entered into without knowledge of the lien if they are to come ahead of a lien creditor. The term "pursuant to commitment" is defined in Revised Section 9–105(1)(k) to cover advances the secured party is bound to make "whether or not a subsequent event of default or other event not within his control has relieved or may relieve him from his obligation." Under Section 1–201(44) "value" is very broadly defined and includes, in addition to a binding commitment, "any consideration sufficient to support a simple contract," which might well cover arguably non-obligatory advances which are in fact made. In most cases a lender who has knowledge of a filed tax lien would almost certainly not make further advances which were not absolutely required by a contract and by business ethics and by the necessity of protecting prior loans—as where more money is needed to complete some processing of raw materials into finished products or else everything is lost, and here some arrangement of priority with the Revenue Service may be feasible. Generally third parties will be no worse off if future advances are given protection, since the security merely offsets the advances, and they may sometimes be in improved positions. Finished goods are worth far more than the incompletely processed parts, and an advance which is protected and, for that reason, made may benefit lien claimants, including the United States.

As defined in the Internal Revenue Code, "commercial financing security" means "(i) paper of a kind ordinarily arising in commercial transactions, (ii) accounts receivable, (iii) mortgages on real property, and (iv) inventory." [81] Leaving real property mortgages to one side, the kinds of security involved in continuous financing arrangements covering changing collateral are arguably provided for; equipment is not. Whether "inventory" is used here in as broad a sense as it is in the Code is unclear, but what is ordinarily thought of as inventory is surely covered. "Accounts receivable" is a broader term than "accounts" in the Code sense, and it should cover contract rights (under the 1962 Code) and most if not all general intangibles. Code chattel paper would be included in "paper of a kind ordinarily arising in commercial transactions," which is an open-ended term on its face.

Section 6323(c)(2)(A) provides:

> The term "commercial transactions financing agreement" means an agreement (entered into by a person in the course of his trade or business)—
>
> (i) to make loans to the taxpayer to be secured by commercial financing security acquired by the taxpayer in the ordinary course of his trade or business, or
>
> (ii) to purchase commercial financing security (other than inventory) acquired by the taxpayer in the ordinary course of his trade or business;
>
> but such an agreement shall be treated as coming within the term only to the extent that such loan or purchase is made before the 46th day after the date of tax lien filing or (if earlier) before the lender or purchaser had actual notice or knowledge of such tax lien filing.

For the purpose of this provision "qualified property" includes only "commercial financing security acquired by the taxpayer" within 45 days after the tax lien is filed.[82] So long as the loan (or purchase) is made within 45 days after the tax lien filing and without knowledge of the lien, it can cover collateral acquired by the taxpayer within the

---

81. 26 U.S.C.A. (I.R.C.1954) § 6323(c)(2)   82. *Id.*, § 6323(c)(2)(B).
     (C).

45-day period even after the loan is made and after the secured party has learned of the lien filing.[83]

As defined in Section 6323(c) (4) (A),

> The term "obligatory disbursement agreement" means an agreement (entered into by a person in the course of his trade or business) to make disbursements, but such an agreement shall be treated as coming within the term only to the extent of disbursements which are required to be made by reason of the intervention of the rights of a person other than the taxpayer.

For the purposes of this provision, "qualified property" includes property subject to the tax lien at the time the lien is filed as well as property acquired after the filing "to the extent that the acquisition is directly traceable to the disbursements . . .," [84] but the disbursements must be made within 45 days after the filing of the lien and without knowledge of the filing.[85]

The 45-day rule on future advances adopted by Revised Section 9-301(4) ties in with the provisions of the Tax Lien Act of 1966 to protect a secured party who comes within the terms of these provisions.

§ 5-17.   Buyers of Goods and Future Advances; The 45-day Rule on Future Advances

Buyers in ordinary course of business [86] take free of security interests in inventory created by their sellers,[87] and this is without regard to when the value was given by the secured party. The situation of a buyer not in ordinary course, in competition with a secured party who has made a future advance after the sale, has not been free from doubt under the 1962 Code. While the debtor may transfer his "rights" in the collateral to such a buyer,[88] the sale will be subject to

---

83. *But see* Texas Oil & Gas Corp. v. United States, 466 F.2d 1040 (5th Cir. 1972).

84. *Id.*, § 6323(c)(4)(B).

85. *Id.*, § 6323(d).

86. § 1-201(9). *See* General Electric Credit Corp. v. R. A. Heintz Const. Co., 302 F.Supp. 958 (D.C.Or.1969). *But see* Hempstead Bank v. Andy's Car Rental System, 35 A.D.2d 35, 312 N.Y.S.2d 317 (1970); Sherrock v. Commercial Credit Corp., 269 A.2d 407 (Del.Super.Ct.1970).

87. § 9-307(1). Buyers of used goods run some risk that the goods they buy may be subject to security interests created by earlier parties. *See* National Shawmut Bank of Boston v. Jones, 108 N.H. 386, 236 A.2d 484 (1967). *Cf.* § 2-403.

88. § 9-311.

an existing security interest, and the obligations covered by the security agreement may include future advances. It would seem, therefore, that such a buyer would take subject to future advances which are made after the buyer has acquired the collateral. These sales are not from inventory, they are not made by persons in the business of selling such goods and existing security interests will be perfected by public filing. Nevertheless, there is some reluctance to allow the enlargement of a security interest after the sale even though the secured party is completely unaware of the transfer, and the secured party who makes a future advance would almost certainly be without knowledge of the sale when an advance was made assuming his sanity and a modicum of business judgment.

Revised Section 9–307(3) is a new provision which states that the buyer will take free of the security interest "to the extent that it secures future advances made after the secured party acquires knowledge of the purchase, or more than 45 days after the purchase, whichever first occurs" but this is subject to an exception if the advance was made "pursuant to a commitment"[89] which was made "without knowledge of the purchase and before the expiration of the 45 day period." If neither an advance nor a commitment to make an advance has been made at the time the secured party learns of the buyer's purchase of the collateral, the buyer will take free of any advances made thereafter if the secured party is so foolish as to make any. But the buyer will in any case take free of advances made more than 45 days after he has acquired the collateral; this obligates the secured party to police the collateral to the extent of being sure the debtor still has it within a limited period before he advances more funds against it.

The term "buyer" is not defined in the Code, although "buyer in ordinary course" is defined in Section 1–201(9), as is "buying" in that context, at least. "Purchase" is broadly defined in Section 1–201(32). While buyers in ordinary course, under the definition, buy "goods" the definition of "goods" in Revised Section 9–105(1)(h) is somewhat more restrictive than the earlier definition and even more restrictive than the definition in Revised Section 1–201(9), at least insofar as the last provision covers sellers of minerals and the like at wellhead on minehead as being "persons in the business of selling goods of that kind."

It would seem that the coverage of Revised Section 9–307(3) should be restricted to goods, and to a sale of goods rather than the

---

89. Revised § 9–105(1)(k).

more all-encompassing "purchase," which includes creation of a security interest.   The title of Section 9–307 is "Protection of *Buyers* of *Goods*" (emphasis added), and if there were a priority conflict between secured parties it should be resolved by Section 9–312.

§ 5–18.   Cross-Collateral Agreements

It is the usual practice in certain kinds of loans for debtors to agree that the collateral will also secure extensions or renewals of the loan and any other indebtedness of the debtor to the secured party. This kind of provision is likely to be found in security agreement forms in common use by banks and finance companies for consumer loans where the notes mature in a limited time and are likely to be extended or renewed rather than in fact paid, or additional borrowings become desirable before full repayment is made or due.[90]

How the problem rises may be illustrated by a bankruptcy case. On November 16, 1965, a bank financed the debtor's purchase of a truck, and the security interest was noted on the certificate of title; the amount financed was $2540, of which $70 remained unpaid on December 12, 1968, when the bankruptcy petition was filed.   On May 23, 1968, the bank loaned the bankrupt $1831, of which $732 was unpaid at bankruptcy.   On October 30, 1968, the bank financed the debtor's acquisition of $3,364 worth of goods but failed to file a financing statement until after bankruptcy, so the security interest in these goods was unperfected under Section 70c of the Bankruptcy Act.   The truck acquired in 1965 was sold by the trustee for $1250, of which all was claimed by the bank but of which the trustee said that the bank was entitled to only $70, the amount then unpaid on the bank's loan on that item of collateral.   The original security agreement covering the truck provided, among other things, that the truck secured not only the money borrowed to buy it but "also any other indebtedness

---

90. Cross-collateral agreements are sometimes used improperly in consumer sales transactions where each item not fully paid for when more goods are bought on time continues to be collateral subject to a security interest securing the consolidated debt.   A particularly flagrant abuse of this kind may be found in Williams v. Walker-Thomas Furniture Co., 121 U.S.App.D.C. 315, 350 F.2d 445 (1965). *See* Dostert, Case Studies in Consumer Fraud, 25 Bus.Law. 153 (Special Issue, 1969).   These transactions may be subject to attack as unconscionable under § 2–302.   Security interests of these kinds should be retired seriatim, as required by § 2.409 of the Uniform Consumer Credit Code, and the provisions of such an act would control over the Code under § 9–204(2), Revised § 9–204(4).   In the absence of a statutory provision requiring application of payments toward retirement of earlier security interests, sellers using add-on clauses may have a problem in claiming a perfected purchase money security interest in the latest consumer goods purchased in the absence of filing. *See In re* Brouse, 6 UCC Rep.Serv. 471 (W.D.Mich.1969) (in bankruptcy).

or liabilities now existing or hereafter arising . . . of the debtor to bank." The court enforced this provision and held that the bank was entitled to $1250.[91]

The bank's security interest in the truck could not have been attacked under any provisions of the Bankruptcy Act, but the issue here was whether the collateral could secure other loans subsequently made. The certificate of title notation of the security interest would not disclose the amount of the loan for which the truck was collateral, nor would any standard form of financing statement disclose such information. Creditors of the bankrupt clearly would have no way of knowing the amount of the loan outstanding unless they had made specific inquiry, so there could have been no reliance on the security interest having been one amount or another.

It is the intention of the Code to provide for the result reached in the case. Section 9–204(5) states: "Obligations covered by a security agreement may include future advances or other value whether or not the advances or value are given pursuant to commitment." It is also fundamental that, as Section 9–201 says, "Except as otherwise provided by this Act, a security agreement is effective according to its terms between the parties, against purchasers of the collateral and against creditors." The security agreement covering the truck provided that the truck would stand as collateral for any other obligations arising between the parties, so that as far as the Code is concerned this agreement should be given effect,[92] even though there was in fact a subsequent security agreement covering additional collateral securing another loan, and there was an apparently otherwise unsecured loan too.

In a business context there would appear to be no objection to cross-collateral agreements, since they are matters of contract between the parties, and at least in the personal property field the agreements have generally been enforced.[93]

91. *In re* White Plumbing & Heating Co., Inc., 6 U.C.C.Rep.Serv. 467 (E.D. Tenn.1969) (in bankruptcy). *Contra, In re* Eshleman, 10 UCC Rep.Serv. 750 (E.D.Pa.1972) (in bankruptcy).

92. But if the secured party acknowledges, despite the provision in the security agreement, that designated collateral is security for one obligation but not others, the secured party may be bound by this admission.

Hancock County Bank v. American Fletcher Nat'l Bank & Trust Co., 150 Ind.App. 513, 276 N.E.2d 580 (1971).

93. *See, e. g.,* In re Riss Tanning Corp., 468 F.2d 1211 (2d Cir. 1972); *In re* Public Leasing Corp., 488 F.2d 1369 (10th Cir. 1973); South County Sand & Gravel Co., Inc. v. Bituminous Pavers Co., 106 R.I. 178, 256 A.2d 514 (1969).

§ 5–19.   Refinancing Without Refiling

While it would seem to be the preferable practice for a security agreement to provide that the collateral will secure any other obligations that may arise, if this is what the parties in fact intend, what happens if the security agreement does not provide for this and subsequent refinancings of the loan take place without filings of new financing statements?   Where the same collateral secures the series of refinanced loans and the security interest was properly perfected in the first place, there should be no question about the enforceability of the security interest.[94]

The Code's filing system gives notice to the world that the secured party claims an interest in the described collateral.   A legitimate issue can be raised, however, as to when the security interest is perfected. In In re Rivet,[95] a leading case involving this problem, Household Finance Corporation had taken a security interest in the bankrupt's household goods and a 250-piece mechanical tool set, and a financing statement had been filed.   The loan was refinanced on four occasions, the last being on April 20, 1966, with bankruptcy adjudication following on September 29, 1966.   New security agreements were executed in each case and new notes were signed with the old notes returned to the borrower "unpaid balance refinanced and included in new note," but no new financing statement was ever filed.   The Court found that

94.   *See, e. g.*, Mid-Eastern Electronics. Inc. v. First Nat'l Bank of Southern Maryland, 455 F.2d 141 (4th Cir. 1970); *In re* Cantrill Construction Co., 418 F.2d 705 (6th Cir. 1969); Burlington Nat'l Bank v. Strauss, 50 Wis.2d 270, 184 N.W.2d 122 (1971); Community Bank of East Peoria v. Meister Bros., Inc., 12 Ill.App.3d 1004, 299 N.E.2d 589 (1973).   *But see* Chattanooga Brick & Tile, Inc. v. Agnew, 18 UCC Rep.Serv. 1063 (Tenn.App.1976) where the first security interest was unperfected and the second security interest was perfected by filing, and after the first loan from the second secured party was paid off, a second loan was negotiated based on the original security.   The court found the first party to have an equitable lien, although it was clearly an unperfected security interest, which was entitled to prevail over the second party whose security interest under the second loan had been perfected by the original filing, on the ground that the second party's financing statement would be considered terminated when the first loan was repaid on the ground that equity "regards that as done which ought to be done."   This is a clear misinterpretation of the Code.   *See also In re* Hagler, 10 UCC Rep.Serv. 1285 (E.D.Tenn.1972) (in bankruptcy) (where the result could be supported on the basis of the security agreement and also on the grounds of estoppel imported through § 1–103).   *Cf. In re* Wilson, 13 UCC Rep.Serv. 1195 (E.D. Tenn.1973) (in bankruptcy).

95.   *In re* Rivet, 299 F.Supp. 374 (E.D. Mich.1969), reversing the referee.   For the referee's opinion *see* 4 U.C.C.Rep. Serv. 1087 (1967).   In accord with the holding in In re Rivet, *see In re* Merriman, 4 U.C.C.Rep.Serv. 234 (S.D.Ohio 1967) (in bankruptcy).   *Contra,* Coin-O-Matic Service Co. v. Rhode Island Hospital Trust Co., 3 U.C.C.Rep.Serv. 1112 (R.I.Super.Ct.1966).   *Cf.,* Safe Deposit Bank & Trust Co. v. Berman, 393 F.2d 401 (1st Cir. 1968).

the security interest in existence at the date of bankruptcy was perfected by the filing in connection with the original loan, although the perfection had taken place only when the events necessary for attachment had occurred in connection with each loan. This result comports with the priority-in-order-of-filing rule of Section 9–312(5), but had the last refinancing been within four months of bankruptcy would there have been a preference? Presumably not, since the transfer was for contemporaneous consideration if it took place within the four-month period. While the proper result was reached in *Rivet*, it would have been easier for the Court if the original security agreement had contained a cross-collateral clause.

Quite apart from the fact that a new filing in connection with each refinancing would be a useless act where the collateral remained the same, the additional cost involved would undoubtedly be passed on, directly or indirectly, to the borrower or to all borrowers from the particular lender. Absent bankruptcy, the priority granted to the first to file is of great importance and might be lost by the filing of a termination statement and the filing of a new financing statement covering exactly the same collateral, as each refinancing took place.[96]

No provisions in the Code expressly cover the refinancing problem. It is, however, fundamental that a financing statement may be filed before a security interest has attached. The most basic priority rule of Section 9–312(5) is that priority goes to the first to file in appropriate cases, and it is clear that filing is not synonymous with perfection. Filing may precede perfection, since a security interest is perfected when the last of the events necessary for attachment *and* perfection has occurred, according to Section 9–303(1).[97] Section 9–303(2) specifically provides that if the steps necessary for perfection are taken before the security interest attaches, "it is perfected at the time when it attaches." Each refinancing would require a new agreement[98]—there would be no question about the debtor having rights in the collateral or the secured party's giving value—and since a filing

---

96. This fact was recognized in Household Finance Corp. v. Bank Commissioner of Maryland, 248 Md. 233, 235 A.2d 732 (1967).

97. *See, e. g.,* Index Store Fixture Co. v. Farmers' Trust Co., 536 S.W.2d 902 (Mo.App.1976).

98. That is, a security interest cannot attach without agreement, under § 9–204(1), Revised § 9–203(1). *See In re Sanelco,* 7 UCC Rep.Serv. 65 (M.D. Fla.1969) (in bankruptcy) (this case relied at least in part on a state statute which was subsequently revised apparently to obviate an erroneous interpretation in *Sanelco,* as to which see Mason v. Avdoyan, 299 So.2d 603 (Fla.App.1974)).

had already been made, perfection would occur at the time the refinancing was consummated.

§ 5–20.   Subordinations of Unsecured Debt

Simply as an aid in identification, subordinations of unsecured loans may be divided into two kinds: *ab initio* and subsequent; that is, rights to payment which are created as subordinated and those which are not so created but at some time after creation are subordinated by contract. These rights to payment may or may not be evidenced by instruments.

Ab initio subordinations include the debt obligations widely issued by finance companies but also by other corporations and even by banks. Such obligations, which have become so important as a means of raising capital, will invariably be evidenced by a note or investment security. In the type of subordinated paper of financial importance in the investment world, the subordination clause becomes operative only on the happening of a specified event, such as insolvency of the common debtor. The fact of subordination will appear on the face of the instrument, and the terms of subordination will either be stated in the instrument or reference will be made to the agreement under which the instrument is issued, where such terms will be set forth at length. If the instrument qualifies as an investment security, the terms are enforceable under Section 8–202(1). If the instrument constitutes commercial paper, the maker's engagement is to pay it according to its tenor at issuance, under Section 3–413(1), and whoever takes it can enforce it only in accordance with its terms (*cf.* Section 3–119(1)), so the subordination provisions should be enforceable without question. If the instrument is not a security and is not commercial paper—i.e., if it is non-negotiable—it should be enforceable only in accordance with its terms including the subordination provision, as a matter of general contract law. Similarly, simply as a matter of enforcing the contract the parties have made, *ab initio* subordinations should be enforceable when no instrument evidences the right to payment.

From time to time there has been some discussion among members of the financial bar about whether a subordination per se created a security interest. The position has been taken that *ab initio* subordinations of the commercially important type did not and could not create security interests.[99] This view was approved by the Perma-

99.   Henson, The Problem of Uniformity, 20 Bus.Law. 689 (1965). *But see* Coogan, Kripke, and Weiss, The Outer Fringes of Article 9: Subordination Agreements, Security Interests in Money and Deposits, Negative Pledge

nent Editorial Board which in 1966 approved a New York proposal [1] as Optional Section 1–209:

> An obligation may be issued as subordinated to payment of another obligation of the person obligated, or a creditor may subordinate his right to payment of an obligation by agreement with either the person obligated or another creditor of the person obligated. Such a subordination does not create a security interest as against either the common debtor or a subordinated creditor. This section shall be construed as declaring the law as it existed prior to the enactment of this section and not as modifying it.

However, a different kind of problem may be presented by subsequent subordinations, which are often called three-party subordinations, perhaps to reflect their restricted, private sphere of application, in contrast to the general, more public aspect so often an integral part of *ab initio* subordination financing. In these subordinations it is possible that, by agreement, no payment may be made on the subordinated debt until the superior debt is fully paid, and quite often no instrument will be involved. These problems can be examined in the context of a recent case. The case which aroused the greatest interest of the financial bar in 1965 is usually called the Wyse case. All commentators agree that the citation is 340 F.2d 719 (6th Cir. 1965), but the case has been referred to by different names. The official report gives two names: first, In the Matter of Wyse, and then, Pioneer-Cafeteria Feeds, Ltd. v. Mack; but at the top of the page in the reports, the name is given as Wyse v. Pioneer-Cafeteria Feeds, Ltd. In the opinion of some lawyers, by whatever name Wyse is called, it, like the rose, smells; others believe it was correctly decided. All agree that the facts and the holding are not really clear, even with the help of two opinions. The decision was based on pre-Code law.

As the minimum the facts were these: Wyse was in the business of raising turkeys and selling turkey eggs in Ohio and other states. In partnership with Campbell, he began a similar operation in Canada, and Pioneer sold feed to this partnership, which was subsequently incorporated in Canada as Northland Turkey Farms, Ltd., with Wyse as

---

Clauses, and Participation Agreements, 79 Harv.L.Rev. 229 (1965); Zinman, Under the Spreading UCC—Subordinations and Article 9, 7 B.C.Ind. & Com.L.Rev. 1 (1965).

1. In First Nat'l Bank of Hollywood v. American Foam Rubber Corp., 530 F.2d 450 (2d Cir. 1976), the court announced that it "anticipated the provisions of § 1–209" by its holding in Cherno v. Dutch American Mercantile Corp., 353 F.2d 147 (2d Cir. 1965).

principal shareholder.   Pioneer then required Wyse, his wife, and Campbell to sign an agreement which contained a continuing guarantee of the liabilities arising between Northland and Pioneer; it also provided that present and future liabilities from Northland to the guarantors were "postponed" to the liabilities of Northland to Pioneer, and that any money the guarantors received would be "received as trustee for you and shall be paid over to you."   Nothing further is heard of Campbell, nor indeed of Mrs. Wyse.   Mr. Wyse filed a bankruptcy petition in Ohio on September 30, 1959 and was adjudicated bankrupt.   Northland filed a voluntary bankruptcy petition in Ontario on November 2, 1959.   Pioneer extended credit to Northland after Wyse filed his petition and until the time Northland filed.   The Canadian bankruptcy of Northland was concluded first.   The claim which Wyse presented, through his trustee in bankruptcy, was allowed, and the dividend to which he was entitled was paid to Pioneer in accordance with the terms of the agreement of guarantee and postponement (i.e., subordination).   In the Ohio bankruptcy of Wyse, Pioneer filed a claim based on Wyse's guarantee of Northland's liabilities to Pioneer. There were, of course, difficulties in liquidating the amount of contingent claims and in selecting the appropriate rate of exchange.   The referee determined that Pioneer was entitled to $94,224 Canadian, but that since Pioneer had received $24,901 Canadian in Northland's bankruptcy based on the turn-over, in accordance with the subordination clause, of Wyse's claim against Northland, and this was 26.43% of Pioneer's claim against Wyse, Pioneer was not entitled to a dividend in the Wyse bankruptcy until Wyse's other unsecured creditors had received 26.43% of their allowed claims.

The court made some point of the fact that the guarantee was unrecorded, apparently thinking this made it rather fraudulent against creditors of the guarantor and, hence, enforceable in only a limited way.[2]   There was no suggestion, however, that there was any place to file a notice of a guarantee in Ohio.   Of course, a guarantee is not a secured transaction, any more than an unqualified indorsement on a note or check is.   To the extent that the court thought the guarantee "unperfected" or unenforceable because unrecorded, the court was clearly wrong, but it is not at all obvious that this point was pertinent to the decision.   While subject to reasonable doubt, the decision was probably correct in the circumstances, but the language of the opinions should certainly be restricted to the improbable reoccurrence of

---

2. *In re* Wyse (Pioneer-Cafeteria Feeds, Ltd. v. Mack) 340 F.2d 719, 725 (6th Cir. 1965).

a similar case, and such double bankruptcies are almost unknown in the reports. It is not true that Pioneer lost in Wyse's bankruptcy what it had won in Northland's, although this conclusion has been reached by some analysts of the case. Pioneer kept what it had received; it simply did not receive a double helping. After all, it was making two claims based on the same contract, emphasizing one aspect of the contract in the first case and another in the second.

Does this case have any implications for what may be called, for want of a better name, commercial *ab initio* subordinations? Clearly not. Let us assume a normal situation where a finance company had issued superior, senior subordinated, junior subordinated, and capital notes in addition to preferred and common stock. Guarantees by subordinated creditors are never involved in such financing. If the common debtor becomes bankrupt, this will normally trigger the subordination clauses involved, for the junior creditors have a right to payments prior to default, and the holders of superior debt will have a right to a distribution which would otherwise be payable to the holders of subordinated debt. If a holder of subordinated debt goes into bankruptcy before the common debtor, holders of superior debt have no claim on his assets, because they have already received whatever of his they were entitled to in the common debtor's bankruptcy, for these clauses have, on various theories, been properly enforced in almost every case.[3] Subordinated debt serves roughly the same function in the obligor's capital structure as preferred stock, and in financial circles, subordinated debt is, for some purposes, treated as part of the borrower's equity base. One of the reasons for the development of large-scale subordinated financing was the restriction on stock ownership to be found in the insurance company investment laws of various states—the income tax laws have had an impact here, too—and subordinated debt may be looked on merely as a sort of superior preferred stock.

What implications does the Wyse case have for the so-called subsequent or three- party subordination cases? Let us suppose a "simple" case where a principal owner of a business agrees to subordinate[4] his

---

3. *See e. g., In re* Credit Industrial Corp., 366 F.2d 402 (2d Cir. 1966). *See generally*, Calligar, Subordination Agreements, 70 Yale L.J. 376 (1961); Everett, Subordinated Debt—Nature and Enforcement, 20 Bus.Law. 953 (1965); Calligar, Purposes and Uses of Subordination Agreements, 23 Bus. Law. 33 (1967); Everett, Analysis of Particular Subordination Provisions,

23 Bus.Law. 41 (1967); Leiby, Enforcement and the UCC, 23 Bus.Law. 57 (1967). *See also* Chase Manhattan Bank v. First Marion Bank, 437 F.2d 1040 (5th Cir. 1971); First Nat'l Bank of Hollywood v. American Foam Rubber Corp., 530 F.2d 450 (2d Cir. 1976).

4. Where there is security, should the subordination agreement be in writ-

claims against the business to debts due or to become due to a third party,[5] which might be a bank or, as in the Wyse case, a trade creditor. In no case does the event of subordination of itself create a secured transaction, but in many instances the debt due the principal owner may be evidenced by a note which can be pledged with the third party, and it would be good business practice, affording maximum protection, to require this where practical; in some cases this is not feasible, as in Wyse or where the debt is between a parent and a subsidiary for goods or funds supplied on a fluctuating basis. In any event, where the common debtor goes into bankruptcy first, there should be a turnover to the third party of the distribution due the principal owner. This was done in the Northland bankruptcy in Canada; it would certainly be done in the United States. If the principal owner goes into bankruptcy after the common debtor, in whose bankruptcy the subordination agreement was duly enforced, then there can be no claim by the third party creditor, in the absence of a guarantee. It was only because of the guarantee in Wyse that Pioneer could present any claim in Wyse's bankruptcy, after having received Wyse's distribution in Northland's earlier bankruptcy. If the principal owner becomes bankrupt first, his trustee is likely to argue that an asset was transferred for security when the subordination was entered into and that, unless perfected, this "transfer" is not valid against lien creditors and consequently is unenforceable. As a practical matter in these circumstances the third party holding a pledged note is obviously in a much stronger position in a bankruptcy proceeding than one simply having an agreement to subordinate claims. For maximum protection, where a note cannot be used, the third party creditor could require, if the transaction can be so cast, a security agreement to be executed between the principal owner and common debtor (which may be a parent corporation and its subsidiary), a financing statement could be filed,

---

ing? *See, e. g.,* First Security Bank of Utah v. Zions First Nat'l Bank, 537 P.2d 1024 (Utah, 1975). A telephone conversation may be inadequate. *See* H. & Val. J. Rothschild, Inc. v. Northwestern Nat'l Bank of St. Paul, — Minn. —, 242 N.W.2d 844 (1976). But an oral subordination agreement was enforced in Williams v. First Nat'l Bank & Trust Co. of Vinita, 482 P.2d 595 (Okl.1971), relying in part on the broad definition of agreement in § 1–201(3). *See also* Percival Constr. Co. v. Miller & Miller Auctioneers, Inc., 532 F.2d 166 (10th Cir. 1976); Hillman's Equipment, Inc. v. Central Realty, Inc., 144 Ind.App. 18, 242 N.E. 2d 522 (1968), reversed on other grounds 253 Ind. 48, 246 N.E.2d 383 (1969); A–W–D, Inc. v. Salkeld, — Ind.App. —, 372 N.E.2d 486 (1978) (dictum).

5. In *In re* Thorner Mfg. Co., Inc., 4 UCC Rep.Serv. 595 (E.D.Pa.1967) (in bankruptcy), an agreement to subordinate was enforced for the benefit of a subsequent lender who was not a party to the agreement. *See* Grise v. White, 355 Mass. 698, 247 N.E.2d 385 (1969) for a general discussion of the law relating to subordinations.

and an assignment of the secured party's interest could be shown of record, either on the face of the original financing statement, as permitted by Section 9–405(1), or on a separate assignment, as allowed by Section 9–405(2). While an assignment of a perfected security interest need not be filed to continue its perfected status against creditors of the original debtor, under Section 9–302(2), filing is required against creditors of the original secured party, the principal owner in our hypothetical example.

These problems may be further complicated if the "principal owner" is a domestic corporation, the common debtor is a foreign subsidiary, and the third party is a United States creditor. The law of this country cannot govern the insolvency of the common debtor in these circumstances, but optional Section 9–103(5) [6] may have some vitality. It provides that where an assignor of accounts or contract rights keeps his records outside the jurisdiction of the United States but the accounts or contract rights are within the jurisdiction of the Code state or the transaction which creates the security interest bears an appropriate relation to the Code state, Article 9 governs the validity and perfection of the security interest, and perfection is by notification to the account debtor rather than by filing in the jurisdiction where the assignor's records are kept. The usual situation to which this provision would apply requires a foreign seller, a domestic buyer, and a domestic financer. In our problem the domestic corporation is more likely to be a seller, while the foreign subsidiary would be the buyer. If so, the transaction could be perfected under the Code against creditors of the seller. The collateral would probably be accounts or contract rights.[7] If the subordinating domestic corporation supplies capital funds rather than goods, it may be impractical for many reasons to obtain a note which can be pledged, and if this corporation becomes bankrupt, the third party creditor may be simply one more lender who made a bad guess. Neither the Code nor any other law can "guarantee" repayment of all debts.

Every transaction that can be properly labeled "subordination agreement" does not involve the same problems and should not be handled in the same way. A certain amount of confusion has arisen by a failure to discriminate among different kinds of situations. In no sense has the Code brought about any problems here, although it

---

6. *Cf.* Revised § 9–103(3)(c). The term "contract right" has been eliminated from Revised Article 9.

7. Under Revised Article 9, with the elimination of the term "contract right" whatever would have been a contract right will be an account or a general intangible. *See* Revised § 9–106.

has caused a re-examination of some basic legal problems in this area as well as in others. Cogent arguments can be advanced to support the proposition that no subordination agreements of the kinds discussed involve security interests in any aspect. But the arguments become a bit subtle in some of the three-party subsequent subordination situations, and the suggestions for handling these cases as secured transactions are aimed at preserving the bargain of the parties in bankruptcy, where complicated arguments may be unappealing. Of course, due enforcement of subordinations in the common debtor's bankruptcy does not affect general unsecured creditors in any way, since the superior creditors are getting only what the subordinated creditors would otherwise be entitled to, both groups being simply unsecured creditors in the bankruptcy proceeding.

If it is assumed that any kind of a subordination agreement creates a security interest, some interesting issues may arise if the subordinated creditor has previously borrowed money under a loan agreement containing a negative pledge clause. While they are drafted in various ways, most negative pledge clauses in substance contain a promise not to encumber assets or not to have assets which are subject to encumbrances (which is a different matter) or else a promise that if a security interest is granted to another creditor, the beneficiary of the negative pledge will be equally and ratably secured. Property which may be encumbered without violating the clause, if any, will usually be listed. In no sense should these clauses be read as creating security interests in themselves; they are merely contractual promises for whose breach an action for damages, or perhaps, in one type of clause, specific performance, would lie. The argument that they may create security interests is based largely on an imaginative and surely unwarranted extension of Coast Bank v. Minderhout,[8] which in any case involved real estate.

A promise not to encumber assets could by no means be construed as the creation of a security interest. A negative pledge with an affirmative aspect superficially looks as if it might create a problem, but there is no intention[9] to create a present security interest— quite the opposite, in fact; the promise is to grant a security interest in the future for the benefit of the promisee if one is granted for the benefit of another. Admittedly the beneficiary of the negative pledge

---

8. 61 Cal.2d 311, 38 Cal.Rptr. 505, 392 P.2d 265 (1964).

9. Article 9 applies, with exceptions as noted, to transactions which are in-

tended to create a security interest. See § 9–102(1)(a), (2), Revised § 9–102 (1)(a), (2).

may require a financing statement to be filed, covering Code collateral, even though the security interest is not intended to attach until a later date, if at all; but if this is done, then what purpose is served by the negative pledge? Could it properly be called a "negative" pledge at all? A filing would presumably transform the (unsecured) loan agreement into a security agreement with peculiar consequences. The security interest would supposedly not attach (but when it attached it would be perfected as to collateral covered by the Code) until a security interest is granted to another lender, who would perfect by filing. Depending on draftsmanship, the first lender might have priority over the second, under Section 9–312(5)(a), yet this original unsecured lender was entitled only to equal and ratable security, that is, to have parity but not priority.

Surely no one could seriously contend that the purchase of an *ab initio* subordinated note creates any kind of security interest. Nothing whatsoever is transferred. The difficulties mount with some very practical situations involving the subsequent subordination of existing and future obligations. Perhaps the answer to the riddle lies in draftsmanship. More fundamentally, the value and function of negative pledge clauses may deserve a new look. Those providing affirmatively for equal and ratable security for an originally unsecured obligation, in the event security is given for a new obligation, might perhaps be abandoned on the twin bases that if the original unsecured lender had wanted security he should have taken it in the first place and that the clauses are a misleading hybrid of no real value to the lender, an annoyance to indenture trustees and counsel, and a potential trap for unwary future creditors.

CHAPTER 6

PROCEEDS

Table of Sections

§ 6–1. Basic Concepts

The term "proceeds" includes whatever is received on the sale, exchange, collection, or other disposition of collateral or proceeds.[1] Proceeds are either cash proceeds or non-cash proceeds. Cash proceeds are money, checks, deposit accounts (under revised Section 9–306(1)), and the like; anything else is non-cash proceeds.[2]

Where collateral has been disposed of without authorization from the secured party, the security interest continues both in the collateral and in identifiable proceeds received by the debtor,[3] but there can, of course, be only one satisfaction of the obligation which the collateral secures.

1. § 9–306(1). The first sentence of this subsection was restated in the revised draft to correct a grammatical error in the 1962 Code; no change of substance was made. (The provision formerly said: ". . . proceeds is . . . ." The noun "proceeds" has no acceptable singular form in current English usage. The term "collateral" is used in § 9–306(1) and that term is defined in § 9–105(1)(c) to include accounts, contract rights (which term has been dropped in the revision of Article 9), and chattel paper which have been sold, so that the possible net that "proceeds" casts is in some instances meaninglessly broad, but this does not appear to be of practical consequence. A contract to sell, under which no further action is taken, is not a "sale, exchange or other disposition." Weisbart & Co. v. First Nat'l Bank of Dalhart, 568 F.2d 391 (5th Cir. 1978).

2. § 9–306(1), Revised § 9–306(1). *See* Revised § 9–105(1)(e) for the definition of "deposit account." A security interest was recognized to continue in a deposit account, under the 1962 Code, in *In re* JCM Cooperative, Inc., 8 UCC Rep.Serv. 247 (W.D.Mich.1970) (in bankruptcy).

3. § 9–306(2). *See* O. M. Scott Credit Corp. v. Apex, Inc., 97 R.I. 442, 198 A.2d 673 (1964).

In the case of inventory collateral, the security agreement would normally authorize [4] the debtor to sell the collateral to buyers in the ordinary course of business,[5] and such buyers would take free of the security interest.[6] It is thus essential for the inventory financer to have a security interest in the proceeds arising on the sale of the goods,[7] and this is given by Section 9–306. The security interest in the proceeds is continuously perfected from the time of the perfection of the security interest in the inventory,[8] and the proceeds may consist, for example, of traded-in goods, a check, cash, a conditional sale contract, an account, or a combination of these kinds of proceeds.[9]

The security interest automatically continues in proceeds for ten days after their receipt by the debtor, under the 1962 Code and under the revised version of Article 9.[10] This is clearly stated in Section 9–306(3), but there has been some confusion because Section 9–203(1)(b) has stated that in a security agreement the word "proceeds" is sufficient to cover proceeds of any character, and the form of financing statement set out in Section 9–402(3) has a place to indicate whether proceeds are claimed.[11]   (Both of these provisions are dropped in

---

4. Authorization to sell has occasionally been found in a course of dealing even though the security agreement prohibited sale. *See, e. g.,* Hedrick Savings Bank v. Myers, 229 N.W.2d 252 (Iowa 1975), relying particularly on Clovis Nat'l Bank v. Thomas, 77 N. M. 554, 425 P.2d 726 (1967), but these cases involved agricultural collateral where there may be peculiar circumstances. *Contra,* Garden City Production Credit Assn. v. Lannan, 186 Neb. 668, 186 N.W.2d 99 (1971) also involving agricultural collateral. *See also* Wabasso State Bank v. Caldwell Packing Co., 308 Minn. 349, 251 N.W.2d 321 (1976), which places particular emphasis on § 1–205(4), where the express terms of an agreement are stated to control a course of dealing and usage of trade, when the course of dealing or usage of trade cannot be construed as consistent with the express terms of the agreement.

5. "Buyer in ordinary course of business" is defined in § 1–201(9).

6. § 9–307(1), Revised § 9–307(1).

7. *See, e. g.,* In re Mid State Wood Products Co., 323 F.Supp. 853 (N.D.Ill. 1971).

8. *See, e. g.,* Biggins v. Southwest Bank, 490 F.2d 1304 (9th Cir. 1973).

9. *See, e. g.,* Commercial Credit Corp. v. National Credit Corp., 251 Ark. 541, 473 S.W.2d 876 (1971).

10. § 9–306(3), Revised § 9–306(3). Where the secured party takes possession of the proceeds within 10 days, the security interest is continuously perfected. Feldman v. Philadelphia Nat'l Bank, 408 F.Supp. 24 (E.D.Pa. 1976). The security interest continues into proceeds even though a claim to "proceeds" is not made in the security agreement or in the financing statement. Fort Collins Production Credit. Ass'n v. Carroll Dairy, —— Colo.App. ——, 553 P.2d 95 (1976).

11. Under § 9–302(1)(b), no filing is required to perfect a security interest in proceeds for the ten-day period specified in § 9–306(3). The basic reason under the 1962 Code for a reference to proceeds in the security agreement is enforceability against the debtor, as the reason for a reference to proceeds in the financing statement is enforceability against third parties.

Revised Article 9.) [12] The only period these two provisions could meaningfully refer to is beyond ten days following receipt of the proceeds by the debtor. For a security interest in proceeds to continue beyond ten days, Section 9–306(3) requires that proceeds be claimed in the filed financing statement which covered the original collateral or the security interest in the proceeds must be perfected within the ten-day period,[13] which the secured party might accomplish either by taking possession [14] or by filing.[15]

The definition of "proceeds" in Section 9–306(1) says the term "includes whatever is received" but it does not say by whom the proceeds must be received. Section 9–306(2) states that the security interest "continues in any identifiable proceeds including collections received by the debtor." This provision is capable of being read to say that proceeds, which include collections, must be received by the debtor, or that the proceeds need not be received by the debtor but the security interest will in any event continue in identifiable proceeds regardless of who receives them and it will also continue in collections received by the debtor. While there is some ambiguity here, perhaps the proper resolution of the problem is to recognize the continuing security interest in proceeds even though they are not "received by the debtor," [16] since they would not be received by the

---

12. The security interest in proceeds has always been automatic for ten days *after receipt* of the proceeds following a disposition of the collateral by the debtor. The requirement of a filed financing statement covering proceeds applied only beyond the ten-day period. *See* §§ 9–306(2), (3). With modifications, this requirement is continued in Revised § 9–306(3). Section 9–203 (1), which specified that a security interest was not enforceable against the debtor or third parties unless the debtor had signed a security agreement describing the collateral, had a sentence stating that the word "proceeds" was sufficient to cover proceeds of any "character." This presumably could only have applied to the period following ten days after the receipt of the proceeds. While it has usually been assumed that 9–203(1) (b) required a reference to proceeds in the security agreement if proceeds were to be claimed, if this provision is read carefully, the assumption may be debatable. In no event is such a reference necessary under Revised § 9–203(3). The confusion resulting from the relationship between "agreement"

as used in §§ 9–203(1) and 9–204(1) has led to a consolidation of these provisions in Revised § 9–203(1) so that it is now unmistakably clear that the agreement necessary for attachment is a written security agreement, except for pledges. The form of the financing statement specified in § 9–402(3) has been changed in several respects, and Revised § 9–402(3) eliminates any reference to proceeds. The revision of § 9–203(3) reads: "Unless otherwise agreed a security agreement gives the secured party the rights to proceeds provided by Section 9–306". This emphasizes the consensual element in the security.

13. *See, e. g., In re* Dubman, 5 UCC Rep.Serv. 910 (W.D.Mich.1968) (in bankruptcy).

14. § 9–305.

15. § 9–402(2)(b).

16. *See* Baker Production Credit Ass'n v. Long Creek Meat Co., Inc., 266 Or. 643, 513 P.2d 1129 (1973), where the court points out that under Revised

debtor in some sense if they were deposited directly in a special account, or if a receiver or trustee were appointed and such a person actually received the proceeds, or if the appointment of a receiver or trustee resulted in the secured party's withholding amounts due pending a determination of entitlement or payment into court.[17] In these unusual circumstances when the security interest in proceeds is needed most strongly by the secured party, it would be anomolous to cut off the security interest because of inartistic drafting which is at best ambiguous. In any event, where the security interest in proceeds "continues," this has the effect of dating the perfection of the interest in proceeds back to the date of the security interest in the primary collateral.[18]

§ 6–2. Basic Changes in Revised Article 9

Under Revised Article 9 the security interest in proceeds beyond ten days after their receipt is automatic: if the secured party filed a financing statement covering the original collateral and a security interest in the proceeds involved could be perfected by a filing in the same office and, if the proceeds are acquired with cash proceeds, the collateral described in the financing statement indicates the types of property constituting the proceeds; or if the proceeds are identifiable cash proceeds where a filed financing statement covered the original collateral; or if the security interest in the proceeds as such is perfected before the end of the ten-day period [19] which may be done by the secured party's taking possession of the proceeds [20] or by filing a financing statement, describing the original collateral, if the security interest in the original collateral was perfected, and only the secured party need sign the financing statement.[21]

Security agreements routinely provide for a security interest in proceeds even though it is highly unlikely that the collateral will be sold and even though it would be a default if it were. Financing statements contain boxes to check if a security interest in proceeds is intended and, aside from inadvertent clerical omissions, this box is always checked unless the form comes with a printed check in the box. Proceeds are always claimed, absent error, in accounts and inventory financing, and all third parties are aware of this, both as a practical

§ 9–306(2) the disposition of the collateral need not be by the debtor. *Cf.* American East India Corp. v. Ideal Shoe Co., 400 F.Supp. 141 (E.D.Pa. 1975).

17. *See, e. g.,* Farnum v. C. J. Merrill, Inc., 264 A.2d 150 (Me.1970).

18. *See, e. g.,* Bogus v. American Nat'l Bank of Cheyenne, 401 F.2d 458 (10th Cir. 1968).

19. Revised § 9–306(3).

20. Revised § 9–305.

21. Revised § 9–402(2) (b).

matter and constructively or actually because of filed financing statements. In other words, Revised Article 9 is simply recognizing as a matter of law what everyone recognizes as a fact of life.

The specific recognition of an automatic interest in proceeds in no sense creates a statutory lien within the Bankruptcy Act.[22] Statutory liens arise apart from contract.[23] In this case the statute recognizes and states that if the parties by contract create a security interest in designated collateral, that security interest extends to the identifiable proceeds of the collateral if it is disposed of.[24] This is simply a specific statutory recognition of pre-Code common law [25] and statutory law.[26] The Code provision is in accord with the understanding that everyone has in these cases: if third parties have no claim to the collateral, they know they have no claim to its proceeds. Absent bankruptcy and the hope of a windfall, third party non-reliance creditors are perfectly aware of this.

In the 1962 Code, quite apart from the ten-day rule the right to proceeds is open-ended and apparently without limit.[27] The claim, if made in the security agreement and in the financing statement, would perfect a security interest in certain kinds of collateral as proceeds when a security interest in that collateral as original collateral could not have been perfected by filing. For example, a security interest in instruments as such expressly can be perfected only by pledge [28] (ex-

---

22. The Bankruptcy Act's definition of "statutory lien" says that it is "a lien arising solely by force of statute upon specified circumstances or conditions, but *shall not include any lien* provided by or *dependent upon an agreement to give security,* whether or not such lien is also provided by or is also dependent upon statute and whether or not the agreement or lien is made fully effective by statute." Bankruptcy Act, § 1(29a), 11 U.S.C.A. § 1(29a) (1964) (emphasis added). While this definition seems clearly on its face not to apply to the 1962 or revised proceeds provisions, a suggestion that the revised Code does create a statutory lien is contained in Countryman, Code Security Interests in Bankruptcy, 75 Com.L.J. 269, 272 (1970).

23. *See generally* V. Countryman, Cases and Materials on Debtor and Creditor 458–70 (1964); Kennedy, Statutory Liens in Bankruptcy, 39 Minn.L.Rev. 697 (1955).

24. § 9–306(2), (3); Revised § 9–306(2), (3).

25. *See, e. g.,* Hamilton Nat. Bank v. McCallum, 58 F.2d 912 (6th Cir. 1932), certiorari denied 287 U.S. 619, 53 S. Ct. 19, 77 L.Ed. 537 (1932); *In re* James, Inc., 30 F.2d 555 (2d Cir. 1929).

26. *See, e. g.,* Taylor v. Quittner, 218 F. 2d 549 (9th Cir. 1954); Commerce Union Bank of Nashville v. Alexander, 44 Tenn.App. 104, 312 S.W.2d 611 (1957); Annot., 36 A.L.R. 1379 (1925).

27. There may be problems with proceeds of proceeds where a consumer sells collateral subject to a perfected security interest and replaces it, under the federal Truth-in-Lending Act, 15 U.S.C.A. § 1601 et seq. and Regulation Z, 12 C.F.R. 226 et seq., where the collateral claimed is too broad. *See, e. g.,* Tinsman v. Moline Beneficial Finance Co., 531 F.2d 815 (7th Cir. 1976).

28. § 9–304(1).

cept for temporary perfection as permitted by Sections 9–304(4) and (5) and for proceeds), and yet if the instruments are received as proceeds, apparently the security interest can continue indefinitely under the 1962 Code. Since the term "instrument" includes negotiable instruments and securities [29] and "proceeds" includes proceeds of proceeds,[30] some difficult problems can be hypothesized.

It has always been theoretically possible to claim a security interest in a Chagall painting acquired with the proceeds arising from the wrongful sale of a dealer's financed stock of automobiles, although no such far-fetched example appears to have arisen outside the classroom. This will not be possible under Revised Article 9 where the security interest in the proceeds must have been capable of perfection by filing in the same office where the original financing statement was filed.[31] Of course, if an important instance of this kind should arise, it is theoretically still possible for the secured party to learn of the disposition and file an appropriate financing statement covering the proceeds within ten days after their receipt.[32] A further refinement is that if the proceeds are acquired with cash proceeds, as they almost certainly will be in a commercial context, the description of the collateral on the financing statement must indicate the types of property constituting the proceeds.[33] If a bank is financing a merchant's "inventory", either in general or of a specific, described kind, this clearly accords with the intent of the parties. Should a merchant sell his financed inventory and purchase a Renoir, there are other ways of reaching it if an innocent third party purchaser has not already acquired it by the time the secured party wakes up.

---

29. § 9–105(1)(g). Revised § 9–105(1)(i).

30. § 9–306(1).

31. Revised § 9–306(3) (a). A dealer's stock of automobiles would be "inventory" under § 9–109. While most theoretical examples of the type in the text assume that the expensive painting bought with the proceeds of inventory would be "consumer goods," it is not impossible that such a painting would turn out arguably to be "equipment" in an era when many businesses of various kinds indulge in art displays, perhaps to improve the public image of the business or perhaps to gratify a whim of a principal in the business. If the painting turned out to be equipment, the security interest would be perfected by a filing in the same office in which the inventory financing statement was filed. In any case the security interest in the painting as identifiable proceeds would be good for ten days if the painting were traded for cars which is unlikely, and if the painting was acquired with cash proceeds then the collateral described in the financing statement must have indicated this type of property, or else the security interest in the painting as proceeds must have been perfected before the end of the ten-day period after the cash proceeds were received. *See* Revised § 9–306(3)(a), (c). Neither situation is likely to occur.

32. Revised § 9–306(3) (c); 1962 Code § 9–306(3) (b).

33. Revised § 9–306(3) (c); *See* note 20 *supra.*

There is no restriction, nor has there been, on tracing the security interest into identifiable proceeds within ten days after their receipt by the debtor, but the special problem dealt with arises beyond that time. The Revised Code does not purport to continue the security interest in all conceivable proceeds merely because a filed financing statement makes a claim to proceeds in general. It will no longer be possible to claim a proceeds security interest in instruments alone (other than checks) beyond ten days after their receipt because they are not "cash proceeds" and it is not possible to perfect an interest in instruments as such by filing.[34] Possession can be taken, of course. If the proceeds are chattel paper (of which the secured party does not take possession) or accounts, a filing will be required in the appropriate jurisdiction,[35] rather than being automatically perfected by a claim to proceeds in the original financing statement.[36]

It must be emphasized that the changes in Article 9 affecting proceeds are not, as a practical matter, significant. Both the 1962 Code and the 1972 Code provide for a security interest to continue in "identifiable proceeds including collections received by the debtor."[37] The 1962 Code gave a continuing security interest beyond the ten-day period when the filed financing statement expressly covered proceeds or when there was an appropriate filing within that period.[38] The revised version continues the possibility of perfecting a security interest in any kind of proceeds within the ten-day period but eliminates the continuation into proceeds of *any* kind because of an original filing as to collateral and proceeds in favor of restricting the continuing automatic interest in two ways: one, the interest continues in identifiable cash proceeds of the original collateral where there is a filed financing statement, which as a practical matter is not likely to be an important situation because identifiable cash proceeds are not likely to remain on hand very long;[39] and, two, where the proceeds are collateral in which the security interest could have been perfected by filing in the same of-

---

34. § 9–304(1). But note the specific recognition of a "proceeds" interest in instruments under Revised § 9–304 (1), which specifically includes §§ 9–306(2), (3).

35. *Compare* Revised § 9–103(6) with § 9–103(1). There is no specific conflict of laws rule covering chattel paper in § 9–103.

36. *Compare* § 9–306(3) (a) with Revised § 9–306(3) (a).

37. § 9–306(2), Revised § 9–306(2). According to Domain Industries, Inc., v.

First Security Bank & Trust Co., 230 N.W.2d 165 (Iowa 1975), the 1972 version of § 9–306 provides that "bank accounts to the extent they include identifiable proceeds from the sale of collateral are now subject to the lien which originally encumbered the collateral itself."

38. § 9–306(3) (b).

39. Revised § 9–306(3) (b).

fice where the original financing statement was filed, which is rather limited to trade-in cases, or if the proceeds are acquired with cash proceeds the originally described collateral must also indicate the types of collateral which the proceeds constitute.[40] This permits financing inventory or accounts on a continuing basis.

The "proviso" to Revised Section 9–306(3) is quite significant for it states that except as otherwise provided, "a security interest in proceeds can be perfected only by the methods or under the circumstances permitted . . . for original collateral of the same type." Note that the provision refers to "type," not "item or type." A reference to "item or type" appears both in the 1962 Code in Section 9–312(3)(c) and in Revised Section 9–312(3)(d) in connection with inventory financing priorities; the reference to "item" will normally be meaningless since inventory will usually be described simply by type, but within the provisions of Section 9–306 "type" is clearly broader than "item." Be that as it may, it will be necessary for the secured party to take possession of instruments if the security interest in them is to continue beyond the ten-day period, and if trade-ins are not likely to be of the same type as the original collateral, policing will be of even more value than would often be the case.

Without serious question, the proceeds provisions of the Code are of routine but primary importance only in accounts or inventory financing. (These provisions are also of importance when a debtor is dishonest or when any collateral is destroyed and insurance proceeds are payable, but these are exceptional situations.) It is vital that this kind of financing be given a firm base for operation, and the Code is designed for this purpose.

The Revised Code may make a change in a problem arising from a typical consumer transaction. Under the 1962 Code, if, for example, a consumer buys a refrigerator on time and no financing statement is filed, the seller (and his assignee) may have a perfected purchase money security interest in the refrigerator, and, if it is sold, in its proceeds, but that interest would not extend beyond ten days and into a new refrigerator bought with the proceeds arising from the sale of the old one, unless a financing statement claiming proceeds had been filed.[41] If a financing statement has been filed and the refrigerator is

---

40. Revised § 9–306(3)(a).

41. See §§ 9–302(1), 9–306(3); Revised §§ 9–302(1)(d), 9–306(3). Both the 1962 Code and the revised version require a filed financing statement to claim proceeds of collateral beyond ten days after their receipt. The only difference in this case is that the financing statement under the revised version need not state that proceeds are covered; in both versions a security in-

traded in on a new one which is sold on a conditional sale contract, in the event of default the resolution of the priority conflict—admittedly a minor one—is not clear.   It is obvious that the new conditional seller has a purchase money security interest, but it is not clear whether the first seller also has such an interest in the second refrigerator.

The Code has never explicitly resolved the priority between a conditional seller and a purchase money financer who provides the balance of the purchase price of consumer goods, at least if neither interest is filed.   It has been generally thought that these financers ranked equally, in proportion to their financial interests, since neither was entitled to priority.

The Revised Code now provides that a purchase money security interest, in collateral other than inventory, has priority over a conflicting security interest in that collateral *or its proceeds*, if the purchase money security interest is perfected when the debtor gets possession of the collateral, as is true in the case of purchase money security interests in consumer goods, or within ten days thereafter.[42] It is not obvious how or whether this provision applies to our problem. The first seller, who filed, has a purchase money security interest and it carries through into the proceeds and is entitled to priority over a conflicting security interest.   But the second security interest is also a purchase money security interest in our example.   If this case is not resolved by Section 9–312(4), and probably it is not, then priority is determined by "priority in time of filing or perfection"[43] and "a date of filing   .   .   .   as to collateral is also a date of filing   .   .   .   as to proceeds,"[44] which appears to give priority to the first financer. There may be nothing wrong with this result as a practical matter, but it is arguably a change from the 1962 Code.   If this result can be reached in the case of consumer goods, it can also be reached in appropriate cases involving equipment.   In other words, the Revised Code seems to enact a priority for collateral other than inventory, in purchase money situations, which could have been implied from the 1962 Code, although some would not have done so and vehemently would not have done so in the case of inventory.

terest in proceeds can be perfected by a filing within the ten-day period, and only the secured party need sign the financing statement.   § 9–402(2) (b); Revised § 9–402(2) (b).   No financing statement is required to perfect a purchase money security interest in most consumer goods, but in the absence of filing certain purchasers will take free of the security interest.   §§ 9–302(1) (d), 9–307(2).

42.   Revised § 9–312(4).

43.   Revised § 9–312(5) (a).

44.   *Id.* § 9–312(6).

Some changes have been made in Section 9–306(4) which restrict the secured party's interest in proceeds in the event of insolvency. The changes are technical rather than substantive. The enforceability of Section 9–306(4) under the 1962 Code has not been open to serious question.[45]

§ 6–3. Proceeds in Inventory Financing: The Mississippi River Theory

Proceeds may arise on the disposition of any collateral; as defined in the Code the term "includes whatever is received when collateral or proceeds is [*sic*] sold, exchanged, collected or otherwise disposed of." [46] The tracing of proceeds is, of course, of great importance, especially in the case of normal inventory financing where the secured party's interest in the collateral terminates on sale [47] but continues in the identifiable proceeds.[48]

Initially all proceeds are identifiable but some rapidly become unidentifiable in a specific sense, such as money placed in a cash register. However, where inventory of a store is being financed, it is entirely possible that the contents of the cash register are all in some sense, identifiable proceeds of collateral sold, and where the money is placed in a designated bank account, that account may be said to be identifiable proceeds. This proceeds interest in a deposit account is recognized in Revised Section 9–104(1).[49] If there is no requirement that the debtor must deposit the proceeds of sale into a segregated account,[50] there may be a problem in claiming that the deposit ac-

---

45. *See, e. g.*, Howarth v. Universal C. I. T. Credit Corp., 203 F.Supp. 279 (W.D.Pa.1962); *In re* Security Aluminum Co., 9 UCC Rep.Serv. 47 (E.D. Mich.1971) (in bankruptcy); *In re* Morris, 8 UCC Rep.Serv. 593 (W.D. Okl.1970) (in bankruptcy); *In re* JCM Cooperative, Inc., 8 UCC Rep.Serv. 247 (W.D.Mich.1970) (in bankruptcy); *In re* Gibson, 6 UCC Rep.Serv. 1193 (W.D. Okl.1969) (in bankruptcy); *In re* C. E. Pontz & Son, Inc., 2 UCC Rep.Serv. 1120 (E.D.Pa.) (in bankruptcy), affirmed 7 UCC Rep.Serv. 1131 (E.D.Pa. 1965); Farnum v. C. J. Merrill, Inc., 264 A.2d 150 (Me.1970); Girard Trust Corn Exch. Bank v. Warren Lepley Ford, Inc. (No. 3), 25 Pa.D. & C.2d 395, 1 UCC Rep.Serv. 531 (C.P., Phil. County 1958) (involving the predecessor of the present section 9–306(4) (d).

46. § 9–306(1). This provision has been restated in Revised § 9–306(1) to eliminate the grammatical error in the 1962 Code.

47. § 9–307(1).

48. § 9–306(2).

49. *See, e. g.*, Domain Industries, Inc. v. First Security Bank & Trust Co., 230 N.W.2d 165 (Iowa 1975). A financer claiming accounts and proceeds was held to have a right to the funds in the debtor's bank account which was entitled to priority over the bank's right of set-off in Commercial Discount Corp. v. Milwaukee Western Bank, 61 Wis.2d 671, 214 N.W.2d 33 (1974).

50. And a covenant by a debtor to deposit proceeds is not a self-fulfilling promise. *See In re* Security Aluminum Co., 9 UCC Rep.Serv. 47 (E.D. Mich.1971) (in bankruptcy), a case

count contains identifiable proceeds,[51] although it has been held by good authority that proceeds commingled in a bank account do not become unidentifiable.[52]   One theory used to maintain the proceeds security interest is the trust doctrine that where funds are commingled, the trustee is presumed to be using personal funds and the proceeds being traced are presumed to remain idle in the account,[53] although this is clearly a fiction.[54]

The Code provides a very simple means of financing inventory. There can be no question about the economic necessity for such financing nor about the power of a state to provide for it by appropriate means.   However, if the Code's liberties of non-accountability by the debtor are fully used, questions about the possible vulnerability of inventory security interests in bankruptcy may be raised, largely because of the constantly changing corpus of collateral vis-a-vis the spector of antecedent debt.[55]   The conceptual problem involved here is at least 2500 years old.

The paradox of Heraclitus is applicable to the flow of inventory into proceeds and back again: you cannot step twice into the same river.[56]   Doubtless this would have seemed absurd to Huck Finn as he waded into the Mississippi, but to the philosophically minded, a river is constantly changing in its flow toward the sea; so is its observer. The paradox suggests the process of change in all life.   However, admitting that we cannot step twice into the same stage of a river does not require a corresponding admission that we cannot step twice into the Mississippi River, whether it is in flood stage or sluggish flow;

where the debtor promised to hold the proceeds in trust for the secured party but nevertheless commingled the proceeds with other funds in a general bank account.

51.   *See, e. g.*, Independence Discount Corp. v. Bressner, 47 A.D.2d 756, 365 N.Y.S.2d 44 (1975).

52.   Brown & Williamson Tobacco Corp. v. First Nat'l Bank of Blue Island, 504 F.2d 998 (7th Cir. 1974) (opinion by Mr. Justice Clark, sitting by designation.)

53.   Michigan Nat'l Bank v. Flowers Mobile Home Sales, Inc., 26 N.C.App. 690, 217 S.E.2d 108 (1975); Associates Discount Corp. v. Fidelity Union Trust Co., 111 N.J.Super. 353, 268 A.2d 330 (1970).   *See also* Universal C. I. T. Credit Corp. v. Farmers Bank of Portageville, 358 F.Supp. 317 (E.D.Mo.

1973) where the "lowest intermediate balance" theory was used.

54.   Under § 4–208(2), dealing with a collecting bank's security interest in items, accompanying documents, and proceeds, "credits first given are first withdrawn," and the "first in, first out" principle ought normally to be applicable.

55.   The conceptual problems of accounts financing in this context are substantially similar to those of inventory.

56.   The paradox has been stated and interpreted in a variety of ways. *See, e. g.*, Muller, The Uses of the Past 373 (1952); Quine, From a Logical Point of View 65–68 (2d ed. 1961); Quine, Methods of Logic 210 (Rev. ed. 1959); Russell, History of Western Philosophy 63 (1946).

for obviously we can.[57] Our intelligence provides a physical referent for the verbal term. And obviously common sense and ordinary usage of language provide a comparable referent when we speak of the flow of inventory and proceeds. No one could possibly be misled by a filed financing statement covering all of the inventory of a named debtor located at a specific address.[58] Of course the inventory changes— but any collateral changes. Sales and replacements of automobiles in a dealer's showroom are simply more obvious than submicroscopic changes in a pledged stock certificate, whose value on the exchange may fluctuate wildly, though perhaps in an intangible fashion. It is curious that some lawyers have difficulty in conceiving of inventory as a financible unit when no one has any problem in identifying the Mississippi River as a conceptual unit. Indeed, this calls to mind Jeremy Bentham's aphorism: "Jurisprudence is the art of being methodically ignorant of what everyone knows." [59]

The Code requires for the perfection of a security interest in inventory that an agreement for the security must be made, the secured party must give value, the debtor must have rights in the collateral,[60] and a financing statement must be filed.[61] The Code's definition of inventory is also quite simple and straightforward:

> Goods are . . . "inventory" if they are held by a
> person who holds them for sale or lease or to be furnished un-

57. What is now sometimes called the Mississippi River theory of inventory and accounts financing was (at least) named in Henson, "Proceeds" Under the Uniform Commercial Code, 65 Colum.L.Rev. 232 (1965), from which this account is taken.

58. *See In re* Goodfriend, 4 CCH Installment Credit Guide ¶ 98977 (E.D. Pa. May 1, 1964), where the description "inventory of merchandise to be maintained in an amount not less than $10,000 . . . contained in the Kiddy and Women's Wear Shop" was held adequate to maintain a security interest in the entire inventory; since all inventory was covered, there was no problem in identifying the goods intended to be secured. *See also* Thomson v. O. M. Scott Credit Corp., 28 Pa.D. & C.2d 85 (C.P.1962); *In re* Little Brick Shirthouse, Inc., 347 F. Supp. 827 (N.D.Ill.1972). On accounts receivable, *see* Industrial Packaging Prods. Co. v. Fort Pitt Packaging Intern., Inc., 399 Pa. 643, 161 A.2d 19 (1960).

In a case arising under the New Hampshire Factors Lien Act, the New Hampshire Supreme Court observed: "These explicit provisions plainly indicate the intent of the parties that after acquired goods should be subject to the lien. It seems improbable that our Legislature intended that a general store borrower, for example, must separately consign each spool of thread, can of beans or package of gum to a lender bank in order to maintain the lien." Colbath v. Mechanicks Nat. Bank, 96 N.H. 110, 113, 70 A.2d 608, 610 (1950); *see* N.H.Laws 1949, ch. 156, § 1. *See also In re* Comet Textile Co., 15 F.Supp. 963 (S.D.N.Y. 1936), affirmed mem., 91 F.2d 1008 (2d Cir. 1937).

59. Quoted in Hinsley, Psephology, Parliament, and the State, 71 The Listener 945 (1964).

60. § 9–204(1); Revised § 9–203(1). Unless the collateral is in the secured

61. See note 61 on page 207.

der contracts of service or if he has so furnished them, or if they are raw materials, work in process or materials used or consumed in a business.[62]

This definition may seem a bit Hydra-headed, but actually it includes only what could obviously be expected plus "materials used or consumed in a business," which should be financible, although probably not included under prior law, and goods held for lease, which must be covered because they constitute a growing source of collateral. While goods held for lease are clearly not held for immediate sale, as is the case with what is usually thought of as inventory, the economic incidents are much the same whether a sale or a lease is involved, and, in any event, leases are often disguised conditional sales.[63]

As defined, inventory includes a merchant's stock in trade as well as a manufacturer's raw materials, work in process, and finished products. Although it would be possible to identify specifically every financed automobile in a dealer's showroom, it clearly is not feasible to attempt such specificity in the case of a clothing producer's manufacturing operation. Under the Code, any description is sufficient if it reasonably identifies what is described;[64] a rather general description of inventory (or of any portion of "inventory" as defined) is considered adequate to put other secured parties and general creditors on notice.

Within our terms of reference, "a security agreement may provide that collateral, whenever acquired, shall secure all obligations covered by the security agreement."[65] This is in line with the pre-

party's possession, the debtor must have signed a security agreement containing a description of the collateral. When the three events cited in the text have occurred, the security interest is said to have attached.

61. § 9–302(1). It is possible, in circumstances not considered here for the secured party to acquire an interest in inventory through documents of title or under a field warehousing arrangement, and perfection in those cases dates from the time "possession" is taken. See §§ 9–304(3), 9–305, 9–312 (6).

62. § 9–109(4).

63. The Code does not set up definitive criteria to determine when a lease is intended as security, but certain guides are set out in § 1–201(37). *See In re* Royer's Bakery, Inc., 4 CCH Inst.Cr.Guide ¶ 99,274 (E.D.Pa.1963); Tishman Equip. Leasing, Inc. v. Levin, 152 Conn. 23, 202 A.2d 504 (1964); United Rental Equip. Co. v. Potts & Callahan Contracting Co., 231 Md. 552, 191 A.2d 570 (1963).

64. § 9–110. For a model decision construing this section, *see* National Cash Register Co. v. Firestone & Co., 346 Mass. 255, 191 N.E.2d 471 (1963). *See also In re* United Thrift Stores, Inc., 363 F.2d 11 (3rd Cir. 1966).

65. § 9–204(3); *see In re* Newkirk Mining Co., 54 Berks County L.J. 179 (E.D. Pa.1962); Thomson v. O. M. Scott Credit Corp., 28 Pa.D. & C.2d 85, (C.P. 1962); Erb v. Stoner, 19 Pa.D. & C.2d 25 (C.P.1959). *See also* § 9–204(4);

Code law of many states in various areas, and raises no significant problems. It is true that a security interest cannot attach until the debtor has rights in the collateral.[66] Once the interest attaches, however, when the collateral is inventory (as inventory would normally be understood), it very clearly continues, although the quantity and possibly even the quality of the inventory may, as does Huck Finn's river, undergo constant change. If anyone wishes to consider this the "unitary" concept of inventory, there surely can be no objection to the label; certainly in substance the concept represents the only realistic approach to this category of collateral. While Judge Magruder is sometimes credited with a "sophisticated" concept of inventory for having enunciated the "unitary" idea,[67] this is not truly a sophisticated but rather a simple common-sense approach that has long been accepted, though not in name, by decisions and statutes. In the context of the Code's recognition of "inventory" as a category of collateral, the "unitary" concept must be accepted on its own terms—outside of bankruptcy without any question, and in bankruptcy as long as no provision of the Bankruptcy Act specifically forbids it.

A provision of the Code which is especially useful here, though it states only what would be true in any event,[68] is Section 9–108:

> Where a secured party makes an advance, incurs an obligation, releases a perfected security interest, or otherwise gives

Mattes v. American Acceptance Corp., 204 F.Supp. 26 (M.D.Pa.1961), affirmed mem., 301 F.2d 908 (3d Cir. 1962).

66. § 9–204(1).

67. *See* Manchester Nat. Bank v. Roche, 186 F.2d 827 (1st Cir. 1951) (dictum). To the effect that the provisions of the Code cannot be construed to embrace the unitary or entity theory of inventory, see Gordon, The Security Interest in Inventory Under Article 9 of the Uniform Commercial Code and the Preference Problem, 62 Colum.L. Rev. 49, 53–56 (1962). Mr. Gordon apparently feels that this theory is "too novel and extraordinary a doctrine to have been left to implication," id. at 56, but his argument ignores the fact that the Code specifically covers "inventory" financing and that the unitary concept is a modern, businesslike approach to this kind of financing. It should be the aim of commercial law to provide a firm, legal basis for sound

business practices—this is, in fact, a purpose of the Code. *See* § 1–102(2). Excessive legalisms bring the law into disrepute and serve no worthwhile purpose insofar as they frustrate legitimate transactions. In any case, an attack on the validity of the unitary concept must be grounded on the Bankruptcy Act, and not on any alleged deficiencies in the Code, and such an attack has not been successful. *See* §§ 7–6 through 7–12 *infra*.

68. Objections have occasionally been made that this section serves no purpose: it either states what is otherwise obvious or else presents a conclusion that cannot be supported, and in either case it is pointless. That it states a conclusion which is amply supported by authority seems to me to be beyond reasonable doubt, and it is inherent in the concept of a code that it should state a complete framework of law for the subject covered. The same objections would have just as

new value which is to be secured in whole or in part by after-acquired property his security interest in the after-acquired collateral shall be deemed to be taken for new value and not as security for an antecedent debt if the debtor acquires his rights in such collateral either in the ordinary course of his business or under a contract of purchase made pursuant to the security agreement within a reasonable time after new value is given.

This Section provides that in our situation, where a financer has put new money into a debtor's business to finance constantly changing collateral, the security interest in the new collateral is taken for new value where the debtor's rights are acquired in the ordinary course of business,[69] because as far as individual items of "inventory" are concerned the secured party's rights are lost when the items are sold. In effect, the Section is simply a provision for recognizing substituted collateral.   The secured party's interest in specific items of collateral, where specific items are being financed, cannot, of course, attach until the debtor has rights in that collateral—to state otherwise would

much merit and just as little relevance if they were applied to § 9–110 stating a guide to determine what is a sufficient description of collateral.

Mr. Gordon finds two principal problems in § 9–108: Whether the section has "any bearing on the perfection of a security interest under the Code," and whether it "has any effect on creditor's rights in general, apart from its effect in bankruptcy." Gordon, *supra* note 50, at 58.   The section clearly has no bearing directly on the perfection of a security interest.   The technical rules for perfection of a security interest in different kinds of collateral are set out in various places in Article 9.   Filing would normally be required for perfection. § 9–302.   If filing precedes the occurrence of the events necessary for attachment, then perfection occurs when the last of the events necessary for attachment and perfection has occurred. § 9–303(1). A technically perfected security interest is, however, not to be entitled to priority against all the world, for there may be conflicting perfected security interests in the same collateral. *See* § 9–312.   On Mr. Gordon's second point, he is probably correct that § 9–108 has no importance in inventory financing outside of bankruptcy or

state insolvency proceedings.   If the problem covered by this section could not arise in other contexts, then there can hardly be any objection to its lack of a broader application.   See Friedman, The Bankruptcy Preference Challenge to After-Acquired Property Clauses Under the Code, 108 U.Pa.L. Rev. 194, 197–214 (1959), for an excellent review of this problem in pre-Code days, including how it was handled under various factor's lien acts, where a similar concept was necessarily involved (though many commentators, including Mr. Gordon, seem to give little or no weight to this obvious analogy).   Section 9–108 is not an effort by a state statute to legislate a new definition for the benefit of bankruptcy proceedings; if it were, it certainly would not be given any effect in bankruptcy.   But it is a statutory recognition of what has been accepted by bankruptcy courts in appropriate cases in times past, and it is properly included in a code.

69. Under the continuing arrangement discussed in the text, the last alternative in § 9–108 would probably not be applicable after the initial stage of the financing was completed.

be creating a fiction. But where inventory qua inventory is the collateral, the interest in the property is "deemed" to be taken for new value on the theory that the security interest in the inventory (and not the individual items composing it) relates back to the time of original attachment and perfection, when new value was given.[70] Tracing the continuous substitutions would be difficult, if not impossible; it should also be unnecessary.

§ 6–4. Financing Patterns

As inventory is sold, proceeds arise. A financer can demand—as was required before the Code—that such proceeds be paid over in specie and then, if necessary, that a new loan be negotiated as new inventory is acquired. There are perfectly adequate business reasons for such practices [71] quite regardless of what the Code allows the parties to do in relaxing these standard pre-Code requirements. Unsecured creditors, however, will be in exactly the same position whether the credit arrangement is revolving or stationary—that is, whether the loan balance fluctuates daily (although over any extended period it is relatively constant) or is a fixed maximum. In one case we are requiring the paying over in specie and then the negotiation of a new loan—time consuming and unnecessary acts—and in the other we are not. Both patterns of financing reach the same end. In neither case is the security interest effective for more than the outstanding balance of the loan, even though the value of the collateral may be greatly in excess of that balance. In both cases whatever is left after the secured claim is paid, is available for other creditors.

The Code provides for a security interest to continue in proceeds [72] as inventory is sold. This intermediate step of "proceeds" is the factor which seems so often ignored by those who argue that as inventory is sold it must be contemporaneously replaced. Under

---

70. Inter Mountain Ass'n of Credit Men v. The Villager, Inc., 527 P.2d 664 (Utah 1974).

71. As a model of good—and safe—business practice under pre-Code law, *see In re* New Haven Clock & Watch Co., 253 F.2d 577 (2d Cir. 1958).

72. § 9–306(2). Proceeds consisting of traded-in goods present no particular problems. The proceeds with which we are basically concerned here are cash, accounts, and chattel paper. Contract rights and general intangibles, defined in § 9–106, cannot arise on re-

tail sales of inventory. It is possible that contract rights, which ripen into accounts, might arise in the context of a wholesale supplier's contracts with dealers, but these problems are not considered here. Moreover, since the Code does not distinguish between sales and transfers for security of accounts, contract rights, and chattel paper (except on default; *see* §§ 9–502, 9–504(2)), no distinction will be made here. Excluded transactions are listed in § 9–104(f). In any case, contract rights as such are eliminated in Revised Article 9. For other changes, *see* § 6–2 *supra*.

the Code, an interest also continues in whatever is received upon the disposition of the proceeds; in this way, a continuous, perfected security interest is provided—inventory, proceeds, inventory again, more proceeds, and so on.[73] In short, to say that a debtor and secured party legally need not engage in a continuing turnover, pay-over arrangement to have a perfected, non-attackable transaction is simply to recognize that modern facts of life do not require needless acts of no benefit to other creditors. The Code merely allows the financer and debtor to accomplish by a simple means what they could unquestionably do by a more elaborate arrangement. The recognition of substituted collateral in Section 9–108, is a result that would necessarily be reached, independently of the Section, by any referee or judge. To require further tracing would be to demand a futile act. With a filed financing statement of record, no one is misled in this kind of financing.

The Code provision that after disposition of the collateral the security interest "continues" in identifiable proceeds eliminates a question that might otherwise be raised if an interest were claimed in proceeds received within four months of bankruptcy. The interest in the proceeds, which are substitute collateral, dates back to the original perfection of the security interest in the financed collateral, but this interest ceases to be perfected ten days after the proceeds are received unless the filed financing statement included proceeds, or the security interest in the proceeds is perfected within the ten-day period.[74] If the interest can be perfected by filing a financing statement, the secured party may file without the cooperation of the debtor because only the secured party's signature is required on the statement.[75] In some instances—for example, instruments—possession of

---

73. If the security interest in inventory was a purchase money security interest originally, it continues to be a purchase money security interest in the replacement inventory, according to Holzman v. L. H. J. Enterprises, Inc., 476 F.2d 949 (9th Cir. 1973).

74. § 9–306(3). *But see* Revised § 9–306 (3) and § 6–2 *supra*.

75. § 9–402(2)(b), Revised § 9–402(2) (b). A continuing security interest in accounts can be perfected only by filing. § 9–302(1). Section 9–204(2), which has been dropped from revised Article 9, provides that the debtor has no rights in an account until it comes into existence, which means that as to an in-

dividual account, a security interest in it cannot attach or be perfected until the account arises. However, where inventory and proceeds are being financed, the security interest carries over into proceeds, and the account replaces the item sold, so that there is a continuing, perfected interest. If accounts alone are being financed, this provision creates no problem on an individual basis where there is separate financing for each account; if there is a "revolving" arrangement, new value will be paid as each account is assigned; if there is a "stationary" arrangement, with the amount of the loan remaining constant, then the newly assigned accounts are simply sub-

the proceeds will be necessary for perfection.[76] It should be noted that a conflict may arise between an inventory financer claiming proceeds and a financer of certain proceeds alone, in which case the only practicable solution is a subordination agreement between the competing lenders.[77]

§ 6–5.   Conflicting Claims to Proceeds

Conflicts may arise between financers of inventory, or between a financer of inventory and a financer of accounts or chattel paper. While the 1962 Code is not explicit on the point, conflicting claims to proceeds asserted by competing inventory financers should be resolved on the basis of their priority in the original inventory financing.[78] This would normally mean that the first financer to file would be entitled to priority unless the problem arose with a subsequent purchase money financer who complied with Section 9–312(3).

Such a resolution is supported by the Code's stipulation that the security interest in collateral continues in the identifiable proceeds

stitute collateral for paid-down accounts.

76. §§ 9–304(1), 9–309. The "twenty-one-day" rule of §§ 9–304(4), (5) is inapplicable in this context.

77. The validity of contractual subordination is recognized by § 9–316. On subordination problems, *see* § 5–20. *See also* Funk, Banks and the Uniform Commercial Code 82–84 (1962).

78. *See* Gilmore, The Purchase Money Priority, 76 Harv.L.Rev. 1333, 1383–84 (1963). Theoretical priority problems have received a considerable amount of attention. *See, e. g.,* Kripke, Practice Commentary to N.Y. UCC § 9–312 (McKinney 1964); Coogan & Gordon, The Effect of the Uniform Commercial Code Upon Receivables Financing— Some Answers and Some Unresolved Problems, 76 Harv.L.Rev. 1529, 1551–66 (1963); Note, 68 Yale L.J. 751 (1959). Judging from reported cases, the problems do not arise with frequency, however, possibly because lenders in this field are unusually sophisticated. One of the most interesting cases which has arisen under the Code was an arbitration proceeding, reported by the arbitrator in Funk, Trust Receipt v. Warehouse Receipt—Which Prevails When they Cover the Same Goods?,

19 Bus.Law. 627, 628–35 (1964). *See also* Thomson v. O. M. Scott Credit Corp., 28 Pa.D. & C.2d 85 (C.P.1962); Hartford Acc. & Indem. Co. v. State Pub. School Bldg. Authority, 26 Pa.D. & C.2d 717 (Dauphin County Ct. 1961). While the Code does not, and in fact could not, answer every conceivable priority question, it does appear that these questions can be resolved without undue difficulty by bearing in mind the Code's preference for purchase money security interests and by accepting at face value the Code priority rules in § 9–312, read with other applicable sections, together with the provision of § 9–303(2) for continuous perfection. That is, if read as a whole, the Code sets out a reasonably clear, comprehensive scheme for regulating conflicting claims to collateral; like any other meaningful collection of words, what it "means" depends to some extent on what an interpreter wants it to mean, as Biblical exegetes attest. In this area some problems have been overanalyzed. An article of special importance in understanding the Article 9 revisions is Kripke, Suggestions for Clarifying Article 9: Intangibles, Proceeds and Priorities, 41 N.Y.U.L.Rev. 687 (1966). *See also* Henson, Countersuggestions Regarding Article 9: A Reply to Professor Kripke, 42 N.Y.U.L.Rev. 74 (1967).

and is continuously perfected.[79] Within our terms of reference, there could not be a purchase money financer of, for example, accounts arising from sales of inventory. There could well be financers of proceeds, however, who expect to have a claim which is superior to that of the inventory financer, and who might be correct if their claim is to chattel paper which is claimed by the inventory financer "merely" as proceeds.[80] It is not unreasonable to expect a financer of inventory alone to watch his debtor closely—to attempt to collect proceeds that the debtor receives from the disposition of the sale proceeds, or else bear the price of his neglect. That is, if the debtor sells his accounts, what he gets for them should go to pay the alert inventory financer; if the latter does not want his loan paid down, then no problem exists in day-to-day operations. The Code does not expressly resolve the potential conflict between a financer of accounts and a subsequent purchase money inventory financer who may have complied with section 9–312(3) insofar as it is applicable. Nonetheless by inference the inventory financer's priority should carry through into the proceeds under Section 9–306(2).

The resolution of the priority conflict between a financer of accounts and a subsequent financer of inventory who claims proceeds, including accounts, has been the subject of some disagreement. For the reasons stated above, it seems probable that a conflict should be resolved in favor of the inventory financer whose collateral must have existed before accounts could arise on its sale and whose security interest would carry through into the proceeds, continuously perfected, thus giving the accounts financer a subordinate interest. Depending on where we start in the cycle, however, it is possible to suggest that if the accounts financer is first in the picture, his security interest carries over into inventory and back into accounts. This is feasible so long as there is no subsequent inventory financer in the pattern but it becomes less attractive at such a point. It is true that inventory may in a sense be proceeds of accounts, but it is more likely to be proceeds of proceeds; that is, cash is the usual proceeds of accounts and the cash must be turned into inventory in time.

An alternative resolution of the conflict is a simple application of the first-to-file rule of Section 9–312(5). If the accounts financer filed first, he is not then pre-empted as to accounts arising from the sale of inventory financed by a subsequent secured party claiming in-

79. §§ 9–306(2), (3) ; Revised §§ 9–306(2), (3).

80. § 9–308, Revised § 9–308. *See, e. g.,* Commercial Credit Corp. v. National Credit Corp., 251 Ark. 541, 473 S.W.2d 876 (1971) ; Associates Discount Corp. v. Old Freeport Bank, 421 Pa. 609, 220 A.2d 621 (1966).

ventory and proceeds, including accounts. Whether this rule can be implied from the 1962 Code is debatable. The Code states no definitive answer.

The revised version of Section 9–312 (5) is intended to state that when there are conflicting security interests in the same collateral, as in accounts in this context, they rank according to priority in time of filing or perfection.[81] (Filing may well pre-date perfection in important financing transactions, for no money may be advanced by the secured party before a filing is made and the files checked to be sure that there are no earlier filed financing statements claiming a security interest in the same collateral.) If the accounts financer files first, he will not be cut off by a later filing as to inventory and accounts.

If a financer of a merchant's inventory and proceeds or accounts and proceeds had a perfected security interest in such collateral and the merchant sold an item of inventory resulting in the creation of an account, the security interest in the account would clearly then be perfected. But if the merchant subsequently persuaded the account debtor—that is, the purchaser—to issue a promissory note for the amount of the account, the account would be extinguished and the security interest would continue in the note as proceeds. Should the merchant then negotiate the note to another financer who met the requirements of a holder in due course, this financer would take priority over the earlier perfected security interest in the note as proceeds.[82] Or if the sale resulted in a conditional sale contract which was sold to a financer who purchased it in the ordinary course of business, the purchaser of this chattel paper would take priority over the inventory financer's perfected security interest in the chattel paper as proceeds.[83]

§ 6–6. Returned or Repossessed Goods

Conflicting claims to returned or repossessed goods are resolved by the Code on the basis of the reasonable expectations of the opposing financers. There is no problem where the secured party financed both the inventory and the proceeds arising on its sale. In

---

81. The first-to-file financer of inventory and proceeds was given priority in certain accounts over a subsequently filed accounts financer in *In re Mary Grey Hosiery Mills, Inc.,* 20 UCC Rep.Serv. 1060 (W.D.Va.1976) (in bankruptcy), apparently with some reliance on § 9–308 which is not applicable in this situation.

82. § 9–309, Revised § 9–308. *See* Citizens Valley Bank v. Pacific Materials Co., 263 Or. 557, 503 P.2d 491 (1972).

83. § 9–308, Revised § 9–308. *See, e. g.,* Bank of Beulah v. Chase, 231 N.W.2d 738 (N.Dak.1975).

this case, the returned goods would fall back under the original security interest;[84] the security interest in the goods would be traced through the proceeds into the returned collateral and the question of continuous perfection would not arise. If, however, chattel paper or accounts arising on a sale were transferred to a second secured party, a conflict of interests could arise on return or repossession of the goods, since the chattel paper or account would presumably then be valueless.[85] While the unpaid transferee of an account has a security interest in the goods as against the transferor, this interest is subordinate to the interest of an unpaid financer of the goods whose security interest again attaches and continues to be perfected.[86] This is a reasonable result because the accounts financer was not lending on chattel security and doubtless maintained a margin of reserves for such a contingency. If the goods were reacquired within four months of bankruptcy, we could expect a trustee to try to invalidate the secured transaction as to the specific goods. He would not, however, challenge the entire financing transaction inasmuch as the rule of *Benedict v. Ratner* [87] is no longer in effect under the Code. If the security interest in this particular inventory had in fact been retired under a revolving arrangement with the funds paid by the accounts financer, the inventory financer would, of course, have no interest in the goods; the interest of the accounts financer would be paramount, provided it had been perfected.[88] Although the accounts financer might not have wished to perfect and thus claim an interest in the goods, if perfection took place, the goods would be substituted for the account and the security would not be vulnerable in bankruptcy. Nor could the trustee successfully challenge the provision that the unpaid financer's security interest in the goods attaches again and continues to be perfected. This problem is no different than that of replacement inventory first acquired during the four-month pre-bankruptcy period.[89] The security interest in inventory clearly covers returned

---

84.   § 9-306(5)(a).

85.   *See* International Harvester Credit Corp. v. Associates Financial Services Co., Inc., 133 Ga.App. 488, 211 S.E.2d 430 (1974).

86.   § 9-306(5) (a).

87.   268 U.S. 353, 45 S.Ct. 566, 69 L.Ed. 991 (1925). Benedict v. Ratner purported to state and apply New York law. The so-called "dominion" rule of that case is abolished by § 9-205.

88.   *See* §§ 9-306(5) (c), (d).

89.   Where goods are bought on open account, creditors of our debtor (the seller) could not levy on them while they are in the possession of the account debtor (the buyer), and the fact that creditors of the account debtor could have levied on them is no more in point than is the fact that creditors of the original supplier could have levied on them before they reached our debtor and became inventory in his hands.

goods and is continuous from the time of the original attachment and perfection.

A transferee of chattel paper does presumably take an interest in the specific goods that are the subjects of the paper involved,[90] and a purchaser of chattel paper who gives new value and takes possession of the paper in the ordinary course of business has priority over a security interest "claimed merely as proceeds of inventory subject to a security interest . . ."[91] This is true even though the purchaser of the chattel paper knows that the paper is subject to a claim by the inventory financer (whether or not the filed financing statement claims proceeds) so long as the latter has not, by a new transaction, acquired a specific interest in the paper.[92] However, this security interest in the goods must be perfected for protection against creditors of the transferor.[93] As long as it is perfected, no preference argument could be maintained because the transaction clearly represents a substitution of property. If it has not been perfected, on the other hand, there is a problem because the security interest has priority over the interest of an unpaid inventory financer, yet at the same time is not good against creditors of the debtor.[94] Here the trustee should have the rights of the transferee of the chattel paper, and under Section 70e(2) of the Bankruptcy Act he should prevail over the inventory financer.

90. Chattel paper by definition is a "writing or writings" evidencing "both a monetary obligation and a security interest in or lease of specific goods." § 9–105(1) (b).

91. § 9–308, Revised § 9–308. While § 9–306(5) (b) speaks of a "transferee" of chattel paper and § 9–308 refers to a "purchaser" of such paper, the difference in terminology is of no significance. "Purchaser" is defined as a "person who takes by purchase" and " 'Purchase' includes taking by sale, discount, negotiation, mortgage, pledge, lien, issue or reissue, gift or any other voluntary transaction creating an interest in property." §§ 1–201(32), (33). "Transferee" is not a defined term.

92. § 9–308. It should be noted that § 9–308 deals with two problems. The second sentence covers a conflict between a subsequent purchaser and a secured party with a prior claim to chattel paper claimed merely as proceeds of inventory. The first sentence gives priority over a security interest in chattel paper perfected by filing to a purchaser who gives new value and takes possession in the ordinary course of business without knowledge that the specific paper is subject to a security interest. Where the paper is, as it may be for various reasons, left with the account debtor, it can be stamped to show an assignment, so that a financer who perfects by filing can retain his priority. This provision is an instance of the various uses of "perfected" and "perfection" in the Code, for while they never mean less than an interest good against lien creditors (and a trustee in bankruptcy), they may not mean that the perfected interest is good against other secured parties. There may, of course, be conflicting perfected security interests in the same collateral. Revised § 9–308 extends the same treatment to chattel paper and instruments, both negotiable and nonnegotiable.

93. § 9–306(5) (d).

94. §§ 9–306(5)(b), (d).

§ 6–7. Proceeds in Insolvency

Perhaps the most interesting proceeds problems arise from Section 9–306(4):

> In the event of insolvency proceedings instituted by or against a debtor, a secured party with a perfected security interest in proceeds has a perfected security interest *only in the following proceeds:*
>
> (a) in identifiable non-cash proceeds[;] *and in separate deposit accounts containing only proceeds;*
>
> (b) in identifiable cash proceeds in the form of money which is [not] *neither* commingled with other money [or] *nor* deposited in a [bank] *deposit* account prior to the insolvency proceedings;
>
> (c) in identifiable cash proceeds in the form of checks and the like which are not deposited in a [bank] *deposit* account prior to the insolvency proceedings; and
>
> (d) in all cash and [bank] *deposit* accounts of the debtor [if other cash] *in which* proceeds have been commingled *with other funds,* [or deposited in a bank account,] but the perfected security interest under this paragraph (d) is
>
> (i) subject to any right of set-off; and
>
> (ii) limited to an amount not greater than the amount of any cash proceeds received by the debtor within ten days before the institution of the insolvency proceedings [and commingled or deposited in a bank account prior to the insolvency proceedings less the amount of cash proceeds received by the debtor and paid over to the secured party during the ten day period,] *less the sum of (I) the payments to the secured party on account of cash proceeds received by the debtor during such period and (II) the cash proceeds received by the debtor during such period to which the secured party is entitled under paragraphs (a) through (c) of this subsection (4).*

As shown above, deletions from the 1962 Official Text are shown in brackets, and language added in the 1972 Official Text is in italics.

The impact of this Section is, of course, broader than bankruptcy situations. "Insolvency proceedings includes any assignment for the benefit of creditors or other proceedings intended to liquidate or rehabilitate the estate of the person involved." [95]   The Section is not, therefore, subject to attack on the ground that it applies only in bankruptcy.[96]   But does the Section do more than state what is otherwise obvious?   To a limited extent, it does.   A security interest in inventory is normally [97] cut off as to the goods when they are sold and continues in the identifiable proceeds.   When insolvency proceedings are impending, however, it is likely that instead of paying over cash proceeds (in a "revolving" credit transaction) or reinvesting cash proceeds in new inventory (in a "stationary" credit arrangement) the debtor may misuse funds that in fact belong to the secured party. Nothing in the Bankruptcy Act forbids tracing proceeds, which are substitute collateral, regardless of the form of those proceeds.

In fact, it has been said that the provisions of Section 9–306(4) (d) of the Code give a secured party the "right to a debtor's cash proceeds received in the 10-day period" before insolvency in lieu of the "right to trace which a secured party had prior to enactment of the Code." [98]   It is to be noted that this perfected security interest in cash and bank accounts, where the funds have been commingled or deposited and cannot be directly traced, is subject to the bank's right of set-off as determined by state law.[99]   Moreover this interest is lim-

95. § 1–201(22).

96. If the section stated an order of distribution effective only in bankruptcy, it would not be recognized in a bankruptcy proceeding. *See* Bankruptcy Act § 64a.

97. It may be helpful to note once more that the definition of inventory in § 9–109(4) includes goods held for lease, and as to them, a security interest presumably might not be cut off if they were sold since such a purchaser might not qualify as a "buyer in ordinary course of business" under the definition of § 1–201(9), and it is only when goods are purchased by such a buyer that a perfected security interest is lost under § 9–307(1). When goods are held for sale, it would be anomalous for the security agreement to prohibit sale, so the subtle implication of § 9–307(1)—that the buyer takes free of the security interest if he knows it exists but does not know the sale violates the security agreement—is inapplicable here. Nor can the dual interest provided in § 9–306(2) exist here, since the sale of inventory must be authorized by the secured party in one way or another, in which case the security interest in the goods is lost on sale and only the interest in the proceeds continues.

The dual security interest continues principles generally recognized under chattel mortgage law: if the mortgagor sold mortgaged property without the mortgagee's consent, the mortgagee could enforce his security interest against the specific property or claim the proceeds, and the proceeds could even be claimed from a purchaser of the property who subsequently sold it. *See* Annot., 36 A.L.R. 1379 (1925).

98. Girard Trust Corn Exch. Bank v. Warren Lepley Ford, Inc. (No. 2), 25 Pa.D. & C.2d 395, 405 (C.P.1958) (referring to the predecessor of § 9–306(4) (d)). The only Code state which has made a substantive change in § 9–306 (4) is California. The California provision was the model for Revised § 9–306(4). The secured party has a perfected security interest in identifiable noncash proceeds on hand at insolvency. § 9–306(4) (a).

99. § 9–306(4) (d) (i). *See* Middle Atlantic Credit Corp. v. First Pa. Bank-

ited to the amount of cash proceeds that were received by the debtor and deposited in a bank account within the ten-day period before the commencement of insolvency proceedings, less the amount of such cash proceeds that were paid to the secured party during the ten-day period. The term "cash proceeds" is defined in broader terms than merely cash and includes checks "and the like." [1]

It has been held that the bank's right of set off cannot be exercised against proceeds in the debtor's bank account in which the secured party has a perfected security interest, without regard to the bank's actual knowledge or lack of knowledge of the secured party's interest.[2] This seems to be the correct result, since the bank's set off should only be available against its depositor's funds, and not against funds in its depositor's account in which a secured party has a security interest duly perfected by filing of which the bank certainly has constructive notice and very likely has actual notice, although very little in Article 9 in fact depends on actual notice. This priority problem is not in terms dealt with in Article 9, and the extent and nature of the right of set off are left to other law.[3] However, the right of set off arises here because there are mutual debts. If a depositor owes a debt to a bank because of a loan made by the bank, the bank is also a debtor of the depositor to the extent of funds on deposit. If the funds on deposit in fact are the proceeds of collateral, so that the secured party has a security interest in the proceeds, it seems a bit inequitable to allow a set off by a bank against funds which do not, in some sense, belong to the depositor. And there are occasions when the behavior of bank officers is so flagrantly wrong that almost anyone's instincts would suggest that the bank should lose.[4] The difficulty with reacting instinctively is that the legal basis for the decision may be a bit unclear, but it is notoriously true, as the old proverb has it, that hard cases make bad law.[5] However,

---

ing & Trust Co., 199 Pa.Super. 456, 185 A.2d 818 (1962).

1. § 9–306(1). *See In re* Security Aluminum Co., 9 UCC Rep.Serv. 47 (E.D. Mich.1971) (in bankruptcy). There is a problem under the 1962 Code in claiming proceeds in a bank account if they are not commingled, but this has been clarified in Revised § 9–306(4) (a), and the 1972 Code introduces into this section the term "deposit account," which is defined in Revised § 9–105(1) (e).

2. Commercial Discount Corp. v. Milwaukee Western Bank, 61 Wis.2d 671, 214 N.W.2d 33 (1974); Associates Discount Corp. v. Fidelity Union Trust Co., 111 N.J.Super. 353, 268 A.2d 330 (1970). *See also* Morrison Steel Co. v.

Gurtman, 113 N.J.Super. 474, 274 A. 2d 306 (1971).

3. According to § 9–104, "This Article does not apply . . . (i) to any right of set-off." The right of set-off is recognized in the Bankruptcy Act, § 68, 11 U.S.C.A. § 108.

4. *See, e. g.,* Brown & Williamson Tobacco Corp. v. First Nat'l Bank of Blue Island, 504 F.2d 998 (7th Cir. 1974).

5. And, as Mr. Justice Holmes said, "Great cases like hard cases make bad law." Northern Securities Co. v. United States, 193 U.S. 197, 400 (1904).

there are sound legal bases for denying the right of set off where the funds do not really belong to the depositor in whose account they may be found.

The progenitor of Section 9–306(4)(d) was Section 10(b) of the Uniform Trust Receipts Act, which provided:

> Where, under the terms of the trust receipt transaction, the trustee has no liberty of sale or other disposition, or having liberty of sale or other disposition, is to account to the entruster for the proceeds of any disposition of the goods, documents or instruments, the entruster shall be entitled, to the extent to which and as against all classes of persons as to whom his security interest was valid at the time of disposition by the trustee, as follows: .   .   .   .

> (b) to any proceeds or the value of any proceeds (whether such proceeds are identifiable or not) of the goods, documents or instruments, if said proceeds were received by the trustee within ten days prior to either application for appointment of a receiver of the trustee, or the filing of a petition in bankruptcy or judicial insolvency proceedings by or against the trustee, or demand made by the entruster for prompt accounting; and to a priority to the amount of such proceeds or value;   .   .   .   .

It should have been perfectly clear that this Section was intended to create an enforceable security interest or lien on proceeds. At the time the Act was promulgated in 1933 this undoubtedly was the case. The Section concluded, however, with a statement that it gave a "priority"—and in 1938, the Bankruptcy Act was amended to eliminate state-created priorities.

In *In re Harpeth Motors, Inc.,*[6] the first of two leading cases involving Section 10(b) of the Uniform Trusts Receipts Act, a federal district court correctly concluded that despite the use of "priority" the Act was intended to create a lien and that this lien was good in bankruptcy. (As a result of this decision, Section 9–306(4) of the Code was redrafted to state the interest in terms of perfected security interest rather than priority).[7]   The second case, *In re Crosstown Mo-*

---

6. 135 F.Supp. 863 (M.D.Tenn.1955), 34 Chi.-Kent.L.Rev. 294 (1956), 69 Harv.L. Rev. 1343 (1956); *see* Note, 66 Yale L.J. 922, 930 (1957).

7. *Compare* § 9–306(4), with Uniform Commercial Code § 9–306(2) (Official Draft, 1952), and ALI Editorial Bd., 1956 Recommendations for the Uniform Commercial Code § 9–306(4) (1957).

tors, Inc.,[8] proceeded on the assumption that "priority" was used in 1933 in exactly the same sense as it was used in 1959. This may not be a novel but is certainly a benighted approach to statutory construction. It is equivalent to a modern court finding that the federal government may not regulate railroads because the draftsmen of our Constitution could not have intended to include railroads—since they had not yet been invented—within the power to regulate commerce. [9]

Words do not have fixed meanings,[10] and in any event distinctions between "liens" and "priorities" in the legal dictionary are far less clear than a casual observer might suppose.[11] Even if the Bankruptcy Act no longer directly enforces state-created priorities, it does so indirectly whenever conflicting claims to collateral must be resolved on the basis of state law. Obviously, such a resolution involves a question of priorities and, of course, Section 64 of the Bankruptcy Act has its own set of priorities for the distribution of assets.

A complete absence of appreciation for the subtleties of meaning and the vicissitudes of usage is evidenced by virtually every line of the opinion in *Crosstown Motors.* In that case the Seventh Circuit was reasonably accurate in stating that Section 10(b) of the Uniform Trust Receipts Act gave "to the entruster a priority ahead of general creditors upon insolvency of the trustee," [12] since this is one purpose of a

---

8. 272 F.2d 224 (7th Cir. 1959), certiorari denied 363 U.S. 811, 80 S.Ct. 1246, 4 L.Ed.2d 1152 (1960); accord, Universal C. I. T. Credit Corp. v. Thursbay Chevrolet Co., 136 So.2d 15 (Fla.1961) (dictum); *see* Duesenberg, Lien or Priority Under Section 10, Uniform Trust Receipts Act, 2 B.C. Ind. and Com.L.Rev. 73 (1960); 35 N.Y.U.L.Rev. 948 (1960).

9. A well known statement, made in a different context, by Mr. Justice Holmes is apropos: "We agree to all the generalities about not supplying criminal laws with what they omit, but there is no canon against using common sense in construing laws as saying what they obviously mean." Roschen v. Ward, 279 U.S. 337, 339, 49 S.Ct. 336, 73 L.Ed. 722 (1929). *See generally,* Frankfurter, Some Reflections on the Reading of Statutes, 47 Colum.L.Rev. 527 (1947); Friendly, Mr. Justice Frankfurter and the Reading of Statutes, in Felix Frankfurter: The Judge 30 (Mendelson ed. 1964).

10. This statement may seem to be obvious but apparently it is not, and the problem involved is of paramount importance in modern law. The subject is discussed briefly and citations to some leading materials are given in Henson, A Criticism of Criticism: In re Meaning, 29 Fordham L.Rev. 553 (1961). *See also* Henson, The Prospective Effect of the Uniform Commercial Code on Commercial Financing, 1962 U.Ill.L.F. 349, 363–371 (1962).

11. *See* Henson, Liens—Seen Through a Glass, Darkly, 2 B.C.Ind. & Com.L.Rev. 85 (1960); MacLachlan, Improving the Law of Federal Liens and Priorities, 1 B.C.Ind. & Com.L.Rev. 73 (1959).

12. 272 F.2d 224, 226 (7th Cir. 1959). The court was, of course, indulging in pure fiction when it ascribed to the Illinois legislature any particular intent with regard to "priority" versus "lien." *Id.* at 226–27. Moreover, it was fiction compounded to assume, as the referee did, that the Illinois legis-

security interest. However, the court held that the purpose of the act was defeated by the use of the word "priority." This leads one to conclude that if the word "priority" were changed to "lien" [13] or "perfected security interest" [14] then an equivalent interest, differing only in name, would be recognized and enforced.

The recognition that the *Crosstown Motors* opinion has been given in legal writings is perhaps not as much a compliment to the court as a commentary on the commentators. Whether a secured party has an enforceable security interest in unidentifiable cash proceeds is not a matter of earthshaking consequence; what is of great importance is the attitude of judges and writers in this area. When leading members of the bench and bar have promulgated a statute after thorough study,[15] the attitude should be that the statutory provisions are valid and enforceable within the ordinary understanding of their aims and terms. It is shocking to find every available means employed to show why the provisions should not be recognized in bankruptcy. The assumption should be that the Code provisions are enforceable in bankruptcy unless the Bankruptcy Act clearly forbids them.

It is not the purpose of the Bankruptcy Act to frustrate legitimate secured transactions. While it might be within the power of Congress to invalidate every secured transaction in bankruptcy, it is unlikely that such a bill would ever be introduced and inconceivable that it would be passed. Surely it is not the function of bankruptcy courts to accomplish indirectly what they are not empowered by Congress to do directly.

In general, the Bankruptcy Act, though not well drafted, is not particularly difficult to read and apply, nor are most of the interpretative cases troublesome in this area. Since the perfection of secured transactions and the concomitant incidents of perfection are deter-

---

lature had a different intent from the Tennessee legislature (by way of getting around the earlier Harpeth case) in enacting a uniform act, particularly in view of § 19 of the Uniform Trust Receipts Act which provides, "This Act shall be uniformly so interpreted and construed as to effectuate its general purpose to make uniform the law of the states which enact it." *See In re* Crosstown Motors, Inc., No. 57 B 3879, N.D.Ill.1959, reported in 33 Ref.J. 58 (1959) (Referee's memorandum opinion); Smith-Hurd Ill.Ann.Stat. ch. 121½, § 184 (1960).

13. This was done in Tennessee. *See* Tenn.Pub.Acts 1961, ch. 250.

14. §§ 9–306(3), (4).

15. On the background on the Uniform Commercial Code, *see* Malcolm, The Uniform Commercial Code in the United States, 12 Int'l & Comp.L.Q. 226 (1963); Schnader, The New Movement Toward Uniformity in Commercial Law—The Uniform Commercial Code Marches On, 13 Bus.Law. 646 (1958). *See also* Schnader, Pennsylvania and the Uniform Commercial Code, 37 Temp.L.Q. 265 (1964); Schnader, Looking Ahead at the Uniform Commercial Code, 19 Bus.Law. 771 (1964).

mined by state law, bankruptcy cases are to be found in support of almost any imaginable legal proposition. A chattel mortgagee's security interest in after-acquired chattels was recognized or not, depending on the state law involved; an assignee's security interest in assigned accounts receivable was recognized or not, depending on the state law involved. This situation is not surprising. Nor is it to be deplored. It does, however, mean that a conscientious court tries to give effect to state law in the field of secured transactions so that the reasonable expectations of the parties are fulfilled. The result of this variable past experience is that judicial support is available to buttress the provisions of the Code, though because of the state statutes involved, decisions to the contrary can probably also be found. It is not essential to the effectiveness of the Code, however, that every provision in it have had a counterpart, judicially approved, in some prior law. Such an unacceptable and unsupportable theory would make legal progress impossible. Indeed, it would be disastrous if the law were to be inextricably tied to *Twyne's Case* [16] or the like; legal attitudes must change with the times—in the commercial as well as in the criminal field.

What provisions of the Bankruptcy Act could Section 9–306(4) be said to offend? Not Section 70e [17] because when we are dealing with a perfected security interest, as *ex hypothesi* we are, no actual creditor can avoid the transaction, and thus neither can the trustee. Not Section 70c [18] because no hypothetical creditor could obtain a superior

---

16. 3 Co. 80b, 76 Eng.Rep. 809 (Star Chamber 1601). Singling out Twyne's Case for opprobrious citation may be a bit unfair, but if the late Professor Hanna, after teaching the case for thirty years, was unsure what it stood for, then there is perhaps no reason to assume it stands for anything of particular relevance in the eighth decade of the twentieth century. *See* Hanna, The Secured Creditor in Bankruptcy, 14 Rutgers L.Rev. 471, 474 n. 7 (1960). However, this is merely an example. There is no more reason why current commercial law practices should be tied to totally inapplicable nineteenth century (or earlier) doctrines than for a modern physician to tie himself to Harvey's theory of the circulation of blood. This peculiar legal tie to the past, without regard for changed conditions, was cogently criticized by Dean Pound over sixty years ago. Pound, Mechanical Jurisprudence, 8

Colum.L.Rev. 605 (1908). The article could have been written yesterday.

17. *See* Hogan, Financing the Acquisition of New Goods Under the Uniform Commercial Code, 3 B.C.Ind. & Com.L. Rev. 115, 134 (1962). *See* § 7–2 *infra*.

18. *See* Lewis v. Manufacturers Nat. Bank, 364 U.S. 603, 81 S.Ct. 347, 5 L.Ed.2d 323 (1961). Section 9–306(4) (d) gives a security interest in unidentified cash and bank accounts in lieu of the right to trace which would exist except for insolvency. This limits the right the secured party would otherwise have had to trace the proceeds by any means of proof available. The security interest in proceeds of whatever kind is superior to the rights of attaching creditors, in or out of insolvency situations. If it were not, it would be meaningless. The Code is clearly intended to create an enforceable in-

lien on the proceeds at the date of bankruptcy, since only the debtor's rights in the collateral can be reached and they are subject to our security interest. Not Section 67c [19] since Article 9 does not create or, in general, deal with statutory liens [20] but only consensual liens.[21] The security interest in proceeds is either a direct or a derivative security interest depending on the security agreement, but it is clearly an incident of a contractual secured transaction which does not arise solely by virtue of a statute, as does, for example, a landlord's lien. Finally, the provision does not offend Section 60, for a great many reasons which are discussed elsewhere.[22]

This discussion of Section 9–306(4)(d) is, however, based on a showing that proceeds went into a bank account. Where a creditor claimed $19,505.27 in the debtor's bank account but could show only that $10 of that amount was proceeds of collateral, the secured party could not claim the entire account.[23] This matter of proof of the

vulnerable security interest and there is no reason why this cannot be done by the use of appropriate language. No actualized hypothetical creditor can come ahead of a perfected security interest. Note the ten-day grace period for purchase money security interests perfected by filing in § 9–301(2) (as against transferees in bulk and lien creditors) and in § 9–312 (4) (for collateral other than inventory as against conflicting security interests) where the stipulated conditions are met. If duly perfected within the ten-day period, the interest would be good despite intervening bankruptcy. *See, e. g.*, Hertzberg v. Associates Discount Corp., 272 F.2d 6 (6th Cir. 1959), certiorari denied 362 U.S. 950, 80 S.Ct. 861, 4 L.Ed.2d 868.

If a security interest is not perfected, then it is subordinate to the rights of those who become lien creditors without knowledge of the interest and before it is perfected. § 9–301(1)(b); *see* United States for the Use of Greer v. G. P. Fleetwood & Co., 165 F.Supp. 723 (W.D.Pa.1958); *In re* Luckenbill, 156 F.Supp. 129 (E.D.Pa.1957). *See generally* Kennedy, The Trustee in Bankruptcy Under the Uniform Commercial Code: Some Problems Suggested by Articles 2 and 9, 14 Rutgers L.Rev. 518, 521–27 (1960). *See* § 7–3 *infra.*

19. On the purposes of this section, *see* H.R.Rep.No. 2320, 82d Cong., 2d Sess. 13 (1952); S.Rep.No. 1395, 82d Cong., 2d Sess. 7 (1952).

20. § 9–103(2) provides, "This Article does not apply to statutory liens except as provided in Section 9–310." § 9–310 resolves certain conflicts between secured parties and lienors who have furnished services or materials with respect to the goods and who have retained possession of them. *See also In re* Einhorn Bros., 171 F.Supp. 655 (E.D.Pa.), affirmed 272 F.2d 434 (3d Cir. 1959).

21. § 9–102(2): "This Article applies to security interests created by contract . . . ." *See generally* Epstein, "Proceeding" Under the Uniform Commercial Code, 3 U.C.C.L.J. 318 (1971).

22. *See* § 7–6 *infra.* The basic problem here is discussed, with a thorough review of the conflicting cases, in Friedman, The Bankruptcy Preference Challenge to After-Acquired Property Clauses Under the Code, 108 U.Pa.L. Rev. 194 (1959); *see also* Schwartz, The Effect of the Uniform Commercial Code on Secured Financing Transactions and Bankruptcy, 38 St. John's L.Rev. 50 (1963); Hogan, Games Lawyers Play with the Bankruptcy Preference Challenge to Accounts and Inventory Financing, 53 Cornell L.Rev. 553 (1968).

23. *In re* Gibson Products of Arizona, 543 F.2d 652 (9th Cir. 1976).

source of funds in a bank account may often be troublesome but it seems impossible to avoid. In the *Gibson Products* case [24] the amount in excess of traceable proceeds was treated as a voidable preference, and the transfer to the creditor was said to be for antecedent debt.[25] In this area, as in others, the results may depend on which issues are raised and how they are raised in the plaintiff's complaint.[26]

But the problems that for some years have been raised about Section 9–306(4)(d) may be somewhat in abeyance. If the growing trend to treat commingled bank deposits as identifiable proceeds continues, then the significance of this provision diminishes, and the proceeds interest can be resolved under Sections 9–306(2) and (3). While the secured party and debtor may agree that the proceeds of inventory sold or accounts collected shall be deposited in a special account containing only proceeds, when a debtor gets into financial difficulty the debtor may not comply with the requirement and the funds may be commingled in a general account.[27] If the deposited and commingled proceeds can be traced to the court's satisfaction, then presumably the ten-day limitation and the other limitations can be disregarded, and the secured party can claim whatever can be traced.

Traditionally it has been considered difficult to trace deposited proceeds, and Section 9–306(4)(d) was drafted to avoid the necessity of tracing, although it has the severely limiting ten-day rule. If the view is accepted that these deposited proceeds are analogous to trust funds, then the secured party's interest is perhaps easier to establish, and the proceeds may be said to be identifiable, perhaps somewhat fictitiously. In a proceeds case it was said by Justice Clark that " .   .   . it is clear in the different, but probably analogous, case of a fund impressed with a trust, such fund may be traced into a fund of commingled money .   .   . and it is conclusively presumed in equity that a trustee dissipates or spends his own funds first, before encroaching upon a trust fund." [28] In another case, Judge Webster stated, "The mere fact that the proceeds from the sales of the six automobiles were commingled with other funds and subsequent with-

---

24. *Id.*

25. *See also* Fitzpatrick v. Philco Finance Corp., 491 F.2d 1288 (7th Cir. 1974).

26. *See, e. g.,* Independence Discount Corp. v. Bressner, 47 A.D.2d 756, 365 N.Y.S.2d 44 (1975), where the plaintiff unsuccessfully sued in conversion to recover proceeds deposited in a general bank account, and the account had always been in excess of the amount due to plaintiff. This would not appear to have been a fact situation where conversion could properly apply,

but it is a situation where the plaintiff perhaps could have recovered on a trust theory. See text following this note.

27. This was said to have happened in *In re* Security Aluminum Co., 9 UCC Rep.Serv. 47 (E.D.Mich.1971) (in bankruptcy). *See generally* Skilton, The Secured Party's Rights in a Debtor's Bank Account Under Article 9 of the Uniform Commercial Code, 1977 So.Ill. U.L.J. 120.

28. Brown & Williamson Tobacco Corp. v. First Nat'l Bank of Blue Island, 504 F.2d 998, 1002 (7th Cir. 1974).

drawals were made from the commingled account does not render the proceeds unidentifiable . . . "[29] He went on to state that the general rule in tracing commingled funds presumes "that any payments made were from other than the funds in which another has a legally recognized interest. This is commonly referred to as the 'lowest intermediate balance' rule." [30] The effect of this rule ordinarily will be that where funds are commingled by a trustee, the beneficiary cannot recover more of the account than the lowest intermediate balance, where there have been deposits by the trustee of both trust funds and personal funds and the withdrawals of funds for personal use have depleted the account below the level of trust funds deposited even though subsequent deposits of personal funds may have resulted in a balance larger than the amount of the trust fund at the time an equitable lien is sought to be enforced.[31]

If an amount at least equal to the claimed proceeds has always been in the debtor's bank account, despite continuous withdrawals and deposits, then a tracing rule can be applied so that the "proceeds from the sale of original collateral would thus be 'identifiable,' because it is presumed that they remained untouched in the bank from the day of their deposit to the day the checking account was seized. The proceeds in the account thus remained subject to [the perfected] security interest." [32]

§ 6–8. Insurance Proceeds as "Proceeds"

To ask whether insurance proceeds are "proceeds" under Article 9 is to frame too broad a question. But in an appropriately restricted fact situation, the fair answer is yes.

The problem begins with Section 9–306(1) which says: " 'Proceeds' includes whatever is received when collateral or proceeds is sold, exchanged, collected or otherwise disposed of." When collateral has been "lost" or destroyed in an insured event, has it been "disposed of?" It clearly has not been "sold, exchanged [or] collected" so that those verbs do not fit the facts. Several cases have now said that the Code's definition of "proceeds" does not apply to what has been called an "involuntary conversion" but only to a voluntary disposition of collateral.[33]

---

29. Universal C. I. T. Credit Corp. v. Farmers Bank of Portageville, 358 F. Supp. 317, 324 (E.D.Mo.1973). This opinion deserves a careful reading. It may prove to be of seminal importance in this area of the law.

30. *Id.* at 325.

31. Restatement of Trusts, Second, § 202, Comment j.

32. Michigan Nat'l Bank v. Flowers Mobile Home Sales, Inc., 26 N.C.App. 690, 217 S.E.2d 108, 111 (1975). *See also* Associates Discount Corp. v. Fidelity Union Trust Co., 111 N.J.Super. 353, 268 A.2d 330 (1970).

33. Quigley v. Caron, 247 A.2d 94 (Me. 1968); Universal C. I. T. Credit Corp. v. Prudential Inv. Corp., 101 R.I. 287,

In this connection we must also examine Section 9–306(2), which provides: "Except where this Article otherwise provides, a security interest continues in collateral notwithstanding sale, exchange or other disposition thereof by the debtor unless his action was authorized by the secured party in the security agreement or otherwise, and also continues in any identifiable proceeds including collections received by the debtor." If we assume that loss or destruction of the property was not authorized by the secured party, must we also assume that "disposition" in this provision also relates only to a voluntary transfer? Would a court boggle at finding a continuing security interest in a truck wrecked by a debtor if the truck had been subject to a security interest before its destruction? Yet the collateral has been "disposed of," and the Code provides that the security interest continues in the collateral and in identifiable proceeds, which insurance proceeds could certainly be. If these provisions relate only to a voluntary disposition, the security interest would not continue in the wrecked truck, and that would seem to make no sense at all.

The situation is somewhat less clear, based solely on the language of the Code, when the truck is wrecked by the action of a third party or if it is stolen. In neither case is that a "disposition by the debtor" and yet the collateral has, in a sense, been disposed of and the security interest would surely be held to continue in it, for whatever that is worth. If Section 9–306(2) does not compel this result, no other section of the Code explicitly does so, but the result seems to be self-evidently correct even though the Code's language requires stretching to reach it.

If the collateral is destroyed, is there any reason why the insurance proceeds should not be considered "proceeds" and therefore substitute collateral? The language of the Code speaks of proceeds "received by the debtor." [34] The receipt may, of course, be constructive in

---

222 A.2d 571 (1966); *In re* Levine, 6 UCC Rep.Serv. 238 (D.Conn.1969) (in bankruptcy). *Contra*, Fireman's Fund American Ins. Co. v. Ken-Lori Knits, Inc., 399 F.Supp. 286 (E.D.N.Y. 1975); *In re* Hunter, 9 UCC Rep.Serv. 928 (S.D.Ohio 1971) (in bankruptcy).

34. § 9–306(2). In *In re* Waltman, 18 UCC Rep.Serv. 576 (S.D.Ala.1975) (in bankruptcy), a car subject to a security interest was "totalled" *after* the debtor filed a voluntary bankruptcy petition. Neither the security agreement nor the financing statement contained any reference to proceeds. The secured party was, nevertheless, named loss payee "as interest may appear" on the insurance policy covering the car. The claim draft was made payable jointly to the debtor and the secured party, but the draft was turned over to the trustee by the debtor. It was held that the secured party's interest was only in the automobile and not in the proceeds. However, it would seem that § 70a of the Bankruptcy Act, which apparently was the source of the trustee's rights, would have established those rights as of the date of bankruptcy, at which time the car was in existence and the

a sense. This event need not be visualized in terms of John Smith physically receiving money or a check; the concept clearly is more difficult if posed in terms of General Motors, but it need present no serious problem. However, the debtor can in no sense be said to receive insurance proceeds if a third party, not the secured party, has been named loss payee on the policy of casualty insurance, and in fact gets the proceeds, so that the issue which has often been raised—that this is purely a matter of insurance law—becomes academic on such facts. The problem we are principally concerned with arises where the debtor is himself entitled to the insurance proceeds, under the terms of the policy, and the conflicting claims are those of the secured party and other creditors.

Where insurance proceeds are clearly payable it is immaterial to the company which party receives them and they can be paid into court for a determination as between third parties. If the security agreement provides that the secured party is entitled to the insurance proceeds, as will normally be the case, this provision should be effective so far as third parties, who are not parties to the insurance contract, are concerned. The Code clearly provides for this.[35] In old-fashioned insurance terminology, this gives the secured party an "equitable" interest in the proceeds, whereas it would have been a "legal" interest if the secured party had been named loss payee.[36] If the security agreement provides for insurance payable to the secured party and the financing statement shows that the secured party claims "proceeds", this should establish a "legal" interest in them.[37] It would be of no value to anyone to require that a claim to "insurance proceeds" be made specifically on a financing statement,[38] since this would simply result in

trustee's rights were clearly subordinate to the secured party's interest. The opinion suggests the result would be different under Revised § 9–306(1), but it ought to have been different in any event as a matter of both insurance law and the Bankruptcy Act.

35. § 9–201: "Except as otherwise provided by this Act a security agreement is effective according to its terms between the parties, against purchasers of the collateral and against creditors." No other provision in the Code governs this problem or provides otherwise.

36. *See* Michigan Fire & Marine Ins. Co. v. Genie Craft Corp., 224 F.Supp. 636 (D.Md.1964). Insurance cases can be found to support practically any proposition, as the standard treatises

will confirm, perhaps unintentionally. Those who are interested should consult 5 J. Appleman, Insurance Law and Practice § 3341 (1941); Couch on Insurance §§ 1936–38 (1931); Couch on Insurance §§ 29:63–29:112 (2d ed. 1960). *See also* Annot., 9 A.L.R.2d 299 (1950).

37. The distinction between "legal" and "equitable" is often tenuous at best, but recording or filing seems to have a magic effect; that is, the interest becomes "legal" on this happening.

38. There is arguably a conceptual inconsistency between §§ 9–203(1)(b) and 9–402(3) on the one hand and § 9–306 (2) on the other. Section 9–203(1)(b) appears to require a claim to proceeds in the security agreement to enforce the security interest against the debt-

such a claim being made on the form in every instance even though the claim might be meaningless.

It is anomalous for third party creditors, whether general or lien, to have a claim to insurance proceeds of collateral when they can claim no interest in the collateral itself,[39] and this is equally so whether the controversy arises in or out of bankruptcy. The insurance proceeds stand in place of the collateral,[40] and the secured party's interest should be equivalent, whether or not the secured party is named as loss payee in the policy, a matter as to which the third parties will have no knowledge or interest unless a windfall appears to be possible after the property is destroyed. It may be doubted that any unsecured third party creditor would attempt to assert a claim against the collateral if, for example, a truck were destroyed and the insurance proceeds were received and used to purchase a replacement which was on hand when financial disaster struck the debtor.

It begs the question and answers nothing to say that "[i]nsurance moneys or proceeds flow from the insurance contract and not from the property insured."[41]

That may in a sense be true, but there could be no such insurance contract if it were not for the property, and the loss will be measured by the value of the property, not the face amount of the policy, in most cases, at least if the collateral is depreciable. This is the same sort of vacuous circularity involved in asking whether the chicken or the egg came first.

Article 9 expressly does not apply "to a transfer of an interest or claim in or under any policy of insurance."[42] This exclusion may have been politically pressured, but the official comment to the section sug-

---

or, and § 9–402(3) appears to require a notice on the financing statement for the interest to be effective against third parties (under § 9–301(1)), and yet § 9–306(2) provides for the automatic continuance of the security interest into identifiable proceeds when the collateral is disposed of. A failure to check the proceeds box on the financing statement form is usually an oversight of no consequence to third parties in fact, and in Revised Article 9 the interest in proceeds has been restated as automatic, without requiring anything on the financing statement. *See* Revised § 9–203(3).

39. In PPG Industries, Inc. v. Hartford Fire Ins. Co., 531 F.2d 58 (2d Cir. 1976), the secured party prevailed over a federal tax lien where the security

interest in inventory and equipment was perfected before the tax lien was filed, but the property was subsequently destroyed. *See also* Aetna Ins. Co. v. Texas Thermal Industries, 436 F.Supp. 371 (E.D.Tex.1977); Distributor's Warehouse, Inc. v. Madison Auto Parts & Service Corps., 8 UCC Rep.Serv. 569 (Wis.Cir.Ct.1970).

40. This is true of any other proceeds, too. There seems to be no valid reason for treating insurance proceeds differently.

41. Universal C. I. T. Credit Corp. v. Prudential Inv. Corp., 101 R.I. 287, 222 A.2d 571, 575 (1966), quoted in Quigley v. Caron, 247 A.2d 94, 96 (Me.1968).

42. § 9–104(g). *Cf.* Revised § 9–104(g).

gests that it was intended to apply basically to life insurance policies,[43] where provisions for policy loans are apparently satisfactorily arranged by the companies involved. On its face, however, the exclusion would also apply if an insurance claim were assigned under a casualty policy. But this is not necessarily precisely our situation.

If a secured party is named as loss payee in a policy, the insurance company's requirements will be met; this act in itself does not create any kind of security interest [44] and Article 9 does not apply to it; [45] and in the event of an insured loss, the proceeds are payable according to the terms of the policy with Section 9–306 merely stating the security consequences of the payment, if any.

If the security agreement requires an assignment of insurance but none is made and a loss occurs, whether the secured party can claim the proceeds as against the debtor is a matter of insurance law and is not resolved by the Code, but if the debtor receives the proceeds—a fortiori if the secured party receives them—they are clearly proceeds of the collateral under Section 9–306 as against the claims of third parties who have no prior interest in the collateral. This result is required by the Code [46] and has nothing to do with insurance law.

If the security agreement does not require an assignment of insurance and if the secured party is not named loss payee but the collateral is destroyed in an event covered by insurance, the proceeds should be payable to the debtor in whose hands they are "proceeds" under Section 9–306, in which the secured party has a continuing security interest if the filed financing statement claimed proceeds or if the security interest in the proceeds is perfected within ten days after the debtor receives them.[47]

---

43. § 9–104, Comment 7. *See* 1 G. Gilmore, Security Interests in Personal Property § 10.7, at 315 (1965).

44. The security interest is in the collateral itself. Merely naming a secured party as loss payee transfers nothing at that time because there is nothing whatsoever to transfer. The debtor can have no right in non-existent insurance proceeds to which a security interest could even attach, under § 9–204(1).

45. § 9–104(g).

46. § 9–306(2). However, in *In re* Parks, 19 UCC Rep.Serv. 334 (E.D. Tenn.1976) (in bankruptcy), where collateral was destroyed by fire and the debtor had not performed its promise to have the secured party named loss payee under the fire insurance policy, the secured party's claim to the insurance proceeds was unsuccessful, apparently on the basis that insurance proceeds are not proceeds under § 9–306(1) of the 1962 Code. The court relied particularly on Universal C. I. T. Credit Corp. v. Prudential Investment Corp., 101 R.I. 287, 222 A.2d 571 (1966) and Quigley v. Caron, 247 A.2d 94 (Me.1968), discussed *infra* in this section, and also on *In re* Waltman, 18 UCC Rep.Serv. 576 (S.D.Ala.1976) (in bankruptcy), discussed *supra* at n. 34.

47. § 9–306(3).

The provisions of the Code create no problems under insurance law, and insurance law creates no problems under the Code.

A number of cases have involved, obliquely or directly, the problem under discussion. The question was rather squarely faced in *Quigley v. Caron*.[48] Here the debtor entered into a security agreement covering a crop of potatoes, and the security interest was duly perfected. The potatoes were destroyed in a fire, and the $13,000 loss was covered by insurance, although the secured party's interest was not disclosed. Then a third party sued the debtor, recovered a judgment for $8,000, and in the principal case apparently sought to enforce the lien of the earlier judgment against the debtor and the insurance companies as trustees of the fund payable. The court noted that the insurance companies had no interest in the outcome of the case.[49]

The Maine Supreme Judicial Court felt that Section 9–306(1) referred only to a "voluntary disposal"[50] of the collateral, so the insurance proceeds could not be "identifiable proceeds" of the collateral under Section 9–306(2). Therefore, the secured party had no claim on the insurance proceeds. It is not clear from the court's opinion what happened to the balance of the insurance proceeds in excess of the third party's claim. Nor is it ever stated whether the secured party claimed an interest in proceeds of the collateral, although a failure to do so would be inexplicable in crop financing and cannot be assumed.

The court was of the opinion that a fire insurance contract was a "personal contract"[51] (whatever that is) between the insured and the insurer in which a secured party, merely by virtue of being such, could claim no interest. Up to a point there is no objection to this analysis, but beyond a point there is. We reach the point of objection when the funds are clearly payable and the question is whether the secured party can claim them as substitute collateral or whether a totally unrelated third party creditor, with no interest in the collateral or its insurance, can come ahead. This is not a matter of insurance law. This is the point where the provisions of the Code determine the answer.

Maine has a statute, which the court referred to, under which a mortgagee of real or personal property can impose a statutory lien on fire insurance procured by a mortgagor.[52] The fact that the se-

---

48. 247 A.2d 94 (Me.1968).

49. *Id.*

50. *Id.* at 96.

51. *Id.* at 95.

52. Me.Rev.Stat.Ann. tit. 24, §§ 1521–25 (1964).

cured party made no effort to enforce such a lien may have influenced the court, although it is doubtful. The court seemed to be most strongly swayed by the Rhode Island case of *Universal C. I. T. Credit Corp. v. Prudential Investment Corp.*[53]

The Rhode Island case involved an agile debtor whose machinations are perhaps not worth going into in detail, but the court did announce that insurance proceeds are not "proceeds" within the meaning of Section 9–306(1): " 'Proceeds' by definition under the code arises [*sic*] from either a sale, exchange, collection or other disposition of either the collateral or proceeds. Insurance moneys or proceeds, however, arise and are paid as the result of a contract." [54]

From this one might infer that a sale or exchange of property does not involve a contract. There are many distinctions to be drawn between an insurance contract and a sale or exchange contract, but they are all "contracts," and that label is as applicable to the one as to the other. It is odd that a court would find a difference between the proceeds of a contract of sale and the proceeds of a contract of insurance based on a label erroneously applied.

The concept of proceeds is of particular value in financing sales of inventory,[55] and no doubt any court, if certain mechanical steps were followed, would enforce a security interest in the proceeds of such a sale even though it was admitted by one and all that the secured party was not a party to the sale contract and had no interest in its terms beyond his right to proceeds. Indeed, the secured party would have no security interest in the specific goods once they were sold and could rely solely on a continuing security interest in the proceeds. But if we change the matrix of the proceeds from a contract of sale to a contract of insurance, we get bogged down in shibboleths and a meaningful analysis of the facts seems so often to be impossible.

To say that the Rhode Island court was wrong in its interpretation of the Code on the proceeds point is not the same as saying the decision was wrong. On its facts the decision was correct. The first secured party to have its claim satisfied was listed as a loss payee in

---

53. 101 R.I. 287, 222 A.2d 571 (1966), noted in 19 Ala.L.Rev. 565 (1966); 52 Iowa L.Rev. 1219 (1967); 65 Mich. L.Rev. 1514 (1967).

54. 222 A.2d at 574 (1966).

55. These problems are discussed from various angles in Henson, "Proceeds" Under the Uniform Commercial Code, 65 Colum.L.Rev. 232 (1965); Kripke, Suggestions for Clarifying Article 9: Intangibles, Proceeds, and Priorities, 41 N.Y.U.L.Rev. 687 (1966); Henson, Countersuggestions Regarding Article 9: A Reply to Professor Kripke, 42 N.Y.U.L.Rev. 74 (1967); Weiss, Original Collateral and Proceeds: A Code Puzzle, 42 N.Y.U.L.Rev. 785 (1967).

the casualty policy. This payment was proper.[56] The argument was between two other secured parties, the first of whom claimed proceeds on its financing statement and the second of whom did not, but did manage to have the debtor execute an assignment of the debtor's interest in the insurance proceeds after the loss had occurred. This assignment is a transaction to which the Code does not apply,[57] and this assignee's claim was in fact more than the excess proceeds available after the loss payee's claim was satisfied. Therefore, no insurance proceeds were ever "received by the debtor," which Section 9–306(2) arguably may require in order for the secured party to have a continuing security interest in them.[58]

To some extent the Rhode Island court relied on a decision by the Court of Common Pleas of Allegheny County, Pennsylvania, in the case of *Hoffman v. Snack*.[59] Here again, the court was wrong in its view that the proceeds at issue could not be proceeds under the Code, but the court may well have been correct in its decision that the secured party, the financer of the debtor's automobile, had no right to intervene under the Pennsylvania rules of civil procedure in an action brought by the debtor against a man who had apparently run into and demolished the debtor's uninsured automobile. Again, no proceeds had been received in which the security interest could continue, and the requirements of Section 9–306(2) were not met. The Pennsylvania court was wrong in its assumption that the secured party's interest in proceeds depended on an unauthorized sale, exchange, or other disposition of the property, but even so the Code's triggering factor—the receipt of proceeds—had not taken place, and the case involved trial procedure.

Despite some ambiguity in the language of Section 9–306, it seems clear that the insurance proceeds are simply substituted for the original collateral, and that the security interest in the insurance proceeds is a continuously perfected security interest when those pro-

56. The Code does not apply to this situation, under § 9–104(g) and Revised § 9–104(g), and the Code's proceeds provisions may apply only where the debtor receives the proceeds, which he cannot be said to do when they are by contract payable to another. See § 9–306(2) and Revised § 9–306(2) which provide that the security interest "continues in any identifiable proceeds including collections received by the debtor." The absence of commas makes it arguable whether the proceeds must be received by the debtor or only the collections. There is no requirement of receipt *by the debtor* in § 9–306(1) or Revised § 9–306(1). The requirement of receipt should not be read into § 9–306(2), according to Farnum v. C. J. Merrill, Inc., 264 A.2d 150 (Me.1970).

57. § 9–104(g).

58. *See* note 56 supra.

59. 113 Pitt.Legal J. 206, 2 UCC Rep. Serv. 862 (1964).

ceeds are received by the debtor or secured party. The erroneous interpretations of various counts on this point led to the insertion of a sentence in Revised Section 9–306(1) which states: "Insurance payable by reason of loss or damage to the collateral is proceeds, except to the extent that it is payable to a person other than a party to the security agreement."

Since casualty insurance could not, presumably, be payable to one who does not have an insurable interest in the goods, the class of claimants would normally be restricted to the debtor and various secured parties. (After loss, the right to payment might be assigned by a person entitled to it.) If a senior secured party was not named loss payee on a policy but a junior secured party was, in the event of loss the insurance proceeds would not be proceeds subject to the senior interest to the extent that the junior party was entitled to them in satisfaction of his security interest. If the senior secured party was named loss payee but the junior party was not, then the senior security interest would be satisfied before any surplus became proceeds subject to the junior interest.[60] When the insurance proceeds are paid to a secured party presumably those proceeds cease to be proceeds under Article 9 because the obligation is paid and the security interest is retired.[61]

The result required by Revised Section 9–306(1) could be reached under the 1962 Code by judicial statesmanship.[62]

60. *See* Distributor's Warehouse, Inc. v. Madison Auto Parts & Service Corp., 8 UCC Rep.Serv. 569 (Wis.Cir. Ct.1970).

61. *See In re* Platt, 58 Berks Co.L.J. 86, 3 UCC Rep.Serv. 275 (E.D.Pa.1966) (in bankruptcy), vacated on other grounds, 257 F.Supp. 478 (E.D.Pa.1966).

62. *See* PPG Industries, Inc. v. Hartford Fire Ins. Co., 531 F.2d 58 (2d Cir. 1976); First Nat'l Bank of Highland v. Merchant's Mutual Ins. Co., 89 Misc.2d 771, 392 N.Y.S.2d 836 (1977).

CHAPTER 7

RIGHTS OF LIEN CREDITORS, INCLUDING THE TRUSTEE IN BANKRUPTCY

Table of Sections

§ 7–1. Rights of Lien Creditors in General

Conflicts between secured parties and lien creditors claiming interests in the same collateral are resolved in Section 9–301 of the Uniform Commercial Code, and some important changes were made in Section 9–301 by the Article 9 Review Committee.

Certain parts of the 1972 version of Section 9–301 are set out below with deletions from the 1962 Code shown in brackets and with additions underscored:

(1) Except as otherwise provided in subsection (2), an unperfected security interest is subordinate to the rights of

. . .

(b) a person who becomes a lien creditor [without knowledge of the security interest and] before [it] *the security interest* is perfected;

. . .

(2) If the secured party files with respect to a purchase money security interest before or within ten days after the *debtor receives possession of the* collateral [comes into possession of the debtor], he takes priority over the rights of a transferee in bulk or of a lien creditor which arise between the time the security interest attaches and the time of filing.

235

(3) A "lien creditor" means a creditor who has acquired a lien on the property involved by attachment, levy or the like and includes an assignee for benefit of creditors from the time of assignment, and a trustee in bankruptcy from the date of the filing of the petition or a receiver in equity from the time of appointment. [Unless all the creditors represented had knowledge of the security interest such a representative of creditors is a lien creditor without knowledge even though he personally has knowledge of the security interest.]

Perhaps the first thing to observe about Section 9–301(1) is that the basic rule is stated in terms of subordination, not priority. Aside from the purchase money situation treated in subsection (2), an unperfected security interest is subordinate to the rights of a person who becomes a lien creditor before the security interest is perfected.[1] In addition, under the 1962 Code, the lien creditor must have become a lien creditor without knowledge of the unperfected security interest.[2] All of the important terms in the preceding sentences are defined in the Code, and the definitions are crucial.

A lien creditor is defined in Section 9–301(3). This person is not to be confused with a judgment lien creditor.[3] The status of a judgment lien creditor is ordinarily determined by state statutory law

---

1. K.N.C. Wholesale, Inc. v. AWMCO, Inc., 55 Cal.App.3d 43, 127 Cal.Rptr. 208 (1976), vacated 56 Cal.App.3d 315, 128 Cal.Rptr. 345 (1976). The security interest is subordinated; it is not void. *See In re* Estate of Hinds, 10 Cal.App.3d 1021, 89 Cal.Rptr. 341 (1970). If the security interest is perfected, the subsequent lien creditor is subordinated. Estate of Cook, 64 Cal.App.3d 852, 135 Cal.Rptr. 96 (1976); Raleigh Industries of America, Inc. v. Tassone, 74 Cal.App.3d 692, 141 Cal.Rptr. 641 (1977); Cibro Petroleum Products, Inc. v. Fowler Finishing Co., Inc., 92 Misc.2d 450, 400 N.Y.S.2d 322 (1977). This is true even if the United States is the subsequent lien creditor. Streule v. Gulf Finance Corp., 265 A.2d 298 (D. C.App.1970). If the security interest is perfected at the time the lien creditor's rights arise, the security interest is clearly entitled to priority. *In re* Chase Manhattan Bank (N.A.) v. State of New York, 48 A.D.2d 11, 367 N.Y.S.2d 580 (1975). Under § 9–311 a lien creditor can reach only the debtor's equity in the goods over and above the interest of the secured party.

Shaw Mudge & Co. v. Sher-Mart Mfg. Co., Inc., 132 N.J.Super. 517, 334 A.2d 357 (1975). *See also* Smith v. Guzman, 16 UCC Rep.Serv. 852 (N.Y.Sup. Ct.1975). *Cf.* Maryland Nat'l Bank v. Porter-Way Harvester Mfg. Co., 300 A.2d 8 (Del.1972).

2. *See, e. g., In re* McClain, 447 F.2d 241 (10th Cir. 1971); *In re* De'Cor Wallcovering Studios, Inc., 8 UCC Rep.Serv. 59 (E.D.Wis.1970) (in bankruptcy); General Lithographing Co. v. Sight & Sound Projectors, Inc., 128 Ga.App. 304, 196 S.E.2d 479 (1973). Provisions similar to § 9–301(1)(b) and related subsections were contained in the Uniform Trust Receipts Act § 8 (2), and the Uniform Conditional Sales Act § 5.

3. Judgment liens are recognized in all states except Kentucky, Michigan, and the New England states aside from Connecticut. Riesenfeld, Creditors' Remedies and the Conflict of Laws —Part One: Individual Collection of Claims, 60 Colum.L.Rev. 659, 665 (1960).

and the requirements for achieving that status are variable. In most states the judgment lien initially reaches only real property, not chattels, and it may arise on the rendition of a judgment, although some other act, such as docketing, may be required.[4] Enforcement of the lien will usually be by levy of execution and sale. But in order to qualify as a "lien creditor" under Section 9–301(3), the judgment creditor will have to go through whatever procedures state law requires (such as attachment, levy, creditors' bill, or supplementary proceeding) to obtain a lien on personal property.[5] In this area, local law may lead to different results in the various states, and a "lien creditor" under Section 9–301(3) will turn out to be quite different in most, if not all, states from "a creditor with a lien on the real estate subsequently obtained by judicial proceedings" under Section 9–313(4)(b) dealing with fixtures.[6] In general terms, Section 9–313 (4) refers to a simple judgment lien creditor while Section 9–301(3) denotes a judgment lien creditor who has taken additional steps to acquire an interest in the Code collateral or to a creditor who has proceeded against the collateral under the local rules governing attach-

4. *Id.* at 666. *See generally* Conard, An Appraisal of Illinois Law on the Enforcement of Judgments, 1951 U.Ill. L.F. 96; Kratovil & Harrison, Enforcement of Judgments Against Real Property, 1951 U.Ill.L.F. 1; Meachum, Enforcement of Judgments Against Personal Property, 1951 U.Ill.L.F. 38; Riesenfeld, Collection of Money Judgments in American Law—A Historical Inventory and a Prospectus, 42 Iowa L.Rev. 155 (1957); Souers, Judgment Liens in Ohio, 16 Ohio St.L.J. 1 (1955); Note, Creditors' Rights—Enforcing a Judgment—When Is a Lien Created on Property of Judgment Debtor?, 45 Ky.L.J. 304 (1957).

5. *See, e. g.,* Asher & Vandenburgh v. United States, 570 F.2d 682 (7th Cir. 1978); Massachusetts Mutual Life Ins. Co. v. Central Penn Nat'l Bank, 372 F.Supp. 1027 (E.D.Pa.1974), affirmed 510 F.2d 969, 970; Bank of Broadway v. Goldblatt, 103 Ill.App. 2d 243, 243 N.E.2d 501 (1st Dist. 1968); Levine v. Pascal, 94 Ill.App. 2d 43, 236 N.E.2d 425 (1968); Stumbo v. Paul B. Hult Lumber Co., 251 Or. 20, 444 P.2d 564 (1968); Rocky Mountain Ass'n of Credit Management v. Hessler Mfg. Co., —— Colo.App. ——, 533 P.2d 840 (1976). *Cf.* Texas Oil & Gas Corp. v. United States, 466 F.2d 1040 (5th Cir. 1972), certiorari denied 410 U.S. 929 (1973). On the

United States as a lien creditor, after a notice of a tax lien is filed *see*, *e. g.,* United States v. Trigg, 465 F.2d 1264 (8th Cir. 1972), certiorari denied 410 U.S. 909 (1973); L. B. Smith, Inc. v. Foley, 341 F.Supp. 810 (W.D.N.Y. 1972); Fred Kraus & Sons, Inc. v. United States, 369 F.Supp. 1089 (N.D. Ind.1974). A temporary restraining order was held to create lien creditor status in Massachusetts Mutual Life Ins. Co. v. Central Penn Nat'l Bank, 372 F.Supp. 1027 (E.D.Pa.1974). Compare the definition of "lien creditor" in § 9–301(3), with the definition in Uniform Trust Receipts Act § 1 (1933): "'Lien creditor' means any creditor who has acquired a specific lien on the goods, documents or instruments by attachment, levy, or by any other similar operation of law or judicial process, including a distraining landlord." There are special rules covering attachment of goods covered by a negotiable document in § 7–602 and attachment or levy on investment securities in § 8–317 and Revised 8–317. As to investment securities, see U. S. Industries, Inc. v. Gregg, 540 F.2d 142 (3d Cir. 1976). *See also* Shaffer v. Heitner, 433 U.S. 186, 97 S.Ct. 2469 (1977).

6. In Revised Article 9, the comparable provision is § 9–313(4)(d).

ment.[7] Section 9–301(3) speaks of "a creditor who has acquired a lien on the property involved by attachment, levy or the like" and "creditor" is defined to include a general creditor, a secured creditor, and a lien creditor, along with representatives of creditors,[8] so that a "lien creditor" could be a general creditor who has secured an attachment covering the collateral although he has not yet obtained a judgment.[9]

The term "lien creditor" also includes "an assignee for benefit of creditors from the *time* of assignment, and a trustee in bankruptcy from the *date* of the filing of the petition or a receiver in equity from the *time* of appointment." [10] Since judicial proceedings are, in some sense, involved in the case of a receiver or trustee,[11] the time of appointment will be verifiable. Of course, in the phrases quoted above, "time" is used twice and "date" once, which could lead to a nice question if a security interest were perfected by filing at 9 a. m. and a bankruptcy petition were filed by or against the debtor at 10 a. m. on the same date. It ought to be clear, however, that if the security interest is perfected as of the time the bankruptcy petition is filed, the trustee's rights as a lien creditor are subordinate.[12] An assignment for the benefit of creditors is, however, a less notorious act and

---

7. Attachment and garnishment remedies have undergone considerable change in recent years as a result of such decisions as, *e. g.*, North Georgia Finishing, Inc. v. Di-Chem. Inc., 419 U.S. 601, 95 S.Ct. 719, 42 L.Ed.2d 751 (1975), and Randone v. Appellate Department, 5 Cal.3d 536, 96 Cal.Rptr. 709, 488 P.2d 13 (1972), certiorari denied 407 U.S. 924 (1972).

8. § 1–201(12). The filing of a notice of lis pendens was held not to give the filer priority over a subsequently perfected security interest in National Bank of Sarasota v. Dugger, 335 So. 2d 859 (Fla.App.1976). Clearly the mere filing of a complaint will not give that plaintiff the status of a lien creditor, and such a plaintiff cannot prevail over even an unperfected security interest in view of § 9–201. United States Shoe Corp. v. Cudmore-Neiber Shoe Co., Inc., 20 UCC Rep. Serv. 1036 (D.S.D.1976).

9. *See* Joint Holdings & Trading Co., Ltd. v. First Union Nat'l Bank of North Carolina, 50 Cal.App.3d 159, 123 Cal.Rptr. 519 (1975). On attachments, see Riesenfeld, *supra* note 5,

at 664–65. "Attachment" as used here refers to the judicial remedy. The term "attachment," however, was constantly used by commentators to describe the effect of the happening of all the events required in § 9–204(1) (an agreement, value given, and the debtor has rights in the collateral). Yet, the word "attachment" was not used in the 1962 Official Text except in the sense of the judicial remedy in § 9–301(3). The use of the term in two different senses leads to occasional confusion. The Revised Article 9 included the word "attachment" in the caption of Revised § 9–203 and according to § 1–109, "Section captions are part of this Act."

10. § 9–301(3) (emphasis added).

11. *See, e. g.*, Heights v. Citizens Nat'l Bank, 463 Pa. 48, 342 A.2d 738 (1975).

12. Aside from any infelicity of language in § 9–301(3), this result is mandated by § 9–301(1)(b). *See In re* Buschmann, 4 UCC Rep.Serv. 260 (E. D.Wis.1967) (in bankruptcy). In this context the trustee's rights are derived from § 70c of the Bankruptcy Act.

where state law requires formalities such as a filing or the posting of a bond, it may not be clear what point in time the definition requires. If under applicable state law the assignment is effective as of the time of its execution, assuming other statutory formalities are ultimately complied with, then the time of the execution of the assignment is presumably the time intended.[13]

Sections 9–301(1)(b) and (3) of the 1962 Code contain knowledge provisions which have been dropped in Revised Article 9. In the first subsection cited, the requirement was that a person must be without knowledge at the time of becoming a lien creditor in order to take priority over an unperfected security interest.[14] Section 9–301(3) provided that unless all represented creditors had knowledge of the unperfected security interest, their representative—an assignee for the benefit of creditors, trustee, or receiver—was a lien creditor without knowledge even though he personally knew of the security interest.[15] The reason officially given for the change in Section 9–301 (3) was to conform that provision to revised Section 9–301(1)(b), and the reason for changing the latter provision was that the 1962 version of the section "denied the lien creditor priority even though he had no knowledge when he got involved by extending credit, if he acquired knowledge while attempting to extricate himself. It was completely inconsistent in spirit with the rules of priority between security interests, where knowledge plays a very minor role."[16] The reason for the change in Section 9–301(3) is understandable, but the reason for the change in Section 9–301(1)(b) may be thought a bit thin, considering the length of time that may well be involved between the date when credit is extended, a default occurs, the creditor files

13. *In re* Federal Wholesale Meats & Frozen Foods, Inc., 43 Wis.2d 21, 168 N.W.2d 70 (1969).

14. *See, e. g.*, Stanley v. Fabricators, Inc., 459 P.2d 467 (Alaska 1969); Ford Motor Credit Co. v. Patchogue Truck & Equip. Co., 5 UCC Rep.Serv. 1272 (N.Y.Sup.Ct.1969). Conversely, if the creditor does have knowledge of a perfected security interest at the time he becomes a lien creditor, the perfected security interest is clearly entitled to priority. Marco Finance Co. v. Solbert Industries, Inc., 534 S.W. 2d 469 (Mo.App.1975). The burden of proving the lien creditors' knowledge is on the holder of the unperfected security interest. Massachusetts Mutual Life Ins. Co. v. Central Penn Nat'l Bank, 372 F.Supp. 1027 (E.D.Pa.1974).

15. *See In re* Dennis Mitchell Indus., Inc., 419 F.2d 349 (3d Cir. 1969); Columbia International Corp. v. Kempler, 46 Wis.2d 550, 175 N.W.2d 465 (1970); Central Nat'l Bank v. Wonderland Realty Corp., 38 Mich.App. 76, 195 N.W.2d 768 (1972); *In re* Anthony Kitchens, Inc., 12 UCC Rep.Serv. 563 (N.Y. Suffolk County Ct.1973). The knowledge of all creditors, when shown, has sometimes been of crucial importance. *See, e. g., In re* Komfo Prods. Corp., 247 F.Supp. 229 (E.D.Pa. 1965).

16. Revised § 9–301, 1972 Official Text with Comments, Reasons for 1972 Change. On knowledge under Article 9 of the 1962 Code, see Felsenfeld, Knowledge as a Factor in Determining Priorities Under the Uniform Commercial Code, 42 N.Y.U.L.Rev. 246 (1967).

suit, recovers judgment (or attaches the collateral), and becomes a lien creditor.

While there could never have been any question about the enforceability of these state law provisions in state proceedings, there has been some feeling that a trustee in bankruptcy should not be affected by the knowledge requirement even if all creditors knew of the unperfected security interest. It is, however, somewhat questionable (in some sense, at least, and regardless of any supposed "bankruptcy" view of the matter) that a representative of creditors should have greater rights than any of the creditors he represents and for whose benefit he supposedly is acting.

There is, it may be acknowledged, generally no particular reason to benefit a secured party who did not properly perfect his security interest. Still there are times when a secured party has in good faith done his best to file in the proper places and simply has not managed to do so. This can happen, for example, in those states which have adopted dual filing in the third alternative of Section 9–401(1)(c).[17] Here it seems unfair for a person with knowledge of the contents of the filed financing statement to be able to take advantage of the secured party's innocent failure to do all that he ought to have done. Therefore, the Code provides that a filing made in good faith in an improper place is "effective" against persons with knowledge of the contents of the financing statement.[18]

What is meant by "knowledge of the contents of such financing statement" is by no means clear. If such knowledge had to be gained by personal examination of the improperly filed statement, few would ever be able to take advantage of the provision for it would be un-

17. § 9–401(1)(c), Third Alternative, provides:

   (1) The proper place to file in order to perfect a security interest is as follows:
   (c) . . . in all other cases, in the office of the [Secretary of State] and in addition, if the debtor has a place of business in only one county of this state, also in the office of . . . of such county, or, if the debtor has no place of business in this state, but resides in the state, also in the office of . . . of the county in which he resides.

See, e. g., P. S. Prods. Corp. v. Equilease Corp., 435 F.2d 781 (2d Cir. 1970); In re Kalinoski, 13 UCC Rep.Serv. 387 (W.D.Wis.1973) (in bankruptcy). In re Kalinoski involved a situation in which the debtor's place of business was in Cuba City, most of which was

in Grant County but a small portion was in LaFayette County, and the debtor's place of business was in the small portion. The postal directory, the State of Wisconsin Blue Book, and the official Wisconsin highway map located Cuba City entirely in Grant County. Relying on the postal directory, the creditors involved filed in Grant County as well as centrally, for dual filing is required in this situation in Wisconsin. Their security interests were held to be unperfected. Section 9–401(2) is not mentioned in the opinion.

18. § 9–401(2). Of course, if the competing secured party has no actual knowledge of the misfiled financing statement's contents, the improperly filed statement has no effect. First State Bank in Talihina v. United Dollar Stores, 571 P.2d 444 (Okl.1977).

usual for a secured party to physically examine the files in these circumstances. Knowledge means actual knowledge under Section 1–201 (25). Could this knowledge come from the report of a search of the files issued by a filing officer under Section 9–407(2) or by a private agency or by the secured party's attorney? The answer is probably yes.[19] If the secured party is orally told of the competing, improperly filed interest, is that knowledge? It should be, because the information is just as meaningful as if conveyed in writing, and it is accurate or else an issue could not be raised in these circumstances; that is, there must in fact be an improperly filed financing statement for this priority problem to exist.[20] It is necessary for a financing statement to have been filed, even if erroneously, to bring an issue of knowledge via Section 9–401(2) into the priority world of Section 9–312. Mere knowledge of an earlier security interest, if no proper filing has been made, will not affect the rights of a subsequent secured party who files or perfects first.[21]

If "effective" filing means anything in this context, it must be relatively synonymous with "perfected security interest." Yet this was not the interpretation reached in *In re Babcock Box Co.*,[22] in which a trustee in bankruptcy was given priority even though he had personal knowledge of the contents of a financing statement filed properly centrally but not filed in the proper local office, and it was not shown that all creditors had knowledge. Although the result in *Babcock Box* was probably correct, the court's interpretation of the term "effective" was incorrect. The decision did not discuss whether a trustee, as a representative of creditors, is intended to come within the definition of "person," [23] which is the term used in Section 9–401

19. *See* Ford Motor Credit Co. v. Patchogue Truck & Equipment Co., 5 UCC Rep.Serv. 1272 (N.Y.Sup.Ct.1969).

20. *See In re* Davidoff, 351 F.Supp. 440 (S.D.N.Y.1972); Franklin Nat'l Inv. Corp. v. American Swiss Parts Co., 42 Mich.App. 211, 201 N.W.2d 673 (1972).

21. §§ 9–312(5)(a), (b); Revised § 9–312 (5)(a). *See* Bloom v. Hilty, 427 Pa. 463, 234 A.2d 860 (1967); *In re* County Green Limited Partnership, 438 F. Supp. 701 (W.D.Va.1977). Official Comment 5 to § 9–401 skirts the issue raised here. It was held in Nat'l Bank of Royal Oak v. Frydlewicz, 67 Mich.App. 417, 241 N.W.2d 471 (1976) that an unperfected (because filed in the wrong office) security interest was, despite § 9–301(1)(c), entitled to priority over a transferee in bulk where the requirements of Article 6

—Bulk Transfers had not been complied with.

22. 200 F.Supp. 80 (D.Mass.1961). *Contra* (on the perfection point) Chrysler Credit Corp. v. Bank of Wiggins, 358 So.2d 714 (Miss.1978). *Cf.* First Nat'l Bank & Trust v. First Nat'l Bank of Greybull, —— F.2d ——, 24 UCC Rep. Serv. 461 (10th Cir. 1978).

23. § 1–201(30): " 'Person' includes an individual or an organization (See Section 1–102)." "Organization" is defined in § 1–201(28). The word "person" is also used in § 9–301(1) to describe those entitled to priority, but the usage is consistent with a restriction to individuals or organizations rather than their representatives for in § 9–301(3), where representatives are encompassed, the term is expanded and expressly "includes" the representatives.

(2) for those against whom an improperly filed financing statement may be effective.

In *Babcock Box* Judge Ford resolved the problem in favor of the trustee under Section 9–301 whose subsection (1)(b) subordinates an unperfected security interest to the rights of a lien creditor in stated circumstances. The basis for giving the trustee priority was principally the statutory language of "unperfected security interest" in Section 9–301(1), and Judge Ford felt that proper filing was required for perfection under Section 9–303(1). Section 9–401(2) "merely makes the *lien effective*, despite the failure to make proper filing as to persons having actual knowledge of the contents of the financing statement." [24] But that section does not make the lien (*i. e.*, security interest) effective; it makes the filing effective. If the filing is effective, it is difficult to see why the security interest is not perfected, and if the security interest is perfected, Section 9–301 will not subordinate it to a lien creditor.[25]

The revised version of Section 9–301 may support the *Babcock Box* result because all that Section 9–301(1)(b) requires to subordinate an unperfected security interest to a lien creditor's rights is that the person become a lien creditor before perfection occurs (subject, of course, to Section 9–301(2)). The trustee acquires the rights of a lien creditor at the date of filing of the bankruptcy petition, and his rights are not affected by whether all the represented creditors had knowledge of the unperfected security interest. Also, both before and after the 1972 revisions, a fair reading of "person" in Section 9–401(2) is that the term is intended to cover individual or organizational creditors but not their representative, such as a trustee in bankruptcy, so that the "effective" filing provision of that section should not be read into Section 9–301 when a representative of creditors is involved.[26] When only an individual or organizational lien creditor is involved, and the creditor has knowledge of the improper filing or of the filing in one but not all of the required places, that filing might well be held "effective," thus creating a perfected security interest so as to eliminate the application of Section 9–301.

---

24. *In re* Babcock Box Co., 200 F.Supp. 80, 81 (D.Mass.1961) (emphasis added). *Cf. In re* Komfo Prods. Corp., 247 F. Supp. 229 (E.D.Pa.1965). *See also* Sequoia Machinery, Inc. v. Jarrett, 410 F.2d 1116 (9th Cir. 1969).

25. In § 9–403 the word "effective" is repeatedly used to refer to filings of financing statements where the meaning is that the act described perfects the security interest in the usual case.

Of course there may be cases in which a financing statement in proper form may be filed and may be "effective" in some sense, but no security interest will ever be perfected as a result of the filing if the events necessary for attachment never occur.

26. *See* notes 22 and 24 *supra*. *See also In re* Coed Shop, Inc., 435 F.Supp. 472 (N.D.Fla.1977).

Another area of conflict between lien creditors and secured creditors concerns purchase money security interests. Section 9–301(2) provides a 10-day grace period for filing a financing statement to perfect purchase money security interests. If there is a filing before the debtor receives possession [27] of the collateral or within 10 days after that event, the secured party will take priority over the rights of a "lien creditor which arise between the time the security interest attaches and the time of filing." [28] This provision relates solely to priority. It does not relate back the effectiveness of the filing for perfection purposes, and the security interest will be perfected for Article 9 purposes only when the filing is accomplished. [29] For security inter-

---

27. The term "receives possession" appears in § 9–312(4), and it was put in to Revised § 9–301(2) so that the language of both sections would be the same since the concepts involved are the same. "Receives possession" appears to be used in both places to mean "receives actual, physical possession." This definition has created several problems under § 9–312(4). When a person in possession of goods, as lessee or otherwise, subsequently decides to buy them and the unpaid balance is secured by a purchase money security interest, the problem of filing within 10 days after the purchaser "receives possession" is insoluble under Code terminology unless there is repossession and redelivery, which may be thought pointless. It is arguably possible to comply technically with § 9–312(4), by saying there was no "debtor" and there was no "collateral" before the sale, and therefore if there is filing within 10 days after that event, the purchase money secured party is entitled to priority. *See* Brodie Hotel Supply, Inc. v. United States, 431 F.2d 1316 (9th Cir. 1970). *Contra,* North Platte State Bank v. Production Credit Ass'n, 189 Neb. 44, 200 N.W.2d 1 (1972). *Cf. In re* Automated Bookbinding Servs., Inc., 471 F.2d 546 (4th Cir. 1972); Fan-Gil Corp. v. American Hosp. Supply Corp., 49 Mich.App. 106, 211 N.W.2d 561 (1973). *See § 5–3 supra.* The problem of priority for the purchase money secured party when the debtor is in possession, whatever the circumstances, for more than 10 days before a filing is made, or realistically could be made, is a difficult one because the Code apparently requires an answer which sometimes will seem to be wrong.

While a lessor as lessor (rather than as secured party) could file under Revised § 9–408, such a filing would not appear to perfect a security interest subsequently created, when the lease is actually a true lease in its inception. Problems similar to those which have recently arisen under § 9–312(4) may well arise in the future under § 9–301(2) in either version of the Code.

28. § 9–301(2).

29. Section 9–403(1) states an explicit rule on what constitutes filing: "Presentation for filing of a financing statement and tender of the filing fee or acceptance of the statement by the filing officer constitutes filing under this Article." *In re* Royal Electrotype Corp., 11 UCC Rep.Serv. 438 (E.D.Pa. 1972) (in bankruptcy), held that a filing officer's misindexing of a correct and "properly filed" financing statement rendered the security interest unperfected and gave the trustee in bankruptcy priority over the security interest. This puts the burden of the filing officer's failure to perform his duties on the secured party, which is completely insupportable under the statutory language. On the most practical level this would encourage surreptitious payments or holiday remembrances to filing clerks to make sure that they do for some persons what they are required by law to do for all, and this is surely not to be encouraged by the bar. Fortunately this decision has been reversed by the Third Circuit. *In re* Royal Electrotype Corp., 485 F.2d 394 (3d Cir. 1973). *See also In re* Callahan Motors, Inc., 538 F.2d 76 (3d Cir. 1976), certiorari denied 429

ests which are perfected without filing, such as most purchase money security interests in consumer goods, the subsection has no application because Section 9–301(1) begins: "Except as otherwise provided in subsection (2), an unperfected security interest is subordinate to the rights of" designated parties, and these interests will always be perfected simply by attachment. It is only when filing is a necessary or alternative[30] means of perfection that subsection (2) provides priority if its terms are met, but subsection (2) is only providing priority for an unperfected security interest over the rights of lien creditors (and transferees in bulk). Where competing secured parties are concerned, their rights are stated in Section 9–312.

The grace period of Section 9–301(2) is not limited to 10 days from the time of attachment but to 10 days from the time the debtor receives possession of the collateral. A filing within 10 days after receipt of possession provides priority over a lien creditor's rights that arose between the attachment and filing, which might be considerably longer than 10 days. If a seller in California were shipping goods to a buyer in New York, the security interest might well attach in California at or before the time of shipment, depending on the terms of the contract, but a purchase money secured party claiming a security interest in those goods would have 10 days to file after the buyer-debtor received possession of them in New York in order to achieve priority over lien creditors. There may, of course, be further complications in multistate transactions when prior secured parties are claiming interests in after-acquired collateral.[31]

§ 7–2. Reclamation Rights of Sellers Under § 2–702

Under the 1962 Official Text of the Uniform Commercial Code, the portion of Section 2–702 dealing with the reclamation rights of sellers[32] read as follows:

U.S. 987; *In re* Tri-Cities Music Centers, Inc., 22 UCC Rep.Serv. 254 (E.D. Tenn.1977) (in bankruptcy).

30. Section 9–305 provides for possessory perfection of security interests in certain kinds of collateral, but perfection dates only from the time possession is taken and there is no relation back. The kinds of collateral covered by Revised § 9–305 are: letters of credit and advices of credit, goods, instruments, money, negotiable documents, and chattel paper. (Money was added in the 1972 revision of Article 9.) A security interest in money as collateral and not as proceeds of collateral can be perfected only by possession despite the possibility of temporary perfection suggested by Revised § 9–304(1), for temporary perfection is not in fact applicable to money under the language of § 9–304(4) and Revised § 9–304(5) which deal with that problem. This perfection problem is probably of interest only to numismatists and their financers. *See In re* Midas Coin Co., 264 F.Supp. 193 (E.D.Mo.1967), affirmed *sub nom.* Zuke v. St. Johns Community Bank, 387 F. 2d 118 (8th Cir. 1968).

31. *See generally* Chapter 9 *infra* and particularly § 9–4.

32. The language of section 2–702(3) was officially unchanged from 1952 to 1966. For the history of this pro-

(2) Where the seller discovers that the buyer has received goods on credit while insolvent he may reclaim the goods upon demand made within ten days after the receipt, but if misrepresentation of solvency has been made to the particular seller in writing within three months before delivery the ten day limitation does not apply. Except as provided in this subsection the seller may not base a right to reclaim goods on the buyer's fraudulent or innocent misrepresentation of solvency or of intent to pay.

(3) The seller's right to reclaim under subsection (2) is subject to the rights of a buyer in ordinary course or other good faith purchaser or lien creditor under this Article (Section 2–403). Successful reclamation of goods excludes all other remedies with respect to them.

In 1966 the Permanent Editorial Board recommended the deletion of the words "or lien creditor" from subsection (3),[33] and the Section with that deletion now appears in the 1972 Official Text of the Code, which is the present authoritative version.

In the 1962 Code it was by no means clear what was meant by the phrase in subsection (3) "or lien creditor under this Article (Section 2–403)." The only reference to lien creditors in Section 2–403 contained a cross-reference to Articles 9, 6, and 7, and the only section in Article 9 dealing with the rights of lien creditors dealt only with

vision, see Braucher, Reclamation of Goods From a Fraudulent Buyer, 65 Mich.L.Rev. 1281 (1967).

33. Uniform Commercial Code, Permanent Editorial Board, Report No. 3, p. 3 (1966). The change reflected the same deletion in California, Cal. Comm.Code § 2702(3) (West 1964); Connecticut, Conn.Gen.Stat.Ann. § 42a–2–702(3) (Supp.1974); Illinois, Ill. Ann.Stat. ch. 26, § 2–702(3) (Smith-Hurd 1963); Maine, Me.Rev.Stat.Ann. tit. 11, § 2–702(3) (1964); New Jersey, N.J.Stat.Ann. § 12A:2–702(3) (Supp. 1974); New Mexico, N.M.Stat.Ann. § 50A–1–702(3) (1962); and New York, N.Y.U.C.C. § 2–702(3) (McKinney 1964). Other states have followed suit: Arkansas, Ark.Stat.Ann. § 85–2–702(3) (Supp.1973); Kansas, Kan.Stat.Ann. 84–2–702(3) (Supp.1974); Minnesota, Minn.Stat.Ann. § 336.2–702(3) (Supp. 1974); North Carolina, N.C.Gen.Stat. § 25–2–702(3) (Supp.1974); North Dakota, N.D.Cent.Code 41–02–81(3) (1968); Oklahoma, Okl.Stat.Ann. tit. 12A § 2–702(3) (Supp.1974); Wisconsin, Wis.

Stat.Ann. 402.702(3) (Supp.1974); Wyoming, Wyo.Stat.Ann. § 34–2–702(3) (Cum.Supp.1973).

It may be assumed that the deletion of the words "or lien creditor" had the blessing of Professor Karl N. Llewellyn, Chief Reporter for the Code, who was Professor of Law at the University of Chicago at the time Illinois enacted the Code with the deletion. The change was made because of the decision in In re Kravitz, 278 F.2d 820 (3d Cir. 1960), which at first glance emasculated the seller's right of reclamation in bankruptcy. There were, of course, differing views on the advisability of the deletion. Compare Hawkland, The Relative Rights of Lien Creditors and Defrauded Sellers—Amending the Uniform Commercial Code to Conform to the Kravitz Case, 67 Com.L.J. 86 (1962) with Shanker, A Reply to the Proposed Amendment of UCC Section 2–702(3): Another View of Lien Creditor's Rights vs. Rights of a Seller to an Insolvent, 14 W.Res.L. Rev. 93 (1962).

conflicts between lien creditors and secured parties, not unpaid sellers of goods on credit.[34] This was not, however, the only confusing reference in the text of the Code to a section which was not apparently on point. Another example is Section 9–307 where subsection (2), dealing with buyers of consumer goods who take free of certain perfected security interests, contains a confusing cross-reference to fixtures and to Section 9–313, when that section does not deal wtih conflicts between buyers and fixture secured parties; the cross-reference is deleted in the 1972 Official Text.

It has been generally thought that the 1962 version of Section 2–702(3) had the effect of referring the resolution of conflicts between lien creditors and unpaid sellers to non-Code law, and this interpretation has led to various results depending on the supposed non-Code law of the state where the conflict arose.[35]

Certain requirements of Section 2–702(2) must be emphasized. The section does not deal with a cash sale where a bouncing check is given in payment for the goods.[36] The basic requirement is a sale

34. The first subsection of section 2–403 deals with the title acquired by purchasers of goods. "Purchaser" is broadly defined in section 1–201(33) but it includes only voluntary transactions. Section 2–403(2) deals with buyers in ordinary course of business where there has been an "entrusting" of the possession of goods to a merchant who deals in that kind of goods, and subsection (3) defines "entrusting." Subsection (4) states: "[T]he rights of other purchasers of goods and of lien creditors are governed by the Articles on Secured Transactions (Article 9), Bulk Transfers (Article 6) and Documents of Title (Article 7)." Nothing in articles 6 and 7 touches the problem of lien creditors versus reclaiming sellers. With the deletion of "or lien creditor" from section 2–702(3) the cross-reference makes sense, since section 2–403 covers the general problems of buyers in ordinary course and good faith purchasers. It is true, however, that the definition of "purchaser" includes a secured party, and it raises the possibility of the buyer's after-acquired property being subjected to a perfected security interest which is entitled to priority over the reclaiming seller. *See In re* Daley, Inc., 17 UCC Rep.Serv. 433 (D.Mass. 1975) (in bankruptcy); *In re* Hayward Woolen Co., 3 UCC Rep.Serv. 1107 (D. Mass.1967) (in bankruptcy); First-Cit-

izens Bank & Trust Co. v. Academic Archives, Inc., 10 N.C.App. 619, 179 S. E.2d 850 (1971). *Cf. In re* American Food Purveyors, Inc., 17 UCC Rep. Serv. 436 (N.D.Ga.1974) (in bankruptcy).

35. Compare *In re* Kravitz, 278 F.2d 820 (3d Cir. 1960) and *In re* Eastern Supply Co., 1 UCC Rep.Serv. 151 (W. D.Pa.1963), affirmed, 331 F.2d 852 (3d Cir. 1964) with *In re* Mel Golde Shoes, Inc., 403 F.2d 658 (6th Cir. 1968) and *In re* Royalty Homes, Inc., 8 UCC Rep.Serv. 61 (E.D.Tenn.1970) (in bankruptcy). *See generally* Kennedy, The Trustee in Bankruptcy under the Uniform Commercial Code: Some Problems Suggested by Articles 2 and 9, 14 Rutgers L.Rev. 518, 521–27 (1960). *See also* Kennedy, The Interest of a Reclaiming Seller Under Article 2 of the Code, 30 Bus.Law 833 (1975); Edelman and Weintraub, Seller's Right to Reclaim Property Under Section 2–702(2) of the Code Under the Bankruptcy Act: Fact or Fiction, 32 Bus. Law. 1165 (1977).

36. Section 2–507(2) states:
Where payment is due and demanded on the delivery to the buyer of goods or documents of title, his right as against the seller to retain or dispose of them is conditioned upon his making the payment due.

of goods on credit to a buyer who is insolvent at the time the goods are received. While the Code's definition of when a person is "insolvent" encompasses the Bankruptcy Act's definition,[37] the Code also includes those who cannot pay debts in the ordinary course of business or those who cannot pay debts as they become due.[38] The triggering event of the seller's right of reclamation is not the buyer's insolvency (in the Code sense), but the receipt of goods while insolvent. The seller's right of reclamation must be exercised by a demand made within ten days after the goods are received by the buyer—and here, as elsewhere in the Code, "receipt" apparently means actual and not constructive receipt of the goods—unless a misrepresentation of solvency has been made in writing to this seller within three months before the goods are delivered. This statutory remedy is exclusive, and in the event of successful reclamation, all other remedies with respect to the goods are excluded.

How the demand must be made is not explicitly stated, but there must be some kind of demand.[39] An oral request may not be adequate.[40] The statute does not expressly state what is required for a written misrepresentation of solvency to the seller within three months before delivery in order to extend the ten-day period, nor is it required in terms that the misrepresentation be made [41] directly by the buyer to the seller, thus leaving open the possibility of a communication from a credit-reporting agency,[42] which might or might not be grounded on information provided by the buyer. If the ten-day limitation does not apply, no other time limitation is stated. While there has been some disagreement about what constitutes a misrepresentation of solvency,[43] it seems to be rather generally accepted that there must

---

Section 2–511(3) states:

Subject to the provisions of this Act on the effect of an instrument on an obligation (Section 3–802), payment by check is conditional and is defeated as between the parties by dishonor of the check on due presentment.

37. The Bankruptcy Act states:
A person shall be deemed insolvent within the provisions of this Act whenever the aggregate of his property, exclusive of any property which he may have conveyed, transferred, concealed, removed, or permitted to be concealed or removed, with intent to defraud, hinder, or delay his creditors, shall not at a fair valuation be sufficient in amount to pay his debts. Bankruptcy Act, § 1(19), 11 U.S.C.A. § 1 (19).

38. § 1–201(23).

39. *In re* Helms Veneer Corp., 287 F. Supp. 840 (W.D.Va.1968); *See In re* Kirks Kabinets, Inc., 15 UCC Rep. Serv. 746 (N.D.Ga.1974) (in bankruptcy).

40. *See In re* Behring & Behring, 5 UCC Rep.Serv. 600 (N.D.Tex.1968) (in bankruptcy).

41. "Made" refers to the time when the statement is presented, not to its date. *In re* Bel Air Carpets, Inc., 452 F.2d 1210 (9th Cir. 1971). On this point, the second paragraph of Official Comment 2 to § 2–702 appears to be clearly in error.

42. *See* Manly v. Ohio Shoe Co., 25 F. 2d 384 (4th Cir. 1928).

43. It has been held that purchase orders submitted by a buyer to a seller

be some demonstrated reliance by the seller (or possibly a person in the position of a seller) on whatever the writing is.[44]

While it may be arguable whether a check is a written representation of solvency, it seems to be ordinarily believed by those who accept checks in payment for goods that the issuers are at least solvent enough that the particular checks will be paid by the payor banks when presented. In fact, the issuer of a check "engages" that if it is dishonored and if he is given "any necessary notice of dishonor or protest he will pay the amount of the draft to any holder or to any indorser who takes it up." [45] It is difficult to see why this engagement is not a misrepresentation of solvency if the check is not paid because of insolvency on presentment.

Some of the problems connected with Section 2–702 are exemplified by the Bankruptcy Court's opinion in *In re Federal's, Inc.*[46] Here Panasonic sold and delivered goods to Federal's, Inc. on August 10; Federal's filed under Chapter XI of the Bankruptcy Act on August 16; and on August 18 by letters and telegrams to the buyer and to the receiver Panasonic asserted its right to reclaim the goods pursuant to Section 2–702. The right of reclamation was denied in the Bankruptcy Court.

After pointing out that "the drafters must have been aware that Article 2 was intended to be a complete revision and modernization of the Uniform Sales Act . . . ." [47] the court went on to state:

> [I]f I were free to do so, I would hold that rights of a reclaiming seller as against a lien creditor is [sic] to be determined solely by reference to the Uniform Commercial Code and the Bankruptcy Act and I would further hold that since by reference to the Code a defrauded seller's right to reclaim is divest-

---

did not constitute misrepresentation of solvency, *In re* Regency Furniture, Inc., 7 UCC Rep.Serv. 1381 (E.D.Tenn. 1970) (in bankruptcy), although common sense might suggest that one who orders goods impliedly warrants an ability to pay for them. A letter admitting inability to pay bills as they matured was not a misrepresentation of solvency; it was, in fact, the reverse. *In re* Units, Inc., 3 UCC Rep. Serv. 46 (D.Conn.1965) (in bankruptcy).

44. *See In re* Bar-Wood, Inc., 15 UCC Rep.Serv. 828 (S.D.Fla.1974) (in bankruptcy); *In re* Fairfield Elevator Co., Inc., 14 UCC Rep.Serv. 96 (S.D.Iowa 1973) (in bankruptcy); *In re* Haugabook Auto Co., Inc., 9 UCC Rep.Serv. 954 (M.D.Ga.1971) (in bankruptcy), af-

firmed 9 UCC Rep.Serv. 1095 (N.D.Ga. 1971), where the writing was a financial statement; Theo. Hamm Brewing Co. v. First Trust & Savings Bank, 103 Ill.App.2d 190, 242 N.E.2d 911 (1968), where checks were given.

45. § 3–413(2). *See* Amoco Pipeline Co. v. Admiral Crude Oil Corp., 490 F.2d 114 (10th Cir. 1974).

46. 12 UCC Rep.Serv. 1142 (E.D.Mich. 1973) (in bankruptcy), affirmed 402 F. Supp. 1357, reversed *sub nom. In re* Federal's Inc. v. Matsushita Electric Corp. of America, 553 F.2d 509 (6th Cir. 1977).

47. 12 UCC Rep.Serv. at 1146 (footnote omitted).

ed by a lien creditor, the trustee, since he is given the right of a lien creditor by Section 70c of the Bankruptcy Act must prevail. However, since the Sixth Circuit Court of Appeals in In re Mel Golde Shoes, Inc. held to the contrary, I am permitted no such freedom.[48]

As was noted, the Sixth Circuit in Mel Golde looked to non-Code Kentucky law to hold that the reclaiming seller prevailed over the lien creditor.[49] Under non-Code Michigan law, the referee thought that

[a] seller was entitled to rescind and recover goods sold by the buyer's bankrupt estate only if he established that the buyer did not intend to pay for the purchased goods. . . . [50]

Since the buyer was apparently conceded to have intended to pay for the goods, Panasonic's right of reclamation under non-Code Michigan law would have been defeated, but it was felt that the Code estab-

---

48. *Id.* at 1148 (footnotes and citation omitted).

49. 403 F.2d at 660.

50. 12 UCC Rep.Serv. at 1150, citing John Heidsik Co. v. Rechter, 291 Mich. 708, 289 N.W. 304 (1939) and Elbro Knitting Mills v. Schwartz, 30 F.2d 10 (6th Cir. 1929).

The court stated, quoting from the Heidsik case, that:

the mere failure of a vendee to disclose to his vendor the fact that he is insolvent, and not able to pay his debts, does not constitute fraud entitling the vendor to reclaim the goods from the trustee in bankruptcy.

291 Mich. at 710, 289 N.W. at 305. This quotation is inaccurate, however. It is not clear from the facts of the case whether the unpaid seller attempted to replevy the goods before or after the filing in bankruptcy. It is clear that the seller neither asked for nor received any financial report from the buyer at the time the sale was contracted, and that the buyer may have been solvent at that time but insolvent at the time of receipt of the goods. It is conjectural whether this case stands for anything today; the statement of facts is very hazy. It seems impossible that any court would ever have allowed an insolvent buyer to retain goods as against the

unpaid seller, and it is uncertain when the filing in bankruptcy took place, for if it did not occur before the replevin action it is difficult to see how the trustee's rights would have been greater than the buyer's; the basis for the trustee's right is unstated. In Elbro it was clear to the court of appeals, despite the referee and district court to the contrary, that the unpaid seller was entitled to prevail over the trustee in bankruptcy as to the proceeds of the goods received by the buyer shortly before bankruptcy. (The goods were sold by consent at a receiver's sale.) From a detailed recital of facts the court concluded that

we are constrained to believe that an analysis of the evidence makes it clear to a moral certainty at least that the bankrupt, without intention or expectation of paying therefor, induced petitioner to part with his goods by concealing both his insolvency and his intention.

30 F.2d at 10. A fair reading of the opinion shows that the buyer's "intention" was divined by the court from actions which could only be presumed to show the fraudulent intent of not paying for the goods, because it was obviously impossible for the buyer to have any sensible expectation of being able to pay for them. The opinion suggests that a seller would be entitled to rely on a report issued by a credit reporting agency.

lished "an irrebuttable presumption of fraud from the mere receipt of purchased goods while insolvent. . . ." so that "in the absence of other defenses . . . the court would be compelled to grant the reclamation petition."[51]

This analysis ignores the non-Code Michigan law on the rights of lien creditors versus reclaiming sellers, which is what subsection 2–702(3) of the 1962 Code (then in force in Michigan) is about. The thrust of subsection 2–702(2) is toward the conflict between the seller and the buyer where the third parties enumerated in subsection (3) have not intervened. That is, the receipt of goods by an insolvent buyer might give the seller an unqualified right to reclaim as against the buyer, regardless of fraud, but where the rights of third parties have intervened, the seller's rights of reclamation may be qualified.

> The court then went on to state that
> the Receiver contends that the aforementioned Code pro-
> vision attempts to confer a priority in violation of Section
> 64A [sic] of the Act and that such provision also creates a
> lien that is invalid as against the trustee by virtue of Section
> 67(c)(1)A of the Act. . . .[52]

It was felt that section 2–702 "literally and practically gives to a specified class of creditors a priority over general creditors upon the insolvency of a debtor . . .."[53] In a footnote to this portion of his opinion, it was stated:

> The event that generally triggers the demand for recla-
> mation is the filing of a petition in bankruptcy. In all but one
> of the reclamation petitions filed in this case the demand for
> the reclamation was not made until after the filing of the peti-
> tion in bankruptcy.[54]

It may be that the bankruptcy filing brought Federal's insolvency to the attention of creditors and thereby precipitated the filing of the reclamation petitions, but the statutory right of reclamation (subject to the rights, if any, of lien creditors) was triggered by the debtor's receipt of goods on credit while insolvent, and not by the subsequent bankruptcy filing.

---

51. 12 UCC Rep.Serv. at 1150. Official Comment 2 to section 2–702 states in part: "Subsection (2) takes as its base line the proposition that any receipt of goods on credit by an insolvent buyer amounts to a tacit business misrepresentation of solvency and therefore is fraudulent as against the particular seller." Uniform Commercial Code § 2–702, Comment 2. No doubt what the Comment states is entirely in accord with the ordinary view of such a transaction, and it is difficult to see how any other view could reasonably be taken.

52. 12 UCC Rep.Serv. at 1151.

53. *Id.*

54. *Id.* at 1152 n. 22.

The court, then, relying on cases arising under the civil law of Louisiana and Puerto Rico,[55] found the seller's reclamation right under Section 2–702(2) to be a statutory lien which was invalid under Section 67c(1)(A) of the Bankruptcy Act. As was stated:

> Since the provision of the Uniform Commercial Code in issue here is in conflict with the Bankruptcy Act it has no application in this proceeding. Panasonic's right to reclaim its property therefore must be determined by reference to Michigan law other than the Code. Under such law reclamation was permitted only if the seller established that the buyer did not intend to pay for the goods . . .. Since Panasonic concedes that Federal's did not have any intention not to pay for the purchased goods Panasonic's reclamation petition is denied.[56]

In fact, it is not Section 2–702(2) which is involved here, for there is no federal question involved in determining the rights between seller and buyer. It is subsection (3) of Section 2–702 which is at issue and it is this subsection which gives rights to lien creditors. While it is difficult to be at all certain about what the court really held, if the import of the decision is to hold invalid the seller's reclamation right as against the lien creditor under subsection 2–702(3), then the lien creditor—the trustee in bankruptcy here—would have no rights, because the lien creditor under Section 70c has rights determined by state law, and if the state law giving those rights (if any) is invalid, then there are no rights. There cannot be any federal question raised about a state statute giving rights to an unpaid seller to reclaim goods from a buyer. The only problem arises where, as here, the rights of a lien creditor intervene; what, if any, those rights are must be determined by state law.

Section 67c(1)(A) of the Bankruptcy Act invalidates, as against the trustee,

> every statutory lien which first becomes effective upon the insolvency of the debtor, or upon distribution or liquidation of his property, or upon execution against his property levied at the instance of one other than the lienor.[57]

55. *In re* Trahan, 283 F.Supp. 620 (W.D.La.1968), affirmed, 402 F.2d 796 (5th Cir. 1968), certiorari denied 394 U.S. 930 (1969); *In re* Nieves & Co., 446 F.2d 188 (1st Cir. 1971). It is perhaps an unintentional commentary on the general law in this area that the only two cases that could be found to support the decision were from Puerto Rico and Louisiana, and whether those cases are supportive may be conjectural.

56. 12 UCC Rep.Serv. at 1153 (citations omitted).

57. Bankruptcy Act § 67c(1)(A), 11 U.S. C.A. § 107(c)(1)(A).

The term "statutory lien" is defined to mean

> a lien arising solely by force of statute upon specified circum-
> stances or conditions, but shall not include any lien provided
> by or dependent upon an agreement to give security, whether
> or not such lien is also provided by or is also dependent upon
> statute and whether or not the agreement or lien is made
> fully effective by statute.[58]

It may be conceded that, unfortunately, the language of the Code
and the Bankruptcy Act may not effectively mesh. The Code does
not use the term "lien" except in the general sense of "mechanic's
lien"; [59] the term is "security interest" when a consensual arrangement is meant. But this Code usage does suggest that the seller's
right of reclamation under Section 2–702 is not intended to be a
security interest, since it is not so denominated, and the transaction is
on open credit so that clearly no security is contemplated.

If it could be said that a "statutory lien" is created by the seller's
right of reclamation in Section 2–702, then some difficult problems
arise as a matter of statutory interpretation. Clearly the seller's right
is not dependent on the buyer's agreement to give security (or the
seller's retention of title in a conditional sale contract). But if Section 2–702 creates (unintentionally) a Code security interest (or a
Bankruptcy Act lien), then Section 9–113 comes into play. This section provides that if a security interest (i. e., lien under the Bankruptcy Act) arises solely under Article 2, then no security agreement
is necessary, no filing is required for perfection, and the secured
party's rights on default are governed by Article 2—so long as the
debtor does not have or does not lawfully obtain possession of the
goods. For the seller to claim a right of reclamation, the buyer must
have possession of the goods, but there can be an issue about whether
the possession was "lawfully" obtained. While this test is vague, the
smell of fraud is in the air when a debtor acquires goods on open credit
at the verge of applying for insolvency relief. While one may occasionally hesitate to question publicly the bona fides of an insolvent who
files for relief, in bankruptcy or otherwise, it simply surpasses belief
that a buyer can honestly expect—quite apart from any presumed intention—to pay for goods while insolvent, and no seller would knowingly deliver goods in such circumstances. There is an overwhelming
aura of fraud here, whether it is actual or constructive or however one
wishes to characterize it. The situation smells. The possession of

---

58. Bankruptcy Act § 1(29a), 11 U.S.
C.A. § 1(29a).

59. § 9–310. § 9–102(2) states:
"This Article does not apply to statutory liens except as provided in Section 9–310."

goods in some sense cannot be "lawfully" obtained,[60] and nothing in federal law says that it is.

It has been traditionally held that where buyers acquired goods while insolvent, sellers might reclaim those goods on the basis of fraud. A trustee in bankruptcy of a fraudulent buyer had no right to hold those goods as against the unpaid seller.[61] The seller's right of reclamation was not treated as creating a lien; it was not a preference,[62] and it certainly was not a priority. Liens traditionally attach to designated goods giving lienors rights in the goods, while priorities arise in the distribution of funds.[63] The bankruptcy problem with state-created priorities was just that they were priorities in the distribution of funds arising on insolvency, even though they might have been designated as liens. They did not arise from lien interests in property which antedated insolvency. It was in part this problem with which Congress attempted to cope in enacting the current version of Section 67c of the Bankruptcy Act.[64]

No one had in mind the unpaid seller's right of reclamation when Section 67c was drafted. The effect of Section 2–702 is probably to cut back the unpaid seller's rights, since successful reclamation probably excludes other remedies such as claims for a deficiency and costs of reclamation.[65] A buyer who receives goods on credit within ten days of bankruptcy has no sensible expectation of paying for them, regardless of any presumed intention. If the seller cannot reclaim

---

60. *See, e. g.*, McAuliffe & Burke Co. v. Gallagher, 258 Mass. 215, 154 N.E. 755 (1927), where a reclaiming seller of goods to a fraudulent buyer prevailed over an intervening attaching creditor; the buyer did not "lawfully obtain possession."

61. *See, e. g.*, Manly v. Ohio Shoe Co., 25 F.2d 384 (4th Cir. 1928), where Judge Parker stated:
Where goods are obtained by fraud of the bankrupt, the seller may rescind the contract of sale and reclaim them if he can identify them in the hands of the trustee. This is on the theory that fraud renders all contracts voidable, and that neither in law nor in morals would the trustee be justified in holding goods obtained by the fraud of the bankrupt for the benefit of other creditors . . . .

Id. at 385. *See also* California Conserving Co. v. D'Avanzo, 62 F.2d 528 (2d Cir. 1933) (L. Hand. J.).

Can a traditional remedy become an invalid "statutory lien" the moment it

is—and simply because it has been—embodied in a statute?

62. *See* Manly v. Ohio Shoe Co., 25 F.2d 384 (4th Cir. 1928).

63. *See, e. g.*, Elliott v. Bumb, 356 F.2d 749 (9th Cir. 1966). *See generally* Henson, Liens—Seen Through a Glass, Darkly, 2 B.C.Ind. & Com.L.Rev. 85 (1960).

64. Bankruptcy Act § 67(c), 11 U.S.C.A. § 107(c). *See generally* Kennedy, The Bankruptcy Amendments of 1966, 1 Ga.L.Rev. 149 (1967); King, Statutory Liens—1966 Amendments of Section 67 of the Bankruptcy Act, 55 Ky.L.J. 542 (1967); Marsh, Triumph or Tragedy? The Bankruptcy Act Amendments of 1966, 42 Wash.L.Rev. 681 (1967); Seligson, Treatment of Statutory Liens in Bankruptcy—The 1966 Amendments of Section 67b and c. 27 Fed.B.J. 111 (1967).

65. § 2–702(3) (1972 version) (second sentence). See Countryman, Buyers and Sellers of Goods in Bankruptcy, 1 N.M.L.Rev. 435, 451 (1971).

the goods, its remedy is essentially nil in either straight bankruptcy proceedings [66] or in rehabilitation proceedings.[67]   To pretend that there is any benefit to ordinary trade creditors in straight bankruptcy by depriving unpaid sellers of the right of reclamation,[68] or to suggest that there is any reason to benefit trade creditors, is to ignore the facts of life.   Goods supplied on open credit to buyers on the verge of bankruptcy will presumably be sold to benefit basically everyone except unsecured creditors, and principally to benefit those persons involved in the administration of the estate.[69]   As a social policy, this result is insupportable.

Aside from the incongruity of suddenly finding the seller's right of reclamation to be a statutory lien in spite of a long history to the contrary, Section 67c(1)(A) invalidates only statutory liens which first become effective on the insolvency of the debtor,[70] and clearly "insolvency" is used in its defined sense:

A person shall be deemed insolvent within the provisions of this title whenever the aggregate of his property, exclusive

66. For the fiscal year ending June 30, 1969, there were 184,930 bankruptcies filed, of which 15,430 were business bankruptcies. Administrative Office of the United States Courts, Tables of Bankruptcy Statistics, 4 (1969). A total of 190,742 cases were closed during that year, of which 22,355 were asset cases in which there was some distribution to some class of creditors; 23,777 were nominal asset cases in which there was no distribution to creditors, and 107,481 were no-asset cases. *Id.* at 9–10. In asset cases a distribution of 76.4 percent was paid on secured claims, while the distribution was 7.8 percent on unsecured claims. *Id.*, Table F6. If an unpaid seller could not reclaim the goods and had to present an unsecured claim, the seller in an average asset case would receive less than eight cents per dollar claimed, and about 90 percent of all bankruptcies are no-asset cases.

67. The plight of some secured creditors in rehabilitation proceedings was forcefully impressed on the bar in *In re* Yale Express System, Inc. 250 F. Supp. 249 (S.D.N.Y.), reversed and remanded 370 F.2d 433 (2d Cir. 1966), affirmed 384 F.2d 990 (2d Cir. 1967). *See* particularly the dissent of Judge Lumbard, 370 F.2d at 439.

68. In asset cases concluded during the fiscal year ending June 30, 1969, se-

cured claims totaling $49,082,828 were allowed and $37,499,860 was paid on these claims. Unsecured claims in the amount of $397,152,793 were allowed, and $30,810,542 was paid on these claims. Administrative Office of the United States Courts, Tables of Bankruptcy Statistics, Table F6 (1969). If all secured claims were invalidated and became unsecured claims, then the unsecured (including the formerly secured) claimants would still be getting less than sixteen cents per dollar claimed.

69. The problem of administrative expenses, which ordinarily consume about 25 percent of realizations in asset cases, has long been a matter of concern. See Warren, Address, 37 Ref.J. 4 (1963). Chief Justice Warren's suggestion of a bankruptcy administrative office outside the judicial branch found favor with the Commission on the Bankruptcy Laws of the United States. See Kennedy, Restructuring Bankruptcy Administration: The Proposals of the Commission on Bankruptcy Laws, 30 Bus.Law. 399 (1975). *See generally* D. Stanley and M. Girth, Bankruptcy: Problem, Process, Reform (1971).

70. Bankruptcy Act § 67c(1)(A), 11 U.S.C.A. § 107(c)(1)(A).

of any property which he may have conveyed, transferred, concealed, removed, or permitted to be concealed or removed with intent to defraud, hinder, or delay his creditors shall not at a fair valuation be sufficient in amount to pay his debts.[71]

The right of reclamation under Section 2–702 arises when the buyer has received goods on credit while insolvent in the Code sense, and the Code definition covers inability to pay debts as they mature and a failure to pay debts in the ordinary course of business, as well as the Bankruptcy Act's test.[72]   Therefore, the seller's right does not necessarily become effective only at the date the bankruptcy petition is filed, or, more properly, it never becomes effective at that time. The right exists from the time the buyer received the goods, if insolvency in the Code sense existed at that time, and it is in no sense dependent upon the initiation of any insolvency proceedings.   If the trustee could ever show the buyer was in fact solvent when the goods were received, despite a bankruptcy filing within ten days thereafter, the right of reclamation would be defeated.   No doubt this can never be shown because it would be contrary to fact, and in many cases unfortunate sellers are alerted to their buyers' financial condition only by bankruptcy filings.

Of course, the seller's right of reclamation is dependent in part on the buyer's insolvency, and the Code's definition of insolvency is considerably broader than the Bankruptcy Act's definition.   There is, however, no statistical evidence of the frequency with which the right of reclamation is exercised in other than bankruptcy proceedings; nor, for that matter, is there any way of knowing how often the right is exercised in bankruptcy.   The reported cases are few in number.

Similarly there is no way of knowing, under the 1962 version of Section 2–702(3), how often lien creditors other than trustees in bankruptcy attempted to prevent reclamation by sellers.   The term "lien creditor" is defined to include creditors who have acquired liens on the property by attachment, levy, or the like, and assignees for the benefit of creditors are included as well as trustees in bankruptcy.[73]

The effect of accepting this expanded statutory lien view would probably be to invalidate as a statutory lien the seller's right to stop goods in transit, a right that has existed so long that it ought to be beyond question.[74]   Section 2–705 gives a seller the right to stop de-

71. Bankruptcy Act § 1(19), 11 U.S.C.A. § 1(19).

72. § 1–201(23).

73. § 9–301(3).

74. The right of stoppage *in transitu*, as it used to be called, was contained in section 57 of the Uniform Sales Act, promulgated in 1906, and section 57 was based on the English Sale of

livery of goods in possession of a carrier or other bailee when the seller discovers that the buyer is insolvent, provided the conditions of the section are met. The provision is not conditioned on a sale on credit or a cash sale (for which a bad check might have been or could be given); but if the seller had in fact been paid, there would be no reason to stop the shipment. Nevertheless, the operative requirements of the section are that the buyer is insolvent and that the goods are in a bailee's possession.[75] Here again, insolvency in the Code sense cannot be equated merely with bankruptcy. But if courts cannot read the Code more carefully in the future than some have in the past, a valuable seller's right will go down the drain with no compensating advantage to society. And, moreover, what is in fact a change in the Bankruptcy Act will be achieved without the amendment of the Act by Congress.

Similarly, what happens to the seller's right to reclaim the goods in the case of a cash sale where the buyer gives a bad check—if by chance the buyer quickly becomes involved in bankruptcy proceedings? The buyer has no right to retain the goods as against the seller.[76] Is the seller's reclamation right to be treated as a statutory lien? The seller's right is not in terms dependent on the buyer's insolvency, but it may well be the case that insolvency precipitates the dishonor of a check simply because of inadequate funds on deposit. Alternatively, payment may be refused by the bank because bankruptcy has intervened,[77] so that in either case insolvency is in fact a triggering factor of the seller's rights. Section 2–507 states no ten-day or other limit on the exercise of the seller's right to reclaim,[78] although any unnecessary delay in exercising the right might be construed as a waiver.[79]

A problem with Section 2–507 is that it does not state the unpaid seller's remedy, so that recourse to Section 2–702 may in fact be

---

Goods Act, § 44. 1A U.L.A. § 57, Commissioners' Note. It has been said to be "declaratory of settled existing law." *In re* Stork & Co., 271 F. 279, 280 (2d Cir. 1921).

75. § 2–705.

76. §§ 2–507, 2–511(3).

77. Under section 70a of the Bankruptcy Act, 11 U.S.C.A. § 110(a), it would appear that a bank has no right to pay prebankruptcy checks issued by its depositor which are presented for payment after bankruptcy, but this rigorous rule is apparently tempered by equitable considerations. Bank of Marin v. England, 385 U.S. 99, 103, 87 S.Ct. 274, 277, 17 L.Ed.2d 197 (1966).

78. The official comment to this section states: "The provision of this Article for a ten day limit [§ 2–702(2)] within which the seller may reclaim goods delivered on credit to an insolvent buyer is also applicable here." Uniform Commercial Code § 2–507 Comment 3. There is no statutory basis for this assertion. It has, however, been accepted by some courts. *See, e. g., In re* Helms Veneer Corp., 287 F.Supp. 840 (W.D.Va.1968). *Cf. In re* Bell Oldsmobile, Inc., 4 Bankr. Ct.Dec. 702 (1978).

79. *In re* Colacci's of America, Inc., 490 F.2d 1118, 1121 (10th Cir. 1974).

necessary, although a statutory cross reference ought to have been provided so that the seller's right to reclaim the goods would have a firm basis. All that the section provides on its face is that the buyer's right to retain or dispose of the goods "is conditional upon his making the payment due." If we assume that the unpaid seller has a right of reclamation and that the ten-day period of Section 2–702(2) is applicable, then a seller who has made a timely demand should be able to get its goods back from the buyer.[80] However, a good faith purchaser for value would cut off any right of the seller to pursue the goods,[81] and when the goods come into the buyer's possession they might be subjected to the rights of a prior secured party claiming an interest in after-acquired collateral,[82] but a lien creditor would ordinarily be able to reach only the buyer's equity, which in this case would presumably be nothing, in the absence of payment.[83] Nothing in Section 2–507 speaks of the rights of lien creditors, nor does anything in Revised Section 2–702(3) give rights to lien creditors, but even if the earlier version of Section 2–702(3) should be in force, it is difficult to see how lien credtiors could be given greater rights than those possessed by the debtor-buyer. Some distinction should be drawn between goods supposedly purchased for cash and those purchased on credit, when derivative rights are being asserted. As Section 9–311 provides, the debtor's rights in collateral may be reached by attachment, levy, garnishment, or other judicial process, but if the debtor has no rights in goods acquired in a cash sale but in fact not paid for, then there is nothing for the lien creditor to reach.

When the possibility of invalidating the seller's right of reclamation as a statutory lien was first enunciated in the *Federal's* case at the Bankruptcy Court level, this view naturally found some followers

---

80. *In re* Mort Co., 208 F.Supp. 309 (E.D.Pa.1962). Where the demand is long delayed, clearly there should be no right of reclamation. *In re* Samuels & Co., Inc., 526 F.2d 1238 (5th Cir. 1976). *Cf. In re* Richardson Homes Corp., 18 UCC Rep.Serv. 384 (N.D.Ind.1975) (in bankruptcy), where there is some apparent confusion as to the seller's remedies. In Ranchers & Farmers Livestock Auction Co. v. Honey, —— Colo.App. ——, 552 P.2d 313 (1976), the reclaimant was held to be entitled to the proceeds of the goods which had been improperly resold.

81. § 2–403(1)(b).

82. United States v. Wyoming Nat'l Bank of Caspar, 505 F.2d 1064 (10th

Cir. 1974). Even an unperfected security interest was held to have priority over a reclaiming seller in Guy Martin Buick, Inc. v. Colorado Springs Nat'l Bank, 184 Colo. 166, 519 P.2d 354 (1974). *See also* Evans Products Co. v. Jorgensen, 245 Or. 362, 421 P.2d 978 (1966); Stumbo v. Paul B. Hult Lumber Co., 251 Or. 20, 444 P.2d 564 (1968).

83. *In re* Mort Co., 208 F.Supp. 309 (E.D.Pa.1962). However, if after a cash sale the seller recasts the sale into a secured transaction, the reclaiming seller's rights will be subject to the rights of an intervening lien creditor pursuant to § 9–301(1)(b). Ranchers & Farmers Livestock Auction Co. v. First State Bank of Tulia, Texas, 531 S.W.2d 167 (Tex.Civ.App.1975).

elsewere,[84] but this decision was ultimately reversed by the Sixth Circuit[85] in an opinion which is in general agreement with the views of the Ninth Circuit[86] so it is possible that this particular issue is temporarily laid to rest, at least in several circuits.[87] While the seller's right of reclamation may not be considered a statutory lien in some circuits at the present time, an understanding of the background of this issue may provide a basis for understanding the next analogous attack which is certain to occur even though its time, place, and theory may now be unknown.[88] The remedy of reclamation given by Section 2–702 is similar to the common law remedy of rescission, but it is greatly circumscribed as to the time during which it can be exercised, unlike common law rescission. Because reclamation operates only against particular goods, it is distinguishable from the state-created priorities which offend the Bankruptcy Act, and, as Mr. Justice Blackmun said, "It would be unjust to permit general creditors to benefit at the expense of one whose assets come into a bankrupt's possession under conditions which warrant rescission."[89]

§ 7–3. Introduction to Bankruptcy

It is often said that the acid test of a security interest is in the debtor's bankruptcy. Since bankruptcies are common today, a great

84. *In re* Giltex, Inc., 17 UCC Rep.Serv. 887 (S.D.N.Y.1975); *In re* Good Deal Supermarkets, Inc., 384 F.Supp. 887 (D.N.J.1974); *In re* Persky & Wolf, Inc., 19 UCC Rep.Serv. 812 (N.D.Ohio 1976) (in bankruptcy); *In re* Richardson Homes Corp., 18 UCC Rep. Serv. 384 (W.D.Ind.1975) (in bankruptcy); *In re* Watson's Corp., 17 UCC Rep.Serv. 423 (S.D.N.Y.1975) (in bankruptcy). *Contra, In re* Federal's, Inc. v. Matsushita Electric Corp. of America, 553 F.2d 509 (6th Cir. 1977); *In re* Telemart Enterprises, Inc., 524 F. 2d 761 (9th Cir. 1975), certiorari denied 424 U.S. 969 (1976); *In re* American Food Purveyors, Inc., 17 UCC Rep.Serv. 436 (N.D.Ga.1974) (in bankruptcy); *In re* National Bellas Hess, Inc., 17 UCC Rep.Serv. 430 (S.D.N.Y. 1975) (in bankruptcy).

85. *In re* Federal's, Inc. v. Matsushita Electric Corp. of America, 553 F.2d 509 (6th Cir. 1977).

86. *In re* Telemart Enterprises, Inc., 524 F.2d 761 (9th Cir. 1975). Whether the seller's demand was made within ten days after the buyer's receipt of the goods is, or may be thought to be,

unclear from the facts as stated by the court.

87. There have been some bankruptcy court decisions which have refused to follow *Federal's* and *Telemart*, although, of course, not in the Sixth or Ninth Circuits. *See, e. g., In re* Rigby Corp., 3 Bkcy.Ct.Dec. 1310 (D.Kan. 1977) (in bankruptcy). In *In re* Garden State Farm Supply Co., Inc., 3 Bkcy.Ct.Dec. 1195 (D.N.J.1978) (in bankruptcy), the court refused to follow *Federal's* and *Telemart* but held that while § 2–702(2) was invalid in bankruptcy under Bankruptcy Act § 67c(1)(a), this invalidity revived the common law remedy of rescission.

88. Of course, the same facts may be viewed very differently by different persons. A former queen of Spain has been described as "[g]entle and saintly or insipid and religion-ridden, according to one's lights . . . ." D. Bergamini, The Spanish Bourbons: The History of a Tenacious Dynasty 183 (1974).

89. O'Rieley v. Endicott-Johnson Corp., 297 F.2d 1, 9 (8th Cir. 1961).

many security interests are tested and for various reasons some of them do not survive. Occasionally secured parties (or their attorneys) have simply not done the proper mechanical acts which are necessary for perfection. Sometimes security interests have been perfected but may nevertheless be attacked in bankruptcy, perhaps properly and perhaps not so properly. There is, of course, some incentive for a debtor's trustee in bankruptcy to attack the validity of a security interest, for if the security interest can be set aside then the value of the security becomes part of the bankrupt's estate and is a source of funds to pay the costs of administration of the estate as well as a source available to distribute to general creditors—and the formerly secured party becomes one of the class of general creditors if the security interest can be invalidated.

At the time a bankruptcy petition is filed, the trustee in bankruptcy succeeds to the bankrupt's title to property under Section 70a of the Bankruptcy Act unless the property is exempt. In some cases the exempt property is totally exempt and in other cases the exemption may be limited to a dollar amount, but at the present time the law of the bankrupt's state generally determines what is exempt,[90] and the exemptions vary a great deal from state to state.[91] Speaking generally, state statutes governing exemptions state what property a judgment debtor may keep when a creditor who has recovered a money judgment against an individual has execution levied to collect the amount of the judgment by a sale of the debtor's property. Perhaps the most well-known example of exempt property is a homestead, but a considerable amount of personal property may also be exempt from execution. Exemptions are given only to individuals.

But while the trustee succeeds to the bankrupt's interest in property, the Bankruptcy Act gives the trustee various rights which the bankrupt could not assert. In certain circumstances the trustee can avoid—or, if it is more advantageous, the trustee can succeed to— liens obtained against the bankrupt's property by attachment, judgment, levy or other legal or equitable process within four months before the filing of the bankruptcy petition.[92] While in general it might be preferable from the trustee's point of view to avoid a lien obtained within the four month period, it is possible that after the lien was obtained the bankrupt granted an indefeasible security interest to a secured party. In this circumstance, if the lien were avoided, the security interest would be paramount, giving the trustee only the debtor's equity, if any, in the property under Section 70a, so that it is in the trustee's interest to succeed to the interest of the lienor, and this

---

90. Bankruptcy Act, § 6.

91. The Commissioners on Uniform State Laws have drafted and approv-

ed for adoption by the states a Uniform Exemptions Act.

92. Bankruptcy Act, § 67a(1), (3).

succession may have the effect of eliminating the security interest if the value of the property does not exceed the value of the lien.

The Uniform Fraudulent Conveyance Act is in force in about half of the states, and in general terms it allows creditors to avoid or disregard conveyances (including the creation of security interests) when a statutorily insolvent person has conveyed property without fair consideration or when a conveyance has been made with intent to hinder, delay, or defraud creditors. A somewhat similar provision appears as Section 67d of the Bankruptcy Act, and the trustee may ordinarily avoid these conveyances.

The usual traditional sources of attacks on security interests are Sections 70e, 70c, and 60 of the Bankruptcy Act, and some typical problems in those areas will be considered in the following pages.

§ 7–4. The Impact of Section 70e

Section 70e(1) of the Bankruptcy Act reads:

> A transfer made or suffered or obligation incurred by a debtor adjudged a bankrupt under this Act which, under any Federal or State law applicable thereto, is fraudulent as against or voidable for any other reason by any creditor of the debtor, having a claim provable under this Act, shall be null and void as against the trustee of such debtor.

If the transfer is "fraudulent," it is presumably voidable under the law of fraudulent conveyances which covers a lot of ground, beginning with the venerable Statute of Elizabeth and going on to Section 67d of the Bankruptcy Act and the Uniform Fraudulent Conveyance Act. Occasionally other state statutes are utilized.[93] But most of the literary attention paid to Section 70e through the years probably stems from *Moore* v. *Bay*.[94] This opinion is enigmatic in its breadth and brevity, but it is usually thought to stand for the proposition that if there is an unsecured creditor no matter how small his claim, who could under state law have avoided the transfer in question, the secured transaction, no matter how large, can be entirely avoided

---

93. *See, e. g.*, Engstrom v. Wiley, 191 F.2d 684 (9th Cir. 1951) where the preference provisions of a Washington statute were the basis of the trustee's claim which presumably was grounded on § 70e of the Bankruptcy Act. Whether the trustee's claim was proper in the context of this case may be subject to doubt. See V. Countryman & A. Kaufman, Commercial Law—Cases and Materials 200–201 (1970).

94. 284 U.S. 4, 52 S.Ct. 3, 76 L.Ed. 133 (1931). There is no known praise of the opinion. For a critical view *see* J. MacLachlan, Bankruptcy 330–334 (1956). Professor MacLachlan's comments about Mr. Justice Holmes, who wrote for a unanimous court, seem to be too biased to be accepted, but his views about the opinion are perhaps fair.

by the trustee. The gap creditor in *Moore* v. *Bay* apparently came into the picture before the chattel mortgagee involved filed his mortgage, for the filing was late and ineffectual against creditors whose claims accrued prior to filing although it might have been thought to be effective against creditors whose claims arose after filing. This kind of state law provision was not unusual before the Code.[95] It would not have been uncommon for a chattel mortgage act to state that the mortgage was "void," except between the parties, unless there was either a transfer of possession to the mortgagee or a recording of the mortgage "immediately" or within a stated number of days. Late filing might have been completely ineffective against third parties or it might have been ineffective only against claims arising before filing.

A pre-Code application of the gap creditor rule of *Moore* v. *Bay* may be found in *Mercantile Trust Co.* v. *Kahn*.[96] Klein gave a note for $1,678.32 to an automobile dealer, secured by a purchase money chattel mortgage on a new car, on October 18. The note and mortgage were sold to a bank which did not record the mortgage until October 25. On October 16 a shoe company sold Klein a pair of shoes on open account for $4.64; they were delivered on October 20. Klein filed a voluntary bankruptcy petition on February 11 of the following year. The shoe seller filed a claim. A second shoe seller, who sold in similar circumstances, also filed a claim. The Missouri chattel mortgage act was somewhat less than clear on when the mortgage had to be recorded, but a "reasonable" time requirement had been read into the statute by the local courts. Since an employee of the car dealer or bank could have taken the mortgage to the local recorder's office in an hour or two, the court held the delay in recording, which was blamed on the post office, to be unreasonable and the chattel mortgage void as to intervening creditors and therefore void as to the trustee, citing *Moore* v. *Bay*. An unsecured claim for $4.64 was the basis for avoiding a $1,678.32 chattel mortgage.

This possibility does not exist under the Code. Section 9–201 says: "Except as otherwise provided by this Act a security agreement is effective according to its terms between the parties, against pur-

---

95. Such statutes are found in, *e. g.*, Constance v. Harvey, 215 F.2d 571 (2d Cir. 1954), certiorari denied 348 U.S. 913, 75 S.Ct. 294, 99 L.Ed. 716, *overruled* in Lewis v. Manufacturers Nat. Bank, 364 U.S. 603, 81 S.Ct. 347, 5 L.Ed.2d 323 (1961); Hertzberg v. Associates Discount Corp., 272 F.2d 6 (6th Cir. 1959), certiorari denied 362 U.S. 950, 80 S.Ct. 861, 4 L.Ed.2d 868.

These cases involve § 70c of the Bankruptcy Act, however, and not § 70e.

96. 203 F.2d 449 (8th Cir. 1953). The relevant Missouri statute provided that no chattel mortgage would be "valid" except between the parties unless the mortgagee had possession of the property or the mortgage was filed in the required office. *Id.* at 450.

chasers of the collateral and against creditors." Section 9–301 states the rights of third parties who take priority over unperfected security interests.   Lien creditors are given rights,[97] but ordinary unsecured creditors, are given no rights at all.   Since in the circumstances involved here the trustee's rights depend on state law, he has no rights if the applicable law gives none.   Under Section 9–301(2) a purchase money secured party, who files before or within ten days after the debtor receives possession of the collateral, has priority over the rights of a lien creditor which arise between attachment and filing,[98] so that even if the creditor in the Missouri case discussed above had become a lien creditor before the bank filed, the bank would still have had priority as the assignee of a purchase money security interest [99] who perfected within ten days after the debtor got the car. The shoe seller, as a simple contract creditor, would be given no priority rights at all under the Code, and there is no reason why he should have any.   When the shoe seller extended credit he clearly did not rely on the bankrupt's unencumbered ownership of a car he did not then possess; in any event new cars are rarely purchased without security interests, as everyone should be presumed to know.

The Code very pointedly does not make unperfected security interests void or voidable; it subordinates them to the rights of the persons specified in Section 9–301(1).[1]   If a security interest were

97. *See generally* Hawkland, The Impact of the Commercial Code on the Doctrine of Moore v. Bay, 67 Com. L.J. 359 (1962) ; Kennedy, The Impact of the Uniform Commercial Code on Insolvency, Article 9, 67 Com.L.J. 113 (1962).

98. Where certificate of title laws require indication of security interests on the certificates, such procedure is the equivalent of filing. *See* § 9–302 (3), (4). Revised § 9–302(3), (4). Presumably § 9–403(1) is applicable in this context. Mercantile Trust Co. v. Kahn, 203 F.2d 449 (8th Cir. 1953), involved an automobile, and the security interest was evidenced by a chattel mortgage which had to be recorded. Under the Code, certificate of title notation is the usual means of perfection.

99. No provision in the Code expressly says that the assignee of an unperfected purchase money security interest can perfect and have the same priority as the original secured party

would have been entitled to in the same circumstances, but it is ordinarily acceptable law that a person can transfer whatever rights he has, and occasionally even more rights than he has. *See, e. g.*, §§ 2–403, 3–201, 3–202, 3–305. The Code does provide that an assignee of a perfected security interest need not file to continue the perfection against creditors of and transferees from the original debtor. § 9–302(2). To support the proposition in the text in instances not involving certificates of title, the financing statement should show the seller as secured party and the bank as assignee. Where certificates are involved, the applicable state law must be checked, but it would be an inane triumph of form over substance to require two writings where one would do. Automobile dealer financers will be able to master the local rules, no doubt. *Cf.* § 9–318, Revised § 9–318.

1. *See, e. g.*, General Lithographing Co. v. Sight & Sound Proj., Inc., 128 Ga.App. 304, 196 S.E.2d 479 (1973).

perfected late and a lien creditor acquired rights in the collateral during the period prior to perfection, the security interest would not necessarily be totally avoided; that is, if the lien creditor's claim was $1000 and the security interest was $10,000 in collateral worth that much money, if the lien creditor's claim arose within four months of bankruptcy, the trustee could succeed to the lien creditor's claim under Section 67a(1) of the Bankruptcy Act but the trustee would be entitled to $1000, not to the entire value of the collateral. If the collateral was worth more than the claims of the lien creditor and the secured party, the trustee could get the balance under Section 70a of the Bankruptcy Act, since the trustee succeeds to whatever interest the bankrupt has in the property above the value of the indefeasible claims against it.

The doctrine of *Benedict v. Ratner* [2] enjoyed a certain vogue for a period of years in some states. While no fraud in fact was found, the Court decided that under the law of New York it was fraudulent in law for an assignor of accounts to retain the right to exercise dominion over the collateral, and the trustee was entitled to the proceeds of the accounts. Whether or not Mr. Justice Brandeis read the law of New York correctly, the rule of the case has been reversed by the Code. This is the express purpose of Section 9–205:

> A security interest is not invalid or fraudulent against creditors by reason of liberty in the debtor to use, commingle or dispose of all or part of the collateral (including returned or repossessed goods) or to collect or compromise accounts, contract rights, or chattel paper, or to accept the return of goods or make repossessions, or to use, commingle or dispose of proceeds, or by reason of the failure of the secured party to require the debtor to account for proceeds or replace collateral.

In accounts or inventory financing under the Code, public notice is given by filing, but this would not necessarily have been true in pre-Code days.

§ 7–5. The Impact of Section 70c

The so-called "strong-arm" clause of Section 70c gives the trustee as of the date of bankruptcy the rights and powers of:

> (1) a creditor who obtained a judgment against the bankrupt upon the date of bankruptcy, whether or not such

2. 268 U.S. 353, 45 S.Ct. 566, 69 L.Ed. 991 (1925).

a creditor exists, (2) a creditor who upon the date of bankruptcy obtained an execution returned unsatisfied against the bankrupt, whether or not such a creditor exists, and (3) a creditor who upon the date of bankruptcy obtained a lien by legal or equitable proceedings upon all property, whether or not coming into possession or control of the court, upon which a creditor of the bankrupt upon a simple contract could have obtained a lien, whether or not such a creditor exists.

The primary impact of this section vis-a-vis the Code is in the rights given to hypothetical lien creditors at the date of bankruptcy.[3] The rights lien creditors have are stated in Section 9–301.

According to Section 9–301(3), the term "lien creditor" means a creditor who has acquired a lien on the property involved by attachment, levy or the like and includes an assignee for benefit of creditors from the time of assignment, and a trustee in bankruptcy from the date of the filing of the petition or a receiver in equity from the time of appointment.

This definition in the 1962 Code goes on to say: "Unless all the creditors represented had knowledge of the security interest such a representative of creditors is a lien creditor without knowledge even though he personally has knowledge of the security interest." This provision ties in with the provision in Section 9–301(1) (b) of the 1962 Code which gives a lien creditor priority over an imperfected security interest if he "becomes a lien creditor without knowledge of the security interest and before it is perfected." The knowledge requirement has usually been considered questionable,[4] and it has been dropped from both provisions in the revised version. It probably might as well be considered deleted, for practical reasons, in the 1962 Code when bankruptcy is involved.

While the Bankruptcy Act gives the trustee the rights of a lien creditor, what those rights are must be determined by state law, in this case the Code. So long as the security interest is perfected at the date of bankruptcy, the Code gives no right of priority to a lien creditor, actual or hypothetical.[5] There is no penalty for filing any number of days after the security interest is created, nor is the inter-

---

3.   Lewis v. Manufacturers Nat'l Bank of Detroit, 364 U.S. 603, 81 S.Ct. 347, 5 L.Ed. 323 (1961) established that the trustee's rights were to be determined at the date of bankruptcy and not at any earlier point in time.

4.   *But see* In re Komfo Products Corp., 247 F.Supp. 229 (E.D.Pa.1965). *Compare* In re Babcock Box Co., 200 F.Supp. 80 (D.C.Mass.1961).

5.   Conversely, if the security interest is not perfected, the trustee in bank-

est "void" if the filing is delayed. There is a ten-day grace period for filing in the case of purchase money security interests, and this period extends for ten days after the debtor receives possession of the collateral. If filing takes place before the end of the period, the secured party has priority over the rights of a lien creditor (or bulk transferee) which arise between the time of attachment and the time of filing (which may be a considerably longer period than ten days).[6] If bankruptcy occurs during the ten-day period and before the filing, but filing takes place before the end of the ten days, the trustee would acquire no priority because a lien creditor would have none.[7]

It perhaps should be emphasized that the ten-day grace period is in fact a grace period; there is no relation back for perfection given by Section 9–301(2), and Section 9–303(1) makes clear that perfection occurs only when a security interest has attached and the applicable steps required for perfection have been taken.

The ten-day grace period has no application to those purchase money security interests in consumer goods where no filing is required for perfection.[8] Since these security interests are automatically perfected on attachment, there is never a time during which a lien creditor could acquire priority because the security interest is never unperfected.[9]

In the normal course of events if a seller wants a purchase money security interest in consumer goods, he will retain one when the goods are sold, probably on conditional sale. This is not quite what Section 9–107 requires, however, for it simply speaks of a purchase money security interest "taken or retained by the seller." Since before the Code, a seller might have "retained" a conditional seller's interest or "taken" a chattel mortgage depending on the location of "title," it would seem reasonable to limit a purchase money security interest to one which arose at the time of sale. (This would seem to be required

---

ruptcy, having the rights of a lien creditor under § 70c of the Bankruptcy Act, is clearly entitled to priority over unperfected security interests under § 9–301(1)(b). *See, e. g.,* York v. Ottusch, 412 F.Supp. 819 (E.D.Wis. 1976). An assignment of a general intangible to secure an obligation requires filing if the assignee is to prevail over the trustee in bankruptcy under § 70c and § 9–301(1)(b). *In re* Joseph Kanner Hat Co., Inc., 482 F.2d 937 (2d Cir. 1973).

6. If the last event necessary for attachment is that the debtor must have rights in the collateral, when we are dealing with goods this may occur some time before the debtor receives them, under Article 2.

7. *See* Kennedy, *The Trustee in Bankruptcy Under the Uniform Commercial Code: Some Problems Suggested by Articles 2 and 9,* 14 Rutgers L.Rev. 518, 527–529 (1960).

8. *See* § 9–302(1)(d), Revised § 9–302 (1)(d).

9. § 9–301(1)(b).

by Section 9–107 if the financer is a third party.) It has been held, however, that where a seller sold goods on open credit and 30 to 60 days later persuaded the consumer to execute a conditional sale contract, the seller had a purchase money security interest in consumer goods perfected without filing which was not subject to attack under Section 70c.[10]

> On June 1, A lends $5,000 to X, an individual. X grants to A a security interest in a Renoir etching hanging in X's living room. X lives on a farm mostly located in F County but the house is located on a portion of the farm located in G County. A files a financing statement in F County on June 2.

> On June 20, B lends $3,500 to X. X tells B that the Renoir etching is subject to A's security interest but B nevertheless takes a security interest in the etching, having checked the Code files in G County and found no filing. B files a financing statement in G County on June 21.

While the etching is consumer goods,[11] neither security interest is purchase money [12] and filing is required for perfection.[13] If X is unable to repay the loans, is B entitled to priority over A? Assuming that filing in the county of the debtor's residence is required for perfection,[14] A has not perfected his security interest. Since both interests are not perfected by proper filing, B is entitled to priority because he is the first to perfect—if section 9–312(5)(b) is read to cover a case where both interests are not technically perfected.[15]

But this answer does not take into account the application of section 9–401(2) which makes a good faith filing "in an improper place

---

10. *In re* Robertson, 6 UCC Rep.Serv. 266 (E.D.Tenn.1969) (in bankruptcy). The Referee relied strongly on arguments advanced by Professor Hogan in 2 P. Coogan, W. Hogan & D. Vagts, Secured Transactions, § 19.02.

11. § 9–109(1).

12. § 9–107.

13. § 9–302(1)(d).

14. § 9–401(1)(a) (assuming the Second or Third Alternative subsection is in force).

15. Section 9–312(5)(a) provides for priority "in the order of filing if both are perfected by filing," while § 9–312(5)(b) specifies priority "in the order of perfection unless both are perfected by filing" which arguably does not apply unless the competing interests are both perfected. But if only one interest is perfected and therefore entitled to priority by implication and regardless of the sure application of any § 9–312 provision, that priority can be derived from § 9–301(1)(a). *See* Bloom v. Hilty, 427 Pa. 463, 234 A.2d 860 (1967), involving a problem falling into this murky area. Presumably, this sort of issue is more clearly resolved by Revised § 9–312(5)(a) which ranks security interests according to priority "in time of filing or perfection," leaving a possible issue in the case of improper filing by the first of the competing secured parties when both have filed.

. . . effective with regard to collateral covered . . . against any person who has knowledge of the contents of such financing statement." Does B have knowledge of the contents of the financing statement? If B saw a copy of the financing statement, it would probably disclose the names of the parties and their addresses, and it would describe the collateral as a Renoir etching with perhaps a title added—and all of this information was imparted to B by X, so it could reasonably be said that B has actual knowledge of the contents of the financing statement. If this is so, and the improper filing is therefore "effective" against B, how is the problem resolved? It would seem that in these circumstances the language of section 9–401(2) would be meaningless unless "effective" meant perfected, and if A's security interest is said to be perfected, then A is entitled to priority as the first to be filed.

Suppose X defaulted under both loan agreements and filed a bankruptcy petition. If A's interest is unperfected, it is subject to the trustee's rights as a lien creditor.[16] Yet B's interest is entitled to priority over the trustee because it is perfected. If A is entitled to priority over B under section 9–401(2) because A's interest is "effective" and yet it is still not "perfected," then we have a circular priority problem: A has priority over B, B has priority over the trustee, the trustee has priority over A. This circuity problem will result if the rationale of *In re Babcock Box Co.*[17] is accepted as correct.[18] The proper result under the 1962 code, however, is reached by reading "effective" as meaning "perfected" and thus permitting A to prevail over both B and the trustee. But under Revised Article 9, even though all represented creditors have knowledge of an unperfected security interest, that knowledge does not affect the trustee.[19] Thus the recently weakened strong-arm clause of section 70c may be regaining its eminence under Revised Article 9.

§ 7–6. Filing: Grace Periods: Section 60

For purposes of determining when a transfer takes place, two grace periods may have an effect, one in the Code and one in the Bankruptcy Act.

Section 9–301(2) provides:

> If the secured party files with respect to a purchase money security interest before or within ten days after the collateral comes into possession of the debtor, he takes priority over the rights of a transferee in bulk or of a lien credi-

---

16. Bankruptcy Act § 70c, 11 U.S.C.A. § 110(c); § 9–301(1)(b).

17. 200 F.Supp. 80 (D.Mass.1961).

18. *See* § 7.1 *supra*.

19. Revised §§ 9–301(1)(b), (3).

tor which arise between the time the security interest attaches and the time of filing.

The provision does not penalize late filing in any way. It simply establishes a priority when its terms are complied with. The grace period extends for ten days after the debtor "receives possession" of the collateral as the provision is phrased in Revised Section 9–301 (2), but the effectiveness of the filing to establish priority may extend for a longer period if the security interest attached before the debtor received the collateral.

Read literally, this section would apply where a secured party filed with respect to a purchase money security interest in consumer goods, as might be done to protect the security interest where a consumer debtor sells to another consumer who might otherwise take free of the security interest under Section 9–307(2). No such filing would be required for perfection, however, and if the section were so read it would imply an absence of priority in the absence of filing. This would be a meaningless implication, since the security interest is perfected at the time of the transfer and no further act is required for Section 60 purposes; nor can lien creditors gain priority under Section 9–301(1) for Section 70 purposes.

For a preference under Section 60, there must have been a transfer, as that term is defined in the Bankruptcy Act.[20] Where applicable law requires perfection by "recording, delivery, or otherwise" for the security interest to be superior to subsequent liens obtainable by legal or equitable proceedings on a simple contract, then Section 60a(7)I provides:

> Where (A) the applicable law specifies a stated period of time of not more than twenty-one days after the transfer within which recording, delivery, or some other act is required, and compliance therewith is had within such stated period of time; or where (B) the applicable law specifies no such stated period of time or where such stated period of time is more than twenty-one days, and compliance therewith is had within twenty-one days after the transfer, the

---

20. Bankruptcy Act § 1(30):
"Transfer" shall include the sale and every other and different mode, direct or indirect, of disposing of or of parting with property or with an interest therein or with the possession thereof or of fixing a lien upon property or upon an interest therein, absolutely or conditionally, voluntarily or involuntarily, by or without judicial proceedings, as a conveyance, sale, assignment, payment, pledge, mortgage, lien, encumbrance, gift, security, or otherwise; the retention of a security title to property delivered to a debtor shall be deemed a transfer suffered by such debtor.

transfer shall be deemed to be made or suffered at the time
of the transfer.

The Code nowhere states any period of time within which filing
is required to be made in order to have a perfected security interest.
Whenever it is made, the filing is effective. The only provisions
as to the time of filing relate to priority, not perfection.

For the purposes of Section 60, so long as filing takes place within 21 days after the attachment of the security interest which is given
for new value, it should relate back to the time of the transfer except
possibly in purchase money situations covered by Section 9–301(2).
It would indeed be anomalous for the favored purchase money security
interests to be treated less favorably than other security interests in
this circumstance, but the language of the Code is susceptible of this
construction. Of course, the argument could be made that there is a
conflict here between state law and the Bankruptcy Act, and that the
Bankruptcy Act should prevail; or it could be said that the Code provision relates solely to priority and hence does not mesh with the
specifications of Section 60a(7), but at first glance the Code does seem
to track with Section 60a(7). An ambiguity arises, however, if the
attachment of the purchase money security interest—the Bankruptcy
Act's "transfer"—takes place some time before the debtor receives
possession of the goods, which is the time when the Code grace period
begins to run. The best solution to the problem would be to say that
in any case, purchase money or otherwise, the Code secured party
has 21 days to file so far as Section 60 is concerned.

§ 7–7. The Preference Problem

Section 60a(1), because of its fundamental importance, warrants
complete quotation:

> A preference is a transfer, as defined in this Act, of any prop-
> erty of a debtor to or for the benefit of a creditor for or on
> account of an antecedent debt, made or suffered by such debt-
> or while insolvent and within four months before the filing by
> or against him of the petition initiating a proceeding under
> this Act, the effect of which transfer will be to enable such
> creditor to obtain a greater percentage of his debt than some
> other creditor of the same class.

Eight elements must coexist before a secured transaction may
be set aside as preferential. Within the frame of reference of a bona
fide secured transaction covering inventory and proceeds it may be
assumed that we have (1) a transfer (by way of security) of (2) the
debtor's property (3) to or for the benefit of a creditor. But was such

transfer (4) made by the debtor while insolvent (5) within four months of bankruptcy (6) on account of an antecedent debt (7) with the effect of enabling the creditor to obtain a greater percentage of his debt than some other creditor of the same class? If so, the transfer may be set aside if (8) the creditor had reasonable cause to believe that the debtor was insolvent when the transfer was made.[21]

While it seems to be generally advantageous to the trustee to set aside preferential transfers, this may not always be the case, and Section 60b of the Bankruptcy Act provides that a voidable preference may be preserved for the benefit of the estate, in which case the preferential security interest will pass to the trustee. It is possible that there may be first a transfer which is a preference, as where there is a security interest which is filed late within four months of bankruptcy, and then there is a subsequent timely perfected security interest, given for new value within four months of bankruptcy and not preferential. If the first security interest were simply avoided by the trustee, the indefeasible security interest would then be the only perfected security interest and entitled to priority, leaving the trustee with only the value of the collateral in excess of this interest. In such a case it ordinarily would be in the interest of the trustee to succeed to the preferential interest, leaving the second and non-preferential security interest to take its proper rank, and then if the collateral has any value in excess of these two interests, that value could be reached by the trustee under Section 70a of the Bankruptcy Act.

If a security interest lapses, a new financing statement will have to be filed, and the time of perfection will be determined by the date of the new filing. A continuation statement filed after the lapse should not be construed to continue the perfection or to re-perfect the security interest, for the continuation statement does not conform to the requirements of an original financing statement. If a security interest is re-perfected within four months of the debtors' bankruptcy, there will be a problem of antecedent debt for preference purposes.[22]

We may assume as a practical matter that both secured and unsecured creditors fall within the same class for purposes of Section 60.[23] This seems rather surprising at first glance, and it is certainly not an interpretation required by the statutory language, which

---

21. Bankruptcy Act, § 60b. *See* Kennedy, The Impact of the Uniform Commercial Code on Insolvency: Article 9, 67 Com.L.J. 113, 118 (1962). *See also* Kennedy, The Trustee in Bankruptcy Under the Uniform Commercial Code: Some Problems Suggested by Articles 2 and 9, 14 Rutgers L.Rev. 518, 543–44 (1960).

22. *In re* Vodco Volume Development Co., Inc., 567 F.2d 967 (10th Cir. 1977).

23. *See, e. g.,* Jentzer v. Viscose Co., 13 F.Supp. 540, 544 (S.D.N.Y.1934), modified, 82 F.2d 236 (2d Cir. 1936); *In re* Star Spring Bed Co., 257 Fed. 176 (D.N.J.1919), affirmed 265 Fed. 133 (3d Cir. 1920). *But see* MacLachlan, Bankruptcy § 256 (1956).

apparently refers to secured and unsecured creditors separately. Of course, if secured and unsecured creditors formed separate classes and if there were but one secured creditor, a transfer to him could not create a preference even though all of the other elements were present, because there would be no other creditor in the same class.

If we are dealing with revolving security such as inventory, it is probable, if not certain, that specific items of inventory and proceeds will change during the four months before bankruptcy, but do these changes constitute transfers? If secured transactions are conceptualized in terms of old-fashioned chattel mortgages, covering only specifically identified chattels, then a transfer will be said to have occurred. But there is no reason why the law should not move with the times. The collateral involved here cannot be treated as the equivalent of specifically mortgaged chattels. If we understand inventory financing to be literally defined—that is, the financing of inventory, whatever items may from time to time compose it—then there is no transfer after the date the original secured transaction has been perfected; this may, of course, have been long in advance of the four months preceding bankruptcy.[24] Perfection would have occurred when the last of four events happened: a financing statement was filed, a security agreement was duly entered into, the debtor had rights in the collateral, and value was given.[25] After-acquired property would

---

24. This has been consistently recognized in the Code cases beginning with Rosenberg v. Rudnick, 262 F.Supp. 635 (D.C.Mass.1967), discussed *infra* at § 7–8. *See also* Rockmore v. Lehman, 129 F.2d 892 (2d Cir. 1942), certiorari denied 317 U.S. 700, 63 S.Ct. 525, 87 L.Ed. 559 (1943). If the financing were entered into within the four-month period, there would be no preference problem if new value were given at the time of the creation of the security interest and if there were a timely filing. The Code does not penalize late filing, although the purchase money priorities of §§ 9–301(2) and 9–312(3), (4) will be lost by not filing within the limits provided. The problem arises under Bankruptcy Act § 60a(7), which provides that if a required filing is not made within twenty-one days of the transfer, there cannot be any relation-back in the effectiveness of the security interest. See Tennessen v. First Nat. Bank, 146 F.Supp. 511 (E.D.Wis.1956).

The conceptual problems involved in accounts financing are much the same as those involved in inventory financing. Inventory problems are dealt with here for purposes of historical development.

25. §§ 9–204(1), 9–302(1), 9–303; revised §§ 9–203(1), 9–302(1). Except in the case of a pledge, the debtor must sign a security agreement describing the collateral. § 9–203(1). In certain circumstances the secured party may have a temporarily perfected security interest which is good for twenty-one days without filing, and security interests in some kinds of pertinent collateral may be perfected by a pledge. §§ 9–304, 9–305. However, it seems most unlikely that a continuing pattern of inventory and proceeds financing would be carried on without filing. *See In re* King-Porter Co., 446 F.2d 722 (5th Cir. 1971); Redisco v. United Thrift Stores, Inc., 363 F.2d 11 (3rd Cir. 1966).

be deemed to be taken for new value because it was acquired in the ordinary course of business,[26] and it would be, in fact, substitute collateral. The property simply is not "transferred" and there is no question of antecedent debt, for new value was necessarily given at the inception of the financing, the time of the transfer.

In a historical context, the problem of "transfer" appears not to have been considered in two important cases involving chattel mortgages with after-acquired property clauses. In *Mason v. Citizens' Nat. Trust & Sav. Bank,*[27] the Court of Appeals for the Ninth Circuit said that the validity of liens authorized by state law (here a chattel mortgage covering after-acquired property of a manufacturer) was not affected by bankruptcy except as expressly provided in the Bankruptcy Act. The lien was good against the trustee. In *Joe Heaston Tractor & Implement Co. v. Claussen,*[28] the New Mexico Supreme Court went surprisingly far in holding that a chattel mortgage covering after-acquired property would have been valid against third parties from the time of filing in New Mexico, and while the instrument at issue was labeled a conditional sale, the court held it to be a chattel mortgage and proceeded to enforce it generously. That is, since New Mexico did not make an unfiled chattel mortgage void as against general creditors,[29] but the "seller" of the goods (the mortgagee, as it turned out) was asking for equitable relief, the court directed foreclosure of the mortgage on after-acquired property, subject to the secured party's waiver of his rights to any property acquired between execution and recording of the mortgage, if any of such goods went into the receiver's hands. It should be noted that in New Mexico a duly filed chattel mortgage on a merchant's stock in trade, including after-acquired property, was valid against a trustee in bankruptcy even though the mortgagor made no accounting to the mortgagee for the proceeds of the goods sold.[30] This is a clear precedent for the kind of financing the Code contemplates as legally permissible.

In the field of accounts receivable financing, the courts seem to have been generally able to look to the purpose of the financing and the necessity for constant change in the accounts, without finding

---

26. § 9–108.

27. 71 F.2d 246 (9th Cir. 1934).

28. 59 N.M. 486, 287 P.2d 57 (1955).

29. Nor does the Code make an unperfected security interest "void" as

against third parties. § 9–301(1) lists those persons to whose rights an unperfected security interest is "subordinate."

30. *See In re* Harnden, 200 Fed. 175 (D.C.N.M.1912).

a preference in accounts coming in just before bankruptcy.[31] This means, at the least, that releases and substitutions are not "transfers" and that the "transfer" took place at the time of the original financing. Nor do the courts always seem to inquire too strictly into the simultaneity of these exchanges.[32] A fixed loan balance may be maintained, collateralized by assigned accounts only roughly constant in aggregate amount.[33]

As to the ten-day security interest in unidentified proceeds, it was specifically held to create a lien in several well-reasoned cases under the Uniform Trust Receipts Act,[34] and conflicts under that Act are now immaterial because of the clear language of the Code in Section 9–306(4)(d).

There is no way to state a legal proposition except in words, despite their notorious inexactitude. If appropriate words are used in a state statute creating a security interest, that interest must be recognized in bankruptcy courts, whatever the predilections of the individual judge. The only conceivable interpretation of the Code provision at issue is that an enforceable security interest is stated to exist. This interest has been recognized outside of bankruptcy.[35] It was enforced even before the Uniform Trust Receipts Act,[36] and it

31. *See, e. g.*, Walker v. Commercial Nat. Bank, 217 F.2d 677 (8th Cir. 1954) ; cf. Wolf v. Aero Factors Corp., 126 F.Supp. 872 (S.D.N.Y.1954), affirmed 221 F.2d 291 (2d Cir. 1955). For cases arising under the Code but outside of bankruptcy, *see* Industrial Packaging Prods. Co. v. State Pub. School Bldg. Authority, 399 Pa. 643, 161 A.2d 19 (1960). Hartford Acc. & Indem. Co. v. State Pub. School Bldg. Auth., 26 Pa.D. & C.2d 717 (C.P.1961).

32. *See In re* Pusey, Maynes, Breish Co., 122 F.2d 606 (3d Cir. 1941).

33. *See* Walker v. Clinton State Bank, 216 F.2d 165 (8th Cir. 1954).

34. *In re* Harpeth Motors, Inc., 135 F. Supp. 863, 867, 868 (M.D.Tenn.1955), 34 Chi-Kent L.Rev. 294 (1956), 69 Harv.L.Rev. 1343 (1956) ; Commerce Union Bank v. Alexander, 44 Tenn. App. 104, 312 S.W.2d 611 (1957) ; cf. Universal Credit Co. v. Citizens State Bank, 224 Ind. 1, 64 N.E.2d 28 (1945) (dictum). *See generally*, Note, 66 Yale L.J. 922 (1957). There is no difficulty

in regard to claiming identifiable proceeds. *See, e. g.*, Taylor v. Quittner, 218 F.2d 549 (9th Cir. 1954) (decided under Uniform Trust Receipts Act) ; Howarth v. Universal C. I. T. Credit Corp., 203 F.Supp. 279 (W.D.Pa.1962) ; Girard Trust Corn Exch. Bank v. Warren Lepley Ford, Inc. (No. 3), 25 Pa.D. & C.2d 395 (C.P.1958). If the entruster did not claim proceeds within ten days of their receipt, then he could not come within the provisions of Uniform Trust Receipts Act § 10 (b), and it would not matter what kind of interest that section created. English v. Universal C. I. T. Credit Corp., 278 F.2d 750 (5th Cir. 1960). Compare § 9–306(4)(d)(ii).

35. See Universal Credit Co. v. Citizens State Bank, 224 Ind. 1, 64 N.E.2d 28 (1945) arising under the Uniform Trust Receipts Act.

36. "As to the used cars taken by the bankrupt in exchange, they were merely *substituted* for the new cars sold. The bankrupt under its limited powers as bailee for the appellants

must be enforced under the Code. There can be no question of a levying creditor coming ahead of the secured party; [37] thus the trustee cannot step into the position of such a creditor. Nor can there be a "gap" creditor, [38] and *Moore v. Bay* [39] can have no effect. Indeed, the ten-day restriction on following proceeds is a restriction on rights the secured party had even before the Uniform Trust Receipts Act was promulgated. [40]

Even those lawyers who think that nothing can be done for the first time will find ample pre-Code precedent for enforcing the Code provisions we have discussed. The fact that cases to the contrary may be found simply illustrates the impact of state law on bankruptcy in this area. Unless the Bankruptcy Act itself forbids the recognition of Code security interests—and it does not at this time—those interests

---

could sell for cash, on time, or for part cash and part exchange. Whatever was received for appellant's cars, *either in the way of money or property*, less profit or commissions, became the property of the appellants . . . . Their claims should have been allowed as secured." Hamilton Nat. Bank v. McCallum, 58 F.2d 912, 914 (6th Cir.), certiorari denied 287 U.S. 619, 53 S.Ct. 19, 77 L.Ed. 537 (1932) (Emphasis added.); see In re James, Inc., 30 F.2d 551, 555, 558 (2d Cir. 1929): "As title to the motor cars was not in the bankrupt, neither was the money received from their sale."

37. Only the debtor's interest in the collateral can be reached. § 9–311. See § 7–3 *supra*. See also Commercial Credit Corp. v. Bosse, 76 Idaho 409, 283 P.2d 937 (1955) where the entruster prevailed over attaching creditors and a federal tax lien on a claim to proceeds, identifiable and promptly claimed under Uniform Trust Receipts Act § 10. The court characterized the entruster's interest as "a property interest and not a lien." 76 Idaho at 416, 283 P.2d at 941.

38. *See* Kennedy, The Impact of the Uniform Commercial Code on Insolvency: Article 9, 67 Com.L.J. 113, 117 (1962). Courts have not always been hospitable to the possibility of "gap" creditors. *See, e. g.,* Emery v. Union Inv. Co., 212 F.2d 183 (6th Cir. 1954); In re Grosse, 24 F.2d 305 (7th Cir. 1928); *cf.* Johnson v. Fulton Nat.

Bank, 201 Ga. 341, 39 S.E.2d 754 (1946). *See* § 7–2 *supra*.

39. 284 U.S. 4 (1931). Of this case, Professor Hanna said: "The rule of Moore v. Bay as now applied to cases under Section 70(c) and (e) is an instance of confiscation of security. Here was a case not properly presented to the Supreme Court, where the Court seemed confused on the facts, made no clear definition of the issues, and gave a Delphic decision. The real issue, upon which the circuits, contrary to what the Court said, were divided, was whether all creditors should share in what was recovered by the trustee when his recovery was based on rights of particular creditors. No one questions the Court's decision that all creditors should share, is correct. If the Court actually meant to hold that the mortgage in question was void entirely it was wrong both as to state and bankruptcy law. The fantastic notion that because under applicable law, usually state law, some creditor has a particular advantage against a security, the security is totally void, has no sound basis in the law of fraudulent conveyances, security, bankruptcy, nor in common sense and justice." Hanna, Cases on Security 11 (1959).

40. See Hamilton Nat. Bank v. McCallum, 58 F.2d 912 (6th Cir.), certiorari denied 287 U.S. 619, 53 S.Ct. 19, 77 L.Ed. 537 (1932); *In re* James, Inc., 30 F.2d 555 (2d Cir. 1929).

are entitled to recognition and proper enforcement in bankrupcy proceedings.

> On February 1, A files and perfects a security interest in the equipment of X. On April 1, B enters into a purchase money security agreement with X to provide desks and chairs for use in X's offices, and the desks and chairs are delivered to X that day pursuant to agreement. On April 4, X files a voluntary petition in bankruptcy. On April 5, B files a financing statement in the proper office or offices.

Because B filed a financing statement within 10 days after X received possession of the collateral, under Section 9–301(2) a lien creditor whose rights arise between attachment and filing will be subordinate to B, and therefore the trustee in bankruptcy here will be subordinate to B since the trustee takes his rights in this context under Section 70c. Under section 60a(7) of the Bankruptcy Act, there is a 21-day relation back in the effectiveness of the filing, so B's interest will not be subject to attack as a preference. Under Section 9–312(4), B will have priority over A, assuming that A's security agreement covered after-acquired equipment and that the financing statement claimed "equipment" [41] or else expressly covered after-acquired equipment, since the filing is within 10 days after the debtor received possession of the collateral.

> Would it matter if B had filed on April 12? From the standpoint of Section 60, it would not matter because the filing was within 21 days of the date of attachment of the security interest and the section would provide for relation back. From the standpoint of Section 70c, the trustee would have the rights of a lien creditor on April 4, and Section 9–301(2) provides no priority in these circumstances for the secured party over a lien creditor because the filing is not within 10 days after the debtor receives possession of the goods. This collateral will be subject to A's security interest, however, and A would be entitled to priority over B under Section 9–312(4). A's security interest would not be subject to challenge under Section 70c, assuming it was perfected on attachment because of an after-acquired property clause in the security agreement and the use of appropriate language in the financing statement, but there might be a challenge under Section 60 because of antecedent debt.

---

41. On the description of collateral in the financing statement, the leading case is National Cash Register Co. v. Firestone & Co., 346 Mass. 255, 191 N.E.2d 471 (1963). While the description in the financing statement cannot enlarge the collateral in which a security interest is granted in the security agreement, the financing statement need only describe the collateral by item or type, under § 9–402(1), and "equipment" is a recognized type of goods under § 9–109.

Had the collateral been inventory in the preceding example, rather than equipment, A would have been entitled to priority over B if B did not file and give A an appropriate notice before X received the goods.   Whether B's filing was on April 5 or April 12, A would have priority over B.   If B's filing were on April 5, B would be entitled to priority over the trustee under Section 9–301(2) and A would have priority over the trustee under Section 70c and over B under Section 9–312(3).   Whether A's interest would be subject to a successful preference challenge is not clear on these facts.   If B's filing were on April 12, A would be entitled to priority over B under Section 9–312(3) and over the trustee under Section 70c and B would be subordinate to the trustee under Section 9–301(1)(b).   A's interest in after-acquired collateral will be perfected when X acquires an interest in it, and the security interest would probably not be subject to a successful preference challenge under Section 60 based on the issue of antecedent debt.[42]

> On January 2, B Co., at the insistence of Bank A, granted to Bank A a security interest in equipment as security for a long-overdue debt of $27,000.   The equipment, otherwise unencumbered, was worth $65,000.   A financing statement was filed in the proper office on January 14.
>
> On February 17, B Co. negotiated a loan from C Finance Co. in the amount of $25,000, granting to C a security interest in equipment.   A financing statement was filed in the proper office on March 4.
>
> On May 3, B Co. filed a voluntary petition in bankruptcy.

Bank A's security interest is perfected when it is filed under Section 9–303(1).   There is no grace period for priority under Section 9–301(2) because this is not a purchase money security interest, and even had it been a purchase money interest, it was not filed within ten days of attachment.   Nor does Section 60a(7) of the Bankruptcy Act provide for relation back of the perfection because this is not a security interest given for "new and contemporaneous consideration."

On the other hand, the security interest of C Finance Co. was given for new value in the form of a contemporaneous loan, even

---

42.   Section 9–108 provides in part that a security interest for after-acquired property "shall be deemed to be taken for new value and not as security for an antecedent debt if the debtor acquires his rights in such collateral either in the ordinary course of his business or under a contract of purchase made pursuant to the security agreement within a reasonable time after new value is given."   Inventory would meet the ordinary course of business requirement whereas equipment probably would not.

though this is not a purchase money security interest, so that the Bankruptcy Act would relate back the perfection to the time of the attachment of the security interest.

Absent bankruptcy, Bank A would have priority over C Finance Co. as the first to file under Section 9–312(5)(a). Since B Co. filed in bankruptcy within four months of the perfection of both interests, it would appear that the security interest of Bank A is a preference (other elements being present) because under Section 60a(2) of the Bankruptcy Act it became "so far perfected that no subsequent lien upon such property obtainable by legal or equitable proceedings on a simple contract could become superior to the rights" of Bank A only when filing took place, which was within the four month period, and the security interest was given to secure an antecedent debt. If Bank A had "reasonable cause to believe the debtor is insolvent" at the time of the transfer, as appears to have been the case, then the transfer by way of a security interest can be avoided by the trustee under Section 60b of the Bankruptcy Act.

But if Bank A's security interest is simply avoided by the trustee, then the security interest of C Finance Co. would be first in line, and C's security interest cannot successfully be attacked as a preference because all of the elements of a preference are not present, the security interest having been given for new value.

In this situation the trustee could succeed to Bank A's interest under Section 60b,[43] then C Finance Co. would come next, and the excess value in the collateral would go to the trustee under Section 70a of the Bankruptcy Act.

Had Bank A's security interest been given for new value, rather than an antecedent debt, Section 60a(7) of the Bankruptcy Act would have provided a 21-day relation back for perfection which would have taken the transfer outside the four-month preference period, so that Bank A's security interest could not have been attacked as a preference.

§ 7–8. Litigation: The *Portland* Case in the Bankruptcy Court

The conceptual problems involved in continuing inventory or accounts financing are similar. Where a loan is secured by accounts then in existence and thereafter arising over a period of time, the concept of a continuing security interest in the accounts is substantially the same as it is in inventory financing, where the collateral is also constantly changing. There is an observable physical difference

---

43. For a somewhat analogous problem under § 67a of the Bankruptcy Act, see First Nat'l Bank of Baltimore v. Staake, 202 U.S. 141, 26 S.Ct. 580 (1906).

when items of inventory are sold and replaced; there is a recordable although perhaps intangible difference when old accounts are paid down or retired and new accounts arise. Determining how a continuing security interest is maintained presents similar issues in both instances.

The first Code case to be decided involving these issues has become familiarly known as the *Portland* case.[44] Predictably the issues were presented in a bankruptcy court hostile to the Code, and the issues were not presented in a typical commercial situation. The principal Code secured party was a corporation formed by 88 labor unions to provide a building to be used by the debtor, a corporation organized by some unions of striking newspaper employees to publish a newspaper to compete with Portland's regular daily papers which continued publication despite the strike. The collateral was accounts arising from display and advertising contracts and from circulation accounts.

To put the matter in a more conventional commercial setting, we may assume that a financer is willing to lend $100,000 for five years against the accounts then existing and thereafter arising in the operation of an ordinary retail store. The accounts are not to fall below $125,000, and it will be an event of default under the loan agreement if they do. Subject to the occurrence of an event of default, the lender is willing for the debtor to exercise dominion over the accounts, to make collections, to accept returned goods and adjust accounts, and to carry on ordinary business transactions. Interest will be paid quarterly on the loan, but no principal will be repaid until the loan matures at the end of five years unless an event of default occurs and maturity is accelerated. A financing statement claiming a security interest in "accounts"[45] is properly filed. Three years after the security interest is perfected the debtor goes into bankruptcy. There are no competing security interests. The accounts subject to the secu-

44. *In re* Portland Newspaper Publishing Co., 3 UCC Rep.Serv. 194 (D.Ore. 1966) (in bankruptcy) (hereinafter cited as *Portland*). A number of issues and parties were involved in this case in addition to those discussed here.

45. That "Accounts" is an adequate description for all accounts covered by the security agreement which arise during the period the financing statement is effective cannot be open to reasonable doubt. *See In re* Platt, 58 Berks Cty.L.J. 86 (E.D.Pa.1966) (in bankruptcy), vacated on other grounds, 257 F.Supp. 478 (E.D.Pa.1966); National Cash Register Co. v. Firestone & Co., 346 Mass. 255, 191 N.E.2d 471 (1963). The Code adopts a system of notice filing, and anyone fluent in the English language would know that a filed financing statement covering "Accounts" could include all present and future accounts arising within the effective period of the filing; no other meaning is sensible.

rity interest have never fallen below $125,000,[46] and the accounts on hand at bankruptcy have all arisen within four months of bankruptcy. Is the security interest entitled to recognition and enforcement in bankruptcy?

Presumably the referee in the *Portland* case would find this security interest a preference and therefore unenforceable in bankruptcy. The reason, subject to some elaboration, would be that the relation back of the security interest in after-acquired property provided by the Uniform Commercial Code will not be recognized in bankruptcy.

It is clear that the hypothesized transaction meets the requirements of the Code for a perfected, enforceable security interest. That is, the security interest attached when the parties made their agreement, the debtor had rights in the collateral, and the secured party advanced funds; [47] it was perfected by filing.[48] The security interest was not impaired by the secured party's failure to exercise any dominion over the collateral,[49] and the Code recognizes a continuing security interest in changing collateral.[50]

In what circumstances may a valid security interest be denied enforcement as a preference? Eight elements must co-exist before a voidable preference exists: there must be (1) a transfer (by way of security) of (2) the debtor's property (3) to or for the benefit of a creditor (4) made by the debtor while insolvent (5) within four months of bankruptcy (6) on account of an antecedent debt (7) with the effect of enabling the creditor to obtain a greater percentage of his debt than some other creditor of the same class,[51] and (8) the creditor must have had reasonable cause to believe that the debtor was insolvent when the transfer was made.[52]

46. It may be pointed out, and perhaps it should be emphasized, that the collateral in *Portland* did not fall below the amount of the loan at any time during the four months preceding bankruptcy. See Exhibit E attached to Stipulation admitted as Exhibit 39 on May 27, 1966, in the record of evidence, *In re* Portland Newspaper Publishing Co., No. B 64–3282, D.Ore., Feb. 9, 1966.

47. § 9–204(1); Revised § 9–204(1).

48. *See* § 9–302(1).

49. § 9–205. This section may be said to repeal the rule of Benedict v. Ratner, 268 U.S. 353, 45 S.Ct. 566, 69 L.Ed. 991 (1925); at all events it eliminates any possible basis for the rule.

The Supreme Court in *Benedict* merely purported to state a rule of New York law, which many states never recognized or abolished by statute even before the Code.

50. §§ 9–204(3), (4); Revised § 9–204(1).

51. Bankruptcy Act § 60a.

52. *Id.* § 60b. The basic problem which the preference provisions of the Bankruptcy Act were designed to meet is the situation where a creditor senses impending doom and grasps security to which he was not previously entitled, thereby diminishing the bankrupt's estate to the detriment of other creditors. This is not the kind of problem involved in the *Portland* case.

The argument to invalidate the security interest usually takes the position that as each new account arises, it is a new transfer when that account becomes subject to the pre-existing security agreement, and, subject to other elements of a preference being found to be present, accounts arising within four months of bankruptcy are voidable preferences.[53] To some extent this argument relies on the Code's stipulation that a debtor has no rights in an account until it comes into existence [54]—a provision which has been dropped from the 1972 Official Text [55]—and of course a security interest cannot attach (or be perfected) before the debtor has rights in the collateral.[56]

---

53. These critics admit, as does the Referee in *Portland*, that the parties could reach exactly the same result provided by the Code by the more expensive and laborious means of revolving credit.

Admittedly if Rose City had retained in its agreement the policing provisions . . . and had insisted upon their observance, it might have avoided the preference challenge. Requirements such as these are insisted upon by sophisticated lenders. They require that all checks, drafts, cash and other remittances in part or full payment of any collateral be deposited in a cash collateral account over which the secured party alone shall have power of withdrawal. . . . It is usually agreed that once each week the secured party will apply the whole or any part of the collected funds in the cash collateral account against the principal or interest of the advances made against the collateral, and new loans similarly are made upon the assignment of new accounts. This revolving credit arrangement enables the secured creditor to keep his financial finger on the business pulse of the debtor. Thus a sound and healthy business relationship may be maintained between creditor and debtor.

Portland, 3 UCC Rep.Serv. 194 at 211. It requires no intellectual sophistication or legal legerdemain to see that where the debtor is allowed to retain collections instead of paying them over to the secured party, the secured party is constantly giving new value to the debtor, just as much as if he had taken the money with one hand and

given it back with the other. As old accounts are paid down, collateral is released, and new accounts come under the security agreement for new value. Section 9–108 says no more than this. To the argument that these substitutions must be strictly "contemporaneous," it may be said that the concept is in fact a practical impossibility, as those who think in terms of events must realize and as those who do not go behind shibboleths will not.

54. § 9–204(2)(d).

55. Revised § 9–204 has dropped all examples of when a debtor may acquire rights in isolated kinds of collateral, such as (to put the matter positively rather than in the negative terms of § 9–204(2)): in the young of livestock on their conception or in fish when caught.

56. §§ 9–204(1), 9–303(1). Professor King seems to feel that these sections *create* the problem, basically because of the concept of attachment. *See* King, Section 9–108 of the Uniform Commercial Code: Does It Insulate the Security Interest from Attack by a Trustee in Bankruptcy?, 114 U.Pa. L.Rev. 1117 (1966). While the concept of attachment is perhaps not an essential one, neither is it new. Under our old chattel mortgage law, for example, we could have had a mortgage "valid between the parties"—*i. e.*, it had "attached"—but invalid as to third parties because there was no recording—*i. e.*, it was not "perfected." The Code provisions at issue here present no difficulty unless one conceptualizes secured transactions in terms of

The simple answer to this so-called problem is in Section 9–108 which provides:

> Where a secured party makes an advance, incurs an obligation, releases a perfected security interest, or otherwise gives new value which is to be secured in whole or in part by after-acquired property his security interest in the after-acquired collateral shall be deemed to be taken for new value and not as security for an antecedent debt if the debtor acquires his rights in such collateral either in the ordinary course of his business or under a contract of purchase made pursuant to the security agreement within a reasonable time after new value is given.

It was unfortunate draftsmanship to include the word "deemed" in this provision. It provides a peg on which to hang the standard objection that this provision is contrary to fact. This provision simply recognizes the standard bankruptcy doctrine that there is no preference when new property is substituted for other property in a secured transaction.[57] The security interest continues and relates back to the

specific mortgages of specific things. To read the Code as some pro-bankruptcy specialists have done, means that accounts and inventory cannot be financed without being vulnerable in bankruptcy unless a revolving credit plan is established; this attitude is insupportable as a social policy or as a legal policy. Professor King suggests that the concept of attachment could be eliminated from the concept of perfection so that "the security interest in after-acquired property could be considered perfected at the time the financing transaction and filing occur without any need to wait for the debtor to acquire the property. There would then be no problem with the section 60(a) four-month period or antecedent debt element." King, *supra* at 1132. Despite whatever possible merit there might have been in this approach, it was not accepted by the Article 9 Review Committee. See Comment of Professor (now Mr. Justice) Braucher in Braucher, Coogan, Davenport, Gilmore, and Kripke, A Look at the Work of the Article 9 Review Committee, 26 Bus.Law. 307 at 328 (1970). This approach has arguably been accepted by certain federal courts, however. See § 7–12 *infra*.

Leaving metaphysics to one side, the Code handles the conceptual problem satisfactorily if one accepts certain basic premises. There is no solution to these problems unless one is willing to accept the necessity of the kind of financing we are concerned with and the statutory provisions which now make it feasible, or any other provisions which may later be used. Any language is capable of more than one interpretation.

57. Where collateral, such as inventory or accounts, is constantly changing, the collateral can be analogized to, *e. g.*, the Mississippi River. In the ordinary usage of English, we think we know what we mean when we say, "Mississippi River," even though that river is not the same at any two moments in time. See *In re* Nickerson & Nickerson, Inc., 329 F.Supp. 93, 96 (D.Neb.1971), affirmed 452 F.2d 56 (8th Cir. 1971). Similarly, when we speak of inventory or accounts of a named debtor we think we know what we are talking about even though that collateral is constantly changing, in tangible or intangible ways. When the collateral changes, we trace the original security interest into the proceeds back into substituted collateral,

original perfection. There is no objection whatsoever to this relation back.

This kind of relation back was not condemned—it was not even involved—in *Corn Exchange Nat. Bank & Trust Co. v. Klauder*,[58] a case which seems to be frequently mis-cited in writings about the Code and the Bankruptcy Act. The *Klauder* case involved a perfectly simple collision between an accounts receivable financer and a trustee in bankruptcy, at a time when Section 60a of the Bankruptcy Act deemed a transfer to take place when no bona fide purchaser from the debtor and no creditor could have acquired rights in the property superior to the transferee. Under Pennsylvania law at that time, an assignee of accounts was required to notify the account debtor, in order to prevail against a subsequent good faith assignee who had given such notice. If no notice was given, and none was in this case, then the transfer was clearly vulnerable under the Bankruptcy Act. Of course, the state law was changed to make the assignment effective when noted on the assignor's books,[59] and the Bankruptcy Act was subsequently amended to incorporate a lien creditor test in place of the bona fide purchaser test.[60] What was apparently disturbing the *Klauder* Court was secret liens,[61] which are impossible under the Code.

In cases decided before the Code was ever dreamed of, as well as in cases arising since it has been effective, courts have recognized continuing security interests covering after-acquired collateral, without even discussing the preference question, when the secured transactions were carried out in accordance with applicable law. Two pre-Code cases [62] were dismissed by the *Portland* referee with the observation that the facts did not disclose that the property in issue was acquired within four months of bankruptcy.[63] This is true, but on the other

and so on, so that the security interest is continuous and continuously perfected. *See* § 9–306(2), Revised § 9–306(2).

58. 318 U.S. 434, 63 S.Ct. 679, 87 L.Ed. 884 (1943). *See* Nunnemaker Transportation Co. v. United California Bank, 456 F.2d 28, 34–35 (9th Cir. 1972). For an example of the mis-citing of *Klauder, see In re* Portland Newspaper Publishing Co., 3 UCC Rep. Serv. 194, 220 (D.Or.1966) (in bankruptcy).

59. 318 U.S. at 436, n. 6, 63 S.Ct. at 681.

60. *See, e. g.,* MacLachlan, Preference Redefined, 63 Harv.L.Rev. 1390 (1950);

Kupfer, The Recent Amendment of Section 60a of the Bankruptcy Act, 24 Ref.J. 86 (1950).

61. *See* Corn Exchange Nat. Bank & Trust Co. v. Klauder, 318 U.S. 434, 63 S.Ct. 679, 87 L.Ed. 884 *passim* (1943). The same problem of secret liens was important in Benedict v. Ratner, 268 U.S. 353, 45 S.Ct. 566, 69 L.Ed. 991 (1925).

62. Mason v. Citizens' Nat. Trust & Sav. Bank, 71 F.2d 246 (9th Cir. 1934); Joe Heaston Tractor & Implement Co. v. Claussen, 59 N.M. 486, 287 P.2d 57 (1955).

63. *Portland,* 3 UCC Rep.Serv. 194 at 222.

hand, nothing indicated that it was not acquired within four months of bankruptcy; and, particularly when we are dealing with inventory, it would appear only common sense to assume that some inventory was received within four months of bankruptcy. A certain number of changing-collateral cases are not treated as preference cases, but this does not mean that the issue could not have been raised; it merely indicates that it was not raised.[64] The cases may be taken to be ambiguous on the point, or they may be taken to support the proposition that at least some bankruptcy courts see it as their duty to enforce security interests in accordance with the state law creating them.

We can find exemplified in the *Portland* case the attitude that the Code simply must not be upheld because its provisions make legitimate secured transactions invulnerable.

> According to these Code sections a merchant by a simple signed agreement, regardless of form, may create a general floating lien for present and future advances on inventory and accounts receivable including future acquisitions. With such an agreement in existence the secured party may leave the merchant in complete control of his business and funds and yet be protected against the claims of other creditors, except purchase money security interests, by filing . . . a financing statement . . . . There is no requirement that it contain any information concerning the limit of the credit to be extended, the amounts advanced or to be advanced or the terms of payment.[65]

Admittedly the referee has grasped the idea of just what the Code does, although it would not have been so shocking to him, perhaps, if he had given some thought to the Uniform Trust Receipts Act.

> Unless the financing statement shows a maturity date of the obligation secured, it remains effective for the five years

---

64. While referees or judges are responsible for what they decide and are entitled to the ensuing praise or blame, it must be remembered that some cases are argued and briefed inadequately by counsel; the issues raised may be a matter of chance; and the fact situations often leave much to be desired.

65. *Portland,* 3 UCC Rep.Serv. 194 at 213. The kind of transaction condemned by the referee was found not to be fraudulent as to creditors who had notice of the financing of inven-

tory because of public recording and who, therefore, must be held to assume a risk at their peril in Etheridge v. Sperry, 139 U.S. 266, 11 S.Ct. 565, 35 L.Ed. 171 (1891). This old case is cited merely to show that some current ideas have respectable antecedents. There is, however, no reason why current commercial law should be saddled with commercial concepts of an agrarian economy of the last century, when such concepts do not accord with modern legislation and the needs of a modern society.

as notice to the world that the secured party may have a
floating lien on the merchant's inventory and receivables.
All other creditors must carry the burden of ascertaining
from time to time the status of his security interests . . . .
It would appear that the secured party is not concerned over
the amount of unsecured credit extended to the debtor.[66]

It is not immediately obvious why "all other creditors" need to
"carry the burden of ascertaining" the limits of the security interest
involved, since they need not become creditors at all. But if they do,
they are creditors with notice. Since the secured party has given
public notice of his interest, surely there is no reason for him to be
concerned with the amount of unsecured credit extended to his debtor
—at least from a legal point of view; from the viewpoint of his interest in seeing the business continue in operation, his concern might be
very real.

> The old-fashioned method of operating a business on the
> strength of equity capital and unsecured bank credit based
> upon the financial integrity of the debtor seems to be giving
> way to the modern trend of financing business operations
> in reliance upon a floating lien on current assets with little or
> no regard for equity capital. Added to this is the more recent
> development of leasing, instead of owning, plant and equip-
> ment. These methods leave the daily suppliers and employees
> in a perilous position. The instant case furnishes a dramatic
> illustration in which the priority labor claims amount to near-
> ly $43,000. Employees furnished the labor to publish and de-
> liver the newspapers that gave rise to the receivables in con-
> troversy. The moneys advanced by the creditors claiming se-
> curity long since had been dissipated in operating losses. If
> these floating liens are valid, the wage claimants may receive
> not more than fifteen per cent on their claims out of the free
> assets.[67]

This is the nub of the case. These transactions must be found
to be invalid so that the erstwhile employees may get more money.
But put in terms of a social problem, it was not quite so simple in the
Portland case. The wage claimants were strikers who started the
defunct newspaper in competition with their former employers, while
Rose City Development Company, Inc., the principal Code secured

---

66. *Portland*, 3 UCC Rep.Serv. 194 at   67. *Id.* at 214.
    213.

party involved, happened to be a corporation formed by 88 labor unions to provide a building for the strikers to use. Moreover, part of the funds Rose City had lent on a secured basis perhaps went to pay the strikers-employees whose work generated the accounts, which secured the capital that may have paid the workers.

Billions of dollars are outstanding in loans against accounts, and these loans are both legal and necessary. It was undoubtedly loans by friendly persons which kept the Portland newspaper going as long as it did. That some security was necessary to obtain the loans is self-evident. The debtor in *Portland* could never have qualified for an unsecured bank loan, which the referee thought a desirable business practice; nor could the debtor have acquired a place to publish the paper free and clear of mortgage debt, which the referee also approved, as a cushion for claims. Times have changed and so have social policies; so has the law.

The referee's opinion in the *Portland* case [68] has been discussed at some length because it is an eloquent defense of an attitude that, in years past at least, has been common among referees. The effect of this attitude manifests itself in many ways in bankruptcy proceedings, and it is important to know it exists and to attempt to understand it. Regardless of the legal merit of the referee's views, there is a practical importance to the outlook those views exemplify.

§ 7-9. **Litigation:** *Rosenberg v. Rudnick*

While the commercial law world was generally aware of the progress of the *Portland* case [69] in the bankruptcy court, the decision of Judge Ford in *Rosenberg v. Rudnick,*[70] approximately a year later, came as a considerable surprise. Here there was a loan of $110,000 secured by equipment, inventory and accounts then owned or thereafter acquired, and a financing statement was filed. When the borrower's financial picture darkened, Rudnick demanded payment of the loan and, when payment was not made, exercised his right of repossession of the collateral given in the security agreement. Bankruptcy followed. The trustee attacked the transaction as a preferential transfer under Section 60 of the Bankruptcy Act, claiming Rudnick's security interest in the inventory arose only as each item of inventory

---

68. The referee's decision was subsequently reversed. See § 7-9 *infra*.

69. *In re* Portland Newspaper Publishing Co., Inc., 3 UCC Rep.Serv. 194 (D.Or.1966) (in bankruptcy).

70. 262 F.Supp. 635 (D.C.Mass.1967).

was acquired by the debtor so that as to inventory coming in within four months of bankruptcy, there was a transfer for antecedent consideration. The transfer was not the repossession but the creation of the security interest in the property.

For purposes of the preference provisions of the Bankruptcy Act, a transfer is "deemed to have been made" when it is "so far perfected that no subsequent lien upon such property obtainable by legal or equitable proceedings on a simple contract could become superior to the rights of the transferee."[71] As Judge Ford pointed out, state law —in this case, the Uniform Commercial Code—determines when the requisite perfection has been reached, and it was held that the transfer took place when the security agreement was executed and a proper filing was made. At that time the security interest was "so far perfected" that it could not be "defeated by a subsequent lien obtainable in proceedings on a simple contract action."[72] This was true even though the Code requires that the debtor have rights in the items of collateral for the security interest to attach to the individual items under an after-acquired property clause. In the case of inventory, which was what the secured party repossessed, the filed security interest was superior to any subsequently arising third party rights except for the rights of buyers in ordinary course of business under Section 9–307(1) and holders of perfected purchase money security interests who complied with Section 9–312(3).

Judge Ford quoted Section 9–108 and noted that it would produce the same result that he had reached. While acknowledging the controversy which that section had aroused, he observed that the Bankruptcy Act did not define antecedent consideration and that, in view of the widespread adoption of the Code, "the definition of § 9–108 should be regarded as generally accepted and in accord with current business practice and understanding and hence applied in bankruptcy."[73]

The trustee apparently argued that the security interest attached separately to each item of after-acquired property as it became part of the debtor's inventory, thus creating constant transfers within the four months preceding bankruptcy. But Judge Ford said that financed inventory should be viewed as a single entity. "The security interest is in the entity as a whole, not in its individual components,

---

71. Bankruptcy Act, § 60a(2).

72. Rosenberg v. Rudnick, 262 F.Supp. 635 at 638 (D.C.Mass.1967).

73. *Id.* at 639. *See also* Nunnemaker Transportation Co. v. United California Bank, 456 F.2d 28 (9th Cir. 1972).

and the transfer of property occurs when this interest in the inventory as an entity is created." [74]

Judge Ford further observed that the transaction was not the kind that Section 60 was designed to avoid. There was no secret lien; a financing statement had been filed. There was no last minute race to get security to the deprivation of other creditors; the security interest was created when the loan was made. No supplier could justifiably claim to have been misled by appearances of ownership by the debtor in view of the filing, and any suppliers who wished security could have obtained it by complying with Section 9–312(3).

§ 7–10. Litigation: The *Portland* Case, Round Two

On review of the *Portland* case,[75] Judge Solomon reversed the referee on the Code issues. The opinion in *Rosenberg v. Rudnick* [76] had now come down. While *Portland* involved accounts and *Rosenberg* involved inventory, the conceptual problems were treated alike. Judge Solomon quoted from Judge Ford's opinion the portion stating that the collateral was to be viewed as an entity; [77] he noted that Judge Ford had held the transfer to have been made when the security agreement was executed and not when each item of inventory was acquired, but that even if the security interest did attach to each item only as acquired, the security interest would be superior to subsequently acquired contract creditors' liens. He also quoted Judge Ford's approval of Section 9–108.

In a statement that has often been quoted, Judge Solomon said: "Good business practice should be good business law." [78] With this he upheld a security interest in changing collateral, making it unnecessary to have daily deposits of collected accounts, with pay-downs of the outstanding loan, followed by new extensions of credit, in order to have an invulnerable security interest in bankruptcy. He noted that the application of Section 9–108 did not diminish the bankrupt's estate, since it provided for a substitution of collateral, and there is no preference when new accounts are substituted for old ones, if they come in in the ordinary course of business.

---

74. *Id.*

75. *In re* Portland Newspaper Publishing Co., 271 F.Supp. 395 (D.C.Or.1967), affirmed sub nom. DuBay v. Williams, 417 F.2d 1277 (9th Cir.).

76. 262 F.Supp. 635 (D.C.Mass.1967).

77. Viewing accounts as an entity avoids any problem with § 9–204(2)(d), which states that the debtor has no rights in an account until it comes into existence, since this provision is critical only if we are dealing with individual accounts. In any event, the provision has been deleted in Revised § 9–204.

78. 271 F.Supp. at 400.

At this point [79] the commercial world's attention moved to the Court of Appeals for the Ninth Circuit where it was assumed that the first opinion at this level would be issued in an appeal of the *Portland* case. As it turned out, the Court of Appeals for the Seventh Circuit was the first federal appellate court to speak.

§ 7-11. Litigation: *Grain Merchants of Indiana*

Grain Merchants [80] involved a security interest in accounts given to secure a bank loan. At issue were proceeds of accounts deposited by Grain Merchants with the bank and proceeds of accounts specifically turned over to the bank shortly prior to bankruptcy but after the bank's last loan was made, and collected by the bank. A preference had been found by the referee, who was reversed by the district court. The district court was affirmed by Court of Appeals.

In a carefully reasoned opinion by Judge Cummings, the Court of Appeals for the Seventh Circuit held that the transfer took place at the time the security agreement was made and the financing statement filed—not when the questioned accounts were turned over to the bank or when deposits were made just prior to bankruptcy—and that for the purposes of Section 60a(2) of the Bankruptcy Act the transfer of future accounts was then "so far perfected" that no subsequent lien creditor could acquire priority. The Court found that this result harmonized with the intent of Congress in enacting the current version of Section 60.

The Court accepted the view that the security interest was in the accounts as an entity, not in the individual accounts, so that the transfer, again, was found to have occurred at the inception of the financing. Judge Cummings observed: "This recognizes business realities, for the business community has depended upon a revolving or flow type of accounts receivable financing for many years." [81]

---

79. Late in 1967 *In re* White, 283 F. Supp. 208 (S.D.Ohio 1967) appeared. In a very terse opinion Judge Hogan sustained a security interest in inventory against an attack under § 60 of the Bankruptcy Act, saying that he could add nothing to the opinions of Judges Ford and Solomon. In mid-1968, *In re* Grain Merchants of Indiana, Inc., 286 F.Supp. 597 (N.D. Ind.1968), affirmed 408 F.2d 209 (7th Cir.), certiorari denied France v. Union Bank & Sav. Co., 396 U.S. 827, 90 S.Ct. 75, 24 L.Ed.2d 78, was decided by Judge Eschbach in a carefully written and thorough opinion which has received far less notice than it deserved because of the timing of its appearance and the rapidity with which the Seventh Circuit heard the appeal and issued its opinion.

80. Grain Merchants of Indiana v. Union Bank & S. Co., Bellevue, Ohio, 408 F.2d 209 (7th Cir. 1969), *certiorari denied* France v. Union Bank & Sav. Co., 396 U.S. 827, 90 S.Ct. 75, 24 L.Ed. 2d 78.

81. 408 F.2d at 216.

The substitution of collateral doctrine was approved and applied. That is, a transfer of collateral by a debtor within four months of bankruptcy is not a preference where there is substantially contemporaneous consideration, as there is where new accounts are substituted for released accounts.   Such a transfer does not diminish the estate of the debtor or enable the creditor "to obtain a greater percentage of his debt than some other creditor of the same class," in the language of Section 60a(1).   The Court found it inappropriate to apply strict rules of contemporaneity to these transfers, in view of Section 9–205.   Since Section 9–108 "merely attempts to codify as state law the substitution of collateral doctrine which is implicit in the provisions of the Bankruptcy Act, with the additional safeguard that such substitution arise in the ordinary course of business," [82] the Court found it unnecessary to resolve any asserted conflict between Section 9–108 and the Bankruptcy Act.

§ 7–12.   Litigation: The *Portland* Case, The Last Round

It was only when the *Portland* case reached the Ninth Circuit that a problem was raised which had been obvious to outsiders from the beginning.   The debtor (of Code importance) on the filed financing statement was the Portland Reporter Publishing Company, Inc. There was a merger thereafter and the debtor became Portland Newspaper Publishing Company, Inc., which was the bankrupt in the case.[83] No new security agreement was entered into—not that there is any substantial basis for requiring one when the new debtor has assumed all of the liabilities of the old one—but no new financing statement was ever filed.   The 1962 Code had no provision covering this point, which was probably not dealt with by any statute, and because the issue was raised only on the appeal, the Ninth Circuit refused to consider it.[84]   (The revised version of Article 9 deals with this problem in Sections 9–402(2)(d) and 9–402(7).)   The Court of Appeals treated the security agreement as if it had been executed by the bankrupt and the filing as if it had been made after the merger.   The basic problem, then, was whether the trustee could set aside as preferential the security interest in accounts arising within four months of bankruptcy.

---

82.   408 F.2d at 218.

83.   *See In re* Portland Newspaper Publishing Co., Inc., 3 UCC Rep.Serv. 194 at 196–198 (D.Or.1966) (in bankruptcy).

84.   DuBay v. Williams, 417 F.2d 1277 at 1286 (9th Cir. 1969).   On a change in the debtor's name after filing, see In-
ter Mountain Ass'n of Credit Men v. The Villager, Inc., 527 P.2d 664 (Utah 1974), holding that the "debtor cannot destroy the perfected security interest of a secured party by merely changing its name or corporate structure" under the 1962 Code.   *See generally* § 4–6 *supra*.

Speaking for the Court, Judge Hufstedler said that the security interest in after-acquired accounts became immune to the preference challenge when the security agreement was entered into and a financing statement was filed. At this point the security interest was "so far perfected" for Section 60a(2) purposes that no subsequent lien creditor could achieve priority over the security interest. This result was found to be in harmony with the intentions of Congress in drafting the preference provisions of the Bankruptcy Act. As Judge Hufstedler pointed out: "If we read section 60a(2) the way the trustee asks us to do, we would defeat, not implement, Congress' intent and we would impair, not promote, the intent of the draftsmen of the Uniform Commercial Code to make security transactions conform to the legitimate needs of commerce, rather than to the common-law lawyer's wish for conceptual nicety." [85]

§ 7–13. Preference Questions for the Future

It seems clear beyond cavil that the federal courts, above the level of the bankruptcy courts, have correctly read the intention of Congress in enacting the present version of Section 60 of the Bankruptcy Act as it applies in the litigated cases. The cases have not, however, dealt with the hard case where the collateral is far below the level of the debt four months before bankruptcy and above the level when bankruptcy comes.[86] Of course this would not always be a "hard" case. Where seasonal inventories are involved as in timber financing transactions, it might well be normal to have little or no collateral on hand when the loan is advanced and a build-up in collateral would be the usual expectation. Regardless of the kind of collateral or its value at any particular points in time, no more than the obligation owing is collectible and excess collateral would be free to satisfy other creditors.

Can the "so far perfected" test be read in a broader context than inventory and accounts financing? The cases to date have been consistent with a substitution of collateral theory and have enforced the provisions of Section 9–108 whether or not the courts have recognized or announced that they have done so. But a substitution of collateral theory would require rough equivalencies in value and rough simul-

85. Id. at 1289. See also In re King-Porter Co., 446 F.2d 722 (5th Cir. 1971); Biggins v. Southwest Bank, 490 F.2d 1304 (9th Cir. 1973).

86. This issue was discussed by Judge Cummings in Grain Merchants of Indiana v. Union Bank & S. Co., Bellevue, Ohio, 408 F.2d 209 at 217–218 (7th Cir. 1969). See Kohn, Preferential Transfers on the Eve of the Bankruptcy Amendments, 2 Prospectus 259 (1968).

taneity in time, and Section 9–108 would require that the substitutions be acquired in the ordinary course of business. There was a time, not very many years ago, when it seemed necessary to explicate these theories and to justify them intellectually and legally in order to insulate after-acquired accounts and inventory financing transactions from attack in bankruptcy.[87]   That fight may have been won through judicial over-kill.

Suppose a security agreement is entered into and a financing statement is filed in February, covering equipment of the debtor at a designated address, including after-acquired equipment. The secured party advances the loan on February 1. The debtor acquires a new item of equipment on July 1, replaces an item of equipment on August 1, and goes into bankruptcy on September 1. While *DuBay v. Williams* [88] should be warily read in an equipment context, if its rationale can be extended at all beyond accounts and inventory, the Court did say that a Section 60a(2) "transfer" is to be "equated with the act by which priority over later creditors is achieved and not with the event which attaches the security interest to a specific account." [89] The Court went on to say that this point was reached when the financing statement was filed, and "[b]ecause Rose City filed its financing statement long before the four-month period anteceding bankruptcy, its security interest is immune from the trustee's preference challenge." [90]

It may be true that the security interest in the after-acquired property, both new and replacement, was "so far perfected" that no subsequent lien creditor would take priority in it at the time the debtor acquired rights in it, but it would be surprising if any court would find the consideration anything other than antecedent or if any court would say that the security interest attached and was perfected on February 1. Nothing in the Code compels or suggests determining the time of the transfer here to be February 1. There is a possibility, however, that the replacement equipment might be said to have been acquired in the ordinary course of business under Section 9–108, so that a "new value" argument could be made as to it, at least if a security interest in the old equipment were released. It is more difficult to come up with such an argument for new, non-replacement equipment when it is acquired some months after the secured party advances funds, unless its acquisition was contemplated when the loan was made.

87.   Indeed that is the purpose of some of the preceding portions of this book.

88.   417 F.2d 1277 (9th Cir. 1969).

89.   *Id.* at 1287.

90.   *Id.* at 1288.

CHAPTER 8

FIXTURES

Table of Sections

§ 8–1. Background

The enactment of the Uniform Commercial Code brought about a renaissance of learning in the field of fixture law. It was the *enactment* of the Code, not its drafting or promulgation, which had this effect. This meant that lawyers learned old-fashioned fixture law at precisely the time when its importance reached its nadir. However, since fixture law was, generally speaking, purely common law in most of the United States, the Code's enactment provided an opportunity for endless discussions and often heated arguments which everyone or anyone could win since no one could provide definitive answers for some of the most elementary questions. That is, of course, a commentary on how important the problems were in fact. Be that as it may, fixtures exist. Quite often their acquisition must be financed on a purchase money basis. There should be some simple answers to common, everyday problems, or what are at least conceivable problems regardless of frequency of appearance in litigation or in fact.

It has often been said that the Code's fixture provisions will not be tested until we have another depression of 1930's dimensions. There may be something in that point of view. Nevertheless, the average number of non-farm mortgage forclosures per year during the period 1930–34 was 215,000; during 1935–39, 156,857; and during 1940–44, 43,709;[1] while comparable figures for 1965 show 116,664 foreclosures and for 1966, 117,473.[2] In 1945, total mortgage

---

[1] 1959 Savings and Loan Fact Book 62.

[2] 1968 Savings and Loan Fact Book at 46. The preliminary estimate of foreclosures, including farm foreclosures, for 1971 was 116,680. Had farms been included in the 1966 figure in the text, the number of foreclosures would have been 134,203. 1972 Savings and Loan Fact Book 50. The Federal Home Loan Bank Board in 1976 discontinued publication of the real estate foreclosure series. 1977 Savings and Loan Fact Book 44. Data for foreclosures by savings and loan associations, which are the major source of residential credit in the United States, show 24,979 foreclosures in 1975 versus 53,788 foreclosures in 1965. *Id.* at 74.

debt on one to four family dwellings was $18.6 billion; the figure rose steadily to an estimated $554.0 billion in 1976.[3] The average construction cost of a private non-farm home was $8,675 in 1950 and $17,400 in 1967,[4] while the median price for new homes sold in 1976 was $44,200.[5] It seems clear that if the current number of home mortgage foreclosures is not up to the 1930's level, it is still shockingly high, and in dollar amount is far in excess of any conceivable figures for the 1930's. Yet fixture litigation is rather sparse, especially in the home field.

One of the most common criticisms of the 1962 Code was that it did not define the term "fixture." [6] It simply said that its special fixture priority rules did not apply to "goods incorporated into a structure in the manner of lumber, bricks, tile, cement, glass, metal work and the like," [7] and further: "The law of this state other than this Act determines whether and when other goods become fixtures." [8] The Code was concerned only with chattels which had lost their discrete quality but which could in appropriate circumstances become ordinary chattels once again. (There was no attempt to interfere with real estate transactions, and fixtures could continue to be mortgaged as part of the real estate.) [9] Aside from local vagaries in just what goods were separately financible as fixtures,[10] there were states where the word "fixture" had a special meaning: goods were fixtures if they were attached to real estate in such a way that they were not

3. 1968 Savings and Loan Fact Book 32. 1977 Savings and Loan Fact Book 30.

4. 1968 Savings and Loan Fact Book 27. The median sales price of new homes was $18,000 in 1963 and $25,200 in 1971. 1972 Savings and Loan Fact Book 28.

5. 1977 Savings and Loan Fact Book 22.

6. See Coogan, Fixtures—Uniformity in Words or in Fact, 113 U.Pa.L.Rev. 1186 (1965), and Shanker, Integrated Financing System for Purchase Money Collateral: A Proposed Solution to the Fixture Problem Under Section 9–313 of the Uniform Commercial Code, 73 Yale L.J. 788 (1964). Probably the three leading articles on the subject of fixtures are: Coogan, Security Interests in Fixtures Under the Uniform Commercial Code, 75 Harv. L.Rev. 1319 (1962); Gilmore, The Purchase Money Priority, 76 Harv.L.

Rev. 1333 (1963); and Kripke, Fixtures Under the Uniform Commercial Code, 64 Colum.L.Rev. 44 (1964).

7. § 9–313(1).

8. Id. See, e. g., In re Factory Homes Corp., 333 F.Supp. 126 (W.D.Ark.1971); In re Plummer, 6 UCC Rep.Serv. 555 (E.D.Mich.1969) (in bankruptcy).

9. §§ 9–313(1), 9–501(4); Revised § 9–313 (3).

10. Doctrines associated with two states are of particular interest. On New Jersey's "institutional doctrine" see, e. g., In re Park Corrugated Box Corp., 249 F.Supp. 56 (D.N.J.1966); On Pennsylvania's "industrial plant doctrine" see, e. g., In re Universal Container Corp., 2 UCC Rep.Serv. 802 (E. D.Pa.1963) (in bankruptcy); In re Kann, 6 UCC 622 (E.D.Pa.1969) (in bankruptcy); General Electric Credit Corp. v. Pennsylvania Bank & Trust Co., 56 Pa.D. & C.2d 479 (1972).

considered to be removable, which is the opposite of the usual American usage of the term.[11] The law of fixtures has been exceedingly varied and complicated and vague, and it was an audacious act to attempt a uniform treatment of the field—and to achieve a treatment which, despite gaps and criticisms, has worked remarkably well.

The 1962 Code did not make any attempt to define "fixture", and the 1972 Code states only that: "Goods are 'fixtures' when they become so related to particular real estate that an interest in them arises under real estate law." [12]

The absence of a definition of a fixture is acceptable. Admittedly the referent of "fixture" will not be obvious in every case, but it never has been and the ambiguity inherent in the concept insures that it never will be. Revised Section 9–313 excludes ordinary building materials incorporated into an "improvement on land," while the 1962 Code excluded "goods incorporated into a structure" unless the structure remained personal property. The difference between "structure" and "improvement" is not immediately obvious, although the latter is a broader term.

Section 9–313 has been omitted from the Codes of several states including California, where the omission appears to have created a serious problem in *Goldie* v. *Bauchet Properties*.[13] This case involved a sale and lease back of real estate, and by the terms of the lease, which was not recorded, the lessor was granted a security interest in a variety of goods, including fixtures and equipment. There was no Code filing. Subsequently the lessee borrowed $10,000 from Goldie, giving Goldie a security interest in a packaging machine then on the leased premises, and a financing statement was filed in the Secretary of State's office. The Court's opinion is thorough, and it illustrates the difficulties inherent in eliminating Section 9–313 and some problems arising from other nonuniform changes in California's Code. While remanded for further proceedings, the court concluded that if the lessor's interest in the machine derived from ownership of the real property, rather than from a grant of a security interest, the problem would be resolved by the state law of real property and fixtures, and the lessor would win; but if the lessor's interest was purely a security interest, then the Code would govern and the perfected security interest in the machine would have priority over the unperfected security interest of the lessor.

11. Perhaps the leading case supporting this view is Teaff v. Hewitt, 1 Ohio St. 511 (1853).

12. Revised § 9–313(1)(a).

13. 15 Cal.3d 307, 124 Cal.Rptr. 161, 540 P.2d 1 (1975). *See generally* Salusky, Uniform Commercial Code Section 9–313: Time for Adoption in California, 27 Hastings L.J. 235 (1975).

Speaking generally and leaving possible local variations aside, if two competing secured parties claim an interest in fixtures and neither interest arises solely as a result of a real estate interest, then the problem is not resolved by Section 9–313 and it goes back to Section 9–312 for solution. Section 9–313 resolves conflicts between real estate interests in fixtures and chattel secured parties with security interest in the same fixtures. Where both claimants are vying for priority in fixtures and their interests arise purely as chattel financing interests, the problem is solved by Section 9–312.

While the terminology is by no means exact, items called "trade fixtures" are probably not in fact considered to be fixtures within the meaning of Section 9–313. Trade fixtures may be installed by a tenant in order to operate a business, and such items are ordinarily removable by the tenant at the end of the lease term, at least if the tenant is not in default, although the lease itself may often need to be consulted in order to determine the rights of the parties, including third parties claiming an interest in the goods.[14] If the trade fixtures are not fixtures within the meaning of the governing law, then a security interest in them will have to be perfected under the Code, presumably in the usual case under the rules covering equipment, if the secured party is to prevail over the claims of third parties. A fixture filing would not be effective to perfect the security interest.[15]

§ 8–2. Basic Provisions

The basic scheme of the 1962 Code's fixture provisions is to give priority to a purchase money financer of a fixture in a contest between the financer and the holder of an interest in real estate whose interest in the fixture is normally derivative.[16] No filing—only attachment—is required for priority over existing real estate interests,[17]

14. *See generally* Goldie v. Bauchet Properties, 15 Cal.3d 307, 124 Cal. Rptr. 161, 540 P.2d 1 (1975).

15. *In re* Factory Homes Corp., 333 F. Supp. 126 (W.D.Ark.1971).

16. *See* Honea v. Laco Auto Leasing, Inc., 80 N.M. 300, 454 P.2d 782 (1969); Blancob Constr. Corp. v. 246 Beaumont Equity, Inc., 23 A.D.2d 413, 261 N.Y.S.2d 227 (1965). Of course, if the item in question is a fixture, § 9–313(3) must be complied with if the fixture secured party wants priority over existing real estate interests; and if the competing interests are claiming the goods as equipment, the provisions of § 9–312(4) must be met if the purchase money financer is to

have priority. *See* Sunshine v. Sanray Floor Covering Corp., 64 Misc.2d 780, 315 N.Y.S.2d 937 (N.Y.Sup.Ct. 1970). *See also* Karp Bros., Inc. v. West Ward Sav. & Loan Assn., 440 Pa. 583, 271 A.2d 493 (1970).

17. § 9–313(2). *See* House v. Long, 244 Ark. 718, 426 S.W.2d 814 (1968); Denis v. Shirl-Re Realty Corp., 4 UCC Rep.Serv. 609 (N.Y.Sup.Ct.1967). In State Bank of Albany v. Kahn, 58 Misc.2d 655, 296 N.Y.S.2d 391 (N.Y.Sup.Ct.1969), a swimming pool was held to be a fixture, and the financer of the pool was held to be subordinate to the real estate mortgagee under § 9–313(3) on the ground that the pool financer's security interest did not attach until the pool was completed and

which merely continues the old situation in those states where no filing was required in conditional sale transactions.[18]　Filing is required for priority over designated, subsequently acquired interests.[19] In most situations these rules undoubtedly worked adequately.　But, of course, the purchase money priority is, so to speak, absolute.　It is available to a seller as against real estate interests even though the buyer is not even in the chain of title.　This supposedly has presented the title companies with a problem, even if it was not as new a problem as they may have thought, and in a number of states amendments were made to the Code requiring that the name of the record owner be shown on a fixture filing.[20]　Of more importance, theoretically at least, is the plight of the home owner who purchases his new home only to learn that a fixture supplier had reserved a good security interest when the bath tubs were sold to the contractor. Moreover, some filing officers have refused to file fixture financing statements in the real estate records because they felt the language of the Code did not absolutely compel it.[21]

The 1972 Code introduces a new term "fixture filing," [22] which means simply a financing statement covering fixtures which the filing officer is required to handle as if it were a real estate mortgage [23] and which, when timely filed, gives priority over real estate interests. If the fixture financer is not concerned with real estate interests, he can in some cases, make a regular chattel filing, if any filing is needed for perfection, which will be good against other third parties.[24]

---

the loan was advanced in reliance on a completion certificate.　The advancing of the loan was the moment when value was given, according to the court, which cut off the financer's claim under § 9–313(2).　This concept of value is arguable in view of the definition of "value" in § 1–201 (44), which is not cited by the court. *See also* Babson Credit Plan, Inc. v. Cordele Production Credit Ass'n, 146 Ga.App. 266, 246 S.E.2d 354 (1978).

18.　*See, e. g.* Sherer-Gillett Co. v. Long, 318 Ill. 432, 149 N.E. 225 (1925).　*See generally* McGraw, Chattel Mortgages and Conditional Sales, 42 Ill.B.J. 738 (1954).

19.　§ 9–313(4).　*See* O'Dell v. Kunkel's, Inc., 49 Okla.Bar Assn.J. 388, 24 UCC Rep.Serv. 227 (1978).

20.　*See, e. g.*, Wis.Stat.Ann. 409.402(1), (3) (1964); *In re* Kahl, 10 UCC Rep. Serv. 1322 (W.D.Wis.1972) (in bankruptcy).

21.　Apparently some country recorders construed the requirement of § 9–401 (1) that a financing statement covering fixtures be filed "in the office where a mortgage on the real estate concerned would be filed or recorded" to be met if the filing were literally in the same office (perhaps in a convenient shoe box) but not in the same file.　This kind of situation has been much commented on, but it is really a trivial variation in the kind of circumstances where it would occur, i. e., rural communities.　So long as the person searching the files is aware of the convention, it is simply a matter of looking in two places rather than one and the inconvenience is minimal. *Cf.* Op.Att'y.Gen. Iowa, 4 UCC Rep. Serv. 125 (1967).

22.　Revised § 9–313(1)(b).

23.　Revised § 9–403(7).

24.　Revised § 9–313(3)(c), (d).　Under this revision, no filing is required for perfection in the case of consumer

Gone, however, is the 1962 Code's concept of priority over existing real estate interests by attachment alone.[25] In a contest between a purchase money security interest and a real estate interest (other than a construction mortgage), the security interest will win *if* the debtor has an interest of record in the real estate or is in possession, and there has been a fixture filing before or within ten days after the goods became fixtures.[26] In the case of a construction mortgage where the mortgage is of record before the goods are affixed, the mortgagee will prevail over the security interest, and if the construction mortgage is refinanced by a permanent lender, the priority goes along with the refinancing mortgage.[27]

These provisions eradicate the problem in the 1962 Code where a fixture financer could come ahead of real estate interests even though the fixture debtor was not in the chain of title. They do not go so far as some real estate lenders would like, however. It appears that some mortgagees want every fixture attached to a building during the life of the mortgage to feed the mortgage.[28] There may be nothing wrong in wanting this, but there would be a great deal wrong if it were allowed. This would, realistically, prevent most mortgagors from keeping their property in good condition through replacements of worn-out fixtures such as furnaces, since no one pays cash for anything anymore and most sellers of fixtures probably want some right, even if they never exercise it, to remove on default. This right has long existed in some states, whether or not it was exercised by conditional sellers and whether or not mortgagees were aware of its existence.[29] The exercise of the right is normally de-

---

goods which become fixtures, but filing is required for priority as specified in Revised § 9–313. Revised § 9–302(1)(d). *See* Funk, The Proposed Revision of Article 9 of the Uniform Commercial Code, Part 1, 26 Bus.Law. 1465, 1468–1477 (1971). Under neither version of Article 9 will a fixture filing perfect a security interest in goods which turn out not to be fixtures. *See, e. g., In re* Kahl, 10 UCC Rep.Serv. 1322 (W.D.Wis.1972) (in bankruptcy).

25. § 9–313(2).

26. Revised § 9–313(4)(a).

27. Revised § 9–313(6). *See also* Revised § 9–313(1)(c).

28. This status seems to have been substantially achieved by Code amend-

ments in Florida and Ohio. *See* Fla. Stat.Ann. § 679.9–313 ; Ohio Rev.Code § 1309.32. In support of this amendatory approach, *see* Pfeiler, Uniform Commercial Code—Adverse Effect on Real Estate Mortgages, 29 Leg.Bull. 201 (1963).

29. *See, e. g.,* National Bank of the Republic v. Wells-Jackson Corp., 358 Ill. 356, 193 N.E. 215 (1934), where the court allowed the removal of a building sprinkling system and said: "The general rule . . . [is] that where the parties to a contract of sale of personal property in which title is reserved in the vendor to the chattel sold, agree that by the annexation of such personal property to the real estate the chattel shall not lose its character as personal property, such contract is enforceable between the par-

pendent on the economics of removal, aside from the possible "spite" case. When, as normally happens, the fixture seller is paid, the fixture will feed the mortgage, but in the meantime the mortgagees need to be restrained in their own (perhaps unrecognized) best interest.

It is possible for a mortgagee to give written consent to the fixture security interest [30] or to disclaim an interest in the goods as fixtures, under section 9–313(3) and revised section 9–313(5)(a), and if this is done the financer has priority regardless of perfection; but such a consent or disclaimer will not be routinely given, and it may not be given at all, which is the basic reason for the Code's rules. The fixture financer's right to remove the fixture on default is his basic right and ultimate weapon. [31]

In any event, the secured party's right is to remove the fixture, and the owner or mortgagee of the real estate (where this person is not the debtor) is not liable for the price of the goods, even though the goods may have been specially made for the premises and would be valueless if removed.[32]

Occasionally a debtor and a secured party will agree in the security agreement that a chattel, which will be affixed to real estate in such a way that it arguably will become a fixture, will be personal property. As a matter of enforcing the contract between the parties,

ties thereto and also against a purchaser or a prior mortgagee, or those occupying similar positions, where the chattel can be removed without material injury to the freehold or the usefulness of the chattel." *Id.* at 364, 193 N.E. at 219. *See also* Holt v. Henley, 232 U.S. 637, 34 S.Ct. 459, 58 L.Ed. 767 (1914); American Laundry Machinery Co. v. Miners Trust Co., 307 Pa. 395, 161 A. 306 (1932); Grupp v. Margolis, 153 Cal.App.2d 500, 314 P.2d 820 (1957). The Code provision is in § 9–313(5), Revised § 9–313(8); there is no substantive difference between the two versions. *See* Honea v. Laco Auto Leasing, Inc., 80 N.M. 300, 454 P.2d 782 (1969); Dry Dock Savings Bank v. De Georgio, 6 UCC Rep.Serv. 1278 (N.Y.Sup.Ct.1969).

30. While *In re* Seminole Park & Fairgrounds, Inc., 502 F.2d 1015 (5th Cir. 1974) was resolved largely on the basis of a Florida amendment to § 9–313, nevertheless it suggests the inadvisability of relying on implied consent based on general agreements rather than receiving specific consent to the

affixation and a specific recognition of the right of removal.

31. It would seem highly unlikely that a financer of aluminum siding attached to a house might wish to remove it, as may be permitted by § 9–313(5) & Revised § 9–313(8), but the threat of removal may have some value as against the mortgagee of the property. *See* Dry Dock Sav. Bank v. De Georgio, 61 Misc.2d 224, 305 N.Y.S.2d 73 (N.Y.Sup.Ct.1969). *See also* Feldzamen v. Paulro Properties, Inc., 4 UCC Rep.Serv. 524 (N.Y.Sup. Ct.1967), where a secured party attempted unsuccessfully to remove electrical wiring from a building, as against a mortgagee, but it would appear that the court relied too strongly on the pre-Code "material injury to the freehold" test rather than the Code rules of § 9–313(5), Revised § 9–313(8).

32. Nu-Way Distributing Corp. v. Schoikert, 44 A.D.2d 840, 355 N.Y.S. 2d 475 (1974).

their characterization should be binding on them, but it should not be effective against innocent third parties if it works to their detriment.[33] If the parties have agreed that a specified item of equipment will be personal property although it may properly be a fixture and they have made a fixture filing, the security interest may not be effective against another secured party who claims the goods under an after-acquired property clause in a security agreement, with a properly perfected security interest in equipment.[34] The intention of the parties should be effective as to them and also effective vis-a-vis third parties when it will benefit the third parties rather than work to their detriment.[35] If the owner of the real estate and the tenant have agreed that fixtures installed by the tenant are to remain personal property and will be removable, the owner of the real estate should not subsequently be able to claim the goods as against the tenant or those asserting rights in the goods which are derived from the tenant.[36]

If there is any reasonable question as to what category an item falls into, the simplest solution is to file twice, once for a fixture and once for equipment or consumer goods, as the case may be. This would eliminate a certain amount of litigation over the correct categorization of the collateral, since the security interest would be perfected regardless of whether the goods were determined ultimately to be fixtures or chattels. In the absence of dual filing a wrong guess will result in an unperfected security interest [37] and possibly an action for malpractice.

§ 8–3. Practical Fixture Problems

Some ordinary fact situations will be hypothesized and briefly analyzed under the 1962 Code and under Revised Section 9–313.

33. Fedders Central Air Conditioning Corp. v. Karpinecz & Sons, Inc., 83 Misc.2d 720, 372 N.Y.S.2d 470 (N.Y. Civ.Ct.1975).

34. The leading early authority for this proposition is Cain v. Country Club Delicatessen, 25 Conn.Super. 327, 203 A.2d 441 (1964).

35. *In re* Nelson, 6 UCC Rep.Serv. 857 (D.Utah 1969). As a matter of historical interest, see Holt v. Henley, 232 U.S. 637, 34 S.Ct. 459 (1914) (opinion by Holmes, J.)

36. In *In re* Petermar, 3 UCC Rep. Serv. 370 (N.Y.Sup.Ct.1966), the assignee for the benefit of creditors of an air conditioning company was entitled to remove certain air conditioning equipment from property where it had been installed for the use of the defaulting buyer-lessee of the real estate, as against the claim of the lessor-owner of the real estate.

37. There seems to have been a needless amount of litigation between trustees in bankruptcy and allegedly secured parties over whether an item is or is not a fixture where the filing was either for fixtures or in the chattel files. *See, e. g., In re* Nelson, 6 UCC Rep.Serv. 857 (D.Utah 1969); *In re* Regency Furniture, Inc., 7 UCC Rep.Serv. 1384 (E.D.Tenn.1970) (in bankruptcy); *In re* Particle Reduction Corp., 5 UCC Rep.Serv. 242 (E.D.Pa. 1968) (in bankruptcy).

1. A buys a new furnace, which we will assume becomes a fixture upon installation, from X Furnace Co. The purchase contract is a conditional sales contract which complies with local state law.[38] X Furnace Co. installs this replacement furnace in A's home.

(a) No financing statement is filed.

(b) A fixture filing is made 15 days after the contract is signed and 9 days after the furnace is installed.

There is a mortgage on A's home. This mortgage was made 12 years ago to finance the construction of the home, and the mortgage covers "fixtures" and their replacements. The mortgagee makes no advances after the furnace is installed. A defaults on the mortgage and on the conditional sale contract. As between the mortgagee and X, who has priority?

Under the 1962 Code it is clear that X has priority whether (a) or (b) is the case. Section 9–313(2) provides for priority of the purchase money security interest over existing real estate interests, such as this mortgage, without any filing for perfection but on the mere attachment of the security interest. For a third party to come ahead of such an interest, the third party must, without knowledge of the security interest and before its perfection, be a subsequent purchaser for value of an interest in the real estate, or a creditor with a lien on the real estate subsequently obtained by judicial proceedings, or a mortgagee who has made subsequent advances.[39] (The 1962 Code speaks of "a creditor with a prior encumbrance of record on the real estate" [40] but such a person would probably be a mortgagee in the usual terminology, and "encumbrance" [41] is a defined term in Revised Article 9 so its usage must be carefully controlled.) No one of the exceptions meets the facts of our hypothetical.

While there is a dearth of pre-Code cases on the point,[42] the 1962 Code's resolution of this problem is probably in line with what would have happened in states like Illinois where the validity of conditional

---

38. While Article 9 will govern security aspects of the transaction, some of the terms of the contract of sale may well be specified in a retail installment sales act, and in the event of a conflict between Article 9 and such act, the act will govern. § 9–203(2), Revised § 9–203(4).

39. § 9–313(4). *See* Meads v. Dial Finance Co. of Gadsden, 56 Ala.App. 84, 319 So.2d 281 (1975).

40. § 9–313(4).

41. Revised § 9–105(1)(g): " 'Encumbrance' includes real estate mortgages and other liens on real estate and all other rights in real estate that are not ownership interests."

42. *See generally,* 2 G. Gilmore, Security Interests in Personal Property, 743–776 (1965).

sales was recognized but no recording or filing was required as a condition precedent to enforceability.[43]   There is no reason why nonreliance third party creditors should get a windfall at the expense of a purchase money financer of fixtures, regardless of filing.

The priority problem is somewhat differently resolved, however, under Revised Article 9.   Revised Section 9–313(4)(a) will give our purchase money fixture financer priority over the real estate mortgagee on these facts if a "fixture filing" is made "before the goods become a fixture or within ten days thereafter," but if no filing is made within this period, the mortgagee will prevail.   This harmonizes with the present priority rule of Section 9–312(4) dealing with collateral other than inventory.   Revised Section 9–302(1)(d)[44] establishes a new rule of automatic perfection of purchase money security interests in consumer goods which become fixtures, but in determining priority between that kind of security interest and a conflicting interest of an owner or encumbrancer, filing is required for priority of the former.[45] In the absence of filing, the security interest is perfectly good against lien creditors.[46]   Under the 1962 Code, if the consumer were to remove a fixture and sell it to a fellow consumer, the purchaser would presumably take his interest subject to the interest of the fixture secured party if filed;   otherwise he would take free of it.[47]   This is apparently thought to be the rule of the 1962 Code[48] but on the basis of the present wording of the subsection, this result is not crystal clear.

Section 9–307(2) states:

> In the case of consumer goods and in the case of farm
> equipment having an original purchase price not in excess of
> $2500 (other than fixtures, see Section 9–313), a buyer takes
> free of a security interest even though perfected if he buys
> without knowledge of the security interest, for value and for

---

43   Sherer-Gillett Co. v. Long, 318 Ill. 432, 149 N.E. 225 (1925).   Cf. Revised § 9–313(4)(d).

44.   § 9–302(1):   A financing statement must be filed to perfect all security interests except the following:
(d) a purchase money security interest in consumer goods;   but filing is required [for a fixture under section 9–313 or for a motor vehicle required to be licensed;] *for a motor vehicle required to be registered; and fixture filing is required for priority over conflicting interests in fixtures to the extent provided in section 9–313.*   (Deleted material is shown in brackets and new material is in italics.)

45.   Revised §§ 9–302(1)(d), 9–313(4)(a). In any event, priority is given to the fixture financer where the fixtures are "readily removable replacements of domestic appliances which are consumer goods."   Revised § 9–313(4)(c).

46.   Revised § 9–313(4)(d).

47.   §§ 9–307(2), 9–301(1)(c).

48.   *See* Comment 3 to § 9–307 in the 1962 Official Text.

his own personal, family or household purposes or his own farming operations unless prior to the purchase the secured party has filed a financing statement covering such goods.

The parenthetical expression is apparently intended to remove fixtures from the operation of the subsection, but, if so, the reference to Section 9–313 is inappropriate because that section determines priorities between fixture financers and real estate interests, not those between fixture financers and consumer buyers. If this possible conflict is not governed by this provision, then it presumably falls within Section 9–301(1)(c) which subordinates an unperfected security interest in goods (which term includes fixtures) [49] to the rights of a good faith buyer not in ordinary course of business who gives value and takes possession before "perfection." We now have a proposed new rule of automatic perfection which is applicable here. A consumer buyer will, presumably, take free of an unfiled purchase money security interest in goods which had been fixtures prior to their removal. It should perhaps be pointed out that the consumer buyer in Section 9–307(2) takes free of a security interest in the specified circumstances without the restriction in Section 9–307(1) that the security interest be created "by his seller." [50]

If the consumer buyer were to buy the fixture by a bill of sale, in connection with a purchase of the real estate, he would have priority over an unfiled fixture security interest under Section 9–313(4)(a) of the 1962 Code. This should continue to be true under Revised Section 9–313 except where the fixtures are readily removable replacements of domestic appliances and the secured party has a purchase money security interest which need not be filed for perfection. [51]

> 2. C Development Co. owns a tract of land which is mortgaged to X Bank. The Bank has agreed to finance the construction of a new office building, making construction advances as the work progresses. When the construction has been completed, Y Insurance Co. has committed itself to make a permanent mortgage. H Construction Co., as the contractor, has subcontracts with J Plumbing Fixtures, Inc. to supply the plumbing fixtures, with K Lumber Co. to supply cement and lumber for the building construction, and with L

49. § 9–105(1)(f).

50. A particularly interesting discussion of these matters may be found in Vernon, Priorities, The Uniform Commercial Code and Consumer Financing, 4 B.C.Ind. & Com.L.Rev. 531 (1963). *See* Everett Nat. Bank v. Deschuiteneer, 109 N.H. 112, 244 A.2d 196 (1968).

51. Revised §§ 9–313(4)(c), 9–313(7).

Wood Co. to supply both ordinary wall paneling and some antique wall paneling for offices of differing quality. Without making dire assumptions of developments, how are some potential problems resolved?

Under the 1962 Code, the suppliers could apparently retain purchase money security interests good against both the construction and permanent mortgagees [52] except for "goods incorporated into a structure in the manner of lumber bricks . . . and the like." [53] However, the construction mortgagee would have priority to the extent of advances made without knowledge of the security interest and before filing,[54] and presumably this priority would be available to the permanent lender.[55] Attachment alone would give the supplier priority over the mortgagee in the absence of future advances, and, of course, over the owner.[56]

52. "A security interest which *attaches* to goods before they become fixtures takes priority as to the goods over the claims of all persons who have an interest in the real estate . . . ." § 9–313(2) (emphasis added). An appealing alternative theory leading to a different result has been proposed by Fairfax Leary, Jr., Esq., of the Philadelphia Bar in a letter to the author dated February 7, 1969. Basically Mr. Leary suggests that the suppliers cannot retain purchase money security interests good against the owner and mortgagees in these circumstances for three reasons. (1) A supplier of fixtures to a contractor knows that the ownership of the fixtures is intended to pass to the owner of the premises, and therefore under § 9–306(2) the security interest does not continue in the goods because they have been disposed of by the contractor-debtor pursuant to the intention of the supplier who has at least "otherwise" agreed to this, even if it is not specifically authorized in the security agreement. (2) The owner of the realty, when the contractor is paid, is really a "buyer in ordinary course" under § 9–307(1) who takes free of a security interest created by his seller; the definition of "buyer in ordinary course of business" in § 1–201(9) does not absolutely rule out this construction. (3) The owner of the real estate is intended by the supplier and the contractor to be the owner of the goods when they are installed, and there-

fore the owner is a "debtor" under § 9–105(1)(d) even though not the person owing payment to the supplier, and under § 9–402(1) the owner must sign the financing statement as debtor if the security interest is to be good against him. *See also* Leary & Rucci, Fixing Up the Fixture Section of the U.C.C., 42 Temp.L.Q. 355, 397–407 (1969).

53. § 9–313(1). Plumbing fixtures may be so integrated into a building as to pass with a conveyance of the real estate and yet they do not lose their distinct identity, so that the fixture financer is entitled to priority over a real estate mortgagee. Denis v. Shirl-Re Realty Corp., 4 UCC Rep.Serv. 609 (N.Y.Sup.Ct.1967).

54. § 9–313(4)(c). *See* House v. Long, 244 Ark. 718, 426 S.W.2d 814 (1968).

55. This would be true in states where it is customary to assign an existing mortgage rather than discharge the old mortgage and execute a new one, but it would be elevating form over substance to reach any other result in any event. Of course a permanent lender might be considered a "subsequent purchaser for value of [an] interest in the real estate," under § 9–313(4), in view of the definitions in §§ 1–201(32), (33).

56. § 9–313(2).

The goods while held in the suppliers' stock would be inventory [57] and could be subject to inventory security interests which would be cut off on a sale to the contractor,[58] even though purchase money security interests might be retained by the suppliers. Because of the intended use of the goods by the contractor, a filing would probably be made, assuming that this is not a cash sale, and the filing would be for fixtures. (Depending on additional facts, the filing might be for equipment or inventory, but in most states it would not matter which the goods were considered since the filing would be central in any case and the goods might not be categorized. Under the 1962 Code but not under Revised Article 9 if such a filing were properly made, it should continue to be effective even though the goods subsequently became fixtures.[59] Assuming that the real estate to which the goods are to be affixed is known and a suitable description is available, it would be shown on the financing statement, but the contractor would be shown as the debtor, and C Development Co. would not be shown at all, even though C is the owner of the land. This would comply with the official version of the 1962 Code, although many states by amendment have required that the name of the record owner be shown on a fixture financing statement, and other states have suggested on officially approved financing statement forms that this information be given.[60]

Under Revised Section 9–313 any security interests retained by the suppliers would be subordinate to the mortgagee's interest. This is spelled out in Revised Section 9–313(6).[61] Under the 1962 Code a security interest may not be retained by the seller in goods which are incorporated into the structure.[62] In Revised Section 9–313(2), the preclusion is stated in terms of "ordinary building materials in-

---

57. § 9–109(4).

58. § 9–307(1). *But see* § 9–306.

59. § 9–401(3) provides that a proper filing continues to be effective even though the use, if that controlled the original filing, changes. This provision is not changed in Revised Article 9, but Revised § 9–313(4)(a) requires that the debtor have an interest of record in or be in possession of the real estate and that a timely fixture filing be made for the security interest to have priority over the real estate interest. In any event, overriding this provision, Revised § 9–313(6) gives priority to a construction mortgage which is recorded before the goods become fixtures if the goods become fixtures before the construction is completed.

If the supplier has not perfected his security interest in goods which are sold to a construction company and eventually installed in an apartment house (assuming that these goods are fixtures on installation), the supplier cannot reclaim as against the building owner's trustee in bankruptcy under § 9–301. *See In re* Beech Street Holding Corp., 10 UCC Rep.Serv. 1294 (E.D.Pa.1972) (in bankruptcy).

60. *See* Kratovil, Financing Statements for Fixture Filings, 23 Bus.Law. 1210 (1968).

61. *See* note 59 *supra*.

62. § 9–313(1).

corporated into an improvement." This would probably eliminate any security interest of K Lumber Co. in cement and lumber, and it would preclude an effective security interest in ordinary wall paneling; antique wall paneling would become part of the real estate and probably could not be removed under the 1962 Code but it might be taken out on default under the revised version. Such paneling might not be "ordinary building materials" [63] which become part of the real estate on incorporation. Surely plumbing "fixtures" would be fixtures under either version.

Revised Section 9–313(6) clearly gives the construction mortgagee priority over a conflicting chattel security interest in a case like ours. We have here a construction mortgagee who is financing the erection of improvements and who has every right to expect that its lien will be superior to any claimed security interests of suppliers, who will probably have to rely on mechanics' liens to enforce their claims. The construction mortgage was of record before the goods were supplied, and in any event the debtor did not have an interest of record in the real estate and was not in possession.

If we were to vary the fact situation and put the problem in terms of a blanket mortgage for the construction of 100 houses on a subdivided tract with individual, unrelated home mortgages subsequently made, the permanent mortgagee would still prevail over the fixture secured party because the debtor (i. e., the contractor) would not have an interest of record in the real estate and would not be in possession.

3. X Railroad decides to install a new microwave transmitting system along its extensive trackage in seven states. How can this be handled on a secured basis?

It may be assumed that the real property of any railroad is subject to a long-term mortgage covering everything that it is possible to cover. Of course a purchase money security interest in the kind of antennas and related equipment involved in a microwave system might well be effective against the mortgagee under the 1962 Code simply because of attachment and without filing,[64] assuming fixture status, but if security is required at all, then filing will also be required by prudent counsel to obviate possible problems which could arise on a sale of the real estate concerned or on the acquisition of liens by creditors through judicial proceedings, or on the making of subsequent advances by the mortgagee.[65] (As to the last problem, there is no re-

---

63. Revised § 9–313(2).

64. § 9–313(2).

65. § 9–312(4).

quirement in the 1962 Code that the future advances by the mortgagee be made against the fixtures; it is sufficient that the advances be made without knowledge of the security interest and before perfection.) If fixture filing is required, where does one file?

Under the 1962 Code fixture filing in these circumstances is extremely troublesome. There is an open question about what kind of description of the real estate is required. Multiple filings are unavoidable. Filing in every county where a fixture is located is necessary.[66] This is the only answer provided by the Code. However, many states have long had separate statutes governing filings for security interests in the property of public utilities,[67] and in a number of states modifications to this end were made in various sections of the Code.[68] There was also a Transmitting Utility Place of Filing Act[69] which tied in with the Code without expressly amending it. In the absence of any extra-Code solution, the transaction may be cast in less traditional terms, of course, and at least the fixture filing problem can be eliminated, but such imaginative devices are beyond the scope of this book.

Revised Section 9–105(1)(n) introduces a new term, "Transmitting utility," whose definition is basically borrowed from the Transmitting Utility Place of Filing Act. A railroad is included in the definition, as are a number of businesses usually thought of as public utilities. Under Revised Section 9–401(5), the proper place to file to perfect a security interest in collateral, including fixtures, of a transmitting utility is the state's central filing office. This central filing constitutes a fixture filing for goods which are or are to become fixtures. No description of the real estate is required,[70] and the financing statement is effective until a termination statement is filed,[71] which eliminates the necessity of periodic re-filings. This is a neat solution for a specialized but troublesome problem.

    4. A buys new bathroom fixtures for his home under a conditional sales contract from Z Plumbing Supply Co. The home is subject to a mortgage held by X Bank.

      (a) Z makes no filing.

---

66. § 9–401(1)(a) or (b), depending on which alternative subsection (1) is adopted by a particular state.

67. *See, e. g.,* Ill.Rev.Stat.1971, ch. 95, § 51.

68. *See, e. g.,* Vernon's Ann.Mo.Stat. § 400.9–302(5); Ga.Code § 109A–9–302 (3)(c).

69. *See, e. g.* Rev.Code Mont.1947, §§ 87A–9–302.1, .2.

70. Revised § 9–402(5).

71. Revised § 9–403(6).

(b) Z makes a timely fixture filing.

(c) Z files in the chattel records.

A goes into bankruptcy a month after the plumbing fixtures are installed.

As between Z and the trustee in bankruptcy, does the trustee prevail?

Under the 1962 Code, a purchase money fixture financer has priority over certain existing third party interests simply by attachment, but filing is required for priority over the interests of certain persons, including lien creditors, subsequently arising.[72] In the absence of filing, the trustee could attack the security interest under Section 70c of the Bankruptcy Act as a creditor who, upon the date of bankruptcy, obtained a lien by judicial proceedings, and who therefore takes priority over an unperfected security interest. Presumably the security interest would be preferential under Section 60 in the absence of filing, if the other elements of a preference were present.[73] If there were a fixture filing within 21 days after the property was transferred to the debtor, there would be no preference because the 1962 Code has no stated time within which a filing must be made for perfection,[74] and any fixture filing made before the date of bankruptcy would preempt the trustee's rights under section 70. A filing in the chattel records would probably not, however, be effective in either case. Bathroom fixtures could not be sold to a consumer for any reasonable purpose other than use as "fixtures" so that the filing would have to be for fixtures to be effective; the possibility of proper filing as a chattel followed by a change of use to a fixture with continued effectiveness of the filing,[75] seems remote.

---

72. §§ 9–313(2), (4).

73. Eight elements are required to set aside a transfer as preferential: (1) a transfer (by way of security) of (2) the debtor's property (3) to a creditor (4) made by the debtor while insolvent and (5) within four months of bankruptcy (6) on account of an antecedent debt (7) with the effect of enabling the creditor to obtain a greater percentage of his debt than some other creditor of the same class; if these seven elements exist, the transfer may be set aside if (8) the creditor had reasonable cause to believe the debtor was insolvent when the transfer was made. Bankruptcy Act, §§ 60a(1), 60b.

74. In substance, under § 60a(7) of the Bankruptcy Act, where filing is required for priority of the security interest as against subsequent liens, the transfer is deemed to take place at the time it was made if an applicable statute requiring filing within 21 days is complied with or, in the absence of a stated time period, if the filing is made within 21 days after the transfer. *See, e. g.*, §§ 9–301(2), 9–312 (4). The only specified time periods for filing in Article 9 relate to priority, not perfection. *But see* § 7–6 *supra.*

75. § 9–401(3).

Where the 1962 Code required filing in the real estate mortgage office for perfection of a security interest in a consumer's fixture,[76] the Revised Article 9 does not. Revised Section 9–302(1)(d) gives automatic perfection to purchase money security interests in consumer goods, requiring a fixture filing only for priority over conflicting interests in the fixture.[77] In the context of our problem, the automatic perfection provision should be helpful. Revised Section 9–313(4)(d) provides that a perfected fixture security interest has priority over a lien on the real estate obtained by legal or equitable proceedings after the security interest was perfected by any permitted method.

Three methods of perfection are available for fixtures under the revised version of Article 9. First, automatic perfection for purchase money security interests in a consumer's fixtures; second, perfection by a fixture filing to gain priority over conflicting real estate interests; and third, perfection by a chattel filing where the secured party is willing to take his chances against competing real estate interests but wants perfection against the rest of the world. In our example, in any of the three circumstances, the security interest should be good against the trustee. Perfection by attachment has always been a feature of the Code in the case of consumer goods,[78] aside from motor vehicles and fixtures, and there is no policy reason for not including fixtures within this ambit. No lien creditor could upset the transaction, under Section 60 or Section 70c, nor should a bona fide purchaser take free of the interest as required by Section 67c. The bona fide purchaser test applicable to real property in Section 60a(2) is not relevant to a contest involving a chattel which has become a fixture but which was financed as a chattel rather than as real estate.

If the debtor in our example were a business corporation buying new bathroom fixtures for an office building which is subject to a mortgage, there would be no automatic perfection on attachment under Revised Article 9, and either a fixture filing or a chattel filing would be necessary if the secured party is to prevail over the trustee; either should be adequate. Revised Section 9–313(4)(a) requires a fixture filing before or within ten days after the goods become fixtures for the security interest in them to prevail over the interest of an owner or encumbrancer [79] (other than a construction mortgagee),[80] but sub-

---

76. §§ 9–302(1)(d), 9–401(1).

77. Revised § 9–302(1)(d). *But see* § 9–307(2), Revised § 9–307(2).

78. § 9–302(1)(d). *See In re* Kretzer, 48 Berks Cty.L.J. 121 (E.D.Pa.1955) (in bankruptcy).

79. The definition of "encumbrance" in Revised § 9–105(1)(g) includes liens on real estate without restriction to contractual liens. The priority provisions of Revised §§ 9–313(4) and (5) are stated with reference to "encumbrancer or owner of real estate."

80. *See* Revised § 9–313(6).

section (d) has no time limitation. So long as the judicial lien is obtained after perfection, the security interest has priority.

> 5. A has leased a one-story building from B for use as a store. The term of the lease is 25 years. All maintenance and replacements of equipment are A's responsibility. The lease is expressly subordinate to the existing mortgage. A installs display counters which are bolted to the floor; X, their seller, has reserved a purchase money security interest in them to secure payment of the balance of the purchase price. Within six months after taking possession of the premises, the furnace must be replaced, and a new furnace is bought on time from Y Furnace Co. which reserves a security interest. B defaults on the mortgage, and the mortgagee institutes foreclosure proceedings.

As between the mortgagee and the conditional sellers, who is entitled to priority?

In so far as the 1962 Code provides for these situations, both sellers have priority over the real estate mortgagee, even in the absence of filing. This is clearly so as to the furnace, which is a fixture, and it is true as to the display counters whether or not they are fixtures. As to fixtures, attachment alone gives priority over existing real estate interests.[81] If the display counters are not fixtures, then the real estate mortgagee probably has no claim to them, but even if he does, the seller's interest arguably attached first and thus may have priority under Section 9–312(5) (c). Of course, the draftsmanship of leases varies considerably—although merely putting some provisions in writing does not make then automatically enforceable, contrary to some lawyers' opinions—and the results might hinge on non-Code law as it impinges on the congeries of contracts and what may be called the "intention of the parties," which is in most circumstances a rather meaningless cliché. Revised Section 9–313(5) (b) clearly states that goods which a tenant has a right to remove are personal property and not fixtures. A normal lease would give the tenant the right to remove his "store fixtures," at least if the tenant is not in default when the lease terminates, but surely not a furnace. As to the furnace, the seller's security interest would have to be perfected by a fixture filing before or within ten days after the furnace was installed, and even then the seller would not have priority unless the tenant was

81. § 9–313(2).

in possession or had an interest of record in the real estate,[82] which would be the case if the lease or a memorandum of lease were recorded.

> 6. B executed a real estate mortgage to X. The recorded mortgage purported to cover real property, fixtures, and all personal property owned by the mortgagor and used on the premises during the existence of the mortgage. B later bought furniture, furnishings, and carpeting on conditional sale from H. No financing statement was ever filed.

The facts stated above are a considerably simplified version of the facts in *United States v. Baptist Golden Age Home.*[83] The court held in that case that the goods supplied by H came under the real estate mortgage, because the security interest of H was unperfected, and the priority conflict was resolved by Section 9–312(4) as to goods which were equipment and by Sections 9–313 and 9–401(1) as to goods which were fixtures. The court's analysis seems to be questionable.

While fixtures may be included in a real estate mortgage, and as a matter of contract between the mortgagor and mortgagee other goods may be covered too, the effect of these provisions on after-acquired property vis-a-vis third parties is a different matter.

Under the 1962 Code, if the mortgagee wishes to cover after-acquired goods other than fixtures, he would have to file a financing statement. The Code expressly covers security interests [84] in personal property.[85] The Code also covers security interests in fixtures, but it is expressly recognized that an encumbrance on fixtures may be created under real estate law.[86] When the fixture is being financed as a chattel, however, Article 9 controls.

Assuming the Code governed the transactions in the *Baptist Golden Age Home* case, attachment alone should have been sufficient to have given the conditional seller of fixtures (which the carpeting may

---

82. Revised § 9–313(4) (a). "Trade fixtures" are covered in Revised § 9–313 (5) (b), which gives priority to the fixture financer if "the debtor has a right to remove the goods as against the encumbrancer or owner" of the real estate, whether or not the security interest in the fixtures is perfected. In any event an encumbrancer or owner of the real estate may consent to the security interest or disclaim an interest in goods as fixtures. § 9–313 (3), Revised § 9–313(5) (a). If the debtor does not have an interest of record in the real estate, Revised § 9–402(3) provides that the name of the record owner should be stated on the financing statement.

83. 226 F.Supp. 892 (W.D.Ark.1964).

84. § 1–201(37).

85. § 9–102(1), (2). As to after-acquired property, *see* § 9–204(3), (4); Revised § 9–204(1), (2).

86. § 9–313(1), Revised § 9–313(3).

have been) priority over the real estate mortgagee. This is the rule of section 9–313(2) of the 1962 Code. (The mortgage in *Baptist Golden Age Home* had, however, been assigned a number of times, and because the last assignment, which was to the United States, occurred after the conditional sale, it is possible that the United States could have been considered a subsequent purchaser for value of an interest in the real estate entitled to priority under Section 9–313(4)(a).) It would ordinarily seem improper to consider a mortgagee by assignment purchasing at its own foreclosure sale as a subsequent purchaser for value, since the interest purchased presumably is the interest originally granted and the purchase price usually will be the amount then due on the mortgage. If a third party purchased at the foreclosure sale, such a person would be considered a subsequent purchaser for value, however; [87] and if the original mortgagee purchased at its own sale, it could not be considered a purchaser for value under Section 9–313(4) of the 1962 Code,[88] but if the mortgagee purchased the property at its foreclosure sale and then sold the property to someone else, the purchaser should qualify for priority under Section 9–313(4) (a).[89] Under revised Article 9, fixture filing before or within ten days after affixation would be required for such priority.[90] As to the goods which remained equipment,[91] rather than becoming fixtures, the mortgagee could not have a perfected security interest in them under an after-acquired property clause in the real estate mortgage because no financing statement had been filed. The conditional seller of the goods likewise could not have a perfected security interest in them because no filing was ever made. This priority problem is not resolved by Section 9–312(4), as the court thought it was, because that provision governs priority only where (1) a purchase money financer

87. § 9–313(4) (last sentence): "A purchaser of the real estate at a foreclosure sale other than an encumbrancer, purchasing at his own foreclosure sale is a subsequent purchaser within this section." *See* Northwest Equipment Sales Co. v. Western Packers, Inc., 543 F.2d 65 (9th Cir. 1976); Tillotson v. Stephens, 195 Neb. 104, 237 N.W.2d 108 (1975).

88. Architectural Cabinet, Inc. v. Manley, 3 UCC Rep.Serv. 263 (Pa.Ct.Com. Pl.1966).

89. Home Savings Ass'n v. Southern Union Gas Co., 486 S.W.2d 386 (Tex. Civ.App.1972).

90. Revised § 9–313(4) (a). While the facts of the case are not pellucid, it is possible that the debtor had possession of the goods including the fixtures, if such they were, for some time before the security agreement was entered into. If so, this raises the possibility that the seller would be entitled to priority as to the fixtures under § 9–313(2) because the secured interest had "attached" under § 9–204(1) but the security interest would not be effective against the debtor or third parties under § 9–203(1). This anomaly is cured by Revised § 9–203(1) (b).

91. The goods were used in business and the debtor was a non-profit organization. § 9–109(2).

of collateral (other than inventory) has filed before or within ten days after the debtor has received the goods and (2) there is a conflicting security interest in the goods. Here there was no such filing. Assuming that the real estate mortgage created a security interest in the after-acquired equipment, the conflict would have to be resolved by Section 9–312(5) which governs cases not otherwise provided for. Since neither interest is perfected under the Code, priority would be determined in the order of attachment.[92] This may be one of those problems which are not resolved in terms by the Code. It is difficult to see how either security interest attached ahead of the other, and if the attachment was simultaneous neither party is entitled to priority, and there is no obvious way to apportion the security interests in the goods. One's sympathies perhaps lie, at least initially, with the conditional seller who is unpaid and who has made acquisition of the goods possible; but he has not filed as he should have done to perfect his security interest. Certainly the real estate mortgagee has no claim at all to the equipment except by reason of the after-acquired property clause in the mortgage, which was arguably overreaching and perhaps unconscionable.[93] It might be possible to construct an argument beginning in Article 2 in support of the seller,[94] but it is by no means clear that in any case any result other than simultaneous attachment could be obtained, because as to both secured parties the debtor presumably obtained rights in the collateral at the same time.

This problem, if the above analysis is acceptable, is not resolved under Revised Article 9. Neither security interest would be perfected, and the issue of simultaneous attachment is not dealt with.[95] The new provision allowing a real estate mortgage to be effective as a fixture filing [96] obviously has no application to equipment which does not become a fixture, and nothing in Revised Section 9–313 determines priorities when goods are not fixtures. Where there is any

---

92. § 9–312(5) (c); Revised § 9–312(5) (b). As to attachment, *see* § 9–204(1), Revised § 9–203(1). Presumably the debtor has signed a security agreement (under § 9–105(1)) in both instances, the secured parties have both given value (as defined in § 1–201 (44)), and the debtor has rights in the collateral. The events necessary for attachment of both interests presumably occur at the same time here.

93. § 2–302 on unconscionability in sales contracts could hardly be im-

ported directly into the real estate mortgage field, but such a doctrine has long been held to exist quite apart from its statutory expression in the Code. *See generally* Davenport, Unconscionability and the Uniform Commercial Code, 22 U.Miami L.Rev. 121 (1967).

94. *See, e. g.,* §§ 9–113, 2–401.

95. *See* Revised § 9–312(5) (b).

96. Revised § 9–402(6).

question about whether a particular item is or is not a fixture, dual filing is a simple solution. To a limited extent Revised Article 9 protects security interests perfected in goods as chattels even though the goods become fixtures,[97] but nothing protects the secured party if there is a fixture filing alone and the goods are held to be chattels and not fixtures.[98]

§ 8–4. Mobile Homes

The rules governing security interests in mobile homes are presently uncertain in general terms and quite apart from how they are handled in a particular state, and Revised Article 9 does not specifically cover this area. If mobile homes are covered by the local motor vehicle act, a security interest in them should be perfected under that act by certificate of title notation,[99] and when they are transported from one state to another, the usual rules of Section 9–103 on multistate certificate of title problems should control. While mobile homes may qualify as consumer goods, under the definition in Section 9–109, a purchase money security interest in them should come within the filing requirement in Section 9–302(1)(d) in essentially all states[1] and a non-purchase money security interest certainly would.

If the mobile homes are in a dealer's possession, even if they are set on foundations and hooked up to septic tanks and electricity, they may be treated as inventory of the dealer for purposes of perfecting a security interest in them, and the inventory financer's claim may be given priority over a real estate mortgagee who claims a real estate interest in them.[2]

Some, or perhaps most, mobile homes are not intended to be mobile once they have been placed on a plot of ground for occupancy. Whether they become fixtures at this point is a difficult issue to resolve. If the debtor owns the real estate on which the mobile home is situated and the home is in fact intended to be permanently located

97. Revised § 9–313(4) (c), (d).

98 *Cf.* Cain v. Country Club Delicatessen, 25 Conn.Super. 327, 203 A.2d 441 (1964).

99. § 9–302(3) (b), Revised § 9–302(3) (b). *See In re* Cahoon d/b/a Bill's Steak House, 4 C.C.H. Sec.Trans. Guide ¶ 51,333 (E.D.Tenn.1971) (in bankruptcy).

1. *See* Albany Discount Corp. v. Mohawk Nat. Bank, 28 N.Y.2d 222, 321 N.Y.S.2d 94, 269 N.E.2d 809 (1971); Recchio v. Manufacturers & Traders Trust Co., 35 A.D.2d 769, 316 N.Y.S.2d 915 (1970). *Cf. In re* Williams, 10 UCC Rep.Serv. 277 (D.Me.1971) (in bankruptcy). A few states eliminated the requirement of filing to perfect a purchase money security interest in a consumer's motor vehicle when the Code was originally passed.

2. Rakosi v. General Electric Credit Corp., 22 UCC Rep.Serv. 204 (N.Y. Sup.1977).

there, it may be a home in the sense that any other home is a home, and therefore part of the real estate which may be subject to a real estate mortgage, so that a real estate mortgagee would have an interest in the home under the mortgage and if the mortgagee were financing the home no Code filing of any kind would be required.[3] In these circumstances it is irrelevant whether the mobile home is considered a fixture or a part of the real estate because the mobile home financer is also the mortgagee of the land. If the contest were between a mortgagee of the land and a financer of the mobile home, it would be essential that the home be considered a fixture. Under the 1962 Code, a purchase money fixture financer would have priority over the existing real estate mortgagee simply by virtue of attachment and regardless of perfection,[4] but in the absence of perfection subsequent interests will have priority if the interests are acquired without knowledge of the fixture security interest.[5] Under the 1972 Code, unless the mortgagee has consented in writing or disclaimed an interest in the fixtures,[6] a fixture filing[7] will be required before or within ten days after the home is attached to the land if the purchase money fixture financer is to have priority.[8]

Under the 1962 Code when the collateral is goods which at the time the security interest attaches are or are to become fixtures, then filing is required in the local mortgage office.[9] This provision is restated in the 1972 Code to apply only where the filing is intended as a fixture filing,[10] since a filing for equipment or consumer goods would be effective for some purposes.[11] If a security interest in a mobile home were perfected by certificate of title notation at the time when the security interest attached and the home was in fact mobile, that perfection should continue even though the home subsequently became relatively permanently attached to land,[12] although this situation clearly can lead to difficult problems.

3. George v. Commercial Credit Corp., 440 F.2d 551 (7th Cir. 1971). Here the mobile home, permanently attached to land, was treated as a fixture in which an interest could be perfected under real estate law, pursuant to § 9–313 (1).

4. § 9–313(2). If the interest is non-purchase money, consent in writing or a disclaimer by the mortgagee will be necessary for the fixture financer to prevail. § 9–313(3). The same is true under Revised § 9–313(5) (a).

5. § 9–313(4).

6. Revised § 9–313(5)(a).

7. Revised § 9–313(1)(b).

8. Revised § 9–313(4)(a).

9. § 9–401(1).

10. § 9–401(1).

11. Revised § 9–313(4) (d).

12. § 9–401(3). Certificate of title notation is presumably the equivalent of

If the "owner" of a mobile home has it placed on land which he has leased for that purpose, a purchase money financer of the home should have priority over the lessor of the land under Section 9–313 (2). This problem is more carefully covered in Revised Section 9–313(5)(b), which gives the fixture financer priority over the lessor, whether or not the security interest is perfected, if the debtor has a right to remove the home as against the lessor, which would normally be the case in such a lease, and if the debtor's right terminates, for whatever reason, the priority of the security interest continues for a "reasonable time."

Problems similar to those with mobile homes (except for certificate of title problems) may arise if prefabricated buildings are financed as fixtures.[13] Ordinary prudence would require the financer of such a building for a lessee to obtain the lessor's written consent or a disclaimer of any interest in the building, and if this were done the financer would have priority over the lessor of the land.[14] This would not seem to be one of those cases to which the "construction mortgage" provisions of Revised Section 9–313 were applicable, and we are not here concerned with following security interests in goods incorporated into a structure under Section 9–313(1).

filing under §§ 9–302(3) and (4) and is expressly such under Revised § 9–302 (4).

13. Apparently buildings which have been moved have occasionally been treated, at least for some purposes, as fixtures. *See, e. g., In re* New Hope & Ivyland Railroad Co., 353 F.Supp. 608 (E.D.Pa.1973).

14. § 9–313(2), Revised § 9–313(5) (a). This result is not clearly required in all circumstances by § 9–313(2) but would probably be reached with the help of § 1–103.

CHAPTER 9

MULTISTATE TRANSACTIONS

Table of Sections

§ 9–1. Basic Provisions on Choice of Law

The 1962 Code's provisions on choice of law have been criticized by a few, little understood by many, and of no consequence to most. Ordinary transactions involve only one state where the debtor, the secured party, and the collateral are all located. Automobiles cross state lines with ease and most collateral is transportable, but the basic honesty of the great majority of debtors minimizes the importance of figuring out which state's law governs certain aspects of any transaction. That choice will normally be obvious.

When the Code was originally drafted, it was by no means certain that it would sweep the country. Some of the provisions were broadly drafted to make the Code cover as many transactions as it could possibly encompass even though the Code might never become law in the majority of the states. The Code's success made a number of refinements possible in the redrafting of Article 9.

The basic choice of law provision in the Code is Section 1–105.[1] This has been made clear in the redraft.[2] It was not so clear in the

1. With 1972 additions underscored and deletions from the 1962 Code in brackets, the section reads:

> **§ 1–105. Territorial Application of the Act; Parties' Power to Choose Applicable Law**
>
> (1) Except as provided hereafter in this section, when a transaction bears a reasonable relation to this state and also to another state or nation the parties may agree that the law either of this state or of such other state or nation shall govern their rights and duties. Failing such agreement this Act applies to transactions bearing an appropriate relation to this state.

2. See note 2 on page 317.

1962 Code and in fact this Section was overridden by the provisions of Sections 9-102 and 9-103 where they were applicable, although their application might occasionally be enigmatic.

Section 9-102 of the 1962 Code is concerned with policy and scope, according to the title of the section. In terms, Article 9 is stated to apply to security interests in any personal property and fixtures within the jurisdiction of the state (and to sales of accounts, contract rights, and chattel paper) unless it is otherwise provided in Section 9-103 on multiple state transactions or unless the transaction is excluded from Article 9 by Section 9-104. The title of Section 9-103 says that it is concerned with accounts, contract rights, general intangibles, equipment relating to another jurisdiction, and incoming goods already subject to a security interest. If the title is accurate, the section may not cover inventory, documents, instruments, or chattel paper. On the other hand, the section does in terms cover goods which are normally used in more than one jurisdiction and which are

Note 1—Continued

(2) Where one of the following provisions of this Act specifies the applicable law, that provision governs and a contrary agreement is effective only to the extent permitted by the law (including the conflict of laws rules) so specified:

Rights of creditors against sold goods. Section 2-402.

Applicability of the Article on Bank Deposits and Collections. Section 4-102.

Bulk transfers subject to the Article on Bulk Transfers. Section 6-102.

Applicability of the Article on Investment Securities. Section 8-106.

[Policy and scope of the Article on Secured Transactions. Sections 9-102 and 9-103.]

Perfection provisions of the Article on Secured Transactions, Section 9-103.

2. This is basically resolved by Revised § 9-102, which follows with 1972 additions underscored and deletions from the 1962 Code in brackets:

§ 9-102. Policy and [Scope] Subject Matter of Article

(1) Except as otherwise provided [in Section 9-103 on multiple state transactions and] in Section 9-104 on excluded transactions, this Article applies [so far as concerns any personal property and fixtures within the jurisdiction of this state]

    (a) to any transaction (regardless of its form) which is intended to create a security interest in personal property or fixtures including goods, documents, instruments, general intangibles, chattel paper or accounts [or contract rights]; and also

    (b) to any sale of accounts [contract rights] or chattel paper.

(2) This Article applies to security interests created by contract including pledge, assignment, chattel mortgage, chattel trust, trust deed, factor's lien, equipment trust, conditional sale, trust receipt, other lien or title retention contract and lease or consignment intended as security. This Article does not apply to statutory liens except as provided in Section 9-310.

(3) The application of this Article to a security interest in a secured obligation is not affected by the fact that the obligation is itself secured by a transaction or interest to which this Articles does not apply.

classified as inventory because they are leased, and Section 9–103(3) professes to deal with "personal property" other than accounts, contract rights, general intangibles, and equipment or other goods classified as inventory because leased where such goods are normally used in more than one state. There are some inherent ambiguities here which cannot be resolved but which are dealt with in the revised version of Article 9.

If we assume that Section 9–103 governs only what the title or the specific language of the subsections covers and we do not take "personal property" in subsection (3) to be inclusive of everything other than fixtures—the preamble to Section 9–102(1) speaks of personal property *and* fixtures—then we have a serious problem when ordinary inventory, for one example, is moved from one state to another. Of course, inventory can be "incoming goods" and could come within the title, but Section 9–103(3) says "personal property" which would include chattel paper. For whatever reasons, inventory has usually been considered included and chattel paper excluded from this section, but this is a dubious answer. Section 9–103(3) speaks of "personal property," not "goods."

Section 9–103 of the 1962 Code contains numerous references to "validity" of the security interest. While no one can be certain what this means, the term is generally taken to refer to "formal requisites." The term has been dropped in Revised Article 9 and if there is a question about validity, the choice of law which determines it will be taken from Section 1–105.

In general terms, Section 1–105 of the 1962 Code provides that, except where Sections 9–102 and 9–103 specify applicable law, if a transaction bears a reasonable relation to more than one state or to another nation, the parties may agree on the law governing their rights and duties.[3] In the absence of such an agreement, the Code "applies to transactions bearing an appropriate relation to this state." Most agreements will state which law governs them; this will be part of the printed form which secured parties operating on a large scale will provide for the transactions they engage in. Where the transaction is large enough to merit a negotiated contract, which may well be printed, the choice of law specified will normally be the state of the counsel for the secured party. This is done for obvious reasons, but in most instances that state will have a sufficient relation-

3. *See, e. g., In re* Yant, 5 UCC Rep. Serv. 645 (W.D.Mich.1968) (in bankruptcy).

ship to the transaction that the choice of law will not be purely arbitrary. That is, New York law will be stated to govern a transaction if New York counsel prepare the papers, but the secured party, or some of the secured parties if a number are involved, may well be located in New York, and the funds will probably be advanced in New York even though the borrower does business only in Hawaii. How much effect this kind of provision will be given in an Article 9 transaction where the collateral is in Hawaii is debatable.[4]

Under the 1962 Code, Section 9-102 would require that the law of Hawaii be applied to collateral located there [5] and assuming that the collateral was goods which were there when the agreement was made and which were never moved, Section 9-103 would not provide otherwise. Under the redraft of Section 1-105(2), the perfection provisions of Hawaii's Article 9 would clearly apply even though other law might govern other aspects of the transaction by agreement of the parties, including a note executed and issued in New York as part of the transaction. But what happens on default? This presumably is one of those situations where, no matter what the parties agreed to, the situation bears no reasonable relation to New York and the law of Hawaii governs.[6]

4. *See, e. g., In re* Kokomo Times Publishing and Printing Corp., 301 F.Supp. 529 (S.D.Ind.1968); *In re* Automated Bookbinding Services, Inc., 336 F. Supp. 1128 (D.Md.1972), reversed on other grounds, 471 F.2d 546 (4th Cir. 1972).

5. *See In re* Laboratory Precision Products, Inc., 4 UCC Rep.Serv. 1139 (S. D.N.Y.1968) (in bankruptcy). In Joint Holdings and Trading Co., Ltd. v. First Union Nat'l Bank of North Carolina, 50 Cal.App.3d 159, 123 Cal.Rptr. 519 (1975), the law of California was applied when goods en route from American Samoa to North Carolina, where a filing had been made, were attached while in Los Angeles. The goods had never been in North Carolina, and there had been no perfection in the jurisdiction where they were located when the security interest attached. *See also In re* Leasing Consultants, Inc., 486 F.2d 367 (2d Cir. 1973).

6. *See, e. g.,* Associates Discount Corp. v. Cary, 47 Misc.2d 369, 262 N.Y.S.2d 646 (N.Y.Civ.Ct.1965). The law of the state where repossession occurs may

well govern the default procedure. *See, e. g.,* Thompson v. Ford Motor Credit Co., 324 F.Supp. 108 (D.S.C. 1971). Professor Gilmore apparently takes the position that § 9-103 equates default rules with perfection rules in determining what law governs. *See* 2 Gilmore, Security Interests in Personal Property 1276-77 (1965). He relies on § 9-103, Comment 7 (third paragraph). Professor Weintraub finds this interpretation "wrong," and says, "No word or phrase in section 9-103 can reasonably be read to include default rights. Instead, choice of law for default rights between a debtor and a creditor is controlled by the situs rule of section 9-102." Weintraub, Choice of Law in Secured Personal Property Transactions: The Impact of Article 9 of the Uniform Commercial Code, 68 Mich.L.Rev. 684, 699 (1970). The redraft of Article 9 appears to agree with Professor Weintraub that § 9-103 relates solely to perfection; the situs test has been deleted from § 9-102; and under § 1-105 it would be surprising if any law were applied other than that of the state where tangible collateral is located on default, if the default pro-

In the redraft of Article 9 there has been deleted the language in Section 9–102(1) which states that Article 9 applies " . . . so far as concerns any personal property and fixtures within the jurisdiction of this state . . . ." The intended effect is to make it clear that it is the function of Section 1–105 to provide general choice of law rules; Section 9–102 no longer will cover jurisdiction questions but only the scope of subject matter coverage. While Section 1–105 allows the parties to choose the law to be applied, if the choice is reasonable, and, further, the Section provides that "failing such agreement" the Code will apply if the transaction bears an "appropriate relation" to the state, no rule is stated to determine applicable law, aside from the perfection rules of Section 9–103, if the parties choose the law of a state which the court concerned feels is unrealistic. This kind of problem is likely to arise when the collateral has been removed from the state where it was located when the security agreement was made and whose law was stated to apply, and a default occurs. Depending on a variety of issues, including the kind of collateral and how the secured party attempts to proceed on default, it is likely that the law of the state where the collateral is located will be applied to default remedies. This is an area where courts will find their own way. If there were a more uniform version of the Code in effect in all states, some possible problems would be relatively academic.

Special circumstances may make the application of the Code's rules uncertain if a problem grows out of a purchase money transaction. Suppose there is a purchase of mobile equipment on conditional sale, the goods are removed from one state to a second state, then the parties agree without consideration on a reduction in monthly payments, and an arguable default occurs, and then the seller demands that the originally agreed payments be made. Is the case governed by Section 1–105 or by Section 9–103? Assuming the parties have not agreed on applicable law, it is possible to say that such a case is divisible; that is, that Article 2 via Section 1–105 may govern the sale aspects of the contract which come within its ambit, such as the provision of Section 2–209(1) permitting modification of a contract without consideration, while Article 9 is limited to questions of perfection (and validity under the 1962 Code). In such a case, if the modification is valid without consideration, then there is no default.[7] This is an appealing solution, and it is implicitly ac-

ceedings are instituted there. *See generally* Juenger, Nonpossessory Security Interests in American Conflicts Law, 26 Am.J.Comp.L. (Supplement) 145 (1978).

7. This was the resolution adopted in Skinner v. Tober Foreign Motors, Inc., 345 Mass. 429, 187 N.E.2d 669 (1963), where an airplane was contracted for

cepted by the 1972 Official Text where Section 1–105 refers to Article 9 only for perfection rules.

§ 9–2. Accounts, Contract Rights, and General Intangibles

Section 9–103(1) states that the validity and perfection of a security interest in accounts and contract rights and "the possibility and effect of proper filing" are governed by the law of the state where the assignor keeps his records concerning them.[8] The law of the state of the debtor's chief place of business similarly governs general intangibles under Section 9–103(2).[9] At least in theory these can be difficult rules to unravel and apply. Since those kinds of collateral are not represented by indispensable pieces of paper, some rule other than the general rule of Section 9–102 is necessary.

The term "validity" is nowhere defined and its meaning is by no means clear. Presumably it refers to "formal requisites."[10] The term recurs throughout Section 9–103, and apparently it may refer, where applicable, to such matters as capacity of the parties, usury, compliance with a retail installment sales act or the provisions of Section 9–203(1) relating to the enforceability of the security interest, for example. The term has been dropped in Revised § 9–103 which is devoted to perfection.

Since it is quite possible for a seller of goods to keep his account records in an improbable state in these computerized days, or indeed to keep no permanent records at all if the accounts are financed by a factor, the provision of Section 9–103 is purely arbitrary and is no longer satisfactory.

and delivered to the buyer in Massachusetts, a Code state, and subsequently removed by the buyer to Connecticut, then not a Code state. There was no issue about validity or perfection here. Perhaps the principal worry of sellers in the conflicts field may be the removal of their goods to Louisiana. The holding in the Skinner case was approved in Weintraub, Choice of Law in Secured Personal Property Transactions: The Impact of Article 9 of the Uniform Commercial Code, 68 Mich.L.Rev. 684, 694 (1970), and disapproved in 2 G. Gilmore, Security Interests in Personal Property 1280 (1965). *Cf.* Cooper v. Cherokee Village Development Co., 236 Ark. 37, 364 S.W.2d 158 (1963).

8. *See* American East India Corp. v. Ideal Shoe Co., 400 F.Supp. 141 (E.D. Pa.1975); Barocas v. Bohemia Import Co., Inc., 33 Colo.App. 263, 518 P.2d 850 (1974). *But see* Miller v. Wells Fargo Bank International Corp., 406 F.Supp. 452 (S.D.N.Y.1975).

9. *See* Estate of Cook, 64 Cal.App.3d 852, 135 Cal.Rptr. 96 (1976).

10. *See* § 9–103, Comment 7. *See* General Motors Acceptance Corp. v. Whisnant, 387 F.2d 774 (5th Cir. 1968). *Compare* In re Zimmardi, 8 UCC Rep. Serv. 1396 (D.Me.1971) (in bankruptcy); In re Erwin, 8 UCC Rep.Serv. 1399 (D.Me.1971) (in bankruptcy).

It was apparently once thought that contract rights turned into accounts as the contracts were performed,[11] but this is not true unless the contract involves sales or leases of goods or the rendition of services.[12] If the collateral for a loan is an assignment of royalties to come due under a contract with a book publisher, such contract rights would become general intangibles as payment is earned (or under Revised Article 9 they would be general intangibles whether earned or unearned), but before payment is made. The rule of Section 9–103(1) is that the security interest in contract rights must be perfected in the state where the assignor keeps his records, while Section 9–103(2) requires perfection in the state where the debtor's chief place of business is located in the case of general intangibles.[13] This is not to say that the security interest is technically lost as royalty payments come in if two states are involved for nothing in Section 9–306 on proceeds distinguishes such a case from any other, either for ten days after receipt of identifiable proceeds in the absence of a filed financing statement claiming proceeds or beyond ten days if there is a filed claim.[14] A financing statement filed in State A could, presumably, perfect a security interest in general intangibles (and their proceeds) as proceeds which, as original collateral, would have to be perfected in State B, and all without regard for where, in fact, the proceeds were "received," which might be in neither state.

This kind of problem might arise if a magazine publisher purchased all rights to books serialized or otherwise printed in the magazine and subsequently entered into a contract with a book publisher providing for royalty payments to the magazine as earned. Assume the corporate publication and editorial offices of the magazine are

---

11. *See* § 9–306(1): "The term [proceeds] also includes the account arising when the right to payment is earned under a contract right." This sentence has been dropped in the revised version of Article 9. *See also* E. Turgeon Const. Co. v. Elhatton Plumbing & Heating Co., 292 A.2d 230 (R.I.1972); Farnum v. C. J. Merrill, Inc., 264 A.2d 150 (Me. 1970); Spurlin v. Sloan, 368 S.W.2d 314 (Ky.App.1963).

12. *See* § 9–106. While the term "contract right" has been eliminated in the redraft and the definition thus dropped from Revised § 9–106, the term "account" has not been broadened to cover more than unearned rights to payment arising from the same kinds of collateral as were previously covered.

13. This example assumes that the right to book royalties may be owned and used as collateral by a business entity, and this can happen. In the case of an individual author, even one working at a job in Chicago and living and keeping his records in Gary where he does his part-time writing, the place of filing is persumably governed by § 9–401. At least this is a common sense solution. This kind of situation is simply overlooked by § 9–103. It is covered by Revised § 9–103(3) (b), (d) which require filing for general intangibles in the state of the debtor's residence in the case of an individual.

14. *See generally* §§ 5–7, 5–11.

in St. Louis, while the circulation records and all business records are kept in Denver or in a nearby cave. If the magazine operation needs more capital and a loan is negotiated with a Santa Fe bank, using the unearned royalties as collateral, where should a financing statement be filed? The loan agreement might specify New Mexico law as governing, although no creditor of the magazine would think of searching there for filed security interests, but Section 1–105 would refer to Sections 9–102 and 9–103. Section 9–102 apparently would not govern because the collateral involved is intangible and has no situs. Section 9–103(1) would require filing in Colorado because the record of the assignment of contract rights would be kept there by the debtor.[15] Since the great value of the royalties as collateral arises when they are earned, there should also be a filing in Missouri under Section 9–103(2) since the debtor's chief place of business [16] is there, for from the time the royalty is earned until the time when it is paid, the collateral is a general intangible, and it is proceeds of the assigned contract rights.

Revised Section 9–103(3) says that in the case of accounts and general intangibles the law (including the conflict of laws rules) of the state where the debtor is located will govern perfection and the effect of perfection or the failure to perfect, and the location of the debtor is his chief executive office if he has more than one place of business. This would specify a Missouri filing, and the law of Missouri

---

15. *See* Industrial Packaging Products Co. v. Fort Pitt Packaging Intern., Inc., 399 Pa. 643, 161 A.2d 19 (1960) (where collateral was accounts and assignor's records were kept in Pennsylvania, Pennsylvania law governed under § 9–103(1) despite agreement of parties that New York law governed; § 1–105 could not override express requirement of § 9–103(1)).

16. The term "chief place of business" is used in § 9–103(2) but is not defined. It could not sensibly mean the state of incorporation when all offices and plants were in other states. No one looks in Delaware for security interests covering collateral of corporations which have no connection with the state except to be incorporated there. Presumably "chief place of business" means "chief executive office," and the latter term is used in Revised § 9–103. The new term at least eliminates any likelihood of argument about

whether the chief place of business is the principal plant or the executive office of a manufacturer. In the case of a few corporations even "chief executive office" may not be free from doubt, but these problems are ordinarily resolvable by no more than two filings at rather minimal cost. Under Revised § 9–103(3) (e), where the debtor's location—in this context, chief executive office—is changed from one state to another, the security interest continues to be perfected for only four months, unless it lapses sooner because its effective period expires before the end of that time, if it is not reperfected in the new state. On the interpretation of "chief place of business," see Tatelbaum v. Commerce Inv. Co., 257 Md. 194, 262 A.2d 494 (1970); Moody Day Co. v. Westview Nat. Bank, 452 S.W.2d 572 (Tex.Civ.App. 1970), refused n. r. e.; In re Brown, 5 UCC Rep.Serv. 401 (W.D.Mich.1968) (in bankruptcy).

would govern this aspect of the transaction. If the parties specify that the law of New Mexico governs the transaction, as they could under Revised Section 1–105, that law may govern all aspects of the transaction except perfection. Perfection affects third parties, or it may do so, and the Code's rules cannot be varied here; as between themselves, the parties may choose the law that applies. Some interesting conflicts may arise if the 1972 Official Text is in force in one state but not in others affected by the kind of transaction hypothesized above, but we survived a transitional period from the time when the Code was the law only in Pennsylvania to the day when it was the law of 49 states, and fortunately conflicts problems are rarely as important or as common as they are interesting.

§ 9–3. Mobile Goods

Section 9–103(2) provides that the law of the jurisdiction where the debtor's chief place of business is located governs "the validity and perfection of a security interest and the possibility and effect of proper filing" if goods are "of a type which are normally used in more than one jurisdiction (such as automotive equipment, rolling stock, airplanes, road building equipment, commercial harvesting equipment, construction machinery and the like) if such goods are classified as equipment or classified as inventory by reason of their being leased by the debtor to others." Perhaps the two most obvious problems here are (1) that the rule applies to goods "normally used" in more than one jurisdiction even though the goods in question need never have been so used [17] and (2) that goods *held* for lease are not covered. In the first case it is not necessarily the law of the state where the goods are located, perhaps permanently, but rather the place of the debtor's chief place of business that governs.[18] Of course, if the goods are covered by a certificate of title, the law of the issuing state governs perfection under Section 9–103(4), and in any case where federal law provides for perfection of security interests, as it does in the case of airplanes and rolling stock,[19] it will override the Code in the manner of perfection.

17. General Electric Credit Corp. v. Western Crane & Rigging Co., 184 Neb. 212, 166 N.W.2d 409 (1969). *See also* General Electric Credit Corp. v. R. A. Heintz Constr. Co., 302 F.Supp. 958 (D. Or.1969).

18. Moody Day Co. v. Westview Nat'l Bank, 452 S.W.2d 572 (Tex.Civ.App. 1970); Foley Machinery Co. v. John T. Brady Co., Inc., 62 Misc.2d 777, 310 N.Y.S.2d 49 (1970). *See also In re* Dobbins, 371 F.Supp. 141 (D.Kan.1973).

Cf. Associates Financial Services Co., Inc. v. First. Nat. Bank of South Central Michigan, 82 Mich.App. 495, 266 N.W.2d 490 (1978).

19. As to airplanes, *see* 49 U.S.C.A. § 1403; as to rolling stock, *see* 49 U.S.C.A. § 20(c). See § 9–302(3), (4), Revised § 9–302(3), (4). For foreign air carriers, *see* § 9–103(2) (optional last sentence), Revised § 9–103(3) (c), (d). Federal law may specify no more than a place to file, in which case state law

The redraft of Article 9 makes no drastic changes here. "Automotive equipment" is deleted, and motor vehicles, trailers, and shipping containers are added to the enumeration of mobile goods, and goods held for lease, as well as goods leased, are covered.[20] The governing law for perfection and its effect will be the law of the place where the debtor is located: his place of business if he has *one*, his chief executive office if he has more than one place of business, and otherwise at his residence.[21] It is made clearer that goods subject to a certificate of title are subject to different rules.[22]

§ 9–4. Other Goods: The Thirty-Day Rule

Section 9–103(3) covers personal property other than that governed by Sections 9–103(1) and (2) which is subject to a security interest when it is brought into "this state." (Certificated motor vehicles are left to one side, in this Section and in this discussion.) The validity of security interests in these kinds of collateral is to be determined by the law (including the conflict of laws rules) of the jurisdiction where the property was located when the security interest attached.[23] On its face this section applies to chattel paper, instruments, documents of title, and goods not classified as mobile (or certificated). Note that the application of the section depends on the location of the collateral at the time of attachment, in determining the validity of the security interest (whatever "validity" may be), but the rules of the

(the Code) should govern other matters such as rights of buyers. *See* Northern Illinois Corp. v. Bishop Distributing Co., 284 F.Supp. 121 (W.D. Mich.1969). *Cf.* Dowell v. Beech Acceptance Corp., 3 Cal.3d 544, 476 P.2d 401, 91 Cal.Rptr. 1, *certiorari denied* 404 U.S. 823, 92 S.Ct. 45, 30 L.Ed.2d 50 (1971). While Revised § 9–103(3) (b) may overstate the matter in saying that the law of the jurisdiction in which the debtor is located governs perfection in these cases, it is probably fair to say, as the Section does, that the law of the debtor's location governs the effect of perfection or nonperfection.

20. Revised § 9–103(3) (a). It has been assumed through the years that goods leased and goods held for lease were both properly classified as inventory under § 9–109(4). The definition of inventory covers goods held for lease (in this connection) but it does not in terms cover goods leased, unless they come within goods "furnished under contracts of service" (whatever that term may mean), although Comment 3 to § 9–109 takes the position that goods leased and held for lease are inventory. From the standpoint of where to file for perfection, it will rarely, if ever, matter whether the goods are classified as equipment or inventory. Regardless of argumentative niceties, goods should be classified as inventory whether they are leased or held for lease.

21. Revised § 9–103(3)(b), (d). For practical purposes here, "chief executive office" replaces "chief place of business" under the 1962 Code. See note 16 supra.

22. *Compare* § 9–103(4) *with* Revised § 9–103(3)(a) (last clause); *see, e. g., In re* Rave, 7 UCC Rep.Serv. 258 (D. Conn.1968) (in bankruptcy).

23. *See, e. g., In re* Washington Processing Co., Inc., 3 UCC Rep.Serv. 475 (S.D.Cal.1966) (in bankruptcy).

section beyond this point depend on whether it was intended that the collateral be kept in "this state" or whether the debtor simply brought it here. The implications may be easier to understand if considered in terms of goods such as equipment or consumer goods, but inventory is included.[24]

Suppose a business in Detroit bought some equipment on conditional sale from a seller in Toledo, for immediate shipment to Detroit. The security interest presumably would attach when the goods were still in Toledo.[25] But it would be pointless to file in Ohio from the standpoint of creditors of the debtor-buyer, for they would check only the files in Michigan. Section 9–103(3) says that if the goods are shipped to the buyer and arrive in Michigan within thirty days after attachment, the "validity" of the security interest is to be determined by Michigan law, and if the security interest was not perfected in Ohio, then perfection in Michigan dates from perfection in "this state." There is, however, a ten-day grace period for filing as to purchase money security interests in equipment from the time the debtor receives possession (not from the time of attachment) under Section 9–301(2) as against transferees in bulk and lien creditors and under Section 9–312(4) for priority over conflicting security interests. If the security interest was perfected in Ohio (although the validity would be determined by Michigan law), the perfection would continue for four months after removal and thereafter if perfected in Michigan before the four months expired. The security interest is not, however, automatically perfected in Michigan for thirty days. The only effect of the thirty-day provision is in deciding which state's law determines validity, and even so it depends on removal within that period for permanent purposes rather than merely interstate transportation if the law of Michigan is to govern.[26]

---

24. A financer of inventory for a debtor doing business in California and Arizona who did not file in Arizona was held to be subordinate as to the Arizona goods to a federal tax lien; the inventory was stationary, and it was located where the parties intended it to be. Interstate Tire Co. v. United States, 12 UCC Rep.Serv. 948 (D.Ariz. 1973).

25. § 9–204(1), Revised § 9–203(1).

26. Assume that the security interest attaches on July 1 in Toledo to a printing press to be shipped to the debtor in Detroit immediately. It is not in fact shipped until July 15 and it arrives at the debtor's place of business on July 20. Judgment liens against the debtor arise in Michigan on July 9 and 29. A financing statement covering after-acquired equipment had been filed in Michigan by T on May 1. Michigan law governs the "validity" of the security interest in Michigan. If filing is within ten days after the debtor receives possession of the goods in Detroit, the secured party will have priority over both judgment liens and the earlier filed financing statement. If there had been a filing in Ohio, it would be effective for four months after the goods reached Michigan and thereafter

While the thirty-day rule of Section 9–103(3) is not tied to purchase money transactions in goods, it is doubtful that the rule has any other practical application. The corresponding rule in Revised Section 9–103(1) (c) is, however, limited to purchase money security interests in goods, and the rule states that the law of Michigan, in our example, "governs the perfection and the effect of perfection or non-perfection" from the time of attachment until thirty days after the debtor receives possession of the goods and Michigan law continues to govern this aspect of the transaction if the goods are taken to Michigan before the end of the thirty-day period. This means, if the debtor's only place of business is in Detroit, that the thirty-day period runs from the time he "receives possession," which may be literally interpreted as meaning actual physical possession. The thirty-day period may in fact be considerably longer than thirty days from the time of attachment. While nice questions may be raised about what "possession" means, nothing in Article 9 suggests that anything less than physical possession by the debtor is meant.[27] That is, the debtor should not be considered to have possession while the goods are being transported to him under a bill of lading, even if it is a straight bill consigning the goods to the debtor. Possession cannot be equated with having rights in the collateral for purposes of attachment.

The thirty-day period is not a grace period and the security interest is not automatically perfected during this period. The ten-day grace periods of Sections 9–301(2) and 9–312(4) apply, however, and a failure to file within ten days after the debtor receives possession of the goods would result in subordinating the secured party's claim to claims of lien creditors and other secured parties (if there are any) which arise between the time of attachment in Toledo and the time of filing in Michigan. Filing in Michigan is required, and a filing in Ohio would not be effective to perfect the security interest if the goods were brought to Michigan as planned; the four-month rule of Revised Section 9–103(1) (d) would not apply. This would be true even if the Detroit debtor also had a place of business in Ohio and took possession of the goods there but it was understood that the goods were to be kept in Michigan. That is, a filing in Michigan is required to perfect a security interest in the goods while they are still in Ohio. If there

if there was a filing within that time in Michigan. If there was no filing in Ohio but a filing in Michigan, it would be effective only from the time of filing, but §§ 9–301(2) and 9–312(4) provide a grace period of ten days after the buyer-debtor receives possession of the goods for filing, as against these lien creditors and other secured parties.

27. § 2–103(1)(c) provides: " 'Receipt' of goods means taking physical possession of them."

were a filing in Michigan but the debtor took possession of the goods in Toledo and, contrary to the parties' original intention, the goods were kept in Ohio and were never brought to Michigan, presumably Ohio law would govern perfection under Revised Section 9–103(1) (b) and filing would be required there. The general rule in this situation is that perfection and its effect are governed by the law of the place where the collateral is located "when the last event occurs on which is based the assertion that the security interest is perfected or unperfected." This leads to the odd result that Ohio law would require following Michigan law, assuming the 1972 Official Text is in force in both states, but a filing in Michigan would be effective for only thirty days from the time the debtor took possession of the goods in Ohio. Clearly a filing in Ohio would seem to be necessary, at least beyond the thirty-day period, and yet it does not quite appear to be required by the language of the section except indirectly: the goods will necessarily be in Ohio when conflicting claims arise, and the issue of perfection will then be raised in that jurisdiction.

The issue created by Revised Section 9–103(1)(b) of "when the last event occurs on which is based the assertion that the security interest is perfected or unperfected" may have some importance in several other possible situations. If there is a filing in State A, where the collateral is then located, but some of the collateral, such as a piece of equipment, is moved to State B before the last event necessary for attachment (such as advancing funds) has occurred, then at the time of the perfection of the security interest under Section 9–303(1), the law of State B will govern as to the removed equipment and a filing in State A will not be effective. This is simply one of the ordinary risks encountered by financers who do not make certain of the existence and location of their collateral when funds are advanced. If there is a filing in State A and funds are advanced there when it is known that some or all of the collateral is in another state and that the debtor will acquire rights in it while it is outside State A so that the security interest will not be perfected at the time the last event necessary for attachment has occurred because of the physical location of the goods at that time, it might be well to invoke Revised Section 9–203(2) and provide for attachment to be postponed under the security agreement (and consequently perfection will be postponed under Section 9–303(1))' until the collateral reaches State A. The concept of postponed attachment is also contained in Section 9–204(1) of the 1962 Code.

§ 9–5. The "Last Event" Test

The "last event" test may be profitably explored in the context of a bankruptcy case. In *In re Miller* [28] a California debtor granted a security interest in goods, which were stated to be equipment, to Ford Motor Credit Company, and the security interest was perfected by filing with the Secretary of State of California prior to April 1, 1973. On April 1, the debtor moved to Oregon and on April 15, the equipment was taken there. On April 24, the debtor granted a security interest to Peerless Pacific Company, and it was duly perfected by filing in Oregon on April 30. Peerless knew of Ford's interest. The goods remained in Oregon until they were removed to California on October 17. The debtor filed a bankruptcy petition in Oregon on October 25, and moved back to California around November 15. On December 10, Peerless filed a financing statement with the Secretary of State of California. At no time did Ford file a financing statement in Oregon, where the equipment was located for over four months.

It was concluded, correctly it would appear, that under the 1962 Code Ford's security interest lapsed four months after the goods were removed to Oregon, that at this time the interest of Peerless was no longer subordinate but was then entitled to priority, and that the priority of Peerless continued when the goods were removed to California. This perfected security interest of Peerless was entitled to priority over the trustee in bankruptcy. The court seemed to say that Ford's security interest, having lapsed in Oregon, was ineffective when the goods returned to California, and while this is surely not true (the California filing being still effective under Section 9–403 (2)), if Ford's interest in California had been recognized as re-perfected when the goods were returned to that state, Ford's interest would no doubt have been a preference under Section 60 of the Bankruptcy Act. There is no comment in the opinion on the effect of the Peerless Code filing in California after the debtor's filing in bankruptcy in Oregon (where a bankruptcy filing would be required under Section 2a (1) of the Bankruptcy Act), and the filing might be thought needless on the theory that rights were frozen at the date of bankruptcy, but in states not having Revised Section 9–403(2) such a filing is probably advisable. [29] Peerless's knowledge of Ford's security interest is immaterial for priority purposes under Section 9–312 (5).

Had these facts occurred in states having Revised Article 9, how would the problem be resolved? There is no question as to the perfection of the Peerless security interest under either version of the

---

28. 14 UCC Rep.Serv. 1042 (D.Or.1974) (in bankruptcy).

29. *Compare In re* South County Motel Corp., 19 UCC Rep.Serv. 1254 (D.R.I. 1976) (in bankruptcy) with Eastern Indiana Production Credit Ass'n v. Farmers State Bank, 31 Ohio App.2d 252, 287 N.E.2d 824 (1972).

Code at the date of bankruptcy. It was entitled to priority in Oregon at the time the goods were removed from that state, and since Ford's interest had then lapsed, the priority of Peerless would continue when the goods were moved to California, assuming that Ford's interest then became reperfected. Nothing in the Code would subordinate the Peerless security interest. Under Revised Section 9–103(1)(b), how is the "last event" test applied? From the point of view of Peerless, the equipment was in Oregon when its security interest attached and was perfected, and Oregon's law will govern the effect of perfection. From Ford's point of view the goods were in California when its security interest attached and was perfected, so that California's law would govern the effect of that security interest's perfection or non-perfection. California law, under Revised Article 9, would provide that the perfected Oregon security interest of Peerless would continue to be perfected for four months after the goods were brought into California (assuming that the perfection of the Oregon interest did not expire sooner under Section 9–403(2)), but since Ford's interest had lapsed, its interest could have been reperfected only when the goods were returned to California. Under Revised Section 9–312 (5)(a), these "conflicting security interests rank according to priority in time of filing or perfection," but priority in time of filing will not work on these facts because there was a gap in Ford's perfection.[30] That leaves priority to Peerless since Ford's perfection at the time of bankruptcy could not have dated back to any time before the goods were returned to California. The draftsmanship of Revised Section 9–312(5) is not such that this answer is free from doubt, but it would seem to be the proper answer on the facts and it is consonant with the purposes of the provision.

If we assume that "event" in the "last event" test means an occurrence, which the dictionary would seem to require the language to mean,[31] and if we assume that the "last event" must refer to one of the requirements for perfection, which requires that the events necessary for attachment have occurred, then it would seem that the test refers us to the law of the jurisdiction where the collateral is located at a particular point in time. This test may have been adopted by the Review Committee with too much haste, for it appears to be subject to some disagreement in its application, and its language may perhaps be a bit infelicitous. To suggest that the test refers to a non-

---

30. *See* Revised § 9–312(5)(a), second sentence.

31. But it has been said on good authority that "the last event supporting a claim of non-perfection . . . will typically be a non-event such as a failure to file or a lapse." Kripke, The "Last Event" Test for Perfection of Security Interests under Article 9 of the Uniform Commercial Code, 50 N.Y.U.L.Rev. 47, 62 (1975). *Compare* this view with Coogan, The New UCC Article 9, 86 Harv.L.Rev. 447, 537–44 (1973). *See also* Haydock, Book Review, 21 Wayne L.Rev. 183, 188 (1974). In agreement with the view that a non-event is an event, see W. Davenport & D. Murray, Secured Transactions 223–225 (1978).

event, such as a failure to file, would warp the statutory language and do violence to ordinary English. On the facts of the *Miller* case, the answer will be the same on either analysis of the "last event" test, however.

While the court in *Miller* viewed the goods as ordinary equipment, it would appear that the goods as described in the opinion might well have been "mobile goods" within the meaning of Section 9–103 (2). Under Revised Section 9–103(3)(a), mobile goods encompass goods of a type normally used (even if not in fact so used) in more than one jurisdiction such as road building and construction machinery, which the goods in question may have been, so that the law of the state of the debtor's location would govern perfection and the effect of perfection or non-perfection of the security interest. The debtor was located in Oregon at the times material to the determination of the priority problem, under Revised Section 9–103(3)(d).

In *In re Dennis Mitchell Industries, Inc.,*[32] a conditional sale contract was entered into covering equipment then located at the seller's plant in New York. The parties agreed in the contract that the goods would be kept at the buyer's plant in Philadelphia until paid for, and the seller filed in the proper offices in Pennsylvania. However, despite the terms of the contract, the buyer had the goods picked up in New York and taken to a plant it operated in New Jersey; the goods were never in Pennsylvania. A bankruptcy proceeding was initiated over a year later, and the seller attempted to reclaim the goods.

While New York law would govern the validity of the security interest under Section 9–103(3), it seems clear that the Pennsylvania filing could not perfect the seller's security interest because the goods were never in that state, and Pennsylvania law could have been effective only if the goods had been taken there. Since the goods were in New Jersey for over a year before bankruptcy, the failure of the secured party to file in that state meant that the security interest was unperfected at the date of bankruptcy, and the trustee would prevail under Section 9–301(1)(b) of the Code and Section 70c of the Bankruptcy Act.

Under the view that the failure to file in New Jersey—a nonevent—is the "last event" referred to in Revised Section 9–103(1)(b), the same result would be reached. Under the view that the last event must be an event, the law of New Jersey would still govern, for it appears from the facts that the goods probably were in New Jersey when the dual filing was completed in Pennsylvania, and the filing was the last event on which the assertion of perfection of the security interest was based, and New Jersey law would not give effect to the filing in Pennsylvania, where the goods had never been located.

---

32. 419 F.2d 349 (3d Cir. 1969).

§ 9–6. Other Goods: The Four-Month Rule

If a security interest is perfected under the law of the place where the collateral is located at the time of attachment, the security interest continues to be perfected for four months after the goods are brought into "this state" [33] and the perfection continues if there is local perfection within the four-month period.[34] There are two very obvious problems here. One is the suggestion, never absolutely explicit, in Section 9–103(3) that a purchase money security interest in consumer goods requires some kind of positive perfection in the state of removal, when clearly none is required.[35] A second is that even though perfection in the first state would expire if the collateral were left there one more day, it continues for four months in the state of removal if timely moved. This result seems improper but it is mandated by statute,[36] and an agile debtor, who would have no interest in doing so, could prolong indefinitely the effectiveness of an otherwise expired financing statement by moving the collateral from state to state just before the end of each successive four-month period.

If the security interest was not perfected in the state from which the goods were removed, there is no perfection to continue in "this state," and if there is no perfection in "this state," the goods are sub-

33. If the security interest is claimed to be perfected by possession under § 9–305 in one state and the goods are released for transportation to and delivery in a second state, this apparently is not the continuing perfection referred to in § 9–103(3). *In re* Automated Bookbinding Services, Inc., 471 F.2d 546 (4th Cir. 1972).

34. *See, e. g.,* Garden City Production Credit Assn. v. Lannan, 186 Neb. 668, 186 N.W.2d 99 (1971); General Motors Acceptance Corp. v. Long-Lewis Hardware Co., 54 Ala.App. 188, 306 So.2d 277 (1974), certiorari denied 306 So.2d 282 (Ala.1974).

35. § 9–302(1)(d), with exceptions for fixtures, which are not intended to be mobile, and automobiles. *Cf.* Revised § 9–302(1)(d). *See* § 9–401(4). *See also* Revised § 9–103(1)(d). It was simply a drafting oversight for § 9–103(3) to say, "If the security interest was already perfected . . . [in the state from which the goods were removed, it] continues perfected in this state for four months and also there-

after if within the four month period it is perfected in this state." No action is required to perfect a purchase money security interest in consumer goods. *Compare* § 9–307(2). *See In re* Marshall, 10 UCC Rep.Serv. 1290 (N.D. Ohio 1969) (in bankruptcy).

36. § 9–103(3). Revised § 9–103(1)(d) makes clear that only if action is required by Part 3 of Article 9 to perfect a security interest must action be taken in the state of removal, and the security interest becomes unperfected whenever it would have expired in the jurisdiction from which the collateral was removed or at the end of four months after removal, whichever comes first, unless reperfected in the state of removal. Under either version of the Code a secured party should file a continuation statement in the state where the security interest is perfected before its effectiveness lapses unless he is aware that the collateral is moved and he knows the state where it is now located and can make a timely filing there.

ject to third party claims which are entitled to priority over the un-perfected security interest.[37]

One of the most interesting cases to arise under the 1962 Code is this: X perfects by filing a purchase money security interest in equipment sold to Y in State A. Without notice to X, Y removes the equipment to State B and within two weeks after removal sells the equipment to Z, who has no notice of X's security interest and who pays value. (Alternatively Z Bank in State B lends money on the security of the equipment as collateral and files in State B.) Six months after the equipment is removed, no payments having been made in the meantime, X locates the equipment. May X proceed against the equipment under Part 5 of Article 9?

The resolution of the problem under the 1962 Code is not self-evident. One resolution is to say that the goods are converted when Z buys them.[38] Nothing that occurs thereafter has any effect. (Or if Z Bank takes a security interest, it is a second security interest and must remain so.) A second resolution is to say that at the end of the four-month period after removal, the security interest of X lapses and while Z may have unwittingly purchased subject to it, he now takes free of it.[39] (Or Z Bank's second security interest now rises to the top and is first.) The second resolution is adopted in revised Article 9.[40] It could be reached under the 1962 Code. There is a conversion when

37. Henson v. Government Employees Finance & Industrial Loan Corp., 247 Ark. 273, 516 S.W.2d 1 (1974).

38. Leaving aside any possible certificate of title problems, this view was taken in First Nat. Bank of Bay Shore v. Stamper, 93 N.J.Super. 150, 225 A.2d 162 (1966) (involving an automobile removed from New York to New Jersey). *See also* Churchill Motors, Inc. v. A. C. Lohman, Inc., 16 A.D.2d 560, 229 N.Y.S.2d 570 (1962). *Cf. In re* Dumont Airplane & Marine Instruments, Inc., 203 F.Supp. 511 (S.D.N.Y. 1962). Professor Gilmore probably would agree with the result in *Stamper* but Professor Vernon would not. *Compare* 1 G. Gilmore, Security Interests in Personal Property 626–28 (1965) *with* Vernon, Recorded Chattel Security Interests in the Conflict of Laws, 47 Iowa L.Rev. 346, 377–78 (1962). Other cases reaching the *Stamper* result include Utah Farm Production Credit Ass'n v. Dinner, 302 F.Supp. 897 (D.Colo.1964) (involving cattle collateral); Pascack Valley Bank & Trust Co. v. Ritar Ford, Inc., 6 Conn.Cir. 489, 276 A.2d 800 (1970). *See* Doenges-Glass, Inc. v. General Motors Acceptance Corp., 175 Colo. 518, 488 P.2d 879 (1971) (based on Colorado Certificate of Title Act). *See also* American State Bank v. White, 217 Kan. 78, 535 P.2d 424 (1975); Community Credit Co. v. Gillham, 191 Neb. 198, 214 N.W.2d 384 (1974); Morris v. Seattle-First Nat'l Bank, 10 Wash. App. 129, 516 P.2d 1055 (1973).

39. United States v. Squires, 378 F. Supp. 798 (S.D.Iowa 1974); Arrow Ford, Inc. v. Western Landscape Constr. Co., Inc., 23 Ariz.App. 281, 532 P.2d 553 (1975) (reaching under § 9–103(3) the result that should have been reached under § 9–103(4), since a vehicle subject to a certificate of title was involved).

40. Revised § 9–103(1)(d)(i). (The term "purchaser" includes a secured party. *See* § 1–201(32), (33).)

the equipment is bought in State B, if a court insists on importing this law into a commercial transaction in these circumstances, but the problem is more properly analysed as a priority question and the effect of lapse should be considered and given due weight. It would be odd indeed if Z were to be considered a converter if he bought the goods one day before the four-month period expired and an unencumbered owner if he bought them one day after, or if Z Bank were to be forever in second place if it lent against the goods the day before the period expired and a holder of a first security interest if it lent two days later.

If the security interest in State A had been a purchase money security interest in consumer goods,[41] it would continue perfected in State B.[42] A secured party in State B who lent against such collateral would not qualify as a buyer under Section 9–307(2) and would take subject to the rights of the purchase money secured party.[43] The term "buyer" is not defined and can mean only what one would ordinarily assume the term to denote in the context of the Code. (The term "purchaser" is defined, and broadly defined, in Section 1–201(33), and it includes a secured party.) If the purchase money secured party had filed in State A, the security interest would be good even against a consumer buyer in State B for four months,[44] but after that time this priority would depend on a refiling in State B within the four month period, or else the refiling would be effective only from the time when it was made.[45]

---

41. That is, a purchase money security interest in consumer goods other than fixtures and motor vehicles subject to the provision in § 9–302(1)(d).

42. This must be implied from § 9–103 (3) (fourth sentence) because it is not explicitly stated. (It is explicit in Revised § 9–103(1)(d). *See In re* Marshall, 10 UCC Rep.Serv. 1290 (N.D. Ohio 1969) (in bankruptcy). *But see In re* Atchison, 6 UCC Rep.Serv. 258 (E.D.Wis.1969) (in bankruptcy) (purchase money security interest in consumer goods purchased in Illinois, where debtor then resided, became unperfected four months after goods were removed to Wisconsin, where amendment to § 9–302(1)(d) required filing for perfection of purchase money security interests in consmer goods having a purchase price over $250 (now $500) and there was no filing in Wisconsin).

43. § 9–307(2).

44. Newton-Waltham Bank & Trust Co. v. Bergen Motors, Inc., 68 Misc.2d 228, 327 N.Y.S.2d 77 (N.Y.Civ.Ct.1971).

45. § 9–103(3), Revised § 9–103(1)(d)(iii). If the filing in State A expired before the end of the four-month period, the security interest would still be effective for four months in State B under the 1962 Code, but it would expire in State B at the same time it expired in State A under the redraft. *Id.* The effect of filing a continuation statement in State A is not resolved under the 1962 Code; in no event would perfection in State A continue beyond four months in State B under the 1972 Official Text, although the filing of a continuation statement in State A might make the perfection last that long where it might originally have expired earlier.

The four-month rule applies and the security interest must be perfected in the state of removal, if re-perfection is required, regardless of whether the secured party knows that the goods have been removed.[46] This requires, of course, that the secured party make some effort to keep track of the debtor and the collateral, and this is not always easy.

§ 9–7. Documents, Instruments, Chattel Paper

Insofar as the title to Section 9–103 is governing, that Section does not deal with documents, instruments, or chattel paper. The title specifies only accounts, contract rights, general intangibles, equipment, and incoming goods. In terms, the first subsection deals only with accounts and contract rights, the second with general intangibles and mobile equipment or leased inventory, the fourth with goods subject to certificates of title, and the fifth with assignors of accounts and contract rights who keep their records outside the United States. That leaves subsection (3) which covers "personal property" other than the kinds dealt with in the other subsections, and arguably it governs the three kinds of collateral not otherwise covered, despite the title to the section.

It is possible to perfect a security interest in negotiable documents, instruments (in some cases), or chattel paper by filing,[47] although the effect of filing is circumscribed. These kinds of collateral involve writings evidencing rights, and in general good faith purchasers for value who take possession of the pieces of paper will have priority over secured parties who have filed.[48] Pieces of paper are transportable, however, and conflicts can arise.

Section 9–102 would require that a security interest in these kinds of collateral be perfected in whatever state they physically were in, either by filing or by taking possession.[49] If a security interest in chattel paper were perfected by filing in State A and the paper was subse-

---

46. *See, e. g., In re* McCormick, 4 UCC Rep.Serv. 1092 (E.D.Tenn.1968) (in bankruptcy); *In re* Welker, 2 UCC Rep.Serv. 169 (W.D.Pa.1964) (in bankruptcy).

47. §§ 9–301(1), 9–304(1). Aside from temporary perfection provided by § 9–304(4) and (5) and an interest in proceeds as provided in § 9–306, a security interest in instruments (which term includes securities, under the definition in § 9–105(1)(g)) can be perfected only by possession unless the instruments are part of chattel paper. If the instruments are part of chattel paper, a security interest can be perfected by filing but almost anyone who would ordinarily buy such paper or take it as security would take priority over a filed interest. See § 9–308.

48. §§ 9–308, 9–309, Revised § 9–308.

49. *See, e. g.,* Fidelity Bank & Trust Co. of New Jersey v. Production Metals Corp., 366 F.Supp. 613 (E.D.Pa.1973) (pledged stock certificates).

quently taken to State B, the secured party should have four months
during which his security interest would continue to be effective in
State B, although the validity of the security interest would be determined by the law of State A. In the unlikely event that the parties
intended that the collateral were to be moved from State A to State
B and this was done within thirty days after the security interest attached, the validity of the security interest would be determined by the
law of State B.[50] If this kind of collateral is considered not to be covered by Section 9–103, then apparently it would fall under Section 9–
102 which would make the governing law that of the state where the
collateral happened to be at any given time. While these kinds of
collateral do not necessarily move around very much, a machinator
could present serious problems to a secured party by moving the paper
out of the jurisdiction where the security interest is perfected and into
any other jurisdiction where it would not be perfected for any period
of time at all, thirty days or four months or otherwise. This would
be an acute problem principally in the event of bankruptcy or if judgment liens arose in the second state, for purchasers of these kinds of
paper would usually take free of a filed security interest in any case.

Under the redraft of Article 9, different rules apply to security
interests in chattel paper depending on whether the security interest
is possessory or non-possessory.[51] If the security interest is possessory,
the rules stated for goods in Revised Section 9–103(1) apply;[52] if
it is non-possessory, the rules for accounts in Revised Section 9–103
(3) apply,[53] except that the security interest cannot be perfected by
notification to the account debtor.[54]

Revised Section 9–103(1) states rules governing documents, instruments, and ordinary goods; and Revised § 9–103(4) states that
these rules for goods apply to possessory security interests in chattel
paper. In general terms, Section 9–103(1) states that the perfection
of the security interest is governed by the law of the state where the
collateral is physically located "when the last event occurs on which
is based the assertion that the security interest is perfected or unperfected." [55] If the collateral is moved from one state to another after
the security interest is perfected in the first state, the perfection continues in the second state for four months, unless it expired earlier in
the first state.[56] It continues perfected in the second state if it is
perfected there before the end of the four month period or before it

---

50. § 9–103(3).

51. Revised § 9–103(4).

52. *See* §§ 9–4, 9–5 *supra.*

53. *See* § 9–2 *supra.*

54. Revised § 9–103(4).

55. Revised § 9–103(1)(b).

56. Revised § 9–103(1)(d)(i).

expired in the second state, whichever period expires first.[57]　When or if the security interest becomes unperfected in the second state, it is then considered "to have been unperfected as against a person who became a purchaser after removal."[58]　This provision is more concerned with ordinary goods, to which the entire subsection also applies, than with paper collateral whose purchasers would normally take priority over a filed security interest in any case,[59] and these provisions cannot apply to a possessory interest in chattel paper for the security interest would continue to be perfected by possession in the secured party.　Nor can the thirty-day rule of Revised § 9–103(1)(c) apply to chattel paper by the reference in Revised § 9–103(4) because this provision applies only where the debtor has possession of goods, and he cannot have possession of the chattel paper here because the cross-reference is only for cases where the secured party has possession of the chattel paper.

If the security interest in chattel paper is perfected by filing rather than possession, the rules applicable to accounts in Revised § 9–103(3) govern.[60]　The law of the jurisdiction where the debtor is located governs perfection and its effect,[61] and for business debtors located in the United States filing will be where the debtor's place of business is, or, if he has more than one place of business, at his chief executive office.[62]

§ 9–8.　Goods Subject to Certificates of Title: 1962 Code

Section 9–103(4) says:

> Notwithstanding subsections (2) and (3), if personal property is covered by a certificate of title issued under a statute of this state or any other jurisdiction which requires indication on a certificate of title of any security interest in the property as a condition of perfection, then the perfection is governed by the law of the jurisdiction which issued the certificate.

There are some questions this subsection answers and there are others that it does not.　Subsection (2) covers goods which are normally used in more than one state if they are classified as equipment or inventory because leased.　Subsection (3) covers other personal prop-

---

57.　Revised § 9–103(1)(d)(ii).

58.　Revised § 9–103(1)(d)(i).

59.　§§ 9–308, 9–309; Revised § 9–308. Note the definition of "purchase" in § 1–201(33).

60.　See § 9–2 supra.

61.　Revised § 9–102(3)(b).

62.　Revised § 9–103(3)(d).

erty, such as consumer goods, not covered by (2). If subsection (4) applies, it appears to supersede any inconsistent provisions in (2) and (3). (These problems are basically, but not totally, limited to automobiles and other motor vehicles.) If (4) covers the facts, then the thirty-day and four-month rules of (3) have no application.

The first thing to note about Section 9–103(4) is that it applies to personal property [63] *covered* by a certificate of title *issued* by "this state" or another jurisdiction which requires certificate of title notation for perfection. If the subsection applies, then perfection is governed by the issuing jurisdiction. [64]

If perfection is governed by (4), then these rules apply "notwithstanding" the subsections dealing with equipment or leased goods normally used in more than one jurisdiction, where perfection depends on the law of the jurisdiction of the debtor's chief place of business, or other goods which have been brought into the forum state. This provision applies if a certificate of title *requires* indication of a security interest for perfection, and if this is the case the law of the issuing state, whether this state or another, governs perfection. It is immaterial whether the goods were brought into this state within thirty days of attachment or how long they have been here.[65] Perfection depends on the law of the jurisdiction issuing the certificate in compliance with this subsection.[66] If this is what the statute means, what problems are there?

For one thing, it is not always clear whether a statute "requires" certificate of title notation for perfection, although Section 9–302(4) states that perfection can be only by notation when a state statute "requires indication" of security interests on certificates of title or,

---

63. While § 9–103(4) applies to "personal property," there is no obvious example of certificated personal property which is not goods. The collateral covered will most commonly be motor vehicles but may be mobile construction equipment, farm machinery, boats and boat trailers, so-called mobile homes, and the like.

64. *In re* Osborn, 389 F.Supp. 1137 (N. D.N.Y.1975); *In re* Price, 5 UCC Rep. Serv. 415 (W.D.Mich.1968) (in bankruptcy); *In re* Edwards, 6 UCC Rep. Serv. 1124 (E.D.Mich.1969) (in bankruptcy). *See also* Seely v. First Bank & Trust, Boynton Beach, Florida, 64 Misc.2d 845, 315 N.Y.S.2d 374 (N.Y. Sup.Ct.1970).

65. *In re* McClintock v. General Motors Acceptance Corp., 23 UCC Rep.Serv. 764 (Ga.1978); *In re* Caraway, 4 UCC Rep.Serv. 1099 (W.D.Mich.1968) (in bankruptcy); *In re* Friedman, 4 UCC Rep.Serv. 890 (D.Conn.1967) (in bankruptcy).

66. Streule v. Gulf Finance Corp., 265 A.2d 298 (D.C.App.1970); Cooper v. Citizens Bank of Gainesville, 129 Ga. App. 261, 199 S.E.2d 369 (1973); Town House Motel, Inc. v. Ward, 2 Ill.App. 3d 699, 276 N.E.2d 809 (1971); *In re* Worsley, 4 UCC Rep.Serv. 1180 (E.D. Mich.1967) (in bankruptcy).

alternatively, if such a notation "can be indicated by a public official." [67] For another, it is not absolutely clear whether the goods must be covered by a certificate when brought into the state, which might have been years before, or when a conflicting claim arises, but it would seem only reasonable to assume the latter is the proper interpretation.[68] The statutory language says "is covered," not "was covered," and in subsection (3) the reference is to "was already perfected" in the third sentence when an earlier point in time is meant.[69]

Since title certificates cannot ordinarily be issued instantly, problems can arise if a purchaser of a vehicle subject to a security interest drives immediately to another state and manages to sell the vehicle before any certificate of title is or could be outstanding. This problem is not precisely covered in Section 9–103(4) where the language says "*is* covered by a certificate of title," but it would appear that the secured party should be protected.[70] If the practical impossibility of instantaneous issuance is ignored and "is covered" is read literally to mean that a certificate must be outstanding when the vehicle is brought into the state, then despite timely issuance of a certificate by the first state, the security interest may be found to be unperfected in the state to which the vehicle is removed.[71] While there may be something to be said for a strict reading of the statute where an innocent consumer-buyer of the vehicle is involved, there is no justification for invalidating the security interest in favor of non-reliance creditors such as trustees in bankruptcy.[72]

---

67. § 9–302(3), Alternatives A and B. The second alternative, if adopted, is intended to convert permissive into mandatory notation.

68. *See, e. g., In re* Singleton, 2 UCC Rep.Serv. 195 (E.D.Ky.1963) (in bankruptcy).

69. These objections to § 9–103(4) and others are made in Rohner, Autos, Title Certificates and UCC 9–103: The Draftsmen Try Again, 28 Bus.Law. 1177 (1972). The answers suggested here are not necessarily Professor Rohner's.

70. *See* Lightfoot v. Harris Trust & Savings Bank, 21 UCC Rep.Serv. 864, (Ala.App.1977), affirmed 12 A.B.R. 914, 23 UCC Rep.Serv. 750 (1978), where the court, having noted Alabama's new certificate of title law, concludes:

"Presumably, Alabama is no longer the sucker state for car thieves and fraud merchants."

71. *See In re* Zimmardi, 8 UCC Rep. Serv. 1396 (D.Me.1971) (in bankruptcy); *In re* Erwin, 8 UCC Rep.Serv. 1399 (D.Me.1971) (in bankruptcy).

72. In *In re* Wolf, 9 UCC Rep.Serv. 177 (W.D.Mich.1971) (in bankruptcy), a security interest was held to be perfected in bankruptcy where, at the date of filing, the vehicle was subject to a Georgia title certificate noting the secured party's interest but the debtor had applied for a Michigan certificate which was not yet issued; since Michigan requires for perfection both title notation and local filing, the security interest would not have been perfected under Michigan law at the date of the bankruptcy filing.

These problems can be examined in the context of what is known as the *Stamper* case.[73] In New York a car dealer sold a used Thunderbird to Stamper and assigned the purchase money security interest to plaintiff bank. Stamper was then a resident of New York, and the security interest was perfected by a New York filing but not by certificate of title notation because New York then had no statute requiring or permitting this. Stamper procured a New York certificate of registration. Not long thereafter Stamper began residing temporarily and then permanently in New Jersey, and he applied for and received, without plaintiff's knowledge or consent, a New Jersey certificate of ownership which showed him as the owner without noting plaintiff's reservation of title, although there was a "Z" at the end of the number on the certificate to show that the vehicle had previously been registered in another state. Three months and one week after purchasing the car in New York, Stamper sold the car in New Jersey to Sharp, apparently an innocent consumer, who received a clean New Jersey certificate of ownership. Shortly thereafter Sharp sold the car to Fitzgerald whose New Jersey certificate showed a lienholder, but not the New York bank, of course. Since Stamper continued making payments for some months after he left New York, it took the bank eleven months after his move to find out that he had moved to New Jersey; shortly thereafter the bank learned that Fitzgerald had the car, and it took another year to find Stamper. Fitzgerald moved "to and fro," according to the court, "between New Jersey, Florida, and now Pennsylvania." The plaintiff bank could not find Stamper and sued Sharp for conversion. Plaintiff bank recovered judgment for the value of the car at the time it was purchased by Sharp.

If the analysis of Section 9–103(4) proposed above is accepted, the New Jersey court was wrong.[74] At the time of Sharp's purchase, the automobile was covered by a New Jersey certificate of title which showed no liens, and so far as appears Sharp bought in reliance on that certificate, and New Jersey law required notation of a security interest on the title for perfection. Section 9–103(4) says that perfection is governed by the law of the jurisdiction issuing the certificate,[75] and the

73. First Nat. Bank of Bay Shore v. Stamper, 93 N.J.Super. 150, 225 A.2d 162 (1966).

New Jersey Supreme Court in 75 N.J. 379, 382 A.2d 1125, 23 UCC Rep.Serv. 756 (1978).

74. This was recognized in IAC, Ltd. v. Princeton Porsche-Audi, 147 N.J. Super. 212, 371 A.2d 84 (1977), which was unfortunately reversed by the

75. *See, e. g., In re* Schoeller, 4 UCC Rep.Serv. 1093 (D.Conn.1968) (in bankruptcy).

New York security interest was therefore not perfected and Sharp should not have bought subject to it.

The New Jersey court relied on Section 9–103(3) and the continuation of the perfection of the New York security interest for four months after the property was brought to New Jersey, so that the purchase by Sharp within that time made him a converter.[76] The importation of tort law is an unnecessary intrusion into a problem otherwise solvable by the Code. Even if Section 9–103(3) covered this case, the New York security interest (based on filing and not on certificate of title notation) ceased to be effective four months after removal, and when it lapsed, the interest of the buyer (Sharp) should have been superior to the then-unperfected security interest of the New York bank.[77] This is a priority problem under the Code, not a matter of the tort law of conversion. Had Stamper waited awhile to buy the car, he would not have been subject to the New York security interest even under the New Jersey court's analysis of the problem. But the New Jersey analysis simply ignores the language of subsection (4) which says it applies "Notwithstanding subsections (2) and (3) . . ." and the court applied (3) notwithstanding (4). This case involved a vehicle moving from a non-title to a title state.

If a certificated vehicle is taken from a title to a non-title state, then so long as the certificate is outstanding it governs perfection under Section 9–103(4).[78] The four-month period of subsection (3) has no application.[79] There is a practical time limit on how long this peri-

---

76. *See also* Community Credit Co. v. Gillam, 191 Neb. 198, 214 N.W.2d 384 (1974); Morris v. Seattle-First Nat'l Bank, 10 Wash.App. 129, 516 P.2d 1055 (1973). *Cf.* Phil Phillips Ford, Inc. v. St. Paul Fire & Marine Ins. Co., 465 S.W.2d 933 (Tex.1971).

77. *See, e. g.,* General Electric Credit Corp. v. Hollywood Bank & Trust Co., 263 So.2d 593 (Fla.App.1972) (involving Chris Craft boat brought from non-certificate of title state into a state where certificate of title was obtained approximately eight months later and boat was purchased in reliance on certificate; court relied on § 9–103(3)).

78. General Motors Acceptance Corp. v. Whisnant, 387 F.2d 774 (5th Cir. 1968); *In re* White, 266 F.Supp. 863 (N.D.N.Y.1967); *In re* Smith, 311 F. Supp. 900 (W.D.Va.1970), affirmed *sub*

nom. Callaghan v. Commercial Credit Corp., 437 F.2d 898 (4th Cir. 1971); *In re* Maxwell, 18 UCC Rep.Serv. 504 (D.Conn.1975) (in bankruptcy); *In re* Fougere, 5 UCC Rep.Serv. 410 (D.Me. 1968) (in bankruptcy); Deposit National Bank v. Chrysler Credit Corp., 48 Ala.App. 161, 263 So.2d 139 (1972). *See also In re* Frye, 11 UCC Rep.Serv. 1254 (M.D.Fla.1972) (in bankruptcy), where the vehicle was taken from one title state to another title state.

79. *In re* Wolf, 9 UCC Rep.Serv. 177 (W.D.Mich.1971) (in bankruptcy). But the four-month period may be applicable if the vehicle is taken from a non-title state to another non-title state. *See* General Motors Acceptance Corp. v. Long-Lewis Hardware Co., 54 Ala.App. 188, 306 So.2d 277 (1974), certiorari denied 293 Ala. 752, 306 So. 2d 282 (1974). *See also* Doenges-Glass, Inc. v. General Motors Acceptance

od will last because the certificate will almost certainly have to be surrendered for registration of the vehicle in the state of removal in order to get new license plates.[80] It sometimes appears to be possible to get a new certificate of title without surrendering an out-of-state certificate.[81] Occasionally the procedures followed by a state's office in charge of title certificates are inexplicable, and there are many variations in state title laws. These problems can scarcely be dealt with by the Commercial Code, and where reliance is to be placed on a certificate of title, as it is in Section 9–103(4), perhaps the ultimate answer is to enforce some kind of liability on the office of the certificating authority for malfunctioning, whether through dishonesty or simple incompetence and whether the loser is a buyer or a secured party who relies on a certificate either for a clean title or for perfection.

Suppose the title to an automobile is represented by a "wild" certificate—that is, a certificate which has been issued by a state which arguably ought not to have issued it—and an issue is subsequently raised about perfection of the security interest. Unless we assume idiocy on the part of a secured party in attempting to protect his security interest—and secured parties normally forward applications for certificates showing their liens and retain the original certificates—no absolutely unrealistic state is likely to be involved.[82] If a certificate is in fact issued and the car is removed or an issue arises in another state, nothing in Section 9–103 gives any option to disregard the outstanding certificate of title even though the certificate might well have been applied for in State B rather than State A.[83]

It is also possible to have a "wild" certificate in the sense that it was applied for fraudulently after the vehicle has been sold. That is,

---

Corp., 175 Colo. 518, 488 P.2d 879 (1971).

80. There may be an exception for transient military personnel. *See, e. g.,* Town House Motel, Inc. v. Ward, 2 Ill.App.3d 699, 276 N.E.2d 809 (1971), where the vehicle was taken from one title state to another.

81. *See In re* Schoeller, 4 UCC Rep. Serv. 1093 (D.Conn.1968) (in bankruptcy). It arguably facilitates fraud for a state to issue a new local certificate for a car brought in from another state without surrender of the original certificate which probably is held by a secured party when it is not surrendered. *See also* General Electric Credit Corp. v. Hollywood Bank &

Trust Co., 263 So.2d 593 (Fla.Dist.Ct. App.1972), involving a certificate of title to a boat, where the court reached the right result without giving the right reasons.

82. In the absence of certificate of title laws, filing in the state where the secured party is located clearly will not perfect a security interest in a vehicle which is, and which clearly is intended to be, kept in another state where the debtor resides. *In re* Van Leeuwen, 15 UCC Rep.Serv. 507 (D.R.I. 1974) (in bankruptcy).

83. *But see In re* Williams, 10 UCC Rep.Serv. 277 (D.Me.1971) (in bankruptcy).

if a vehicle is sold for cash, the buyer may well trust the seller to apply for a certificate of title. If the seller is dishonest, the seller may use the certificate to borrow money for his own purposes, and the lender may in fact then be shown on a new certificate as the secured party. The buyer may have nothing to evidence what was purchased except a bill of sale. If the position is taken that the buyer acquired title at the time the vehicle was delivered, which Section 2–401(2) seems to provide, then arguably the seller had nothing left to which a security interest could attach,[84] and if the interest could not attach, it could not be perfected.[85] Such a certificate may be said to represent nothing,[86] and it is true that automobile certificates of title are not documents of title so that a pledge of the certificate could perfect the security interest, as would be true of a negotiable document.[87] Whatever may be said of this point of view, this situation can be distinguished from a case where a certificate has been issued and reflects the true status of title even though it is issued by a state which perhaps ought not to have issued it.

People do not purchase automobiles in the same way that they may purchase "hot" watches. While some understanding for innocent consumers is desirable, no innocence need be assumed for used car dealers who can be expected to notice out-of-state license plates or dealer's identification insignia of various types which are likely to be prominently displayed, and dealers ought to be held to cognizance of certificate of title laws and compliance with them. In any case, given an even choice, only the reasonably ignorant should be given the benefit of the doubt, and this group does not include trustees in bankruptcy.[88]

A referee in bankruptcy held that a security interest in a truck was subordinate to the debtor's trustee in bankruptcy when the lien was noted on an Indiana certificate rather than on a Michigan certificate, where the debtor operated his trucking business in Michigan but had the vehicle titled in Indiana at his sister's address to save taxes.[89] Apparently the referee's reasoning was that the Code's provi-

---

84. § 9–204(1), Revised § 9–203(1)(c).

85. § 9–303(1).

86. *See* National Exchange Bank of Fond du Lac v. Mann, 81 Wis.2d 352, 260 N.W.2d 716 (1978); Stroman v. Orlando Bank & Trust Co., 239 So.2d 621 (Fla.App.1970).

87. § 9–305.

88. There is absolutely no excuse to require, for the benefit of the trustee in bankruptcy, that the certificate be issued before the vehicle comes into a state, for clerical problems unquestionably do exist and the trustee does not rely on a certificate or the absence of one. *But see In re* Zimmardi, 8 UCC Rep.Serv. 1396 (D.Me.1971) (in bankruptcy); *In re* Erwin, 8 UCC Rep. Serv. 1399 (D.Me.1971) (in bankruptcy).

89. *In re* Brown, 5 UCC Rep.Serv. 401 (W.D.Mich.1968) (in bankruptcy). *Cf. In re* Antonuzzo, 20 UCC Rep.Serv. 180 (E.D.N.Y.1976) (in bankruptcy).

sions for perfection were designed to give notice and a certificate issued in Indiana would not do so. To the extent that this was the basis for the holding, it does not survive examination because a person looking at a certificate of title is equally informed of noted liens regardless of which state issued the certificate, and nothing could be less material in fact in a bankruptcy proceeding where the trustee has relied on nothing. The referee felt that perfection had to be in the "proper" state under Sections 9–103(2) and (3), and that this debtor's chief place of business was in Michigan rather than Indiana, which is immaterial for certificated vehicles under (4), and it was not clear whether Indiana required indication of liens on certificates of title, which was the essential point that ought to have been resolved, for under (4) this is the determining factor. The same referee later felt differently where an individual, not in business, perhaps basically lived in Michigan but was working and to some extent living in Illinois and bought a car titled in Illinois with a lien noted on the certificate. Here the Illinois security interest was properly enforced because it was duly perfected by notation on the certificate.[90]

§ 9–9. Goods Subject to Certificates of Title: 1972 Code

Goods which are covered [91] by a certificate of title are subject to Revised Section 9–103(2) if the certificate is issued by "this state" or by another jurisdiction whose law requires title notation for perfection. This provision continues the present uncertainty, where there is any, about which states' laws "require" notation, but this is an area that is more open to academic disputation than practical argument by practicing lawyers or finance companies who are very likely to be able to resolve problems that academic commentators quibble about.

In general, perfection and the effect of perfection are governed by the law (and conflict of laws rules) of the jurisdiction issuing a title

---

90. *In re* Longnecker, 7 UCC Rep.Serv. 264 (W.D.Mich.1969) (in bankruptcy). This debtor was acknowledged to have no "chief place of business" anywhere and apparently there was no question about the requirement of certificate of title notation in Illinois. Effect was given to § 9–102, applying the law of the location of the collateral to the transaction. *See also* General Motors Acceptance Corp. v. Whisnant, 387 F. 2d 774 (5th Cir. 1968); In re Canter, 8 UCC Rep.Serv. 252 (E.D.Tenn.1970) (in bankruptcy).

91. The language of Revised § 9–103(2) (a)—"this subsection applies to goods covered by a certificate of title . . ."—is subject to the same difficulties as § 9–103(4) where the vehicle is immediately transported from one state to another state before a certificate of title can be issued by the first state, and the car is quickly resold in the second state or the buyer takes bankruptcy there. *See generally* § 9–8 *supra*. *Compare* Lightfoot v. Harris Trust & Savings Bank, 357 So.2d 651 (Ala.App.1977), affirmed 12 A.B.R. 914, 23 UCC Rep.Serv. 750 (1978) with *In re* Zimmardi, 8 UCC Rep.Serv. 1396 (D.Me.1971) (in bankruptcy).

certificate. Subject to the rights of a buyer not in the business of selling such goods, this perfection extends for four months and "thereafter until the goods are registered in another jurisdiction, but in any event not beyond surrender of the certificate." [92] This provision arguably extends perfection beyond the period required by the 1962 Code where it may be maintained that perfection does not exist under the earlier certificate after the goods have become subject to a clean certificate in a new state regardless of when that takes place.[93] This provision adopts a four-month period in line with the general period applicable to other goods which are removed from one state to another; it gives no effect to the fact that certificates of title are relied on for certain goods while they are unknown for other goods. The merits of this approach are debatable. In any case, the security interest is subject to the rights of a buyer who pays value and takes delivery of the goods, if the buyer is not in the business of selling such goods and if the transaction occurs after the issuance of a clean certificate in this state, so long as the buyer has no knowledge of the security interest.[94] This will protect innocent consumers or, in the case of automobiles, anyone except an automobile dealer who ought to be alert enough to know what is going on.

This same kind of buyer is protected to the same extent where goods are brought into State B subject to a security interest which is perfected in any way other than title notation in State A after the goods are covered by a certificate of title in State B. So far as other third parties in State B are concerned, a security interest perfected by filing in State A continues to be perfected in State B until the filing expires in A or until four months after removal to B, whichever period expires first, unless there is perfection in B.[95]

Perfection in State B may or may not present a practical problem. If perfection may be accomplished by filing a financing statement in

---

92. Revised § 9–103(2)(b).

93. *See, e. g., In re* Edwards, 6 UCC Rep.Serv. 1124 (E.D.Mich.1969) (in bankruptcy), where a failure to perfect by meeting dual filing requirements in the state to which the vehicle was removed resulted in an unperfected security interest when the debtor took bankruptcy less than four months after moving to Michigan.

94. Revised § 9–103(2) (d). Illinois, the first state to adopt the 1972 Official Text, deleted the "who" clause in this subsection so that any buyer (not "purchaser") could take free of a foreign security interest after a local clean certificate is issued. While this amendment may have some merit, it was obviously promoted by certain automobile dealer interests. It has the effect of cutting off prior interests as well as protecting present interests, so it cannot be an unmixed blessing to automobile dealers and their financers. They will probably lose in as many cases as they win. A financer is not included in the term "buyer."

95. Revised § 9–103(2) (c).

B, the secured party may do this without the debtor's cooperation. If B is a title state and the vehicle came from State A, also a title state, the debtor's cooperation may be needed so that the certificate can be surrendered and a new one issued showing the security interest. It is conceivable that the debtor will not facilitate this transaction, in which case the secured party's only practical alternative may be to continue perfection by means of taking possession of the vehicle. Removal of the vehicle from the original state of perfection is almost certain to be a default under the security agreement which, at least as a matter of contract between the parties, would permit the secured party to repossess the car.

§ 9–10. Minerals and the Like

The 1962 Code requires in Section 9–203(1)(b) that a security agreement covering oil, gas, or minerals to be extracted must contain a description of the land concerned, although there is no such requirement for a financing statement. This requirement for a land description has been dropped from Revised Section 9–203(1), but a description is required on the financing statement by Revised Section 9–402(5).

The 1962 Code does not cover oil, gas, or minerals before extraction.[96] Prior to extraction, they are part of the real estate. Most of the time this apparently presents no problems, but difficulty can arise in the case of oil and gas interests particularly and also in the case of coal where there may be widely diffused interests arising at the moment of extraction. Investors, or owners if this is the preferred term, may live anywhere, and if their interests are sold or subjected to a security interest at the moment of extraction, the interest involved is normally an account under Section 9–106, and if multiple states are involved Section 9–103(1) presumably requires perfection in the state where the assignor of the accounts keeps his records. If the wellhead is in Texas and the assignors live in Iowa, Idaho, and Rhode Island the problems are obvious.

Revised Section 9–103(5) adopts the rule that the law of the state where the wellhead or minehead is located governs perfection of security interests in minerals and the like (including oil and gas) which are created before extraction and which attach on extraction

---

96. See § 2–107(1). See also the definition of "goods" in § 9–105(1)(f). *Cf.* Revised §§ 2–107(1) and 9–105(1)(h). See generally Vagts, Impact of the Uniform Commercial Code on the Oil and Gas Mortgage, 43 Tex.L.Rev. 825 (1965). *See also* Thomas, Natural Resources and the Uniform Commercial Code, 7 Nat. Resources Law 439 (1974).

or which attach to accounts arising from sales at the wellhead or mine-head. Filing for perfection of these security interests will be required in the real estate records of the county where the real estate is located, whether the security interest is in the minerals or the accounts aris-ing on their sale.[97] It should be noted, however, that these rules apply to production interests attaching on extraction. If the minerals are immediately sold, the buyers are "buyers in ordinary course of busi-ness"[98] and take free of this kind of security interest, although the minerals may be immediately subjected to a security interest in the buyer's inventory, and the security interest created by the investor-seller would continue only in the resulting account.

§ 9–11. International Transactions

In Section 9–103 there is an optional sentence at the end of sub-section (2) to cover security interests in airplanes of foreign debtors and an optional subsection (5) to cover certain transactions in ac-counts and contract rights. Most states have adopted both provi-sions.

The optional sentence in Section 9–103(2) states that the chief place of business of a debtor who is a foreign air carrier under the Federal Aviation Act of 1958, for purposes of determining the validity and perfection of a security interest in an airplane, is the designated office of an agent for service of process. Without this sentence, the reference in the preceding part of the section might be to the law of the country whose airline's planes were involved, and this could be highly unsettled and unsatisfactory. For signatory countries, the Con-vention on the International Recognition of Rights in Aircraft (the Geneva Convention) will supersede state law, and this is recognized in Revised Sections 9–302(3)(a) and (4). These rules are continued in Revised Sections 9–103(3)(b) and (d), except that perfection alone is covered, not validity.

Section 9–103(5) provides that where an assignor of accounts or contract rights keeps his records outside a jurisdiction of the United States but the collateral is within the state's jurisdiction or the trans-action bears an "appropriate relation" to the state, the state's law gov-erns the validity and perfection of the security interest and perfection must be by notification to the account debtor. A foreign seller of goods to a buyer in "this state" might not keep this records here, and if the records were kept abroad subsection (1) would refer to the law of that country for validity and perfection, without the enactment

---

97. Revised § 9–401(1).   **98.** Revised § 1–201(9).

of this provision, although the accounts were assigned for security to a financer in this state. Where this subsection applies, perfection is by notification to the account debtor, not by filing.

Revised Section 9–103(3) (c) provides that where the debtor is not located in the United States (which is defined to include territories, possessions, and Puerto Rico) and the debtor's jurisdiction does not provide for perfection by filing or recording, perfection and its effect are governed by the law of the jurisdiction in this country where the debtor's "major executive office" is located. "Contract rights" as a kind of collateral have been eliminated in Revised Article 9, and this kind of collateral will now be either accounts or general intangibles, and both kinds of collateral along with mobile goods (other than aircraft where the debtor is a foreign air carrier) are covered by the rule stated above. An alternative rule is stated for "accounts and general intangibles for money due or to become due," and where a debtor gives collateral of these kinds and is not located in the United States or Canada, the security interest may be perfected by notification to the account debtor.

CHAPTER 10

DEFAULT

Table of Sections

§ 10–1. Introduction

Defaults are dismal developments. The commonest kind of default arises when a consumer has purchased goods on conditional sale and at some point before the goods are fully paid for either cannot or does not pay an installment as it comes due. While the security interest in the goods could be waived by the secured party in favor of an unsecured claim for the balance of the purchase price, this is an unlikely occurrence because the debtor normally will be unable to pay the debt, and the secured party will have to try to collect the amount due by realizing on the collateral. This means that in some fashion the debtor will lose the right to possess the property and the secured party will become involved in time-consuming and perhaps costly procedures. Except for a few sellers and financers of used automobiles, who are alleged to find constant financings and repossessions of the same automobiles to be profitable, defaults are, in quite different ways, as distasteful to secured parties as to debtors. If the debtors usually lose the goods, the secured parties most of the time lose money. Apart from direct out-of-pocket expenses in repossessing, storing, and disposing of the goods, when new goods are sold with minimal down payments they often depreciate in value more rapidly than the unpaid balance of the purchase price goes down through installment payments. While the practices of some secured parties could not be defended, neither could the practices of some debtors.

Permissible default procedures have been the subject of much discussion through the years and currently are enjoying considerable judicial attention. Unquestionably default procedures have been designed for the benefit of creditors throughout most of our history. This is changing. But if there is no expeditious means of acquiring and disposing of collateral on default, if extensive judicial proceedings are always to be required rather than the traditional self-help, the added costs will be passed on directly or indirectly to consumers because there is no other ultimate source of the funds. Installment selling may not be particularly diminished but sales to persons of questionable ability to pay may be reduced. This is a very delicate and emotional subject of far-reaching ramifications.

By no means are all defaulting debtors consumers. The Code states fairly general guidelines for default procedures in Part 5 of Article 9, and most are applicable to all debtors.

§ 10–2. What Constitutes a Default

The security agreement between the parties will state what constitutes a default.[1] The primary event of default will be a failure to make required payments to the secured party in accordance with the schedule agreed upon. These may be monthly payments, as in the ordinary conditional sale contract, or a single payment on the maturity of a note, or whatever the contract calls for. Beyond this point, the events of default vary depending on the kind of collateral, whether the transaction is purchase money or not, the debtor's business (if the debtor is not a consumer) and so on.[2]

Most security agreements covering equipment, for example, will contain warranties or representations by the debtor, the breach of

1. *See* Honeywell Information Services, Inc. v. Demographic Systems, Inc., 396 F.Supp. 273 (S.D.N.Y.1975). *See also* Feldman v. Philadelphia Nat'l Bank, 408 F.Supp. 24 (E.D.Pa.1976) (filing of petition under Bankruptcy Act was made a default). § 9–501(1) begins: "When a debtor is in default under a security agreement . . . ." Security agreements adaptable for most transactions may be found in Henson & Davenport, 5 Uniform Laws Annotated—Uniform Commercial Code Forms and Materials, 230–589 (1968).

2. Death may be made a default, authorizing acceleration, in consumer transactions. *See* Trust Company Bank v. Johnson, 143 Ga.App. 650, 239 S.E.2d 542 (1977).

which will be a default. These warranties are likely to begin with one warranting that the debtor owns the collateral and that the collateral is subject to no liens or security interest, except the one created by the agreement. There will probably be a warranty that the goods will be used for a specified purpose (and no others) and that the goods will not become fixtures (or if they will, that they will be affixed to described real estate). If the security interest is purchase money, it will probably be warranted to be such.

In addition to promising to pay the obligation which is being secured, the debtor is also likely to promise or agree that the collateral will be adequately insured, that it will be kept in good condition, that it will not be moved to another location without consent, that the collateral will not be disposed of, that the collateral will not be subjected to other security interests or liens of any kind. Breach of these undertakings and others which are agreed upon will be a default.

While it may be made a default if the debtor's rights in the collateral are disposed of voluntarily (as by sale, gift, or the creation of another security interest)[3] or involuntarily (by attachment, levy, or garnishment), the secured party cannot prevent or render ineffective such a disposition.[4] The debtor can transfer what interest he has in collateral, and third party creditors can reach that interest by way of judicial process. What interest the debtor has in collateral will often be difficult to determine, and the Code offers no guidelines toward making that determination.

§ 10–3. Acceleration Clauses

Virtually all installment notes contain clauses allowing the unpaid balance to be accelerated if the debtor fails to make any payment due, either on the date when it is due or within a certain number of days of grace.[5] Security agreements will contain similar provisions, certainly if notes are not used and probably if they are. The unpaid

---

3. It will not be a default if the security agreement does not provide that it is. Production Credit Assn. of Chippewa Falls v. Equity Corp. Livestock Sales Assn., 82 Wis.2d 5, 261 N.W.2d 127 (1977).

4. § 9–311. Production Credit Assn. of Chippewa Falls v. Equity Corp. Livestock Sales Assn., 82 Wis.2d 5, 261 N.W.2d 127 (1977).

5. If there is no acceleration clause, then the unpaid balance cannot be accelerated. General Electric Credit Corp. v. Castiglione, 142 N.J.Super. 90, 360 A.2d 418 (1976); General Electric Credit Corp. v. Bankers Commercial Corp., 244 Ark. 984, 429 S.W.2d 60 (1968). If a debtor issues demand notes waiving presentment to a bank where the debtor has an account, then the bank may exercise its right of set-off against the debtor's bank account without notice or without proceeding against any security. Allied Sheet Metal Fabricators, Inc. v. Peoples Nat'l Bank of Washington, 10 Wash.App. 530, 518 P.2d 734 (1974).

balance will also be subject to acceleration on the happening of any other specified event of default.[6] The acceleration will normally not be automatic but at the option of the holder of the note, if there is a note, or at the option of the secured party, if there is no note.

If the unpaid balance has been accelerated because of a default, tender and acceptance of delinquent installments will not reinstate the original contract, and the secured party's right of repossession, unless otherwise agreed, may still be exercised.[7]

There is no statutory requirement of notice to the debtor when the secured party exercises a contractual right to accelerate the debt, although the security agreement may provide for such notice. The general requirement of good faith would apply, however, pursuant to Section 1–203.

Regardless of where the acceleration clause appears, if it is stated to be effective "at will" or when a party "deems himself insecure," or if similar language is used, this kind of provision will be construed to mean that the determination that payment or performance is impaired must be made in good faith,[8] but the burden of establishing lack of good faith is on the party against whom the acceleration was exercised.[9]

According to Section 1–201 (19), " 'Good faith' means honesty in fact in the conduct or transaction concerned." (This definition is amplified in the case of sales transactions by Section 2–103 (1) (b) which provides, " 'Good faith' in the case of a merchant means honesty in fact and the observance of reasonable commercial standards of fair dealing in the trade." The term "merchant" [10] is not, however, used in Article 9.) If honesty in fact is what we are concerned with, and if "burden of establishing" means "that the existence of the fact is more probable than its non-existence," [11] then it would appear that the debtor will have to prove to the satisfaction of the trier of the facts that the secured party could not reasonably have believed in good faith that its prospect of payment or performance was impaired when the debt was accelerated.[12] It seems fairly likely that a jury would in

6. But if the specified events have not occurred, there is no default and the secured party cannot proceed against collateral even though the debtor is clearly in difficulty. *In re* Levine's Boy's & Men's Shop, Inc., 14 UCC Rep. Serv. 254 (E.D.N.Y.1974).

7. Honeywell Information Services, Inc. v. Demographic Systems, Inc., 396 F.Supp. 273 (S.D.N.Y.1975); Philyaw v. Fulton Nat'l Bank, 139 Ga.App. 28, 227 S.E.2d 811 (1976).

8. Kupka v. Morey, 541 P.2d 740 (Alaska 1975).

9. § 1–208. *See* Universal C.I.T. Credit Corp. v. Shepler, —— Ind.App. ——, 329 N.E.2d 620 (1975).

10. "Merchant" is defined in § 2–104(1).

11. § 1–201(8).

12. *See* Universal C.I.T. Credit Corp. v. Shepler, —— Ind.App. ——, 329 N.E. 2d 620 (1975).

any case apply such a test, rather than attempting to probe the secured party's personal motivation (assuming corporate secured parties may be presumed to have personal motivation), if they were asked to apply the statutory language. The statutory language presumes that the secured party acts in good faith when the debt is accelerated.[13] It would appear that supposed distinctions between subjective and objective tests are more illusory than real and that no court would accept a claim that an acceleration was exercised in good faith—that is, in an honest belief that payment or performance was impaired—when the judge could not conclude that a reasonable person might have believed in good faith that such was the case.[14]

§ 10–4. Security Agreements as Adhesion Contracts

Essentially all security agreements are adhesion contracts in the sense that there is no negotiation of terms. The borrower either accepts the terms presented in the form offered for signature, or he goes elsewhere for accommodation. If the president of America's largest corporation were to borrow funds from his bank, as he probably does, he would sign the same note and security agreement as anyone else and he would very likely sign it without question. The only provision that would probably be negotiable would be the interest rate, and he would no doubt be given the most favorable current rate, not only for business reasons but also because his credit rating is excellent, the collateral is ample, there is no question of his willingness and ability to repay the loan—and in view of all this it really doesn't matter to either party what the security agreement says.

"Adhesion" as a label applied to certain contracts is intended to provoke the automatic response that they are bad, unconscionable, unenforceable. The fact is that there is no conceivable way that ordinary business could get done without form contracts. Millions of loans or sales could not occur daily if every contract had to be separately negotiated. The borrowers or buyers would not understand what features might be objectionable, and most such agreements are not worth consulting a lawyer about. Even if there were enough lawyers to handle the business a consultation would not be worth the lawyer's time from the standpoint of any reasonable compensation, and it would not be worth the borrower's or buyer's time because the chances are great that nothing whatsoever will turn out to be wrong

---

13. *See, e. g.,* Jensen v. State Bank of Allison, 518 F.2d 1 (8th Cir. 1975); Sheppard Federal Credit Union v. Palmer, 408 F.2d 1369 (5th Cir. 1969).

14. *See* State Bank of Lehi v. Woolsey, 565 P.2d 413 (Utah 1977); *Cf.* Farmers Cooperative Elevator, Inc. v. State Bank, 236 N.W.2d 674 (Iowa 1975).

and the loan will be repaid or the goods will be paid for without difficulty.

While telling points can be made about small print, and properly so, and the Code requires certain disclaimers to be conspicuous,[15] it is common knowledge that essentially every buyer or borrower will sign anything put before him. This appears to be true even if the writing is in a language the debtor does not understand,[16] but it is quite likely that it would make absolutely no difference if he did understand it. He would still sign it because he would not read it, or if he did read it and comprehend it, he would assume that the dire consequences would never occur to him.

While most of the points made against adhesion contracts probably will not survive a practical analysis on various grounds, the problems raised are of consequence because of the disparity in bargaining power between the debtor and secured party in almost all instances. Secured parties will demand, as long as they can, that security agreements contain certain terms, even though their meaning may be unclear to everyone, and borrowers will sign the agreements without questioning them, and if they did question them they would not receive legal answers. One cannot expect a sales clerk or a young bank officer to know what certain provision mean, if they mean anything at all.

Since there is no conceivable means of abolishing adhesion contracts in favor of negotiating every contract, if our system of facilitating consumer credit is to be continued, a more realistic approach should be taken to the problem. If certain provisions are thought to

---

15. *See, e. g.*, § 2–316(2) on excluding or modifying the warranties of merchantability and fitness. "Conspicuous" is defined in § 1–201(10).

16. *See* Frostifresh Corp. v. Reynoso, 52 Misc.2d 26, 274 N.Y.S.2d 757 (N.Y. Dist.Ct.1966), *rev'd per curiam* 54 Misc.2d 119, 281 N.Y.S.2d 964 (1966), involving a contract which was surely unconscionable by any standards applied under § 2–302. The terms of the contract were negotiated orally in Spanish but the contract was written in English and not "translated or explained" to the buyers, and there was some implication that they could not read it. It would be surprising if an ordinary contract for the sale of goods in this country had to be in a language ordinarily spoken by the buyers if the language were other than English. If the language of the contract in itself were an unconscionable feature, the probable result would be that those who could not speak English adequately could not buy on time, which would not be a desirable result from the standpoint of such potential buyers. It is unrealistic to expect an ordinary salesman to "explain" the terms of any sales contract to buyers; ordinary lawyers in fact probably could not do that, although they might try. In attempting to reach a fair result in this case, or in others, some courts occasionally are unrealistic in practical ways, and they use broad language which is susceptible of a more encompassing interpretation than is necessary or probably desirable in a wider context than the case being decided.

be harmful to the debtor and unnecessary for the secured party, bills to abolish them should be introduced into the state legislatures or Congress, in accordance with democratic tradition. This is not an area where courts have particular expertise. Many or most judges seem to have little or no background in business problems and business law, and some seemingly meritorious decisions can have unintended consequences. Elaborately prepared Brandeis briefs are not common in law suits where few dollars are involved. The issues which are often raised here are rarely as susceptible of simple solutions, or obviously right solutions, as the proponents on either side may assert.

Most provisions of most security agreements are of minimal consequence to anyone because there will be no defaults which trigger acceleration of the unpaid balance and the utilization of default procedures contained in the agreement or in the Code. Most loans are promptly and properly repaid. This is true in the overwhelming number of secured transactions, whether the debtors are consumers or businesses.

§ 10–5. Proceeding Against Real and Personal Property

A security agreement may cover both real and personal property. This is not likely to happen in consumer transactions but it may occur in corporate loans. Where both kinds of property are included in a security agreement, the secured party may proceed against the personal property in accordance with the provisions of Part 5 of Article 9, or he may proceed against both the real and personal property as the local real estate law allows and Part 5 will not apply.[17] The term "personal property" is not defined. Ordinarily there will be no difficulty in determining whether particular collateral may properly be called personal property, but there is a gray area sometimes. In this provision the gray area is fixtures. Nevertheless, the last subsection in Section 9–313, which deals with priorities of security interests in fixtures, states that a fixture secured party may in certain circumstances remove the fixture "on default, subject to the provisions of Part 5 . . . . "[18] Since the Code remedies are more expeditious than the usual mortgage foreclosure laws, there may be occasions when a mortgagee would choose to remove fixtures under the Code's rules rather than proceed under real property law as to both the real property and fixtures, and this should be possible under the 1962 Code if there has been a Code filing as to the fixtures which are covered in

17. § 9–501(4). *See* Hildner v. Fox, 17   18. § 9–313(5), Revised § 9–313(8).
Ill.App.3d 97, 308 N.E.2d 301 (1974).

the mortgage,[19] or under the 1972 Code where the mortgage is effective as a fixture filing.[20]

If the secured party uses the procedure permitted by Section 9–501(4) and proceeds against personal property of whatever kind under real estate law, a judicial foreclosure or the exercise of a power of sale in the mortgage (or trust deed or indenture) might be involved. While the Code provisions may not be detailed in all respects, they are likely to be more specific than the mortgage foreclosure laws of most states, not only as to the debtor's rights but as to the secured party's rights and remedies as well. This provision is unlikely to be used very often.

§ 10–6. Basic Default Provisions

When default occurs, the rights and remedies of the parties are determined primarily by Part 5 of Article 9 and secondarily by the security agreement.[21] If the secured party is in possession of the collateral, either as pledgee under a security agreement or by reason of having taken possession after default, then Section 9–207 applies.[22]

The default remedies are not dependent on the perfection of the security interest if no third party interests have intervened.[23] Nor is there any requirement that a secured party proceed against the collateral rather than seek a judgment for the amount of the unpaid obligation. Except for those consumer cases covered by Section 9–505(1) where the debtor has paid sixty percent of the obligation, there appears to be no reason why a secured party in possession of collateral could not retain the collateral as security and sue for the obligation without proceeding against the collateral, since the statutory remedies are in general permissive rather than mandatory.[24]

---

19. Section 9–313(1) recognizes that a security interest in fixtures may be created under real estate law but a financing statement covering the fixtures could also be filed, if thought desirable for Code purposes. While the 1972 Official Text continues the right to encumber fixtures in a real estate mortgage in Revised § 9–313 (3), a mortgage may be effective in a fixture filing under Revised § 9–402 (6). It should be noted that the secured party's right to remove fixtures on default is dependent on his having priority over designated interests. Under the 1962 Code he may have this priority and the right to remove even though there has been no Code filing.. See § 8–2 *supra.*

20. *See* Revised § 9–402(6). The term "fixture filing" is defined in Revised § 9–313(1) (b).

21. §§ 9–501(1), (2).

22. *Id.*

23. Kansas State Bank v. Overseas Motosport, Inc., 222 Kan. 26, 563 P.2d 414 (1977); South Division Credit Union v. Deluxe Motors, Inc., 42 Ill. App.3d 219, 355 N.E.2d 715 (1976). *See also* Mazda Motors of America, Inc. v. Southwestern Motors, Inc., 36 N.C. App. 1, 243 S.E.2d 793 (1978).

24. *See* McCullough v. Mobiland, Inc., 139 Ga.App. 260, 228 S.E.2d 146 (1976).

The secured party may reduce his claim to judgment, foreclose, or enforce the security interest by any other available judicial remedy. Where the collateral is documents, the secured party may proceed either against the documents or against the goods.[25] If the secured party reduces his claim to judgment, the execution lien relates back to the time when the security interest in the collateral was perfected;[26] the execution lien is simply a continuation of the original security interest and not a new transfer for an antecedent debt. A judicial sale pursuant to an execution is one means of enforcing the security interest,[27] and such a sale is governed by other state law, not by the Code, and the Code's restrictions on the secured party's buying at a foreclosure sale will not apply.[28]

Certain Code provisions may not be waived or varied to the extent they give rights to the debtor and impose duties on the secured party, except as expressly permitted with respect to compulsory disposition and redemption of collateral, but the parties may agree on the standards to be met in performing those rights and duties if the standards are not "manifestly unreasonable." These provisions, which are contained in Section 9–501(3), are: (a) Sections 9–502(2) and 9–504(2) insofar as they require the secured party to account for any surplus realized on the disposition of collateral securing an obligation;[29] (b) Sections 9–504(3) and 9–505(1) dealing with the disposition of collateral, although the debtor may renounce or modify his rights by a signed statement after default; (c) Section 9–505(2) covering acceptance of the collateral by the secured party as a discharge of the debtor's obligation; (d) Section 9–507(1) covering the liability of the secured

---

25. § 9–501(1).

26. § 9–501(5). *In re* Schindler, 16 UCC Rep.Serv. 252 (E.D.Pa.1974) (in bankruptcy). If there is no execution on the collateral after an in personam judgment is recovered for the debt, § 9–501(5) in terms does not apply. *See, e. g., In re* Wilson, 390 F.Supp. 1121 (D.Kan.1975) where the secured party apparently was held to an election of remedies, having sued on the debt without attempting to foreclose on the collateral, and the judgment was recovered within four months of the debtor's bankruptcy and was dischargeable; the security interest was said not to be enforceable, but in any event the collateral was probably exempt from execution on the facts stated since the security interest was not purchase money. *See also* Garza

v. Allied Finance Co., 566 S.W.2d 57 (Tex.Civ.App.1978) (dictum).

27. An execution sale which does not bring enough money to satisfy the claim does not constitute an election of remedies so as to bar the secured party from seeking further means of collecting the debt secured. Bilar, Inc. v. Sherman, —— Colo.App. ——, 572 P.2d 489 (1977).

28. § 9–501(5).

29. Article 9 covers sales of accounts and chattel paper (and contract rights under the 1962 Code) as well as transfers of these kinds of collateral for security. In the case of a sale, the debtor is entitled to a surplus or liable for a deficiency only if the security agreement so provides. §§ 9–502(2), 9–504 (2).

party who does not comply with the requirements of Part 5 of Article 9. Except for these provisions, the parties may agree on the standards measuring their performance, if not manifestly unreasonable, but the obligations of good faith, diligence, reasonableness, and care prescribed by the Code may not be disclaimed.[30]

The standards measuring performance may appear in the security agreement. While the security agreement must be signed by the debtor,[31] it is quite likely that he has not read the agreement or at least has not read it with comprehension. Nevertheless, the fact is that the debtor could have read the agreement, whether he did so or not, and he is bound by its terms if they are not found to be "manifestly unreasonable." Particularly in business transactions, a course of dealing or usage of trade may be important in giving meaning to the terms of the parties' agreement.[32]

In a provision of general application throughout the Code, Section 1–201(3) states that the *effect* of the Code's provisions may be varied by agreement, except as otherwise provided in the Code and except that prescribed obligations of good faith, diligence, reasonableness, and care may not be disclaimed although standards of performance not manifestly unreasonably may be agreed upon.[33] While this provision is apparently thought to be significant, it is by no means clear. It is said to affirm the principle of freedom of contract.[34] It is also said that the meaning of the statute must be found in its text and in "appropriate extrinsic aids; it cannot be varied by agreement." [35] The Official Comment to this Section goes on to say that private parties cannot by contract make negotiable what is otherwise a non-negotiable instrument, but they can by "an agreement change the legal consequences which would otherwise flow from the provisions of the Act." [36] In the absence of specific examples of how this can be done or what it means, reliance on this Comment would be misplaced. Clearly the rights of third parties cannot be affected by an agreement between

---

30. § 1–102(3). It is expressly stated in § 1–203 that: "Every contract or duty within this Act imposes an obligation of good faith in its performance or enforcement." *See* Skeels v. Universal C. I. T. Credit Corp., 335 F.2d 846 (3rd Cir. 1964).

31. § 9–203(1) (b), Revised § 9–203(1) (a). The statement in the text is not applicable technically in the case of a pledge, but it is true as a practical matter in most pledges.

32. § 1–205. Note the broad definition of "agreement" in § 1–201(3). It is by agreement, not necessarily by the terms of a security agreement, that the standards of performance are measured.

33. § 1–102(3).

34. § 1–102, Comment 2.

35. *Id.*

36. *Id.*

the parties of which they know nothing, nor should a clear Code provision be overriden by a compact of which one of the affected parties presumably has no knowledge.[37] The import of the provision is to allow for changes in practical procedures and not to put the developing law in a strait jacket, but the provision must be gingerly relied on.

Where Section 9–504(3) requires (in most instances) reasonable notice of sale to be sent by the secured party to the debtor before the collateral is disposed of, a general consensus is that five days' notice is all right.[38] In most circumstances it probably is, but if sent on a Friday when July 4 was the following Tuesday and many offices would be closed on Monday, it would certainly be questionable, no matter what the security agreement said.[39] A little common sense and common decency can lessen this possibly unfair application of an otherwise permissible provision in the agreement. But this is the kind of thing a security agreement properly can and ought to provide for.

Section 9–504(2) clearly provides that the debtor is liable for any deficiency remaining after the collateral has been disposed of by the secured party after default. Where the secured party has not carefully adhered to the Code's provisions, there has been a tendency in some courts to refuse to recognize this right to a deficiency on one basis or another.[40] The debtor's Code remedy, where the secured par-

---

37. In West Side Bank v. Marine Nat. Exchange Bank, 37 Wis.2d 661, 155 N.W.2d 587 (1968), in which the question involved arguably was whether a stop payment order came too late and the court did not even cite § 4–303 which deals with that problem, a clearing house rule was allowed to override the very clear rule of Article 4 on the midnight deadline by extending that deadline for 24 hours. Some justification for this can be found (although the decision is clearly wrong on other grounds), in § 4–103(1), which is comparable to § 1–102(3), although it would seem that there ought to be some difference between altering the "effect" of a Code provision and completely rewriting the terms of a provision which governs such a mechanical concept as a midnight deadline. The comments of the draftsman of the principal Code provision at issue are illuminating. *See* Malcolm, Reflections on West Side Bank: A Draftsman's View, 18 Cath. U.L.Rev. 23 (1968). *See also* Rohner, Posting of Checks: Final Payment and the Four Legals, 23 Bus.Law. 1075 (1968).

38. By local amendment California requires five days' notice, among other things, and a notice not stating the "exact date, time, and place of public sale" was held inadequate in J. T. Jenkins Co. v. Kennedy, 45 Cal.App. 3d 474, 119 Cal.Rptr. 578 (1975). *See also* Sears Bank & Trust Co. v. Scott, 29 Ill.App.3d 1002, 331 N.E.2d 607 (1975), holding that the ten-day notice required by the local Retail Installment Sales Act prevailed over the Code's reasonable notice requirement by virtue of § 9–203(2), Revised § 9–203(4).

39. In Levers v. Rio King Land & Inv. Co., —— Nev. ——, 560 P.2d 917 (1977), a notice sent on May 25 of a sale to be held on June 2 was held not to be reasonable; Memorial Day weekend intervened.

40. *See, e. g., In re* Bishop, 482 F.2d 381 (4th Cir. 1973); Leasing Associates, Inc. v. Slaughter & Son, Inc.,

ty has not proceeded properly, is stated in Section 9–507(1). Where the collateral has been improperly disposed of, the debtor is liable for any deficiency but the secured party is liable for "any loss caused by a failure to comply" with the statutory requirements.[41] In the case of consumer goods, the secured party's minimum liability is the credit service charge plus ten per cent of the principal amount of the debt or the time price differential plus ten per cent of the cash price.[42] It appears likely that the Code remedy would often be advantageous to consumers, particularly where the collateral is automobiles, and there appears to be no statutory warrant for the judicial disregard of the Code's provisions, although the earlier cases disregarding the Code may have resulted from an inadequate understanding of the rather complicated statutory provisions, and the later cases may simply be the result of stare decisis. Where the Code's provisions are disregarded, the usual result seems to be to leave the parties where they were, holding the debtor not liable for any deficiency, and holding the secured party not liable for any loss caused the debtor.

§ 10–7. Collateral in Possession of Secured Party

Collateral may be in the possession of the secured party either because it was pledged as security or because the secured party took

450 F.2d 174 (8th Cir. 1971) (interpreting Arkansas cases to require that the secured party must prove "actual value" of collateral at time of sale in order to recover deficiency, relying in part on Norton v. Nat'l Bank of Commerce of Pine Bluff, 240 Ark. 143, 398 S.W.2d 538 (1966) where the court indulged "the presumption . . . that the collateral was worth at least the amount of the debt, thereby shifting to the creditor the burden of proving the amount that should reasonably have been obtained through a sale conducted according to law."); Beneficial Finance Co. v. Reed, 212 N.W.2d 454 (Iowa 1973); Turk v. St. Petersburg Bank & Trust Co., 281 So.2d 534 (Fla.App.1973); Leasco Data Processing Equipment Corp. v. Atlas Shirt Co., Inc., 66 Misc. 2d 1089, 323 N.Y.S.2d 13 (Cir.Ct. 1971); Edmondson v. Air Service Co., 123 Ga.App. 263, 180 S.E.2d 589 (1971); Moody v. Nides Finance Co., 115 Ga. App. 859, 156 S.E.2d 310 (1967). See generally W. Davenport & D. Murray, Secured Transactions 292–297 (1978).

41. See, e. g., United States v. Whitehouse Plastics, 501 F.2d 692 (5th Cir. 1974); Clark Leasing Corp. v. White Sands Forest Products, Inc., 87 N.M.

451, 535 P.2d 1077 (N.Mex.1975) (where the court stated, "The complete denial of a deficiency smacks of the punitive and is directly contrary to Article Nine's underlying theme of commercial reasonableness."); Wirth v. Heavey, 508 S.W.2d 263 (Mo.App. 1974); Community Management Ass'n of Colorado Springs, Inc. v. Tousley, 32 Colo.App. 33, 505 P.2d 1314 (1973) (indulging what appears to be a common presumption that the value of the collateral was the amount of the debt, leaving the secured party to proof of market value where the sale was not conducted according to Code rules); O'Neil v. Mack Trucks, Inc., 533 S.W.2d 832 (Tex.Civ.App.1975) reversed 542 S.W.2d 112 (Tex.1976), recalled and reissued 551 S.W.2d 32 (Tex.1977); Conti Causeway Ford v. Jarossy, 114 N.J.Super. 382, 276 A.2d 402 (1971). For a perceptive discussion of these problems see Hall v. Owen County State Bank, 23 UCC Rep.Serv. 267 (Ind.App.1977). See also Levers v. Rio King Land & Inv. Co., — Nev. —, 560 P.2d 917 (1977).

42. See, e. g., Conti Causeway Ford v. Jarossy, 114 N.J.Super. 382, 276 A.2d 402 (1971).

possession of it after default.[43] In either case, the provisions of Section 9–207, if applicable, will govern.[44]

The secured party is required to use "reasonable care" in the custody and preservation of any collateral which is in his possession.[45] This duty of care cannot be disclaimed although the standard of care, if not manifestly unreasonable, may be agreed upon.[46] Where the collateral is instruments or chattel paper, reasonable care "includes taking necessary steps to preserve rights against prior parties unless otherwise agreed."[47] In the case of instruments which are collateral in themselves or as part of chattel paper, unless the parties have agreed that no such action need be taken, presentment should be made and notice of dishonor (or protest) should be given to prior parties to preserve the right of recourse against them if an instrument is not paid on presentment.[48]

When the secured party has possession of the collateral, unless the parties agree otherwise (which is most unlikely): the secured party is entitled to reasonable expenses (including insurance and taxes)[49] incurred in the custody, preservation, use, or operation of the collateral, and these expenses will be secured by the collateral; the risk of accidental loss or damage is on the debtor if there is any deficiency in insurance coverage; the secured party may hold as additional security any increase or profits other than money (such as stock dividends) but if money (such as cash dividends) is received, it must be applied to reduce the debt unless it is sent on to the debtor; the secured party may commingle fungible collateral but other collateral must be kept identifiable; the secured party may repledge collateral, such as stock, but only on terms which do not impair the debtor's right

---

43. The secured party is not required to take possession of the collateral on default even if requested to do so by the debtor. North Carolina Nat'l Bank v. Sharpe, 35 N.C.App. 404, 241 S.E.2d 360 (1978).

44. § 9–501(1), (2).

45. § 9–207(1). The secured party may have a considerable liability if the collateral is convertible securities. *See, e. g.,* Reed v. Central Nat. Bank of Alva, 421 F.2d 113 (10th Cir. 1970); Tallahassee Bank & Trust Co. v. Bryant, 11 UCC Rep.Serv. 467 (Fla. Dist.Ct.App.1972); Brod-Heim v. Chase Manhattan Bank, 8 UCC Rep.Serv. 89 (N.Y.Sup.Ct.1970); Grace v. Sterling Grace & Co., 30 A.D.2d 61, 289

N.Y.S.2d 632 (1968); Traverse v. Liberty Bank & Trust Co., 5 UCC Rep. Serv. 535 (Mass.Super.Ct.1967).

46. § 1–102(3).

47. § 9–207(1). *See* § 1–102(4).

48. *See* §§ 3–501, 3–507, 3–508, 3–509. Ordinarily presentment and notice of dishonor (or protest) will be waived in notes, and this is entirely permissible. § 3–511(2) (a). The term "instrument" includes securities, under § 9–105(1)(g), Revised § 9–105(1)(i).

49. *See* J. T. Jenkins Co. v. Kennedy, 45 Cal.App.3d 474, 119 Cal.Rptr. 578 (1975) (secured party entitled to claim $6,200 in fuel taxes paid to state in order to clear title for resale).

to redeem.[50]   If the secured party fails to meet these obligations, he is liable for any loss caused by his failure but he will not lose his security interest.[51]

The secured party may use or operate collateral to preserve it or its value, or if permitted by court order, or, except in the case of consumer goods, if and as provided in the security agreement.[52]   This provision allowing operation of the collateral, together with the provision of Section 9–207(2)(a) permitting the expenses of such operation to be charged to the debtor and secured by the collateral, may occasionally be useful.   Official Comment 4 to Section 9–207 states: "Agreements providing for such operation are common in trust indentures securing corporate bonds and are particularly important when the collateral is a going business."   Just how common—or, if common, effective—this provision is in trust indentures may be subject to question, as may the frequency of use of a "going business" (whatever that is) as collateral.[53]

§ 10–8.   Secured Party's Right to Take Possession

Section 9–503 states that the secured party has a right to take possession of the collateral on default,[54] unless the parties have agreed otherwise, which is very unlikely.   It is indeed probable that the contract between the parties—the security agreement—will expressly grant the secured party the right to take possession on default, if he is not already in possession as pledgee.   Probably what the Code provision is intended to say is that except for pledges, the secured party has no right to possession before default unless the security agreement provides for it.   Possession may be taken by self-help if this can be done without a breach of the peace, or judicial process may be utilized.[55]

---

50.   § 9–207(2).

51.   § 9–207(3).

52.   § 9–207(4).

53.   *But see* Hogan, The Secured Party and Default Proceedings Under the UCC, 47 Minn.L.Rev. 205, 213 (1962).

54.   Fairchild v. Williams Feed, Inc., —— Mont. ——, 544 P.2d 1216 (1976). There is no statutory requirement of notice to the debtor before repossession. *See* Fulton Nat'l Bank v. Horn,

239 Ga. 648, 238 S.E.2d 358 (1977); Teeter Motor Co., Inc. v. First Nat'l Bank of Hot Springs, 260 Ark. 764, 543 S.W.2d 938 (1976).

55.   Judicial process will probably be necessary if a third party is in possession of the collateral, but the right to possession is enforceable against third parties. *See* Long Island Trust Co. v. Porta Aluminum Co., 49 A.D.2d 579, 370 N.Y.S.2d 166 (1975). *See also* Riblet Tramway Co. v. Monte Verde Corp., 453 F.2d 313 (10th Cir. 1972).

Perhaps in most cases where debtors are in default because of inability to make the necessary installment payments, the debtors will cooperate with the secured party's repossession of the collateral. Occasionally debtors may claim that there is no default, even though payments have been missed, because there is a breach of warranty which might be thought to justify withholding payments, and such debtors may resist repossession. Then there are some debtors who are unquestionably in default and who have no meritorious defense to repossession but who nevertheless will not, if they have the option, permit repossession, in which case the secured parties will probably utilize expeditious judicial procedures under claim and delivery statutes or the like.[56] It is clear that a secured party cannot repossess without judicial process if this would cause a breach of the peace,[57] and repossessing items of household furnishings might sometimes be impossible. Motor vehicles kept in parking lots or carports or unlocked garages [58] or on the public streets have often been removed by professional repossessors,[59] obviously without informing the debtors of what is going on, although this occupation may justifiably be thought of as hazardous, especially in some cities. So long as the car is removed without objection, whether from the debtor's premises (at least without breaking a lock) or from a public street or wherever else it may be, the repossession is presumably rightful,[60] and the Code has no requirement of prior notice.[61]

---

56. *See, e. g.*, Honeywell Information Systems, Inc. v. Demographic Services, Inc., 396 F.Supp. 273 (S.D.N.Y. 1975). Bringing an action to gain possession of the collateral does not prevent the secured party from bringing a subsequent action for a deficiency following resale. KMAP, Inc. v. Town & Country Broadcasters, Inc., 49 Cal.App.3d 544, 122 Cal.Rptr. 420 (1975).

57. Or if the repossession causes a breach of the peace, the secured party will be liable in damages to the debtor. Nicholson's Mobile Home Sales v. Schramm, —— Ind. ——, 330 N.E.2d 785 (1975). *See also* Deavers v. Standridge, 144 Ga.App. 673, 242 S.E.2d 331 (1978).

58. *See, e. g.*, Pierce v. Leasing International, Inc., 142 Ga.App. 371, 235 S.E.2d 752 (1977); Marine Midland Bank-Central v. Cote, 351 So.2d 750 (Fla.App.1977); Messenger v. Sandy Motors, Inc., 121 N.J.Super. 1, 295 A.2d 402 (1972).

59. In Henderson v. Security Nat'l Bank, 72 Cal.App.3d 764, 140 Cal.Rptr. 388 (1977), where a professional repossessor entered a locked garage to remove a car, the court allowed to stand a jury verdict against the secured party for $1,357.43 in compensatory damages on a claim of conversion but reversed an award of $125,000 in exemplary damages. Less appealing facts in support of any recovery would be difficult to find.

60. *See, e. g.*, Thompson v. Ford Motor Credit Co., 550 F.2d 256 (5th Cir. 1977), where the automobile was repossessed from a garage when it was taken for repairs, and no breach of the peace was found.

61. Georgia once apparently adopted the peculiar rule that a notice of acceleration of the unpaid debt must be given to the debtor before the collateral can be repossessed. *See, e. g.*, Chrysler Credit Corp. v. Barnes, 126 Ga.App. 444, 191 S.E.2d 121 (1972). Or this issue may have arisen because of in-

Repossessed cars are often alleged to have contained small items of considerable value, which items seem always to disappear.[62] Conceivably such claims may occasionally have merit instead of merely nuisance value, but they may be reduced or waived by requiring prompt notice in the security agreement.[63]

The recognition of the secured party's right to self-help repossession in Section 9–503 is merely a statutory embodiment of an ancient common law remedy.[64] While much litigated in recent years, this right does not appear to be subject to Constitutional challenge under the rubric of an action taken under color of state law,[65] but to avoid the assertion of that claim, the secured party's right to repossess can be expressed in the security agreement as a matter of the contract between the parties.

If the debtor has been consistently late in making payments and the secured party has just as consistently accepted the late payments without quibble, it probably will not be feasible to declare a default and accelerate the unpaid balance for one more late payment, unless the debtor has been given reasonable notice that the contract terms will be strictly enforced.[66]

Section 9–503 also authorizes a provision in the security agreement under which the secured party may require the debtor to assemble the collateral and make it available at a reasonably convenient place designated by the secured party. Obviously this is not a self-executing contractual provision, but it may have occasional *in ter-*

artistic drafting of the security agreement. Notice apparently is not required now. Ford Motor Credit Co. v. Hunt, 241 Ga. 342, 245 S.E.2d 295 (1978).

62. *See, e. g.,* Grucella v. General Motors Corp., 10 Pa.D. & C.2d 65 (C.P. 1956). *See also* First Nat'l Bank & Trust Co. in Macon v. State, 141 Ga. App. 471, 233 S.E.2d 861 (1977) (indictment for theft of contents of repossessed vehicle; defendants acquitted).

63. Thompson v. Ford Motor Credit Co., 550 F.2d 256 (5th Cir. 1977). *But see* Jones v. General Motors Acceptance Corp., 565 P.2d 9 (Okl.1977).

64. *See, e. g.,* Hill v. Michigan Nat'l Bank, 58 Mich.App. 430, 228 N.W.2d 407 (1975).

65. *See, e. g.,* Bosse v. Crowell, Collier & MacMillan, 565 F.2d 602, (9th Cir. 1977); Shirley v. State Nat'l Bank

of Connecticut, 493 F.2d 739 (2d Cir. 1974), certiorari denied 419 U.S. 1009, 95 S.Ct. 329, 42 L.Ed.2d 284; Gibbs v. Titelman, 502 F.2d 1107 (3d Cir. 1974), certiorari denied 419 U.S. 1039, 95 S.Ct. 526, 42 L.Ed.2d 316; James v. Pinnex, 495 F.2d 206 (5th Cir. 1974); Turner v. Impala Motors, 503 F.2d 607 (6th Cir. 1974); Bichel Optical Lab., Inc. v. Marquette Nat'l Bank, 487 F.2d 906 (8th Cir. 1973); Nowlin v. Professional Auto Sales, Inc., 496 F.2d 16 (8th Cir. 1974), certiorari denied 419 U.S. 1006, 95 S.Ct. 328, 42 L.Ed.2d 283; Adams v. Southern California First Nat'l Bank, 492 F.2d 324 (9th Cir. 1974), certiorari denied 419 U.S. 1006, 95 S.Ct. 325, 42 L.Ed.2d 282. On "under color of state law," see Flagg Brothers, Inc. v. Brooks, —— U.S. ——, 56 L.Ed.2d 185, 98 S.Ct. 1729 (1978).

66. *See, e. g.,* Lee v. Wood Products Credit Union, 275 Or. 445, 551 P.2d 446 (1976); Raffa v. Dania Bank, 321 So.2d 83 (Fla.App.1975).

rorem value or specific performance might be available.[67] Even without removing equipment, which may be impractical to remove for many reasons, the secured party may render the equipment unusable while leaving it on the debtor's premises, and collateral may be disposed of on the debtor's premises under Section 9–504, which requires that every aspect of the disposition must be "commercially reasonable" so that undue advantage cannot be taken by the secured party.

With the exception of the provision allowing equipment to be made unusable on the debtor's premises, the section broadly refers to collateral. But the collateral must be tangible in some sense, even if it is not goods, for possession to be taken. The section clearly cannot refer to intangible collateral such as accounts.

The Code provision allowing peaceable repossession of the collateral is in line with pre-Code law on the subject.[68] No change in this provision was made in the redraft of Article 9 and apparently no change was suggested to the Review Committee by any individual or group. Nor has any state legislature eliminated this provision.

§ 10–9. Secured Party's Collection Rights

Obligations owing to the debtor are a common form of collateral. Perhaps the simplest example is accounts arising from a store's sales on open credit. These accounts may be used as collateral when the store needs financing and, depending on a variety of circumstances, the assigned accounts may be collected by the secured party from the date of the assignment or in any event on default.[69]

Section 9–502(1) states that the secured party has the right to notify an account debtor or the obligor on an instrument to make payment to him at any time if the security agreement so provides but in any event on default, and he may take control of any proceeds

---

67. Specific performance was granted in Clark Equipment Co. v. Armstrong Equipment Co., 431 F.2d 54 (5th Cir. 1970), rehearing denied 434 F.2d 1039, certiorari denied 402 U.S. 909, 91 S.Ct. 1382, 28 L.Ed.2d 650.

68. Uniform Trust Receipts Act § 6; Uniform Conditional Sales Act § 16. *See generally* Hogan, The Secured Party and Default Proceedings Under the UCC, 47 Minn.L.Rev. 205, 211–212 (1962). *Compare* Cherno v. Bank of Babylon, 54 Misc.2d 277, 282 N.Y.S.2d 114 (Sup.Ct.1967), *affirmed* 29 A.D.2d 767, 288 N.Y.S.2d 862 (1968), *with* Morris v. First Nat. Bank & Trust Co., 21 Ohio St.2d 25, 254 N.E.2d 683 (1970) and Stone Machinery Co. v. Kessler, 1 Wash.App. 750, 463 P.2d 651 (1970).

69. *See* Marine Nat'l Bank v. Airco, Inc. v. Craneways, Inc., 389 F.Supp. 231 (W.D.Pa.1975).

which he is entitled to under Section 9–306.[70] The term "account debtor" means a person obligated on an account, chattel paper, or general intangible (or contract right under the 1962 Code).[71] Instruments may be part of chattel paper or they may be separate.[72]

In any case where third parties owe an obligation which is used as security, the secured party has collateral which is usually self-liquidating and the next best collateral to cash from the standpoint of collectability without unduly difficult realization problems such as goods often present.

Practices vary widely in dealing with such collateral as accounts and chattel paper. A furniture store selling on time, whether the credit is unsecured (that is, accounts for financing purposes) or secured (conditional sale contracts or notes and conditional sale contracts which, if used as security, would be chattel paper in either case) might well use these obligations for its own financing. An assignee of such paper would probably not make direct collection before default; the buyers would pay the store. Automobile dealers, on the other hand, are unlikely to sell on unsecured credit and are quite likely to use a conditional sale contract which shows on its face that it is to be assigned to a finance company or bank, and the buyer will make payments directly to the financer. In these examples, the first might be called non-notification financing and the second notification financing. If royalties under a contract with a book publisher or patent licensee were assigned, these would be general intangibles,[73] and the contract should spell out in detail what the terms of the assignment are.

In "factoring" the assignee of the accounts commonly assumes the credit risk and more or less functions as a credit department for sellers, principally textile sellers.[74] If an account is uncollectible, it is not the responsibility of the assignor to make it good and there is no recourse against him.

All financing arrangements of this kind are matters of contract, generally carefully negotiated contracts, whether recourse or non-re-

---

70. Feldman v. Philadelphia Nat'l Bank, 408 F.Supp. 24 (E.D.Pa.1976); Peters v. Washington Loan & Banking Co., 133 Ga.App. 293, 211 S.E.2d 148 (1974).

71. § 9–105(1)(a).

72. § 9–105(1) (b), (g), Revised § 9–105 (1) (b), (i).

73. § 9–106.

74. See Moore, Factoring—A Unique and Important Form of Financing and Service, 13 Bus.Law. 703 (1959); Greenberg, Inventory and Accounts Receivable Financing, 1956 U.Ill.L.F. 601, 612–18.

course, notification or non-notification financing. The security agreements should spell out in detail what the rights of the parties are. If the secured party (or assignee) may change back uncollected collateral or is entitled to recourse against the debtor (or assignor) for bad debts, then he must proceed in a commercially reasonable manner if he undertakes to collect against the account debtors or obligors, and he may deduct reasonable collection expenses.[75] He has no right to "dump" accounts and attempt to enforce a deficiency. He must behave in a commercially reasonable manner.[76]

These forms of financing may as well involve sales of accounts or chattel paper (or contracts rights under the 1962 Code) as transfers for security. If a sale is involved, the debtor is entitled to a surplus realized or liable for a deficiency only if the security agreement provides for it. If the arrangement is for security, the secured party must account to the debtor if there is a surplus and the debtor is liable for a deficiency unless the security agreement provides otherwise.[77] Whether a transaction involving accounts or chattel paper is a sale or for security, it is likely to be phrased in terms of assignment (for lack of any more exact terminology), and Article 9 applies to both.[78]

§ 10–10.   Secured Party's Right to Dispose of Collateral

"Commercially reasonable" is the key phrase modifying every aspect of the disposition of the collateral by the secured party.[79] While the disposition may be by public sale,[80] there is no requirement that it must be, for often public sales with newspaper or courthouse notices produce only the local vultures, not the most advantageous bids from the standpoint of either the debtor or the secured party, both of whom have an interest in getting the most money out of the collateral. The sale is likely to be the only means the secured party has of getting his money back, if the disposition is by sale, and if there is a surplus, it goes to the debtor (or the holders of subordi-

---

75. § 9–502(2), Revised § 9–502(2).

76. *See* DeLay First Nat'l Bank & Trust Co. v. Jacobson Appliance Co., 196 Neb. 398, 243 N.W.2d 745 (1976).

77. § 9–504(2), Revised § 9–504(2).

78. § 9–102(1), Revised § 9–102(1).

79. § 9–504(3), Revised § 9–504(3). *See* United States v. Terry, 554 F.2d 685 (5th Cir. 1977); C. I. T. Corp. v. Lee Pontiac, Inc., 513 F.2d 207 (9th Cir.

1975); Bryant v. American Nat'l Bank & Trust Co., 407 F.Supp. 360 (N.D.Ill.1976); *In re* Zsa Zsa Ltd., 352 F.Supp. 665 (1972), affirmed 475 F.2d 1393 (2d Cir. 1973); Old Colony Trust Co. v. Penrose Industries Corp., 280 F. Supp. 698 (E.D.Pa.1968), affirmed 398 F.2d 310 (3d Cir. 1968).

80. § 9–504(3), Revised § 9–504(3). *But see* S. E. C. v. Guild Films Co., 279 F.2d 485 (2d Cir.), certiorari denied 364 U.S. 818, 81 S.Ct. 52, 5 L.Ed.2d 49 (1960).

nate security interests).[81]   A deficiency may be the debtor's responsibility,[82] but it is likely to be uncollectible.[83]

The term "debtor" is, of course, more broadly defined than meaning simply the primary obligor.   It includes the owner of the collateral, if he is not the same person who owes payment of the obligation secured.[84]

The requirements of a public sale are nowhere stated in the Code, but at the minimum it would seem that there must be adequate notice, probably by newspaper advertisement, giving a meaningful description of what is to be sold and on what terms and when.[85]   The standard of commercial reasonableness applies, which gives flexibility varying with the different kinds of collateral and other circumstances.[86]

The property may also be disposed of by private sale or by lease "or otherwise," and there may be one or more contracts, but any sale will be subject to Article 2.   The collateral may be disposed of as a unit or sold piecemeal.[87]   In any case, the "method, manner, time, place and terms must be commercially reasonable."[88]   The basic idea is to allow the secured party, who usually will be commercially *au courant*, to get the best possible terms by the best possible means, but he is held only to a "commercially reasonable" standard.[89]   He

81.   § 9–504(1), (2), Revised § 9–504(1), (2).

82.   § 9–504(2), Revised § 9–504(2). *See* Grucella v. General Motors Corp., 10 Pa.D. & C.2d 65 (C.P.1956) for a judicial adjustment of difficult problems in this area.

83.   In Massey-Ferguson Credit Corp. v. Casaulong, 62 Cal.App.3d 1024, 133 Cal.Rptr. 497 (1976), it was held that the four-year limitation of § 2–725(1) barred an action for a deficiency under a conditional sale contract.

84.   § 9–105(1) (d), Revised § 9–105(1) (d).

85.   *See* § 9–504(3), Revised § 9–504(3); Annot., 4 A.L.R.2d 575 (1949) (on "public sale"). *See also In re* Kiamie's Estate, 309 N.Y. 325, 130 N.E.2d 745 (1955), a pre-Code case which probably has continuing vitality.   Public notice given by posting notices on a telephone pole near an entrance to an alley, on a utility pole in an alley, and

on a building wall, was held not to be commercially reasonable in Wilkerson Motor Co., Inc. v. Johnson, 49 Okl. Bar Ass'n J. 115, 580 P.2d 505 (Okl. 1978).

86.   Where the secured party bought the collateral at a "public sale" for $100 and resold it for $10,000, the sale was found not to be commercially reasonable in Levers v. Rio King Land & Inv. Co., —— Nev. ——, 560 P.2d 917 (1977).

87.   §§ 9–504(1), (3), Revised §§ 9–504(1), (3).

88.   § 9–504(3), Revised § 9–504(3). *See* Alliance Discount Corp. v. Shaw, 195 Pa.Super. 601, 171 A.2d 548 (1961).

89.   § 9–507(2).   According to Clark Leasing Corp. v. White Sands Forest Products, Inc., 87 N.M. 451, 535 P.2d 1077 (1975), the secured party must allege and, unless admitted, prove that the sale was commercially reasonable. *See also* Vic Hansen & Sons, Inc. v. Crowley, 57 Wis.2d 106, 203 N.W.2d

does not guarantee that the price obtained will be the highest possible price or that it will satisfy the obligation outstanding, and it is unlikely in many cases involving depreciating goods that the sale price will equal the unpaid balance due by the debtor.

§ 10–11.   Notice of Disposition

The secured party is not required to give any notification [90] of his intended disposition of the collateral in these circumstances: where the collateral is perishable (as in the case of agricultural commodities), or where it threatens to decline speedily in value (as in the case of seasonal goods such as those designed for certain holidays), or where it is of a type customarily sold on a recognized market (such as registered stock),[91] but the disposition must still be commercially reasonable.[91]

In all other cases the 1962 Code requires that reasonable notice be sent by the secured party to the debtor stating the time and place of any public sale [93] or the time after which any other disposition is to be made.[94]   Except for consumer goods, such notice must also be sent to other secured parties who have interests in the collateral evidenced by filed financing statements or who are known by the secured party to have such interests.[95]   While five days' notice is generally consid-

---

728 (1973); Granite Equipment Leasing Corp. v. Marine Development Corp., 139 Ga.App. 778, 230 S.E.2d 43 (1976); Jones v. Morgan, 58 Mich.App. 455, 228 N.W.2d 419 (1975). *Cf.* Fryer & Willis Drilling Co. v. Oilwell, Division of United States Steel Corp., 472 S.W.2d 857 (Tex.Civ.App.1971), reversed 493 S.W.2d 487 (Tex.1973).

90.   § 1–201(26).

91.   Marine Midland Bank-Rochester v. Vaeth, 88 Misc.2d 657, 388 N.Y.S.2d 548 (1976) (stock sold on New York Stock Exchange). A number of courts have held that used automobiles are not collateral "of a type customarily sold on a recognized market." *See,* *e. g.*, O'Neil v. Mack Trucks, Inc., 533 S.W.2d 832 (Tex.Civ.App.1975), reversed 542 S.W.2d 112, Sup., recalled and reissued 551 S.W.2d 32 (Tex.1977).

92.   § 9–504(3), Revised § 9–504(3).   See Bankers Trust Co. v. J. V. Dowler & Co., Inc., 62 A.D.2d 778, 406 N.Y.S.2d 51 (1978).

93.   *See* J. T. Jenkins Co. v. Kennedy, 45 Cal.App.3d 474, 119 Cal.Rptr. 578 (1975); *In re* Webb, 17 UCC Rep.Serv. 627 (S.D.Ohio 1975) (in bankruptcy).

94.   If a debtor authorizes the secured party to dispose of pledged collateral prior to technical default, Part 5 of Article 9 has been held not to apply. Spillers v. Five Points Guaranty Bank, 335 So.2d 851 (Fla.App.1976). *Cf.* O'Neil v. Mack Trucks, Inc., 533 S.W.2d 832 (Tex.Civ.App.1975), reversed 542 S.W.2d 112, recalled and reissued 551 S.W.2d 32 (Tex.1977).

95.   § 9–504(3).   *See* Young v. Golden State Bank, —— Colo.App. ——, 560 P. 2d 855 (1977); Bank of Camilla v. Stephens, 234 Ga. 293, 216 S.E.2d 71 (1975). "Knows" or "knowledge" means actual knowledge under § 1–201 (25). *See* Balzer Machinery Co. v. Klineline Sand & Gravel Co., 271 Or. 596, 533 P.2d 321 (1975), where the filing of a notice of a non-possessory artisan's lien was not notice to the secured party under § 9–504.

ered reasonable and often appears in security agreements;[96] there is no Code requirement that the period begins to run after receipt by the debtor, or for that matter that the notice ever be received, and considering the ever-worsening postal service and the current vogue of long weekends, five days from depositing a notice in the mail may sometimes be unfair and not commercially reasonable.[97]

Where the Code requires that notice be "sent" to the debtor, this presumably means a written communication,[98] but oral notice has been held to be sufficient.[99] This acceptance of oral notification by some courts may be based on the statutory language in Section 9–504(3) stating that "reasonable notification . . . shall be sent," with more reliance on "notification" than on "sent," since "reasonable notification" would not require a written communication.[1] In these cases the fact that the debtor is quite aware of having defaulted and knows that the secured party is taking steps to realize on the security, may be quite influential,[2] since the debtor's objection to the disposition of the collateral is purely technical. In any event, there is no statutory requirement that the notice be received.[3]

The term "debtor" is broadly defined in Section 9–105(1)(d), and it includes not only the person who owes the payment but also the owner of the collateral, where they are not the same person. Where the secured party has a duty to give a notice to the "debtor," the notice must be given to the owner of the collateral, when that person is different from the person owing payment, as well as to the person who has an obligation to pay the debt which has been secured.[4] A somewhat different problem arises where there is a guar-

96. It is permissible for the parties to agree on a reasonable period of notice under § 9–501(3). Section 1–201 (26) distinguishes between notifying or giving a notice or notification and receiving a notice or notification.

97. Notice sent on May 25 announcing a sale on June 2 was held not to be reasonable when Memorial Day weekend intervened in Levers v. Rio King Land & Inv. Co., — Nev. —, 560 P.2d 917 (1977).

98. DeLay First Nat'l Bank & Trust Co. v. Jacobson Appliance Co., 196 Neb. 398, 243 N.W.2d 745 (1976). "Send" is defined in § 1–201(38). See Hall v. Owen County State Bank, 23 UCC Rep.Serv. 267 (Ind.App.1977).

99. Fairchild v. Williams Feed, Inc., 169 Mont. 18, 544 P.2d 1216 (1976); Crest Investment Trust, Inc. v. Alat-

zas, 264 Md. 571, 287 A.2d 261 (1972). See also GAC Credit Corp. v. Small Business Administration, 323 F.Supp. 795 (W.D.Mo.1971).

1. § 1–201(25), (26).

2. See In re Nellis, 22 UCC Rep.Serv. 1318 (E.D.Pa.1977) (in bankruptcy), where the debtor was fully aware of the secured party's actions but received written notice only on the day of the sale; this was held to be reasonable notification. See also Chase Manhattan Bank v. Natarelli, 23 UCC Rep.Serv. 539 (N.Y.Sup.Ct.1977).

3. But see Hensley v. Lubbock State Bank, 23 UCC Rep.Serv. 261 (Tex.Civ. App.1978). Cf. MFT Leasing v. Fillmore Products, Inc., 579 P.2d 924 (Utah 1978).

4. Rushton v. Shea, 423 F.Supp. 468 (D. Del.1976). See also § 9–112.

antor of the obligation that is secured and the guarantor is not the owner of the collateral. Arguably such a guarantor may not come within the definition of "debtor"[5] and therefore would not be entitled to notice prior to disposition of the collateral under Section 9–504(3).[6] If such a person were held to be a debtor entitled to notice, then it would seem that the right to notice could not be waived or varied under Section 9–501(3).[7] However, the ordinary form of guaranty would almost certainly waive the right to notice, just as the ordinary form of note would contain a waiver by the maker and indorsers of the requirements of presentment, notice of dishonor, and so on.[8] It would be peculiar if a guarantor of a secured obligation (who is not the owner of the collateral) could not waive notice and be held to this,[9] and be held to the ensuing liability, when there would be no question of liability in the case of an unsecured note, and the liability would be for the full amount of the note, not merely for a portion of it, as in the case of a deficiency. In any event, if the guarantor pays the loan, the guarantor is entitled to succeed to the secured party's right to enforce the obligation and can proceed against the collateral.[10] If the collateral is transferred to the guarantor, the guarantor has the same rights and duties as the secured party.[11]

The 1972 Code changes these provisions in two ways. First, no notice need be sent to the debtor if he has signed a statement after default renouncing or modifying his right to notice.[12] Probably no

---

5. The second sentence of § 9–105(1)(d) states:

"Where the debtor and the owner of the collateral are not the same person, the term 'debtor' means the owner of the collateral in any provision of the Article dealing with the collateral, the obligor in any provision dealing with the obligation, and may include both where the context so requires." The first sentence states:

" 'Debtor' means the person who owes payment or other performance of the obligation secured, whether or not he owns or has rights in the collateral . . . ." It could be suggested that a guarantor is not an "obligor" in the sense of primary obligor, but see § 3–416. *Cf.* Chase Manhattan Bank v. Natarelli, 23 UCC Rep.Serv. 539 (N.Y. Sup.Ct.1977).

6. *See* First Nat'l Park Bank v. Johnson, 553 F.2d 599 (9th Cir. 1977). The guaranty as such is not a transaction covered by the Code, according to EAC Credit Corp. v. King, 507 F.2d 1232 (5th Cir. 1975). Revised § 9–504(3) allows a renunciation or modification of the right to notification after default.

7. Barnett v. Barnett Bank of Jacksonville, 345 So.2d 804 (Fla.App.1977).

8. This is permissible under § 3–511(2)(a). *See* Cessna Finance Corp. v. Meyer, 575 P.2d 1048 (Utah 1978).

9. *See* Weinstein v. United States, 511 F.2d 56 (6th Cir. 1975). *See also* § 3–606(1)(b).

10. § 9–504(5). *See* KMAP, Inc. v. Town & Country Broadcasters, Inc., 49 Cal.App.3d 544, 122 Cal.Rptr. 420 (1975); Benschoter v. First Nat'l Bank of Lawrence, 218 Kan. 144, 542 P.2d 1042 (1975), appeal dismissed 425 U.S. 928 (1976).

11. § 9–504(5). *See* Reeves v. Associates Financial Services Co., Inc., 197 Neb. 107, 247 N.W.2d 434 (1976).

12. Revised § 9–504(3). *See* Teeter Motor Co., Inc. v. First Nat'l Bank of

consideration is necessary to support this renunciation or modification.[13] · Second, notice need be sent only to other secured parties who have themselves notified the secured party in writing that they claim an interest in the collateral before notice of sale is sent to the debtor or before he has renounced his rights.[14] This eliminates the distinct possibility under the 1962 Code that a subordinated secured party might claim to have given notice orally—a telephone call to an unidentified person in the secured party's office, perhaps—and this kind of claim has a certain nuisance value [15] even if, as is probably ordinarily the case, it is completely fraudulent. If such a person had a legitimate claim, it should be represented by a filed financing statement indexed in the debtor's name. Moreover, there is rarely any surplus in dispositions of collateral. If there were likely to be any, the debtor could have arranged re-financing before the default proceeded quite so far.

§ 10–12. Application of Proceeds on Disposition

So long as whatever is done by the secured party in disposing of the collateral is "commercially reasonable," the Code is quite permissive.[16] Aside from requirements of reasonable notice, the secured party need not hold the collateral for considerable periods, building up storage charges as the property depreciates in the case of goods. The secured party may make the best deal he can without having undue concern about being called to account.[17] The collateral may be sold or leased or otherwise disposed of in its existing condition or after "commercially reasonable preparation or processing." [18] Some equipment might require repair to be salable, or goods in process of manufacture might need more processing, for example, and this is permissible.

The proceeds of disposition must first be applied to "the reasonable expenses of retaking, holding, preparing for sale or lease, selling,

---

Hot Springs, 260 Ark. 764, 543 S.W.2d 938 (1976).

13. In the case of a conditional sale contract or other contract coming within Article 2, *see* § 2–209(1). *Cf* 1–107 which states that no consideration is necessary to waive or renounce a claim or right arising out of an alleged breach if a written waiver or renunciation is signed, and delivered by the aggrieved party. This is the reverse of the situation in the text, but the provision might be applied by analogy. In any case, an obligation of

good faith is imposed on all contracts. § 1–203.

14. Revised § 9–504(3).

15. The liability of a secured party who has not complied with the requirements of the Code in disposing of collateral is stated in § 9–507(1).

16. § 9–504(3), Revised § 9–504(3).

17. *See* § 9–507.

18. § 9–504(1), Revised § 9–504(1).

leasing and the like and, to the extent provided for in the agreement and not prohibited by law, the reasonable attorneys' fees and legal expenses incurred by the secured party." [19] It may be assumed that all security agreements will, as a matter of course, provide for attorneys' fees and legal expenses to be secured by the collateral.[20] When extensive judicial proceedings are required in recovering and disposing of the collateral, the already remote possibility of any surplus begins to reach the vanishing point and the probability of a deficiency looms large.

The second application of the proceeds is to the satisfaction of the indebtedness held by the secured party who is disposing of the collateral.[21] The third application is to the satisfaction of subordinate security interests in the collateral if notice of demand has been received before all proceeds are distributed, and such a subordinate party must furnish reasonable proof of his interest on demand.[22]

If there is any surplus, the debtor is entitled to it, if the collateral secured a debt, and he is liable for any deficiency unless the parties have agreed otherwise.[23] Article 9, in addition to covering security interests, governs sales of accounts and chattel paper (and contract rights under the 1962 Code).[24] Where the transaction was a sale of such collateral, the debtor is not entitled to a surplus or liable for a deficiency unless the security agreement provides for it.[25]

§ 10–13. Rights of a Purchaser at Disposition

A disposition by the secured party transfers to a purchaser for value all of the debtor's rights in the collateral and discharges the security interest under which the disposition was made and all subordinate security interests and liens.[26] The term "purchaser" is far more broadly defined than merely a buyer. It includes anyone acquir-

---

19. § 9–504(1)(a), Revised 9–504(1)(a). *See* Davis v. Small Business Inv. Co. of Houston, 535 S.W.2d 740 (Tex.Civ. App.1976).

20. Presumably the local law governs allowance of attorney's fees, although the statutory provision would suggest that they are recoverable as a matter of contract, if provided for, unless expressly prohibited by state law. *See In re* American Beef Packers, Inc., 548 F.2d 246 (8th Cir. 1977).

21. § 9–504(1)(b).

22. § 9–504(1)(c).

23. § 9–504(2), Revised § 9–504(2).

24. § 9–102(1), Revised § 9–102(1).

25. § 9–504(2), Revised § 9–504(2).

26. § 9–504(4). *See* Levers v. Rio King Land & Inv. Co., — Nev. —, 560 P.2d 917 (1977); T. M. Cobb Co. v. County of Los Angeles, 16 Cal.3d 666, 128 Cal.Rptr. 655, 547 P.2d 431 (1976) (sale free of tax lien); Young v. Golden State Park, — Colo.App. —, 560 P.2d 855 (1977) (sale free of unperfected security interest).

ing an interest in property in a voluntary transaction.[27] "Value" is also quite broadly defined and includes any consideration sufficient to support a simple contract.[28] Any sale is subject to Article 2.[29]

Even though the secured party does not comply with the Code's requirements or the requirements of a judicial proceeding, a purchaser for value will take free of the specified rights in any case other than a public sale if he acts in good faith and in the case of a public sale if he has no knowledge of any defects in the sale and if he does not buy in collusion with the secured party, other bidders, or the person, such as an auctioneer, conducting the sale.[30] The secured party may, however, be liable to the debtor or other secured parties if he has not proceeded in accordance with the Code's provisions.[31] The requirement of good faith in a private disposition means honesty in fact.[32] While there is no requirement of "good faith" for a buyer at a public sale, he certainly will not be protected if he buys in bad faith and it may be doubted that there is in substance any difference between the two standards. What application this Code provision might have in a judicial sale is somewhat uncertain, since a judicial sale is not a Code proceeding.[33] If there is a judicial sale and the secured party purchases, he will take the collateral free of any other requirements of Article 9, such as the notice requirements.[34] If he buys at a non-judicial public sale, he will have to comply with all of the Code requirements.[35] The secured party may buy at a private sale only if the collateral is typically sold in a recognized market or is the subject of widely distributed standard price quotations.[36]

Occasionally a third party may be liable, at least potentially, in case of default by the primary debtor. This commonly happens where conditional sellers of goods require a co-signer or accommodation indorser on the note [37] or when a third party guarantees payment of the obligation.[38] In commercial financing, an automobile dealer might,

---

27. § 1–201(32), (33).

28. § 1–201(44).

29. § 9–504(1).

30. § 9–504(4). *See* Borochoff Properties, Inc. v. Howard Lumber Co., 115 Ga.App. 691, 155 S.E.2d 651 (1967).

31. § 9–507(1). *See* Young v. Golden State Park, —— Colo.App. ——, 560 P. 2d 855 (1977).

32. § 1–201(19). *See* Cooper v. Klopfenstein, 29 Mich.App. 569, 185 N.W.2d 604 (1971).

33. § 9–501(1), (5).

34. § 9–501(5).

35. § 9–504(3), Revised § 9–504(3).

36. *Id.*

37. *See* § 3–415 on the contract of an accommodation party. *See generally* § 10–11 *supra*.

38. If the guaranty is on the instrument, see § 3–416. The guaranty may be a matter of separate contract.

for example, agree to repurchase paper transferred to a financer in the event the buyer ("account debtor" in these circumstances) defaults; on a transfer of this kind of chattel paper, the transferee-financer would become the secured party.

Section 9–504(5) provides that one "who is liable to a secured party under a guarantee, indorsement, repurchase agreement or the like and who receives a transfer of collateral from the secured party or is subrogated to his rights has thereafter the rights and duties of the secured party. Such a transfer of collateral is not a sale or disposition of the collateral under this Article." Where a fact situation fits this provision, a sale technically complying with Article 9 presumably will be a transfer. For example, if an automobile dealer assigns a conditional sale contract to a financer and guarantees payment, and the financer later repossesses the car after the buyer's default and gives notice of intended sale, the sale when held may turn out to be a transfer if the dealer buys the car.[39] On the other hand, if the dealer had repurchased the chattel paper and had himself given the required notice of sale, the sale might be a sale, although it might make a difference whether the sale was public or private.[40]

§ 10–14. Acceptance of Collateral as Discharge of Obligation; Compulsory Disposition

In many cases the debtor will have so little equity in the collateral or its value will have declined or depreciated so much that it will not be advantageous to the debtor to require that it be sold, with the costs of recovering and selling it to be added to the unpaid balance of the obligation.[41] In all cases it is possible for the secured party to retain the collateral in satisfaction of the obligation, either by the debtor's consent or in the absence of objection by those entitled to notice, as the case may be, and where this is done the secured party waives any right to a deficiency.[42]

---

39. *See* Jefferson Credit Corp. v. Marcano, 302 N.Y.S.2d 390, 60 Misc.2d 138 (N.Y.Civ.Ct.1969). *See also* Rangel v. Bock Motor Co., 437 S.W.2d 329 (Tex. Civ.App.1969), refused n. r. e. In the fact situation in the text, the collateral is chattel paper in the transaction between the dealer and the financer, while it is an automobile that is being repossessed and sold. This added complication has been troublesome in the matter of notice. *See* Norton v. National Bank of Commerce, 240 Ark. 143, 398 S.W.2d 538 (1966).

40. *See* Donovan v. Wechsler, 11 Cal. App.3d 210, 89 Cal.Rptr. 669 (1970).

41. *See* § 9–504(1) (a), Revised § 9–504 (1) (a).

42. § 9–505(2), Revised § 9–505(2). *See* Kruse, Kruse & Miklosko, Inc. v. Beedy, — Ind.App. —, 353 N.E.2d 514 (1976). *Cf.* Moody v. Nides Finance Co., 115 Ga.App. 859, 156 S.E. 2d 310 (1967). Retention of stock collateral and claiming a deficiency in absence of notice and formal sale may not constitute a permissible disposition. *In re* Copeland, 531 F.2d 1195 (3d Cir. 1976).

In the situation where a consumer has paid sixty per cent of the cash price, in the case of a purchase money security interest in consumer goods, or sixty per cent of the loan in any other case involving consumer goods, he may sign after default (but not before) a statement renouncing his rights under the default sections of the Code. If he does not do so, a secured party who has taken possession of the collateral must dispose of it under the rules of Section 9–504 within ninety days or the debtor has the option of recovering in conversion or under Section 9–507(1) [43] In the case of a purchase money security interest, sixty per cent of the cash price is not the same as sixty per cent of the amount financed, if the debtor has made a down payment, for when sixty per cent of the cash price has been paid sixty per cent of the amount financed will not have been. This assumes that "cash price" means the price the seller would have accepted for the goods as a lump sum payment. A purchase money security interest may be created by a seller or by a third party financer, under Section 9–107, but even where created by the seller, it may be assigned to a financer, and the problems can become complicated. The provision may be of minimal practical importance.

Section 9–505(2) begins: "In any other case involving consumer goods or any other collateral a secured party in possession may, after default, propose to retain the collateral in satisfaction of the obligation." Presumably this means that if a consumer has paid at least sixty per cent of his debt or the cash price and has waived his right to demand a disposition of the collateral, he need receive no notice of the official proposal by the secured party, which makes sense. It makes less sense that there is no provision in subsection (1) of Section 9–505 stating that the debtor's renunciation of rights satisfies his obligation, but this can properly be imported from subsection (2). The provisions of subsection (2) clearly apply to all business transactions and to those cases where a debtor, regardless of the amount he has paid, has not renounced his rights after default as he may do if he has paid sixty per cent of the cash price or debt, as the case may be.

Where the secured party wishes to retain the collateral in satisfaction of the obligation, under the 1962 Code written notice must be sent to the debtor and, except in the case of consumer goods, to any other secured parties who have duly filed in the state or who are

---

43. § 9–505(1). *See* Michigan Nat. Bank v. Marston, 29 Mich.App. 99, 185 N.W. 2d 47 (1971). As to conversion, *see* Klingbiel v. Commercial Credit Corp., 439 F.2d 1303 (7th Cir. 1971), Margolin v. Franklin, 270 N.E.2d 140 (Ill.App. 1971). *Cf.* Bradford v. Lindsey Chevrolet Co., 117 Ga.App. 781, 161 S.E.2d 904 (1968).

"known" by the secured party in possession to have an interest in the collateral.[44] The secured party must dispose of the collateral under Section 9–504 if the debtor or any other person entitled to notice objects in writing within thirty days after receipt of the notice [45] or if any other secured party objects in writing within thirty days after the secured party obtains possession of the collateral.[46] This provision is objectionable for at least two reasons. Where a security interest in the collateral can be perfected only by filing, those entitled to notice should be limited to secured parties who have filed (in addition to the debtor), to avoid the problems that can arise on possibly spurious claims of telephone notice to a secured party or any other kind of notice which might have been sent but was not received. The period of thirty days after receipt of notice is unrealistically long for objections; it effectively extends the period of waiting and the accumulation of storage charges for forty days or, in view of current mail service, the indefinite future.[47] Strangely enough, however, there is no requirement that the written objection be received.

There would appear to be no basis for continuing to recognize the common law remedy of accord and satisfaction [48] when the Code provides an analogous, but probably more satisfactory, remedy in Section 9–505, when the secured party and debtor are in agreement that the collateral may be retained by the secured party in satisfaction of the debt. Where the remedy of accord and satisfaction has been recognized,[49] it has sometimes appeared probable that the debtor had a more helpful remedy under the Code, in view of the remedy provided by Section 9–507(1) where the secured party did not pro-

---

44. § 9–505(2). If the secured party knows that the collateral is owned by a person other than the debtor, that person is entitled to receive notice and to object to a retention in satisfaction. § 9–112.

45. Waldrep v. Jochum, 337 So.2d 334 (Ala.1976).

46. If the secured party simply retains collateral pledged by a third party without disposing of it or proposing to retain it in satisfaction of a judgment recovered against the debtor, it was said to present a triable issue of fact whether this retention was in satisfaction of the obligation in Shultz v. Delaware Trust Co., 360 A.2d 576 (Del. Super.1976), where the collateral was retained more than five years after judgment was recovered and no execution on the judgment debtor's property was ever made. Except for the con-

sumer cases dealt with in § 9–505(1), no time is stated in the Code within which the collateral must be disposed of.

47. See Davenport, Preface, Uniform Commercial Code Annual Survey— 1968, 23 Bus.Law. 807, 810–811 (1968).

48. See Clark Leasing Corp. v. White Sands Forest Products, Inc., 87 N.M. 451, 535 P.2d 1077 (N.Mex.1975).

49. The remedies of accord and satisfaction and of rescission, neither of which is expressly recognized by the Code, were sought by the debtor in McCullough v. Mobiland, Inc., 139 Ga. App. 260, 228 S.E.2d 146 (1976), but neither was granted by the court for reasons unrelated to the Code's provisions.

ceed in accordance with the Code. Accord and satisfaction has been implied from the action of the parties, thereby discharging the debtor's liability,[50] when in some cases it would appear that the secured party did not take the steps required by Part 5 of Article 9 and therefore should be liable under Section 9–507(1) for "any loss caused by a failure to comply" with Part 5, and in the case of consumer goods the debtor could recover at least the credit service charge plus ten per cent of the principal amount of the debt or the time price differential plus ten per cent of the cash price. This would not be de minimus in the case of automobile loans.

There is no statutory basis for assuming that the secured party has decided to retain the collateral in satisfaction of the debt when the required written notice to that effect has not been sent.[51] If the secured party has not complied with the statute, there is liability under Section 9–507, but the debtor is still liable for a deficiency.

The Code makes no express provision covering the situation where the collateral has depreciated or deteriorated in value below the amount of the outstanding debt and the secured party proposes to retain the collateral in partial, rather than complete, satisfaction of the obligation owing. As a matter of two parties adjusting their differences by an agreement at some time after default, this might be effectively accomplished,[52] but where there are third parties involved, such as subordinate secured parties, it would appear that their express consent would be necessary in the absence of any statutory procedure, or else the secured party may be settling for a law suit.

Under the redraft of Article 9, the notice provisions have been changed. If a debtor has renounced his rights by a signed statement after default he need not be sent a written notice of a proposal to retain the collateral in satisfaction of the obligation. The right to renounce rights (as opposed to failing to object to the notice regarding retention) is now applicable to all debtors, not just to certain consumer debtors. The requirement of sending a notice of the proposal only to the debtor, in the case of consumer goods, is retained and more plainly stated. In other cases, notice must be sent only to other secured parties from whom the secured party has received written notice of a claim of an interest in the collateral prior to the time notice was sent to the debtor or before the debtor renounced his rights.[53] The time

---

50. *See, e. g.,* Moody v. Nides Finance Co., Inc., 115 Ga.App. 859, 156 S.E.2d 310 (1967).

51. Jones v. Morgan, 58 Mich.App. 455, 228 N.W.2d 419 (1975).

52. *See* § 1–107. But the obligation of good faith imposed by § 1–203 is ever

present. There may arguably be an impediment in § 9–501(3). *See* Hall v. Owen County State Bank, 370 N.E.2d 918, 23 UCC Rep.Serv. 267 (Ind.App. 1977).

53. Revised § 9–505(2).

when a renunciation is effective is not stated, but presumably it is effective when given if delivered in person or when deposited in the mail, but there is a slight possibility of an argument here in rare cases, and the most conservative response would be the proper one without regard to technicalities: a notice should be sent to all other secured parties who make even a questionable effort to comply. The secured party must dispose of the collateral pursuant to Section 9–504 if he *receives* a written objection from anyone entitled to notice within twenty-one days after the notice was sent.[54] This effectively reduces the ordinary waiting period to perhaps half of what it was under the 1962 Code; it is not merely a reduction of nine days from thirty to twenty-one because the secured party must receive the notice within the twenty-one day period, where under the 1962 Code other parties had thirty days to object after they had received the notice without regard to how long it took their objections to reach the secured party. There is no magic in a period of twenty-one days, and it might well be further reduced.

§ 10–15. Debtor's Right to Redeem

Unless waived in writing after default,[55] the debtor[56] or any other secured party may redeem the collateral by tendering performance of all obligations secured by the collateral at any time before the collateral has been disposed of or a contract for its disposition has been entered into or before the obligation has been discharged by a timely failure to object to the secured party's proposal to retain the collateral in satisfaction of the debt.[57] Ordinarily default will accelerate the maturity of the unpaid balance of the obligation, and the secured party will also be entitled to reasonable repossession expenses plus storage costs and expenses incurred in preparing the collateral for disposition along with, if not prohibited by law, attorneys' fees and legal expenses.[58] There is no statutory period of redemption, but every aspect

---

54. *Id.*

55. The right of redemption cannot be waived before default, § 9–506. *See* Indianapolis Morris Plan Corp. v. Karlen, 28 N.Y.2d 30, 319 N.Y.S.2d 831, 268 N.E.2d 632 (1971).

56. Here, as elsewhere, the term "debtor" carries the definition provided in § 9–105(1)(d) and includes both the owner of the collateral and the obligor on the obligation when they are not the same person. *See* Security Pac.

Nat'l Bank v. Goodman, 24 Cal.App.3d 131, 100 Cal.Rptr. 763 (1972).

57. § 9–506. Where the collateral is owned by a person other than the debtor, that person has the same right as the debtor to redeem the collateral. § 9–112. *See also* § 9–105(1)(d), defining "debtor."

58. § 9–506. While the debtor is obligated to tender reasonable repossession expenses, these expenses do not include earlier costs incurred by the secured party in collecting delinquent

of the disposition must be commercially reasonable,[59] 'which means that the actions of an over-anxious creditor are always subject to review.

§ 10–16. Liability of Secured Party Who Fails to Comply with Part 5

Where the secured party is not acting in accordance with the Code's default procedures, disposition may be restrained or ordered on appropriate terms and conditions.[60] If the debtor is under the jurisdiction of a bankruptcy court, the secured party may be restrained regardless of the reasonableness of the proceedings when viewed in any other light.[61]

If the collateral has been disposed of to a purchaser for value, he will take free of the claims of the debtor, the secured party, and junior secured parties and lienors,[62] but the secured party will be liable for any loss caused by a failure to comply with Part 5 of Article 9, and this liability runs to the debtor and to other secured parties entitled to notice under Section 9–504(3) because they have filed or whose security interest was "made known" to the secured party before disposition.[63] The words "made known" in Section 9–507(1) tied in with similar language contained in Section 9–504(3) of the 1962 Code which is dropped in the 1972 Code so that this category is probably now subsumed under another rubric or else is nil.

While damages for loss for failure to comply are not circumscribed,[64] minimum damages are set in only one case: where the collateral is consumer goods, the debtor is entitled to at least the credit service charge plus ten per cent of the principal of the debt or the time price differential plus ten per cent of the cash price of the goods.[65]

payments. Owens v. Automobile Recovery Bureau, Inc., 544 S.W.2d 26 (Mo.App.1976).

59. § 9–504(3), Revised § 9–504(3).

60. § 9–507(1).

61. See, e. g., In re Yale Express System, Inc., 370 F.2d 433 (2d Cir. 1966), 384 F.2d 990 (2d Cir. 1967).

62. § 9–504(4).

63. § 9–507(1). See Norton v. National Bank of Commerce, 240 Ark. 143, 398 S.W.2d 538 (1966).

64. Where the secured party has complied with the Code's requirements, the debtor is not entitled to damages merely for loss of use of the collateral. Borg-Warner Acceptance Corp. v. Scott, 86 Wash.2d 276, 543 P.2d 638 (1975).

65. § 9–507(1). In purchase money consumer cases covered by § 9–505(1) if the secured party has not complied with the statute, the debtor may sue in conversion or under § 9–507(1) but may not recover on both grounds. UIV Corp. v. Oswald, 139 Ga.App. 697, 229 S.E.2d 512 (1976). The damages provided in § 9–507(1) are not cumu-

Every part of the disposition must be commercially reasonable but not every aspect of the disposition can be questioned successfully in the light of hindsight. The mere fact that a better price might have been obtained by selling at a different time or by a different method is not sufficient to establish liability for failure to sell in a commercially reasonable manner.[66] Commercial reasonableness is established if the sale conforms with reasonable commercial practices among dealers in similar property, or if the property is sold in the usual manner in a recognized market or if the collateral is sold at a price current in a recognized market at the time of sale. The rules applicable to sales apply to any other type of disposition insofar as they are applicable.[67]

If a disposition is approved in a judicial proceeding, it is conclusively deemed to be commercially reasonable.[68] The same is true when the approval is by a bona fide creditors' committee or a representative of creditors. But no such approval is ever required by the Code, and any failure to obtain such approval does not brand the transaction commercially unreasonable.[69]

§ 10–17. The Federal Courts and Creditors' Remedies: Summary Procedures

For some years the Supreme Court of the United States decided few cases dealing with commercial law. The dam was broken with *Sniadach*.[70] While it seems doubtful, it is possible that the federal courts may now be in the process of revising state civil procedure as they have in the not distant past rewritten state criminal procedure. It is likely that the prod of the Supreme Court will at the minimum result in some of our more adventurous state courts striking out on their own [71] and legislative changes may follow.

---

lative for each violation under Part 5 of Article 9. Crosby v. Basin Motor Co., 83 N.M. 77, 488 P.2d 127 (1971).

66. *See, e. g., In re* Nellis, 22 UCC Rep. Serv. 1318 (E.D.Pa.1977) (in bankruptcy).

67. § 9–507(2).

68. *See* Bryant v. American Nat'l Bank & Trust Co., 407 F.Supp. 360 (N.D.Ill. 1976). *See also In re* Zsa Zsa Limited, 352 F.Supp. 665 (S.D.N.Y.1972), affirmed 475 F.2d 1393 (2d Cir. 1973).

69. § 9–507(2).

70. Sniadach v. Family Finance Corp., 395 U.S. 337, 89 S.Ct. 1820, 23 L.Ed.2d 349 (1969). For a perceptive discussion of this case and its implications, *see* Kennedy, Due Process Limitations on Creditors' Remedies: Some Reflections on Sniadach v. Family Finance Corp., 19 Am.U.L.Rev. 158 (1970).

71. *See, e. g.*, Randone v. Appellate Dept., 96 Cal. 709, 487 P.2d 13 (1971), Jones Press Inc. v. Motor Travel Services, Inc., 286 Minn. 205, 176 N.W.2d 87 (1970). *Cf.* Termplan, Inc. v. Superior Court, 105 Ariz. 270, 463 P.2d 68 (1969).

In *Sniadach* a finance company, utilizing Wisconsin statutory procedure, instituted a garnishment action against the defendant and her employer as garnishee based on a claim of $420 due on a promissory note. The defendant apparently had no defense on the merits but asked to have the garnishment proceedings dismissed for failure to satisfy the due process requirements of the Fourteenth Amendment because notice and an opportunity to be heard were not required by statute before an in rem seizure of wages. The Supreme Court held, in an opinion by Mr. Justice Douglas, that the Wisconsin pre-judgment garnishment procedure [72] violated fundamental principles of due process. Mr. Justice Harlan concurred and Mr. Justice Black dissented.

Mr. Justice Douglas announced: "The question is not whether the Wisconsin law is a wise law or unwise law. Our concern is not what philosophy Wisconsin should or should not embrace . . . . We do not sit as a super-legislative body." [73] To this Mr. Justice Black replied: "Of course the Due Process Clause of the Fourteenth Amendment contains no words that indicate that this Court has power to play so fast and loose with state laws. The arguments the Court makes to reach what I consider to be its unconstitutional conclusion, however, show why it strikes down this state law. It is because it considers a garnishment law of this kind to be bad state policy, a judgment I think the state legislature, not this Court, has power to make." [74] Mr. Justice Black noted that the Court's opinion quoted some "emotional rhetoric" [75] of Congressmen in support of its opinion which he thought might be appropriately addressed to the Congress or the Wisconsin legislature but when used in an opinion of the Supreme Court the result of the language amounted to "a plain, judicial usurpation of the state legislative power to decide what the State's laws shall be." [76]

Mr. Justice Black went on to say:

There is not one word in our Federal Constitution or in any of its Amendments and not a word in the reports of that document's passage from which one can draw the slightest inference that we have authority thus to try to supplement or strike down the State's selection of its own policies. The Wisconsin law is simply nullified by this Court as though the

---

72. This procedure is reviewed in Family Finance Corp. v. Sniadach, 37 Wis. 2d 163, 154 N.W.2d 259 (1967), reversed 395 U.S. 337, 89 S.Ct. 1820, 23 L.Ed.2d 349.

73. 395 U.S. at 339.

74. 395 U.S. at 344.

75. *Id.*

76. 395 U.S. at 345.

Court had been granted a super-legislative power to step in and frustrate policies of States adopted by their own elected legislatures. The Court thus steps back into the due process philosophy which brought on President Roosevelt's Court fight. Arguments can be made for outlawing loan sharks and installment sales companies but such decisions, I think, should be made by state and federal legislators, and not by this Court: [77]

While Mr. Justice Douglas says, "The fact that a procedure would pass muster under a feudal regime does not mean that it gives necessary protection to all property in its modern forms,"[78] the fact is that the procedure was legally perfectly acceptable until the moment the Supreme Court spoke. His comment that "We deal here with wages—a specialized type of property presenting distinct problems in our economic system"[79] has occasionally been thought to limit the holding, [80] and indeed that may ultimately prove to be the case.

Mr. Justice Harlan's carefully worded concurrence states that in his opinion "due process is afforded only by the kinds of 'notice' and 'hearing' which are aimed at establishing the validity, or at least the probable validity, of the underlying claim against the alleged debtor *before* he can be deprived of his property or its unrestricted use." [81]

Following on the heels of *Sniadach*, a three-judge district court sitting in New York found Article 71 of the New York Civil Practice Law and Rules, permitting prejudgment seizure of chattels in a replevin action without an order of a judge or of a court of competent jurisdiction, to be unconstitutional as violating the search and seizure provisions of the Fourth Amendment and the procedural due process requirements of the Fourteenth Amendment.[82] This statute was claimed to descend from the days of Henry III and to have been incorporated into the laws of New York in 1788.[83] While the statute allows a sheriff to repossess goods, even by forcible entry, if the reclaiming party does certain acts including giving an undertaking in at least twice the

77. *Id.*

78. 395 U.S. at 340.

79. *Id.*

80. *See, e. g.,* Reeves v. Motor Contract Co., 324 F.Supp. 1011 (N.D.Ga.1971); Black Watch Farms v. Dick, 323 F. Supp. 100 (D.Conn.1971); American Olean Tile Co. v. Zimmerman, 317 F.

Supp. 150 (D.Hawaii 1970); Young v. Ridley, 309 F.Supp. 1308 (D.C.1970).

81. 395 U.S. at 343.

82. Laprease v. Raymours Furniture Co., 315 F.Supp. 716 (N.D.N.Y.1970). *Cf.* Brunswick Corp. v. J. & P., Inc., 424 F.2d 100 (10th Cir. 1970).

83. 315 F.Supp. at 721, n. 4.

claimed value of the chattels to assure return of the chattels or payment of damages if ultimately ordered, the defendant against whom replevin is sought may recover the goods by in turn posting an undertaking in the same amount as the reclaimant's. The plaintiffs in this case were poor and presumably unable to give the required undertaking. One with a husband and ten children was on welfare, one was receiving Aid for Dependent Children, and one had been working but became ill. The chattels in question were household furnishings such as beds, stoves, chairs, end-tables, a record player. One party "believed" she had a defense on the merits which was not stated in the opinion, but if the other two parties had defenses they are not stated. They were simply unable to pay for the goods and unable to post a bond, and for reasons not specified apparently claimed they were not in default.

The court found the New York procedure to violate the Fourth Amendment in that it permitted seizure of goods without judicial intervention, and this amounted to unreasonable search and seizure. The procedure violated the due process provisions of the Fourteenth Amendment because notice and hearing in advance of seizure were not required. The court did not pass on whether the statutory provision allowing defendants to reacquire the property after seizure by posting a bond violated the Equal Protection Clause of the Fourteenth Amendment because it applied to everyone, including the poor.

The court found that household furnishings were, "like wages in *Sniadach,* a 'specialized type of property presenting distinct problems in our economic system' the taking of which on the unilateral command of an adverse party 'may impose tremendous hardships' on purchasers of these essentials. That it is a temporary taking, does not obviate the objection that it is a taking prior to hearing and notice." [84] The court ultimately said, however, that procedural due process required notice and an opportunity to be heard before seizure "or at least that the creditor present to a judicial officer the circumstances allegedly justifying summary action." [85]

In response to this case the New York legislature amended the replevin provisions in issue, requiring an "order of seizure" from a court which may be granted under these circumstances:

> Upon presentation of the affidavit and undertaking and upon
> such terms as may be required to conform to the due process

---

84. *Id.* at 722–23. The quotations in the opinion are from *Sniadach,* 395 U.S. at 340.

85. 315 F.Supp. at 724.

of law requirements of the fourteenth amendment to the constitution of the United States, the court shall grant an order directing the sheriff of any county where the chattel is found to seize the chattel . . ..[86]

Under this provision the courts are expressly authorized to perform the legislature's former function, although such an express authorization has perhaps not recently been thought to be needed.

We come now to the *Fuentes* case.[87] Here the Supreme Court reviewed two cases, one from Florida and one from Pennsylvania, involving somewhat similar state laws both of which provided for state agents to seize chattels on an ex parte application of one who claims to have a right to them and who posts a bond. Neither statute required a notice to the possessor of the chattels and a hearing prior to seizure. The goods involved in Mrs. Fuentes' case were a gas stove and a stereo set. Most of the chattels involved in the Pennsylvania case were also household goods.[88] Both three-judge district courts had upheld the constitutionality of the state laws involved.[89]

The Court held that the replevin statutes of Florida and Pennsylvania were unconstitutional under the Fourteenth Amendment as working a deprivation of property without due process of law in the absence of providing an opportunity for a hearing before the chattels were repossessed.[90] The Fourth Amendment search and seizure issue was not reached. It was recognized that the seller as well as the buyer had an interest in goods sold on conditional sale and that the buyer's deprivation might be only temporary since the goods could be re-

---

86. McKinney's N.Y.C.P.L.R. § 7102(d).

87. Fuentes v. Shevin, 407 U.S. 67, 92 S.Ct. 1983, 32 L.Ed.2d 556 (1972).

88. One of the four Pennsylvania appellants was divorced from a deputy sheriff who was familiar with local practice, and he used routine forms to obtain a writ ordering seizure of his son's clothes, furniture, and toys in connection with a custody dispute. 407 U.S. at 72. This situation is anamolous and will not be differentiated in the text; it was substantially ignored by the Court.

89. Fuentes v. Faircloth, 317 F.Supp. 954 (S.D.Fla.1970), jurisdiction noted 401 U.S. 906, 91 S.Ct. 893, 27 L.Ed.2d 804; Epps v. Cortese, 326 F.Supp. 127 (E.D.Pa.1971), jurisdiction noted 402 U.S. 994, 91 S.Ct. 2185, 29 L.Ed.2d 159.

90. Mr. Justice Stewart wrote for the Court. Mr. Justice White dissented in an opinion joined by the Chief Justice and Mr. Justice Blackman. Mr. Justice Powell and Mr. Justice Rehnquist did not participate.

The Court recognized that in three cases attachment of property without a prior hearing had been allowed: Ownbey v. Morgan, 256 U.S. 94, 41 S.Ct. 433, 65 L.Ed. 837 (1921); Coffin Brothers & Co. v. Bennett, 277 U.S. 29, 48 S.Ct. 422, 72 L.Ed. 768 (1928); McKay v. McInnes, 279 U.S. 820, 49 S.Ct. 344, 73 L.Ed. 975 (1929); 407 U.S. at 91, n. 23. These cases, along with others, were cited in Mr. Justice Douglas's opinion in Sniadach v. Family Finance Corp., 395 U.S. 337 at 339, 340 (1969) as supporting the proposition that summary procedure may meet due process requirements in extraordinary situations.

covered by those from whom they were taken under the state laws involved. It was also recognized that the buyers might have no defense of any kind on the merits.[91] Moreover, the buyers did not effectively waive their right to a pre-seizure hearing by signing conditional sale agreements which said that in case of default the sellers could "take back" or "retake" or "repossess" the goods. These terms were "in relatively small type and *unaccompanied by any explanations clarifying their meaning.*"[92] The contracts said nothing about waiving a prior hearing nor did they "indicate *how* or *through what process*—a final judgment, self-help, prejudgment replevin with a prior hearing, or prejudgment replevin without a prior hearing—the seller could take back the goods."[93]

Mr. Justice White's dissent made three main points. First, state court proceedings were in progress when the federal actions were filed and decided, and any constitutional objections could have been raised there, so that the district court judgments should be vacated and reconsidered under *Younger v. Harris*[94] and companion cases.[95]

In the second place, Mr. Justice White would not elevate to a constitutional requirement the need for a seller to do more than the state law involved here required. The Justice pointed out that

> in these typical situations the buyer-debtor has either defaulted or he has not. If there is a default, it would seem not only "fair," but essential, that the creditor be allowed to repossess; and I cannot say that the likelihood of a mistaken claim of default is sufficiently real or recurring to justify a broad constitutional requirement that a creditor do more than the typical state law requires and permits him to do . . . . [I]t would not seem in the creditor's interest for a default occasioning repossession to occur; as a practical matter it would much better serve his interests if the trans-

---

91. So far as appears in the case, three of the four appellants seem to have had no defenses, and the fourth appellant's case was arguable. 407 U.S. at 70–72, 87.

92. *Id.* at 94 (emphasis added).

93. *Id.* at 96 (emphasis in original). It would be interesting to see what would happen if there were default and repossession by self-help under an agreement which stated in bold type, with a videotaped and sensible oral explanation to the buyer at the time he

signed the contract, that on default in making a payment, the seller had a right to repossess an automobile "by self-help or by prejudgment replevin without a prior hearing."

94. 401 U.S. 37 (1971).

95. Samuels v. Mackell, 401 U.S. 66, 91 S.Ct. 764, 27 L.Ed.2d 688 (1971); Boyle v. Landry, 401 U.S. 77, 91 S.Ct. 758, 27 L.Ed.2d 696 (1971); Perez v. Ledesma, 401 U.S. 82, 91 S.Ct. 674, 27 L.Ed.2d 701 (1971).

action goes forward and is completed as planned. Dollars and cents considerations weigh heavily against false claims of default . . . . Nor does it seem to me that creditors would lightly undertake the expense of instituting replevin actions and putting up bonds.

. . . I would not construe the Due Process Clause to require the creditors to do more than they have done in these cases to secure possession pending final hearing. Certainly, I would not ignore, as the Court does, the creditor's interest in preventing further use and deterioration of the property in which he has substantial interest. Surely under the Court's own definition, the creditor has a "property" interest as deserving of protection as that of the debtor. At least the debtor, who is very likely uninterested in a speedy resolution that could terminate his use of the property, should be required to make those payments, into court or otherwise, upon which his right to possession is conditioned.[96]

The third point was that the Court's opinion would have little impact on state law for

It would appear that creditors could withstand attack under today's opinion simply by making clear in the controlling credit instruments that they make retake possession without a hearing, or, for that matter, without resort to judicial process at all. Alternatively, they need give only a few days' notice of a hearing, take possession if hearing is waived or if there is default; and if hearing is necessary merely establish probable cause for asserting that default has occurred. It is very doubtful in my mind that such a hearing would in fact result in protections for the debtor substantially different from those the present laws provide. On the contrary, the availability of credit may well be diminished or, in any event, the expense of securing it increased.[97]

Mr. Justice White closed by observing that the procedures struck down by the Court were not a "barbaric hangover from bygone days" [98] but were approved by Section 9–503 of the Uniform Commercial Code, which (unless otherwise agreed) gives the secured party the right to take possession of the collateral on default, without judicial process if this can be done without a breach of the peace, or by action. He

---

96. 407 U.S. at 100–02.

97. *Id*. at 102–03.

98. *Id*. at 103.

further noted no change in this provision was proposed in the revision of Article 9, and he is "content to rest on the judgment of those who have wrestled with these problems so long and often and upon the judgment of the legislatures that have considered and so recently adopted provisions that contemplate precisely what has happened in these cases." [99]

In *Mitchell* v. *W. T. Grant Company* [1] the Supreme Court appeared to retreat from its recent prior holdings in this field. This Louisiana case involved the seller's repossession through a constable of various household appliances which had been sold on time and not paid for, and the seller utilized the Louisiana remedy of sequestration. Apparently under Louisiana law in this kind of transaction an unpaid seller has a vendor's lien to secure the payment of the unpaid balance of the purchase price, and this lien is lost if the buyer sells or transfers possession of the goods to third parties against whom the lien will not be good. This is similar to the Code situation where there is a perfected but unfiled [2] purchase money security interest in consumer goods, and the security interest is lost if the debtor sells to a neighbor who buys in good faith and pays value.[3] The Louisiana writ of sequestration was said not to be issued on conclusory allegations of ownership or possessory rights but "only when the nature of the claim and the amount thereof, if any, and the grounds relied upon . . . clearly appear from specific facts" shown by verified petition or affidavit, and, at least in the particular parish involved, the showing had to be made to a judge. The judicial presence in the process was a distinction from the state procedure relied on in the statutes involved in *Fuentes*.[4] Finding a number of distinctions from earlier precedents, the Court approved the Louisiana procedure.

The Court announced that the Due Process Clause did not guarantee to the debtor "the use and possession of the goods until all issues in the case were judicially resolved after full adversary proceedings had been completed." The Court noted that in the case of consumer goods if the defaulting buyer remained in possession, the goods would be used and would deteriorate without any payments being made to the seller in the interim, and the unpaid seller may have as much or more interest in the goods than the buyer. There was also the problem that if a defaulting buyer could retain possession after notice and until hearing, the buyer might improperly dispose of the goods and destroy the seller's vendor's lien. It was found to comport "with due process to permit the initial seizure on sworn *ex parte* documents,

---

99. *Id.*

1. 416 U.S. 600, 94 S.Ct. 1895, 40 L.Ed. 2d 406 (1974).

2. § 9–302(1)(d).

3. § 9–307(2).

4. Fuentes v. Shevin, 407 U.S. 67, 92 S.Ct. 1983, 32 L.Ed.2d 556 (1972).

followed by the early opportunity to put the creditor to his proof." Here the debtor was entitled to an immediate hearing on the right to possession, but no such hearing was requested. It was emphasized that in this case the unpaid seller had a prior interest in the goods whereas in *Sniadach* [5] the creditor had no earlier interest in the debtor's wages, and wages are "a specialized type of property presenting distinct problems in our economic system." Since the seller had to post a bond, the buyer would have been protected against economic loss if the buyer prevailed.

Following shortly on the heels of *Mitchell* came *North Georgia Finishing, Inc.* v. *Di-Chem. Inc.* [6] Instead of a consumer, it was a business corporation whose assets were garnished at the time a suit was filed for the price of goods sold and delivered in the amount of $51,279.17, and what was garnished was a bank account. The bank as garnishee was dismissed when the debtor filed a bond.

The Georgia statute under which the garnishment was made was found to violate the Fourteenth Amendment, apparently because this property—the bank account—was frozen without notice and without opportunity for a hearing. The writ of garnishment was issuable by a court clerk on the conclusory affidavit of the creditor or its attorney, who might have no personal knowledge of the facts, and no judge was involved. There was no requirement for an early hearing, and it appeared that, absent the filing of a bond, no challenge to the garnishment could be made.

This opinion would appear to be a considerable retrenchment from *Mitchell*. Interestingly enough, the majority opinion was written by Mr. Justice White, who also wrote for the Court in *Mitchell* and who dissented vigorously in *Fuentes*. Citing Mark Twain, Mr. Justice Stewart, who wrote the majority opinion in *Fuentes*, observed: "It is gratifying to note that my report of the demise of Fuentes v. Shevin . . . seems to have been greatly exaggerated." [7]

Mr. Justice Powell, concurring, noted that pregarnishment notice and prior hearing had not been constitutionally required in the past, and he did not interpret the Court's opinion to require them in the future. He thought that procedural due process would be satisfied if the garnishor had to provide adequate security and establish before a neutral officer, not necessarily a judge, some factual basis for resorting to this remedy to prevent removal or dissipation of assets, and there should be a prompt post-garnishment judicial proceeding to establish the need to continue the garnishment, with the opportunity for the debtor to free the assets by posting security.

5. Sniadach v. Family Finance Corp., 395 U.S. 337, 89 S.Ct. 1820, 23 L.Ed.2d 349 (1969).

6. 419 U.S. 601, 95 S.Ct. 719, 42 L.Ed.2d 751 (1975).

7. 419 U.S. at 608.

While the status of pre-judgment remedies is by no means clear at this time, one distinction to be made between the *Mitchell* and *North Georgia* cases is that the pre-judgment remedy was approved in *Mitchell* where a judge was involved in the procedure. This would not seem to be a meritorious distinction, however, for a busy judge might glance over piles of such applications in just as summary fashion as a clerk. Mr. Justice Powell did not agree that a judge should be required to issue the writ of garnishment, but he thought it adequate if there were a prompt post-garnishment hearing before a judge. Another possible distinction can be drawn between an affidavit setting out the facts on which the application for the remedy is based and a conclusory affidavit stating virtually nothing. Moreover, in *Mitchell* the seller had a pre-existing and continuing interest in the assets involved, while in cases where bank accounts are garnished this is not likely to be the case aside from instances of inventory financing where proceeds of sales are deposited in the bank account and the secured party has a perfected security interest in proceeds.

While state procedures vary considerably in their approach to prejudgment garnishment and attachment, it would appear that there is some value in such remedies. They prevent dissipation or secreting of assets which might otherwise be available to satisfy a judgment, and those assets might deteriorate or disappear when left in the debtor's unfettered dominion if prior notice and hearing were required before the assets could be impounded. The posting of a bond by the creditor is a guarantee to the debtor that the property or its value will be available if the creditor's claim is not recognized by a court. The posting of a bond by the debtor allows continued availability of the asset to the debtor while the proceedings go on, but this is perhaps not a viable remedy for consumer-debtors who might not have the money necessary to post a bond. However, even consumers may have no right to retain possession of goods purchased on conditional sale if they have defaulted and have no defense to payment except an inability to pay.

Any attempt to predict the future in this field is subject to a googol of objections. Yet there must be some point of common ground between those who think every consumer is automatically right and those who recognize no right except on the side of the secured party.

The recently litigated cases do not suggest that secured parties are pressing default remedies when defaults do not exist. The cases do suggest that consumers may be pressing rights which may allow them to retain possession of goods for a longer period of time although they probably may ultimately lose the right to possession because the fact is that they are in default and the default cannot be remedied because they simply cannot pay the price they contracted to pay and have no right to retain the goods under the contract of purchase.

This is a hard pill for some advocates of consumer rights to swallow. This is a very difficult issue to rationalize as a matter of social policy, especially when the buyers are on welfare. In too many cases the items purchased turn out to be stereo sets or television sets or eleven-piece dinette sets or something which can hardly be justified as really necessary. There is some feeling that anyone who would sell such goods to a person on welfare deserves to lose the goods and the unpaid balance of the price. Very often such sellers do charge exorbitant prices, although their profits may in fact, for whatever the reasons, be no more than so-called legitimate sellers make.[8] On the other hand, perhaps the alternative is to say that persons on welfare cannot buy such goods on time and that will be the result if sellers have no summary and effective remedies to recover the goods when the price is not paid. The cost of drawn-out court procedures will either be paid by the delinquent purchaser, if he is able, or it will be passed on to other purchasers indirectly. This is one of the facts of life. It is foolish to expect sellers not to pursue their remedies against goods because if one seller abandoned goods in one case, he would have nothing but wholesale defaults the next day. Whatever repossessed goods may be worth, the seller cannot afford to ignore the radiating effect of not enforcing a default.

Most sellers do not pursue their default remedies the day after a default occurs. They send notices, progressively less pleasant, to the buyer in an attempt to secure payment. Some sellers are indeed disreputable, and these sellers are not confined to the ghetto and the term "sellers" may here include manufacturers. But on balance most sellers probably are decent, just as most buyers probably are decent. Unfortunately, however, some buyers just cannot pay for the goods they have bought, whether these goods are necessary or frivolous. If sellers cannot proceed against the goods without undue delay, for the goods will not appreciate in value with use, then other buyers will simply have to pay the additional costs. These costs of collection will be passed on to the poor as well as to the rest, to those who pay in cash as well as to those who pay on time. There is no deep pocket to absorb the ordinary costs of doing business; they are passed on to all buyers. Whether the ultimate social price is worth the candle is a matter for debate in the legislature, not the courts where, notoriously, hard cases make bad law.

8. *See* White, Consumer Credit in the Ghetto: UCCC Free Entry Provisions and the Federal Trade Commission Study, 25 Bus.Law 143, 146–151 (1969).

CHAPTER 11

A SIMPLE SECURITY AGREEMENT: FORM AND CONTENT

Table of Sections

§ 11–1. Introduction

Article 9 of the Uniform Commercial Code sets forth a few minimal requirements for a security agreement. For the security interest to be enforceable against the debtor or third parties, either the collateral must be in the secured party's possession (in which case the security agreement may, but ordinarily will not, be oral), or the debtor must have signed a security agreement containing a description of the collateral, and in some cases a description of the land concerned is also required.[1]

There are no formalistic requirements, such as acknowledgments. There are no magic words that must be used. Any description of real or personal property is sufficient, whether or not it is specific, if it reasonably identifies what is described.[2]

Drafting suggestions can best be offered in a concrete context, but no form should ever be used without careful consideration being given to any necessary adaptations for the transaction at hand. Certain facets of the security agreement are commented on following the form.[3] The numbers of the comments correspond to numbers at the left of certain provisions in the security agreement.

§ 11–2. Security Agreement—Equipment

(1) _____
    (Name)   (Street Address)   (City)   (County)   (State)

(2) ("Debtor"), hereby grants to _____, ("Bank"), a security

(3) interest in the following goods located at _____

_____
(Address or addresses where goods are or are to be kept)

---

1. § 9–203(1). *Cf.* Revised § 9–203(1).

2. § 9–110.

3. This agreement is taken from Henson & Davenport, 5 Uniform Laws Annotated—Uniform Commercial Code Forms and Materials 363–365 (1968).

(4)   *[Description of Goods]*

(5)   together with all parts, fittings, accessories, equipment, special tools, renewals and replacements of all or any part thereof, and other goods of the same class whether now owned or hereafter acquired by Debtor (all hereinafter called "Collateral"), to secure (i) the payment of a note dated _____, executed and delivered by Debtor to Bank, in the sum of $_____, payable as to principal and interest as therein provided; (ii) further advances, to be evidenced by additional notes if such advances are made at Bank's option; (iii) all other liabilities (primary, secondary, direct, contingent, sole, joint, or several) due or to become due or which may be hereafter contracted or acquired, of Debtor to Bank; and (iv) performance by Debtor of the agreements hereinafter set forth.

(6)   Debtor Warrants: (a) Debtor is the owner of the Collateral clear of all liens and security interests except the security interest granted hereby; (b) Debtor has the right to make this agreement; (c) the Collateral is used or bought for use primarily for business purposes and will be kept at the address specified above; (d) the Collateral is being acquired by Debtor with the proceeds of the note identified above, and the Bank is hereby authorized to pay the proceeds of the loan directly to the seller of the Collateral as shown on Bank's records; (e) the Collateral will not be attached or affixed to real estate in such a manner that it will become a fixture. (Delete (d) or (e) if inapplicable, but if (e) is deleted describe real estate concerned and give name of record owner here:

_____—).

(7)   Debtor Agrees that it:

1. Will pay the Bank all amounts payable on the note mentioned above and all other notes held by Bank as and when the same shall be due and payable, whether at maturity, by acceleration or otherwise, and will perform all terms of said notes and this or any other security or loan agreement between Debtor and Bank, and will discharge all said liabilities.

2. Will defend the Collateral against the claims and demands of all persons.

3. Will insure the Collateral against all hazards requested by Bank in form and amount satisfactory to Bank. If Debtor fails to obtain insurance, Bank shall have the right to obtain it at Debtor's expense. Debtor assigns to Bank all right to receive proceeds of insurance not exceeding the unpaid balance under the note, directs any insurer to pay all proceeds directly to Bank, and authorizes Bank to endorse any draft for the proceeds.

4. Will keep the Collateral in good condition and repair, reasonable wear and tear excepted, and will permit Bank and its agents to inspect the Collateral at any time.

5. Will pay as part of the debt hereby secured all amounts, including attorneys' fees, with interest thereon, paid by Bank (a) for taxes, levies, insurance, repairs to, or maintenance of the Collateral, and (b) in taking possession of, disposing of or preserving the Collateral after any default hereinafter described.

6. Will not permit any of the Collateral to be removed from the above-mentioned location without the prior written consent of the Bank.

7. Will immediately advise Bank in writing of any change in any of Debtor's places of business, or the opening of any new place of business.

8. Will not (a) permit any liens or security interests (other than Bank's security interest) to attach to any of the Collateral; (b) permit any of the Collateral to be levied upon under any legal process; (c) dispose of any of the Collateral without the prior written consent of Bank; (d) permit anything to be done that may impair the value of any of the Collateral or the security intended to be afforded by this agreement; or (e) permit the Collateral to become an accession to other goods.

9. Bank is hereby appointed Debtor's attorney-in-fact to do all acts and things which Bank may deem necessary to perfect and continue perfected the security interest created by this security agreement and to protect the Collateral.

(8)   Until default Debtor may retain possession of the Collateral and use it in any lawful manner not inconsistent with the agreements herein, or with the terms and conditions of any policy of insurance thereon.

(9)   Upon default by Debtor in the performance of any covenant or agreement herein or in the discharge of any liability to Bank, or if any warranty should prove untrue, Bank shall have all of the rights and remedies of a secured party under the Uniform Commercial Code or other applicable law and all rights provided herein, in the notes mentioned above, or in any other applicable security or loan agreement, all of which rights and remedies shall, to the full extent permitted by law, be cumulative. Bank may require Debtor to assemble the Collateral and make it available to Bank at a place to be designated by Bank which is reasonably convenient to Bank and Debtor. Any notice of sale, disposition or other intended action by Bank, sent to Debtor at the address specified above, or such other address of Debtor as may from time to time be shown on Bank's records, at least five days prior to such action, shall constitute reasonable notice to Debtor. The waiver of any default hereunder shall not be a waiver of any subsequent default.

(10)   All rights of Bank hereunder shall inure to the benefit of its successors and assigns; and all obligations of Debtor shall bind its heirs, executors, administrators, successors and assigns. If there be more than one Debtor, their obligations hereunder shall be joint and several.

(11)   This agreement is executed on _____, 19__.

(12)

                                            _____

                                                 (Debtor)

                                 By _____

                                 Title:

§ 11–3. Comments on the Security Agreement

(1) There is no requirement that a security agreement begin by naming the parties and giving their addresses, but it is commonly done at the present time. For ease in subsequent identification throughout the body of the agreement, an abbreviated reference ordinarily is given after the complete names. In the form above, the references are simply "Debtor" and "Bank." There is no need to state "hereinafter called the Debtor" or the like; no one could possibly mistake the reference. Outmoded legalisms such as "hereinafter," "whereas," and "witnesseth" are ordinarily to be avoided. Where background recitals detailing the origin of the transaction are thought to be helpful, and occasionally they do serve a purpose, it is sufficient to say, "This transaction is based on these facts," and the facts may

then be given in order; it is not necessary to preface each one with "Whereas," nor to end the recitals and begin the body of the agreement with "Now, therefore, this indenture witnesseth . . ."

(2) It is sufficient for a debtor simply to "grant" a security interest in the goods to the secured party. There are no required words, such as "mortgage and warrant," and a multiplicity of verbs in this instance, as in most others, will do nothing that one word alone does not do.

(3) The collateral's location may or may not be important legally, although its location and existence are of business importance, of course. If we are dealing with ordinary, stationary equipment—i. e., goods used or bought for use by a business—in most states filing is central,[4] so that the exact location may be legally immaterial. However, if the debtor has a place of business in only one county, local filing is also required in some states; or if the equipment is used in farming operations, filing in the county of the debtor's residence may be required, or if the debtor is a non-resident, filing may be required in the county where the goods are kept. There is a warranty that the goods will be kept at the specified address, and a breach of the warranty would be a default, but whether moving the goods from one location to another within the state will require a new filing for continued perfection depends on which alternative subsection (3) of Section 9–401 has been adopted. If the goods are mobile or if they are permanently moved from one state to another, Sections 9–103(2) and (3) must be consulted. If the goods are fixtures, local filing is necessary and a subsequent provision in the form covers this problem.

(4) The Code does not require a so-called serial number description of collateral. Indeed, considering the range of collateral covered by the Code, such a requirement would be unreasonable. Where the collateral is constantly changing, as in the case of inventory or accounts, specificity would be an impossible requirement. However, where the collateral is existing equipment, it would usually be possible to describe the goods in specific terms and this should be done if it is at all feasible. It is clearly improper to claim "equipment" in a filed financing statement where the security agreement covers only one described printing press, and the financing statement cannot enlarge the security interest granted in the agreement. But if a security in-

---

4. There are many local variations in the filing rules of § 9–401(1), but each of the three alternatives in the Official Text provides for fixture filing in the local real estate mortgage office. If it is not certain whether a particular item of equipment is a fixture, filing in both "fixture" and "equipment" filing offices is the proper solution.

terest covers all of the debtor's equipment, then that term is sufficient as a description to cover everything the debtor owns which can be properly classified as equipment.

(5) Because equipment wears out and requires replacement of parts, this contingency should be covered in the agreement, and it is covered here. The obligations described in the balance of the paragraph will probably be broader where a bank is a secured party than in other cases, and there may, although it is doubtful, be some merit in enumerating the various kinds of liabilities in (iii). Collateral may, as (iv) emphasizes, be security for performance, as well as payment, of an obligation.

(6) The purpose of warranties (a), (b), and (c) is obvious. Either or both of warranties (d) and (e) may be inapplicable. If the Bank intends to acquire a purchase money security interest in the collateral and to take advantage of Sections 9–301(2) and 9–312(4), then the Bank must see that the funds advanced do in fact go to pay for the goods, and this is most easily done by paying the seller directly or by paying against documents. Crediting the buyer-debtor's bank account is not generally a satisfactory alternative. If the equipment is to become a fixture, then a filing in the real estate records is necessary to perfect the security interest. Because of local variations in keeping real estate records, it is usually helpful to have a legal description, a common description, and the name of the record owner. While the official version of the 1962 Code does not require that the name of the record owner be shown on a fixture financing statement,[5] many states have specifically adopted this requirement; it may be implied in any case where the information is necessary for proper filing because the real property would not otherwise be reasonably described under Section 9–110.

(7) These promises of the Debtor are fairly standard; failure to perform any of them will result in a default.

(8) It is doubtful that this paragraph states anything that is of special value.[6] Aside from pledges, it is to be expected that the debtor will retain possession of the collateral until default. Naturally the secured party hopes that the use will be lawful and not inconsistent with the terms of any insurance coverage; but a covenant to that effect is not self-executing.

(9) It is not necessary to state in detail the rights and remedies of the secured party on default, for they are specified in Part 5 of

5. § 9–402(1), (3). *Cf.* Revised § 9–402   6. See § 9–503.
  (3), (5).

Article 9.[7] However, the secured party's right to require the debtor to assemble the collateral at a reasonably convenient place does depend on having such a provision on the security agreement.[8] In general, the secured party is required to give reasonable notice before a sale or other disposition of the collateral, after default.[9] The parties may agree on the number of days' notice and this will be binding if not "manifestly unreasonable."[10] While a five-day notice is generally considered to be reasonable, there is a considerable difference between such a notice sent on Monday of an ordinary business week and one sent on Thursday or Friday when Monday is a holiday.

(10) The first sentence of this paragraph is customary surplusage. The second sentence may or may not be useful. In most instances, equipment will be collateral used by a business so that more than one debtor will be unusual. Although this form is not designed for such a situation, it is possible that the owner of the collateral may not be the borrower; the term "Debtor" in Article 9 means both parties, or either of them, as appropriate.[11]

(11) It is not necessary to conclude an agreement by stating "In Witness Whereof, the parties to these presents have hereunto set their hands and seals." Nor does any similar language serve any function. The old style testimonium clause should be relegated to the legal attic. If the agreement is dated in the opening paragraph, then the customary concluding paragraph can be omitted entirely.

(12) The security agreement must be signed by the debtor, but there is no requirement that the secured party sign, although for various reasons this may be considered desirable by some lenders. If the agreement is signed by both parties and contains proper addresses of both, it may be used as a financing statement,[12] although this is not recommended. The standard form financing statement for the state involved should always be filed except in the most exceptional circumstances which certainly will not exist in the situation this form was designed to cover.

---

7. While it would not presently appear to be necessary that the security agreement restate the Code remedies, if they are set out in the agreement then they are a matter of contract between the parties. *See generally* § 10–8 *supra*.

8. *Id.*

9. § 9–504(3), Revised § 9–504(3).

10. § 9–501(3).

11. § 9–105(1)(d).

12. § 9–402(1). Under Revised § 9–402 (1) only the debtor need sign a financing statement or a security agreement filed as a financing statement. Many states quite properly require an additional fee if the financing statement submitted for filing is not a standard form; this practice has been incorporated in Revised § 9–403(5).

APPENDIX

1972 OFFICIAL TEXT SHOWING CHANGES MADE IN FORMER TEXT OF ARTICLE 9, SECURED TRANSACTIONS AND OF RELATED SECTIONS AND REASONS FOR CHANGES

Amendments to Article 1

§ 1—105. Territorial Application of the Act; Parties' Power to Choose Applicable Law

(1) Except as provided hereafter in this section, when a transaction bears a reasonable relation to this state and also to another state or nation the parties may agree that the law either of this state or of such other state or nation shall govern their rights and duties. Failing such agreement this Act applies to transactions bearing an appropriate relation to this state.

(2) Where one of the following provisions of this Act specifies the applicable law, that provision governs and a contrary agreement is effective only to the extent permitted by the law (including the conflict of laws rules) so specified:

Rights of creditors against sold goods. Section 2—402.

Applicability of the Article on Bank Deposits and Collections. Section 4—102.

Bulk transfers subject to the Article on Bulk Transfers. Section 6—102.

Applicability of the Article on Investment Securities. Section 8—106.

[Policy and scope of the Article on Secured Transactions. Sections 9—102 and 9—103.]

Perfection provisions of the Article on Secured Transactions, Section 9—103.

Reasons for 1972 Change

The reference to Section 9—102 has been deleted and a change made in Section 9—102 deleting any reference therein to conflict of law problems, because there is no reason why the general principles of the present section should not be applicable to the choice of law problems within its scope. Section 9—103 continues to govern choice of law questions as to perfection of security interests and the effect of perfection and non-perfection thereof. The usual rule is that perfection is governed by the law of the jurisdiction in which the collateral is when the last event occurs on which is based the assertion that the security interest is perfected or unperfected. Section 9—103 contains special rules for the cases of intangibles which have no situs, certain types of movable goods, goods which the parties intended at the inception of the transaction to be kept in another jurisdiction, goods subject to certificate of title laws, and certain other cases. Section 9—103 also contains local law rules as to reperfection of security interests when collateral is moved from one jurisdiction to another.

§ 1—201. General Definitions [Unchanged except for definitions (9) and (37)]

(9) "Buyer in ordinary course of business" means a person who in good faith and without knowledge that the sale to him is in violation of the ownership rights or security interest of a third party in the goods buys in ordinary course from a person in the business of selling goods of that kind but does not include a pawnbroker. All persons who sell minerals or the like (including oil and gas) at wellhead or minehead shall be deemed to be persons in the business of selling goods of that kind. "Buying" may be for cash or by exchange of other property or on secured or unsecured credit and includes receiving goods or documents of title under a pre-existing contract for sale but does not include a transfer in bulk or as security for or in total or partial satisfaction of a money debt.

(37) "Security interest" means an interest in personal property or fixtures which secures payment or performance of an obligation. The retention or reservation of title by a seller of goods notwithstanding shipment or delivery to the buyer (Section 2—401) is limited in effect to a reservation of a "security interest". The term also includes any interest of a buyer of accounts[,] or chattel paper[, or contract rights] which is subject to Article 9. The special property interest of a buyer of goods on identification of such goods to a contract for sale under Section 2—401 is not a "security interest", but a buyer may also acquire a "security interest" by complying with Article 9. Unless a lease or consignment is intended as security, reservation of title thereunder is not a "security interest" but a consignment is in any event subject to the provisions on consignment sales (Section 2—326). Whether a lease is intended as security is to be determined by the facts of each case; however, (a) the

inclusion of an option to purchase does not of itself make the lease one intended for security, and (b) an agreement that upon compliance with the terms of the lease the lessee shall become or has the option to become the owner of the property for no additional consideration or for a nominal consideration does make the lease one intended for security.

Reasons for 1972 Change of Definitions (9) and (37)

(9) The new language fits in with changes as to minerals in Section 9—103 which are explained in the references to minerals in the Reasons for Change and Comments to that section.

(37) The omission of the term "contract rights" conforms to the elimination of that term from Article 9. See Reasons for Change under Section 9—106. •

Amendment to Article 2

§ 2—107. Goods to Be Severed From Realty: Recording

(1) A contract for the sale of [timber,] minerals or the like (including oil and gas) or a structure or its materials to be removed from realty is a contract for the sale of goods within this Article if they are to be severed by the seller but until severance a purported present sale thereof which is not effective as a transfer of an interest in land is effective only as a contract to sell.

(2) A contract for the sale apart from the land of growing crops or other things attached to realty and capable of severance without material harm thereto but not described in subsection (1) or of timber to be cut is a contract for the sale of goods within this Article whether the subject matter is to be severed by the buyer or by the seller even though it forms part of the realty at the time of contracting, and the parties can by identification effect a present sale before severance.

(3) The provisions of this section are subject to any third party rights provided by the law relating to realty records, and the contract for sale may be executed and recorded as a document transferring an interest in land and shall then constitute notice to third parties of the buyer's rights under the contract for sale.

Reasons for 1972 Change

Several timber-growing states have changed the 1962 Code to make timber to be cut under a contract of severance goods, regardless of the question who is to sever them. The section is revised to adopt this change. Financing of the transaction is facilitated if the timber is treated as goods instead of real estate. A similar change is made in the definition of "goods" in Section 9—105. To protect persons dealing with timberlands, filing on timber to be cut is required in Part 4 of Article 9 to be made in real estate records in a manner comparable to fixture filing.

Amendment to Article 5

§ 5—116. Transfer and Assignment

(1) The right to draw under a credit can be transferred or assigned only when the credit is expressly designated as transferable or assignable.

(2) Even though the credit specifically states that it is nontransferable or nonassignable the beneficiary may before performance of the conditions of the credit assign his right to proceeds. Such an assignment is an assignment of [a contract right] an account under Article 9 on Secured Transactions and is governed by that Article except that

    (a) the assignment is ineffective until the letter of credit or advice of credit is delivered to the assignee which delivery constitutes perfection of the security interest under Article 9; and

    (b) the issuer may honor drafts or demands for payment drawn under the credit until it receives a notification of the assignment signed by the beneficiary which reasonably identifies the credit involved in the assignment and contains a request to pay the assignee; and

    (c) after what reasonably appears to be such a notification has been received the issuer may without dishonor refuse to accept or pay even to a person otherwise entitled to honor until the letter of credit or advice of credit is exhibited to the issuer.

(3) Except where the beneficiary has effectively assigned his right to draw or his right to proceeds, nothing in this section limits his right to transfer or negotiate drafts or demands drawn under the credit.

Reasons for 1972 Change

The change conforms to the deletion of the defined term "contract right" from Article 9.

ARTICLE 9

SECURED TRANSACTIONS; SALES OF ACCOUNTS[, CONTRACT RIGHTS] AND CHATTEL PAPER

PART 1

SHORT TITLE, APPLICABILITY AND DEFINITIONS

§ 9—102. Policy and [Scope] Subject Matter of Article

(1) Except as otherwise provided [in Section 9—103 on multiple state transactions and] in Section 9—104 on excluded transactions, this Article applies [so far as concerns any personal property and fixtures within the jurisdiction of this state]

(a) to any transaction (regardless of its form) which is intended to create a security interest in personal property or fixtures including goods, documents, instruments, general intangibles, chattel paper or accounts [or contract rights]; and also

(b) to any sale of accounts [contract rights] or chattel paper.

(2) This Article applies to security interests created by contract including pledge, assignment, chattel mortgage, chattel trust, trust deed, factor's lien, equipment trust, conditional sale, trust receipt, other lien or title retention contract and lease or consignment intended as security. This Article does not apply to statutory liens except as provided in Section 9—310.

(3) The application of this Article to a security interest in a secured obligation is not affected by the fact that the obligation is itself secured by a transaction or interest to which this Article does not apply.

> **Note:** *The adoption of this Article should be accompanied by the repeal of existing statutes dealing with conditional sales, trust receipts, factor's liens where the factor is given a non-possessory lien, chattel mortgages, crop mortgages, mortgages on railroad equipment, assignment of accounts and generally statutes regulating security interests in personal property.*

403

Where the state has a retail installment selling act or small loan act, that legislation should be carefully examined to determine what changes in those acts are needed to conform them to this Article. This Article primarily sets out rules defining rights of a secured party against persons dealing with the debtor; it does not prescribe regulations and controls which may be necessary to curb abuses arising in the small loan business or in the financing of consumer purchases on credit. Accordingly there is no intention to repeal existing regulatory acts in those fields [.] <u>*by enactment or re-enactment of Article 9.*</u> *See Section 9—203(4) and the Note thereto.*

Reasons for 1972 Change

The omissions in the first paragraph of subsection (1) make applicable the general choice of law principles of Section 1—105 (except for special rules stated in Section 9—103), instead of an incomplete statement in this section.

The omission is clause (1) (b) conforms to the elimination of the term "contract rights" from the Article. See Reasons for Change under Section 9—106.

[§ 9—103. Accounts, Contract Rights, General Intangibles and Equipment Relating to Another Jurisdiction; and Incoming Goods Already Subject to a Security Interest]

[(1) If the office where the assignor of accounts or contract rights keeps his record concerning them is in this state, the validity and perfection of a security interest therein and the possibility and effect of proper filing is governed by this Article; otherwise by the law (including the conflict of laws rules) of the jurisdiction where such office is located.]

[(2) If the chief place of business of a debtor is in this state, this Article governs the validity and perfection of a security interest and the possibility and effect of proper filing with regard to general intangibles or with regard to goods of a type which are normally used in more than one jurisdiction (such as automotive equipment, rolling stock, airplanes, road building equipment, commercial harvesting equipment, construction machinery and the like) if such goods are classified as equipment or classified as inventory by reason of their being leased by the debtor to others. Otherwise, the law (including the conflict of laws rules) of the jurisdiction where such chief place of business is located shall govern. If the chief place of business is located in a jurisdiction which does not provide for perfection of the security interest by filing or recording in that jurisdiction, then the security interest may be perfected by filing in this state. [For the purpose of determining the validity and perfection of a security interest in an airplane, the chief place of business of a debtor who is a foreign air carrier under the Federal Aviation Act of 1958, as amended, is the designated office of the agent upon whom service of process may be made on behalf of the debtor.]]

[(3) If personal property other than that governed by subsections (1) and (2) is already subject to a security interest when it is brought into this state, the validity of the security interest in this state is to be determined by the law (including the conflict of laws rules) of the jurisdiction where the property was when the security interest attached. However, if the parties to the transaction understood at the time that the security interest attached that the property would be kept in this state and it was brought into this state within 30 days after the security interest attached for purposes other than transportation through this state, then the validity of the security interest in this state is to be determined by the law of this state. If the security interest was already perfected under the law of the jurisdiction where the property was when the security interest attached and before being brought into this state, the security interest continues perfected in this state for four months and also thereafter if within the four month period it is perfected in this state. The security interest may also be perfected in this state after the expiration of the four month period; in such case perfection dates from the time of perfection in this state. If the security interest was not perfected under the law of the jurisdiction where the property was when the security interest attached and before being brought into this state, it may be perfected in this state; in such case perfection dates from the time of perfection in this state.]

[(4) Notwithstanding subsections (2) and (3), if personal property is covered by a certificate of title issued under a statute of this state or any other jurisdiction which requires indication on a certificate of title of any security interest in the property as a condition of perfection, then the perfection is governed by the law of the jurisdiction which issued the certificate.]

[[(5) Notwithstanding subsection (1) and Section 9—302, if the office where the assignor of accounts or contract rights keeps his records concerning them is not located in a jurisdiction which is a part of the United States, its territories or possessions, and the accounts or contract rights are within the jurisdiction of this state or the transaction which creates the security interest otherwise bears an appropriate relation to this state, this Article governs the validity and perfection of the security interest and the security interest may only be perfected by notification to the account debtor.]]

§ 9—103. Perfection of Security Interests in Multiple State Transactions

(1) Documents, instruments and ordinary goods.

(a) This subsection applies to documents and instruments and to goods other than those covered by a certificate of title described in subsection (2), mobile goods described in subsection (3), and minerals described in subsection (5).

(b) Except as otherwise provided in this subsection, perfection and the effect of perfection or non-perfection of a security interest in collateral are governed by the law of the jurisdiction where the collateral is when the last event occurs on which is based the assertion that the security interest is perfected or unperfected.

(c) If the parties to a transaction creating a purchase money security interest in goods in one jurisdiction understand at the time that the security interest attaches that the goods will be kept in another jurisdiction, then the law of the other jurisdiction governs the perfection and the effect of perfection or non-perfection of the security interest from the time it attaches until thirty days after the debtor receives possession of the goods and thereafter if the goods are taken to the other jurisdiction before the end of the thirty-day period.

(d) When collateral is brought into and kept in this state while subject to a security interest perfected under the law of the jurisdiction from which the collateral was removed, the security interest remains perfected, but if action is required by Part 3 of this Article to perfect the security interest,

(i) if the action is not taken before the expiration of the period of perfection in the other jurisdiction or the end of four months after the collateral is brought into this state, whichever period first expires, the security interest becomes unperfected at the end of that period and is thereafter deemed to have been unperfected as against a person who became a purchaser after removal;

(ii) if the action is taken before the expiration of the period specified in subparagraph (i), the security interest continues perfected thereafter;

(iii) for the purpose of priority over a buyer of consumer goods (subsection (2) of Section 9—307), the period of the effectiveness of a filing in the jurisdiction from which the collateral is removed is governed by the rules with respect to perfection in subparagraphs (i) and (ii).

(2) Certificate of title.

(a) This subsection applies to goods covered by a certificate of title issued under a statute of this state or of another jurisdiction under the law of which indication of a security interest on the certificate is required as a condition of perfection.

(b) Except as otherwise provided in this subsection, perfection and the effect of perfection or non-perfection of the security interest are governed by the law (including the conflict of laws rules) of the jurisdiction issuing the certificate until four months after the goods are removed from that jurisdiction and thereafter until the goods are registered in another jurisdiction, but in any event not beyond surrender of the certificate. After the expiration of that period, the goods are not covered by the certificate of title within the meaning of this section.

(c) Except with respect to the rights of a buyer described in the next paragraph, a security interest, perfected in another jurisdiction otherwise than by notation on a certificate of title, in goods brought into this state and thereafter covered by a certificate of title issued by this state is subject to the rules stated in paragraph (d) of subsection (1).

(d) If goods are brought into this state while a security interest therein is perfected in any manner under the law of the jurisdiction from which the goods are removed and a certificate of title is issued by this state and the certificate does not show that the goods are subject to the security interest or that they may be subject to security interests not shown on the certificate, the security interest is subordinate to the rights of a buyer of the goods who is not in the business of selling goods of that kind to the extent that he gives value and receives delivery of the goods after issuance of the certificate and without knowledge of the security interest.

(3) Accounts, general intangibles and mobile goods.

(a) This subsection applies to accounts (other than an account described in subsection (5) on minerals) and general intangibles and to goods which are mobile and which are of a type normally used in more than one jurisdiction, such as motor vehicles, trailers, rolling stock, airplanes, shipping containers, road building and construction machinery and commercial harvesting machinery and the like, if the goods are equipment or are inventory leased or held for lease by the debtor to others, and are not covered by a certificate of title described in subsection (2).

(b) The law (including the conflict of laws rules) of the jurisdiction in which the debtor is located governs the perfection and the effect of perfection or non-perfection of the security interest.

(c) If, however, the debtor is located in a jurisdiction which is not a part of the United States, and which does not provide for perfection of the security interest by filing or recording in that jurisdiction, the law of the jurisdiction in the United States in which the debtor has its major executive office in the United States governs the perfection and the effect of perfection or non-perfection of the security interest through filing. In the alternative, if the debtor is located in a jurisdiction which is not a part of the United States or Canada and the collateral is accounts or general intangibles for money due or to become due, the security interest may be perfected by notification to the account debtor. As used in this paragraph, "United States" includes its territories and possessions and the Commonwealth of Puerto Rico.

(d) A debtor shall be deemed located at his place of business if he has one, at his chief executive office if he has more than one place of business, otherwise at his residence. If, however, the debtor is a foreign air carrier under the Federal Aviation Act of 1958, as amended, it shall be deemed located at the designated office of the agent upon whom service of process may be made on behalf of the foreign air carrier.

(e) A security interest perfected under the law of the jurisdiction of the location of the debtor is perfected until the expiration of four months after a change of the debtor's location to another jurisdiction, or until perfection would have ceased by the law of the first jurisdiction, whichever period first expires. Unless perfected in the new jurisdiction before the end of that period, it becomes unperfected thereafter and is deemed to have been unperfected as against a person who became a purchaser after the change.

(4) Chattel paper.

The rules stated for goods in subsection (1) apply to a possessory security interest in chattel paper. The rules stated for accounts in subsection (3) apply to a non-possessory security interest in chattel paper, but the security interest may not be perfected by notification to the account debtor.

(5) Minerals.

Perfection and the effect of perfection or non-perfection of a security interest which is created by a debtor who has an interest in minerals or the like (including oil and gas) before extraction and which attaches thereto as extracted, or which attaches to an account resulting from the sale thereof at the wellhead or minehead are governed by the law (including the conflict of laws rules) of the jurisdiction wherein the wellhead or minehead is located.

Reasons for 1972 Change

The section has been completely rewritten to clarify the relationship of its several provisions to each other and to other sections defining the applicable law. Now that the Code has been adopted in all states but Louisiana and also adopted in the District of Columbia and the Virgin Islands, the emphasis in the revision has been to make clear where perfection of a security interest must take place, rather than on problems of actual conflicts of rules of law.

1. The section now concerns itself exclusively with perfection of security interests and the effect of perfection or non-perfection thereof. The 1962 Code has several references to the "validity" of a security agreement, and these have been deleted. Likewise, a deletion has been made from Section 9—102 of the language which went beyond that section's basic function of defining the scope of Article 9 and purported to state a choice of law rule. These two changes make it clear that Article 9 does not govern problems of

choice of law between the original parties, and that this question is governed by the general choice of law provision in Section 1—105.

2. While most of the substantive materials of the section are in the 1962 Text, the statement thereof and their relationship to each other were not clear. In the revision they are clarified according to the following structure:

The basic rule of this section is that the controlling law, as to perfection of the security interests and the effect of perfection or non-perfection, is the law of the jurisdiction where the collateral is when the last event occurs on which is based the assertion that the security interest is perfected or unperfected (paragraph (1) (b)). There are certain exceptions: (i) In the case of a purchase money security interest in goods, where the parties intended to remove the collateral to another jurisdiction within 30 days after the debtor received possession of the goods, the law of the latter jurisdiction will govern the initial perfection until the expiration of the 30-day period, and thereafter if the goods are removed to the other jurisdiction before the end of the period (paragraph (1) (c)). (ii) Where the collateral is covered by a certificate of title, perfection will be governed by the law of the issuing jurisdiction (subsection (2)). (iii) If the collateral is certain mobile goods or certain intangibles, perfection will be governed by the law of the jurisdiction wherein is located the debtor (subsection (3)).

Where the collateral has been removed from the jurisdiction whose law first governed, the jurisdiction into which it is removed (i. e., "this state") adds a local requirement of re-perfection to the requirements of the state from which the collateral was removed—i. e., refiling is required within 4 months after removal, or within any lesser period during which perfection would have continued in the other jurisdiction (paragraphs (1) (d) and (2) (c)).

3. The two former rules for determining place of perfection as to intangibles (namely, for accounts, the office where the records were kept concerning the accounts; and for general intangibles, the chief place of business of the debtor) have been consolidated into the rule that the filing is at the debtor's location. That location will ordinarily be the office designated in the 1962 Text as "chief place of business," now redesignated as "chief executive office." A new provision (paragraph (3) (e)) has been added to cover the case where that office moves from one jurisdiction to another.

A principal objection to the original rule that the place for filing as to accounts was the place where the debtor kept his records with respect to them was that persons seeking to search records might not know where this place might be, in the case of a far-flung debtor or of multicorporate enterprises with central accounting. Where the debtor assigned his accounts without recourse, as in factoring, he might keep few records with respect to them. Moreover, it was thought undesirable to have one rule for accounts and another rule for general intangibles, because in many financing situations both types of receivables may be involved. See discussion in Reasons for Change to Section 9—106. Therefore, it was decided to adopt for both types of intangibles the rule heretofore applicable to general intangibles.

§ 9—104. Transactions Excluded From Article

This Article does not apply

(a) to a security interest subject to any statute of the United States [such as the Ship Mortgage Act, 1920,] to the extent that such statute governs the rights of parties to and third parties affected by transactions in particular types of property; or

(b) to a landlord's lien; or

(c) to a lien given by statute or other rule of law for services or materials except as provided in Section 9—310 on priority of such liens; or

(d) to a transfer of a claim for wages, salary or other compensation of an employee; or

[(e) to an equipment trust covering railway rolling stock; or]

(e) to a transfer by a government or governmental subdivision or agency; or

(f) to a sale of accounts[, contract rights] or chattel paper as part of a sale of the business out of which they arose, or an assignment of accounts [, contract rights] or chattel paper which is for the purpose of collection only, or a transfer of a [contract] right to payment under a contract to an assignee who is also to do the performance under the contract or a transfer of a single account to an assignee in whole or partial satisfaction of a preexisting indebtedness; or

(g) to a transfer of an interest in or claim in or under any policy of insurance, except as provided with respect to proceeds (Section 9—306) and priorities in proceeds (Section 9—312); or

411

(h) to a right represented by a judgment (other than a judgment taken on a right to payment which was collateral); or

(i) to any right of set-off; or

(j) except to the extent that provision is made for fixtures in Section 9—313, to the creation or transfer of an interest in or lien on real estate, including a lease or rents thereunder; or

(k) to a transfer in whole or in part of [any of the following:] any claim arising out of tort; [any deposit, savings, passbook or like account maintained with a bank, savings and loan association, credit union or like organization.]; or

(*l*) to a transfer of an interest in any deposit account (subsection (1) of Section 9—105), except as provided with respect to proceeds (Section 9—306) and priorities in proceeds (Section 9—312).

Reasons for 1972 Change

Former paragraph (e), excluding railway equipment trusts from the coverage of Article 9, has been deleted. The whole thrust of Article 9 is to eliminate differences based on the form of a transaction, and the equipment trust serves the same function as other purchase money forms of financing. In fact, a form known as the "New York equipment trust" comes closer to a conditional sale contract then it does to a Pennsylvania equipment trust, and thus the former exclusion left substantial uncertainty. Railway financing on rolling stock will continue to be exempt from the filing provisions of Article 9 by virtue of Section 9—302(3) and (4). Thus, the principal purpose of the former exclusion will be retained. There is, however, no reason why the other provisions of Article 9 by virtue of Section 9—302(3) and (4). closure, etc., should not be available to the parties to railway financing, since these problems are not adequately covered in any other statutes.

A new paragraph (e) has been added to make clear that this Article does not apply to security interests created by governmental debtors.

Other changes reflect the elimination of the term "contract rights" and the fact that, while transfers of claims under insurance policies and deposit accounts are in general excluded from the Article by this section, proceeds claims thereto are subject to Section 9—306.

§ 9—105. Definitions and Index of Definitions

(1) In this Article unless the context otherwise requires:

(a) "Account debtor" means the person who is obligated on an account, chattel paper[, contract right] or general intangible;

(b) "Chattel paper" means a writing or writings which evidence both a monetary obligation and a security interest in or a lease of specific goods, but a charter or other contract involving the use or hire of a vessel is not chattel paper. When a transaction is evidenced both by such a security agreement or a lease and by an instrument or a series of instruments, the group of writings taken together constitutes chattel paper;

(c) "Collateral" means the property subject to a security interest, and includes accounts[, contract rights] and chattel paper which have been sold;

(d) "Debtor" means the person who owes payment or other performance of the obligation secured, whether or not he owns or has rights in the collateral, and includes the seller of accounts[, contract rights] or chattel paper. Where the debtor and the owner of the collateral are not the same person, the term "debtor" means the owner of the collateral in any provision of the Article dealing with the collateral, the obligor in any provision dealing with the obligation, and may include both where the context so requires;

(e) "Deposit account" means a demand, time, savings, passbook or like account maintained with a bank, savings and loan association, credit union or like organization, other than an account evidenced by a certificate of deposit;

(f) [(e)] "Document" means document of title as defined in the general definitions of Article 1 (Section 1—201)[;], and a receipt of the kind described in subsection (2) of Section 7—201;

(g) "Encumbrance" includes real estate mortgages and other liens on real estate and all other rights in real estate that are not ownership interests.

(h) [(f)] "Goods" includes all things which are movable at the time the security interest attaches or which are fixtures (Section 9—313), but does not include money,

413

documents, instruments, accounts, chattel paper, general intangibles, [contract rights and other things in action,] or minerals or the like (including oil and gas) before extraction. "Goods" also includes standing timber which is to be cut and removed under a conveyance or contract for sale, the unborn young of animals, and growing crops.

(i) [(g)] "Instrument" means a negotiable instrument (defined in Section 3—104), or a security (defined in Section 8—102) or any other writing which evidences a right to the payment of money and is not itself a security agreement or lease and is of a type which is in ordinary course of business transferred by delivery with any necessary indorsement or assignment;

(j) "Mortgage" means a consensual interest created by a real estate mortgage, a trust deed on real estate, or the like;

(k) An advance is made "pursuant to commitment" if the secured party has bound himself to make it, whether or not a subsequent event of default or other event not within his control has relieved or may relieve him from his obligation.

(l) [(h)] "Security agreement" means an agreement which creates or provides for a security interest;

(m) [(i)] "Secured party" means a lender, seller or other person in whose favor there is a security interest, including a person to whom accounts[, contract rights] or chattel paper have been sold. When the holders of obligations issued under an indenture of trust, equipment trust agreement or the like are represented by a trustee or other person, the representative is the secured party;

(n) "Transmitting utility" means any person primarily engaged in the railroad, street railway or trolley bus business, the electric or electronics communications transmission business, the transmission of goods by pipeline, or the transmission or the production and transmission of electricity, steam, gas or water, or the provision of sewer service.

(2) Other definitions applying to this Article and the sections in which they appear are:

"Account". Section 9—106.

"Attach".   Section 9—203.
"Construction mortgage".   Section 9—313(1).
"Consumer goods".   Section 9—109(1).
["Contract right".   Section 9—106.]
"Equipment".   Section 9—109(2).
"Farm products".   Section 9—109(3).
"Fixture".   Section 9—313.
"Fixture filing".   Section 9—313.
"General intangibles".   Section 9—106.
"Inventory".   Section 9—109(4).
"Lien creditor".   Section 9—301(3).
"Proceeds".   Section 9—306(1).
"Purchase money security interest".   Section 9—107.
"United States".   Section 9—103.

(3) The following definitions in other Articles apply to this Article:

"Check".   Section 3—104.
"Contract for sale".   Section 2—106.
"Holder in due course".   Section 3—302.
"Note".   Section 3—104.
"Sale".   Section 2—106.

(4) In addition Article 1 contains general definitions and principles of construction and interpretation applicable throughout this Article.

Reasons for 1972 Change

A definition of "transmitting utility" has been added to identify a class of debtor with special filing problems on far-flung properties, for which special filing rules are stated in Part 4.

A definition of "deposit account" has been added to facilitate references to such accounts in the section on proceeds (Section 9—306).

A definition of "pursuant to commitment" has been added as the basis for use of this concept in Sections 9—301, 9—307, and 9—312.

Definitions of "encumbrance" and "mortgage" have been added as the basis for the use thereof in Section 9—313.

The definition of "document" has been amended to include therein the kind of receipt issued by a person who is not technically a warehouseman, as described in Section 7—201(2).

The exclusion of "other things in action" from the definition of "goods" has been deleted as unnecessary. "General intangibles", which under Section 9—106 includes "things in action", are themselves excluded from the definition of goods.

Other minor changes reflect the elimination of the classification "contract right" in Section 9—106.

§ 9—106.   Definitions: "Account"; ["Contract Right";] "General Intangibles"

"Account" means any right to payment for goods sold or leased or for services rendered which is not evidenced by an instrument or chattel paper[.], <u>whether or not it has been earned by performance.</u> ["Contract right" means any right to payment under a contract not yet earned by performance and not evidenced by an instrument or chattel paper.] "General intangibles" means any personal property (including things in action) other than goods, accounts, [contract rights,] chattel paper, documents, [and] instruments, <u>and money.</u> All rights to payment earned or unearned under a charter or other contract involving the use or hire of a vessel and all rights incident to the charter or contract are [contract rights and neither] accounts [nor general intangibles].

Reasons for 1972 Change

The term "contract right" has been eliminated as unnecessary. As indicated by a sentence now being eliminated from Section 9—306(1), "contract right" was thought of as an "account" before the right to payment became unconditional by performance by the creditor. But the distinction between "account" and "contract right" was not used in the Article except in subsection (2) to Section 9—318 on the right of original parties to modify an assigned contract, and that subsection has been redrafted to preserve the distinction without needing the term "contract right". The term has been troublesome in creating a "proceeds" problem where a contract right becomes an "account" by performance; in the Code's former denial that there could be any right in an account until it came into existence (former Section 9—204 (2) (d)), notwithstanding a security interest in the pre-existing contract right; and in the danger of inadequate description in financing statements by claiming "accounts" or "general intangibles" when before performance they should have been described as "contract rights"; and in other respects.

"Money" is expressly excluded from the catch-all definition, "general intangible", to preclude any possible reading that a security interest in money may be perfected by filing.

The other changes are conforming changes.

§ 9—114. Consignment

(1) A person who delivers goods under a consignment which is not a security interest and who would be required to file under this Article by paragraph (3) (c) of Section 2—326 has priority over a secured party who is or becomes a creditor of the consignee and who would have a perfected security interest in the goods if they were the property of the consignee, and also has priority with respect to identifiable cash proceeds received on or before delivery of the goods to a buyer, if

    (a) the consignor complies with the filing provision of the Article on Sales with respect to consignments (paragraph (3) (c) of Section 2—326) before the consignee receives possession of the goods; and

    (b) the consignor gives notification in writing to the holder of the security interest if the holder has filed a financing statement covering the same types of goods before the date of the filing made by the consignor; and

    (c) the holder of the security interest receives the notification within five years before the consignee receives possession of the goods; and

    (d) the notification states that the consignor expects to deliver goods on consignment to the consignee, describing the goods by item or type.

(2) In the case of a consignment which is not a security interest and in which the requirements of the preceding subsection have not been met, a person who delivers goods to another is subordinate to a person who would have a perfected security interest in the goods if they were the property of the debtor.

Reasons for 1972 Adoption of New Section

An uncertainty has existed under the 1962 Code whether the filing rule in Section 2—326(3) applicable to true consignments requires only filing under Part 4 of Article 9 or also requires notice to prior inventory secured parties of the debtor under Section 9—312(3). The new Section 9—114 accepts the latter view, and provides in substance that, in order to protect his ownership of the consigned goods, the consignor must give the same notice to an inventory secured party of the debtor that he would have to give if his transaction with the consignee was in the form of a security transaction instead of in the form of a consignment. This new section follows closely the language of Section 9—312(3).

PART 2

VALIDITY OF SECURITY AGREEMENT AND RIGHTS OF PARTIES THERETO

§ 9—203. Attachment and Enforceability of Security Interest; Proceeds; Formal Requisites

[(1) Subject to the provisions of Section 4—208 on the security interest of a collecting bank and Section 9—113 on a security interest arising under the Article on Sales, a security interest is not enforceable against the debtor or third parties unless

    (a) the collateral is in the possession of the secured party; or

    (b) the debtor has signed a security agreement which contains a description of the collateral and in addition, when the security interest covers crops or oil, gas or minerals to be extracted or timber to be cut, a description of the land concerned. In describing collateral, the word "proceeds" is sufficient without further description to cover proceeds of any character.]

(1) Subject to the provisions of Section 4—208 on the security interest of a collecting bank and Section 9—113 on a security interest arising under the Article on Sales, a security interest is not enforceable against the debtor or third parties with respect to the collateral and does not attach unless

    (a) the collateral is in the possession of the secured party pursuant to agreement, or the debtor has signed a security agreement which contains a description of the collateral and in addition, when the security interest covers crops growing or to be grown or timber to be cut, a description of the land concerned; and

    (b) value has been given; and

    (c) the debtor has rights in the collateral.

(2) A security interest attaches when it becomes enforceable against the debtor with respect to the collateral. Attachment occurs as soon as all of the events specified in subsection (1) have taken place unless explicit agreement postpones the time of attaching.

(3) Unless otherwise agreed a security agreement gives the secured party the rights to proceeds provided by Section 9—306.

(4) [(2)] A transaction, although subject to this Article, is also subject to ....*, and in the case of conflict between the provisions of this Article and any such statute, the provisions of such statute control. Failure to comply with any applicable statute has only the effect which is specified therein.

> **Note:** *At * in subsection (4) insert reference to any local statute regulating small loans, retail installment sales and the like.*
>
> *The foregoing subsection (4) is designed to make it clear that certain transactions, although subject to this Article, must also comply with other applicable legislation.*
>
> *This Article is designed to regulate all the "security" aspects of transactions within its scope. There is, however, much regulatory legislation, particularly in the consumer field, which supplements this Article and should not be repealed by its enactment. Examples are small loan acts, retail installment selling acts and the like. Such acts may provide for licensing and rate regulation and may prescribe particular forms of contract. Such provisions should remain in force despite the enactment of this Article. On the other hand if a retail installment selling act contains provisions on filing, rights on default, etc., such provisions should be repealed as inconsistent with this Article[.] except that inconsistent provisions as to deficiencies, penalties, etc., in the Uniform Consumer Credit Code and other recent related legislation should remain because those statutes were drafted after the substantial enactment of the Article and with the intention of modifying certain provisions of this Article as to consumer credit.*

Reasons for 1972 Change

Subsection (1) has been revised to incorporate into the concept of enforceability of a security interest the elements of agreement, value, and rights in the collateral, which formerly were stated in Section 9—204. These are combined with the requirement of written agreement (unless the security interest is evidenced by possession of the collateral by the secured party), and the security interest is said to "attach" when all of the events specified have occurred. This drafting cures the former anomaly that a security interest could attach and be perfected, and yet be unenforceable against anyone for lack of a written security agreement.

The requirement that a security agreement covering oil, gas or minerals to be extracted contain a description of the land concerned has been eliminated since the Article does not recognize a security interest in such collateral until it has been extracted from the land.

The former reference to proceeds in subsection (1) has been eliminated and new subsection (3) added to make clear that claims to proceeds under Section 9—306 do not require a statement in the security agreement, for it is assumed that the parties so intend unless otherwise agreed.

§ 9—204. [When Security Interest Attaches;] After-Acquired Property; Future Advances

[(1) A security interest cannot attach until there is agreement (subsection (3) of Section 1—201) that it attach and value is given and the debtor has rights in the collateral. It attaches as soon as all of the events in the preceding sentence have taken place unless explicit agreement postpones the time of attaching.]

[(2) For the purposes of this section the debtor has no rights

(a) in crops until they are planted or otherwise become growing crops, in the young of livestock until they are conceived;

(b) in fish until caught, in oil, gas or minerals until they are extracted, in timber until it is cut;

(c) in a contract right until the contract has been made;

(d) in an account until it comes into existence.]

[(3) Except as provided in subsection (4) a security agreement may provide that collateral, whenever acquired, shall secure all obligations covered by the security agreement.]

420

[(4) No security interest attaches under an after-acquired property clause

    (a) to crops which become such more than one year after the security agreement is executed except that a security interest in crops which is given in conjunction with a lease or a land purchase or improvement transaction evidenced by a contract, mortgage or deed of trust may if so agreed attach to crops to be grown on the land concerned during the period of such real estate transaction;

    (b) to consumer goods other than accessions (Section 9—314) when given as additional security unless the debtor acquires rights in them within ten days after the secured party gives value.]

<u>(1)</u> Except as provided in subsection (2), a security agreement may provide that any or all obligations covered by the security agreement are to be secured by after-acquired collateral.

<u>(2)</u> No security interest attaches under an after-acquired property clause to consumer goods other than accessions (Section 9—314) when given as additional security unless the debtor acquires rights in them within ten days after the secured party gives value.

<u>(3)</u> (5) Obligations covered by a security agreement may include future advances or other value whether or not the advances or value are given pursuant to commitment (subsection (1) of Section 9—105).

Reasons for 1972 Change

Former subsection (1) has been eliminated. The term "attach" has been moved to Section 9—203 and related to the concept of enforceability of the security interest between the parties to the security agreement contained in that section.

Former subsection (2) has been eliminated as unnecessary and in some cases confusing. Its operation appeared to be arbitrary, and it is believed that the questions considered are best left to the courts.

Former subsections (3) and (5), now subsections (1) and (3), have been rewritten for clarity.

Former subsection (4) is redesignated (2), and clause (a) thereof relating to crops eliminated. That clause provided that no security interest in crops attaches under an after-acquired property clause to crops which become such more than one year after the security agreement, unless the agreement involved certain real estate transactions. The obvious purpose of this provision was to protect a necessitous farmer from encumbering his crops for many years in the future. The provision did not work because there was no corresponding limit on the scope of a financing statement covering crops, and under the Code's notice-filing rules the priority position of a security arrangement covering successive crops would be as effectively protected by the filing of a first financing statement whether the granting clause as to successive crops was in one security agreement with an after-acquired property clause or in a succession of security agreements. On the other hand the clause did require an annual security agreement for crops even when the encumbrance on crops was agreed to as part of a long-term financing covering farm machinery and other assets. The provision thus appeared to be meaningless in operation except to cause unnecessary paperwork, but it did introduce some element of uncertainty as to its purpose.

§ 9—205. Use or Disposition of Collateral Without Accounting Permissible

A security interest is not invalid or fraudulent against creditors by reason of liberty in the debtor to use, commingle or dispose of all or part of the collateral (including returned or repossessed goods) or to collect or compromise accounts [contract rights] or chattel paper, or to accept the return of goods or make repossessions, or to use, commingle or dispose of proceeds, or by reason of the failure of the secured party to require the debtor to account for proceeds or replace collateral. This section does not relax the requirements of possession where perfection of a security interest depends upon possession of the collateral by the secured party or by a bailee.

Reasons for 1972 Change

The change reflects the deletion of the defined term "contract right" from the Article.

PART 3

RIGHTS OF THIRD PARTIES; PERFECTED AND UNPERFECTED SECURITY INTERESTS; RULES OF PRIORITY

§ 9–301. Persons Who Take Priority Over Unperfected Security Interests; Right of "Lien Creditor"

(1) Except as otherwise provided in subsection (2), an unperfected security interest is subordinate to the rights of

  (a) persons entitled to priority under Section 9–312;

  (b) a person who becomes a lien creditor [without knowledge of the security interest and] before [it] the security interest is perfected;

  (c) in the case of goods, instruments, documents, and chattel paper, a person who is not a secured party and who is a transferee in bulk or other buyer not in ordinary course of business, or is a buyer of farm products in ordinary course of business, to the extent that he gives value and receives delivery of the collateral without knowledge of the security interest and before it is perfected;

  (d) in the case of accounts [, contract rights,] and general intangibles, a person who is not a secured party and who is a transferee to the extent that he gives value without knowledge of the security interest and before it is perfected.

(2) If the secured party files with respect to a purchase money security interest before or within ten days after the debtor receives possession of the collateral [comes into possession of the debtor], he takes priority over the rights of a transferee in bulk or of a lien creditor which arise between the time the security interest attaches and the time of filing.

(3) A "lien creditor" means a creditor who has acquired a lien on the property involved by attachment, levy or the like and includes an assignee for benefit of creditors from the time of assignment, and a trustee in bankruptcy from the date of the filing of the petition or a receiver in equity from the time of appointment. [Unless all the creditors represented had knowledge of the security interest such a representative of creditors is a lien

423

creditor without knowledge even though he personally has knowledge of the security interest.]

(4) A person who becomes a lien creditor while a security interest is perfected takes subject to the security interest only to the extent that it secures advances made before he becomes a lien creditor or within 45 days thereafter or made without knowledge of the lien or pursuant to a commitment entered into without knowledge of the lien.

Reasons for 1972 Change

Paragraph (1) (b) has been amended to eliminate the element of knowledge in the conditions under which a lien creditor may defeat an unperfected security interest. Knowledge of the security interest will no longer subordinate the lien creditor to the unfiled security interest. The former section denied the lien creditor priority even though he had no knowledge when he got involved by extending credit, if he acquired knowledge while attempting to extricate himself. It was completely inconsistent in spirit with the rules of priority between security interests, where knowledge plays a very minor role.

The change in subsection (2) is made to conform the language to that of the related provision in Section 9—312(4).

The second sentence of subsection (3) is deleted because the question of knowledge has been eliminated from paragraph (1) (b).

New subsection (4) deals with the question of the extent to which advances made under a perfected security interest after the rights of a lien creditor have attached to the collateral will come ahead of the position of the lien creditor. This subsection should be read with Section 9—307(3) (which deals with the same problem in the case of an intervening buyer) and Section 9—312(7) (which deals with the same problem in the case of a secured party), and paragraph (5) of Reasons for Change under Section 9—312.

In the case of the lien creditors dealt with by this subsection, the rule chosen is crucial to the priority of the security interest for advances over a federal tax lien for 45 days after the tax lien has been filed, as contemplated under section 6323(c) (2) and (d) of the Internal Revenue Code of 1954 as amended by the Federal Tax Lien Act of 1966. The actual importance of the priority rule chosen between a secured party and possible lien creditors during the 45 days is believed to be slight; but the rule chosen is essential to give the secured party the protection against Federal tax liens believed to have been intended by the Federal Tax Lien Act of 1966, the operation of which is made to depend on state law. The rule of state law was not certain before this revision. Accordingly, the priority of the security interest for future advances over the judgment lien has to be absolute for the 45 days, without regard to any knowledge of the secured party that the judgment lien exists. After the 45 days the priority of the security interest depends on the secured party's lack of knowledge of the lien at the time he makes the subsequent advance or commits to do so.

§ 9—302. When Filing Is Required to Perfect Security Interest; Security Interests to Which Filing Provisions of This Article Do Not Apply

(1) A financing statement must be filed to perfect all security interests except the following:

(a) a security interest in collateral in possession of the secured party under Section 9—305;

(b) a security interest temporarily perfected in instruments or documents without delivery under Section 9—304 or in proceeds for a 10 day period under Section 9—306;

[(c) a purchase money security interest in farm equipment having a purchase price not in excess of $2500; but filing is required for a fixture under Section 9—313 or for a motor vehicle required to be licensed;]

(c) a security interest created by an assignment of a beneficial interest in a trust or a decedent's estate;

(d) a purchase money security interest in consumer goods; but filing is required [for a fixture under Section 9—313 or for a motor vehicle required to be licensed;] for a motor vehicle required to be registered; and fixture filing is required for priority over conflicting interests in fixtures to the extent provided in Section 9—313;

(e) an assignment of accounts [or contract rights] which does not alone or in conjunction with other assignments to the same assignee transfer a significant part of the outstanding accounts [or contract rights] of the assignor;

(f) a security interest of a collecting bank (Section 4—208) or arising under the Article on Sales (see Section 9—113) or covered in subsection (3) of this section;

(g) an assignment for the benefit of all the creditors of the transferor, and subsequent transfers by the assignee thereunder.

(2) If a secured party assigns a perfected security interest, no filing under this Article is required in order to continue the perfected status of the security interest against creditors of and transferees from the original debtor.

[(3) The filing provisions of this Article do not apply to a security interest in property subject to a statute

(a) of the United States which provides for a national registration or filing of all security interests in such property; or

Note: *States to select either Alternative A or Alternative B.*

Alternative A—

(b) of this state which provides for central filing of, or which requires indication on a certificate of title of, such security interests in such property.

Alternative B—

(b) of this state which provides for central filing of security interests in such property, or in a motor vehicle which is not inventory held for sale for which a certificate of title is required under the statutes of this state if a notation of such a security interest can be indicated by a public official on a certificate or a duplicate thereof.]

[(4) A security interest in property covered by a statute described in subsection (3) can be perfected only by registration or filing under that statute or by indication of the security interest on a certificate of title or duplicate thereof by a public official.]

(3) The filing of a financing statement otherwise required by this Article is not necessary or effective to perfect a security interest in property subject to

(a) a statute or treaty of the United States which provides for a national or international registration or a national or international certificate of title or which specifies a place of filing different from that specified in this Article for filing of the security interest; or

(b) the following statutes of this state; [[list any certificate of title statute covering automobiles, trailers, mobile homes, boats, farm tractors, or the like, and any central filing statute*.]]; but during any period in which collateral is inventory held for sale by a person who is in the business of selling goods of that kind, the filing provisions of this Article (Part 4) apply to a security interest in that collateral created by him as debtor; or

(c) a certificate of title statute of another jurisdiction under the law of which indication of a security interest on the certificate is required as a condition of perfection (subsection (2) of Section 9—103).

(4) Compliance with a statute or treaty described in subsection (3) is equivalent to the filing of a financing statement under this Article, and a security interest in property subject to the statute or treaty can be perfected only by compliance therewith except as provided in Section 9—103 on multiple state transactions. Duration and renewal of perfection of a security interest perfected by compliance with the statute or treaty are governed by the provisions of the statute or treaty; in other respects the security interest is subject to this Article.

> * **Note:** *It is recommended that the provisions of certificate of title acts for perfection of security interests by notation on the certificates should be amended to exclude coverage of inventory held for sale.*

Reasons for 1972 Change

Former paragraph (1) (c), which created a nonfiling rule for purchase money security interests in certain farm equipment, has been eliminated. The analogy drawn in the 1962 Code of farm equipment to consumer goods (for which a similar nonfiling rule is provided in paragraph (1) (d)) is believed to be inappropriate. The effect of the rule was to make farmers' equipment unavailable to them as collateral for loans from some lenders.

A new paragraph (1) (c) exempts from filing rules security interests created by assignments of beneficial interests in trusts and estates, because these assignments are not ordinarily thought of as subject to this Article, and a filing rule might operate to defeat many assignments.

The requirement of filing for purchase-money security interests in consumer goods which are fixtures has been made applicable only for priority against real estate interests (Section 9—313).

A new paragraph (1) (g) has been added exempting from filing assignments for the benefit of creditors because they are not financing transactions.

Former subsections (3) and (4) have been rewritten into new subsections (3) and (4). The alternatives of former subsection (3) had proved unacceptable formulations in many states. The states adopted non-uniform amendments to use language more closely geared to their certificate of title laws than the uniform alternatives. It is believed that the simplest thing is to have each state specify its statutes intended to be applicable as it adopts the revised Article 9.

Former Alternative B to subsection (3) has been abandoned as no longer serving any purpose: it had been an attempt to convert obsolete non-mandatory certificate of title laws into laws under which notation on the certificate of title was the necessary method of perfection of a security interest.

Subsection (3) continues to carry the thought that was formerly only in Alternative B—namely, that the certificate of title procedure does not control the perfection of inventory or "floor plan" security interests, but instead normal Code filing rules are applicable. Non-uniform variations to the contrary under some state laws are believed to increase operating burdens and it is hoped that the states will abandon them.

References to federal statutes have been broadened to include treaties.

§ 9—304.   Perfection of Security Interest in Instruments, Documents, and Goods Covered by Documents; Perfection by Permissive Filing; Temporary Perfection Without Filing or Transfer of Possession

(1) A security interest in chattel paper or negotiable documents may be perfected by filing. A security interest in <u>money or</u> instruments (other than instruments which constitute part of chattel paper) can be perfected only by the secured party's taking possession, except as provided in subsections (4) and (5) <u>of this section and subsections (2) and (3) of Section 9—306 on proceeds.</u>

(2) During the period that goods are in the possession of the issuer of a negotiable document therefor, a security interest in the goods is perfected by perfecting a security interest in the document, and any security interest in the goods otherwise perfected during such period is subject thereto.

(3) A security interest in goods in the possession of a bailee other than one who has issued a negotiable document therefor

is perfected by issuance of a document in the name of the secured party or by the bailee's receipt of notification of the secured party's interest or by filing as to the goods.

(4) A security interest in instruments or negotiable documents is perfected without filing or the taking of possession for a period of 21 days from the time it attaches to the extent that it arises for new value given under a written security agreement.

(5) A security interest remains perfected for a period of 21 days without filing where a secured party having a perfected security interest in an instrument, a negotiable document or goods in possession of a bailee other than one who has issued a negotiable document therefor

> (a) makes available to the debtor the goods or documents representing the goods for the purpose of ultimate sale or exchange or for the purpose of loading, unloading, storing, shipping, transshipping, manufacturing, processing or otherwise dealing with them in a manner preliminary to their sale or exchange, [;or] but priority between conflicting security interests in the goods is subject to subsection (3) of Section 9—312; or

> (b) delivers the instrument to the debtor for the purpose of ultimate sale or exchange or of presentation, collection, renewal or registration of transfer.

(6) After the 21 day period in subsections (4) and (5) perfection depends upon compliance with applicable provisions of this Article.

Reasons for 1972 Change

The change in subsection (1) corrects an inadvertent omission in the 1962 Text, and makes clear that a security interest in money cannot be perfected by filing.

A provision has been added to subsection (5) making it clear that the 21-day period referred to therein deals only with perfection, but that there must be compliance with the notice provisions of Section 9—312(3) in order to achieve priority over earlier inventory financers. Corresponding clarifying changes have been made in Section 9—312(3).

§ 9—305. When Possession by Secured Party Perfects Security Interest Without Filing

A security interest in letters of credit and advices of credit (subsection (2) (a) of Section 5—116), goods, instruments, money, negotiable documents or chattel paper may be perfected by the secured party's taking possession of the collateral. If such collateral other than goods covered by a negotiable document is held by a bailee, the secured party is deemed to have possession from the time the bailee receives notification of the secured party's interest. A security interest is perfected by possession from the time possession is taken without relation back and continues only so long as possession is retained, unless otherwise specified in this Article. The security interest may be otherwise perfected as provided in this Article before or after the period of possession by the secured party.

Reasons for 1972 Change

The change corresponds to the change in Section 9–304 to clarify the special position of money.

§ 9—306. "Proceeds"; Secured Party's Rights on Disposition of Collateral

(1) ["Proceeds" includes whatever is received when collateral or proceeds is sold, exchanged, collected or otherwise disposed of. The term also includes the account arising when the right to payment is earned under a contract right.]

"Proceeds" includes whatever is received upon the sale, exchange, collection or other disposition of collateral or proceeds. Insurance payable by reason of loss or damage to the collateral is proceeds, except to the extent that it is payable to a person other than a party to the security agreement. Money, checks, deposit accounts, and the like are "cash proceeds". All other proceeds are "non-cash proceeds".

(2) Except where this Article otherwise provides, a security interest continues in collateral notwithstanding sale, exchange or other disposition thereof [by the debtor] unless [his action was] the disposition was authorized by the secured party in the security agreement or otherwise, and also continues in any identifiable proceeds including collections received by the debtor.

(3) The security interest in proceeds is a continuously perfected security interest if the interest in the original collateral was perfected but it ceases to be a perfected security interest and becomes unperfected ten days after receipt of the proceeds by the debtor unless

  [(a) a filed financing statement covering the original collateral also covers proceeds; or]

  (a) a filed financing statement covers the original collateral and the proceeds are collateral in which a security interest may be perfected by filing in the office or offices where the financing statement has been filed and, if the proceeds are acquired with cash proceeds, the description of collateral in the financing statement indicates the types of property constituting the proceeds; or

(b) a filed financing statement covers the original collateral and the proceeds are identifiable cash proceeds; or

(c) [(b)] the security interest in the proceeds is perfected before the expiration of the ten day period.

Except as provided in this section, a security interest in proceeds can be perfected only by the methods or under the circumstances permitted in this Article for original collateral of the same type.

(4) In the event of insolvency proceedings instituted by or against a debtor, a secured party with a perfected security interest in proceeds has a perfected security interest only in the following proceeds:

(a) in identifiable non-cash proceeds[;] and in separate deposit accounts containing only proceeds;

(b) in identifiable cash proceeds in the form of money which is [not] neither commingled with other money [or] nor deposited in a [bank] deposit account prior to the insolvency proceedings;

(c) in identifiable cash proceeds in the form of checks and the like which are not deposited in a [bank] deposit account prior to the insolvency proceedings; and

(d) in all cash and [bank] deposit accounts of the debtor [if other cash] in which proceeds have been commingled with other funds, [or deposited in a bank account,] but the perfected security interest under this paragraph (d) is

(i) subject to any right of set-off; and

(ii) limited to an amount not greater than the amount of any cash proceeds received by the debtor within ten days before the institution of the insolvency proceedings [and commingled or deposited in a bank account prior to the insolvency proceedings less the amount of cash proceeds received by the debtor and paid over to the secured party during the ten day period,] less the sum of (I) the payments to the secured party on account of cash proceeds received by the debtor during such period and (II) the cash proceeds received by the debtor during such period to which the secured party is entitled under paragraphs (a) through (c) of this subsection (4).

(5) If a sale of goods results in an account or chattel paper which is transferred by the seller to a secured party, and if the goods are returned to or are repossessed by the seller or the secured party, the following rules determine priorities:

(a) If the goods were collateral at the time of sale, for an indebtedness of the seller which is still unpaid, the original security interest attaches again to the goods and continues as a perfected security interest if it was perfected at the time when the goods were sold. If the security interest was originally perfected by a filing which is still effective, nothing further is required to continue the perfected status; in any other case, the secured party must take possession of the returned or repossessed goods or must file.

(b) An unpaid transferee of the chattel paper has a security interest in the goods against the transferor. Such security interest is prior to a security interest asserted under paragraph (a) to the extent that the transferee of the chattel paper was entitled to priority under Section 9—308.

(c) An unpaid transferee of the account has a security interest in the goods against the transferor. Such security interest is subordinate to a security interest asserted under paragraph (a).

(d) A security interest of an unpaid transferee asserted under paragraph (b) or (c) must be perfected for protection against creditors of the transferor and purchasers of the returned or repossessed goods.

Reasons for 1972 Change

The first sentence of subsection (1) is rewritten for clarity.

The former second sentence of subsection (1) is omitted consistently with the abandonment of the term "contract right" in Section 9—106.

The new second sentence of subsection (1) is intended to overrule various cases to the effect that proceeds of insurance on collateral are not proceeds of the collateral. The "except" clause is intended to say that if the insurance contract specifies the person to whom the insurance is payable, the concept of "proceeds" will not interfere with performance of the contract.

Heretofore an apparent inconsistency and ambiguity has existed between the last sentence of Section 9—203(1) (b) of the 1962 Code, which indicated that a claim to proceeds had to be an express term of a security agreement, and Section 9—306(2), which indicated that a right to proceeds was automatic without reference to a term of a security agreement. This ambiguity has been clarified in favor of an automatic right to proceeds, on the theory that this is the intent of the parties, unless otherwise agreed. Further, there has been eliminated the requirement of claiming proceeds in a financing statement, which had resulted in a checking of a box on each financing statement in order to claim proceeds. Instead, the filed claim to the original collateral is treated as constituting automatically a filing as to proceeds. To this principle, a limitation has been stated: Where the filing as to the original collateral is an inappropriate means of perfection as to proceeds of certain types, or is made at a place that is inappropriate as to such proceeds, the filed claim to the original collateral perfects the claim to proceeds for only 10 days. One example of this is negotiable instruments as proceeds, as to which filing is inappropriate under Section 9—304(1). Another example is the case of accounts as proceeds of inventory, as to which under the rules of Section 9—103 the state of filing for the accounts might be different from the state of filing for the inventory.

The revised subsection (4) is a clarification based on the California revision. It makes clear that the claim to cash allowed in insolvency is exclusive of any other claim based on tracing.

§ 9—307. Protection of Buyers of Goods

(1) A buyer in ordinary course of business (subsection (9) of Section 1—201) other than a person buying farm products from a person engaged in farming operations takes free of a security interest created by his seller even though the security interest is perfected and even though the buyer knows of its existence.

(2) In the case of consumer goods [and in the case of farm equipment having an original purchase price not in excess of $2500 (other than fixtures, see Section 9—313)], a buyer takes free of a security interest even though perfected if he buys with-

out knowledge of the security interest, for value and for his own personal, family or household purposes [or his own farming operations] unless prior to the purchase the secured party has filed a financing statement covering such goods.

(3) A buyer other than a buyer in ordinary course of business (subsection (1) of this section) takes free of a security interest to the extent that it secures future advances made after the secured party acquires knowledge of the purchase, or more than 45 days after the purchase, whichever first occurs, unless made pursuant to a commitment entered into without knowledge of the purchase and before the expiration of the 45 day period.

Reasons for 1972 Change

The change in subsection (2) is a conforming change made necessary by the deletion of Section 9—302(1) (c) of the 1962 Code, which provided in substance that a purchase money security interest in farm equipment having an original purchase price not in excess of $2500 need not be filed. The omission of that provision in Subsection 9—302(1) makes any corresponding reference unnecessary in the present section.

Subsection (3) is one of three new provisions clarifying the extent to which future advances under a security interest may outrank an intervening right. See Sections 9—301(4) and 9—312(7) and paragraph (5) of Reasons for Change under Section 9—312.

§ 9—308. Purchase of Chattel Paper and [Non-Negotiable] Instruments

[A purchaser of chattel paper or a non-negotiable instrument who gives new value and takes possession of it in the ordinary course of his business and without knowledge that the specific paper or instrument is subject to a security interest has priority over a security interest which is perfected under Section 9—304 (permissive filing and temporary perfection). A purchaser of chattel paper who gives new value and takes possession of it in the ordinary course of his business has priority over a security interest in chattel paper which is claimed merely as proceeds of inventory subject to a security interest (Section 9—306), even though he knows that the specific paper is subject to the security interest.]

A purchaser of chattel paper or an instrument who gives new value and takes possession of it in the ordinary course of his business has priority over a security interest in the chattel paper or instrument

(a) which is perfected under Section 9—304 (permissive filing and temporary perfection) or under Section 9—306 (perfection as to proceeds) if he acts without knowledge that the specific paper or instrument is subject to a security interest; or

(b) which is claimed merely as proceeds of inventory subject to a security interest (Section 9—306) even though he knows that the specific paper or instrument is subject to the security interest.

Reasons for 1972 Change

The section has been rewritten for clarity.

Another purpose of the changes is to make the rules of this section applicable to negotiable instruments. Heretofore, the holder of a negotiable instrument was under some circumstances in a less protected position against competing claims than the holder of chattel paper. The holder of a negotiable instrument had protection only if he achieved the holder in due course status referred to in Section 9—309, which status would not be achieved if the holder had knowledge of a conflicting proceeds claim. In contrast, the holder of chattel paper who met the stated conditions was protected under the second sentence of Section 9—308 of the 1962 Code even if he had knowledge of the conflicting proceeds claim. Under the changes, the holder of a negotiable instrument who may not qualify as holder in due course may nevertheless qualify for the protections of this section.

§ 9—312. Priorities Among Conflicting Security Interests in the Same Collateral

[(1) The rules of priority stated in the following sections shall govern where applicable: Section 4—208 with respect to the security interest of collecting banks in items being collected, accompanying documents and proceeds; Section 9—301 on certain priorities; Section 9—304 on goods covered by documents; Section 9—306 on proceeds and repossessions; Section 9—307 on buyers of goods; Section 9—308 on possessory against non-possessory interests in chattel paper or non-negotiable instruments; Section 9—309 on security interests in negotiable instruments, documents or securities; Section 9—310 on priorities between perfected security interests and liens by operation of law; Section 9—313 on security interests in fixtures as against interests in real estate; Section 9—314 on security interests in accessions as against interest in goods; Section 9—315 on conflicting security interests where goods lose their identity or become part of a product; and Section 9—316 on contractual subordination.]

(1) The rules of priority stated in other sections of this Part and in the following sections shall govern when applicable: Section 4—208 with respect to the security interests of collecting banks in items being collected, accompanying documents and proceeds; Section 9—103 on security interests related to other jurisdictions; Section 9—114 on consignments.

(2) A perfected security interest in crops for new value given to enable the debtor to produce the crops during the production season and given not more than three months before the crops become growing crops by planting or otherwise takes priority over an earlier perfected security interest to the extent that such earlier interest secures obligations due more than six months before the crops become growing crops by planting or otherwise, even though the person giving new value had knowledge of the earlier security interest.

[(3) A purchase money security interest in inventory collateral has priority over a conflicting security interest in the same collateral if

(a) the purchase money security interest is perfected at the time the debtor receives possession of the collateral; and

(b) any secured party whose security interest is known to the holder of the purchase money security interest or who, prior to the date of the filing made by the holder of the purchase money security interest, had filed a financing statement covering the same items or type of inventory, has received notification of the purchase money security interest before the debtor receives possession of the collateral covered by the purchase money security interest; and

(c) such notification states that the person giving the notice has or expects to acquire a purchase money security interest in inventory of the debtor, describing such inventory by item or type.]

436

(3) A perfected purchase money security interest in inventory has priority over a conflicting security interest in the same inventory and also has priority in identifiable cash proceeds received on or before the delivery of the inventory to a buyer if

(a) the purchase money security interest is perfected at the time the debtor receives possession of the inventory; and

(b) the purchase money secured party gives notification in writing to the holder of the conflicting security interest if the holder had filed a financing statement covering the same types of inventory (i) before the date of the filing made by the purchase money secured party, or (ii) before the beginning of the 21 day period where the purchase money security interest is temporarily perfected without filing or possession (subsection (5) of Section 9—304); and

(c) the holder of the conflicting security interest receives the notification within five years before the debtor receives possession of the inventory; and

(d) the notification states that the person giving the notice has or expects to acquire a purchase money security.interest in inventory of the debtor, describing such inventory by item or type.

(4) A purchase money security interest in collateral other than inventory has priority over a conflicting security interest in the same collateral or its proceeds if the purchase money security interest is perfected at the time the debtor receives possession of the collateral or within ten days thereafter.

(5) In all cases not governed by other rules stated in this section (including cases of purchase money security interests which do not qualify for the special priorities set forth in subsections (3) and (4) of this section), priority between conflicting security interests in the same collateral shall be determined [as follows:

(a) in the order of filing if both are perfected by filing, regardless of which security interest attached first under Section 9—204(1) and whether it attached before or after filing;

(b) in the order of perfection unless both are perfected by filing, regardless of which security interest attached first under Section 9—204(1) and, in the case of a filed security interest, whether it attached before or after filing; and

(c) in the order of attachment under Section 9—204(1) so long as neither is perfected.]

according to the following rules:

(a) Conflicting security interests rank according to priority in time of filing or perfection. Priority dates from the time a filing is first made covering the collateral or the time the security interest is first perfected, whichever is earlier, provided that there is no period thereafter when there is neither filing nor perfection.

(b) So long as conflicting security interests are unperfected, the first to attach has priority.

[(6) For the purpose of the priority rules of the immediately preceding subsection, a continuously perfected security interest shall be treated at all times as if perfected by filing if it was originally so perfected and it shall be treated at all times as if perfected otherwise than by filing if it was originally perfected otherwise than by filing.]

(6) For the purposes of subsection (5) a date of filing or perfection as to collateral is also a date of filing or perfection as to proceeds.

(7) If future advances are made while a security interest is perfected by filing or the taking of possession, the security interest has the same priority for the purposes of subsection (5) with respect to the future advances as it does with respect to the first advance. If a commitment is made before or while the security interest is so perfected, the security interest has the same priority with respect to advances made pursuant thereto. In other cases a perfected security interest has priority from the date the advance is made.

Reasons for 1972 Change

(1) The change in subsection (1) is primarily a simplification of statement.

(2) Changes have been made in subsection (3) to answer unresolved questions under the 1962 Code.

(a) One change answers the question how often a notice must be given under that subsection. The period of five years has been chosen by analogy to the duration of a financing statement.

(b) Another change answers the question of the priority status of the security interest in inventory temporarily perfected for 21 days without filing or perfection in a situation which begins with release of a pledged document under Section 9—304(5). The answer provided is the usual rule that the purchase-money claimant to preserve his priority resulting from the document must give the required notice before the debtor receives possession of the inventory. If the secured party fails to give timely notice, he loses his priority under this subsection.

(c) One of the most widely discussed questions under the 1962 Code was the question of the priority between a person claiming accounts as proceeds of inventory and a person claiming the accounts by direct filing with respect thereto. One issue was whether the special position of an inventory financer as a purchase money financer or as the first financer in the business cycle of the debtor gave him any special position as to accounts resulting from the inventory. In general, as revised, a negative answer has been given, and a prior right to inventory does not confer a prior right to any proceeds except identifiable cash proceeds received on or before the delivery of the inventory (i. e., without the intervention of an account). Other aspects of this issue are discussed under subsection (5) of this section.

(3) A different answer has been given in subsection (4) relating to purchase money security interests in collateral other than inventory. Here, where it is not ordinarily expected that the collateral will be sold and that proceeds will result, it seems appropriate to give the party having a purchase money security interest in the original collateral an equivalent priority in its proceeds. The 1962 Code was unclear on this point.

(4) Existing subsection (5) contains two principal rules. Paragraph (a) is a first-to-file rule where both competing security interests are perfected by filing. Paragraph (b) is a first-to-perfect rule when either of the security interests is or both of them are perfected otherwise than by filing. A traffic rule is provided by existing subsection (6) to the effect that a continuously perfected security interest shall be treated for the purpose of the foregoing rules as if at all times perfected in the manner it was first perfected. The problems raised have been the subject of an enormous legal literature. They are complicated by the unforeseeable effect of the temporary perfection of security interest in proceeds without filing under Section 9—306, and by speculation as to whether a secured party could claim that his security interest was originally perfected without filing under this rule even though the security interest in proceeds was claimed in his filing as to the original collateral. They are further com-

plicated by the question whether different rules would apply when a financing statement was drawn to cover, e. g., inventory and its proceeds (which would include accounts) and when it was drawn to cover inventory and accounts.

To settle these questions it is proposed to replace the present paragraphs (a) and (b) of subsection (5) by a single rule, subsection (5), and to eliminate existing subsection (6). Together with this treatment should be noted the fact that a filing as to proceeds automatically arises from a filed security interest in original collateral under the proposed revision of Section 9—306(3), subject to limitations therein discussed. New proposed subsection (6) makes it clear that subject to these limitations the time of filing or perfection as to original collateral is the time of filing or perfection as to proceeds.

The rule of proposed subsection (5) ranks conflicting perfected security interests by their priority in time, dating back to the respective times when without interruption the security interests were either perfected or were the subjects of appropriate filings.

Perhaps the most debated subject under Article 9 has been the question whether between conflicting security interests a priority as to original collateral confers a priority as to proceeds. As indicated above, in the case of collateral other than inventory, e. g., equipment, it seems clear that the policy favoring the purchase money secured party in Section 9—312 (4) should give him the first claim to the proceeds. This is so even though the security interests will have been perfected simultaneously when the proceeds arise and the debtor acquires rights therein.

Proper policy is much less clear when the collateral involved is inventory and proceeds consisting of accounts. (Policy as to other types of receivables as proceeds is expressed in Sections 9—308 and 9—309). Accounts financing is more important in the economy than the financing of the kinds of inventory that produce accounts, and the desirable rule is one which makes accounts financing certain as to its legal position. Therefore, the rule proposed is that where a financing statement as to accounts is filed first (with or without related inventory financing), the security interest in accounts should not be defeated by any subsequent claim to accounts as proceeds of a security interest in inventory filed later. There is therefore no provision in Section 9—312(3) carrying forward to accounts any priority right in inventory, and proposed subsections (5) and (6) adhere firmly to the principle that a date of filing as to original collateral also defines the date of filing as to proceeds. Correspondingly, a financing statement as to inventory (carrying with it a claim to proceeds) which is filed first will under the same provisions have priority over a later-filed security interest in accounts.

(5) The priority of future advances against an intervening party has been the subject of much discussion and disagreement. Where both interests are filed security interests, the first-to-file rule of present Section 9—312(5) (a) or the corresponding proposed revision is clearly applicable. Under the 1962 Code, the position of an intervening pledgee in reference to a subsequent advance by an earlier-filed secured party is debatable. The proposed unified priority rule of subsection 9—312(5) would indicate that subsequent advances by the first-filed party have priority, and subsequent advances under a security interest perfected by possession likewise have priority over an intervening filed security interest. These priority rules are expressly stated in proposed subsection (7). That proposal also deals with the rare case of the priority position of a subsequent advance made by a secured party whose security interest is temporarily perfected without either filing or possession, against an intervening secured party. Since there is no notice by the usual methods of filing or possession of the existence of the security interest, the subsequent advances rank only from the actual date of making unless made pursuant to commitment.

Different but related problems exist with reference to the status of subsequent advances when the intervening party is a judgment creditor. He is not directly part of the Code's system of priorities. It seems unfair to make it possible for a debtor and secured party with knowledge of the judgment lien to squeeze out a judgment creditor who has successfully levied on a valuable equity subject to a security interest, by permitting later enlargement of the security interest by an additional advance, unless that advance was committed in advance without such knowledge. Proposed Section 9—301(4) provides that a lien creditor does not take subject to a subsequent advance unless it is given or committed without knowledge, but there is an exception protecting future advances within 45 days after the levy regardless of knowledge. The 45-day period corresponds to a provision on protection of advances made after the filing of tax liens in the Federal Tax Lien Act of 1966.

A similar problem arises where the intervening party is a buyer of the collateral subject to the security interest. While buyers must necessarily take subject to rights of secured parties, the buyer should take subject to subsequent advances only to the extent that they are given "pursuant to commitment" or within the period of 45 days after the purchase but not later than the time that the secured party acquires knowledge of the purchase. It is so proposed in Section 9—307(3). A definition of the quoted phrase appears in Section 9—105.

§ 9—313.　Priority of Security Interests in Fixtures

[(1) The rules of this section do not apply to goods incorporated into a structure in the manner of lumber, bricks, tile, cement, glass, metal work and the like and no security interest in them exists under this Article unless the structure remains personal property under applicable law. The law of this state other than this Act determines whether and when other goods become fixtures. This Act does not prevent creation of an encumbrance upon fixtures or real estate pursuant to the law applicable to real estate.]

[(2) A security interest which attaches to goods before they become fixtures takes priority as to the goods over the claims of all persons who have an interest in the real estate except as stated in subsection (4).]

[(3) A security interest which attaches to goods after they become fixtures is valid against all persons subsequently acquiring interests in the real estate except as stated in subsection (4) but is invalid against any person with an interest in the real estate at the time the security interest attaches to the goods who has not in writing consented to the security interest or disclaimed an interest in the goods as fixtures.]

[(4) The security interests described in subsections (2) and (3) do not take priority over

(a) a subsequent purchaser for value of any interest in the real estate; or

(b) a creditor with a lien on the real estate subsequently obtained by judicial proceedings; or

(c) a creditor with a prior encumbrance of record on the real estate to the extent that he makes subsequent advances

if the subsequent purchase is made, the lien by judicial proceedings is obtained, or the subsequent advance under the prior encumbrance is made or contracted for without knowledge of the security interest and before it is perfected. A purchaser of the real estate at a foreclosure sale other than an encumbrancer purchasing at his own foreclosure sale is a subsequent purchaser within this section.]

(1) In this section and in the provisions of Part 4 of this Article referring to fixture filing, unless the context otherwise requires

(a) goods are "fixtures" when they become so related to particular real estate that an interest in them arises under real estate law

(b) a "fixture filing" is the filing in the office where a mortgage on the real estate would be filed or recorded of a financing statement covering goods which are or are to become fixtures and conforming to the requirements of subsection (5) of Section 9—402

(c) a mortgage is a "construction mortgage" to the extent that it secures an obligation incurred for the construction of an improvement on land including the acquisition cost of the land, if the recorded writing so indicates.

(2) A security interest under this Article may be created in goods which are fixtures or may continue in goods which become fixtures, but no security interest exists under this Article in ordinary building materials incorporated into an improvement on land.

(3) This Article does not prevent creation of an encumbrance upon fixtures pursuant to real estate law.

(4) A perfected security interest in fixtures has priority over the conflicting interest of an encumbrancer or owner of the real estate where

(a) the security interest is a purchase money security interest, the interest of the encumbrancer or owner arises before the goods become fixtures, the security interest is perfected by a fixture filing before the goods become fixtures or within ten days thereafter, and the debtor has an interest of record in the real estate or is in possession of the real estate; or

(b) the security interest is perfected by a fixture filing before the interest of the encumbrancer or owner is of record, the security interest has priority over any conflicting interest of a predecessor in title of the encumbrancer or owner, and the debtor has an interest of record in the real estate or is in possession of the real estate; or

(c) the fixtures are readily removable factory or office machines or readily removable replacements of domestic appliances which are consumer goods, and before the goods become fixtures the security interest is perfected by any method permitted by this Article; or

(d) the conflicting interest is a lien on the real estate obtained by legal or equitable proceedings after the security interest was perfected by any method permitted by this Article.

(5) A security interest in fixtures, whether or not perfected, has priority over the conflicting interest of an encumbrancer or owner of the real estate where

(a) the encumbrancer or owner has consented in writing to the security interest or has disclaimed an interest in the goods as fixtures; or

(b) the debtor has a right to remove the goods as against the encumbrancer or owner. If the debtor's right terminates, the priority of the security interest continues for a reasonable time.

(6) Notwithstanding paragraph (a) of subsection (4) but otherwise subject to subsections (4) and (5), a security interest in fixtures is subordinate to a construction mortgage recorded before the goods become fixtures if the goods become fixtures before the completion of the construction. To the extent that it is given to refinance a construction mortgage, a mortgage has this priority to the same extent as the construction mortgage.

(7) In cases not within the preceding subsections, a security interest in fixtures is subordinate to the conflicting interest of an encumbrancer or owner of the related real estate who is not the debtor.

(8) [(5)] When [under subsections (2) or (3) or (4) a] the secured party has priority over [the claims of all persons who have interests in] all owners and encumbrancers of the real estate, he may, on default, subject to the provisions of Part 5, remove his collateral from the real estate but he must reimburse any encumbrancer or owner of the real estate who is not the debtor and who has not otherwise agreed for the cost of repair of any physical injury, but not for any diminution in value of the real estate caused by the absence of the goods removed or by any necessity of replacing them. A person entitled to reimbursement may refuse permission to remove until the secured party gives adequate security for the performance of this obligation.

Reasons for 1972 Change

As the Code came to be widely enacted, the real estate bar came to realize the impact of the fixture provisions on real estate financing and real estate titles. They apparently had not fully appreciated the impact of these provisions of Article 9 on real estate matters during the enactment of the Code, because of the commonly-held assumption that Article 9 was concerned only with chattel security matters.

The treatment of fixtures in pre-Code law had varied widely from state to state. The treatment in Article 9 was based generally on prior treatment in the Uniform Conditional Sales Act, which, however, had been enacted in only a dozen states. In other states the word "fixture" had come to mean that a former chattel had become real estate for all purposes and that any chattel rights therein were lost. For lawyers trained in such states the Code provisions seemed to be extreme. Some sections of the real estate bar began attempting with some success to have Section 9—313 amended to bring it closer to the pre-Code law in their states. In some states, such as California and Iowa, Section 9—313 simply was not enacted.

Even supporters of Article 9 and of its fixture provisions came to recognize that there were some ambiguities in Section 9—313, particularly in its application to construction mortgages, and also in its failure to make it clear that filing of fixture security interests was to be in real estate records where they could be found by a standard real estate search.

Section 9—313 and related provisions of Part 4 have been redrafted to meet the legitimate criticisms and to make a substantial shift in the law in favor of construction mortgages. The specific changes are described in the 1972 Comments to Section 9—313, and the Comments to the several sections of Part 4.

§ 9—318. Defenses Against Assignee; Modification of Contract After Notification of Assignment; Term Prohibiting Assignment Ineffective; Identification and Proof of Assignment

(1) Unless an account debtor has made an enforceable agreement not to assert defenses or claims arising out of a sale as provided in Section 9—206 the rights of an assignee are subject to

(a) all the terms of the contract between the account debtor and assignor and any defense or claim arising therefrom; and

(b) any other defense or claim of the account debtor against the assignor which accrues before the account debtor receives notification of the assignment.

(2) So far as the right to payment or a part thereof under an assigned contract has not been fully earned by performance, [right has not already become an account,] and notwithstanding notification of the assignment, any modification of or substitution for the contract made in good faith and in accordance with reasonable commercial standards is effective against an assignee unless the account debtor has otherwise agreed but the assignee acquires corresponding rights under the modified or substituted contract. The assignment may provide that such modification or substitution is a breach by the assignor.

(3) The account debtor is authorized to pay the assignor until the account debtor receives notification that the [account] amount due or to become due has been assigned and that payment is to be made to the assignee. A notification which does not reasonably identify the rights assigned is ineffective. If requested by the account debtor, the assignee must seasonably furnish reasonable proof that the assignment has been made and unless he does so the account debtor may pay the assignor.

(4) A term in any contract between an account debtor and an assignor [which] is ineffective if it prohibits assignment of an account [or contract right to which they are parties is ineffective] or prohibits creation of a security interest in a general intangible for money due or to become due or requires the account debtor's consent to such assignment or security interest.

Reasons for 1972 Change

The principal changes conform to the elimination of the term "contract right" in Section 9—106.

Minor changes in subsections (3) and (4) eliminate technical difficulties in the 1962 Code which arose out of the fact that the term "account debtor" used in these subsections is defined to include debtors under general intangibles and chattel paper, and is therefore broader than the term "account" heretofore used in these subsections. Subsection (4) is broadened to apply to general intangibles for money due as well as to accounts.

PART 4

FILING

§ **9—401.**   **Place of Filing;   Erroneous Filing;   Removal of Collateral**

First Alternative Subsection (1)

(1) The proper place to file in order to perfect a security interest is as follows:

   (a) when the collateral is timber to be cut or is minerals or the like (including oil and gas) or accounts subject to subsection (5) of Section 9—103, or when the financing statement is filed as a fixture filing (Section 9—313) and the collateral is goods which [at the time the security interest attaches] are or are to become fixtures, then in the office where a mortgage on the real estate [concerned] would be filed or recorded;

   (b) in all other cases, in the office of the [[Secretary of State]].

Second Alternative Subsection (1)

(1) The proper place to file in order to perfect a security interest is as follows:

   (a) when the collateral is equipment used in farming operations, or farm products, or accounts [, contract rights] or general intangibles arising from or relating to the sale of farm products by a farmer, or consumer goods, then in the office of the . . . . in the county of the debtor's residence or if the debtor is not a resident of this state then in the office of the . . . . in the county where the goods are kept, and in addition when the collateral is crops growing or to be grown in the office of the . . . . in the county where the land [on which the crops are growing or to be grown] is located;

   (b) when the collateral is [goods which at the time the security interest attaches are or are to become fixtures] timber to be cut or is minerals or the like (including oil and gas) or accounts subject to subsection (5) of Section 9—103, or when the financing statement is filed as a fixture filing (Section 9—313) and the collateral is goods which are or are to be become fixtures, then in the office where a mortgage on the real estate [concerned] would be filed or recorded;

(c) in all other cases, in the office of the [[Secretary of State]].

Third Alternative Subsection (1)

(1) The proper place to file in order to perfect a security interest is as follows:

(a) when the collateral is equipment used in farming operations, or farm products, or accounts [, contract rights] or general intangibles arising from or relating to the sale of farm products by a farmer, or consumer goods, then in the office of the .... in the county of the debtor's residence or if the debtor is not a resident of this state then in the office of the .... in the county where the goods are kept, and in addition when the collateral is crops growing or to be grown in the office of the ...... in the county where the land [on which the crops are growing or to be grown] is located;

(b) when the collateral is [goods which at the time the security interest attaches are or are to become fixtures] timber to be cut or is minerals or the like (including oil and gas) or accounts subject to subsection (5) of Section 9—103, or when the financing statement is filed as a fixture filing (Section 9—313) and the collateral is goods which are or are to become fixtures, then in the office where a mortgage on the real estate [concerned] would be filed or recorded;

(c) in all other cases, in the office of the [[Secretary of State]] and in addition, if the debtor has a place of business in only one county of this state, also in the office of ...... of such county, or, if the debtor has no place of business in this state, but resides in the state, also in the office of ...... of the county in which he resides.

Note: *One of the three alternatives should be selected as subsection (1).*

(2) A filing which is made in good faith in an improper place or not in all of the places required by this section is nevertheless effective with regard to any collateral as to which the filing complied with the requirements of this Article and is also effective with regard to collateral covered by the financing statement against any person who has knowledge of the contents of such financing statement.

(3) A filing which is made in the proper place in this state continues effective even though the debtor's residence or place of business or the location of the collateral or its use, whichever controlled the original filing, is thereafter changed.

Language in double brackets is Alternative Subsection (3)

[[(3) A filing which is made in the proper county continues effective for four months after a change to another county of the debtor's residence or place of business or the location of the collateral, whichever controlled the original filing. It becomes ineffective thereafter unless a copy of the financing statement signed by the secured party is filed in the new county within said period. The security interest may also be perfected in the new county after the expiration of the four-month period; in such case perfected dates from the time of perfection in the new county. A change in the use of the collateral does not impair the effectiveness of the original filing.]]

(4) [If collateral is brought into this state from another jurisdiction, the] The rules stated in Section 9—103 determine whether filing is necessary in this state.

(5) Notwithstanding the preceding subsections, and subject to subsection (3) of Section 9—302, the proper place to file in order to perfect a security interest in collateral, including fixtures, of a transmitting utility is the office of the [[Secretary of State]]. This filing constitutes a fixture filing (Section 9—313) as to the collateral described therein which is or is to become fixtures.

(6) For the purposes of this section, the residence of an organization is its place of business if it has one or its chief executive office if it has more than one place of business.

Note: *Subsection (6) should be used only if the state chooses the Second or Third Alternative Subsection (1).*

Reasons for 1972 Change

The several alternatives for subsection (1) have been rewritten to provide for filing in the real estate records of security interests intended to give a priority as a "fixture filing" under Section 9—313.

This requirement for filing in real estate records applies only if the priority advantages of Section 9—313 are desired. If the secured party is not concerned about priority against real estate parties, he can file for a fixture as for an ordinary chattel, in the chattel records, omitting the filing in the real estate records, and he will have a security interest perfected against everyone but real estate parties. In the case of a purchase money security interest in consumer goods, he need not file at all. See Section 9—313(1) (d). For the question of the effect of the regular chattel filing in lieu of fixture filing in the event of the debtor's bankruptcy, see Comment 4(c) to Section 9—313.

This requirement for filing in real estate records applies also to timber to be cut and to minerals or the like (including oil and gas) financed at the wellhead or minehead or accounts resulting from the sale thereof.

This filing is not merely in the *office* where a mortgage of real estate would be recorded, but it is intended that it be filed *in the real estate records*. This is made clear by the model form in Section 9—402(3) which recites that the financing statement is to be filed for record in the real estate records, the required recital in Section 9—402(5), and the provision of Section 9—403(7) requiring the indexing thereof in the real estate records. Thus, it is intended that these filings will be readily disclosed on any real estate search and they can be treated like any real estate encumbrance so disclosed.

A new subsection (5) makes clear that a financing statement filed against a "transmitting utility" (Section 9—105) need be filed only in the office of the [Secretary of State] and not locally. Special provision had to be made for filing where these far-flung utilities were debtors. If the problem were only on non-fixtures, not more than one local filing would have been necessary under any of the alternative versions of subsection (1), but the problem was more difficult in the case of fixtures, where the standard rule would require filing with real estate descriptions in every county where there were fixtures.

There has been some difficulty in the concept that one files against farmers at their residences, in view of the number

of incorporated farms. A new subsection (6) is therefore
added to define the residence of an organization. Subsection (6) is also needed if the provision of the Third Alternative Subsection (1) for double filing against local business
debtors is adopted.

§ 9—402. Formal Requisites of Financing Statement; Amendments; Mortgage as Financing Statement

(1) A financing statement is sufficient if it gives the names
of the debtor and the secured party, is signed by the debtor [and
the secured party], gives an address of the secured party from
which information concerning the security interest may be obtained, gives a mailing address of the debtor and contains a statement indicating the types, or describing the items, of collateral.
A financing statement may be filed before a security agreement
is made or a security interest otherwise attaches. When the
financing statement covers crops growing or to be grown [or
goods which are or are to become fixtures], the statement must
also contain a description of the real estate concerned. When
the financing statement covers timber to be cut or covers minerals or the like (including oil and gas) or accounts subject to
subsection (5) of Section 9—103, or when the financing statement is filed as a fixture filing (Section 9—313) and the collateral is goods which are or are to become fixtures, the statement must also comply with subsection (5). A copy of the security agreement is sufficient as a financing statement if it contains the above information and is signed by [both parties.] the
debtor. A carbon, photographic or other reproduction of a security agreement or a financing statement is sufficient as a
financing statement if the security agreement so provides or if
the original has been filed in this state.

(2) A financing statement which otherwise complies with
subsection (1) is sufficient [although] when it is signed [only]
by the secured party instead of the debtor if it is filed to perfect
a security interest in

   (a) collateral already subject to a security interest in another jurisdiction when it is brought into this state, or
   when the debtor's location is changed to this state. Such
   a financing statement must state that the collateral was
   brought into this state or that the debtor's location was
   changed to this state under such circumstances; or

(b) proceeds under Section 9—306 if the security interest in the original collateral was perfected. Such a financing statement must describe the original collateral; <u>or</u>

(c) <u>collateral as to which the filing has lapsed; or</u>

(d) <u>collateral acquired after a change of name, identity or corporate structure of the debtor (subsection (7)).</u>

(3) A form substantially as follows is sufficient to comply with subsection (1):

Name of debtor (or assignor) ....

Address ....

Name of secured party (or assignee) ....

Address ....

1. This financing statement covers the following types (or items) of property:
   (Describe) ....

2. (If collateral is crops) The above described crops are growing or are to be grown on:
   (Describe Real Estate) ....

[3. (If collateral is goods which are or are to become fixtures) The above described goods are affixed or to be affixed to:
   (Describe Real Estate) ....]

3. <u>(If applicable) The above goods are to become fixtures on*</u>

* Where appropriate substitute either "The above timber is standing on . . . . ." or "The above minerals or the like (including oil and gas) or accounts will be financed at the wellhead or minehead of the well or mine located on . . . . ."

(Describe Real Estate) ....
<u>and this financing statement is to be filed [[for record]] in the real estate records. (If the debtor does not have an interest of record) The name of a record owner is</u>
....

4. (If [proceeds or] products of collateral are claimed) [Proceeds—] Products of the collateral are also covered.

<u>(use</u>   ⎧ ....
<u>whichever</u> ⎥   Signature of Debtor (or Assignor)
<u>is</u>   ⎥ ....
<u>applicable)</u> ⎩   Signature of Secured Party (or Assignee)

(4) <u>A financing statement may be amended by filing a writing signed by both the debtor and the secured party. An amend-</u>

ment does not extend the period of effectiveness of a financing statement. [The term "financing statement" as used in this Article means the original financing statement and any amendments but if] If any amendment adds collateral, it is effective as to the added collateral only from the filing date of the amendment. In this Article, unless the context otherwise requires, the term "financing statement" means the original financing statement and any amendments.

(5) A financing statement covering timber to be cut or covering minerals or the like (including oil and gas) or accounts subject to subsection (5) of Section 9—103, or a financing statement filed as a fixture filing (Section 9—313) where the debtor is not a transmitting utility, must show that it covers this type of collateral, must recite that it is to be filed [[for record]] in the real estate records, and the financing statement must contain a description of the real estate [[sufficient if it were contained in a mortgage of the real estate to give constructive notice of the mortgage under the law of this state]]. If the debtor does not have an interest of record in the real estate, the financing statement must show the name of a record owner.

(6) A mortgage is effective as a financing statement filed as a fixture filing from the date of its recording if (a) the goods are described in the mortgage by item or type, (b) the goods are or are to become fixtures related to the real estate described in the mortgage, (c) the mortgage complies with the requirements for a financing statement in this section other than a recital that it is to be filed in the real estate records, and (d) the mortgage is duly recorded. No fee with reference to the financing statement is required other than the regular recording and satisfaction fees with respect to the mortgage.

(7) A financing statement sufficiently shows the name of the debtor if it gives the individual, partnership or corporate name of the debtor, whether or not it adds other trade names or the names of partners. Where the debtor so changes his name or in the case of an organization its name, identity or corporate structure that a filed financing statement becomes seriously misleading, the filing is not effective to perfect a security interest in collateral acquired by the debtor more than four months after the change, unless a new appropriate financing statement is filed before the expiration of that time. A filed financing statement remains effective with respect to collateral transferred by the debtor even though the secured party knows of or consents to the transfer.

(8) [(5)] A financing statement substantially complying with the requirements of this section is effective even though it contains minor errors which are not seriously misleading.

Note: *Language in double brackets is optional.*

Note: *Where the state has any special recording system for real estate other than the usual grantor-grantee index (as, for instance, a tract system or a title registration or Torrens system) local adaptations of subsection (5) and Section 9—403(7) may be necessary. See Mass. Gen. Laws Chapter 106, Section 9—409.*

Reasons for 1972 Change

Certain changes are conforming changes to new requirements of Section 9—401 that certain financing statements covering such collateral as timber and minerals be filed in the real estate records. Persons interested in real estate have complained with some justice that the provisions of the 1962 Code failed in several ways to tie the fixture filings to the real estate search system. Among these was the absence of clear specification that the fixture security interest was to be indexed in the real estate records. On this point, a responsive change has been made in Section 9—403. Other objections related to the adequacy of the real estate description and to the fact that the debtor might not be an owner of an interest of record in the real estate. The optional language in subsection (5) is designed to meet the objection as to real estate descriptions but without imposing on a fixture-secured party the duty of obtaining a "legal description" unless the state's recording system requires it. While no doubt a full "legal description" is proper practice in conveyancing, it is believed that something significantly less, like a street address, would be adequate in most states, and would frequently be a guide to a recorded map. Where a state has a tract index system or other special system not dependent on a grantor-grantee index, special adaptations may be required and no attempt is made in the Code to deal with all such situations.

Another objection of real estate parties has been that the name of the debtor might not be in the real estate chain of title and there have been numerous non-uniform amendments to Sections 9—401, 9—402, or 9—403 designed to require the showing of the name of the record owners of the real estate in the financing statement. Since Section 9–313(4) (a) and (b) permit fixture filing against persons in possession of the real estate who do not have interests of record, Section 9—402 requires the naming of an owner of record of the real estate in such cases, and Section 9—403(7) requires indexing the fixture filing against the name.

Subsection (6) makes it possible for a real estate mortgage to serve as a financing statement, and a related change in Section 9—403(6) makes it unnecessary to file continuation statements for such a financing statement.

Subsection (1) has been changed to require only the signature of the debtor rather than that of the secured party. The requirement of signatures of secured parties has sometimes misled secured parties, who are accustomed to pre-Code practice and real estate practice under which only the debtor, not the secured party, need sign such instruments as chattel mortgages and real estate mortgages. Thus, when the security agreement was used as the financing statement, it might have been defective under the 1962 Code for failure to have the signature of the secured party. This change also fits in with the provisions of Section 9—403(6), under which a real estate mortgage (customarily signed only by the debtor) may be effective as a financing statement.

Changes in the form of financing statement in subsection (3) conform to the foregoing and are also intended to have the secured party make clear when a financing statement is intended to be filed in real estate records. This had been a matter of some concern when the parties used the term "fixture" loosely in their description of goods.

Certain of the changes in Section 9—402 are not related to real estate filings. The changes in paragraph (2) (a) conform to Section 9—103(3), which requires refiling when the debtor's location changes. Additions in subsections (2) (d) and (7) relating to the problem of the name of the debtor against which a filing should be made and the effect of transfer are discussed in the related Comments.

§ 9—403. What Constitutes Filing; Duration of Filing; Effect of Lapsed Filing; Duties of Filing Officer

(1) Presentation for filing of a financing statement and tender of the filing fee or acceptance of the statement by the filing officer constitutes filing under this Article.

(2) Except as provided in subsection (6) a [(2) A] filed financing statement [which states a maturity date of the obligation secured of five years or less is effective until such maturity date and thereafter for a period of sixty days. Any other filed financ-

ing statement] is effective for a period of five years from the date of filing. The effectiveness of a filed financing statement lapses [on the expiration of such sixty day period after a stated maturity date or] on the expiration of [such five] the five year period [, as the case may be] unless a continuation statement is filed prior to the lapse. If a security interest perfected by filing exists at the time insolvency proceedings are commenced by or against the debtor, the security interest remains perfected until termination of the insolvency proceedings and thereafter for a period of sixty days or until expiration of the five year period, whichever occurs later. Upon [such] lapse the security interest becomes unperfected, unless it is perfected without filing. If the security interest becomes unperfected upon lapse, it is deemed to have been unperfected as against a person who became a purchaser or lien creditor before lapse. [A filed financing statement which states that the obligation secured is payable on demand is effective for five years from the date of filing.]

(3) A continuation statement may be filed by the secured party [(i) within six months before and sixty days after a stated maturity date of five years or less, and (ii) otherwise] within six months prior to the expiration of the five year period specified in subsection (2). Any such continuation statement must be signed by the secured party, identify the original statement by file number and state that the original statement is still effective. A continuation statement signed by a person other than the secured party of record must be accompanied by a separate written statement of assignment signed by the secured party of record and complying with subsection (2) of Section 9—405, including payment of the required fee. Upon timely filing of the continuation statement, the effectiveness of the original statement is continued for five years after the last date to which the filing was effective whereupon it lapses in the same manner as provided in subsection (2) unless another continuation statement is filed prior to such lapse. Succeeding continuation statements may be filed in the same manner to continue the effectiveness of the original statement. Unless a statute on disposition of public records provides otherwise, the filing officer may remove a lapsed statement from the files and destroy it[.] immediately if he has retained a microfilm or other photographic record, or in other cases after one year after the lapse. The filing officer shall so arrange matters by physical annexation of financing statements to continuation statements or other related filings, or by other means, that if he physically destroys the financing statements of a period more than five years past, those which

have been continued by a continuation statement or which are still effective under subsection (6) shall be retained.

(4) Except as provided in subsection (7) a [(4) A] filing officer shall mark each statement with a [consecutive] file number and with the date and hour of filing and shall hold the statement or a microfilm or other photographic copy thereof for public inspection. In addition the filing officer shall index the statements according to the name of the debtor and shall note in the index the file number and the address of the debtor given in the statement.

[(5) The uniform fee for filing, indexing and furnishing filing data for an original or a continuation statement shall be $......]

(5) The uniform fee for filing and indexing and for stamping a copy furnished by the secured party to show the date and place of filing for an original financing statement or for a continuation statement shall be $.......... if the statement is in the standard form prescribed by the [[Secretary of State]] and otherwise shall be $........, plus in each case, if the financing statement is subject to subsection (5) of Section 9—402, $......... The uniform fee for each name more than one required to be indexed shall be $.......... The secured party may at his option show a trade name for any person and an extra uniform indexing fee of $......... shall be paid with respect thereto.

(6) If the debtor is a transmitting utility (subsection (5) of Section 9—401) and a filed financing statement so states, it is effective until a termination statement is filed. A real estate mortgage which is effective as a fixture filing under subsection (6) of Section 9—402 remains effective as a fixture filing until the mortgage is released or satisfied of record or its effectiveness otherwise terminates as to the real estate.

(7) When a financing statement covers timber to be cut or covers minerals or the like (including oil and gas) or accounts subject to subsection (5) of Section 9—103, or is filed as a fixture filing, [[it shall be filed for record and]] the filing officer shall index it under the names of the debtor and any owner of record shown on the financing statement in the same fashion as if they were the mortgagors in a mortgage of the real estate described, and, to the extent that the law of this state provides for indexing of mortgages under the name of the mortgagee, under the name of the secured party as if he were the mortgagee thereunder, or where indexing is by description in the same fashion as if the financing statement were a mortgage of the real estate described.

Note: *In states in which writings will not appear in the real estate records and indices unless actually recorded the bracketed language in subsection (7) should be used.*

Reasons for 1972 Change

The change in subsection (2) makes every financing statement (except those described in subsection (6)), effective for a full five years, thus changing the rule of the 1962 Code that a financing statement which showed a maturity less than 5 years was effective only for the period until maturity plus 60 days. This limitation could have been easily evaded simply by not showing a maturity, even though there was one. The change facilitates renewals or extensions up to a maximum combined duration of five years, without the danger of the financing statement ceasing to be effective.

Subsection (2) also recognizes that financing statements might expire during an insolvency proceeding. While the prevailing line of decisions is to the effect that the situation is frozen at the moment of bankruptcy without an obligation to refile, there are contrary decisions, and this situation might prove an inadvertent trap to a secured party who failed to refile or file a continuation statement during a bankruptcy. The change continues the validity of the financing statement until the end of the insolvency proceedings and for 60 days thereafter, or until the expiration of the five-year period, whichever is later. Ordinarily, if the secured party expects that the secured debt may continue in existence after the end of the insolvency proceedings, he should file a continuation statement on the normal schedule, to preserve the filing for use at the end of the insolvency proceeding and to preclude any discontinuity of the filings.

Subsection (2) also clarifies the effect of lapse, a matter on which there has been some dispute among writers on the subject. Compare also Section 9—103(1) (d).

Subsection (5) is intended to adopt non-uniform amendments made in some states giving the filing officer authority to charge extra fees if the financing statement does not conform to a uniform prescribed size and content. It also permits the secured party to show a trade name at his option and to have it indexed for an extra fee.

New subsection (6) deals with transmitting utilities (Sections 9—105 and 9—401(5)) and also with real estate mortgages which are effective as financing statements under Section 9—402(6). In these special cases a financing statement is good indefinitely and its validity is not limited to five years. The filing in real estate records of a financing statement which is also a real estate mortgage will give notice to persons searching the record as to this continuing validity and will not interfere with the purpose of the Code's standard rule of five-year validity for financing statements. The name of a transmitting utility should give equivalent notice in filings against that kind of company.

The purpose of the standard rule is to permit the files to be self-clearing, so that whether or not termination statements have been filed, the filing officer can clear the files after a suitable period after the five-year validity expires, unless the duration of the financing statement has been continued by a continuation statement.

Various technical changes in this section are designed to facilitate the handling of financing statements by filing officers in reference to the use of microfilm, etc., and to carry out the principle of the self-clearing nature of the files after five years.

New subsection (7) deals with a point in reference to fixtures on which the 1962 Code was properly subject to criticism, namely, that it was not explicitly stated that the fixture filing in the county where a real estate mortgage would be recorded was intended to be made and be indexed in the *real estate records*. This principle is now stated and is also made applicable to timber to be cut and to minerals and the like (including oil and gas) financed at the wellhead or minehead or accounts resulting from the sale thereof.

The other minor changes coordinate with the addition of subsection (7) to Section 9—402.

§ 9—404. Termination Statement

(1) If a financing statement covering consumer goods is filed on or after ...., then within one month or within ten days following written demand by the debtor after there is no outstanding secured obligation and no commitment to make advances, incur obligations or otherwise give value, the secured party must file with each filing officer with whom the financing statement was filed, a termination statement to the effect that he no longer claims a security interest under the financing statement, which shall be identified by file number. In other cases whenever [Whenever] there is no outstanding secured obligation and no commitment to make advances, incur obligations or otherwise give value, the secured party must on written demand by the debtor send the debtor, for each filing officer with whom the financing statement was filed, a termination statement to the effect that he no longer claims a security inter-

est under the financing statement, which shall be identified by file number. A termination statement signed by a person other than the secured party of record must [include or] be accompanied by [the assignment or] a separate written statement of assignment signed by the secured party of record [that he has assigned the security interest to the signer of the termination statement. and] complying with subsection (2) of Section 9—405, including payment of the required fee. [The uniform fee for filing and indexing such an assignment or statement thereof shall be $........] If the affected secured party fails to file such a termination statement as required by this subsection, or to send such a termination statement within ten days after proper demand therefor he shall be liable to the debtor for one hundred dollars, and in addition for any loss caused to the debtor by such failure.

(2) On presentation to the filing officer of such a termination statement he must note it in the index. [The filing officer shall remove from the files, mark "terminated" and send or deliver to the secured party the financing statement and any continuation statement, statement of assignment or statement of release pertaining thereto.] If he has received the termination statement in duplicate, he shall return one copy of the termination statement to the secured party stamped to show the time of receipt thereof. If the filing officer has a microfilm or other photographic record of the financing statement, and of any related continuation statement, statement of assignment and statement of release, he may remove the originals from the files at any time after receipt of the termination statement, or if he has no such record, he may remove them from the files at any time after one year after receipt of the termination statement.

(3) If the termination statement is in the standard form prescribed by the [[Secretary of State]], the uniform fee for filing and indexing [a] the termination statement [including sending or delivering the financing statement] shall be $........, and otherwise shall be $........, plus in each case an additional fee of $........ for each name more than one against which the termination statement is required to be indexed.

Note: *The date to be inserted should be the effective date of the revised Article 9.*

Reasons for 1972 Change

The additions to subsection (1) require the filing of termination statements in the case of consumer goods even without a demand by the consumer. It is believed that consumers will frequently not understand the importance of making demand in order to clear the files. The scope of the change is not as great as might first appear, because (1) filing is not required for purchase money security interests in consumer goods, except in the case of motor vehicles (Section 9—302(1) (d)); and (2) perfection of security interests in most motor vehicles is governed by certificate of title laws, not by the provisions of Article 9.

The other changes are purely formal and tie in with corresponding changes in filing mechanics in other sections.

§ 9—405. Assignment of Security Interest; Duties of Filing Officer; Fees

(1) A financing statement may disclose an assignment of a security interest in the collateral described in the financing statement by indication in the financing statement of the name and address of the assignee or by an assignment itself or a copy thereof on the face or back of the statement. [Either the original secured party or the assignee may sign this statement as the secured party.] On presentation to the filing officer of such a financing statement the filing officer shall mark the same as provided in Section 9—403(4). The uniform fee for filing, indexing and furnishing filing data for a financing statement so indicating an assignment shall be $........ if the statement is in the standard form prescribed by the [[Secretary of State]] and otherwise shall be $........, plus in each case an additional fee of $...... for each name more than one against which the financing statement is required to be indexed.

(2) A secured party may assign of record all or part of his rights under a financing statement by the filing in the place where the original financing statement was filed of a separate written statement of assignment signed by the secured party of record and setting forth the name of the secured party of record and the debtor, the file number and the date of filing of the financing statement and the name and address of the assignee and containing a description of the collateral assigned. A copy of the assignment is sufficient as a separate statement if it complies with the preceding sentence. On presentation to the filing officer of such a separate statement, the filing officer shall mark such separate statement with the date and hour of the filing. He shall note the assignment on the index of the financing statement, or in the case of a fixture filing, or a filing covering timber to be cut, or covering minerals or the like (including oil and gas or ac-

461

counts subject to subsection (5) of Section 9—103, he shall index the assignment under the name of the assignor as grantor and, to the extent that the law of this state provides for indexing the assignment of a mortgage under the name of the assignee, he shall index the assignment of the financing statement under the name of the assignee. The uniform fee for filing, indexing and furnishing filing data about such a separate statement of assignment shall be $...... if the statement is in the standard form prescribed by the [[Secretary of State]] and otherwise shall be $......, plus in each case an additional fee of $...... for each name more than one against which the statement of assignment is required to be indexed. Notwithstanding the provisions of this subsection, an assignment of record of a security interest in a fixture contained in a mortgage effective as a fixture filing (subsection (6) of Section 9—402) may be made only by an assignment of the mortgage in the manner provided by the law of this state other than this Act.

(3) After the disclosure or filing of an assignment under this section, the assignee is the secured party of record.

Reasons for 1972 Change

The changes are all conforming changes connecting with changes in mechanics in other sections of Part 4; with the addition of timber and minerals or the like (including oil and gas) at wellhead or minehead and accounts resulting from the sale thereof to the groups of collateral which must be filed and indexed in the real estate records; and with the provision (Section 9—402(6)) that a mortgage of real estate may act as a financing statement of fixtures.

§ 9—406.   Release of Collateral; Duties of Filing Officer; Fees

A secured party of record may by his signed statement release all or a part of any collateral described in a filed financing statement. The statement of release is sufficient if it contains a description of the collateral being released, the name and address of the debtor, the name and address of the secured party, and the file number of the financing statement. A statement of release signed by a person other than the secured party of record must be accompanied by a separate written statement of assignment signed by the secured party of record and complying with subsection (2) of Section 9—405, including payment of the required fee. Upon presentation of such a statement of release to the filing officer he shall mark the statement with the hour and date of filing and shall note the same upon the margin of the index of the filing of the financing statement. The uniform fee for filing and noting such a statement of release shall be $...... if the statement is in the standard form prescribed by the [[Secretary of State]] and otherwise shall be $........, plus in each case an additional fee of $........ for each name more than one against which the statement of release is required to be indexed.

Reasons for 1972 Change

The changes are merely conforming changes to changes in other sections.

[[§ 9—407.   Information From Filing Officer]]

[[(1) If the person filing any financing statement, termination statement, statement of assignment, or statement of release, furnishes the filing officer a copy thereof, the filing officer shall upon request note upon the copy the file number and date and hour of the filing of the original and deliver or send the copy to such person.]]

[[(2) Upon request of any person, the filing officer shall issue his certificate showing whether there is on file on the date and hour stated therein, any presently effective financing statement naming a particular debtor and any statement of assignment thereof and if there is, giving the date and hour of filing of each such statement and the names and addresses of each secured party therein. The uniform fee for such a certificate shall be $....... [plus $....... for each financing statement and for each statement of assignment reported therein.] if the request for the certificate is in the standard form prescribed by the [[Secretary of State]] and otherwise shall be $........ [plus $....... for each financing statement and for each statement of assignment reported therein.] Upon request the filing officer shall furnish a copy of any filed financing statement or statement of assignment for a uniform fee of $....... per page.]]

Reasons for 1972 Change

The change in this optional section is merely a conforming change to the changes in other sections.

Note: *This section is proposed as an optional provision to require filing officers to furnish certificates. Local law and practices should be consulted with regard to the advisability of adoption.*

§ 9—408. Financing Statements Covering Consigned or Leased Goods

A consignor or lessor of goods may file a financing statement using the terms "consignor," "consignee," "lessor," "lessee" or the like instead of the terms specified in Section 9—402. The provisions of this Part shall apply as appropriate to such a financing statement but its filing shall not of itself be a factor in determining whether or not the consignment or lease is intended as security (Section 1—201(37)). However, if it is determined for other reasons that the consignment or lease is so intended, a security interest of the consignor or lessor which attaches to the consigned or leased goods is perfected by such filing.

Reasons for 1972 Adoption of New Section

This new section adapts the filing system of the Article to consignments and leases. Filing of consignments is required under certain conditions (Sections 2—326(3), 9—114). Filing of true leases which are not security interests (Section 1—201(37)) is not required; but because the question whether a lease is a true lease may be a close one, filing is permitted for leases.

PART 5

DEFAULT

§ 9—501. Default; Procedure When Security Agreement Covers Both Real and Personal Property

(1) When a debtor is in default under a security agreement, a secured party has the rights and remedies provided in this Part and except as limited by subsection (3) those provided in the security agreement. He may reduce his claim to judgment, foreclose or otherwise enforce the security interest by any available judicial procedure. If the collateral is documents the secured party may proceed either as to the documents or as to the goods covered thereby. A secured party in possession has the rights,

remedies and duties provided in Section 9—207. The rights and remedies referred to in this subsection are cumulative.

(2) After default, the debtor has the rights and remedies provided in this Part, those provided in the security agreement and those provided in Section 9—207.

(3) To the extent that they give rights to the debtor and impose duties on the secured party, the rules stated in the subsections referred to below may not be waived or varied except as provided with respect to compulsory disposition of collateral (subsection (3) of Section 9—504 and [(subsection (1) of] Section 9—505) and with respect to redemption of collateral (Section 9—506) but the parties may by agreement determine the standards by which the fulfillment of these rights and duties is to be measured if such standards are not manifestly unreasonable:

  (a) subsection (2) of Section 9—502 and subsection (2) of Section 9—504 insofar as they require accounting for surplus proceeds of collateral;

  (b) subsection (3) of Section 9—504 and subsection (1) of Section 9—505 which deal with disposition of collateral;

  (c) subsection (2) of Section 9—505 which deals with acceptance of collateral as discharge of obligation;

  (d) Section 9—506 which deals with redemption of collateral; and

  (e) subsection (1) of Section 9—507 which deals with the secured party's liability for failure to comply with this Part.

(4) If the security agreement covers both real and personal property, the secured party may proceed under this Part as to the personal property or he may proceed as to both the real and the personal property in accordance with his rights and remedies in respect of the real property in which case the provisions of this Part do not apply.

(5) When a secured party has reduced his claim to judgment the lien of any levy which may be made upon his collateral by virtue of any execution based upon the judgment shall relate back to the date of the perfection of the security interest in such collateral. A judicial sale, pursuant to such execution, is a foreclosure of the security interest by judicial procedure within the meaning of this section, and the secured party may purchase at the sale and thereafter hold the collateral free of any other requirements of this Article

The change is purely technical, to clear up an ambiguity as to whether a debtor could after default agree on the time within which a sale might be held or the time after which a secured party might keep the goods in lieu of a sale.

§ 9—502. Collection Rights of Secured Party

(1) When so agreed and in any event on default the secured party is entitled to notify an account debtor or the obligor on an instrument to make payment to him whether or not the assignor was theretofore making collections on the collateral, and also to take control of any proceeds to which he is entitled under Section 9—306.

(2) A secured party who by agreement is entitled to charge back uncollected collateral or otherwise to full or limited recourse against the debtor and who undertakes to collect from the account debtors or obligors must proceed in a commercially reasonable manner and may deduct his reasonable expenses of realization from the collections. If the security agreement secures an indebtedness, the secured party must account to the debtor for any surplus, and unless otherwise agreed, the debtor is liable for any deficiency. But, if the underlying transaction was a sale of accounts [, contract rights,] or chattel paper, the debtor is entitled to any surplus or is liable for any deficiency only if the security agreement so provides.

Reasons for 1972 Change

The change is only the deletion of the term "contract rights", which is being eliminated as a defined term under the Article.

§ 9—504. Secured Party's Right to Dispose of Collateral After Default; Effect of Disposition

(1) A secured party after default may sell, lease or otherwise dispose of any or all of the collateral in its then condition or following any commercially reasonable preparation or processing. Any sale of goods is subject to the Article on Sales (Article 2). The proceeds of disposition shall be applied in the order following to

    (a) the reasonable expenses of retaking, holding, preparing for sale or lease, selling, leasing and the like and, to the extent provided for in the agreement and not prohibited by law, the reasonable attorneys' fees and legal expenses incurred by the secured party;

(b) the satisfaction of indebtedness secured by the security interest under which the disposition is made;

(c) the satisfaction of indebtedness secured by any subordinate security interest in the collateral if written notification of demand therefor is received before distribution of the proceeds is completed. If requested by the secured party, the holder of a subordinate security interest must seasonably furnish reasonable proof of his interest, and unless he does so, the secured party need not comply with his demand.

(2) If the security interest secures an indebtedness, the secured party must account to the debtor for any surplus, and, unless otherwise agreed, the debtor is liable for any deficiency. But if the underlying transaction was a sale of accounts [, contract rights,] or chattel paper, the debtor is entitled to any surplus or is liable for any deficiency only if the security agreement so provides.

(3) Disposition of the collateral may be by public or private proceedings and may be made by way of one or more contracts. Sale or other disposition may be as a unit or in parcels and at any time and place and on any terms but every aspect of the disposition including the method, manner, time, place and terms must be commercially reasonable. Unless collateral is perishable or threatens to decline speedily in value or is of a type customarily sold on a recognized market, reasonable notification of the time and place of any public sale or reasonable notification of the time after which any private sale or other intended disposition is to be made shall be sent by the secured party to the debtor, if he has not signed after default a statement renouncing or modifying his right to notification of sale. In the case of consumer goods no other notification need be sent. In other cases notification shall be sent to any other secured party from whom the secured party has received (before sending his notification to the debtor or before the debtor's renunciation of his rights) written notice of a claim of an interest in the collateral [and except in the case of consumer goods to any other person who has a security interest in the collateral and who has duly filed a financing statement indexed in the name of the debtor in this state or who is known by the secured party to have a security interest in the collateral]. The secured party may buy at any public sale and if the collateral

467

is of a type customarily sold in a recognized market or is of a type which is the subject of widely distributed standard price quotations he may buy at private sale.

(4) When collateral is disposed of by a secured party after default, the disposition transfers to a purchaser for value all of the debtor's rights therein, discharges the security interest under which it is made and any security interest or lien subordinate thereto. The purchaser takes free of all such rights and interests even though the secured party fails to comply with the requirements of this Part or of any judicial proceedings

> (a) in the case of a public sale, if the purchaser has no knowledge of any defects in the sale and if he does not buy in collusion with the secured party, other bidders or the person conducting the sale; or

> (b) in any other case, if the purchaser acts in good faith.

(5) A person who is liable to a secured party under a guaranty, indorsement, repurchase agreement or the like and who receives a transfer of collateral from the secured party or is subrogated to his rights has thereafter the rights and duties of the secured party. Such a transfer of collateral is not a sale or disposition of the collateral under this Article.

Reasons for 1972 Change

Under the 1962 Code the secured party giving notice of sale had to notify (except in the case of consumer goods) not only every other person who had duly filed a financing statement indexed in the name of the debtor in the state and who still had a security interest in the collateral, but also any other person known by the secured party to have an interest in the collateral. This meant that the secured party had to search the records in every case of notice of sale, to ascertain whether there were any other secured parties with financing statements that might be deemed to cover the collateral in question. Moreover, he ran the risk that some informal communication by letter, or even orally, might be deemed to have given him knowledge of the interest of that other party. These burdens of searching the record and of checking the secured party's files were greater than the circumstances called for because as a practical matter there would seldom be a junior secured party who really had an interest needing protection in the case of a foreclosure sale. Therefore, a change is made requiring notice to persons other than the debtor only if such persons had notified the secured party in writing of their claim of an interest in the collateral before he sent his notification to the debtor or before the debtor's renunciation of his rights. Express provision is made to recognize the right of a debtor to renounce or modify his right to notice after, but not before, default. A corresponding change is made in Section 9—505.

§ 9—505. Compulsory Disposition of Collateral; Acceptance of the Collateral as Discharge of Obligation

(1) If the debtor has paid sixty per cent of the cash price in the case of a purchase money security interest in consumer goods or sixty per cent of the loan in the case of another security interest in consumer goods, and has not signed after default a statement renouncing or modifying his rights under this Part a secured party who has taken possession of collateral must dispose of it under Section 9—504 and if he fails to do so within ninety days after he takes possession the debtor at his option may recover in conversion or under Section 9—507(1) on secured party's liability.

(2) In any other case involving consumer goods or any other collateral a secured party in possession may, after default, propose to retain the collateral in satisfaction of the obligation. Written notice of such proposal shall be sent to the debtor [and except in the case of consumer goods to any other secured party who has a security interest in the collateral and who has duly filed a financing statement indexed in the name of the debtor in this state or is known by the secured party in possession to have a security interest in it. If the debtor or other person entitled to receive notification objects in writing within thirty days from the receipt of the notification or if any other secured party objects in writing thirty days after the secured party obtains possession the secured party must dispose of the collateral under Section 9—504.] if he has not signed after default a statement renouncing or modifying his rights under this subsection. In the case of consumer goods no other notice need be given. In other cases notice shall be sent to any other secured party from whom the secured party has received (before sending his notice to the debtor or before the debtor's renunciation of his rights) written notice of a claim of an interest in the collateral. If the secured party receives objection in writing from a person entitled to receive notification within twenty-one days after the notice was sent, the secured party must dispose of the collateral under Section 9—504. In the absence of such written objection the se-

cured party may retain the collateral in satisfaction of the debtor's obligation.

Reasons for 1972 Change

Under subsection (2) of this section the secured party may in lieu of sale give notice to the debtor and certain other persons that he proposes to retain the collateral in lieu of sale. Under the 1962 Code the other persons were the same as those who were entitled to notice of sale under Section 9—504(3), and such other persons are limited by the change in the same fashion as they were limited in Section 9—504(3) and for the same reasons. See the Reasons for Change under Section 9—504.

TABLE OF CASES

References are to Pages

TABLE OF CITATIONS
TO THE
UNIFORM COMMERCIAL CODE

*

INDEX